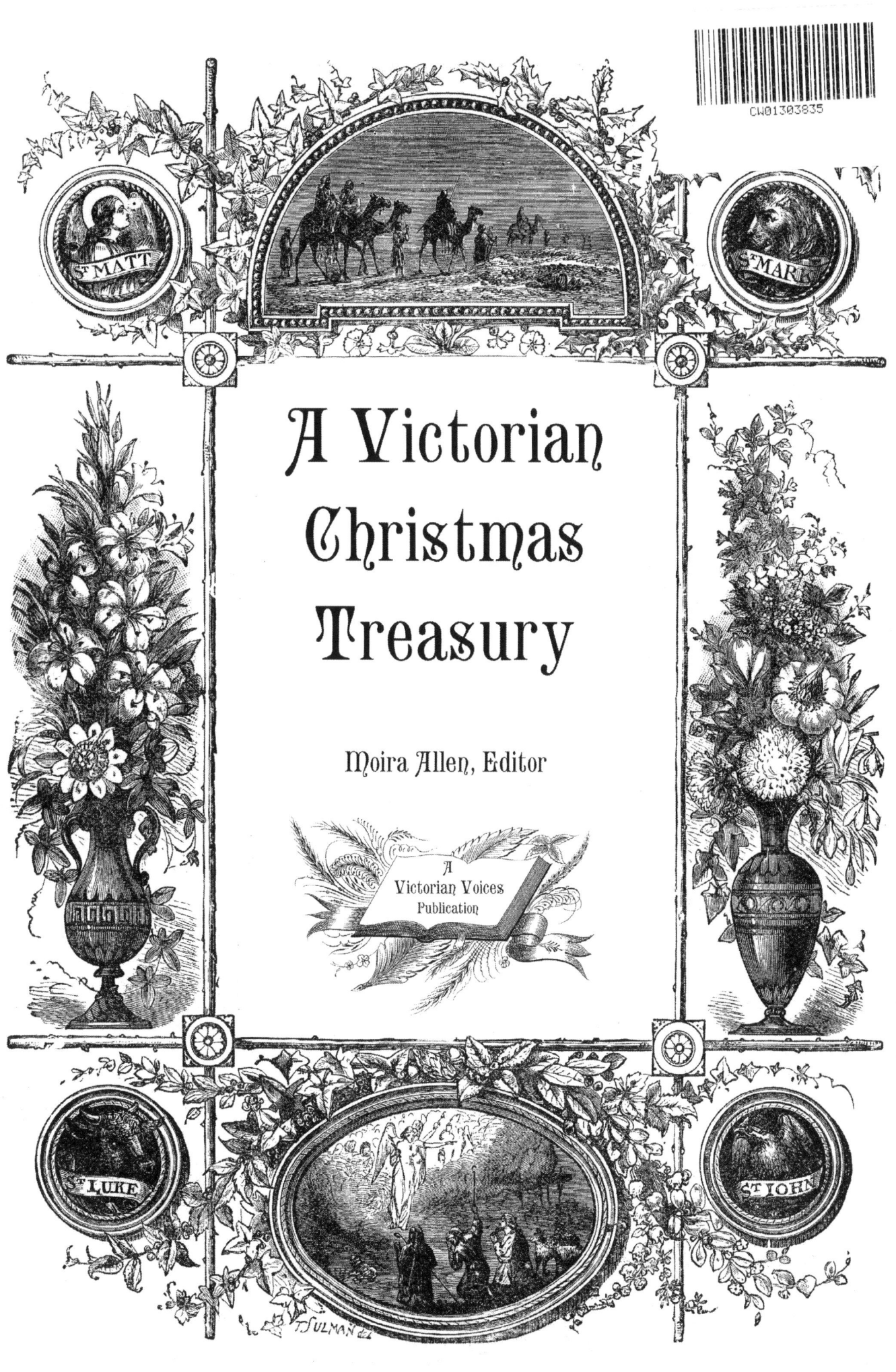

Also available from VictorianVoices.net:

*Graveyard Humor:
A Collection of Quaint and Curious
Inscriptions and Epitaphs*
By W. Fairley

Needle-Crafts from a Victorian Workbasket
Moira Allen, Editor

Bits About Animals: A Treasury of Victorian Animal Anecdotes
Moira Allen, Editor

Visit http://www.VictorianVoices.net/books/index.shtml for details

Victorian Times
A free monthly journal of Victoriana!

Visit http://www.VictorianVoices.net/VT/index.shtml to subscribe,
download back issues, read excerpts, or access the print edition

Copyright © 2014 Moira Allen
Published by Moira Allen via CreateSpace
All rights reserved. This book may not be reproduced or transmitted in any form or by any means, electronic or mechanical, including photocopying, recording, or by any information storage and retrieval system, without the written permission of the editor, except where permitted by law. For reprint permission, contact Moira Allen at editors@victorianvoices.net.

Contents

5   **Introduction**, by Moira Allen
7   **If You Love Christmas, Thank a Victorian**, by Moira Allen
9   **Christmas**, by His Grace the Archbishop of Canterbury *(GOP,* 1881)*
11 **Letters to Santa Claus**, by Mary K. Davis *(The Strand, 1897)*
16 **Christmas Fare for Rich and Poor**, by Lucy Yates *(GOP, 1896)*
17 **Christmas in History** *(GOP, 1896)*
21 **How to Make an Ice Sledge** *(GOP, 1896)*
22 **A Page of Puddings** *(GOP, 1896)*
23 **The Christmas Tree** *(Illustrated London Almanack, 1853)*
25 **Our Christmas Decorations** *(Cassell's Family Magazine, 1885)*
27 **A Christmas Box from "Medicus,"** by Gordon Stables *(GOP, 1892)*
28 **Model Menu for December**, by Phyllis Browne *(GOP, 1893)*
31 **Private Christmas Cards**, by Gleeson White *(GOP, 1896)*
33 **Christmas Day in a London Hospital** *(GOP, 1889)*
34 **Something New** [An Entertainment], by Somerville Gibney *(GOP, 1889)*
35 **Country Scenes: December**, by Thomas Millier *(Illustrated London Almanack, 1848)*
37 **Music: Sweet Christmas Bells** *(Cassell's Family Magazine, 1892)*
39 **Christmas Crackers** *(The Strand, 1891)*
47 **Fiction: The Christmas Tree**, by Lizzie McIntyre *(Godey's Lady's Book, 1860)*
49 **Christmas in Old London**, by Sir Walter Besant *(Cassell's Magazine "Great Christmas Number," 1900)*
58 **Carols and Carol Singers** *(The Home Magazine, 1898)*
59 **December: Christmas Waits**, by Thomas Miller *(Illustrated London Almanack, 1849)*
61 **Home-Made Sweetmeats**, by Edith Brodie *(GOP, 1890)*
63 **Christmas in the New Hospital for Women** [London], by Sophia Caulfield *(GOP, 1884)*
65 **What We Used to Do at Christmas**, by Ruth Lamb *(GOP, 1883)*
69 **Poem: The Return**, by Sydney Grey *(GOP, 1885)*
69 **Christmas With Our Poets**, by T.F. Thiselton Dyer *(GOP, 1885)*
71 **Christmas at Court**, by the Hon. Mrs. H. Armytage *(GOP, 1883)*
73 **Dishes for a Christmas Season**, by Phyllis Browne *(GOP, 1889)*
74 **Poem: Christmas Day on Dartmoor**, by Charles Johns *(GOP, 1885)*
75 **How I Spent Christmas in the Fatherland** *(Cassell's Family Magazine, 1888)*
79 **Christmas in the German Fatherland** *(GOP, 1887)*
80 **Christmas in a French Boarding-School** *(GOP, 1887)*
81 **Christmas Gifts**, by B.C. Saward *(GOP, 1887)*
82 **Chocolate Dates** *(GOP, 1899)*
83 **Music: The Girl's Own Carol**, by Joseph Barnby *(GOP, 1884)*
85 **Swiss Cakes, and How to Make Them**, by L. Stanton *(GOP, 1890)*
86 **Poem: The Plea of the Tom-Tit**, by Jetty Vogel *(GOP, 1885)*
87 **Christmas Card Poets**, by W.J. Wintle *(Windsor Magazine, 1897)*
100 **Poem: In the Olden Time** *(GOP, 1885)*
101 **Useful Hints** *(GOP, 1882)*
101 **Health Recreations: Skating** *(GOP, 1880)*;
103 **Useful Hints: Welcome Guest Pudding** *(GOP, 1880)*
104 **Poem: Greetings**, by Sydney Grey *(GOP, 1883)*
104 **Tobogganing**, by Richard Patterson, J.P. *(GOP, 1890)*
107 **Our Christmas Decorations** *(GOP, 1884)*
108 **Useful Hints** (Recipes) *(GOP, 1880)*
109 **December** *(Illustrated London Almanack, 1845)*
110 **Music: The Angels' Song**, by Frances Ridley Havergal/C.H. Purday *(GOP, 1883)*
111 **Poems: Merry Christmas** - A poetry selection from around the world *(Demorest's Magazine, 1880)*

*GOP = *The Girl's Own Paper/The Girl's Own Annual*

Page	Title
114	**Christmas Dinner Menus/Puddings and Pies for Christmas** *(Demorest's Magazine, 1880)*
117	**Christmas Throughout Christendom** *(Harper's New Monthly Magazine, 1873)*
135	**Poem: Christmas Hymn** *(GOP, 1883)*
135	**Useful Hints** *(GOP, 1883)*
135	**Our Yule-Tide Evergreens,** by Sophia Caulfield *(GOP, 1883)*
138	**Poem: The Frost Spirit,** by Whittier *(GOP, 1889)*
139	**Fiction: The Touching Tale of a Plum Pudding,** by Beatrice Molyneux *(Windsor Magazine, 1897)*
143	**Useful Hints** (Recipes) *(GOP, 1895)*
143	**Music: See, the Dawn from Heaven Is Breaking!** by Thomas More & W.G. Cusins *(GOP, 1886)*
147	**Hints for Christmas Decorations** *(GOP, 1881)*
149	**Useful Hints**
149	**Christmas in Italy** *(GOP, 1887)*
150	**Christmas Day Festivities in Italy** *(GOP, 1897)*
151	**Popular Christmas Festivities in Naples** *(GOP, 1896)*
153	**Our Novel Christmas-Tree** [including a charade], by Ruth Lamb *(GOP, 1880)*
158	**Useful Hints** (Recipes) *(GOP, 1880-1882)*
159	**A Christmas Mystery in the 15th Century,** by Theodore Child *(Harper's New Monthly Magazine, 1888)*
176	**Poem: December** *(Chatterbox, 1873)*
177	**Christmas Sweet Dishes,** by Constance *(GOP, 1892)*
179	**Reminiscences of Christmas,** by An Anglo-Canadian *(GOP, 1891)*
180	**Christmas Parties,** by the Rev. T.F. Thiselton Dyer, M.A. *(GOP, 1889)*
183	**Poem: The Little Christmas Spy,** by Helen Gray Cone *(St. Nicholas Magazine, 1888)*
184	**Christmas Day on the Pavement** *(Illustrated London Almanack, 1855)*
185	**The Queen's Christmas** *(The Home Magazine, 1898)*
186	**Music: A Christmas Carol,** by Cotsford Dick *(GOP, 1882)*
187	**Plum Pudding and Other Receipts for Christmas** *(Godey's Lady's Book, 1863)*
190	**Christmas Table Decorations** *(GOP, 1897)*
191	**Chats About the Calendar: December** *(GOP, 1883)*
193	**Christmas in the Olden Time** *(Peterson's Magazine, 1879)*
197	**Christmas Poultry and Game, and How to Cook It** *(GOP, 1892)*
199	**Christmas Customs Here and Elsewhere,** by William Cowan *(GOP, 1895)*
201	**Music: A Christmas-Tide Remembrance,** by Mrs. Norton/C.A. Macirone *(GOP, 1888)*
204	**December** *(Illustrated London Almanack, 1846)*
205	**The Story of Santa-Claus** *(Little Folks Magazine, 1878)*
207	**The Ancient and Original Mummery of St. George and the Turkish Knight** *(Little Folks Magazine, 1878)*
209	**The Children's Party-Supper** [Recipes], by Lucy Yates *(GOP, 1897)*
211	**Poem: The Christmas Snow,** by Louise W. Tilden *(Young People's Scrapbook, 1884)*
212	**Poem: The Flight of Winter** *(Young People's Scrapbook, 1884)*
213	**The Mistletoe,** by Sutherland Walker *(The Home Magazine, 1898)*
214	**Poem: A Vision of St. Nicholas,** by Clement Moore *(The Strand, 1891)*
217	**Poem: A Vision of Santa Claus,** by Christian Burke *(GOP, 1902)*
217	**Some Curious Christmas Pies and Other Pasties** *(GOP, 1897)*
219	**Christmas Day at Sea** *(Little Folks Magazine, 1878)*
221	**Christmas Fare for Rich and Poor,** by Lucy Yates *(GOP, 1896)*
221	**All About Oranges,** by Phyllis Browne *(GOP, 1892)*
224	**Music: An Old Christmas Carol** [The First Noel] *(GOP, 1881)*
225	**An Original Charade** *(GOP, 1881)*
228	**Diamond Cut Diamond: A Christmas Entertainment,** by Somerville Gibney *(GOP, 1896)*
231	**The Christmas Kalends of Provence,** by Thomas Janvier *(Century Magazine, 1897)*
249	**New Year's Eve,** by Nora Chesson *(GOP, 1902)*
250	**Poem: A Happy New Year,** by Helen Marion Burnside *(GOP, 1894)*
251	**Recipe Index**

Introduction

I confess, I'm addicted to Christmas. I love the lights, the baubles, the sparkle and glitter. I love revisiting my tin of heirloom ornaments. I love finding "the perfect gift;" I even love composing the annual Christmas letter. I also love Victoriana—which leads to, quite naturally, a love of "Victorian Christmas."

I've wanted to put this book together since I first began collecting Victorian magazines. It's one thing to be *told* about Victorian Christmas celebrations in articles written by researchers and enthusiasts; it's quite another to actually *experience* the holiday season as the Victorians did, in their own words and images. In Victorian Britain and America, this was a truly sacred season, beloved and respected.

This book is packed with glimpses into Victorian homes and hearts, giving a rare look at how Christmas was celebrated not just in the fine houses but throughout Victorian society. Who would have imagined that the nurses at a London hospital would take time to make "bran pies" (mock pies stuffed with bran and holding small gifts) for their patients? In this volume, you'll discover Christmas celebrations in Victorian England and America—and in other countries as well. (At the very last minute I made the serendipitous discovery of the article on the "Kalends of Provence" that appears near the end of the volume—a delightful look at French holiday traditions!)

The articles and stories in this collection are drawn from dozens of Victorian magazines, ranging from the 1840's through the end of the century. They come from women's magazines, general-interest publications, even children's magazines. Most of the publications are British, but some (*Godey's, Harper's, Century Magazine, Demorest* and *Peterson's*) are American.

Surprisingly, Victorian magazines weren't actually packed with holiday articles as are our publications today. "Christmas" features tended more toward fiction and poetry than nonfiction "how-to" pieces. Much of the focus during the holiday season was upon morally improving and uplifting literature. I've featured a handful of short stories in this collection, including a delightful look into the life of a rather pompous plum pudding. The story "The Christmas Tree," from *Godey's Lady's Book*, is a good example of the type of story magazines fancied during this season of hope and reconciliation; I include it because it also offers a charming glimpse of just how a Christmas tree would be set up and decorated—and adorned with gifts—for the children of the household.

Nor is every feature in this collection specifically a "Christmas" article. I've included many pages of recipes that would have been welcome at any Victorian holiday celebration, even if they were published at other times of the year. The article on oranges actually appeared in the summer, as oranges were a very seasonal fruit in Victorian times—but today, they are so much a part of our holiday celebrations that I thought it would be lovely to offer some Victorian uses for the fruit. I've ended the collection with a piece on New Year's traditions, because New Year's Day marked the end of the Victorian Christmas "season"—and also because Christmas and New Year's traditions had considerable overlap. On either "eve," one might wassail the apple trees, sing carols, entertain mummers, or attempt to divine whom one's future spouse might be!

Finally, I have sought to make this a true treasury of "presents"—a constantly unfolding selection of surprises, like so many packages beneath the tree. With each turn of the page, you'll find something new: A carol, a poem, a collection of recipes, an account of Christmas folklore from around the world, an explanation of how Christmas crackers are made, a selection of actual letters from Victorian children to Santa Claus. Most of these pieces have never been anthologized before (though you will undoubtedly recognize "A Visit from St. Nicholas"!).

If you love Victoriana—or Christmas—this treasury will be a source of delight and inspiration for years to come. Use it to plan your own special Victorian Christmas—or simply as a way to "travel back in time" to witness this most sacred of holidays in the world of Dickens and Ebenezer Scrooge.

May your Christmas be merry and your New Year be bright!

—Moira Allen
December 2014

SANTA CLAUS.

The Strand, 1891

If You Love Christmas, Thank a Victorian...

What do you love most about Christmas? Is it the tree, with its lights and glittering baubles? Is it "decking the halls" with garlands and greens, until every surface is a magical wonderland? Is it the cards, sent to and received from distant friends, as a reminder and renewal of valued connections? Is it the gifts—and the joy of playing "Santa Claus" for your little ones, ensuring that their stockings are filled and their holiday dreams come true? Is it the food—the special, "let's forget the diet for a week" treats that we make only at this time of year? Is it the joy of gathering with family? Or do you, perhaps, harbor a guilty addiction to Hallmark Christmas fantasy movies, including endless variations on the theme of Dickens' Scrooge?

If you said "yes" to any of these, chances are that your favorite Christmas traditions have been shaped by the Victorian era. While Christmas (obviously) goes back far beyond the 19th century, and many of its traditions date back for centuries, the Victorian period had a huge influence on shaping and moulding the customs that we still practice today. Not so many of us, nowadays, practice such ancient traditions as wassailing the apple trees or carrying in the boar's head (or stuffed peacock) as an essential part of our holiday feast. But a great many of us can't wait to put up the tree, bring out our favorite heirloom ornaments, hang swags of holly and evergreen from the mantel, and send out our holiday greetings near and far.

The Victorians didn't *invent* Christmas—but they *did* manage to *redefine* it. They helped spread the notion that Christmas and Christmas celebrations were for everyone, not just the lord of the manor (i.e., those who could afford boar's heads and stuffed peacocks). Many of our current traditions did indeed find their roots in the Victorian period—Prince Albert, for example, was instrumental in bringing the German "Tannenbaum" to Britain, giving us our brightly lit Christmas tree with all its baubles. (In fact, ironically, Americans have returned the favor, by introducing Germans to the concept of multi-colored lights—the German tradition having been, until the 1980's, to use only clear lights on their trees.) The first Christmas card designed for public consumption was designed in 1843—in part to take advantage of the Victorian development of the "penny post" that made it possible, for the first time, for people to send cards and packages inexpensively throughout Britain.

The Victorians also brought us some of our most cherished Christmas "themes"—from jolly old St. Nick to the beloved Ebenezer Scrooge. These two figures have become the icons of Christmas today—a means by which the "spirit of Christmas" can be expressed and brought alive even for those who prefer not to observe Christmas as a religious holiday. Charles Dickens' *A Christmas Carol* was first published in 1843. Clement Moore's "A Visit from St. Nicholas" actually predates the Victorian period a wee bit (it was first published in 1822)—but its depiction of the "jolly old elf" with his belly "like a bowl full of jelly" helped inspire Thomas Nast's Civil War and post-Civil War drawings of Santa Claus in *Harper's Weekly* (the most iconic being that of 1881). It's thanks to Moore and Nast that, today, we envision Santa as chubby, red-cheeked and red-clad, traveling by a reindeer-drawn sleigh. (Even Moore assumed, however, that Santa might get a bit sooty coming down the chimney!)

With so many of our traditions coming from the Victorian period, it's easy to imagine that what we think of as a classic "Victorian Christmas" was, in fact, the sort of holiday the Victorians themselves celebrated. If you could travel back in time to visit a Victorian family on the eve of this most sacred holiday, however, you might be a bit surprised by what you'd see!

And that's exactly what this book is designed to do: To give you a chance to "travel through time" and experience a true Victorian Christmas. Whether you'd like to learn new ways of Victorian decorating, or discover some authentic Victorian Christmas treats (there are over 200 recipes in this book!), or whether you'd like to get a glimpse of how the Victorians themselves experienced Christmas, it's all here. This is your magical Victorian Christmas tour guide, drawn from the pages of dozens of Victorian magazines from England and the US.

Magazines... Now, right there is one key difference. Today, the magazine shelves are packed with bright volumes promising us new ways to celebrate the holidays—new ways to make wreaths, new decorations, new gifts, new recipes. Since Christmas was such a beloved holiday in Victorian times, I rather expected that Victorian magazines would be similarly packed with articles on how to make the most of the occasion. Instead, Victorian writers and editors used this time to celebrate the *meaning* of Christmas—and December "numbers" were packed with holiday-themed stories and poetry, much of which was rather heavily laden with a moral message.

In reality, "Victorian Christmas" was very much a "work in progress." I've said that the era helped define and mould the traditions that we cherish today—but that moulding process was spread over several decades. Some articles in contemporary magazines seem to indicate that the popularity of Christmas waxed and waned over the 19th century; not everyone, it seems, chose to make a "big deal" out of it. Some looked back with a bit of nostalgia for what was, then, the "old traditional" Christmas (wassail and boar's heads) and wondered a bit about these "newfangled" traditions (Christmas trees and cards).

While the Victorians introduced Christmas cards, for example, we'd probably not recognize many of their favorites as being traditionally "Christmassy." Favorite Victorian Christmas card themes included bouquets of spring and summer flowers, birds, and other decidedly unwintery images. One prize-winning line from Raphael Tuck featured a series of owls in summery landscapes—because apparently nothing says "Victorian Christmas" like an owl on a fencepost!

The Christmas stocking was almost unknown in England; this was primarily an American tradition. In England, gifts were literally hung *on* the Christmas tree. I wondered about this until it dawned on me... No wrapping paper! It wasn't possible yet to produce our colorful, inexpensive paper ("colorful" and "inexpensive" were not words used together in Victorian printing days)—so smaller gifts were placed on the branches of the Christmas tree. Quite often the tree itself was small and stood upon a table; the huge floor-to-ceiling tree was generally reserved for grander, wealthier homes. The Christmas tree itself was almost never decorated (or even brought into the home) until Christmas Eve; then, after the younger children were put to bed, it would be "decked" and the gifts placed on its boughs, to greet the children in its full glory when they awoke on Christmas morning.

Even though Moore and Nast had introduced the concept of a jolly, round Santa with his reindeer, older images of Santa (also known as St. Nicholas or Father Christmas) endured well into the early 20th century. In these older versions, St. Nick is generally depicted as a tall, lean, solemn gentleman, dressed in elegant robes. I have one turn-of-the-century postcard that shows him in a lovely green German hunter's outfit! He is usually, but not always, bearded, and his robes may be just about any color; green, blue and purple (not red!) are the most popular. Reindeer are rarely a part of his ensemble, and if he rides anything, it's often a white horse. Even more interesting is the image that appears just before this introduction; it comes from *The Strand* in 1891, and is titled "Santa Claus"—but shows a glowing child, more reminiscent of the Christkindle (Christ child) who brings gifts in parts of Europe.

Victorian Christmas was very much a DIY experience—part of the joy was creating your own decorations and gifts. Those of us who enjoy decorating with more natural elements would have found kindred spirits amongst Victorian girls, who scoured the woods for pine cones and holly and other "found" items to create their decorations. (City dwellers could purchase all manner of greenery brought to "town" for the occasion.) Glitter hadn't been invented yet, so to bring sparkle to the décor, decorators either ground up glass bottles "saved for the purpose," or, on the safer side, soaked their greens and then sprinkled them with Epsom salts. And yes, lighting the tree meant... lighting dozens of tiny candles!

If you could ask a Victorian about the "meaning" of Christmas, however, you'd find that trees and wreaths and Christmas cards are not the only traditions that the Victorians have passed along to us. For them, these were simply the trappings. The "meaning" lay far deeper. As one article puts it, Christmas was a time that "brought peasant and peer together"—it transcended class boundaries, and reminded its participants of the duty owed by those who "had" to those who "had not." Christmas was a time of giving—not just of filling the stockings of one's own children, but of ensuring that children who had no stockings might actually have a pair of shoes, or a warm meal. St. Nicholas and Ebenezer Scrooge brought the same message, then as now, on this day of days, reminding celebrants that this was meant to be a season of giving, not just getting.

In that, I believe, we stand united with the past. Lighting the neighborhood is lovely; lighting hearts is lovelier still. It is the season of "Peace on earth, good will to men"—and as Tiny Tim would remind us, "God bless us, everyone."

—Moira Allen
December 2014

Christmas.

By HIS GRACE THE ARCHBISHOP OF CANTERBURY.

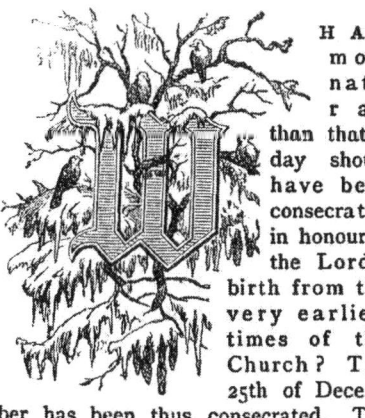

WHAT more natural than that a day should have been consecrated in honour of the Lord's birth from the very earliest times of the Church? The 25th of December has been thus consecrated. The date of the first observance of this day cannot indeed be given with certainty; neither can we tell now on the authority of what tradition or history its consecration rests. It may or may not have been engrafted on the Jewish Festival of the Dedication, which was in the winter; or have been made to take the place of a Roman holiday which marked the closing year. The Christians of the Western Church adopted the observance at that season very early, though some uncertainty prevails as to the exact day. It would seem that for a time in the East the commemoration of the birth of Christ and of His manifestation to the wise men were combined. But dismissing minute antiquarian questions, we can have no doubt that our present Christmas Day has been hallowed by the worship of fourteen centuries.

Not an unimportant thought is thus suggested. Are we thankful to know that the doctrines preached to us now and here in England are those which the Apostles derived straight from the Lord Himself? Do we prize the two Sacraments as gracious gifts direct from Christ, which have nourished spiritual life in the Church since He first appointed them? Is it well that we should remember that the facts embodied in the Church's creed are the very same which we find in the four Gospels? Still, we shall be unwise not to prize also, according to the degree of their importance, many words expressing doctrines and many forms of worship which come to us indeed without directly divine sanction, but the value of which has been proved by their being helps to piety for many centuries.

There are many divisions amongst Christians in the present day, and many things divide us here in England in this 19th century from the Christians of the old times. Yet all the faithful in Christ in all ages form one body through their union with Him; and every word, or rite, or ceremony is to be prized which has become venerable as the means of keeping up this union. When, therefore, we gather together in church on the 25th of December, it will be well to think what a multitude of redeemed spirits have, in all lands and in all ages during this long time, been helped, by the observance of Christmas Day, better to express their thankfulness for that wonderful condescension which brought the Eternal Son of God to begin His life on this lower earth as a helpless infant that He might redeem us.

Is there joy in every family when a child is born into the world? And does it please us to keep our own and our friends' birthdays, notwithstanding all the uncertainty of coming happiness or misery which must throw some shadow over the brightest mere human life? And is it not right that we should celebrate with joy and thankfulness the birthday of Him whose coming upon earth has dispelled so many sorrows and opened to all of us such bright hopes of joy eternal? Every ordinance, then, and arrangement of our worship which helps us better to realise the greatness of the gift to man of Christ's birth is much to be prized.

In Roman Catholic countries it is common to exhibit in church at the Christmas season some outward image of the Holy Babe and His Mother and Joseph, with the shepherds and the oxen standing round. To our English and Protestant ideas there seems to be a childishness and even a coarseness in such representations which we do not think suitable to the simple majesty of the worship due to the great mystery of the Incarnation. It is true that unlettered Italian peasants, whose whole life and training has been very different from our own, may have the truths of the Gospel forced on their imaginations by such sights; and young children can probably admire them, feeling that the Christ thus represented in His infancy is brought very near to their simple minds.

After all, these representations may, in a certain stage of knowledge and feeling, have much the same effect as some noble picture of the Holy Family executed by a great painter has on the educated and refined. It is not denied that under quite different circumstances to ours they may be helps to devotion. What is to be guarded against in such representations is, not their setting forth a vivid image of the sacred history, but, first, their tendency to give a somewhat low idea of what the Lord Jesus Christ is in His Divine Majesty; and, secondly, that they may be used, as these certainly have been in some countries, to withdraw the mind from Christ Himself to the worship of the human mother, to whom the Heavenly Babe was subject.

But though we may not feel any inclination to imitate this kind of representation by which Roman Catholics seek to recall the history of Christ's birth, we are right to mark the Christmas season by such decent alterations in our churches as custom and the manner of our worshp approve as suitable. There has been a great change in this respect in our churches of late years. We are not necessarily the better for this—but certainly we are not the worse—and we may well be the better if we use the signs of an outward adornment to impress more vividly on our minds the reality and importance of heavenly truths. We are not to make too much of these things either in opposing or approving of them. They are things indifferent which may have a very good use.

I remember when I first went to live in the extreme north of England there was scarcely a single church within many miles of our cathedral city in which any green boughs or other decorations were allowed to mark the Christmas season. I do not think the people in that district were either better or more staunch in the reformed faith because their churches, usually very poor edifices, carelessly kept in order, were thus bare. There always seemed something cheering when I came to the south again about the Christmas season, and found every church in its simple way getting ready to proclaim in all our villages that there ought to be thankful joy for the birth of Christ. Let these things never be matters of contention. Let them be used to express that our religion is full of happiness and to help us to think more of its doctrines and the practical lessons they teach. Thus shall we use these outward symbols aright.

Was Christ once a little child? This speaks to us of the blessedness of a holy childhood, reared in a holy home, and taught with its dawning reason to welcome holy thoughts.

Did He not afterwards call little children to Him? Did He not take them in His arms and bless them? Did He not tell us that in simplicity His disciples must become as little children?

Christmas is the festival of the childhood. All who have to deal with children may learn many special lessons from it besides its general lessons for us all.

The Girl's Own Paper, 1881

"UNDER THE MISTLETOE." BY A. HUNT.—FROM "THE ILLUSTRATED LONDON NEWS."

The Illustrated London Almanack, 1867

Letters to Santa Claus.

By Mary K. Davis.

SOME years back a little boy wrote a letter to Santa Claus asking for a box of paints. The letter was addressed as shown below.

The postman, unfortunately, did not know where Santa lived, so he took the letter to the post-office, and, in course of time, the little boy received the box of paints. Nothing, I think, could more clearly prove that Santa, by some mysterious means, is accessible to all children through the mail.

Children certainly think so. Every year Santa's post-bag is filled with letters from boys and girls in all parts of the Christian world, and the wonder is, not how Santa can find time to read them all in so many different languages, but how they ever get to him. Santa's address has never been divulged. The little old man with the grey beard and fur-coat, who comes from somewhere in one short night and leaves something nice in the stocking of every good boy and girl, disappears as quickly as he comes, and for a whole year lives in seclusion, where no person can reach him. So far as is known, there is one man in the post-office who knows the correct address. How else would the boy have got his box of paints? But this man will not tell his secret. Some think, I believe, that Santa calls in person once a year at the post-office to receive his mail, but as no one has ever seen him, the supposition must be abandoned as untrue.

With the whereabouts of Santa I have, of course, little to do, but it seems to me that the safest way for small boys and girls to reach him by mail is to let father or mother act as amanuensis. The letter will then be written, stamped, and directed in the best possible manner, and no delay will take place in the mails. The girl who addressed the envelope shown at the foot of this page, "Blaes letter-man give this to Santa Cause", was greatly disappointed at not getting an answer from Santa on Christmas Eve, but the New York letterman who picked it out of the box took such a long time trying to find Santa's address in the directory, that Santa did not get the letter until after he had started on his trip.

In every well-regulated post-office there is a corps of "guessers" and directory searchers, who are kept for the express purpose of finding out where people live, when addresses are carelessly or not fully written out. Last year a letter came to the post-office, post-marked New York, with the superscription "To Santa Claus, 263, Goat Street." There is no Goat Street in New York, so the letter was stamped "misdirected," as in the reproduction above, and sent to Washington, where, it was supposed, Goat Street might be found. The clerks thought that fuller directions might be discovered inside, so they opened the envelope, and found the following letter:—

Dear Santa,—When I said my prayers last night I told God to tell you to bring me a hobby horse. I don't want a hobby horse, really. A honestly live horse is what I want. Mamma told me not to ask for him, because I probably would make you mad, so you wouldn't give me anything at all, and if I got him I wouldn't have any place to keep him. A man I know will keep him, he says, if you get him for me. I thought you might like to know. Please don't be mad.—Affectionately, JOHN.

P.S.—A Shetland would be enough.

P.S.—I'd rather have a hobby horse than nothing at all.

I am very sorry to say that John did not get the horse. Little boys who don't do as their mothers tell them find little favour with Santa Claus.

The desires of some children are not very great, and Santa is always pleased with modest children. Down in Norfolk there is a family containing four of the brightest boys and girls to be found within many a mile, and these children lately sent off a batch of letters to Santa, which were admirable, and pleased Santa very much. I quote them together:—

Dear Santa Claus
I should very much like a teaset will you kindly send me one please I should be so thinkful if you would sed me from Yours truely Rosa

dear Santa claus pleas will you send me a nice doll with black eyes nice cloas on it from Maretta

dear Santa Claus i should realy like a tin wistle with red marks on it
Yours truly
Charlie

dear Santy clawes i should lik a nice little doll with brown eys black hear will you let me have one please from Marion

An interesting story is told about the following envelope, which passed through the New York Post Office on December 16th of last year. One of the officials was standing with the envelope in his hands, and turning round to another official, he said, "Here is a

letter to Santa Claus, addressed to Air Street. Where is Air Street?" "Why, don't you know?" answered the second official, who had children at home. "Air Street's in the town where the sun rises." The letter was duly delivered.

On this page two superscriptions are reproduced, which show how ideas regarding Santa's address differ. The first, addressed to the North Pole, Siberia, was evidently written by a father at the child's dictation, and failed in reaching its destination because

the father had neglected to stamp it. Note the round mark on the envelope, with "Held for Postage" stamped thereon by some assiduous post-office clerk. The second letter was addressed to the Green Mountains, Vermont, probably because Vermont is one of the many places in the United States where the Christmas trees come from. "Where," thought this little one, "should Santa live but in the land of Christmas trees?"

There is a little London boy who wrote a rather pathetic note to Santa trying to

appease him for having eaten up a pot of jelly which some kind lady had given to the said boy when he had the measles. Here is what he wrote :—

My dear Santa Claus

Christmas will soon be here, and I spect you are very busy geting your presents ready. You did not forget me last year and the things you brought me were booful. How did you stweze down our small chimley the toys were not a bit smuty. Dear Santa Claus my mama says you only come to good boys and girls. I had the meesels wonce and a kind lady gave me a pot of jelly. I thot I would help my self and ate it all up at wonce. I hope dear Santy Claus you will forget this cos I did like that jelly. Plese bring me a bicykel You cant put that in my stocking or through the chimley but I will ask my daddy to put the door open for you to come in Plese bring a monkey on a stick for my baby brother and a walking stick for my daddy. He has a lot of walking about and his air is getting gray. My stocking is big so plese pop in sweets and nuts and a big pot of jelly. I wont eat it all at wonce. I hope dear Santy Claus you will not have a bad cold or the meesels, and not be able to come.

My name is
Percy ——

I haven't the slightest doubt that Santa Claus would look with favour on this appeal, and we all hope that Santa will never have the "meesels."

A dear little six-year-old girl, who lives not many miles from Charing Cross, also put her wishes on paper, which is, after all, one of the safest ways to get what you want. I wish we could reproduce the pages of the original letter, but the letter has been passed on to Santa. Here is our copy of it:—

My dear Santa Claus.
I hope you are twite well and hab dot a sack full ob nice toys to dive away. You didnt fordet me last Twismas. You brought me a horse and tart and a lot of buns, nuts and sweets. Pwease, dear Daddy Twismas, will you bwing me a lantern this Twismas, will you bwing me a big ball and some sweets. I tink you will be able to queeze em frough de shimney. Will you bwing my baby sister a wag dolly wiv long close and a lot ob sugar ticks. My dear dada would yike a bicycle to dow to work wiv, he has de scrumatics in his bid toe and has to walk wid a stick. My bedroom hab dot a berry bid shimney I tink dere will be woom for you to det down. I will sut my eyes tight and be fast asleep while you are bwinging dem down frou de shimney. So dont fordet. Dood-bye, dear Daddy Twismas, I am longing for you to tum from Jack in the box.

Another letter, written by a girl of seven, who is sometimes "norty," was sent off some time ago, in order that Santa might have a good opportunity to get the doll's baby carriage and the "squeak cat for the baby."

My Dear Santa Claus.
I hope you are quite well. I have got a great big stocking reddy to hang up at Xmas. There is only one big hole in it at the top for you to put the things in. Plese bring me a dolls pram. If it is too big to put in my stocking plese tie it outside where I can see it. Dear Santa Claus I do like butter scotch, plese not forget to bring some, also some nuts and oranges. My teacher tells me you will look at my face to see if I have been good. I am norty some times but plese dont forget me, and bring a horse and cart for my little Tommy and a squeak cat for the baby. I love you very much and ope you will not forget poor little Jimmy who lives at Hope Cottage.

For individuality, and expression of a sweet womanly nature, the following letter, written by an eleven-year-old girl, could hardly be surpassed:—

My Dear Santa Claus
I have been counting up the weeks to Christmas and am longing for the time to come. You have put something in my stocking lots of times so please Dear Santa Claus remember me again. Last year I wanted a dear little baby a real live one you know but I suppose it was too cold and besides I did not write to you as I am doing now, so it did not come. Please bring me one this year. a little girl if you can. I have saved money enough to buy a cradle, and I can get plenty of flannelette to keep it warm. Dear Santie a dear lady gave me your photo. It is hanging in my bedroom, and when I look at it I think you must be

Dear Santa Claus
I'se havent seen you for a wery, wery long time, and i want Chistmas to come fast. i shall hang my

great great grandi father's stocking up, so you will be able to bring me a doll a boat, and house and lots of buns and sweets and tarts. Deer Daddy

> Christmas do bring me a likle funny live doggie to mind my daddy's house. Who are you Santie? I nebber sees you tumming down the chimberley. Do you ebber see de beglers when you walk on the roof. I spects you does but nebber mind Santie I loves you a great big lump. Please bring my things in your sack to
>
> Diney Dumpling
> Long Alley

getting very old, and I am sure your legs must ake a good deal at Christmas, when you have to get up and down so many chimneys. If you find the inflewenza coming on, drink a good big glassful of hot lemon water and nosset yourself up or a lot of little boys and girls will be disappointed. As babies are so expensive I will not ask for anything else for myself, but kindly remember my dear Dad by popping in a pair of woollen socks to keep his toes warm when he goes to church, and a warm comfort to tie round his mouth to keep the fog from getting down his throat. Please bring a chooky pig for my little Clement. He will be nearly two years old then. Good-bye dear Daddy Christmas, with my best love, hoping you will not forget little Gertie.

P.S.—If you really do manage to bring the baby, please not forget the feeding bottle.

Most children, when they write, sign nicknames, thinking, perhaps, that Santa will recognise them more quickly by their pet names than by their more formal appellations. The five-year-old girl who wrote the interesting letter reproduced in facsimile above is down on the register of births as Dinah Denton, but little Dinah preferred to sign her pet-name. I know that Santa Claus will not forget Long Alley on his rounds, and that Diney, on Christmas morning, may be the happy possessor of a doll, even if her daddy doesn't get "a likle funny live doggie" to mind his house.

CHRISTMAS FARE FOR RICH AND POOR.

A Turkish Fig-Pudding.—One pound of best figs finely chopped, one pound of breadcrumbs, half a pound of suet, finely shred, quarter of a pound of moist sugar, two ounces of candied peel, one ounce of ground almonds, half a nutmeg grated, three eggs well beaten, and a wineglassful of sherry. Boil—or steam —for two hours and a half, and serve with wine sauce.

Now let us look at some Christmas cakes. Still remembering the poor and needy, here is a cake that cuts up splendidly for school-parties, and one that is a capital stand-by for the home table also.

School-Treat Cake.—To each pound of flour add half a pound of mixed fruit, currants, raisins, and sultanas, two ounces of shred candied peel, a quarter of a pound of brown sugar, six ounces of butter or good beef-dripping, half a teaspoonful of spice, one teaspoonful and a half of baking-powder, half a teaspoonful of salt, and cold milk to mix to the consistency of soft dough; no eggs.

Beat together the sugar and the butter, mix first all the dry ingredients, then work in the butter and make up with the milk. Make up into rather large cakes, and let them be nearly a week old before using. Above all bake gently, but in a good hot oven, and test them with a skewer to make sure they are done through.

The two following recipes are for cakes that are somewhat uncommon, but essentially appropriate for Yule-tide. The first pre-supposes the possession of a bottle of elderberry wine, which most country households are sure to have in stock.

A Seasonable Cake.—The excellence of this will depend upon the care exercised in its mixing and baking. Beat to a cream six ounces of fresh butter and the same weight of moist sugar (brown). Add to these three well-beaten eggs and a tumblerful (half pint) of elderberry wine, beat together, then stir in gradually twelve ounces of flour, to which has been added half a pound of rich raisins, stoned and cut small, a quarter of a pound of candied orange peel, and a large teaspoonful of powdered allspice. It is important that the dry ingredients should have been well-mixed together. Stir lightly, then pour into a shallow tin well-buttered, and bake in a moderate oven for quite an hour. It should be a rich-brown colour, and if carefully made is little inferior to wedding-cake.

Almond Simnel Cake.—Make two separate mixtures, one of cake and one of almond icing. For the former beat together six ounces each of butter and sugar, then add four eggs (beaten), two ounces of rice-flour, six ounces of dry flour, and two ounces of mixed candied peel cut very fine. Mix well, then pour half the quantity into a round buttered cake tin, put in half an inch layer of almond icing, then the remainder of the cake mixture. Bake in a moderate oven for forty minutes, test it to see if it be cooked through, and then spread the top with another layer of almond icing, and when that is set, cover the cake all over with sugar icing. Keep two days before cutting.

For the almond icing pound together six ounces of blanched sweet and one ounce of bitter almonds, two ounces of castor sugar and the whites of two eggs.

We all admire *Cherry Cake*, but we cannot all make it for ourselves; the following is a reliable recipe. Half a pound of butter beaten to a cream, half a pound of castor sugar, the yolks of five eggs, quarter of a pound of ground rice, half a pound of flour, two ounces of candied peel cut in shreds, half a pound of candied cherries and the whites of the eggs whisked stiff. Mix the ingredients in the order given above. Bake gently and ice the top, decorating according to fancy.

When the boys and girls are home from school it becomes necessary to have some cake always at hand, but it need not to be a rich or costly one. A plum cake made with yeast is so wholesome and good that it invariably finds itself a warm welcome in the play-room; it is at its best when a fortnight old, and should, therefore, be made in good time.

Yeast Plum Cake.—To four pounds of flour, one pound of butter and dripping mixed together (rubbed into the flour), one pound of brown sugar, one pound of stoned raisins, one pound of dried currants, quarter of a pound of candied peel, two ounces of treacle, large teaspoonful of mixed spice, same of ground ginger, three ounces of yeast, two eggs, and a pint and a quarter of milk.

Rub together flour, butter, a teaspoonful of salt, the spice, sugar and fruit. Make a well in the centre, into which pour the dissolved yeast, the eggs, and a teacupful of milk; with these make a "sponge," and when that has risen work up the cake, using the remainder of the milk. It should be a little softer than bread dough. Let it rise for two or three hours, then make into cakes and bake in a moderately quick oven. Should yield ten pounds of cake.

But a truce to cakes and sweet things; let us consider something savoury. Here is a *Game Pie* that is made without game; and a very useful and excellent dish it is.

First of all a forcemeat must be prepared from half a pound of calf's liver and the same quantity of fat bacon; both cooked until thoroughly tender in a covered vessel, then pounded to a paste in a mortar. When thoroughly reduced add a good teaspoonful of mixed savoury herbs, half a teaspoonful of black pepper, mustard and mace and salt, also a few bread-crumbs, mix quite smoothly with two yolks of eggs. Make some good raised-pie crust, and shape or line a tin mould, place a few strips of fat bacon at the bottom, then a layer of this forcemeat, fill up with boned joints of fowls, rabbits, or anything available at the time.

Fill up all the spaces with forcemeat, lay a little more bacon at the top, then put on the top crust, garnish and bake. When the pie is nearly done it should be taken out of the tin, brushed all over with beaten egg and put back to become richly browned. This may be eaten hot, but it is better cold; a little strong gravy added after it has finished baking is an improvement.

Another excellent savoury dish for a large family (or a substantial dish for the poor man's supper party, we have borne in mind all along) is *Beef à la Mode.*—For this the ribs rolled round, or a piece off the "round" of beef is the most suitable part. If the latter, lard it with long strips of salted pork by the aid of a larding-needle. At the bottom of an earthen stew-pan lay a slice or two of fat bacon, then several small onions left whole, two carrots cut in rounds, a few pepper-corns and a bunch of savoury herbs. Lay the meat upon this and place more vegetables and bacon above and around that, pour a teacupful of water over and half a teacupful of vinegar. Cover closely, set in the corner of the oven and cook gently for three or four hours. When intended for eating cold it should be left untouched in the vessel until almost cold, then lifted out, the gravy drawn away from the fat and clarified, adding a little dissolved gelatine to it and the meat glazed with it at intervals. The rounds of carrot should be stamped out into patterns and furnish a garnish for the dish with tufts of parsley and horse-radish.

While we have puff-paste about when making our mince-pies, we may usefully employ a portion for some

Savoury Patties.—For the filling of these the remains of cold game, poultry, or very nice meat with ham or cooked bacon, if cut very small and gently simmered in strong thick gravy and highly seasoned will prove excellent; or cold boiled fish, flaked and heated in white sauce, or picked shrimps in sauce that is flavoured with anchovy, may be used instead. A teaspoonful of the "filling" is sufficient for each patty. These are capital for breakfast, luncheon, or supper.

The mention of mince-pies reminds us that our page of Christmas fare will not be thought complete unless it include a recipe for mincemeat, although that has, doubtless, been given nearly every previous year.

Mincemeat.—Made four weeks in advance. Six pounds of russet apples, pared, cored, and finely chopped, two pounds of minced beef suet, three pounds of well-washed currants, two pounds of stoned raisins, half a pound of lemon and orange peel, nutmegs, cinnamon, and mixed spice, two teaspoonfuls of each, three teaspoonfuls of ground ginger, one teaspoonful of salt, two pounds of brown sugar, half a pint of brandy.

A frequent stirring is desirable for the first week after making this, then it may be put up in jars and tied down. It will keep good for three months at least.

The above quantities will be sufficient for a hundred moderate pies.

L. H. YATES.

CHRISTMAS IN HISTORY.

To judge by the slight references made to the subject in the magazines and newspapers of the last century, Christmas was not so very much thought of in England until, as husband of the present Queen, Prince Albert came over from Germany to revive its popularity. It would have been quite reasonable if a German family, on settling down in this insular home, had brought their national customs with them, and if this had been so Christmas-trees would have struck root in the English national affection more than a century earlier than is found to have been the case. We are probably still somewhat behind the Germans in our enthusiasm for observing this season, but in a degree which could hardly have been understood by our ancestors, we have learned to make Christmas pre-eminently the season for the enjoyment of children and young people. A century and a half ago, under the rule of the foreign King George II., London at the approach of Christmas would not have shown any such enlivening spectacle as is the case to-day. The butchers and the grocers might have shown greater supplies than usual, but there were no Christmas numbers or annuals as we understand them; and only short and casual notices of the season occurred in the newspapers, if, indeed, anything at all was said about the subject. The keeping of Christmas seems even to have declined since the preceding century, for under the Stuarts before the Revolution the festival appears to have been observed with an enthusiasm and a splendour surpassing anything to be seen in any other of the nations of Europe.

As we try to realise what Christmas in the abbey or the baronial castle in pre-Reformation days was, we may recall a few of those old-time sayings which were once, as it were, current coin. Thus, "After Christmas comes Lent," reminded those who were disposed to be too roystering or convivial, that fasting might really be better for them than feasting. On the other hand, those who looked too lingeringly on the joys that were gone, that "Another year will bring another Christmas." The French had a proverb, "Christmas is talked of so long it comes at last." In the reign of Elizabeth, old Tusser gave forth his ringing couplet—

"At Christmas play, and make good cheer;
For Christmas comes but once a year."

The saying, "A green Christmas a white Easter," was probably taken seriously in a day when those who had mastered the arts of reading and writing were naturally supposed also to possess the gifts of the seer. The supposition that mild weather in midwinter was unhealthy, was of course founded in mere prejudice. What we know is, that "A green Christmas" is more healthy than a frosty and foggy one, such as occasionally afflicts modern London.

In the year that William I. made the conquest of England, Christmas Day fell on Monday, and being the antipodes of Midsummer the Saxons called the festival Midwinter Day. That was the time that the Conqueror chose for his coronation. As the Saxon chronicle tells, Archbishop Aldred consecrated the king at Westminster, and at the same time gave him possession of "the books of Christ" as well as of the kingdom. It being Christmas Day, the churchman may have thought that, in a sense, he occupied vantage-ground. At all events, before he would consent to place the crown on the king's head, he made him swear that he would govern the land as well or better than

DISTRIBUTING THE MISTLETOE.

CANDLEMAS

any ruler who had preceded him. It was a strange kind of ceremony altogether which took place in the Abbey on that winter day. In the first place Aldred of York was selected for the ceremony because Stigand of Canterbury was then engaged in quarrelling with the Pope. Though the people and nobles had no choice in the matter when William had won his place by conquest, the archbishop was apparently as particular to have both sides agreed as to the new era, as if he had before him a coy bride hesitating to accept a rough husband who was eager to possess her. When he asked the native nobles if they would give their allegiance to their new king, the affirmative response was so hearty, that the Norman guards outside mistook the noise for a growl of discontent. Houses were set on fire and many lives were lost, so that it was a woful Christmas night for London.

The great abbey of St. Albans was one of the most magnificent buildings of mediæval England, and on Christmas Day, 1115, when the then new structure was consecrated, one of the most imposing spectacles which that age could afford was witnessed, the king, Henry I., and his wife, Matilda of Scotland, being among the guests. Abbot Richard, who held office during the building, must on that occasion have felt somewhat of the satisfaction of an ambitious ecclesiastic who had realised to the utmost his fondest day-dreams. The queen was there not only as a guest, but as a benefactress who had given two manors to the abbey, and to meet her and the king were the Archbishop of Rouen, a number of Anglican bishops, nobles, and other eminent persons. The festivities, which commenced on Christmas Day, were kept up for nearly a fortnight, or until January 6, our present Old Christmas Day. In *The Golden Book of St. Albans* in the British Museum, and described as "a kind of conventual album," containing a list of benefactors and the amount of their donations, is to be seen the only portrait existing of Matilda.

Anybody rambling around St Albans, and visiting the church, will be thankful that this portion of the ancient abbey is so well preserved. In connection with Abbot Richard's great Christmas party in 1115, we should bear in mind that the older structure had become ruinous at the time of the Conquest, and despite the barbarous character of the times, the whole was now rebuilt with a magnificence which might well inspire our modern builders with despair.

Christmas appears to have been much thought of in those rough days when kings and nobles seemed to regard war as their natural occupation. Thus, two years later, when the king had to leave England to put down a revolt in Normandy, he and his son thought it worth their while to pay a hasty visit to England in order to keep Christmas with the queen. Father, mother and son then met for the last time. As regards Henry I., however, the Saxon annals make further reference to his Christmas merry-making in later life. Thus, in 1126, we find him observing the festive season at Windsor in accordance with his own tastes, his chief table-companion then being his second Queen, Adelicia of Louvaine, otherwise the Fair Maid of Brabant.

"Boxing Day" as we understand it was probably unknown in the twelfth century; but December 26th being the feast of St. Stephen, the successor of Henry I. chose to be crowned on what he called his "Name-day." This was in 1135, and it is one of the most sunny memories of Stephen's inauspicious reign. Twelve years later, or in 1147, the season was observed by Stephen and his queen with a greater degree of splendour, however. The reason of this extra outlay was the fact that amid snow and wintry blast a few nights previously, the Empress Matilda, the claimant to the throne and therefore the troubler of Stephen's peace, had left Oxford Castle for the Continent. The king and queen happened to be at Lincoln, and among the superstitious prophecies current in that day—the midnight of the mediæval age—was one to the effect that some unknown evil would happen to any king of England who should presume to appear in Lincoln Cathedral on Christmas Day dressed in royal robes and wearing the crown. Notwithstanding the seers, and "against the advice of his sagest counsellors, both temporal and spiritual," as Agnes Strickland tells us, the king attended service in state and returned home unscathed. With all his faults, Stephen may have been in advance of the follies of a time when the highest ecclesiastics and the greatest politicians were the slaves of superstitious fears.

In times of semi-barbarism and of abounding ignorance, extreme splendour in dress was so far removed from being any indication of moral worth, that low or even degraded natures might be seen as the chief slaves of such weakness. Probably few of us have any higher appreciation of the character of King John than his own nobles had when, with ominous threats in their scowling eyes, they compelled him to sign Magna Charta; but, however small the attractions of this precious adventurer may have been in other respects, Miss Strickland declares he was "the greatest fop in Europe." If we ask how so, the answer is that, "At one of his Christmas festivals he appeared in a red satin mantle embroidered with sapphires and pearls, a tunic of white damask, a girdle set with garnets and sapphires, while the baldric that crossed from his left shoulder to sustain his sword was set with diamonds and emeralds, and his white gloves were adorned, one with a ruby and the other with a sapphire." This seems to present to us a curious side of John's degraded character. He liked to honour Christmas-tide; and we have to think of such an exquisite sitting-down to a feast, compared with which our modern elegant repasts would show but a meagre provision. Thus the kitchens of a royal castle would then have fireplaces and appliances for roasting oxen whole—an appetising royal dish, indeed, if the cook were only master of his art, and also knew how to prepare a seasonable piquant sauce. As regards the necessity for thus roasting oxen whole, it may have been found in the immense consumption of beef at a great feast in those days, when a multitude would need to be fed at once such as would never enter into our modern calculations. Take, by way of example, the feast given by the Archbishop of York at Christmas, 1251, when his guests included the royal families of England and Scotland. Alexander III. of the latter kingdom, aged twelve, was married to Margaret, daughter of Henry I. and Eleanor of Provence. There was a great Christmas party, at which, according to the old chronicler, 600 oxen were eaten at one repast. When we realise that 2000 persons would not dine amiss if they were now to consume an ox, this looks like exaggeration; but mediæval oxen were not such as ours, and the common people when they sat down to a feast probably attacked the viands with the appetites of cannibals.

The Scottish nation has never taken to Christmas so cordially as the English; and although in these times we might go to Scotland at Christmas-tide, we should hardly think of going thither to keep Christmas. In 1304 Edward I. and his wife, Marguerite of France, kept Christmas Day at Dunfermline, under very exceptional circumstances. The unhappy

As a Royalist Evelyn has a somewhat doleful entry for Christmas Day, 1654, when the season was supposed to be "abolished" by the Puritans of the Commonwealth. As no churches were open or public assembly allowed, Evelyn says, "I was fain to pass the devotions of that blessed day with my family at home." As might have been expected, it was afterwards found that the love of Christmas was so engrafted on the public mind that it could not be put aside, notwithstanding the penalties to which those persons exposed themselves who kept the season after the old English manner. It was on Christmas Day, 1655, that Evelyn makes his most mournful entry in regard to what he regarded as the iron rule then prevailing:

"I went to London, where Dr. Wild preached the funeral sermon of preaching, this being the last day; after which Cromwell's proclamation was to take place, that none of the Church of England should dare either to preach or administer sacraments, teach schools, etc., on pain of imprisonment or exile. So this was the mournfullest day that in my life I have seen, or the Church of England herself, since the Reformation, to the great rejoicing of both Papist and Presbyter. So pathetic was his discourse, that it drew many tears from the auditory. Myself, wife, and some of our family received the communion; God make me thankful, who hath hitherto provided for us the food of our souls as well as bodies. The Lord Jesus Christ pity our distressed church, and bring back the captivity of Zion."

A year later, or in 1656, Evelyn attended "an assembly of devout and sober Christians" at Dr. Wild's lodgings.

We find that a man like Evelyn would have money given him to distribute in charity at the festive season. Christmas, 1683, was remarkable for its excessive cold, and also for a severe epidemic of small-pox. It was one of those phenomenal winters to which we may in any year be exposed in this high latitude, but of which a person may grow old and know nothing. The ice on the Thames became sufficiently strong for streets of booths to be set up upon it. The river was really frozen over before Christmas Day; and early in January Evelyn says: "I went across the Thames on the ice, now become so thick as to bear not only streets of booths, in which they roasted meat and had divers shops of wares quite across, as in a town, but coaches, carts, and horses passed over." A little later we find Evelyn going to Sayes Court to look into the condition of his garden. "I found many of the greens and rare plants utterly destroyed," he says. "The oranges and myrtles very sick, the rosemary and laurels dead to all appearance, but the cypress likely to endure it." At the time that was supposed to have been the coldest winter which had ever occurred in the memory of man. Evelyn sent a report of the season to the

pleasant, fine, and delicate," remarked the young Virgin Queen, "and henceforth I will wear no more cloth stockings."

Passing from the sixteenth to the seventeenth century, we find several references to the festive season in Evelyn's Diary and Correspondence. Being in Rome on Christmas Eve, 1644, he tells how he walked about all night, going from one church to another "in admiration at the multitude of scenes and pageantry which the friars had with much industry and craft set out to catch the devout women and superstitious sort of people." On Christmas Day the Pope sang Mass, while a representation of the cradle of Christ was exhibited.

northern kingdom was supposed to be completely subdued, and the king was desirous that the queen should undertake the journey from England, in order to judge of the thoroughness of his work. The war, indeed, had been so successful, that the great patriot, William Wallace, was a captive soon to be judicially murdered; but the roads through which Marguerite was obliged to pass were infested with armed desperadoes, which rendered them extremely dangerous. We do not envy Edward his merrymaking under such conditions, for we seem to think that there must have been mocking spectres at the feast.

Philippa of Hainault, queen of Edward III., was welcomed by the Londoners to her adopted country on December 23, 1327, and on Christmas Day, and for some days afterwards, there were feasts and rejoicings in the old city on the royal bride's account. We find that a great number of the clergy, in "solemn procession," went before when she entered the city; and then the Lord Mayor, on behalf of the guilds he represented, presented a service of plate of the value of £300 —no mean offering when money was worth many times over what it is to-day. Some months previously a commercial treaty between England and the Low Countries, and which promised to be profitable to the Londoners, had been completed, the prospect of its advantages no doubt stimulating the loyalty of the merchants, the smaller traders, and their apprentices.

We pass from the fourteenth to the fifteenth century, and, while doing this, it may be interesting to remember that from one Christmas Day to another, from the beginning of a century to its end, the wax-lights at the tomb of Edward I.'s beloved Eleanor have been kept burning night and day, and that they will burn on until put out by the light of the Reformation in the sixteenth century. The scene we now look upon is at Eltham, and the time is the Christmas of 1413, where in the old suburban palace Henry IV. and Jane of Navarre are spending their last Christmas together. It was a sombre, or even a sorrowful, occasion; for, in addition to an accusing conscience, the king had become so afflicted in body that his days on earth were fast drawing to a close. Henry was an epileptic, and the eruptions on his face, which sorely disfigured his once comely countenance, were declared by some to be a judgment on him for many misdeeds. There was good reason for keeping the season in seclusion; and the crown, once so eagerly desired, was now found to press heavily on the brow, if it was not actually the symbol of cares almost too grievous to be borne.

The idea of spending Christmas in the Tower of London is to us sufficiently doleful, and the conditions under which Elizabeth of York, otherwise the Good, there passed the days preceding the Christmas of 1502 were such as might have frightened away a fair woman, whose family associations of that place were terrible in their tragic interest. Just before Christmas Day we find the queen adjourning to old Richmond Palace, where the presents bestowed on various people reveal to us how Christmas was observed in days close upon four hundred years ago. In those days great personages were especially fond of minstrels, and such of these as were not regularly employed would have a special gift made to them at Christmas. The minstrels included the reciters, whose performances would sometimes take the form of several acting their parts; and anyone who gave more than common satisfaction would receive an extra gift. Thus the sum of 13s. 4d., which Elizabeth of York gave to one William Cornish, "for setting the carol on Christmas Day," was not a small fee when money was so much more valuable than now. A dancer was supposed to be well rewarded with 4s. 4d., and a fool with 6s. 8d. A few weeks after this merry Christmas, and on her birthday, the queen passed away at the age of thirty-seven.

The son of Elizabeth of York, Henry VIII., was even more partial than his mother to festive occasions and imposing pageants. He was proud of his knightly prowess, and in the early days of his married life, when he seems to have been happy with Catherine of Arragon, he had a craze for suddenly leaving the company and soon reappearing in some strange disguise. Thus it was at Christmas 1509 that the young king "stole from the side of the queen during the jousts, and returned in the disguise of a strange knight, astonishing all the company with the grace and vigour of his tilting." The court shows, as well as the street pageants, were then more costly or picturesque than now; but as was also in keeping with the times, they may also have been more childish. What is more surprising is, that the commonalty from the City would crowd into one end of the great state-apartment, then called the White-hall, when anything more than ordinarily striking was to be witnessed. Occasionally there would be a scramble for mementoes of a court pageant, and persons of title have even lost jewels and ornaments in a *mêlée*, the distinguished company being literally despoiled of their valuables by the vulgar herd of sightseers from London.

Years pass on, and we are enabled to see some of the attendant circumstances of Christmas 1523, when the Reformation time of transition had hardly come on in England, though some far-sighted seer may have thought that he descried its dawn. The king and queen dined at old Eltham Palace on that Christmas Day, now exactly three hundred and seventy-one years ago; and one of the chief topics of conversation would be the foundation of the great college at Oxford, named after Christ. Wolsey was then at the height of his prestige, and Henry VIII. was so proud of the achievement of his favourite, that during the holidays of that Christmas he introduced Langland, Bishop of Lincoln, to the queen, with the memorable words: "Madame, my lord of Lincoln can show my lord cardinal's college at Oxford, and what learning there is and shall be." Langland's account of what further happened is in his own handwriting in the Cottonian MSS.:—"And so the king departed, and I showed the king's grace the effect of all, and what great good should come of the same, likewise in the exposition of the Bible; and expressed to her grace the number of the house, the divine service of your college, and of the great suffrages of prayer ye have made her participant of." That was perhaps as pretty a Christmas scene as can be found in history; but only seven Christmas Days onward how wofully the outlook had changed. The queen was then discarded by her husband, the English Bluebeard, and the great Wolsey had just died in disgrace.

Greenwich appears to have been a favourite place in the time of the Tudors at which to spend Christmas. Thus, in December 1536, we find the court removing from Richmond to the old palace in the nearer suburb, there to spend the holidays. Only just before, the Princess Mary was again received into the good graces of her father, King Bluebeard, after an estrangement, and Bluebeard gave his daughter some gold bordering for a dress, which cost the recipient nearly £5 to have altered into the fashion. What is especially noteworthy is, that the young royal lady lost a greater number of angels "at the cards" than appeared to be quite decorous, according to our modern notions, each angel being a coin of the value of 7s. 6d. On the other hand, her grace gave alms to the poor in a right royal manner, and, consequently, passed as a good Catholic in a credulous age, when a good deed was superstitiously supposed to counterbalance a bad one. A year later Mary is found travelling by water from Windsor to Richmond to keep Christmas, giving the boatman 5s. for his trouble. Then as the Christmas diversions were aided by "Jane the fool," that young woman had to be suitably rewarded. There were many other calls to which a royal lady was expected to make a proper response; and to do this was not always convenient when the allowances of such dames were commonly quite out of keeping with their brilliant expectations. It was not the golden age, though the artistic work of ladies in the royal palace made it appear an industrious one, while the learning of courtly dames was considered to be in their case a commonplace characteristic. The presents they gave to other dames of rank oftentimes were evidences of their taste as well as their skill. Thus silken hose ornamented with gold, "a gown of carnation satin," sleeves for other gowns worked with silver or gold. In the early part of the sixteenth century oranges were served up with the Christmas dessert. The fruit was ten a penny—hardly so cheap as they are now, when due allowance is made for the difference in the value of money.

The marriage of Queen Mary with the worthless and fanatical Philip II. of Spain, in 1554, boded no good either to the bride or her country; but on account of the wedding festivities being postponed until the end of December, the Christmas of that year was particularly brilliant, and one that was long remembered as a red-letter day in our English annals. The season appears to have been observed at Whitehall, where hundreds of coloured lamps were made to produce a kind of magical effect on Christmas Eve. The Princess Elizabeth and a great gathering of English and foreign nobles were present. The only drawback was to those who had to provide the entertainment, the restriction which the queen put upon their enterprise from economic motives. Carden, the master of the ceremonies, insisted that he had already shown his novelties, and needed resources for new inventions. Master Carden's genius found plenty of scope for its exercise; and the mention of some of his devices shows that the inventions of the sixteenth century were just of the kind which would be appreciated by grown-up children in the nineteenth. Thus, by means of rabbits'-skins apes were well counterfeited, and, sitting in a row, they played various musical instruments, and thus were made to appear like minstrels of the most comical kind. Dozens of cats'-tails were also in request, "a masque of cats," with an accompanying recitation, causing great merriment. Plays representing the condition of Ireland, Venice, etc., were also produced at considerable cost. A great book, painted by Holbein, for the royal diversion at Christmas-tide would now be a relic of the Tudor era, which would command a high price.

In regard to the Reformation in England, Christmas Day ought to be held in some account, for it was on that day in the year of her accession, 1558, that Queen Elizabeth is supposed formally to have broken away from the Romish Mass. As the public opinion supported her in her action, the English service took the place of the Romish Latin in the Chapel Royal and all other churches. Perhaps it may not be generally known that silk stockings came in with the Reformation. Henry VIII. wore cloth hose, which were certainly too good for him; Edward VI. appears to have had a pair of Spanish silk ones "sent him as a great present;" but in 1559 Queen Elizabeth commenced the wear of silk stockings, which was afterwards continued. "I like silk stockings well, because they are

Royal Society, and it is to be found in their "Transactions."

Master Samuel Pepys was also an admirer of Christmas, as observed after the old English manner, and next to a good dinner he seems to have liked an able sermon. After morning church on Christmas Day, 1660, went "home to dinner, where my brother Tom, who this morning came to see my wife's new mantle put on, which do please me very well." The dinner consisted of "a good shoulder of mutton and a chicken," which being succeeded by a dull sermon at afternoon church "made me sleep." Each Christmas Day seems to have had its own particular characteristics. Thus, in 1664, Pepy's went "to Mr. Rawlinson's church, where I heard a good sermon." Nor was that all; for in the same place was found "very great store of fine women . . . more than I know anywhere else about us." On Christmas Day of the year following, or in 1665, Pepys witnessed "a wedding in the church," an unusual spectacle for the season. What also struck him was seeing "the young people so merry one with another!" It was also "strange to see what delight we married people have to see these poor fools decoyed into our condition, every man and woman gazing and smiling at them." On Christmas Eve Mrs. Pepys would sit up until four in the morning, "seeing her maids make mince-pies," and these, with " good ribs of beef roasted," as well as " plenty of good wine of my own," Master Pepys considered to be good seasonable fare.

On Christmas Eve, 1667, Pepys is found going in a coach "to see the ceremony's . . . at the Queen's Chapel;" but he was disappointed, and fearful that his pocket would be picked. The sight being "nothing but a high masse," he might well have stayed at home, and we find him exclaiming: "What an odde thing it was for me to be in a crowd of people, here a footman, there a beggar, here a fine lady, there a zealous poor Papist, and here a Protestant, two or three together, come to see the show." In the small hours of morning, the moon shining brightly, he returned home, not forgetting to drop money at several places about the City, "which I was the willinger to do," says Pepys, "it being Christmas Day, and so home, and there to find my wife in bed, and Janie and the maid making pyes." The last Christmas Day which Mrs. Pepys passed on earth appears to have been that of 1668, when, with her husband at her side and a boy to read, she was employed all day in "altering and lacing a noble petticoat."

Probably it will be thought that Christmas in the *Spectator* would be Christmas in fiction rather than in history, otherwise reference might be made to the efforts which were made by Sir Roger de Coverley to make the Christmas season a gladsome time for the farmers and cottagers on his estate. Then, though it was not very much written about, some illustration of the way in which Christmas was observed in different parts of the country might be gathered from the periodicals of the last century. The customs greatly varied in country places in days when the provinces had far less intercommunication than now. Of course elderly persons thought that the times of their youth had been more favourable for the worthy keeping of Christmas than the then present times. That was a too common delusion which still survives however; Christmas is properly the festival of youth, and those who have grown older can never again look upon it with the eyes of early days, nor ever again enjoy its diversions with equal zest.

G. H. P.

HOW TO MAKE AN ICE SLEDGE.

The advent of ice is always a time of rejoicing to the young who can figure about on skates. But the pleasure would be half lost if dear mother could not come and view with pride the sporting of her young flock, and many a time have I seen her with praiseworthy patience beating the cold out of her feet on the borders of the pond. Now I think it is high time something should be done for her, and, coming home from the ice at 4 o'clock, I determined to have a sledge ready by the next morning. I will give you a short account of how I set about to accomplish it. I reckon it was six hours' work, and cost me 4s. The first thing of importance was to borrow from the house or garden an ordinary wicker-chair, then cut two lengths of ordinary flooring-boards six inches by two inches in lengths of five feet, curve them upwards towards the front, and round off the sharp corner at the back. Plane them along the base taking off a slight bevel towards the inner edge, now you have your "runners." Set them apart at a convenient distance, being guided by the width of your chair. Board over two-thirds with some of the flooring-boards, take an angle off the front of the runners and nail a piece of the flooring across.

You will now have a pretty firm platform for your chair, which you can fix down with one-and-a-half-inch iron staples, but, before fixing this, turn your runners over and strengthen them midway with a pair of iron brackets to keep them from splaying out at the base. These must be placed to get clear of the snow. The board across the front acts as a set off for snow, and can be ornamented at the two corners by carved wood trusses, 8d. each at any wood carver's or turner's; nail or screw them round side downwards. These give quite an elegant finish. The sledge can now be painted any colour to suit the fancy, bright green or sealing-wax-red looks the best. At any time the staples can be drawn and the chair taken off and put back in its place, and the runners hung up in an out-house until the next frost. There is nothing cumbersome about it—always an objection to a sledge. "What shall we do with it all the summer?" Utilising the chair obviates this, and it is one of the most *chic* things one can have.

By twelve o'clock the next day we packed mother in a nest of rugs and furs, and we boys and girls flew over the ice with her, her cheeks all aglow, looking by far the most youthful of our party. Then in the evening decorated with Japanese lanterns—— But there, I must leave something to my readers' imaginations.

	s.	d.
16 feet of floor boarding, 6 by 2 at 1½d.	2	0
Pair of carved wood trusses	1	4
Staples and nails	0	4
Pair of iron brackets	0	4
	4	0

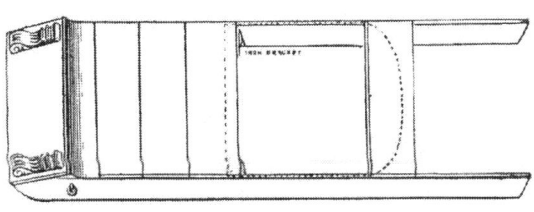

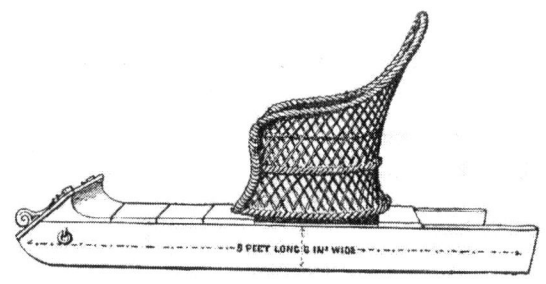

The Girl's Own Paper, 1896

A PAGE OF PUDDINGS,

EVERY ONE OF WHICH IS TRIED AND TRUE.

The Queen of Puddings.—One teacupful of fine white sugar, two teacupfuls of dry breadcrumbs, a tablespoonful of fresh butter, a pint of boiling milk, pinch of salt, and the beaten yolks of three eggs. The grated rind of a fresh lemon should be added to the first-named ingredients, to the which are put first the boiling milk, and, when cool, the yolks of the eggs. Mix well and pour into a shallow buttered fireproof china dish, or an enamelled pie-dish, bake in moderate oven until set firm and a pale brown colour. Spread over the surface a little choice preserve without stones, and heap upon that a *méringue* of the whites of the eggs beaten with a tablespoonful of sugar and same of cream. Return to the oven to slightly colour the top, then remove at once. Good either hot or cold.

Lemon Méringue Pudding.—A quart of boiling milk poured over two teacupfuls of fine breadcrumbs, when well soaked add two ounces of castor sugar, the grated rind of a fresh lemon, two ounces of butter, and lastly the yolks of four eggs with the juice of half the lemon. Bake in gentle oven to a pale brown colour, then cover with a *méringue* sweetened and flavoured with the remaining lemon-juice. This also is good to eat cold.

Orange pudding may be made in the same way.

Newark Pudding.—One cupful of breadcrumbs soaked in a pint of milk, a tablespoonful of ground rice, a quarter of a pound of raisins, the stones removed and cut in two, a few drops of vanilla or almond essence, two tablespoonfuls of melted butter, a pinch of salt and half a teaspoonful of carbonate of soda. Separate the yolks and whites of two eggs; add the yolks to the other ingredients first, then lastly stir in lightly the whites; pour the mixture into a buttered dish and bake in gentle oven one hour.

Winter Raspberry Pudding (most delicious).—Two ounces of butter, two eggs, a pound pot of raspberry jam, half a pound of breadcrumbs, a quarter of a pound of brown sugar. Beat the butter and eggs separately, to the butter add the sugar and jam, then the eggs.

Butter a plain mould, sprinkle crumbs all around it and a layer at the bottom, then put in a layer of mixture, then more crumbs and more mixture, until the mould is full. Cover with a buttered paper and bake from three-quarters to one hour in moderate oven. Serve with sweet wine or cream sauce.

Apple Custard Pudding, for eating cold.—Pare, core and slice up four or five good cooking apples, add a little water to them and cook until they will beat up smoothly; sweeten well and flavour. Put them into a buttered pie-dish and carefully pour on the top half a pint of custard made from half a packet of custard powder (sweetened), grate a little nutmeg over, and let the pudding stand in a cool place.

Marmalade Pudding.—Half a pound each of breadcrumbs, beef suet (chopped) and sugar, six ounces of marmalade added. The whole well worked together with three or four well beaten eggs (no other moisture). Boil in a mould for two hours. Best made over-night.

Curates' Puddings.—Put into a saucepan one pint of milk, a few lumps of sugar and a bit of lemon rind, let it nearly boil, remove to cool. Whisk three eggs light, beat into them three spoonfuls of flour, add the sweetened milk by degrees, beat to a smooth batter. Pour into cups, only half filling them, and bake.

Cocoanut Pudding.—Half a pint of milk, quarter of a pound of cocoanut, two tablespoonfuls of cake-crumbs or fine breadcrumbs, two ounces of castor sugar, two ounces of butter, three eggs, one teaspoonful of vanilla.

Simmer the cocoanut in the milk in a saucepan, cream the butter and sugar together. Beat up the eggs, yolks and whites separately. When the cocoanut is tender take the saucepan from the fire and stir into it the butter and sugar. Add the yolks of eggs and vanilla, stirring well; and lastly the whites whipped to a stiff froth; stir lightly and thorougly and pour into a buttered pie-dish and bake half an hour.

Fig Pudding (superior).—Half a pound of fine grated breadcrumbs, half a pound of good figs cut small, quarter of a pound of beef suet chopped fine, quarter of a pound of moist sugar, two ounces of candied peel shred fine, one ounce of sweet almonds or a little of the essence, half a nutmeg grated.

Mix the dry ingredients well together with a pinch of salt, then moisten the whole with two well whisked eggs and, if wished, a glass of sherry or light wine.

Butter a plain mould or basin, and pour in the mixture, cover the top with a thin paper, tie a cloth tightly over and boil for three hours. Turn out and serve with sweet sauce.

Exeter Pudding (choice).—Make a mixture of the following ingredients—six tablespoonfuls of fine bread-crumbs, two tablespoonfuls of fine sago, three tablespoonfuls of finely chopped suet and three tablespoonfuls of soft sugar. Beat two eggs well, adding half a cup of milk and a little lemon flavouring. Pour over the dry ingredients and mix thoroughly.

Now butter a pudding mould and put in a layer of sponge rusks at the bottom, cover these with a layer of the mixture, next another layer of rusks. On these spread a layer of delicate jam, then a layer of mixture, and so proceed until the mould is full; the top layer must be one of mixture. Bake in the oven for forty minutes or steam for an hour and a half. Serve with sauce made by boiling two or three tablespoonfuls of jam with a little water and straining it.

Nice Chocolate Pudding.—Take a quarter of a pound of stale sponge cakes or rusks in crumbs, two ounces of sugar, three ounces of butter and a quarter of a pound of mild chocolate, three eggs and three quarters of a pint of milk. Rub the butter and sugar to a cream, add the egg yolks well beaten, dissolve the chocolate in the milk and stir altogether, lastly stir in the whites well beaten to a froth. Bake in a deep round tin or steam in a mould about one hour.

Ginger-Bread Pudding.—Excellent for cold weather. Rub together in a basin eight ounces of breadcrumbs and four ounces of flour with six ounces of suet, one teaspoonful of baking-powder, and one teaspoonful each of ground ginger and mixed spice, also half a teaspoonful of salt. Warm well six ounces of treacle. Beat up one egg with a quarter of a pint of milk and stir well into the warm treacle. Pour over the dry ingredients and mix all well together. Pour into a greased mould leaving a little room to swell. Boil steadily for three hours. A few chopped figs or dates can be added to this pudding by way of change.

Swiss Apple Pudding.—Ingredients: Half a dozen large baking apples and half a pound of finely grated breadcrumbs. Butter a pie-dish and cover the bottom with a layer of crumbs, then a layer of sliced apples; sprinkle over these a large spoonful of moist sugar and a little grated nutmeg and lemon rind. Fill the dish with these alternate layers, letting crumbs form the upper and lower layers. Place little pieces of butter here and there over the top of the pudding, or, if liked, a sprinkling of fine suet crumbs, which is better for children. Pour into the dish half a cupful of water and bake gently in a moderate oven until the apples are tender; about half an hour.

Raisin Pudding.—Into one pound of flour rub a teaspoonful of baking-powder and a pinch of salt. Grate the rind of a fresh lemon into it, and add eight ounces of finely shred beef suet, also half a pound of good raisins stoned and cut small. A little spice may be added to flavour if liked. Work into a rather stiff paste with an egg and a cupful of milk.

Butter a plain mould and three parts fill it with the mixture, tie over it a buttered paper and steam the pudding for four hours. Serve with a sauce made by mixing one ounce of cornflour with half a pint of water, one ounce of butter, three ounces of sugar, the grated rind and juice of a lemon. Boil to a cream.

Pembleton Pudding.—Take equal quantities (a teacupful) of breadcrumbs, chopped suet, raisins, currants, sugar, a little shred lemon peel and pinch of salt. Mix with two beaten eggs and a little milk. Bake in well-buttered pie-dish until well set. Make a custard with two more eggs, half a pint of milk sweetened and flavoured, and pour on the top, baking until the custard is firm.

The Girl's Own Paper, 1896

THE CHRISTMAS TREE.

CHERISH how fondly soever we may the relics of those essentially national associations which heralded in the Christmas season in years gone by, we are not the less disposed, when mourning the gradual disappearance of these our own time-honoured observances, to welcome the introduction of any foreign custom which may promise, in some degree, to compensate for their loss by adding lustre and interest to our cherished festival. It is true that many amongst us may not cease to sigh for the merry days of old, and the boisterous revelry of which time has enhanced the charm and veiled the disadvantages. They may regret that the boar's head should have ceased to be either a desirable or attainable addition to our good cheer; that the masques and pageantry in which princes once condescended to take part should have been long deemed unworthy the advancing intellect of the age; that the principles of order should be so powerful an element in our constitution as to forbid the reign of Misrule, even for that brief span which formerly witnessed its authorised dominion; and as they look back to the pastimes which it will never be their lot to enjoy, may feel, be their prepossessions Royalist or Roundhead, that the Puritans did us ill-service in waging a war of extermination against the merry-makings of old Christmas. Others, again, there may be, who, without any antiquarian respect for the habits and manners of the real olden times, or any desire to awaken them from their long rest, may yet lament the departure of those familiar relics which were endeared by their own youthful associations; they may long once more by the light of the yule-log, to be half-amused, half-terrified by mummers; may grumble that their rest is less and less frequently disturbed by the harmony of the waits; and grieve that we are becoming too refined to admit the privileges of the sacred mistletoe. But let them not be unjust to the present, and the enjoyments it provides. If the lordly boar's head no longer smokes in the centre of our modern dinner-table, have we no lordly baron or knightly sirloin to supply its place? If no gay pageant assembles eager crowds to witness its magnificence, has not each homestead its own individual gala, its festival of affection? And last, but not least, what matter though the mistletoe be banished, if we have the Christmas Tree, whose fruits, far less evanescent, will, undoubtedly purchase many a kiss, not stolen, but given as a free-will offering.

For this last picturesque innovation, now so completely a feature of our English Christmas, we are indebted to Germany, where it has held the same high position in general favour for years, we might almost say for ages; indeed, if we may credit the testimony of a well-known foreign print, representing Christmas in the household of Martin Luther, the illuminated tree afforded amusement to the children of our great reformer himself. The first instance generally known of the importation of the custom to our own country was during the embassy of Prince Talleyrand, who neglected no means of rendering himself popular and prominent amongst us; the reputation of the splendid tree which commemorated Christmas in his household spread far and wide at the time, and is no doubt still remembered by many. It was not, however, until the Royal marriage had established a kind of brotherly relationship between ourselves and our German neighbours—and by rapidly increasing the intercourse between the two nations, had rendered their habits and manners familiar to us—that this characteristic of a German Christmas was decidedly engrafted on our own. Since then it has gradually taken root in England; Royal example having given it fashion, and its own merits ensured it favour. There are now probably not very many families of which the elder branches are moderately enterprising, that do not establish a Christmas Tree; which, though ostensibly for the gratification of the younger scions, proves a source of interest and pleasure to all. There are, of course, various degrees both in the beauty of these trees and in the amount of enjoyment derived from them (two points wholly independent of each other); and though each one must have a certain individuality of its own, yet they may be generally divided into two classes. First, perhaps, in splendour, are those summoned up without even the exertion of a thought through the potent intervention of Messrs. Fortnum and Mason. We know there are persons in the world who eschew trouble even when it takes the guise of pleasure. Happily for them many pleasures are to be purchased "ready-made," and our now popular Christmas diversion is of the number. There was a time when the annual display of Twelfth-cakes was esteemed well worthy a visit of inspection, but their attractions sink into complete insignificance before the curiosities and novelties in the form of, Christmas Trees with their adornments, a glimpse of which at the right season fills up an idle half hour very pleasantly.

For the advantage of those whose sphere of personal observation may be limited, but who may have their own reasons for feeling interested in the subject, we shall notice a few of the improvements which have been recently introduced: the benefit of them is chiefly confined to our first class of merrymakers—those who enjoy the result, but have nothing to do with the means. First, then, it must be understood that the Christmas Tree is by no means invariably one that Nature would acknowledge for her own production; indeed, the greater number of those that are supplied, ready dressed, are imitations—very good ones, be it understood—formed of painted tin. Hitherto, the comely and symmetrical fir-tree has served as a model; but, in the coming season, a novelty is to be introduced consisting of imitative palm-trees, varying from two to six feet in height, in which the hand of Nature has not been disgraced by that of the artificer. There is the notched and gracefully tortuous stem, overhung with the long green pendent leaves, which fall so judiciously over each other as to provide for the proper distribution of the lamps, or ornamented tapers which are attached to the points; a row of hooks, placed on the under side of every leaf, enables the ornaments to be disposed in close proximity, without injury to the general outline. Another design, equally new and pretty, represents a vine trained on a trellis, bearing large bunches of grapes, composed of coloured glass, but not on this account less tantalizing to the eye. Of half the elegancies and grotesqueries which are invented for the dressing of this elaborate groundwork, it would be impossible to make mention, for their name is legion. All are, however, receptacles for bon-bons, but so curious and ornamental in themselves that their original destination might be easily overlooked. We can have boxes in the semblance of dogs' heads, and may even choose between the aristocratic greyhound, surly mastiff, and faithful Newfoundland; or, for those who may prefer fac-similes of their own genus, there are half-length figures of sailors in their glazed hats, Saracens in turbans, crusty old men, good-tempered young ones—in fact, characters of every kind, to whom the hand of the Nuremburg workman has imparted a degree of expression that is really marvellous: but all these form receptacles for a store of good things, which are exposed to view by the process of decapitation. The tree is not, however, to be overloaded with these oddities; amongst them are dispersed pretty miniature representations of familiar objects, as book-cases, guitars, balloons, &c.; also, gelatine flowers of great beauty, with gold leaves, made in Paris for this very purpose; and any odd corners are filled up with artificial fruit and similar trifles. To each of these articles is attached a number, and their possession is determined by lot. The principal and best manufactory, both for the trees themselves and for their adornments, is acknowledged to be Nuremburg, which has long enjoyed an established reputation for the ingenuity of its toys, many of which are made by the nimble fingers of children. The prices charged by the importers for the decorated trees range from one to thirty guineas, according to their size and the number and value of the articles which are placed upon them. All are in their degree tasteful and pretty, and can be said to lack nothing, except that particular interest which can only be purchased at the expense of a little trouble.

We must now glance at the second class of Christmas Trees; those of home growth; and ascertain if they have not some peculiar advantages of their own, to counterbalance their inferiority in elegance. In contradistinction to those individuals who do not make acquaintance with their tree until it has assumed its full dress, are a large proportion of aspirants for enjoyment, who would on no account relinquish the preparations to professional hands. They embark in the undertaking with the sensible resolution of extracting from it all the pleasure which it is capable of affording; and the amount, in a large family especially, is by no means contemptible. On our domestic tree comparatively little money is expended, for it is soon discovered that the trouble and ingenuity so willingly bestowed, go very far to supply its place. It may occasionally be made the medium of conveying handsome presents destined for many a year to recall the memory of the day to their possessors, but these can scarcely be considered as part of the legitimate expenses; and, as a principle, the productions of the tree are of an inexpensive character—often labours of love. For weeks before the long-looked-for day, the leisure occupations of those who may have taken upon themselves the responsibility of the affair, have reference to its success. Many an hour is stolen from sleep and the social circle, for the secret manufacture of these same presents, half the charm of which would be lost to the donor if the glance of admiration with which they are received be not equally one of gratified surprise. Many a walk is taken for the purpose of choosing the pretty bon-bons and ornaments which cannot be made at home, or dispensed with altogether. Even amongst the children there is an unwonted cessation of noisy activity, for they, too, have their own important affairs to arrange. They have to select from their own toys those that are to grow on the tree for the benefit of the little cousins who will be of the merry Christmas party; their generous impulses being no doubt rather quickened by the prospect of fresh acquisitions for themselves. They have to determine the division and employment of the hoarded half-crown, and pay many a visit to the bazaar ere it is laid out to the best advantage. Lastly, there are the book-marks, intended to minister to the intellectual tastes of papa and mamma, to be completed and delivered in to the authorities on the eve of the great day. It will in truth be fortunate if its arrival do not surprise them ere the various plans are fully matured and realised. We should here observe that the time selected for the lighting up and grand exhibition of the Tree depends on individual taste; but as it most usually forms the crowning pleasure of Christmas Day itself, when the circle of assembled friends and relatives supplies a meet audience, we may conclude that the preliminary arrangements are made on the preceding evening. A select committee, consisting of those who are recognised authorities in matters of taste, closet themselves, with the various appliances of their business, in the back drawingroom, or wherever else may be the theatre of exhibition. How gaily they enter on their appointed task of decking the dark spreading branches of the vigorous young fir-tree, which, to afford full scope for their genius, should be some six feet in height. The first step is to attach the coloured tapers, by means of large pins, or any better expedient that can be devised. It may, perhaps, prove no easy matter to persuade them to maintain their appointed attitudes, and avoid all the risk of the illumination progressing into a conflagration; but if the candles do not look quite as much at home on our tree as on those of a more artificial character, they will at least give as good a light. Then the bon-bons, sweetmeats, flowers, and any other pretty things that may have been provided, are suspended from various parts of the tree, with those presents that are of a sufficiently light and ornamental description. The residue are gracefully strewed around, as though they had been showered down by the benevolent hand of some good fairy. During these proceedings, which have occupied considerably more time than their description, general curiosity has been exhibited outside the door to ascertain the progress of affairs; for, be it understood, there is "no admission for any one excepting on business." Idlers would only interfere with the industrious; and for the children, above all, the *coup d'œuil* is reserved until to-morrow; they would not have half the respect for the marvellous tree if they had beheld it unadorned, and discovered that it differed in no respect from those which they often carelessly passed in their country walks. The appeals of little eager voices for "just one look" are therefore entirely disregarded, and the plots laid by mischievous brothers to steal in on some specious pretext are disappointed by wary caution on the part of the besieged. It is ordained that all shall wait till to-morrow, and, fortunately, there is too much excitement going on in every household on Christmas Eve for the delay to be very irksome, or the interval to seem very long.

There are, we should hope, not very many who do not wake to the dawn of the Christmas Day morning with an indistinct consciousness that something pleasant is about to happen; and with the children this something speedily assumes the form of the Christmas Tree. Its prospective glories will present themselves to the best-regulated juvenile minds during church time, and not even the unwonted pleasure of dining with parents, aunts, uncles, and all the dignitaries of the family, is sufficient to prevent many an exclamation of joy when this preliminary is at last over and the moment of fruition arrived. The tapers lighted, and finishing touches given, the folding-doors are opened or curtain raised, and the Christmas Tree, in all its dazzling magnificence, is exposed to view. The admiration is so absorbing, that for many minutes it shines and glitters in undisturbed glory; but at length there is an evident desire to realise the existence of the treasures by actual possession, and to the most humorous of the party is entrusted the duty of distributing to every one their allotted portion, with appropriate remarks of his own.

Now are all those mysteries and hours of seclusion explained and accounted for to the general satisfaction. Every one would seem to have had his own especial secret; even the heads of the family have privately added at the last moment love tokens to their children, whose surprise they not a little enjoy. There may be (we say not that there is) a watch for him whose ambition it has so long been to possess one; a concertina or drawing-box for her whose tastes may render such a gift acceptable; and so munificent an assortment of dolls, with every appliance for their comfort, that the little ones forget to breathe one sigh of regret as they see their own generous intentions realised, and treasures, once the most cherished, pass into other hands. Nor are the juniors without their own moments of triumph; how pleased is the affectionate mother, when the beautiful, braided table-cover worked by the hands of her daughters is presented to her; and yet it scarcely meets with more consideration than the book-marks and the needle book. We must certainly relinquish all idea of enumerating a tithe of the gifts that are interchanged, for it really seems that each one has remembered everyone else, and has been by them as carefully remembered. Finally, the bon-bons are distributed as a *bonne-bouche*, but the tree must not be entirely dismantled on this occasion; some time should elapse before it ceases to be an object of interest; and surely another Christmas will be almost at hand ere its glories fail to prove an agreeable and ever-fruitful topic of conversation.

We have endeavoured to give some little idea of the distinctive characteristics of the two classes of Christmas Trees, as we see them in England; and now without offering any ungracious comparisons, we bid farewell to our readers of every age, desiring for them all possible enjoyment from their own Christmas diversions, be they foreign or be they of home growth; and, in the time-honoured words of our ancestors, wishing them each and all

"A MERRY CHRISTMAS AND A HAPPY NEW YEAR!"

AST Christmas we made our decorations on a much more elaborate scale than formerly. All the members of our family were to be united, including our sailor-boy; two uncles, an aunt, and some cousins were also to make an addition. We therefore determined that we would spare no pains to make their visit enjoyable, and made arrangements—subject to circumstances—for the season to be one of consecutive "felicities." Hence, our home decorations were to be superfine. In the hope that my account will prove practically helpful and suggestive to others, I will explain how we very successfully transformed the appearance of the interior of our "modest mansion."

First, however, I must own that during the autumn time our eyes and hands had industriously exerted themselves in fields, lanes, and woods, for materials. I commend this plan to those who love to see their homes wear a Christmas-like aspect; and, besides, it is very pleasant to be ever on the look-out for nature's wealth.

Having collected a goodly store of material, one person — the elder sister — was in our case elected superintendent, and by her directions we pursued our work orderly and well, no incongruities ensuing. Many leaders spoil effect. I advise that when any decorative project is intended, the leader be elected a reasonable time in advance, so that she may make her plans and allow them to mature. It is advisable for a leader to write out a list of purposed schemes beforehand; having a programme for reference, all may glide smoothly. Five of us, besides Enid, our superintendent, helped to decorate last year. A special task (say a motto, or bordering) was assigned to the responsibility of each; and then, with concentrated thoughts, we strove to emulate each other. Our work was apportioned out more than a week before Christmas, a spare room was devoted to our accumulated paraphernalia, and there in leisure moments we pursued our "labour of love." On difficulties arising, we always referred to Enid. We had dining-room and sitting-room—both comparatively large places—to specially decorate. We expended the more care on the latter.

Round the top of the room, close under the ceiling, ran the words—

> "Gather ye rosebuds while ye may,
> Old Time is still a-flying;
> And this same flower that smiles to-day,
> To-morrow will be dying."

The first line occupied the wall over the window; the second was over the fireplace, and so on, the final line being over the door. We used crimson paper—twelve inches deep—for the background, and white jeweller's cotton for the letters, which were first cut out in stout paper, then covered with the cotton. Our letters were plainly and clearly designed, and were not "fancy" ones. This is a first essential in mottoes. In cutting out letters, a rule and measure should be well used, for it quite ruins effect if they are not uniform in height. For bordering, we made on broad black tape long wreaths of mixed material—box, bay, tiny bits of holly, oats, grasses, everlasting flowers, cotton grass, &c. These were comparatively slight wreaths, as thick and heavy ones might have hidden our beautiful words in some degree not desired. Our work, being light, was fastened on the walls at each edge of the crimson paper, with pins—which are less injurious to paper than tacks. A few tacks only as mainstays were used. Enid the tasty undertook the mantel-piece. She made a charming hanging for it, of stiff calico, covered luxuriously on the outer side with white wadding. The sentence it bore was "A HUNDRED THOUSAND WELCOMES." The letters were sweetly pretty, being made on cardboard by layers of tapioca, dyed red (using Judson's dye) to resemble coral. The letters needed three layers, and were each

Cassell's Family Magazine, 1885

time left till the gum had quite dried. The border was carefully made with mixed mosses and lichens, arranged somewhat unevenly. Along the lower border, a few fern-fronds, dried grasses and flowers, and silver leaves — from Table Mountain — were arranged as though growing up from behind the lichen boundary. All had previously been pressed and dried, after the manner of preserving for a herbarium, and were kept upright by means of a few stitches. As our mantelpiece was rather high, the heat of the fire was quite harmless. A scattering of cotton grass was finally distributed about the afore-mentioned edging. Above the mantel-piece hung a pier-glass, at either side of which some long sprays of trailing ivy were placed. Some truant pieces reflected in the mirror enhanced the beauty. From the summit of the glass a fox's head (stuffed) snarled down, and the expedient of sticking a spray of holly and mistletoe with a few suspicious barn-yard feathers in Reynard's mouth was hit upon. At the top of the glass, bulrushes, teasel-heads, oats, thorn-apple capsules, and pampas grass were also arranged, together with a little holly. The mantelpiece held some busts and statuettes, upon which we tied jeweller's cotton where snow might be supposed to rest. The entire shelf was treated in this way, and we pulled our artificial snow into natural likeness, some pieces drooping over our lambrequin. The cotton grass in the valence-border was a very good imitation of snow-flakes, and looked well in conjunction with the work above it.

For several large pictures we made wreaths from our autumn gatherings, using wire (which, owing to its bending properties, is so useful for pictures and suchlike articles) to work upon. Our wreathing rested on the top ledges of pictures without further adjustment. We bordered two pictures with bright-berried holly, after frosting it with Epsom salts (fearing crushed glass, on account of children's feet); we intermingled cotton grass with the holly. The crystallisation was lovely, and the snow-flakes—cotton grass—against the dark holly perfect in effect. We composed six little bannerettes to hang in the too neglected places. One bearing our father's monogram was placed on the wall on one side of the pier-glass, and another bearing mother's on the other side. They quite matched. In making them, we cut cardboard the desired shape and size (some good hints may be gained by procuring a printed sheet of the banners and flags extant), and covered it with crimson cloth. *All* our bannerettes were covered alike. The monograms were fastened in the centre, after we had made the letters separately in different colours, gold and white. We gleaned some good straws from a stack-yard for the frame, lengthy ones to edge the entire sides first, and then made little straw stars on the top of these, at equal distances apart. The two remaining bannerettes bore unique Christmas cards, which were framed prettily with cotton grass before fixing. These banners were edged with frosted holly.

We inlaid our window-ledge — an old-fashioned thing — with moss, and afterwards partially embedded a few tiny pots of cut flowers with pleasing effect. Our Christmas roses were much admired.

We decorated the dining-room but slightly. "A HAPPY CHRISTMAS" was the motto we made for the mantel-piece, using tiny pink everlasting flowers for the letters, white wadding for the background, and mixed evergreens for the border. On the mantel-piece we arranged berried holly, &c., in lustres and vases. For the picture-framing we wove on wire some slight greenery of mixed evergreens crystallised with crushed glass. The wreathing was arranged to only border each picture at the top, and part way down each side, but we made some to wind round the hanging cards. In each corner of the room, about half-way up, we fixed a picture, each being completely environed with holly and cotton grass. The subjects were entitled, "The Mistletoe Bough," from Sir Roger de Coverley; "Arrival of Santa Claus;" "Christmas in the Fifteenth Century," boar's head predominating; and "Christmas in the Nineteenth Century," chief fare, plum-pudding. Over the room-door rested a scroll, on which one of us had illuminated, "GLORY TO GOD IN THE HIGHEST, AND ON EARTH PEACE, GOODWILL TOWARDS MEN." This was enclosed within a border of holly-leaves, one leaf-point laid over the base of another, and two rows of leaves placed side by side, as a single row looks too scanty. (*Three* rows of leaves even might be an improvement.) The scroll and bordering were tacked on laths, the corners crossing like an Oxford frame.

We did little more; all the cut flowers we could muster were fitted into suitable places, as well as pot plants, as we needed them. Enid made a motto to surmount the sitting-room door in the hall; it was another Shakspearian scrap, "PRAY YOU, WALK IN," made of tinfoil letters on a dark fawn-coloured paper ground, and edged with dried green moss, in which at equal distances a small sprig of berried holly was secured. Enid's thoughts were ever capital ones, and a more appropriate prelude to her "Hundred thousand welcomes" than the hall invitation, "Pray you, walk in," it would be difficult to suggest. Around the socket inside our hall-lamp, lichens and holly-berries were placed, making it pretty when lighted.

Nothing further remains for me to tell, except that when *we* had folded our arms, judging our work to be completed, Enid was exercising a pirouette in the kitchenery regions, distributing evergreens in likely places; "for," said she, "such an important part of the house shall *not* be slighted." Let it not be thought that our work was executed in a day. We commenced many little things fully a fortnight before Christmas, leaving, of necessity, the more perishable materials until last. I strongly advocate "taking Time by the forelock" in decorations for Yuletide, for nothing is so annoying as to have the prospect of much work at the last moment, say on Christmas Eve, when a hundred and one little duties are sure to require attention. If our tasks master us, do we not feel provoked? Then let us order our affairs well, so that we may wear smooth and happy faces when ushering in that glad festival, our Christmas Day.

E. E. A.

CHRISTMAS-BOX FROM "MEDICUS."

By HIMSELF.

Here we are again, as merry as a May cricket and as happy as a sand-boy! And why shouldn't I, or why shouldn't you, or any of us, be happy in this bright world of ours if we feel like being so? For, mind you, nothing will ever make me believe that there isn't far more of joy than sorrow on earth, far more of good than bad, far more of sunshine and moonlight and star gleams, than of murky skies, darkness, or gloom. I don't care a bit what pessimists may tell me to the contrary. They may point to the wind-tossed rain-filled clouds, and ask me where the sunshine is.

"Away behind those very clouds," I'll answer; "and somewhere else as well—in the heart."

Well, now, girls, you'll be reading these lines some time in what is called "bleak December," but I am writing them in sunny September.

By-the-way, though, why should December always, or nearly always, be called bleak? I'm sure I for one never saw any very great amount of bleakness about it. In my opinion December is an honest month, and a very decided one to boot. December bears a bad character, but doesn't seem to break its heart on this account. It is a reckless, rollicking, happy-go-lucky sort of a month, and we have to take it just as it comes. And this is doing what we ought to do. Perhaps a cold Norland wind goes shrieking and howling through the leafless trees, or across the fields all waste and bare, when we first start out of a morning; but we can walk and keep warm. And thanks to our own industry, we are warmly clad and comfortably shod. Have we not also made an excellent breakfast, good digestion waiting on appetite, and bounding health on both?

What though it rains as well as blows! What though the breeze sweeps round the corners in gusts and squalls, and tries to blow us off the foot-path! Battling with the wind on a December morning is the finest fun out, and if Boreas is determined we sha'n't hold up an umbrella, why, we can wrap our plaids or mackintoshes around us and laugh in his face.

Then at eventide, as we journey homewards, December may bring all his battery to bear upon us, and mingle sleet and hail with rain, and blow at us and roar at us from every direction of the compass; but even then, in the darkness and gloom, glad visions of a cosy fireside not far away, of a comfortable curtained room, of a well-laid supper-table, with a kettle on the hob and a cat on the hearth, will rise up before our mind's eye, and we will quicken our steps till imagination at length merges into reality.

But when December does make up its mind to be good, it is very good indeed. Think of the calm bright days to which we are often treated during this month; the ground so hard that it rings under our feet; the sprinkling of snow; the sea-green skies of the gloaming hour; the moonlight that follows; and the glorious stars. So whatever anyone else may say, I shall always have a good word to say for December.

But it is September with me as I write. Oh, of course there has been rain; I'm not going to think of that now it is past and gone. I am writing by the roadside on a wooden bench, in a wide space where three roads meet at upper Bognor. In the centre of this triangle is a large circular grass plot, from which tower skywards seven splendid trees, forming a dome far aloft, where their branches interlace like the roof of some grand cathedral aisle. Each of the roads that radiate from this space is a cool green avenue, or lovers' lane.

The trees above me are graceful as well as tall; the sunshine is shimmering and falling in patches all around. Every broad green leaf is a transparency in the marvellous light, and the breeze is making such sweet low music through the foliage that were I reading instead of writing I might be lulled to sleep. Just one little glimpse of the blue sea is needed to complete this picture; and lo! yonder it is. My faithful companion, Queen (the Newfoundland), is seated beside me, leaning her great honest head on the bench, so I am not quite alone.

Not far off is my camp; not an extensive one —simply the caravan "Wanderer," and a snow-white tent. But very pretty they look in that quiet green meadow surrounded by waving trees and hedges all trailed over with bramble. The greenery of the field is starred over with the orange of autumnal hawk-bit and patched with the purple bartsia.

But in a day or two, after I have finished this paper, I shall strike camp and go wandering homewards through the prettiest parts of Sussex, Surrey, Kent, and Berks. Is it not pleasant, reader, even in December, to look back to a summer holiday well spent, and while doing one's best to enjoy the winter, hug to one's heart the thought that summer will come again?

"Spring will return,
And birds and lambs again be gay;
And blossoms clothe the hawthorn spray.

* * * *

The daisy's flower
Again shall paint your summer bower;
Again the hawthorn shall supply
The garlands you delight to tie.
The lambs upon the lee shall bound,
The wild birds carol to the sound;
And while you frolic light as they,
Too short shall seem the summer day."

* * * *

But now to change the theme. For once in a way, then, I, your Medicus, am transformed. Hey! presto! and I stand forth in the garb and likeness of old St. Claus. I have donned a long white beard, a cap of fur, and a coat all covered with snowflakes. My cheeks, that are usually sicklied o'er with the pale cast of thought, I have tinged with rouge and eke my noble brow, and I have assumed my jolliest smile. I have got into your house somehow—either down the chimney or through the key-hole. No matter—here I am, and here is my wallet, cram-full of good things for this joyous and festive season. There is no deception, mind you. I carry with me no nasty drugs—not even a pill. Physic for the nonce I have thrown to the dogs, and the dogs know better than to touch it.

Where did you hang your stocking, miss? I wish you wouldn't throw your boots down anywhere for poor St. Claus to tumble over and make a noise. I'm sure I don't want to be shot for a burglar by that big brother of yours.

Oh, here is your stocking! I declare you've hung out two. Never mind, I have plenty to fill them, and if you store up and make use of the receipts I am going to give you, they will aid you in becoming quite a little treasure of a housekeeper.

The receipts then are all useful and *seasonable*, so here goes.

1. I suppose you know that men folk often come in off the ice, or from a long winter's ramble feeling very thirsty, and that ordinary ale or beer is heating. Well, why not make some *spruce* beer. It is best made of the branches of the spruce, but for these in winter you have to substitute the essence. But all you want is, say, four and a half gallons of boiling water; in this you dissolve three pounds of treacle or sugar, and when cool, two ounces of spruce essence and about half a pint of yeast. Let it work as ginger beer does, and bottle off. This is not only a most refreshing drink, but it is also tonic and wholesome, and quite suited for Christmas drink.

2. Did ever you try making *Orange Marmalade*? Mind, you never know what you can do till you try. Take a sufficient number of Seville oranges and half the quantity of nice juicy sweet ones. Great care must be taken that they are clean and skinned, ripe and good. Peel them, take off the inside white skin from the peel, cut the peel in pieces, and boil till tender, then slice very thin. Meanwhile, squeeze out the juice and remove the pips from the pulp. Now put all together and weigh, and add the same weight of pure white sugar. Boil for half an hour, skimming well. Then put in jars, and cover down when it is quite cold. This is the Aberdeen plan. A little clear honey is sometimes added, and sometimes only the bitter oranges are used.

3. Sago, arrowroot, and tapioca are all very nice and nutritious, but receipts for cooking

these you will find in any cookery book. *Iceland Moss* is also very good. Steep half an ounce of the best picked moss in hot water for ten minutes, strain, and boil in a pint of fresh water till it is reduced to four ounces; add some liquorice root, and boil a little longer.

4. *Gruel* is a very nutritious and wholesome drink, and will lie on a sick stomach sometimes when nothing else will. Yet few know how to make it well. Most people make it too thick or too thin. I think that which is made from *good* oatmeal is the best. The oatmeal ought to be the medium sort. When buying it, taste it. A shopkeeper may assure you it is fresh when it is far from it. Put a pinch or two in the mouth, and if it has the slightest "bite," or feeling of bitter warmth, it is unfit for human food. Mix two tablespoonfuls with four of cold water. Pour on a pint of boiling water, and boil the whole for three minutes, stirring all the time. Pass through a sieve, and add butter, sugar, and spices to taste. Serve hot.

5. *Beef Tea.*—When really good beef is not to be had, Liebig or Bovril may be used instead. Bovril is malted, and easily digested. Beef tea can hardly be made too strong. Remove every particle of fat from the meat and cut up or mince; put in a jelly jar and cover with cold water. Tie a piece of paper over the jar with pin-holes in it, and place the jar in a pannikin of boiling water. Let it simmer till well done. Any meat—chicken, rabbit, veal, etc.—may be used to make tea in the same way; but it should be served hot, and eaten with toast or bread-crust, for really the tea itself is little more than a stimulant.

6. Although I have made and cooked almost everything, I have never manufactured *Gingerbread*. The following, however, seems to me to be a good receipt. It is taken from an old medical book. Take half a pound of fine flour, and, putting it on the baking-board, thoroughly mix it with a quarter of a pound of treacle—golden syrup is best—working it into a paste. Add ground ginger to a portion of this according to taste; mix extra well, roll out, then bake till crisp. A little butter greatly improves the whole, and probably a dust of baking-powder would make it lighter.

7. *Curry Powder* is one of the finest and most wholesome condiments we possess. We seldom get a really good dish of curry set before us in this country. Like all officers who have served in India or the seas around, I flatter myself I *can* make a good curry. My teacher was an Arab in Zanzibar; he taught me also how to make coffee. One reason why curry in this country is seldom of great excellence is that the powder is not so fresh as it ought to be; another reason is that few cooks dream of adding cocoa-nut milk to it. I do not mean the cocoa-nut water you find in the green cocoa-nut. Let me tell you how Suleiman, my Arab, used to curry my fowl in the bush at Boo-boo-boo. He grew the turmeric in his wild wee garden, in his cocoa-tree patch, and I think he also cultivated most of the other seeds, etc.; so everything was fresh as peas new-gathered on a May morning. Well, he solemnly cleaned and prepared the fowl by tearing it all in pieces. Meanwhile, the chattee was on the clear fire, and therein was floated a sliced onion in a well of butter or *gee*. When this was done brown he threw in the fowl, and stirred the pieces about until they were partially cooked, the aroma that arose causing my mouth to water. He had already mixed his curry ingredients, and he had grated down half an old cocoa-nut on a hair sieve; through this he poured water, and lo! rich, creamy milk was the result. Then he added the curry paste and this milk, and stewed the whole till tender. The little black girl had boiled the rice, and to complete the curry stew Suleiman thickened the gravy with a little flour. It was then ready to dish up. Mind you, the rice was placed on one dish and the fowl curry on another, not served up in the messy English fashion, with the rice all round the edge of the dish, to get cold and look ugly. So if ever you make curry, whatever you do, forget not the cocoa-nut milk.

If you don't choose to make your own curry powder, buy it from the best Italian warehouse you know of. You may not be able to get what will suit your taste at first, but when you do succeed in obtaining a good brand, take a note of it, and never get any other.

8. Here is a receipt for what is called *Indian Curry Powder*. I have not tested it nor tasted it, but it seems to be genuine, and it is not at all difficult to make. First catch your hare—that is, catch your coffee-mill—and have it thoroughly cleaned, because I don't think the flavour of Mocca would improve a true Indian curry. Now take half an ounce each of turmeric, fresh ground ginger, and coriander seeds, half a drachm each of black pepper and poppy seed (called *maw* seed in the shops), ten or fifteen grains of cinnamon, a morsel of garlic, six cloves, and two chillies. Mix, and grind all together, and keep in a well-stoppered bottle.

9. *Chutney* is such a delightful relish that I wonder housekeepers do not make it more often than they do. To buy the real Indian chutney becomes expensive. Besides, there is always the danger of a shock to the nervous system from finding what seem, and probably are, cockroaches' legs in it. But most of the so-called Indian chutney is made in England. Here is a receipt on a large scale—you can make less in the same proportions:—Equal parts—say a pound and a half—of apples, chillies, ginger, sultana raisins, and salt; add to this three-quarters of a pound of grated garlic, and one pound of loaf sugar, and five bottles of best vinegar. The chillies are first soaked in the vinegar for a couple of hours, then all the ingredients are mixed and ground to a pulp.

10. *Tarragon Vinegar* is greatly relished by some epicures, and although dear in shops, it is *so* easily made. You simply steep the leaves of tarragon in vinegar, according to taste, and there you have it after a maceration of fourteen days. In the same way vinegar from many fragrant herbs may be made.

11. *Curry Vinegar* is made by adding two ounces of best curry powder to a pint of vinegar and keeping it in a warm place for a few days, then straining.

12. It is not generally known that cods' liver may be nicely cooked and relished by invalids who can hardly bear to take the oil itself. You see, it is ever so much fresher thus. I need scarcely dilate here on the benefits that accrue from a long course of cod-liver oil to those who are in any way below par, or whose lungs may not be so strong as they might be.

Many ladies suffer very much from cold during the winter months, and really dread the coming of January, which is undoubtedly the bitterest month in this country. The taking of cod-liver oil in pretty large doses, and the wearing of rather loose warm clothing, is the cure, for by this means cold is set at defiance.

Potatoes—nice floury ones—are steamed till cooked, then a nice portion of cod's liver placed over them, cut in pieces to let the oil exude, and steamed again. The liver itself is eaten with some relish or condiment, and this makes a most nutritious meal. Rice or tapioca is also cooked and then treated with cod's liver. I think many will thank me for giving this treat.

I shall finish my paper by giving one or two other receipts from my wallet, then retire.

13. What so refreshing as *Toilet Vinegar*, either to damp the brow or hair with when one has a headache, or to put in the water to lave the face, arms, and hands, or to throw into the cold or tepid bath, or use in a sick room as a perfume. But to buy, it is very dear.

On the other hand, it is both easily and cheaply made. Here is the receipt in a single sentence:—Otto of roses, one hundred drops; rectified spirits of wine, twelve ounces; acetic acid (dilute), forty-five ounces. Shake, and it is made; but some add four or five ounces of dried rose leaves, and macerate for fourteen days; then strain.

14. *Cold Cream* is not difficult to make, and is very useful for chapped hands or lips in winter. Eight ounces of oil of almonds are melted in an earthen vessel with two ounces of pure white wax, and as soon as it gets cool—not cold—stir in six ounces of rose water.

15. Just one more delightful preparation—the *Cream of Lemons*. An ounce of spermaceti and half an ounce of oil of almonds, to which, as it cools, add eight drops of the oil of lemons.

And now St. Claus takes up his wallet and once more escapes up the chimney or through the keyhole. Before he goes, however, he breathes a blessing on his readers, and says from his heart—Girls all, I wish you a happy Christmas and *such* a jolly New Year!

MODEL MENU FOR DECEMBER.

Menu.

Tomatoes and Sardines.

Soup Brunoise.

Cutlets of Cod à la Genoise (or with Genoese Sauce).

Turkey Poult.

Turnips.   Potato Snow.

Plum Pudding.   Castle Puddings.

Cheese.

At this time of year we are accustomed to think that we ought to have tolerably substantial dinners to fortify us against the cold and dreariness of winter. The spirit of the season is also somewhat festive. In December friends drop in to dinner almost as a matter of course; and it is particularly desirable that we should give them not only a hearty welcome, but acceptable fare. Let us, then, see what can be done; and while studying our menu, let us remember that, concerning a dinner, we may say of the food what a great vocalist once said of the human voice in singing: "It is a detail. The manner of its presentation is everything."

Tomatoes and Sardines.—A very tasty and acceptable appetiser may be made of the fillets of sardines freed from skin and bone, and arranged upon a slice of tomato laid upon a little piece of toasted crumb of bread about two inches in diameter. This savoury can be served either hot or cold. If it were preferred hot, the rounds would need to be put in a hot oven for two or three minutes. One sardine would furnish fillets for two *hors d'œuvres*. The tomato would have to be cut with a sharp knife into slices a quarter of an inch thick. Little sprigs of parsley might be employed as a garnish.

Soup Brunoise is simply the name given in these days to clear, pale soup, in which are floating vegetables cut either into dice or into small round balls of the size of peas. It is a very pretty soup, especially when the vegetables employed for making the balls are of different colours. Thus, white balls can be composed of turnip, yellow balls of carrot; and if a spoonful of preserved green peas can be added, they will be a valuable addition, although we can do without them if more convenient. The balls are most readily formed when there is at hand a vegetable-cutter, or turner, as it is sometimes called; a little instrument, which can be bought at a first-class shop for a few pence. Housekeepers who have never used a vegetable-cutter are apt to think it a costly utensil, difficult to manage. It is really quite a simple affair, very cheap, and with its aid it would be easy to stamp out as many balls as would be needed for a dish of soup in a few minutes. Ladies, therefore, who have resolved to improve the family fare, are advised very early in the proceedings to purchase a plain, round vegetable-turner, the end of which is of the size of a pea. While doing so, they may as well buy also a second one with a cutter about the size of a marble. This will also be most useful. We shall find occasion for it before we have gone through our model menu. The vegetable balls may be cut out and boiled some time before they are wanted. They will then merely need to be put into the tureen, and have the boiling soup poured over them. About six or eight little balls should be given with each plate of soup.

Clear Soup is usually very acceptable at the commencement of dinner. When well flavoured and well made it is very appetising; it is light, and easy of digestion, and yet is sufficiently sustaining to take away the feeling of faintness with which so many busy people sit down to dinner. It is satisfactory also, because by merely altering the garnish it can be presented in many forms, all with a different name. Thus it comes about that the cook who can make clear soup properly has at her disposal a dozen soups. If she likes to have the garnish of vegetables cut in long thin slices, and fried in a little butter, then drained, she has *Julienne Soup*. A garnish of young carrot and turnip cut into flat round pieces produces *Printanier Soup*; another of homely vegetables cut into cylindrical pieces makes *Soupe à la Jardinière*, or *Soupe à la Macedoine*; another of brussels sprouts produces *Flemish Soup*; another of bread cut into fancy shapes and fried till crisp makes *Croûte au Pot*; a garnish with threads of vegetables floating in it is *Soupe Xavier*; *Soupe à la Royale* is soup garnished with savoury custard, and *Soupe à la Princesse* is soup garnished with quenelles; while *Nudeln Soup* and *Profiterolles Soup* are merely clear soups to which the distinctive garnish has been added. Practically, the soups just named are all the same soup, the differences between them lying in the garnish. When once we realise this fact how desirable we feel it to be that our cook should be able to make clear soup readily.

There are two or three ways of making clear soup, and we may as well confess that the orthodox high-class method is both troublesome and expensive, so that we cannot wonder that people are afraid of it. On the other hand, the common "easy" way of making clear soup furnishes a food that is so little tempting in taste that we must sympathise with individuals who consider it objectionable. A great deal of the clear or gravy soup prepared for hungry diners is positively distasteful. Its colour is produced from burnt sugar; its strong taste is a combination of dissolved gelatine and Liebig's Extract. Whatever else it is, it is not agreeable. We read that a well-known authority used to say that, "Soup is to a dinner what a portico is to a palace, or an overture to an opera—it is not only the commencement of the feast, but gives an idea of what is to follow." If this be true, there is no doubt that a person of cultivated taste, having partaken of clear soup as prepared by the majority of cooks, would gain an idea that the dinner was going to be a fraud.

According to the orthodox high-class method of making clear soup, a pound of undressed meat is allowed for each pint and a quarter or so of water. The meat is simmered with vegetables for about five hours; it is then strained, and clarified with more raw meat and vegetables; and when the recipe for making it is followed exactly it is perfect. It is clear as spring water, bright as sherry, and its taste is excellent. But then, what has it cost? Think of the money and time which have been spent upon it! It must be made on the day it is wanted, for if kept long it goes cloudy. Except as an occasional luxury we cannot afford to make soup thus.

According to the ordinary easy method of making soup, stock made in the usual way, from scraps and odds and ends, and flavoured with vegetables, is clarified with white of egg, which means that the soup is first made boiling hot and skimmed well; then it has white and crushed shell of egg (one white to a quart of stock) which has been whisked with a little water, and stock mixed with it; it is stirred quickly until it nearly boils, when it is put to the side of the fire and allowed to stand until the egg-white, having drawn to it the particles which cloud the stock, separates therefrom, and lies in a mass on the top. This point being reached, the stock can be strained through a cloth, and after once or twice straining, it is almost sure to be clear. Unfortunately, the process which separates from the stock the cloudy particles, separates also the flavouring particles, and thus it comes about that clear soup made of stock clarified with white of egg is too often sadly deficient in flavour. It may be that the cook will discover this before sending it to table, and, by way of mending matters, she adds a little burnt sugar to make the soup look strong of gravy. The effect of her effort is that she entirely destroys any little delicacy and flavour that might still remain, and serves a soup that tastes of nothing but burnt sugar and salt. Let it be understood, therefore, that if we want to make clear soup successfully, burnt sugar should for the time be banished from the kitchen. It is a most dangerous ingredient, and yet it is in constant and daily use. If our clear soup, when ready for the tureen, is not quite all that it ought to be, let us add a quarter of a teaspoonful of Liebig's Extract, and boil a piece of burnt onion in the soup before it is strained. This will impart a flavour that is at least not objectionable. Burnt onion can be bought, or, if there is none at hand, it is easy to make it by putting a small onion in the oven or on the hot-plate, and turning it often until it is browned well, but not charred; if charred, it will spoil the soup.

When, however, there is not time to make clear soup properly, or if fresh meat for making it is not available, it is wise to boil the vegetables that would be used for flavouring in water for an hour and a half or so, then strain the liquid and dissolve a little Liebig's Extract in it until it is pleasantly coloured, and tastes of meat, when salt and pepper can be added. Soup produced by this method is not bad. It is not as good as soup correctly made, but it is by no means to be despised. At any rate, it is far superior to soup clarified with white of egg and coloured with burnt sugar.

The following is the best easy way of making Clear Soup:—Take two pounds of fleshy beef, without fat (silver-side or buttock), and tie the meat into a compact shape. Take also two pounds of bones which have been broken up, and are quite free from marrow. (If any marrow or fat get in, it will be most difficult to make the soup clear.) Put the meat into a saucepan and set it on a moderate fire for about ten minutes, to draw out the juice and brown it. Be careful not to let it burn; to prevent its doing so, shake the pan once or twice, and turn it once during the ten minutes, sticking a large fork well into it to make the gravy flow. When the meat is brown, put the bones under it, pour on three pints of cold water, and add a small tablespoonful of salt. Let it come slowly to the boil, skim it well, and throw in a wineglassful of cold water; bring to the point of boiling again, and skim once more. Do this three times, or till no more scum rises. The object of throwing in the cold water is to keep the soup from boiling until all the scum has risen. Scum rises to the surface when soup is on the point of boiling. After boiling, the scum melts and sinks, and if not removed the soup is never so clear.

When no more scum forms, but not before, put into the soup two carrots, a turnip, four bay leaves, two onions, one leek, a bunch of parsley, and four cloves. Draw the pan back, and simmer gently for four hours. When wanted, strain the soup through muslin (twice if necessary), and serve. If successfully made, this soup will be clear and bright, and very tasty. It should be served very hot, and to secure its being so, the tureen in which it is sent to table should be made hot beforehand, and should not be over large for the measure of soup that is to be served in it. When soup sufficient only for a small party is put into a large tureen, it is certain to get cold quickly, and lukewarm soup leaves much to be desired.

When soup made according to the recipe just given is not what we should like it to be, the failure is generally attributable to one of three causes. Either the saucepan was in fault, or the soup was boiled quickly, not simmered, or else the cover was left on the pan; whereas the rule should be, that until the soup is quite clear the pan should remain uncovered. The best saucepan for making clear soup is an earthenware one, such as is used by the French for their *pot-au-feu*. Such pans stand well at the side of the close stoves that are now common, but they are not often found in our kitchens. Next best is a copper saucepan tinned inside, and retinned frequently; next in point of excellence is a white enamelled saucepan, provided this is quite whole and perfect. It is, however, just as well to understand that it is hardly possible to make clear soup successfully in an iron saucepan which has been used for making stews and all sorts of things. Good workmen never quarrel with their tools, it is said, but a cook who is expected to make clear soup in a saucepan of this kind is justified in making a protest.

It will have been noticed that to make clear soup in the way described, it was necessary to use undressed meat. There is, however, no occasion for either soup or vegetables to be wasted. The latter may be put into the stock-pot (for they will be full of flavour), or they may be made into a salad. In order to get as much value as may be out of them, it will be well to take them out of the soup as soon as tender. If they are boiled too much they will interfere with the clearness of the soup. The meat may be cut into slices and served cold with salad, or it may be minced, and garnished with poached eggs. If simmered without ceasing it will be excellent food.

When fresh meat is not allowed, soup called "clear" is frequently made of scraps and odds and ends. Even this soup is not to be despised, provided always that the odds and ends are of a varied nature, and sufficient in quantity, and that the soup is made the day before it is wanted. The way to make it is to collect whatever scraps there may be, look them over, cut away everything that is not quite sweet and good, break up the bones, and carefully remove all fat and skin. Now put the material into a stewpan; cover with cold water, add a few rinds of bacon scalded and scraped, an onion stuck with one or two cloves, and a bunch of herbs. Stew well for some hours, leave the pan uncovered, and carefully remove the scum as it rises, throwing in cold water once or twice as in the last recipe, to assist it to rise. When the bones are clear, strain the soup through muslin, and leave it all night. Next day take the fat from the top, and pour the soup gently into the stewpan, being careful to leave behind any sediment that may have settled at the bottom. Prepare the vegetables used in the last recipes. Boil these in about a pint of water for an hour, then strain the liquor into the soup. Boil up and serve. Soup thus made will be fairly clear. The longer it boils the stronger it will be; but it will probably need to have a little Liebig put with it. When in the souptureen it will appear cloudy, but a spoonful in a plate will not look bad. Its excellence will depend very much on the thoroughness with which it is skimmed.

Cutlets of Cod à la Genoise.—In the winter season there is not a great choice of fish. It is true that in large towns—London especially—almost every variety of fish can be had nearly all the year round; but still there are periods when special sorts are specially excellent and abundant, and winter is the period when the finer sorts of fish are expensive. Cod, however, is then at its best, and consequently it is a valuable resource. Yet it needs to be carefully chosen, for there is no fish that comes to market that varies so much in quality. When it is blue and semi-opaque it is to be avoided; it should be white, firm, elastic, and close.

Old-fashioned housekeepers have a great respect for boiled cod. They have the head and shoulders, or a handsome piece from the middle, boiled, with an accompaniment of oyster sauce, and then feel that they have done well for the family. So they have. Boiled cod with oyster sauce is a munificent dish—a dish fit to set before a king. Yet there is a good deal of it. If provided for a small family there would be a large piece left, and this would have either to be warmed up or wasted. Also, it would be a costly dish. We should be fortunate if we obtained fish, sauce, and garnish for less than five or six shillings.

When, therefore, cod is wanted for a small dinner, it is advisable to eschew the head and shoulders and the middle of cod, and modestly to purchase about two pounds of the tail-end of a cod. This is the cheapest part, and generally regarded as inferior; yet a very tasty and inviting dish can be made of it, particularly if it is garnished with potatoes; and it is to be remembered that cod is one of the few fish which may correctly be garnished with potatoes. Here is the recipe :—Divide the cod into neat slices about an inch thick. Sprinkle pepper and salt over these, and let them lie for an hour; then drain them. Put them in a single layer in a saucepan of boiling water slightly salted, and boil gently for about five minutes. Drain well, and have the sauce hot and ready in a small saucepan. Lay the pieces of fish in very carefully, and stew gently for another five minutes, or till the flesh will leave the bone. When sufficiently cooked, dish the cutlets in a circle, coat them with the sauce, and put potato-balls in the centre.

The Genoese Sauce is made as follows :—Melt an ounce of butter in a small stewpan, and fry in it a piece of carrot, a piece of turnip, and a shalot or small onion, all of which have been cut into thin slices. Stir over a sharp fire for five minutes, then add three quarters of an ounce of flour, and fry this also. Pour in half a pint of stock, also a teaspoonful of good mushroom ketchup and half a teaspoonful of anchovy. Stir the sauce till it boils, if not dark enough add a little *pastille charpentier*, strain it, and it is done. It may be made before it is wanted, and kept in a gallipot surrounded with boiling water till the fish can be placed in it. Or an easier way still—the fish can be boiled till done in the water, and the sauce poured over it in the dish. People accustomed to use wine in sauces would think it necessary to add claret to this sauce. Without wine, however, it is not to be despised.

Potatoes Tossed in Butter.—Peel four large kidney potatoes and cut them into square plugs the length of the little finger. Put them into cold water and let them get half cooked, then drain them. Thus far the potatoes may be made ready beforehand. A few minutes before they are wanted melt two ounces of butter in a small saucepan, season the potatoes slightly with pepper and salt, and throw them into the hot butter. Let them cook gently, and shake the pan every now and again. When sufficiently cooked, serve them in the centre of the cutlets. A little chopped parsley may be sprinkled over them. These potatoes will be excellent if they are cooked as directed. If the butter is stinted, or if they are not half boiled before being thrown into the butter, they will probably prove a disappointment. These are not fried potatoes, it will be understood. Fried potatoes would be very good, but it would disturb the equanimity of the average good plain cook to have a pan of fat on the stove and be called upon to fry potatoes while both sauce and fish had to be looked after. Cooked thus, however, the stewpan containing the potatoes can be set at the side. If shaken now and again they will be all right. Kidney potatoes are preferred to regents for this dish, because kidneys are firmer, and less likely to break with cooking.

Turkey with Turnips and Potato Snow.—Turkey is the dish *par excellence* for Christmas; and as Christmas Day approaches it begins to be exceedingly high in price. About Christmas also, if the truth may be told, turkeys are sometimes more abundant than acceptable. People who are in the way of having them get too much of them, although people who are not in the way of having them consider them a luxury, and buy them when they are at their dearest. Surely this is not good management. Quite early in December small turkeys are often to be had at a very reasonable price, and they are most delicious food. Would it not be an advantage if housekeepers would have the courage to dispense with the large turkey for Christmas Day, and provide a small bird once or twice early in the month, when the dish would be less common and more likely to be enjoyed?

A turkey is all the better for hanging three or four days before being cooked, although it should never be in the least "high." It should be trussed and cooked like a fowl, and have rolls of bacon, or small sausages, or slices of tongue, or a border of watercress, round the dish as a garnish. Bread sauce and good gravy are the usual accompaniment to it. The bird may be stuffed or not—probably the decision on this point will depend on its size. It is, however, not usual to put forcemeat into a small roast turkey; a little onion and a slice of butter placed in the crop are all that are considered necessary. The flesh should be well basted or it will be dry. To prevent dryness, it is an excellent plan to put a slice of bacon over the breast whilst it is being cooked. This should be removed during the last half-hour, or the skin may not be properly browned.

Turnips, when daintily prepared, are quite a delicacy. Unfortunately, they seldom are daintily prepared. They are watery, and rather strong in taste. They need to be carefully cooked. Peel them thickly down to the white part. If the peel is taken off too thinly they are sure to be bitter. Put them into cold water slightly salted, and bring this to the boil; then pour it off and substitute fresh boiling water. Remove the scum as it rises, and boil the turnips until tender enough to pass through a sieve. Let them stand for an hour in a colander or on a sieve, that the water may drain from them. (Some cooks put the pulp into a cloth and wring it, to get the water from it.) Turn the pulp into a stewpan. With each quart thereof put a good lump of butter, a tablespoonful of milk or cream, and a little pepper and salt. Stir over the fire, and while doing so dredge in a tablespoonful of flour. When hot, smooth, and free from moisture, the turnips are ready. They will be altogether a different thing from turnips as usually served.

Plum Pudding.—Of late years there has arisen a prejudice against plum pudding. It has been pronounced unwholesome and indigestible, and all sorts of charges have been brought against it. For the most part these charges are unfounded. Probably the reason why it is so badly spoken of is, that it is usually served at the end of a heavy Christmas dinner, and thus it happens that it has to bear blame which does not properly belong to it. This much may be said in its favour—that the materials of which it is composed are all valuable and sustaining; raisins, especially, are believed to be as sustaining as wine, without being harmful; and not long ago a physician of high repute said that, far from thinking plum pudding injurious, he had found it to be very excellent food for healthy persons, and that in his own experience, when he had specially exhausting work to do he frequently fortified himself with a slice. Moreover, the dish is very convenient.

Five or six puddings can be mixed together and boiled together in separate moulds, and they can be readily warmed as wanted. Like turkey, plum pudding is generally enjoyed more in the early days of December than at the orthodox time.

It is probably scarcely necessary to give a recipe for plum pudding, for proved recipes are in the possession of every family.

Castle Puddings.—These simple puddings are well known, though they appear under various names. They are generally liked, however, and very easily made, and by exercising a little taste they can be made to look very pretty. They are very much like small sponge cakes in taste, and the only thing we have to be careful about when making them is, not to mix them until just before they are wanted, because if allowed to stand they will be less light than they ought to be. As they can be mixed in a few minutes, this condition is easily met.

To make them, take any number of eggs (let us say, in this instance, two), and their weight, when unbroken, in sugar, butter, and flour. Beat the butter and sugar to a cream, then add the flour gradually, with the addition of a pinch of salt and a few drops of vanilla flavouring, or, if preferred, a little grated lemon rind. Last of all add the eggs, well whisked. Have ready some small tins well greased with butter, half fill with the mixture, and bake in a moderate oven. Ornament in any way that is pretty. If four pennyworth of cream may be allowed, this can be whipped till firm. Then put in large knobs on the top of each pudding, a *glacé* cherry being dropped into each. *Glacé* cherries are to be bought of any high-class grocer. They cost about eighteenpence a pound, and a quarter of a pound will ornament a good many puddings. They will keep for an indefinite period in a box or covered tin. If cream is considered unnecessary, the puddings may have a little desiccated cocoanut sprinkled over them. In this case a little sauce should be served with the pudding, which sauce may be made as follows :—

Pudding Sauce.—Put a quarter of a pint of water, an inch or two of thin lemon rind, and a tablespoonful of white sugar, and boil. Mix half a teaspoonful of arrowroot or cornflour smoothly with a little cold water; stir the boiling water into it; boil up once more, and add the strained juice of a large fresh lemon. By the way, it may be added that if these little puddings can be baked in fluted tins they will look all the prettier. PHYLLIS BROWNE.

PRIVATE CHRISTMAS CARDS.

THE origin, full popularity and gradual abandonment of a widely spreading social custom usually covers many generations; but the rise of the Christmas card, its rapid acceptance and the signs of its waning hold upon public taste, all fall well within half a century. Nor, trivial as it may appear by the side of matters affecting morals or health, does its little history fail to reflect many far more important movements that were its contemporaries. It has been said of modes, that when once a garment is recognised as "the fashion," it is a proof that it has really ceased to be fashionable. But the affectation of superiority which would limit a fashion to a few aristocratic leaders, cannot be urged against the Christmas card. It came into being with a new recognition of the beauty of the Christmas festival, and was in its intention a formal expression of the settling of quarrels, the balancing of social accounts, wiping off old debts, and at least professing to be in amity with all men as befits the season. Nor was it a movement confined to any particular class, all ranks of people were alike anxious to forward, by its help, kindly greetings to their friends. Nor, curiously enough, although in idea distinctly the outcome of an ecclesiastical feast, did it attract those only whose creed implies formal recognition of certain appointed days. As in far Japan the New Year's exchange of very similar cards of greeting was observed by non-christian peoples, so in England the feast of Christmas was interpreted in the sense of the angels' message to include all men of good-will, Jews, infidels, Turks and heretics alike. How the pleasant and graceful courtesy grew to overwhelming proportions, so that which was at first a sincere message became a purely formal courtesy, need not be retold here. Nor need one dwell on the inane and inappropriate designs which, accompanied with more or less unsuitable words, usurped the simpler cordiality of the earlier cards. The tawdry elegance of the ornate varieties, and the would-be æsthetic attractions of others, alike have failed to maintain their supremacy. So in recent years, people whose sense of good taste is their most cherished possession, have abandoned the design prepared for anybody and everybody who cares to buy copies, in favour of a plainer card specially printed with a personal greeting; too often as vague and stilted in its phrases as the ordinary established formula of a printed invitation or its equally trite acceptance. For if you have to strike an average message that shall suit the more distant acquaintance as well as the dearest friend, it is the lowest mean average that is usually struck.

Thanks to the growth of various new economic processes which enable a special design to be prepared for lithographic, or still better, for ordinary letter-press printing, at a price out of all proportion to older methods of engraving, it is now possible for anyone of quite moderate means not merely to have a

The Girl's Own Paper, 1896

So much for the commercial side of the affair, which is always best got out of the way as soon as possible. The artistic side is not so easily settled. This, for two or three reasons. First, people's tastes differ, or they think they do, to an alarming extent. But if you look close into the matter, few people have much of their own. What passes for taste is merely (as a rule) the selection of sombody else's taste to imitate. We all imitate more or less; those who are careful to choose great examples reap the reward. For although it sounds like a paradox when put in plain words, we are generally more original when consciously following another's lead than when we believe we are initiating something no one ever thought of doing before. In the first case, the unconscious personal element so modifies our intended imitation, that the subtle difference is often enough to give a distinctly individual character to the work. When we purposely try to be absolutely original, we either produce some hideous thing that all well-conducted minds had rejected before, or it turns out to be a plagiarism that the trickster memory had supplied us with, and not recalled the source at the same time.

specially printed card bearing the name and address of the sender, but the text itself embodied within a graceful design. The cost of a block for such a card should not exceed five shillings; the charge for printing fifty or one hundred ought certainly not to be more than half-a-crown, so that you may get a hundred cards from your own design at about the cost of the penny card of economic courtesy.

Of course, if an artist is commissioned to produce a design for you, he or she must be paid, but even then the price of the cards will not be very high, and the pleasure of possessing a unique publication to send to friends is surely worth a trifle extra expense.

People who are satisfied with cards at a penny a dozen will hardly change for these unless they send many hundreds (as some folks do), when the special card would be no more costly. But the more generous heart that expands in collections, or seasonable benevolence, to a silver threepenny bit for each purpose, may essay more ambitious flights than the course I have quoted.

For designs, we may go far afield, and yet find someone has been there before. When one realises the really stupendous fact that in England alone about 200,000 designs have been published for Christmas and New Year's cards, the chances of getting hold of a new idea at once suitable and in good taste appears somewhat remote.

As we may take it that the cost and technical knowledge involved in the preparation of a colour design limits us to black and white, we will only consider that class. I need not say that the conventional expression "black and white" includes any single colour on any single colour. It is, in fact, merely the vernacular for "monochrome," which sounds rather like a text-book.

So in choosing your design, do not be afraid of selecting a good model, and adapt it exactly to please your taste. If gifted with artistic talent, you prepare the design yourself, whatever colour you elect to have it printed, the drawing should be in absolutely black ink—ebony wood-stain, costing sixpence a bottle, or the liquid Indian ink, sold by artists' colourmen, or perhaps, best of all, waterproof American Indian ink, which costs a shilling a bottle. If you use the latter, you can make any corrections in Chinese white, which is a great advantage, hence its superiority to purely soluble inks.

The design is best if drawn about half as large again as the intended impression. One warning is of the first importance, namely, to use as few lines as possible, and those strong and clearly defined. Never employ a dozen fine lines when one thick one will do as well. To be simple is much harder than people suppose; in drawing a detail, a dozen scratches all somewhere near the exact place of the contour gives a specious air of careless abandon. In the hands of a master it may not only do this honestly, but at the same time impart a sense of movement; but in the hands of a novice it implies carelessness merely, which is not quite the same thing as careless power. If you are not sure of your prowess in figure-drawing, treat the doubt as a certainty that you are unequal to tackle the most difficult of all subjects. But even this need not keep you limited to still-life forms, because any old

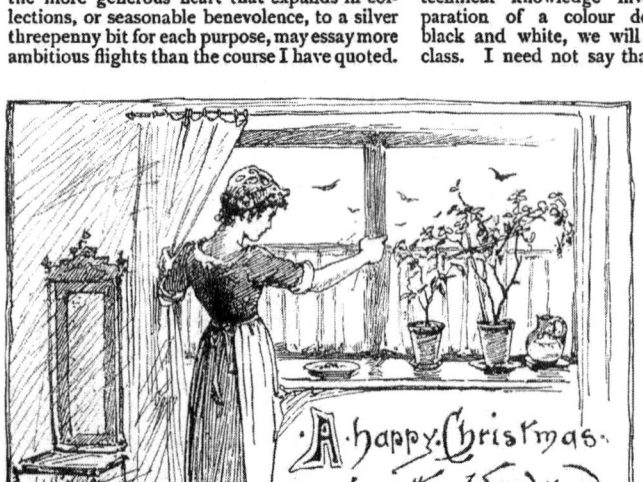

woodcut or engraving may be pasted on your card, and a border, with appropriate lettering, added. I say any old engraving, because the copyright laws forbid you to make copies of modern work. For this purpose dozens of old woodcuts of the Nativity and other suitable subjects, and many exquisite etchings and engravings of the Old Masters, are both admirable and available. As copyright extends forty-two years, after the publication, or seven years after the artist's death (whichever be the longer), it is safer to consider nothing since 1840 as open to indiscriminate reproduction. If, however, you will be entirely original, first think out your subject well, and sketch it in pencil, then add the lettering. Now to draw a design may be a thing not within the power of everybody to acquire, but to letter well means only good taste and infinite patience. If your lettering is poor, the whole result will be feeble; but really firm, well-placed inscriptions will add dignity to a poor design. In fact it is hardly overstating the case to say that the importance of the lettering is far and away beyond that of all the rest. In the reproduced designs, the charming fancy of Mr. F. G. Jackson's card would seem ten times as good, did bolder and better-placed lettering fill up the space at the lower right-hand corner.

In "Fortune's Wheel," by Mr. Alan Wright, a design made for Dr. Harrison Low (who reproduced it in most marvellous carbon photographs), the lettering is entirely good; so in Mr. Arthur Gaskin's "Hodson" card, the lettering, rough as it is, is admirably planned. In the delightful little silhouette, the placing of the wording is so good, that one overlooks the fact of its being just hasty —but quite consistent—printing.

The mottoes available are legion. It is best to hunt up an unhackneyed one, or invent a pleasant greeting of your own, not too coldly formal in its wishes.

If your artistic power can only design a few sprigs of flowers, see that the sprigs are placed well on the card, and study to arrange the wording so that the design is improved by it. To know what to avoid, one has but to look at the cheap illuminated texts, where gigantic and hideous ornamental letters, so-called, ruin the effect of the decoration, which is often quite decent in its way.

Do not be afraid of simplicity, better three simple sprigs in a row, with plain type-letters below, than a formless, shapeless mass. If possible enclose all you design within a strong border-line (not necessarily rectangular), it brings the whole into unity, and yields a decorative effect.

Did but space permit, a hundred designs might be reproduced here, in proof of the popularity this pleasant innovation has already won.

A last word of warning, to prepare these things well before the time; the block will take a few days to make, the printer also will require one or two clear days. Everybody is pushed to the extreme limit of busy-ness at Christmas-time, and by planning in advance you will save yourself anxiety, and refrain from adding to that of others. It is always a pity when any pleasure is gained at the cost of another's worry or pain, so this little homily may be forgiven at a season when the ruling sentiment of all should be one of thoughtful consideration for the happiness of others, in small things as well as great.

GLEESON WHITE.

CHRISTMAS DAY IN A LONDON HOSPITAL.

CHRISTMAS Day in a hospital! How dreadful! We shall pity you, poor dear!"

So said all my friends last year on my announcing to them that I should be unable to join the family circle on the fast approaching Christmas Day.

I had only recently entered one of our London hospitals to be trained as a nurse, and I confess that my own heart sank when I found I should not get leave of absence for Christmas.

"We shall want all the help we can get," said the lady-superintendent. "It is a busy day here, and I think you will find it a happy one."

So I made up my mind to be as cheerful as possible under the circumstances; but "happy it cannot be for me," I thought. Such a sad contrast to the bright faces and merry firesides I had been accustomed to associate with the thought of Christmas. I had yet to learn that in blessing others we ourselves are blessed.

Preparations had been going on for some days, and all our time off duty had been devoted to dressing dolls and making decorations for the Christmas tree. In the wards the patients had begun to talk among themselves about the coming festivities; the children especially asking many eager questions as to the treat in store for them, their little faces brightening and eyes sparkling at the bare mention of the Christmas tree. Many little patients in our children's ward had never seen one, and forgot their pain and weariness while they speculated as to its size, and what sort of presents each one would get off it. And how hard they all tried to get well! Medicine was readily swallowed and painful dressings submitted to without a murmur, because, "it will help to make you strong enough to go down to the tree."

This eagerness was not confined to the children's ward alone. I was astonished and touched to find even the men putting the constant question, "Nurse, will I be well enough to go down to the tree?"

The day came at last. We rose an hour earlier than usual, and hastily swallowing our breakfast, hurried to the top ward of the hospital to begin the day with a short service and singing the Christmas hymn.

The winter morning had scarcely begun, but the wards look bright and cheerful with the firelight dancing on the holly and wreaths which adorned the walls, and lightening up the faces of the patients sitting up in their beds, arrayed in new scarlet flannel jackets, and we standing in two lines down the long ward in our spotless caps and aprons, hymn-books in our hands, waiting for our chaplain to join us. A harmonium had been wheeled into the ward, and as soon as he entered we began the sweet old hymn—

"Hark! the herald angels sing."

Nearly every patient joined in, some heartily, some only at intervals in weak low tones, but all with evident enjoyment, and many eyes filled with tears. One or two poor women even sobbed aloud before we had ended. "Oh, it wor that beautiful! Just like angels a-singing. I did feel sort of heaven-like!" said one old woman to me afterwards.

The hymn ended, our chaplain spoke a few earnest words, and offered up a short prayer with the collect for Christmas Day. This little service was repeated in every ward in the hospital, finishing just in time for us to go on duty at our usual hour. The rest of the morning passed in the usual way—hospital work must be done, however festive the day.

Dinners were served at one o'clock, and all those well enough had a plentiful supply of roast beef and plum pudding, extra delicacies being provided for the greater invalids. At three o'clock the hospital was thrown open to visitors, who had been collecting long before this hour in the courtyard, and came thronging in with eager feet, seeking out their relatives with little delay, except to pause to admire the various decorations of the wards as they passed by.

At the tea hour the hospital presented a very gay and festive scene. Each ward had vied with another in preparing the smartest table. There was no lack of good things. Cakes, jam, oranges, etc., had been sent in abundance, as well as flowers and plants, by the kind subscribers and those interested in the hospital, and great taste had been displayed in arranging the dainties. What a buzz of conversation and laughter as the well-filled plates and cups were handed round by the willing helpers!

Anyone looking into the wards might have wondered what had become of the poor "suffering patients," for all seemed so glad and gay. Those patients whose cases were too serious to be allowed to join in the feast, seemed quite content to watch their more fortunate companions, and enjoy what little they were allowed to partake of. Not one murmur escaped any lips; pain and weariness seemed for the time banished, the weak ones getting their full share of tender service and kindly sympathy, and the stronger patients never forgetting to keep their mirth within bounds, so as not to jar on the nerves of their more suffering neighbours.

At six o'clock the great event of the day came off. The board room, which had been closed all day, was thrown open, and there in the middle stood the noble tree, towering up to the ceiling, radiant with dozens of tiny lights, and almost weighted down with its load of treasures; the large dolls forming a picturesque group round the base of the tree. Dolls formed the greater part of the presents, and were received with delight, not only by the children, but by the men and women—all were anxious to get one; the men particularly received them with great joy.

"For my little 'un at home, nurse!"

Forms and couches had been arranged carefully about the room, so as to accommodate all who were able to come down.

Many walked in, some with the aid of sticks and crutches, some leaning on a kind strong arm. Children were carried down by the doctors or students, for everyone seemed eager to do all in their power to help make merry, and lastly came those who were unable to be raised from their beds; these were carried bodily upon their mattresses, and laid carefully on the couches or forms. When every available part of the room was filled, it presented a strange sight; it reminded one of the Pool of Bethesda, for there were the halt, the lame, and the blind, young and old, all more or less afflicted and suffering, assembled in a group round one centre-piece—the Christmas tree.

Quick hands soon stripped the branches of their treasures, each one receiving something. Perfect order was maintained throughout, no snatching or clamouring; their quiet and good behaviour was remarkable, considering the untutored rank to which the majority belonged.

When the tree was quite stripped the senior surgeon addressed a few kind words to the patients, and dismissed them with the wish that none would be the worse and many the better for their Christmas Day's entertainment.

It must not be supposed that those patients

The Girl's Own Paper, 1890

who were unable to attend the gathering round the tree were forgotten. Business meanwhile had been going on gaily in the half-deserted wards. Bran pies and lucky tubs were handed round from bed to bed, so that even the most feeble shared in the distribution. Each patient, too, received some substantial present.

In one ward, for instance, each woman received a warm petticoat or jacket, while the men got knitted vests and socks, and each gift was accompanied with an illuminated text, bearing sweet words of comfort and peace.

Surely many a heart, hardened with the struggle and battle of life, must have been touched and softened on that day, while some, I sincerely trust, will carry away with them the remembrance of their Christmas in a hospital, which, doubtless, many had dreaded as much as I myself had done, but where they learned to understand a little of what is meant by "Peace on earth, goodwill towards men."

"To think so much should be done for the like of we!" exclaimed one old man with tears in his eyes. "Why, they seems to glory in waitin' on us, and fussin' us up!
But t'aint themselves as does it, it be the Lord in their hearts."

But was it not also a joy to us to make these weary ones joyful! Let any who doubt it just try the experiment on this coming Christmas Day. Let them give up their usual part in the family gathering and all the luxury of their rich homes, and go for once among their poor brethren—the sick and sad of our great city. Let them see the glad smiles light up the wan faces and hear the words of gratitude, and I, from my own experience, can tell what will be their answer to the question, "Did you spend a happy Christmas?"

SOMETHING NEW.

By SOMERVILLE GIBNEY.

Now, girls, a word or two with you respecting Christmas entertainments; for though no doubt papa and mamma are the real givers of the party, yet you probably consider yourselves in a great measure responsible for its success, and this is quite as it should be. Papa finds the needful, mamma sees after the culinary arrangements, and you superintend the preparation of the house and the amusements—a fair division of labour. I have no doubt that many times during this joyous season, when the giving of a party is being discussed, the wish for something new and out of the common in your department will be expressed, something that will provide your guests with pleasant recollections to carry away with them, and that will stamp your party as the party of the season. Now I want to give you a few hints how this wish may be made to end in a triumph at the cost of very little beyond slight trouble and the exercise of good taste. But in order to prevent disappointment, let me inform you at once that I am not going to tell you of any new form of entertainment in one sense of the word. The old ones that have served for so many years have still plenty of life in them, and will serve for many more yet. The standing dish may be the same you have served on many previous occasions. I am going to speak about the trimmings, and you who interest yourselves in these matters will know what value attaches to these. A daintily-arranged lobster salad is much more appetizing than one carelessly thrown together, without any attempt at a picturesque appearance, though the ingredients be just the same in each—and so it is with a party. There are parties and parties. Coming back from one you say, "Oh, it was very nice and pleasant—the usual thing, you know." Coming back from another you exclaim, "It was charming; everything was so pretty and well arranged." And this is what I should wish may be said of yours, and what will be said if you carry out my instructions.

Let me imagine, by way of illustration, that you live in a house that has a small outer hall opening into a more commodious one, and that the drawing-room where the party proper is to be held opens out of this, as also the dining-room, where the supper is laid, while the tea-room and ladies'-room are upstairs. The evening has arrived, and with it your guests. They enter the hall, and are startled and delighted to find they have stepped into the midst of the realms of the Frost Queen, from which, for comfort's sake, the personal presence of Jack Frost has been excluded, although his handiwork is everywhere apparent. They discover the floor is thickly coated with snow. The walls, which they believed to have been covered with some dark wall paper, are now white, with ivy creeping up them, whose leaves glisten and sparkle in the light. Snow lies piled up against the foot of the stairs, as if swept out of the way. The stairs themselves are white and snow-covered, while the balustrades have patches of snow in all their crannies. Fir trees have suddenly sprung up in corners where they certainly gave no promise of growing a few days ago. Robin Redbreasts are perched here and there, as if about to sing, and the whole fairy-like scene is flooded by a crimson glow which does away with any idea of coldness. On going upstairs to the tea-room, you find the snow-storm has raged as violently there as down below, and has produced an equally picturesque effect. And now let me explain how this has been managed, and, remember, I am speaking of what has been done, not what might be done. This is no wild impracticable theory, but an accomplished fact, in which I had a hand, or rather both hands; so do not have any doubt about the result, but follow the directions, and the outcome will be success.

To begin with the floor. The snow we managed with large white dust sheets—very white. It did not matter about them fitting the shape of the hall, because where they were too big we turned them under, and the unevenness gave the idea of the snow lying thicker against the walls. The stairs were treated in the same way, the whole of the steps being covered, and also the landing on which the tea-room opened. For the walls, which were distempered a dark colour, we got several rolls of common white paper and fastened these with paste just below the ceiling, and again on the skirting-board against the floor. In this manner we covered the whole of the walls, and when it came to taking the paper down, a little warm water and a sponge removed all marks of the paste in a few moments, and the walls were not damaged in the slightest. Against this paper, which of course hung somewhat loosely, we pinned long creepers of ivy, having previously drawn them through water and dipped them in flour. We carried these creepers up about five or six feet, and, when fixed, ornamented them further with Epsom salts and tufts of cotton wool. The handrail on the stairs had a thick covering of the same, bound on with thin white string, and some was also placed in the corners and angles of the balustrades. In most of the angles of the walls we placed small fir trees in pots, the pots of course being hidden beneath cotton wool, and the trees themselves sprinkled with flour and salts. The doorways, from which the doors had been removed, had looped-up curtains of crimson muslin, and above them were large bunches of ivy and evergreens, in which were seated stuffed birds, as if singing. The gas lamps were not turned up too high, and each of them had a crimson cover, so that all the light that was shed on the scene was of a warm red colour. The gas stove in the hall was treated in the same way, and the gleam of red light lying athwart the mimic snow was most picturesque.

Every one of the guests was loud in his admiration, and declared the experiment a complete success. It was something so new and at the same time so pretty. There was one drawback, and the gentlemen were quick to discover it. If they happened to brush up against or even touch any of the numerous patches of cotton wool with their coats, they carried away some of it on their backs, and it was no easy matter to get rid of it, it adhered so closely to the cloth. But this after all was a minor matter. Finally, when the party was over, and it came to setting the house in order the following day, other advantages of our scheme made themselves apparent. We first of all unpinned and took down the ivy, then the cotton wool was collected, and the white paper from the walls, which was carefully rolled up to serve for another occasion; and lastly, instead of the carpets having to undergo a thorough sweeping, the white dust sheets were gathered together with all the litter in them and carried outside, leaving the floors as neat and tidy as if nothing extraordinary had taken place. That, girls, was our plan, and I would advise you to try it if during this party-giving season you are on the look out for something new.

COUNTRY SCENES.—DECEMBER.

Full knee-deep lies the winter snow,
 And the winter winds are wearily sighing
Toll ye the church-bell sad and slow
And tread softly, and speak low,
 For the old year lies a-dying.
                                TENNYSON.

Those who have read that exquisite little song of Shakspeare's, at the close of 'Love's Labour Lost'—and who is there that has not?—can never forget the perfect and finished wintry picture which every line presents. The icicles are first seen hanging beside the wall like great long, cold, bright-pointed spear-heads, which, only to look at, causes Dick, the shepherd, to blow his tingling nails more eagerly; to stamp, and jump, and shake off the clouted snow from his heavy shoes, as he beats his numbed feet upon the ground. Tom, who is seated beside the large old yawning kitchen fire-place, jumps up as if he were struck, by the head of a cross-bolt, when he sees Marian enter, with her nose "red and raw," her milk starred and frozen, in the clean white pail, running down over the bright, cold, polished hoops, on which it has congealed, like beaded pearls. Tom wants no summoning; but, leaping up, with a "God a mercy," hurries off to the log-house, and, shouldering a couple of such mighty blocks as could only be burnt in the huge old-fashioned fire-places of Shakspeare's day, rushes into the large hall without ceremony, well nigh stumbling over the great shaggy stag-hound, which lies stretched out at the foot of the old Knight, who, seated in his high-backed oaken chair, watches the sparks, as they go dancing above the quaintly-fashioned hand-irons, up the wide dark chimney, and rubs his hands for very cold. Without, the wind is blowing, bleak and bitter, whistling round the gable-ends of the ancient mansion, yet scarcely turning the frozen weathercock, while beside the hedges, which stretch along the "foul ways," the birds sit shivering and brooding in the snow—cold, with all their feathers, and scarcely able to peck the frozen berries, though their pointed beaks are rendered sharper by hunger. Sunday comes, and in the old, cold, grey country church, where the figures of Knights are freezing in icy mail, as their grim effigies lie stretched out with folded hands, the old Knight, having left his hall, and his log fire, can scarcely hear a word the parson says, for the loud and incessant coughing. One aisle coughs against the other; north answers south—the sound is contagious; it is caught in the chancel, and all the rounded periods of the old Divine are lost amid that never-ceasing chorus; and the old Knight is thankful when he again places his feet upon his own hearth, and sees his bowl of smoking lambs-wool placed before him, on the surface of which the roasted crabs bob and hiss, as they are popped in hot, from the red logs which Tom had piled upon the fire. Outside, the staring owl is crying "To-whit, too-whoo," somewhere about the red-bricked twisted chimnies. Such is the picture which the immortal Poet has drawn of Winter in twelve brief lines, each of which would form a text for a longer passage than we have written as a summary of the whole.

Now the brief days are cold, cheerless, and gloomy; the woods are naked and desolate; there is a sad, leaden, melancholy colour about the sky; the open country is silent, the fields are empty, the lanes abandoned by the village children, and, excepting the robin, you hear not the voice of a bird amid the whole landscape. You wander on in the direction of the village, and there, upon the large frozen pond, surrounded by a few aged willows, you behold a group of hardy rustics amusing themselves with the healthy exercise of sliding, and making a strange, hollow, and unearthly sound, as they run upon the ice. You see the sportsman far off, with his dogs and gun, and behold the white smoke rolling beside the hedge in the valley, while the report awakens the low and sleeping echoes. Further on, along the frozen and cheerless road, you see the village carrier's grey tilted cart, rocking between the naked hedgerows, as it moves slowly on past the cold white guide-post, by the embankment which is covered with withered and hoary grass, beside the long plantation where the snow is piled *beneath the dark green* fir trees, past the reedy pool where the flags stand with their sharp frozen edges, looking as if they would cut like a sabre, so cold, keen, and piercing do they appear.

Dreary would December be, did it not bring with it merry Christmas, with its holly, and ivy, and mistletoe, through the leaves of which peep the scarlet, and purple, and dull white berries, giving a green and summer appearance to our rooms, and throwing a cheerfulness around our hearths. We see the laden coach rolling past our window, piled high with game, hares, and pheasants, and great white geese, and black turkeys, whose plumage the wind blows back as they swing suspended from the roof; conjuring up visions of huge comfortable fires, well-spread tables, and happy faces, all congregated to do honour to good Old Christmas, whom Southey has beautifully drawn as seated beside the high-heaped hearth in his great armed-chair, watching the children at their sports, or pausing at times to stir the huge fire, and every now and then sipping the bright brown ale. For nights before the happy season arrives, we hear the village bells, awakening the surrounding silence by their silver music, and throwing a cheerful sound over the wild wintry landscape. When the morning of that old and holy day arrives, we hear the rustic waits chanting some simple Christmas carol, as they stand in the grey moonlight, at the front of the picturesque parsonage-house, telling how Christ was on that day born, and that while shepherds were attending their flocks by night, the Angel of the Lord descended, and proclaimed tidings of peace and good-will to all mankind. How plaintive and tremulous do those old chants fall upon the ear, sinking noiselessly and peacefully into the heart, and filling the soul with a holy and reverential awe; and, while the cock from the neighbouring farm makes answer to the carol of the village waits, we recall that exquisite passage of Shakspeare, in which, alluding to some old superstition, he says:

Some say, that ever 'gainst that season comes
Wherein our Saviour's birth is celebrated,
This bird of dawning singeth all night long.

Or we turn to those bye-gone times, so beautifully and feelingly described by Irving, who says:—"Christmas seemed to throw open every door, and unlock every heart. It brought the peasant and the peer together, and blended all ranks in one warm generous flow of joy and kindness. The old halls of castles and manor-houses resounded with the harp and the Christmas carol, and their ample boards groaned with the weight of hospitality. Even the poorest cottage welcomed the festive season with green decorations of bay and holly; the cheerful fire glanced its rays through the lattice, inviting the passenger to raise the latch and join the gossip knot huddled round the hearth, beguiling the long evening with legendary jokes and oft-told Christmas tales."

In our eye, Christmas never looks so beautiful as when it has been ushered in by snow, and frost, and rime; when the thatched roofs of the cottages are whitened over, and the branches of the trees are laden with feathery flakes; when the ivy that covers the grey and weather-beaten church-porch is half buried beneath the weight of accumulated snow, as if

Nature, in awe to Him,
Had doffed her gaudy trim,
With her great Master so to sympathise,
Hiding her guilty front with innocent snow.

Such a scene, witnessed under one of those cold, clear, blue skies which sometimes hangs over the earth in December, with the cottage chimnies sending up their columns of pale silver smoke, and a group of happy faces emerging from the ancient village church, sighing or smiling alternately as they recognise a child or a relation who has walked miles to bid them a merry Christmas—or, as they glance at the surrounding graves, and think of those who will never more sit at the high-piled table, over which the mistletoe branch again hangs, as it did in the days of old. Scott, in the following lines, has graphically described these ancient festivities:—

The fire, with well-dried logs supplied,
Went roaring up the chimney wide;
The huge hall-table's oaken face,
Scrubbed till it shone, the time to grace
Rose then upon its massive board
No mark to part the Squire and Lord.
Then was brought in the lusty brawn
By old blue-coated serving-man
Then the grim boar's head frowned on high,
Crested with bays and rosemary.

England was merry England when
Old Christmas brought his sports again:
'Twas Christmas broached the mightiest ale,
'Twas Christmas told the merriest tale;
A Christmas gambol oft would cheer
The poor man's heart through half the year.

Those who have looked upon the shadows of the trees as they are reflected upon the ground at this season of the year, cannot fail at being struck by the beautiful forms which they present. Every twig and branch is as clearly made out as if drawn with a dark pencil upon white paper; there you see endless patterns for embroidery and netting—open-work, square, or diamond-shaped threads, that seem to run into squares and ovals, crossing and turning in every imaginable form. In frosty weather, almost every object we look upon is beautifully marked, from the ragged flakes that hang upon the moss-covered boughs—the crimson berries, that seem encrusted with the whitest silver—the dark leaves of the evergreens, along which run pearly lines of frost-work—the bladed grass, sprinkled all over with minute pearls, down to the starry and diverging rays, which every little hollow that contained water has assumed,—all are beautiful. But pick up the skeleton of a leaf, when only the fine fibres are left; hold it between your eye and the light, and you will confess that never did lady wear a lace collar woven in the finest frame, of so fine and delicate a texture as the network of the fallen leaf; and the graceful cup-moss, when closely examined, is shaped in the forms of the most delicate cups, and urns, and vases, pale and dark green, and chased with silver, and all as neatly wrought as if they had come from the hand of the most finished artist.

Sometimes, on a fine day in December, when the snow has disappeared, there is a green Spring-look about the meadows, where the grass has sprouted up afresh beneath the Autumn rains, especially in those pastures from which the cattle were driven away early in the season. Under the hedgerows, and among the shady copses, peeping from amid the fallen foliage, we see the hardy leaves of the primrose and the violet, looking as green and fresh as if it were already the first month of Spring, for neither frost nor snow has power to destroy them in these sheltered places. Near spring-heads, which seldom freeze, we see the little wagtail, the smallest bird that walks, planting one leg before the other, and surveying everything his sharp eye alights upon, in his busy endeavour to pick up a meal. The larks huddle together in small parties, and seem, by their wistful looks, to wish that the air was warm enough to sing in; and if an unusually fine day should break out by the close of the next month, they will be seen trying their wings a little way up amongst the trees, and scattering around a few stray notes; and sometimes, at this season of the year, we see the porch of a cottage wreathed with the China rose, whose pale blossoms throw out a faint sweet perfume, and, with the green foliage, form a Summer-like scene amid the gloom, and cloud, and darkness of mid-Winter. The author of "Waverley" has left us a most graphic picture of the *ennui* which sometimes besets the hardy sportsman at this season. It is full of minute and excellent painting, and abounds in those little touches which tell that it has been struck off from the life, and is worthy of a place beside the little gem which we have commented upon at the opening of the present month.

When dark December glooms the day,
And takes our Autumn joys away;
When short and scant the sunbeam throws
Upon the weary waste of snows
A cold and profitless regard,
Like patron on a needy bard
When sylvan occupation's done,
And o'er the chimney rests the gun,
And hang in idle trophy, near,
The game, pouch, fishing-rod, and spear
When wiry terrier, rough and grim,
And greyhound with his length of limb
And pointer, now employed no more,
Cumber our parlour's narrow floor
When in his stall the impatient steed
Is long condemned to rest and feed;
When from our snow-encircled home,
Scarce cares the hardiest step to roam,
Since path is none, save that to bring
The needful water from the spring;
When wrinkled news-page, twice conned o'er
Beguiles the weary hour no more,
And darkling politician crossed,
Inveighs against the lingering post;
And answering housewife sore complains
Of carriers' snow-impeded wains;—
When such the country cheer, I come,
Well-pleased, to seek our city home.

The kitchen garden is worth peeping into at this time, when there is so little to be seen in the out-of-door world. The earthed-up celery beds have a fresh and green appearance, and the lettuces which were planted late, wear a healthy Spring look; while cauliflowers, kale, brocoli, cabbages, and green's of every description, have now a crispy and tempting tenderness, which is fully appreciated when they come to throw their odour around the table, as they are placed beside the red and juicy ham, and the well-fed pullets. If a hare or rabbit cross our path, we scarcely regard them with the eye of a naturalist now, but think what a flavour there would be about the one jugged, and the other, with a few accessories, wrapt up under the comfortable crust of a pie.

The rosemary flowers this month; and there were few plants held in higher esteem than this by our ancestors. They used it to stir up the spiced Christmas tankard; it was also dipped in their drinking cups at weddings, and borne before the bridal party as they went to church. It was strewed upon the dead; and Herrick, in allusion to these customs, says that the rosemary

Grows for two ends, it matters not at all,
Be it for my bridal or my burial.

I shall conclude the description of this month by a snow-scene, taken from my "Pictures of Country Life," descriptive of a ride over a cold, cheerless common:—"The snow had fallen all night long, and continued throughout the day without ceasing. Over the wide, bleak, unsheltered common, it lay deep and untrodden, blown here and there into wild, fanciful ridges, just as the ground rose and fell, or where the wind had whirled it; and it was only by some white-covered hillock of stones, a furze bush of taller growth, the remains of an aged hawthorn, and the relics of an old finger-post, that a practised eye was enabled to trace the winding of the road. All around hung the low, dull, leaden-coloured sky, so low, that, as far as the eye could stretch, it seemed to rest everywhere upon the snow, save where, on the furthest rim of the horizon, the level monotony of the line was broken by a steep slate roof, now covered with snow; and that was all which stood visible of the Union Workhouse, for the rest of the building was lost in the distance. It was so cold and cheerless a day, that not even a donkey—the hardiest defier of wind and weather—was to be seen in the whole wide range of the sky-bounded common, for even he had sought a shelter in some unseen hollow; nothing stirred amid the wild solitude of that wintry scene."

The close of December brings with it one great consolation—the shortest day is past, and, after a few more evenings, we shall see them slowly lengthen; and when the snow-drop appears, we know that

The storms of Wintry time will quickly pass,
And one unbounded Spring encircle all.

(Country Scenes for every Month in this Almanack are written by Thomas Miller.)

Sweet Christmas Bells!

Words by Samuel S. McCurry.
Music by Gerard F. Cobb.

Sweet Christ-mas Bells! Your voi-ces bring Blest mus-ings while ye glee-ful ring; Far up the vale your an-them swells, And mu-sic wakes the snow-clad dells, Where mute is ev-'ry liv-ing thing: Sweet Christmas Bells! Sweet Christmas Bells! Long years a-go on

Cassell's Family Magazine, 1892

seraph wing Bright angels came on earth to sing, And still your tongue their story tells—Sweet Christmas Bells! Sweet Christmas Bells!

Into sad hearts your gladness fling, Where shades of sin and sorrow cling; Let your true message work its spells, In dreary homes where discord dwells: Then shall Messiah reign as King—Sweet Christmas Bells! Sweet Christmas Bells!

Christmas Crackers.

IF there is one thing inseparable from Christmas in general and the little ones' seasonable gatherings in particular, it is —a cracker. With what a delightful look of expectation they have waited for it to go "bang," and how they have screamed as they scrambled after the surprise which came in response to the explosion, and revelled in a complete outfit in the way of paper garments, hats and caps, jewels, toys, puzzles, and what not. But there are others who love the cracker. Have you not seen them? She is merry eighteen, and he with just enough moustache to twirl. They each seize an end of that convenient little cracker—"bang" it goes. Why doesn't he pick up the gaily decorated paper cap, or she the piquant little apron with the blue bows? Simply because there is a tiny slip of paper inside, and they are eager to read it. That little scrap of paper may say:

"The sweet crimson rose with its beautiful hue
Is not half so deep as my passion for you.
'Twill wither and fade, and no more will be seen
But whilst my heart lives you will still be its queen!"

and the next moment they are in the quietest corner of the room. It was Cupid himself who hopped out of that cracker. Christmas crackers have much to answer for.

Considering the many moments of merriment which these small rolls of paper will surely bring, and the countless chats

"BANG."

The Strand, 1891

on courting topics they are sure to give rise to, we are inclined to hasten from romance to reality, and take a peep in upon the workers whose busy fingers provide the crackers—in short, to find out exactly how they are made, from the moment the paper arrives at the factory to the time the completed article is ready to be packed up in dozens and sent away. Messrs. Tom Smith & Co., of Wilson-street, Finsbury, are really the creators of the Christmas cracker as we now know it. About forty years ago a sweetmeat and love-motto was wrapped in a piece of fancy paper, and in those days answered the same purpose as Christmas crackers do now. They were called "Kiss Mottoes." Then it got converted into "Somebody's Luggage," and finally the elaborately got up Christmas Cracker of to-day. Oscar Wilde did much, however, for its welfare. Even the crackers caught the æsthetic movement and became wrapped up in æsthetic colours. Messrs. Tom Smith & Co. manufacture eleven millions in a single season. Our own country will claim some eight or nine millions of these, and the remainder will get scattered over the world, India claiming a big parcel.

The first room visited at their immense factory was on the ground floor. Here is a miniature quarry. Hundreds of stones imported from Germany are stacked everywhere. Men are busy in the far corner grinding and grinding them until a perfectly pure and level surface is obtained. If you feel inclined you might endeavour to raise from the floor the largest litho stone used. It measures sixty inches by forty, and would turn the scale at a ton. The stones are then passed on to the litho artists, for lithography plays a most important part in the manufacture of a Christmas Cracker. Upstairs is the artists' room. Clever artists are constantly engaged in making fresh designs year in and year out, and it is nothing extraordinary for some of them to spend weeks in completing a single set of designs. The literary work, too, is no small item, and a man who can write good verse can earn good money. Ladies seem to be the most adept at this sort of thing, which is paid for at so much a set of verses. Mr. Walter Smith, who accompanied us on our tour, goes to a desk and takes out a handful of sheets on which all sorts and conditions of bards have written. Some of them are very funny. Here is one, which is immediately waste-paper basketed:—

"Whilst sweets are eaten, and crackers cracked,
   Naughty boys are sure to be whacked."

The poet asked five shillings for this, and offered to supply them in unlimited quantities at the same price.

The next one is a gem, and is at once accepted:—

"Half hidden 'neath the spreading leaves,
   A purple violet bent its head;
Yet all around the moss-grown path
   In love its fragrance softly shed.
My living violet, whisper low,
   That o'er my life your fragrance sweet
Will make a garden of my life,
   Where love its counterpart may meet!"

We now pass through innumerable avenues of Christmas crackers, all in huge parcels. In one stack alone there are no fewer than 50,000 boxes in a line one hundred feet long and ten feet wide.

"GRINDING LITHOGRAPHIC STONES."

This represents a month's work, and every one is sold. We can quite realise this when we are told that one retail firm alone in London will send in such an order for crackers that it would take sixteen of the largest delivery vans built to convey them, with 1,200 boxes packed away in each van. It is no unusual thing for an order of £500, £1,000, or £1,500 worth of Christmas crackers to be received, the biggest of all totalling up to £3,000, the highest in the trade. This reminds us of the number of cardboard boxes which must be needed. The box-making is a distinct industry. A plant of machinery for their manufacture costs anything between £2,000 and £5,000, and during a busy week 30,000 would be made and used in that time. The card is all cut to shape and stacked away, and the patterns are many, for there are over 150 varieties of boxes. Just look at this pile of sacks in the corner. It is all waste cuttings, and often ten and fifteen bags will come down the lift in the course of a day.

On the floors above, the printing is going on. A number of litho machines are running, for the most part presided over by men assisted by girls, who certainly take off the sheets with marvellous rapidity. One machine is printing funny faces to go outside the crackers, another is turning out sheets with hundreds of flowers on it, and yet another is giving us countless little Cupids. Every rose and Cupid is cut out, and it is the same with any other picture with which it is intended to decorate a cracker.

We shall be safe in saying that the contents of crackers come from every part of the world, and a peep into the store-room where they are kept in huge bins and great boxes, will substantiate this. On one corner of the counter are thousands of tiny pill boxes. These are filled with rouge and powder,

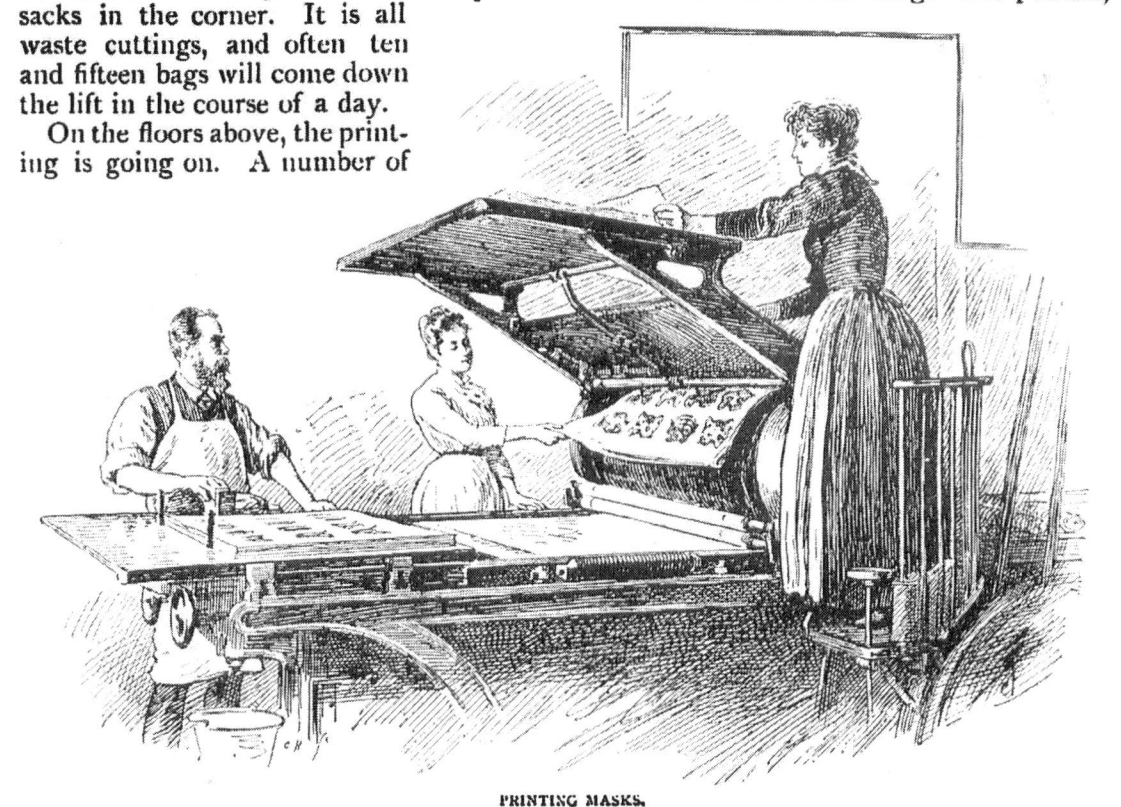

THE PARCEL DEPARTMENT.

PRINTING MASKS.

with a little puff thrown in. Such are the contents of one of the "Crackers for Spinsters," those estimable single ladies also being allotted faded flowers, a night-cap, a wedding ring, and a bottle of hair dye. This pile of bracelets came from Bohemia, fans from Japan, toys from Christiania, with little wooden cups and saucers from the same place, scarf-pins from Saxony; the little miniature pipes, as played on by the accompanist to a Punch and Judy show, are made by Parisians; Jews' harps come from Germany, and tiny wooden barrels from America. The familiar flexible faces which can be squeezed and pulled into every conceivable shape are made in London. Hundreds of little glass bottles are here, supposed to be filled with a certain intoxicant known as gin. A young girl is filling them with the very reverse of anything intoxicating, although the label on the bottle says "A 1,000,000 overproof." Italy, Turkey, India, China, and South Africa all contribute to the store. The sight would set a child pining with pardonable envy to play about this part of the factory.

To enumerate every item which

"FROM ALL QUARTERS OF THE GLOBE."

finds its way inside the crackers would call for a catalogue the size of THE STRAND MAGAZINE.

We are now on our way to the top of the building where the Christmas cracker is really made. First, there is the giving-out counter. Here come the girls and receive into their hands a certain quantity of what is wanted to make the particular part on which they are engaged. Every strip of paper is counted. Close by the giving-out counter a number of young women are fringing the edges of the paper to be rolled. This is done on a small machine capable of taking four thicknesses of ordinary paper and six of the brighter-looking gelatine. The material to be fringed is put against the teeth of the apparatus, the girl stamps it, and it is ready to give a neat and gay appearance to either end of the body of the cracker.

The main workroom presents a busy sight. It is nearing one o'clock, when the dinner bell will ring, and the hands are

FRINGING.

working at high speed so as to finish their self-allotted task ere the bell tolls. Four hundred feet of benches are ranged from end to end of the room, and here are scores of girls sitting in front of partitioned-off spaces ranged along the lengthy counters. Every girl has her glue-pot by her side. Turn round and look at the immense stove where twenty pots are being constantly warmed up, so that as soon as a worker's glue cools down she has only to cross to the stove and there is another pot ready at hand for her. It is noticeable how cheerful the young women are and to what a superior class they apparently belong. A good cracker hand can easily earn 14s., 16s., and at a busy time 18s. a week, and the cracker trade of this firm alone means the constant employment, directly and indirectly, of close upon 1,000 people.

One young woman is rolling the paper — paper of all the colours of the rainbow are before her, and dozens of completed crackers are arranged in front waiting to be carried away, and the manufacture of them booked to her credit. The paper is rolled on a brass tube, so that a trim appearance is obtained. Coloured string ties it up, and the gelatine is quickly placed round it. The girl we were watching said she could roll two dozen "best work" in a quarter of an hour, though she could do commoner work much quicker. Her next door companion was blessed with busy fingers. First she took a slip of paper—this was the inner lining; round this she wrapped the gelatine, added two decorating ends or fringes, and then put in the detonator, the explosive paper tape, and it was ready to receive its contents. She could do a gross an hour. Her fingers travelled faster than the pencil in our note-book. Passing girl after girl, we find them all surrounded by the brightest of colours in gelatine and paper. One is making paper dresses for a doll, a neat little white tissue frock trimmed with red braid. This formed part of rather a novel box of crackers. A good-looking doll is placed in the box, and each cracker has some article of attire inside, so that when every one was "pulled" the doll could be provided with a complete outfit. Others were making hats and caps. The paper is rolled round a tin to shape, pasted together, and there is your *chapeau*. All is very simple, but nothing could be more effective when the article is completed.

The cardboard alone used in the manufacture of the empty boxes in which the crackers are packed exceeds a hundred tons in weight during a single season, and the tiny strips of card constituting the detonators over five tons. Twenty tons of glue and paste, between 6,000 and 7,000

CUTTING THE PAPERS.

reams of coloured and fancy papers are used, whilst the total weight of the thin transparent sheets of coloured gelatine, which add so much to the brilliancy of a Christmas cracker, amounts to nearly six tons.

The process by which gelatine is manufactured is a most interesting one. The raw gelatine comes over in five hundred-weight casks from Switzerland. It arrives on these shores in thick, rough sheets, measuring six feet by three feet, weighing about three to four ounces each. It is then reduced to a liquid by steam power; water being added, it is clarified, and while in its liquid state dyes of the richest hues are poured in to render it of the shade of colour desired. While the gelatine is thus in a liquid form, it is poured upon frames of glass, measuring twenty-four inches by eighteen inches, much resembling window panes. Workmen, by the movement of the glass, allow the melted gelatine to spread over it, and so form a sheet of uniform thickness. These sheets of glass are then arranged in stacks, and the film of gelatine allowed to set. When the gelatine sheets are hard upon the glass, they are then transferred to a room in which a strong current of air is allowed to pass in and out, to complete the drying process. This takes from twelve to eighteen hours, after which a knife is run round the edges of the gelatine, which then being cut with a knife peels easily off the glass, and is now ready for use.

We were curious to know what was the biggest cracker ever made. Crackers are made three feet long, containing a full-sized coat, hat, collar, frill, whiskers, umbrella, and eye-glass. A story is told of a well-known

MAKING CRACKERS.

MAKING CAPS.

member of the aristocracy who entered a West-end shop one day and saw one of these gigantic crackers. He inquired the size, and when he heard it, exclaimed:

"Three feet! Not big enough for me. Just you order me three dozen crackers, each six feet long!"

The six feet crackers were made and delivered. Whether the nobleman congratulated himself on the fact that he had obtained the largest cracker up to date we do not know, but the biggest of all was that made every night for Harry Payne as clown to pull with the pantaloon in the pantomime at Drury Lane. It was seven feet long, and contained costumes large enough for the merry couple to put on, and a multitude of crackers, which were thrown amongst the children in the audience.

THE CHRISTMAS TREE.

Godey's Lady's Book, 1860

THE CHRISTMAS TREE.

BY LIZZIE M'INTYRE.

(*See plate.*)

Dr. Grantley sat alone in his office, his head resting on his hands, thinking deeply. He had not been thus solitary many minutes, for a frail, delicate girl had just left him, his eldest daughter and his darling, who had filled the place of mother, and sister, too, to the younger children of the Doctor. Marion Grantley carried from this interview a heavy heart. It was the old, old story—she loved, was beloved, and her father frowned upon her lover. There was no personal dislike between Dr. Grantley and Morton Loring; but, in years long past, Amos Loring, the young man's father, and George Grantley, rivals in love, had sworn an undying, bitter hatred, and for this old quarrel, though Amos Loring was numbered with the dead, Dr. Grantley was breaking the heart of his gentle, dutiful child. Her last words, as she left him, uttered in low, pleading accents, were: "Father, you know I will never disobey you; but it is Christmas Eve; for the day's sake, by the memory of my mother, who was taken into heaven seven years ago this evening, by the love I have ever tried to show you, forget this old quarrel. Let me bring to you one who, for my sake, will be a son in your old age, who loves and respects you. Father, do not break my heart!"

In reply, the Doctor merely waved his hand toward the door, and quietly, sadly, with no violent outbreak of passion to tell her bitter grief, Marion passed out. From the office, across the entry, she went into the parlor. There was a blaze of light there, and round the centre-table were clustered four little sisters and one brother, her mother's legacy to Marion. Grace, the one next Marion, a pretty blonde, just entering her nineteenth year, looked up as her sister entered. There was no discontented, fretful glance to throw back her loving one; gentle, serene, and tender, Marion smiled upon the group, stifling back her own sorrow to give them a Christmas greeting.

"Oh, I wish it was to-morrow!" cried Eddie, the youngest, a boy of eight years old, the pet and darling of all the five sisters.

"To-morrow evening!" said Fannie, the next in order, "to-morrow evening! O such fun! A Christmas tree!"

"I am sorry I did not have it this evening," said Marion, "if you are so impatient; but Aunt Lizzie's box of presents from New York always comes on Christmas day, and we can make a much prettier tree if its contents are hung upon it."

"Won't it be fun to dress it!" whispered Grace, who was to be the only one admitted to this delightful task.

"Oh, Marion, will it have my work-box?" cried Hester.

"And my doll?" said Fannie.

"And my set of china tea things? You know you promised me a new set." And, fairly started, all the children joined in the list of demands, making a perfect Babel of the parlor.

The little mantel clock struck nine. As the last stroke died away, Marion pointed with a smile to the clock, and the children rose, kissed their sisters, and went merrily up stairs to bed, Fannie leading Eddie, while Hester and Lizzie, little girls of eleven and twelve, went up arm in arm.

"There is so much to do to-morrow, Gracie," said Marion, as the chamber door closed, shutting out the sound of the merry voices, "there are so many things to attend to that I think we will dress the tree this evening. We can shut the folding doors, and keep the children from the back parlor to-morrow, and it will not take many minutes to hang Aunt Lizzie's presents upon the tree, when they arrive in the morning."

"O yes, we will dress it now. I'll call father." And the young girl danced off to the office, humming a merry tune. Marion, in the mean time, went out to a closet in the entry, and brought in a large baize covering for the centre of the floor. It was green, and meant for the foundation of the beautiful show Marion's tree always made. Grace and the Doctor soon came in, and the process of making a Christmas tree commenced in good earnest.

The square of green baize being tacked down, a large stone jar was placed in the middle of it, and in this the tree stood nobly erect. Damp sand was put round the stem till the large green tree stood firmly in its place. A flounce of green chintz round the jar concealed its stony ugliness, and over the top, round the tree, was a soft cushion of moss. It was a large evergreen, reaching almost to the high ceiling, for *all* the family presents were to be placed upon it. This finished, the process of dressing commenced. From a basket in the corner, Marion drew long strings of bright red holly-berries, threaded like beads upon fine cord. These were festooned in graceful garlands from the boughs of the tree, and while Marion was thus employed, Grace and the Doctor arranged the tiny tapers. This was a delicate task. Long pieces of fine wire were passed through the taper at the bottom, and these clasped over the stem of each branch, and twisted together underneath. Great care was taken that there should be a clear space above each wick, that nothing might catch fire. Strings of bright berries, small bouquets of paper flowers, strings of beads, tiny flags of gay ribbons, stars and shields of gilt paper, lace bags filled with colored candies, knots of bright ribbons, all homemade by Marion's and Grace's skilful fingers, made a brilliant show at a very trifling cost, the basket seeming possessed of unheard-of capacities, to judge from the multitude and variety of articles the sisters drew from it. Meantime, upon the wick of each little taper the Doctor rubbed with his finger a drop of alcohol, to insure its lighting quickly. This was a process he trusted to no one else, for fear the spirit might fall upon some part of the tree not meant to catch fire.

Marion, unconscious that her father's eye followed her in every movement, tried to keep up a cheerful smile, for her sister's sake, yet sometimes a weary sigh would come from her overcharged heart as the contrast between these gay preparations for festivity and the weight of her own sorrow struck her. At last, all the contents of the basket were on the tree, and then the more important presents were brought down from an upper room. There were many large articles, seemingly too clumsy for the tree, but Marion passed around them gay-colored ribbons till they formed a basket work, and looped them over the branches till even Hester's work-box looked graceful. Dolls for each of the little girls were seated on the boughs, and a large cart for Eddie, with two horses prancing before it, drove gayly amongst the top branches, as if each steed possessed the wings of Pegasus. On the moss beneath the branches Marion placed a set of wooden animals for Eddie, while from the topmost branch was suspended a gilded cage, ready for the canary-bird Dr. Grantley had purchased for the pet-loving Lizzie.

Various mysterious packages, wrapped in paper and marked Grace, Marion, or Papa, were put aside, that all the delicious mystery of Christmas might be preserved.

At length all was ready, and, carefully locking the doors, the trio went up to their respective rooms.

It was Christmas evening. All the presents were on the tree, and Marion was alone in the back parlor, waiting for the Doctor's return from a professional visit, before she lighted the tree. The children were in the sitting-room, and their eager, merry voices came faintly to her as she sat sadly waiting there.

Hark! A voice in the entry. The door of the large closet opened and shut again, and then her father's voice summoned her to open the door.

"Marion," he said, taking her hands in his own, "you have thought for all the others this Christmas evening; I have a gift for you."

She said "Thank you," quietly smiling, yet without much appearance of interest.

I wish to place it on the tree myself, and then this year I will play lamplighter. You bring the children into the next room."

Dancing feet soon sounded on the stairs, and eager voices shouted "Merry Christmas," as the little ones followed Marion into the front parlor. It was entirely dark. Standing them in a row, at some distance from the folding-doors, Marion spoke to tell her father all was ready. The doors flew open. The tall tree, one blaze of light, covered with tasty gifts, stood in the middle of the room, and behind it was a figure which Marion at first took for her father; only for a moment. Dazzled and confused as she was by the sudden blaze of light, a second glance sent a full tide of happiness to her heart.

"My Christmas gift," she said, softly, stepping forward.

"And I claim mine," was the reply, in a deep, manly voice, from behind the tree, and Morton Loring came forward to where Marion had paused, awaiting him.

Christmas was surely not a time for quarrels, sanctified, too, as it was to the Doctor and Marion, and Dr. Grantley repaid long years of devotion to himself and his children by making Marion happy on Christmas.

CHRISTMAS IN OLD LONDON

BY SIR WALTER BESANT.

THE first point to be observed, in speaking of London at any season of the year, is that, if feasting, merriment, music, and cheerfulness can by any excuse be connected with the time of year, the good people of London will take advantage of that excuse. Fortunately, there have always been plenty of excuses for holding high festival at Christmas. It was both a pagan festival and a Christian festival; it was the greatest festival of the year; the longest; the most joyful; the most natural. It stood at the end of one year and the beginning of the next; it was held in those halcyon days when—as they believed—all Nature was hushed and the kingfisher hatched her eggs in a nest that floated under a still sky upon still waters; the sun had reached his lowest and had already begun to return; the short days and the frosts forbade much work; the long and the cold nights made the people gather round the fire; the harvests of the year were gathered in, even to the latest October apple; and the season commemorated the event which, of all the Christian Year, appealed most strongly to the hearts of the people.

Again, in this time of frost and snow; of the sharp frost and the silent snow; of the short days and the long evenings; it was necessary that folk should keep up their hearts with feast and song. Think only what the depth of winter meant to our forefathers. The working day, the day of daylight, was not eight hours long; the evening set in before four o'clock; in the narrow lanes of London, with the tall, gabled houses overhanging on either side, there was no brightness of sun and sky, but only twilight which lasted all the day; outside reigned Winter, cold and wet: the shops were closed, the stalls were cleared, the workshop fires were raked out, at sunset; there followed a long evening to be faced; the deserted streets were as black as the night; there were no books to read; there were no theatres; there were no amusements of any kind; for light, there was the fire on the hearth; what could they do to get through the long and weary evening but feast and drink, on days of festival, and gather in the halls of their Guild to dance and sing and dress up and play antics?

To dress up: to become mummers: to play antics: to act and pretend: the staple amusement was to do this or to see others doing it. That unfortunate sovereign, Edward the Second, used to beguile his journeys by laughing at his Tom Fool who fell off his horse every five minutes and pretended to break his bones. He was a king, however, and could afford to keep this kind of Christmas all the year. His subjects, less fortunate, had to become their own Tom Fools and to perform their own Tomfoolery for themselves; and, oh! only to think of the comic actors, the funny men, the men who could not speak without causing the whole audience to hugh, that the generations in their following produced! They had their day and their fame and their reward, and they are long since forgotten. To every age its comic mime and its own sense of humour: we have ours and are, I hope, properly grateful therefor. We may be quite sure that the comic muse was encouraged as much when the Edwards ruled as when Victoria reigns.

The Christmas festivities, then, consisted, first, of the gathering together in house and Hall: merely to feel one of a company is something; then, of feasting, with an attention to the wine cup which would, literally, stagger humanity of the present day; with minstrels playing continually; with singing —the people always had their songs in their own tongue, Saxon, Old English, Middle English, or whatever the scholars call it; with dancing; and with mumming—always with mumming, which included juggling and tumbling, and feats of skill and strength. A mediæval feast, after the dinner, on which I will presently enlarge with pleasure, very much resembled the performance at a modern music hall with its successive "turns" and its favourite performers.

The "making up" began in the Church. First, they prepared the manger and acted in dumb show, while the choir sang carols and Psalms, the Nativity, and the arrival of the three kings from the East. This was one of the simple dramas by which the people who could not read learned the essentials of the Gospel history. In the same way they learned and realised the meaning of the Resurrection; of the Raising of Lazarus; of the doubts of Thomas; and so on.

In addition to this sacred drama, however, Christmas provided the entertainment of the Boy Bishop. Attempts have been made to

"THE BOY BISHOP AND HIS FOLLOWING RODE ABOUT THE STREETS OF LONDON IN STATE."

show what the Church intended by this extraordinary custom: my own opinion is that the Church intended nothing; but that the people in the Church, whether reverend divines or irreverent deacons, just endeavoured to make the time one of topsy-turvydom. The way was this. I take the custom at St. Paul's Cathedral to stand for all.

On the Day of St. Nicholas—December 6th—the children of the choir elected one of themselves to hold office as Bishop until Childermass or the Day of Holy Innocents, on December 28th. St. Nicholas, it may be remembered, was the admirable Saint who restored to life the three children who had been murdered and cut to pieces and put in pickle by the inn-keeper. You may see

CENTUM QUADRAGINTA.

the mothers; the Bishop gave his benediction paternally; they received gifts and they made good cheer.

On the evening of St. John's Day — December 27th — after vespers, the Boy Bishop and his clerks, all duly arrayed, left their places in the choir, and with lighted tapers in their hands—would that I were an artist to paint this scene!— they walked in procession singing the words beginning "Centum Quadraginta," from Rev. xiv. 1, down the darkening Church to the Altar of the Blessed Trinity, which the Boy Bishop censed. Then they sang an anthem: this done, the Boy Bishop recited certain prayers commemorative of the Holy Innocents. Going back to the Choir, the boys took the stalls of the Canons, while these Reverend Fathers served in their place, humbly carrying candles, thurible, and book. The service finished, the Boy Bishop rose in his throne, and, holding the pastoral staff in his left hand, pronounced the Benediction, all kneeling. After this he made the sign of the Cross over the kneeling crowd, saying:—

Crucis signo vos consigno; vestra sit tuitio.
Quos nos emit, et redemit, suæ carnis pretio.

pictures of the boys, restored to life and joined together, standing up in their tubs. Assistants or clerks to the Bishop were also chosen by the choristers. It must be borne in mind that, so far as the Church was concerned, everything was done in due order and without any burlesque. Only things must be topsy-turvy. The Boy Bishop was attired in pontificals duly preserved among the Vestments of the Church: he wore a white mitre adorned with flowers; he carried a pastoral staff, and he was dressed in such robes as belong to a Bishop. The Bishop's attendants wore copes and stoles like the Canons and Prebendaries. For three weeks the Boy Bishop and his following rode about the streets of London in state; the Dean found a horse for the Bishop; the Canons residentiary found horses for the clerks; they called at the houses of the merchants; they sang their carols; they were caressed and welcomed by the girls and

The next day, that of the Holy Innocents, was the last day and the grand day of this brief elevation. On that day the Boy Bishop preached his sermon in the Cathedral. This sermon, a perfectly serious discourse, was written for him. Dean Colet ordered that the boys of St. Paul's should attend the sermon; he himself wrote at least one of the sermons; Erasmus wrote one; two others have been preserved and published. After the sermon followed a feast provided by the Dean, or one of the canons, for his two chaplains, his taper bearers, his clerks and two of the Church servants. Then my Lord Boy-Bishop, with tears, put off his mitre and his *pontificalia*, and went back to the Cathedral school and to the Choir— and oh! how flat, for many and many a day, did life become in thinking of the glories and the splendours of that brief Translation!

Once the boy died while he was still a

Bishop; they buried him with episcopal ceremonies, keeping up the topsy-turvydom even to the funeral service; and they erected a marble monument to his memory which you may see in Salisbury Cathedral. In the year 1542, Henry VIII. abolished the custom. Queen Mary revived it—and Queen Elizabeth finally abolished it. How far it was observed in the parish Churches I know not. In the inventory of vestments belonging to St. Peter's, Cheapside, there are copes and vestments for the "child"; which looks as if there was a Boy Bishop in that Church as well. I incline to think, however, that the parish churches of the City merely took part in the election and in the provision of copes and vestments, and that St. Paul's, in the matter of the Boy Bishop, acted for the whole city.

It has sometimes been objected, as against the dignity of Royalty, that Sovereigns and Princes have always been fond of looking on at a mumming of all kinds, and especially at merry making and tomfoolery. I have remarked on the deplorable example of Edward II. James I. was also accused of unseemly merriment when alone with jesters, buffoons, and comic persons. Those who object should consider the weakness of human nature. No man, not even one born to it, and trained for it, can endure the Royal Highness and the Gracious Majesty always. There must be moments of relaxation. Let His Majesty's moments of unbending be respected and remain unknown. Therefore we find a Fool always in attendance upon the King; you may be sure that he was not such a Fool as to intrude himself when he was not wanted. Therefore, also, we find a Lord of Misrule appointed every Christmas in the Court to conduct the festivities of the season. The Rule of the Misrule was that everything, save that which pertained to the dignity of the Sovereign and the great people of the Court, was to be turned topsy-turvy. The King kept open house: in the Norman days he wore his Crown throughout the Christmas Feast; every day there were performances of minstrels and mummers; every day there was feasting for all; music for all; merriment for all. But since the dignity of the Court must be maintained in public, however much the Sovereign might unbend in private, the entertainment of the evening was always some kind of drama, taking, in the 16th and 17th centuries, the form of the Masque.

Bacon says of Masques, "These things are but toys—but yet, since princes will have such things it is better they should be graced with elegancy than daubed with wit." He proved his taste by the attention he gave to the production of a Masque.

The Lord of Misrule at the Court of Queen Elizabeth during the last ten years of her reign was George Ferrers, one of the authors of the "Mirror for Magistrates." The Masque was a performance with set scenes of the most elaborate character, contrivances of trap doors and side scenes, for surprises and vanishing. The characters were dressed in

"MY LORD BOY BISHOP PUT OFF HIS MITRE."

the most sumptuous and elaborate apparel; the parts were taken, not by the humble players, but by the courtiers themselves and even by members of the Royal Family; the "book" was written by Ben Jonson, Beaumont, or by one of the recognised poets of the time. The poem was allegorical or moral, generally the former. With its setting and its acting it was the actual forerunner of the play as we understand it. That is to say, while the Elizabethan dramas were acted in the yards of inns; or on rough stages with hangings for scenery and not much expenditure in mounting or in dress, these pieces were staged and mounted in the best fashion possible for the time; a Masque as performed before James I. and his Court would appear splendid even to those of us who know how a piece can be produced at the Lyceum or Her Majesty's. There were songs and dances set to music composed for the occasion; the unravelling and following of the Allegory, which, it must be confessed, was generally tedious and sometimes trivial, occupied the mind of the audience while the scenery and the dresses pleased their eyes. It was common to present the Heathen Deities on the stage; Angels, Fairies, Spirits, Elves, Demons, with Muses and Graces came down hill-sides; sprang up from the nether regions; emerged from caves; or floated down a river. Everybody recognised Diana or Venus, Minerva or Juno; everybody knew a Dryad from a Naiad, and a Satyr from a Centaur; everybody understood the Latin tags and verses which were curiously interjected: you will not find them in Ben Jonson, but they were put in by some of the actors.

"WHEN THE JUDGES AND BENCHERS AROSE AND DANCED ROUND THE GREAT FIRE."

If you will look at the map of London, say, about the end of the seventeenth century you will remark that between what we now call the West End, which was then gradually filling up, and the City, there is a broad belt occupied entirely by the lawyers. They had the Temple on the North, with Clements Inn, Lyon's Inn, New Inn, Serjeant's Inn, Clifford's Inn, Lincoln's Inn, Staple Inn, Barnard's Inn, Gray's Inn, and Furnival's Inn. They formed a quarter to themselves; they were quite a separate class: I believe, but I have no proof, that a good many lawyers were the sons, grandsons, fathers and grandfathers of lawyers. However that may be, the lawyers lived in this quarter and they lived very much together and apart from the merchants on one side and their neighbours the great Lords on the other side. Now, when Christmas came the lawyers like the rest of the world unbent;

they elected their Lord of Misrule; this Prince reigned with splendour during the whole of the festive season; he was surrounded with the outward show of Royalty; he had his officers of State, his Lord Keeper; his Treasurer, his Guard of Honour, and two Chaplains who preached before him. As in the case of the Boy Bishop there is a curious blend of seriousness even in the midst of pretence. The first command of the Lord of Misrule was to lay aside all their wisdom and dignity—Judges, Masters, Benchers, King's Counsel, Serjeants, Readers, Barristers, all alike laid down their gravity and their wisdom and became, so to speak, boys again. The capacity of the age, in all classes, and at every time of life, for mirth and merriment and antics is to us truly wonderful. Prynne —the acidulated Prynne—says, mournfully, that this time was spent "in revelling, epicurisme, wantonesse, idlenesse, dancing, drinking, stage plaies, masques, and carnal pomps and jollity." True. Very true. And a most delightful time it was! Think only of the evening in Gray's Inn when the Judges and the Benchers arose and danced round the great fire under the Louvre in the middle of the Hall! This would be a delightful spectacle could it be repeated. And the Tudor dance was not a mere walk round, mind you! There were shakings of leg and cuttings of capers: there were sprightly turns and pointings of toes, with wreathed smiles on learned faces, not to speak of unwonted invitations of hand and inclining of body. "Carnal pomp and jollity," indeed!

In the year 1561, there was kept a very noble Christmas at the Temple, the chief person, or Lord of Misrule, was Lord Robert Dudley, afterwards Earl of Leicester, who had with him four Masters of the Revels, a Master of the Game, and all the proper Officers of State, as Lord Chancellor, Lord Treasurer and so forth, duly dressed for their parts. What they did, with what state and ceremony they kept up the performance, is set forth at length in Nicholl's "Progresses of Queen Elizabeth." I will take part of the ceremonies for St. Stephen's Day. After the first course of dinner had been served, the Constable Marshal, with the Lieutenant of the Tower, in "complete harness," with drums and fifes before and Trumpeters following after, marched three times round the fire and then knelt before the Lord Chancellor and proffered their services. The Master of the Game, attired in green, and with him the Rangers of the Forest, next came in, with their attendants, and marched round the fire. They were followed by a Huntsman with a fox and a cat and nine or ten couples of hounds, and, amid the blowing of horns and the shouts of the company, the fox and the cat were chased in the Hall and killed by the hounds.

At the second course the Common Serjeant made a speech. Then "the ancientest" of the Masters of the Revels sang a song, followed by others. The evening closed with minstrelsy, mirth, and dancing. The entertainment, you will observe, consisted chiefly of make up and of acting. I should like to describe the great doings at Gray's Inn at the Christmas of 1594, when the Lord of Misrule performed the

"THEN 'THE ANCIENTEST' OF THE MASTERS OF THE REVELS SANG A SONG."

"THERE MUST BE MOMENTS OF RELAXATION"

performed it before Her Majesty the Queen. The following is the last verse in that entertainment:

The hours of sleepy night decay apace;
And now warm beds are fitter than this place:
All time is long that is unwilling spent;
But hours are minutes when they yield content.
The gathered flowers we love that breathe sweet scent,
But loathe them, their sweet odour being spent.
   It is a life is never ill
   To lie and sleep in roses still.

The full report of all the doings of this magnificent Lord of Misrule fill nearly one hundred pages of a goodly quarto. There are paradoxes; learned burlesques; songs and dances; dialogues; orations and parodies. But I must not linger over this incomparable Christmas Feast.

There was also a Lord of Misrule elected at Cambridge; but I have not by me any account of his doings; part of his duty, however, as *Præfectus Ludorum*, was the superintendence of the Latin plays performed by the students.

Let us pass eastward and visit the city.

Every house is decorated with green branches and sprigs of holm, ivy, bay, holly, and all the evergreens that grow. The craftsmen and the 'prentices go about asking for Christmas boxes. The children run from house to house singing carols in the morning; in every house the Yule Log is laid on the

"Gesta Grayorum." He was a Lord of many titles. "Prince of Purpoole" (Gray's Inn Lane was once Portpool or Purpool Lane), "Duke of Stapulia and Bernardia," Staple Inn and Barnard's Inn—"Duke of High and Nether Holborn," and so on, for five or six lines. Then was performed much lawyer-like, learned, and scholarly fooling, ending with dances—"thirty couples," we read, "danced the old measures and the galliards and other kinds of dances, revelling till it was very late."

They performed also burlesque ceremonies. Tenures of strange and wonderful character— I believe they had read Rabelais for the occasion—were recited; the Prince pronounced a General Pardon; he received Ambassadors; he heard mock petitions which satirised and exposed the weak places in the practice of the lawyers themselves; he instituted an Order of Knighthood, the rules of which are excellent fooling; he went in Procession through the City to dine with Sir John Spencer, Lord Mayor, at Crosby House; he received Letters of Advice from various parts of his dominions, even from distant Clerkenwell. He produced a Masque and

"THE CHILDREN RUN FROM HOUSE TO HOUSE SINGING CAROLS."

fire; no house so poor that cannot afford some kind of Christmas fare.

As to the Christmas fare itself, we know pretty well what it was. In the houses of the better sort, the Boar's head was the principal dish: brawn and mustard always formed part of the feast. Among the rich people the great Christmas dish was the peacock. The bird was first killed and then skinned with the feathers adhering to the skin. He was then roasted and stuffed with spices and sweet herbs, and basted with yoke of egg; the skin and feathers were then put on him again and so, with the splendour of his displayed feathers, he sat royally in the dish, served with abundance of gravy. One would think that the gravy would spoil the feathers; one would ask how the bird within those feathers could be carved at all. One detail is pleasing: the peacock was brought in by the ladies of the house, preceded by maids carrying wax tapers, and was set before the principal guest. When the banquet was less splendid, the peacock, without the feathers, went into a pie. In addition to this noble bird, they served at Christmas pheasants "drenched with ambergrease"; and pies of carps' tongues. It was not, however, everybody who could afford peacocks and pies of carps' tongues. For them there were capons and geese—remark that no mention is made of beef and mutton at the mediæval feasts; they were meats too common for festivals and banquets. The Christmas dinner in most houses began with plum pottage or plum broth, which must not be confounded with plum porridge. It consisted of plain mutton or beef broth, thickened with brown bread, and enriched by the addition of raisins, currants, prunes, cloves, mace, and ginger. It seems as if it would be good. Mince pie or "shred" pie was also a necessary part of a Christmas feast.

Nor must one forget furmenty, a dish of wheat boiled in broth, and served with milk and the yoke of egg; nor plum porridge, which was the predecessor of the immortal plum pudding. Other pies there were: fish pie, goose pie, pigeon pie; and there was the wonderful dish called Apple Florentine. You would like to try an Apple Florentine next Christmas? Pray do. If it were revived, it would probably become once more a national dish, popular especially with Temperance Societies. Take a large pewter dish; fill it with good baking apples; put in plenty of sugar and lemon; cover it with pastry. When it is baked, take off the cover,

"THE PEACOCK WAS BROUGHT IN BY THE LADIES OF THE HOUSE."

pour in a quart of well spiced ale, cover it up again, and serve.

As for drinks, they drank what they could afford and as much as they could afford, white wine, for choice, with sugar in the cup; or, indeed, red wine, for they were catholic in their love of the grape; or cider, or perry, or metheglin, but always returning or harking back to the national beverage, the good, strong ale that the Briton has always loved. And, indeed, can there be a finer drink than honest beer? Pepys says that after a feast at the New Year they ended the evening with ale and apples out of a wooden cup. There was great medicinal virtue in a wooden cup; it was made of elm, box, maple, or holly; Pepys, however, does not tell us the material of his cup nor the properties it possessed. As for the apples, they were first baked and then dropped into the beer, to which they imparted a flavour delicate and a feeling festive. These customs, with certain modifications, continued almost to the present day. The Lord of Misrule vanished from the Court and the Inns of Court when the Puritans got the upper hand. When the King came back, the people had lost the power of mumming. Dignity was preserved even at Christmas. The Lord of Misrule appeared on the stage in the Christmas Pantomime introduced by Rich in 1713. The people—alas!—had lost, besides their old powers of merriment and mumming, the arts of music and singing in which they had formerly so greatly excelled. Lute and theorbo and guitar were put away, and the madrigal and the four part song were no longer heard in the taverns, and the barbers' shops, and the private houses; but never, never, never, did the good folk of London forget how to feast and to drink. And, as a part of the Christmas feast—a sad degeneration of manners is indicated!—cards took the place of mumming, dancing, and singing. The game of Primero was followed by that of Maw; with both flourished the games of All Fours and Noddy; Ombre displaced Maw, and was itself displaced by Basset and by Quadrille. Finally, Whist alone remained the King of games for the elders, while for the frivolous there is offered Nap or Loo or Vingt-et-un.

Looking back upon the old festivities and the old mumming, I should like to have seen the Boy Bishop, in his white mitre, surrounded by his boy Canons, as innocent to look upon as the angels on the painted wall, blessing the people; I should like to have seen the judges and the serjeants and the Revellers holding up their petticoats and dancing round the central fireplace in Gray's Inn; I should like to have seen a City feast at Christmas in a Company's Hall; I should like to try a slice of that roast peacock, with a little of the stuffing; I should like to taste that dish called Apple Florentine; and I should like to have heard the children's carols, in the streets—oh! so very, very much better than our own performances—on the cold morning of Christmas Day.

"THEY ENDED THE EVENING WITH ALE AND APPLES OUT OF A WOODEN CUP."

CAROLS AND CAROL SINGERS

THE origin of Christmas Carols is wrapped in obscurity, and the authors of the older ones are unknown. A carol is a sort of sacred ballad, or narrative song, based principally on St. Luke's account of the birth of Christ, which is practically versified in "While shepherds watched their flocks by night." The term Carol was originally applied to songs intermingled with dancing, and came afterwards to signify festive songs, such as were sung at Christmas. One powerful influence, which did much to shape the old Christmas Carol, is to be found in the mysteries or sacred dramas, which for centuries formed one of the most popular entertainments at the church festivals, particularly at Christmas. These mysteries are said to have been introduced about the end of the eleventh century; and although they present many Gospel scenes in confused form, they did much to spread religious thought and feeling. Those who have witnessed the wonderful realism of the Ober-Ammergau passion play can understand this. The Mystery Plays were, probably, accountable for the many curious traditions embodied in old Christmas Carols. Some of these can be traced to the Apocryphal Gospels; in other cases the source is lost. The old carol of "The Camel and the Crane," thirty stanzas long, abounds in incongruities and anachronisms, and is descriptive, among other things, of the Flight into Egypt. The maternal delight and affection of the mother of Christ for her Son is an unfailing subject in old carols.

Most of the ordinary popular carols show by their style that they have at all events received their present form from the hands of less educated singers than those of the choir of the Chapel Royal. For many years it was the duty of this choir to produce a carol at Christmas, before the King or Queen went to supper; and it is probable that many of the higher class of carols owe their existence to this custom, or to a similar usage in houses of the nobility. Many carols were directly intended to be the means of obtaining gifts of money from wealthier neighbours. Sometimes they assumed a religious, sometimes a convivial tone.

Besides religious and legendary carols, there is a large miscellaneous class which treats rather of the accidental circumstances of the Christmas season than of the events which it commemorates. The cold, snow, boar's head, boar-hunt, holly and ivy, and the feasting and merrymaking, which have always belonged to the Christmas holidays, have all furnished matter for a variety of old Christmas carols. Numerical carols, too, are not uncommon. Besides "The Joys of Mary," which are variously fixed at five, seven, and twelve in different versions, there is "A New Dyall," ending with "Twelve make our creed." "The dial's done," and others are to be met with during research.

The first printed collection of carols came from the press of Wynkyn de Worde in 1521. A unique fragment of it is still extant, containing the famous "Boar's Head Carol," which is still sung at Queen's College, Oxford, on Christmas Day. The Jovial Carols were issued in a small black-letter collection in 1642, another in 1661, and yet another in 1688. These are of the highest rarity, and contain curious specimens of the songs that were sung by shepherds and ploughmen at Christmas entertainments in farmhouses. The inmates never failed to regale the singers with plum-cake and hot spiced ale. The Puritans did their best to discourage carol singing, but the practice revived at the Restoration, and continues to the present day.

In France the singing of "Noëls" was common at an early date, and collections were published as early as the 16th century. Russian literature is very rich in carols and religious songs, many of the singers being beggars and lame people who wander about singing for charity. Many of the legends in these Russian carols are of great antiquity. The Isle of Man has a large store of carols, or "caroal," but very few are in print. Wales, too, has her "Book of Carols" containing quite a number.

For some time past it has been a growing practice to sing carols in churches instead of in the open air, as in bygone days, and the old fantastic carols are in consequence fast falling out of remembrance. The great obstacles to the general revival of really ancient carols are the obsolete and sometimes irreverent language, the irregularity of the versification, extreme length of many, and often the loss of the original tunes.

A very pleasant way of keeping up the old custom of carol-singing to some degree, is to form a party of friends of congenial tastes, possessed of good voices, who will meet for a few rehearsals when well-known favourite carols should be practised. Shortly before Christmas week appropriate notice-cards may be circulated among friends and acquaintances, announcing that the carol-singers purpose calling and singing a few carols, either in the cause of charity or of friendship. Substantial sums may be collected in this way for a good cause. If preferred, the party may organise a "Carol Concert" at a hall or house of a friend. The idea is capable of much variation, and may not only be made productive of help to the destitute, but may also afford pleasant opportunities of social intercourse among those who carry it out.

The Home Magazine, 1898

DECEMBER.—CHRISTMAS WAITS.

Good Christians, rise; this is the morn
When Christ, the Saviour, He was born;
All in a stable so lowloe,
At Bethlehem, in Galilee.
Rejoice! our Saviour He was born
On Christmas-day in the morning.—*Old Christmas Carol.*

Hush! hush! Those are the village waits, not your noisy musicians, whose clamour arouses a whole neighbourhood, but those who bring no other instruments excepting their voices—who go from hamlet to hamlet all night long, chanting such carols as our pious forefathers loved to listen to in those good old days when Christmas was not only a holiday, but a holy time. Let us uplift the corner of the white blind gently. Although they hope that all are listening, they would but feel uneasy to know that they were overlooked. We shall be very glad to see them on boxing-day, when they will come round and simply announce themselves as the waits; then we can reward them for the pleasure they have afforded us. A few old-fashioned doors will be opened, where they will be cheered with elder wine, spiced ale, and plum cake; they know the houses. There are those who make a point of sitting up to receive them; cold although the night may be, they will not lack bodily comfort. How sweetly the moonlight sleeps upon the untrodden snow; it kept falling until twelve o'clock; and then the queen of the stars came out adorned with more than her usual brilliancy. It is just such a Christmas morning as a lover of old customs would crave for—cold, frosty, and bright. How the snow will " crunch" beneath the feet at daylight! But they are gone; you can just hear their voices at intervals, sounding faintly over the snow, when the red cock that crows from the far-off farm is silent, for they are now singing at the lonely grange beside the wood. The old farmer who resides there would never fancy that it was Christmas unless he heard the waits. Rumour, who is a slanderer, does say that when they have left his old-fashioned parlour they never again sing in tune—that bass is heard in place of tenor, and treble gets over his part before the others have well begun—and that, when complaints are made the next morning, the only answer is, " Christmas comes but once a year."

Then comes the church service in the morning; nobody either thinks or cares about the sermon on that day—all feel good enough without it. No! their thoughts are with the friends they hope to meet; they need no other sermon than the snow which lies on the graves of those who are still dear to them in memory—the dead, who, perhaps, only the year before, were guests at the Christmas board—those whom

The breezy call of incense-breathing morn,
The swallow twittering from the straw-built shed,

The Illustrated London Almanack, 1849

The cock's shrill clarion, or the echoing horn,
No more shall rouse them from their lowly bed.

For them no more the blazing hearth shall burn,
Or busy housewife ply her evening care;
No children run to lisp their sire's return,
Or climb his knees the envied kiss to share.

In vain are the beloved portraits decorated with holly and ivy: the same calm faces look down upon the Christmas festival, but the eyes no longer brighten, neither do the lips move, nor will the merry laugh that rung like music over the scene ever more be heard.

High up the vapours fold and swim,
Above him floats the twilight dim,
The place he knew forgetteth him.—TENNYSON.

They mistake Christmas who state that it is a merry day; on the contrary, a Christmas dinner is more often a solemn assemblage of those who live, and whose thoughts are occupied with those who have departed. In England, with but few exceptions, it seldom consists of more than members of the family. If a friend drops in it is generally one who has no other friends to meet; or if he has, they lie too far and wide away for him to visit them. It is a time when grandchildren and grandfathers and grandmothers meet together; when old times and old scenes are recalled; when the hidden household gods are brought forth; and the young bride, often for the first time, meets the family of which she is now a member; when old crusty men, who after much persuasion have at last agreed to attend, shovel off the cold crust from their hearts, as the good old port comforts them, go home, and alter their will, and sleep more comfortably after it than they have ever done for years before; when hands which have never been clasped for many a long day lie enfolded within each other, and marvel however they came to be separated. No! Christmas is not a merry season; it makes a man think of how few such days he can remember, and how few more he can hope to see. He begins to think that a brief year of days spent so happily, dating from the time he first slept an infant in the cradle, and but kept up once a week, would tell him that he had lived beyond half a century; and he feels no wish to number as many more, although he knows that

In the grave there is no company.

"From the first introduction of Christianity into these islands," says the Book of Christmas, "the period of the Nativity seems to have been kept as a season of festival, and its observance recognised as a matter of state. The Witenagemots of our Saxon ancestors were held under the solemn sanction and beneficent influence of the time; and the series of high festivities established by the Anglo-Saxon kings appear to have been continued with yearly increasing splendour and multiplied ceremonies under the monarchs of the Norman race. From the Court the spirit of revelry descended, by all its thousand arteries, throughout the universal frame of society, visiting its furthest extremities and most obscure recesses, and everywhere exhibiting its action, as by so many pulses, upon the traditions, and superstitions, and customs which were common to all or peculiar to each. The pomp and ceremonial of the Royal observance were imitated in the splendid establishments of the more wealthy nobles, and far more faintly reflected from the diminished state of the petty baron. The revelries of the baronial castle found echoes in the hall of the old manor-house, and these were again repeated in the tapestried chamber of the country magistrate, or from the sanded parlour of the village inn: merriment was everywhere a matter of public concernment, and the spirit which assembles men in families now congregated them by districts then."

Such, indeed, was the merry Christmas of the olden time. The whole wide country was then filled with rejoicing: in the bannered hall the long tables were spread; on the ancient armour and the antlers of the wild deer, holly, and ivy, and mistletoe were placed; the huge yule log went roaring up the wide old-fashioned chimnies, and cold although it might be without, all was warm and comfortable within. The large wassail-bowl—a load of itself when full—was passed round, and each one before he drank, stirred up the rich spices with a sprig of rosemary, while the cooks (says an old writer) "looked as black and greasy as a Welsh porridge-pot." Roast goose and roast beef, minced pies, the famous boar's head, plum porridge, and plum pudding, together with no end of sausages, and drinks of every description, but, chief of all, the "bowl of lamb's wool," seemed to have formed the staple luxuries of an old Christmas dinner. But even more than two hundred years ago the cry was raised, "Is old, good old Christmas gone?—nothing but the hair of his good, grave, old head and beard left!"

Were I to paint a December day, such as I wandered out in last year (1847), it would read more like a description of spring than winter. The sky was intensely blue, and the sun shone with a summer brightness. The wide Downs which lie to the left of Sanderstead seemed to bask in the sunlight of May. On either hand, between the woods, the holly and ivy hung aloft in the richest green, while hips and haws glittered in the hedgerows in thousands, like beads of the brightest coral. The woodlark (which, it is well known, sings nearly the whole of the year, and is only silent in June and July), and the robin were singing as cheerfully as if it were a fine day in February; and, unless my ear deceived me, I caught the notes of the thrush. The day was, indeed, so beautiful that I could not resist the temptation of venturing into the wood, for there was a dryness about the fallen leaves such as I had but rarely seen in winter. Wandering onward, I arrived at a little dell. One side was in shade; on the other the golden sunshine slept. Strange, there was also a rich yellow light on the shady side of the dell. On a nearer approach, I saw hundreds of primroses in full flower. Pale and beautiful, there they stood, throwing a sweet fragrance all around; the new green leaves and the old ones, brown and decayed, all adhering to the same root. Such a discovery would have been a little fortune to a London flower-seller; and had they been dug up by the roots, and offered for sale in Cheapside (which is not more than twelve miles from Sanderstead), no doubt the whole dell-full might have been disposed of in one day, for it was just upon the verge of Christmas.

At no season of the year is the hare in better condition than now. He has got over his full autumn feeding, and there is a firmness about the flesh which will be lost after January. Hare hunting takes the precedence of the fox chase. It was followed by the ancients, and we have a description of it by Xenophon, long before the Christian era. By many it is also considered to afford more true hunting than the fox chase. The hare is no sooner found than it starts off and makes a circle; and as the scent is very weak until the hare is warmed, the harriers are often at fault, and driven over, and sometimes run backward instead of forward, hunting, as it is termed, "heel-ways." The hare should never be pressed upon too closely when first found, nor should the hounds be followed too near, as they sometimes turn back to regain the lost scent. Besides, by remaining behind, the motions of the hare can be better observed at a reasonable distance, and all her foils and doubles detected. It is wonderful what doubles the hare will sometimes make, when the scent has become warm: instances are on record of her feats on a dry road, when, having run all sorts of intricate ways, she will at last make a clear spring several feet from the spot, which occasions many a fault; and while the harriers are beating widely about, or are far ahead, she will lie motionless in the very spot where she at one spring threw herself until the hounds have passed, when she will return again to her old starting point. When the hare begins to make more contracted circles, it is a sure proof that the hunt is pretty well over, for it is sure to come soon within the "spread of the pack," and it will not then be long before her death-cry is heard. Although the hare sleeps, the eyes are never closed: it is the same with fishes—they also sleep with the eyes open.

The following description of winter, written about three hundred years ago, will be new to thousands of our readers; it was written by a good old Scotch bishop, named Gavin Douglas, and first rendered familiar to English readers by the poet Warton, to whom we are indebted for the following beautiful modern version:—"The fern withered on the miry fallows; the brown moors assumed a barren mossy hue; banks, sides of hills, and bottoms, grew white and bare; the cattle looked hoary from the dank weather; the wind made the red reed waver on the dyke. From the crags and the foreheads of the yellow rock hung great icicles, in length like a spear. The soil was dusky and grey, bereft of flowers, herbs, and grass; in every holt and forest the woods were stripped of their array. Boreas blew his bugle-horn so loud that the solitary deer withdrew to the dales; the small birds flocked to the thick briars, shunning the tempestuous blast, and changing their loud notes to chirping; the cataracts roared, and every linden tree whistled and bowed to the sounding wind. The poor labourers, wet and weary, draggled in the fen, the sheep and shepherds lurked under the hanging banks or wild broom. Warm from the chimney side, and refreshed with generous cheer, I stole to my bed, and lay down to sleep, when I saw the moon shed through the window her twinkling glances and wintry light; I heard the horned bird, the night-owl, shrieking horribly with crooked bill from her cavern; I heard the wild geese, with screaming cries, fly over the city through the silent night. I was now lulled to sleep, till the cock, clapping his wings, crowed thrice, and the day peeped. I waked and saw the moon disappear, and heard the jackdaws cackle on the roof of the house. The cranes, prognosticating tempests, in a firm phalanx pierced the air, with voices sounding like a trumpet. The kite, perched in an old tree fast by my chamber, cried lamentably, a sign of the dawning day. I rose, and half opening my window, perceived the morning, livid, wan, and hoary; the air overwhelmed with vapour and cloud; the ground, stiff, grey, and rough; the branches rustling; the sides of the hills looking black and hard with the driving blasts; the dew-drops congealed on the stubble and rind of trees; the sharp hailstones, deadly cold, and hopping on the thatch." We know no description of winter so beautiful as the above; nearly every word is a picture, every epithet is well chosen, and the whole as fine a piece of word-painting as ever appeared in descriptive poetry.

We have again arrived at the close of another year, and in our journey through it have glanced at many of the old manners and customs which are fast fading away. The railroads, that have cut up the ancient highways of England, will soon uproot the few rude and rural customs that remain: the rapid interchange will revolutionise the habits of our simple villagers, and they will become ashamed of following the ancient amusements, which for centuries have been the delight of their ancestors. As for ourselves, we seem to have lived on the verge of important changes. We have with our own eyes beheld the old May-games, harvest-homes, sheep-shearing feasts, wakes, statutes, Plough-Mondays, Palm-Sundays, and other ancient festivals and ceremonies, as they have no doubt existed for at least three or four centuries. We have also been dragged at the rate of two or three miles an hour in the creeping market-boat and heavy stage-waggon, and been wafted fifty miles in the same space of time in an express train. We can also just remember when a steam-boat was a marvel, and the banks of the river were lined for miles with wondering spectators. What changes another generation may witness, the future can alone unravel; if they keep pace with those that have marked the last memorable quarter of a century, scarcely a feature of the England which we have here depicted will remain. All the wonders of the "Arabian Nights" sink into insignificance beside our iron roads and electric telegraphs. As for Puck's exploit in the "Midsummer Night's Dream," of "putting a girdle round about the earth in forty minutes," we shall ere long be able to send a message around the same circle in less time than the fairy boasted of.

(The Descriptions of the Twelve Months are from the pen of Thomas Miller.)

HOME-MADE SWEETMEATS.

I THINK to most young folks the sweetstuff made by themselves at home tastes indescribably better than that which comes from what Scotch children call a "sweetie" shop. It has, at any rate, the merit of being more wholesome. With this idea I have written out some successful recipes, which have been duly tried and approved of by an appreciative circle of girl friends, and I think, if you carefully follow them, you also will be pleased with the results.

My first shall be for that time-honoured favourite, *Toffee.* Take one pound of brown sugar, two ounces of butter, and half a teacupful of cream or milk. Put these materials into a nice clean pan, and boil, without stirring, for twenty minutes. At the end of that time find out if it is sufficiently boiled, by dropping a little into cold water, when, if it "sets," the mixture should be poured into a buttered dish or tin. The addition of five or six drops of essence of vanilla, just before it is poured out, is a great improvement.

Toffee Balls are made by taking a little of the toffee off the buttered dish before it gets too cold, and rolling small pieces tightly into balls in your fingers. When you have thus shaped the balls, roll them about on a cold plate until they are perfectly hard and cold.

If you want to have *Almond Toffee,* blanch four ounces of almonds, split them into strips, and throw them into the toffee just before it is dished, omitting the vanilla flavouring. To blanch the almonds, throw them into a basin of slightly salted boiling water, and leave them to soak for two or three minutes. Then pour off the water, and you will find the skins slip off between your fingers. Drop each almond into clear cold water, then strain and lay them in a shallow dish to dry slowly in front of the fire before using.

Everton Toffee.—For this, half a pound of golden syrup, half a pound of Demerara sugar, lemon juice to taste, and from five to six ounces of butter are required. Mix carefully the sugar and syrup, and then add the butter in little bits, stirring slowly till it is all thoroughly mixed. Then cease stirring, or the toffee will "sugar," let it boil gently till a tiny bit thrown into cold water sets. If everything is satisfactory it will be beautifully crisp, and the whole should then be poured into a tin previously well rubbed with sweet oil or butter. When it is half cold, mark it into squares.

Butter Scotch.—Put into a very clean pan one pound and a half of soft sugar, two ounces of butter, half a teaspoonful of cream of tartar, and half a teacupful of cold water. Let the whole boil for about ten minutes without stirring, then dip a spoon in cold water, pop it into the pan, and back again with its contents into cold water, when if the mixture hardens it will do. You may add, if you like, a little powdered ginger or vanilla essence just before pouring it out. Mark it into neat squares when it cools a little.

Marzipan.—Procure half a pound of almonds, two ounces of bitter almonds, and half a pound of sugar. Blanch the almonds and pound them in a mortar; clarify and cook the sugar slightly, then remove it from the fire and stir into it the almonds. Warm all together, stirring well, and taking the greatest care that it doesn't burn. When it is cooked enough (that is, when it won't adhere to the fingers), pour it out on a board sprinkled with sugar. As soon as it is cool cut it into tiny fancy shapes, stars, rings, and fingers; and, if you are anxious to make it a very "swell" goody, decorate it with preserved cherries or other dried fruits.

Chocolate Creams.—Take one pound of loaf sugar, put it into a saucepan, and pour some good milk or thin cream over it, as much as the sugar will absorb. Let the latter dissolve, then boil it gently for a time, until when you drop a little into cold water it candies. Do not boil it too long, or, in place of smoothly creaming, the sugar will go into minute sand-like grains. Be most careful, too, that it doesn't stick to the pan, but do not stir it till it is taken off, when it must be continually stirred until it creams. Then beat until cool, when it has to be rolled into little balls, which form the inner cream of the sweetmeat. Now put half a pound of vanilla chocolate into a jar, and place over a saucepan of boiling water to dissolve; when melted, dip the creams into it, and place them on a buttered paper to get cool.

Cocoa-nut Tablet.—Get a small fresh cocoa-nut, open one of the holes at the top, and pour out the milk into a cup; crack the shell, take out the kernel, and pare all the skin from it, then grate about half of the kernel. Dissolve half a pound of loaf sugar in a large cupful of cold water, and when it is dissolved put it on a clear moderate fire, without flame or smoke, to boil; a little of the cocoa-nut milk may be added. Allow it to boil for five or six minutes, carefully removing every particle of scum that rises, when the sugar should look like a thick white cream; then add the grated cocoa-nut, and let it boil for a few minutes longer, stirring it continuously from the bottom with a wooden spoon to prevent it catching. Try if it is ready by pouring a teaspoonful into a cup of cold water, when if you can gather a little soft lump at the bottom of the cup, it is sufficiently boiled. Remove it from the fire, pour it out upon a buttered plate, or sheet of clean, common note-paper previously laid in front of the fire to warm. When it is thoroughly set, but not quite cold, cut it into neatly shaped blocks. If you would like the tablet to be pink, add some drops of cochineal to the syrup while boiling, stirring to see the required tint.

Barley Sugar.—For this you require one pound and a half of fine loaf sugar broken into very small lumps and boiled over the fire in a pint of water. Keep on skimming it carefully till it looks like glue, and becomes so brittle when dropped into cold water that it snaps. Now add the juice of a lemon, and a few drops of essence of lemon, and boil the sugar up once. Stand the pan in a basin of cold water till the contents have somewhat cooled, when they may be poured out upon a shallow buttered tin; to prevent the sweetmeat spreading too much, draw it together with a knife. When it has cooled sufficiently to be handled, cut it into small pieces, and roll them into round sticks, which you can twist a little so as to make them look more like the barley sugar one buys in shops. All that remains to be done is to sift sugar lightly over the sticks when they have become perfectly cold and hard.

Fig Rock.—For this take one cupful of sugar, three-quarters of a cupful of water, and a quarter of a teaspoonful of cream of tartar. Boil till the mixture becomes an amber colour, but do not stir during the process; add the cream of tartar just before taking from the fire. Wash the figs, split them in half, and lay them flatly on a dish, pour the mixture over them, and let it stand till cold.

EDITH A. BRODIE.

The Girl's Own Paper, 1890

The Girl's Own Paper, 1883

CHRISTMAS IN THE NEW HOSPITAL FOR WOMEN.

A HOSPITAL almost entirely under the management of women, and solely for the benefit of that sex, must have a special interest for those of our girls whose hearts are capable of sympathetic feeling towards the afflicted with bodily sufferings. Such an institution is that at 222, St. Marylebone-road, London, and to it I desire to call the attention of those who so often inquire where a gift of their own handiwork would prove a much-needed boon.

I have just made a little tour through the two united houses, seen the patients—consisting of both ladies and women in a humbler position—some prostrate, but others sitting up in bed and engaged in reading, writing, drawing, or working. They were, apparently, as cheerful as sufferers could be, under the thoughtful, kindly auspices of those directing the household and the nurses in personal attendance. Notwithstanding the dread of painful curative treatment, present pain, and that most weary waiting for better days, how many brave hearts—unknown to the world outside—beat time to those "songs in the night" heard only of God and the angels around them! I need not explain what songs those are, nor that they are born of that peace-giving Faith and Hope that sees in the far distance the borders of that land "where the inhabitant shall not say, I am sick."

I made my circuit of all the wards, the waiting, consulting, and operating rooms, the dispensary, office, etc. Some convalescent had left a pleasing memorial behind her of recovered strength, having decorated the lower panes of some of the windows with paintings of flowers representing a window-garden. Screens decorated with coloured pictures and cards on one side, and black and white ones on the other, were in great requisition; and one poor girl, who was laid up with bronchitis, actually cried because a dark, unadorned screen was placed between her and the window, and she had to be solaced with another gay with bright groups of figures, landscapes, and flowers placed on the other side of her bed. Truly nothing is a trifle when strength is wasted, nerves are weak, and "griefs are many, while joys are few!" Then,

"A little thing is but a toy—
With hey, ho! the wind and the rain!"

And the wind and rain make but doleful music outside the casement of an infirmary, when wintry weather prevails within!

A bright glow of natural sunshine does much to raise the spirits, whether you be sick or well; and in this smoky city, and at this ungenial time of the year, a little artificial

The Girl's Own Paper, 1884

brightness should be created by those in happier circumstances. You amongst my readers to whom "the lines have fallen in pleasant places," "lend me your ears," and kindly accept a few suggestions with regard to this hospital.

As a preface to these, I must tell you of the efforts made by the ladies who hold office in this hospital, to make a Christmas for those dwelling amongst strangers as home-like as possible; and you will be glad to hear that some of our girls' deft little fingers unknowingly contributed to the brightness of the occasion, both last year and the year before. It is scarcely necessary that I should explain how you took part in this charitable work, as you all know well that the articles you send in to our needlework competitions are ultimately designed for the benefit of the needy in hospitals and homes.

In reply to my inquiries, I was told by the lady who has the chief management of the institution that, on the evening of Christmas Day, the largest of the wards is illuminated with Chinese lanterns, and gaily decked with evergreens; and that a "Father Christmas" is extemporised out of the wicker-work sides of a vapour-bath, standing about four feet high. A pole is secured in the centre of this, and a stick placed across it at the top of the wicker sides to form shoulders, from which some appearance of arms may depend. On the top a bearded and whitened head is affixed, an appropriate mask having been procured for the purpose. Drapery is hung round the lower part of the figure; and in form it resembles that of the "Green Man," or "Jack o' the Green," paraded in the streets on May Day. A hole is left in the old gentleman's back, which renders the hollow in the middle of his body available for the insertion of the various gifts, clothing, and other articles contributed by the benevolent. These are all numbered, and tickets with corresponding numbers are drawn by everyone in the house—the nursing and the nursed.

Whatever objection may reasonably be urged to the removal of certain patients from their beds upstairs, or whatever the difficulties to be encountered, when bad legs with cradles over them must be taken into consideration, the doctors' scruples and anxieties are set aside for that pleasant evening, and the promoters of the fête are willing to bear all the responsibility of danger incurred. In fact, the refreshment of the change to weary eyes, and to the brain so engrossed by one most harassing train of thought, is known to counteract many disadvantageous results, and to do more good than harm.

The grizzly old "father," attracting so much of interest in the little community, has a very capacious inside, and articles of considerable size find space within his wooden ribs. Amongst the gifts that produced the most lasting impression were some beautifully made flannel petticoats, which elicited the admiration of all, and were sent by the Editor of THE GIRL'S OWN PAPER, the winter before last, from the Needlework Competition of our young readers.

I inquired of the secretary what articles were the most acceptable, and she gave me the following list. Knitted woollen night-socks (very particularly), and every description of article for wear; plants (especially ferns), vases, and fancy flowerpots. These plants and vases, of course, would be placed out of sight on Christmas Day behind the old gentleman's drapery. Those of you who have read that charming Italian story, "Picciola" (the little prison flower), will understand the truth of the secretary's remark to me: "Something that is growing is always such a pleasure to the patients, and they are so interested in the springing up of the new fronds of the ferns, which thrive better than almost anything else in the wards." But any little gift would be welcomed—such as workboxes, needle-books, thimbles, scissors, packages of pencils, boxes of cottons, tapes, and pins; ribbons, spectacles ("clearers"), books (especially those illustrated), bottles of Eau de Cologne—in fact, almost anything. Bed-rests, to support the back when sitting up in bed, made of light woodwork, and also horsehair cushions, not very hard, I think would be very valuable.

I have written so far without telling my readers certain other particulars that may interest them respecting the management of this hospital, and the special claims which it has on their consideration. I said it was "almost entirely under the management of women;" for although the "general" and

A QUIET CONVERSATION.

"managing" committees are composed of both men and women, the four "visiting physicians" and the "house doctor," as well as the "dispenser," the hon. treasurer, hon. secretary, and the acting secretary and housekeeper, are all women. In fact, this is the only hospital in London thus completely "officered" by them. This is a great boon to many whose peculiar circumstances and individual feelings cause them to prefer female medical attendance, and that in a hospital where there are no male medical students.

This institution commenced with twelve beds, increased to fifteen, and now provides twenty-six. But out-patients are likewise attended to. Upwards of 2,000 patients were of this latter class during the past year, and about 200 are annually admitted as in-patients. Payment by the latter is not compulsory, for very necessitous cases are taken in free of charge; but as a general rule the patients are expected to pay from 2s. 6d. and upwards weekly. The out-patients pay an entrance fee of sixpence, and twopence for every succeeding visit.

All the nurses are taken from St. Thomas's Hospital, and the lady superintendent and secretary, Miss Hunt, was trained at the "Nightingale School," at the same hospital. At her special request, I invite any of our London readers, not too far removed from the locality, to pay a visit to the hospital. On any day, excepting Saturdays, they would be welcome between the hours of 2 and 5 p.m. Saturdays are reserved for the visits of the friends of the patients.

Lastly, this New Hospital for Women is entirely dependent on voluntary contributions, and the promoters, managers, and all the officers connected with it look forward without apprehension, not only to a continuance of support—such as that with which the good Providence of God has already blessed their labours—but to a further increase of the same. May I not cause a more widespread interest by far in commending their cause to the kindly remembrance of "Our Girls"? I appeal to that "charity," the loveliest of Christian graces, which, like mercy,

" Droppeth as the gentle rain from heaven
  Upon the place beneath. It is twice blest—
  It blesseth him that gives and him that takes."

S. F. A. CAULFEILD.

WHAT WE USED TO DO AT CHRISTMAS.

By RUTH LAMB.

"AUNT JOE can remember lots of things about Christmas and New Year, and can tell us what she used to do when she was a little girl. Of course, I mean *old New Years*," added Jack Swainson, by way of giving a particularly lucid explanation of his speech.

Aunt Josephine, or "Joe," was Mrs. Rivers, and Mr. Swainson's only sister. She had been many years married, but having no children was equally beloved and tyrannised over by those of her brother, on whom she bestowed the affection which might have been given to her own, had they lived to claim it.

Christmas would have seemed dull, and the New Year of as little account as the old one, had not Aunt Joe and her equally popular husband formed members of the family party at these seasons.

"Well, tell us about Christmas and New Year, aunt."

"Ah! we did a great many things, and were pleased with some very simple ones which you children would laugh at now. But, then, *I* can remember my first ride on the first railroad made. I can remember being taken out—in fact, we children all went, solemnly and with quite awe-stricken faces—round the town to see the effect of gas for the first time, just as some of you will be able to speak to your children of the first electric light you saw. It was Christmas time, and though I am sure the gas was very poor, and the lamps few and far between, it was *the* sight of the season, to us children especially. We were all allowed to stay an hour later when we went out to tea that Christmas on account of the increased safety insured by the improved lighting. Before that we had a dim oil lamp per quarter-mile or so, when there was no vestige of a moon visible. At other times no pretence at lighting."

"How did the church look?" asked one of the girls.

"It had large, square pews, in which little people were quite extinguished, unless the elders kindly mounted them on the seats, and so brought their heads into view. Boys were not generally mounted thus, and I am afraid that, as they could neither see nor be seen, they occupied much of their time, when unaccompanied by their elders, in cutting their names and drawing, sometimes, objectionable hieroglyphics on the woodwork.

"Woe betide the sacrilegious artists if the old sexton caught them! He was a tall, old man of severe aspect, and something peculiarly awesome about the eyes, the lids of which were unnaturally elongated, and looked as if they were turned inside out. He used to pace solemnly round the church at intervals, walking softly, and carrying a long cane. His height enabled him to look down into the pews as he passed, and the youngsters who saw him coming would be still as mice, and keep their eyes steadily turned towards the part whence the voice of the preacher proceeded.

"If he caught a carver busy at his work, down would come the cane on his devoted head, with a 'swish' that could be heard all through the church.

"If a cry followed, a scuffle was certain to come next, and the shutting of a door told that the offender had been bundled out of the sacred edifice. I had a great awe of the old sexton, and so had your father, Jack, when we were children. In later years we knew him as a trustworthy and useful old fellow, who, out of church, had nothing terrible about him.

"There was no heating apparatus, except a little stove in the vestry by which to warm the parson's fingers—no light except what came from a central chandelier, and here and there a candle stuck in a tin socket of primitive pattern, and attached to the woodwork of the pews. The church was of great size, and you may fancy how we shivered through the services during an old-fashioned Christmas.

"As to our decorations! They corresponded in style with the system of lighting. The clerk did them, and his method was to stick in a good branch of holly, laurel, or other evergreen wherever there was a hole in the woodwork into which he could insert a stem. The tops of the pews appeared to have bushes growing thereon at irregular intervals, and of equally varied shapes and sizes.

"The decorators never scrupled to enlarge the holes in the woodwork by a vigorous use of the pocket-knife. The effect of their operations may be imagined when rendered fully visible by the removal of the withered evergreens at Candlemas. This mode was appropriately termed 'sticking the church.'

"As to the clergyman, his head looked out from a perfect thicket, it being considered correct to make the pulpit a complete bower of greenery. Somebody irreverently compared him to an owl looking out of an ivy bush. I am sure the dear good man's hands sometimes suffered amongst the holly, which, on account of its gay berries, was lavishly used on desk and pulpit.

"Had we plenty of bell-ringing, did you say? I should think so. Not only at Christmas, but for weeks and weeks beforehand. It was the custom to practise ringing for Christmas, so for three nights in each week the musical old peal of eight bells was kept on a continual jingle. The ringers tried firing salutes, change ringing, and even played Christmas hymn tunes on the bells. We, however, not only had the result of all this painstaking when the time came, but we had been hearing all the blunders and their gradual correction for at least six weeks beforehand.

"There were two ringers for each of seven bells, but it was an article of faith with us that there was only one man who could ring the biggest. He was leader, teacher, and tyrant all in one, and the bells made pleasant melody under his guidance. Still, his fourteen subordinates often grumbled, and vowed that, after the New Year had once been rung in, they would stand no more of Dick's 'ordering ways.'

"But they always forgot this threat when they came to receive contributions and to be complimented on their fine ringing on New Year's morning. At length the day came when they sorrowfully rang a muffled peal for their chief, and another stepped into Dick's vacant place. The biggest bell was not silent, but sounded much the same as of old—another proof that however much we may think of ourselves, we can be done without, and the world goes on as before."

Aunt Joe paused and looked thoughtful. Somebody whispered the words—

"CAROL SINGING."

A smile came on Aunt Joe's face.

"We had the Waits, of course, as we have now. But I always want to laugh when I think of a woman who used to come round when I was a little girl. She carried a wooden box under her arm, suggestive of a small coffin, smuggled beneath her shawl. She used to fling open the street door, and standing in the doorway, commence the old carol—

' God rest you, merry gentlemen,
  Let nothing you dismay;
  Remember Christ, our *Sa-vi-or*,
  Was born on Christmas-day.'

"I presume she called her performance singing, but it was simply indescribable. She jerked out each syllable in a nasal shriek with a touch of howl in it, and I never heard a second verse myself, or of any person who could endure more than the four lines, which would be got through whilst someone reached the scene of the performance.

"She 'shut up,' as you would say, Jack, so far as the carol was concerned, when we children made our appearance, and, throwing aside her shawl, brought out the box, opened the lid, and displayed a wax doll dressed in white and adorned with artificial flowers.

"I suppose it was meant to typify the infant Saviour, and we looked at it with a certain amount of awe, chiefly, I think, because it suggested a dead baby in a coffin rather than a living one either in cradle or manger.

"Then mother would give the least amongst us a silver coin to pass to the exhibitor, who bobbed a curtsey, shut the box, and passed on to fling open the next door and repeat her performance."

The youngsters here asked if Aunt Joe could give them an imitation of the style of singing. She began, but after a line or so her voice was drowned in shouts of laughter, and the youngsters declared it was no wonder that a second verse was never called for.

"On Christmas Eve, in my native county, everybody baked hot currant, or *plum cakes*, as we called them. The oven was heated by the blazing yule-log, and the hot cakes were served with spiced ale and cheese for supper, all comers being invited to partake thereof. It used to be one of our local superstitions that for every sample of Christmas or Yule cake that we tasted, we should have a happy month in the coming year. Of course, everybody wished to taste in at least twelve different houses, so as to ensure a year of perfect felicity.

"We used to ask each other how many cakes had been tasted, and condole with those who had not made up their dozen.

"The same thing is sometimes said about mince pies, which are in certain localities counted equally lucky and indigestible.

"There was a great deal of pig killing at this season, and it was customary, and I daresay is still in my native county, for little presents to be sent by those who did kill to those who did not. A little maiden would carry a basket neatly covered with a snowy cloth, and deliver the same 'with mother's love, and she has sent you a taste of *pig cheer*.'

"*Lift the cloth*, and mince pies proportioned to the number of the family, links of sausages, a highly-ornate raised pork pie, or perchance a spare-rib would be revealed. And all this was done with the simplest kindness, and the plenty of the one household overflowed into the homes of the neighbours who were not pigkeepers.

"We had our superstitions, too, at which you youngsters would only laugh to-day. Amongst these was a desire to have a lucky person as

'THE FIRST FOOT ON NEW YEAR'S MORNING.'

"I once heard a gentleman declare that were a woman or a fair-haired man to endeavour to be the first to enter his house on New Year's morning, he should be ready to use force, if needful, to hinder such an unlucky 'first-foot.' Dark-haired men were supposed to bring luck; and it was not the poor and untaught who said this, but the richest and best educated people in country communities at that time.

"Some would sit up for the ringers, who would be the first to enter. Others had a member of some particular family who would come long before daylight and do duty as 'first-foot.' Of course he received hospitable entertainment and a New Year's gift, in proportion to the means of those he visited.

"I can remember stealing downstairs, as a little toddles, in very unsufficient garments, to see our 'first foot' admitted before there was a ray of morning light. I was scolded, bundled up in a warm shawl, and allowed to remain by the kitchen fire whilst he partook of the usual refreshments.

"He always brought with him a large stick, which he placed in a corner of the parlour. This was in obedience to the old saying, that something should always be brought into the house on New Year's morning, before anything was taken out, to insure plentiful supplies during the year. Every inmate of the house was expected to fetch in some article, which was duly placed in a fitting corner or on a shelf, and not stirred until the following day, for fear of ill luck.

"I do not know what calamity would have been expected had one of these articles been inadvertently removed; but, as masters and servants were equally superstitious, and children solemnly warned not to touch, nothing was ever disturbed.

"Sometimes people would play tricks by bringing in some lumbering article and placing it where it would be in every person's way. All the same, it had to stay there.

"You look as though you would like me to give you an instance, children, so I will. A waggon laden with corn was standing under the shed ready for starting on January 1st. It had been made ready overnight, but the men who should have gone with it wanted a holiday on New Year's day. Knowing their master's superstitious feeling about the removal of any article that might be first carried into the house, they propped up the waggon, took off a hind wheel, and carrying it into the great kitchen, placed it in the very centre of the floor.

"The farmer knew why the trick had been played, but he would not have the wheel moved. He only laughed good-humouredly, and gave the men the wished-for holiday.

"There was another thing which was deemed unlucky, and that was the paying of money on New Year's day. 'Never do it,' said an old woman, in my hearing. 'If you begin the year by paying money, you will be doing it all the year through. You will pay much and take little.'

"In like manner it was said that, in whatever occupation we spent the first day of the year, we should also pass the greater portion of the remaining 364; so we were warned to be cautious, and employ its hours wisely and well.

"Let me see. What else did we do? We took off the yule-log before it was quite consumed, and extinguished the fragment in a pail of water. This was carefully preserved and used to light up next year's log.

"Parties of mummers used to go about dressed up in all sorts of tags and ribbons. I think I see St. George with his wooden sword, swaggering up and down a farmhouse kitchen, attended by an impossible dragon, and repeating an old rhyming jingle that had been handed down from generation to generation, for many past centuries. These exhibitions, and the superstitions I have told you of—familiar to the country folk of half a century ago—are gradually dying out. The mummers, guisers, and plow-jags, or jaggers, on whose coming we children used to count, are no longer seen. Many of the old customs that are still kept in mind are regarded in a very different light from what they used to be, and happily so, since they were usually the outcome of gross superstition."

"But what did you do before Christmas trees were invented?" inquired a small girl.

"We did without and never missed them. They are becoming old-fashioned institutions to many of you young people, and every year there are fresh contrivances to surprise and amuse you. Still, I think no little people would like Christmas trees to be abolished. In my young days everybody—that is, all who were acquainted—invited everybody else out to tea at Christmas time, when we played the games which our great-grandmothers had delighted in, and were abundantly satisfied therewith."

At this moment Uncle Tom made his first remark during the sitting. "I can tell you," he said, "that of all the girls I ever heard about, Aunt Joe was the very naughtiest."

There was an indignant protest from the whole assembly, and several voices insisted loudly that Aunt Joe might have been fond of tricks and fun, but *real wicked!* Never!!

"That is what I meant. She played tricks on everybody, but they were such as the victim could laugh at as heartily as could the lookers-on. She was a great taleteller too in those days."

"Tell us a proper tale, Aunt Joe."

"About one of your tricks."

"A Christmas trick, Aunt Joe," shouted a chorus of voices.

Aunt Joe complied with suspicious promptitude, and there was a mischievous twinkle in her eye as she began:—

"When I was a girl of twenty, I was one of a number of young guests at a delightful country house. The owners had no children, so they invited as many guests as they could accommodate at Christmas and New Year, and then called together the neighbours of similar age to meet them.

"Country neighbours often live several miles apart, so guests that had a distance to drive used to leave early. After their departure we still had a pretty long evening before us, often extended, too, beyond the usual bedtime. I used to be treated then much as I am now by you children—pounced upon and made to do as I was bid. Our dear, kind hostess would stay with us, though I am bound to confess that the stories which pleased the children, often had the effect of sending her to sleep in her chair.

"It was on New Year's Eve—how well I remember it! I had been telling tales for hours. Amongst my hearers was a gentleman of about five-and-twenty, the youngest brother of our dear hostess. He had no business amongst us. He ought to have been with the gentlemen, instead of sneaking off in that objectionable manner, and leaving our host and his friends, in order to listen to stories never intended for his ears.

"The children resented his presence. As a matter of course, one's tales were interfered with by that grown-up wet blanket. How could I talk nonsense properly with that dreadful, whiskered individual sitting glowering at me and taking in every word?

"He was so atrociously quiet, too! and I dare say he thought that would be a recommendation, and entitle him to a good-conduct certificate and unlimited toleration in the listeners' circle. We all regarded it as an additional aggravation. Perhaps the most annoying thing of all was that, when we had forgotten his presence for the moment, the tiresome creature would break out all at once into a chuckling laugh, which showed that he had taken in every word of the story. Then, as if afraid of consequences, he would become as silent and sober-looking as though the laugh were all a mistake, or somebody else was the guilty party."

"What a nuisance of a fellow!" said Jack.

"We thought him so; and the youngsters wondered how we might contrive to keep him out of our snuggery. But we had to be careful, for Mr. John—I will call him—was our dear hostess's favourite brother, and we would not have pained her for the world.

"'If Mr. John comes to our room to-morrow evening I shall either leave it or remain silent!' said I, at the close of our sitting.

"This resolution did not suit the youngsters, who clamoured against it.

"'If we could only send Mr. John to bed!' they said.

"A happy thought seized me.

"'I *will* send him to bed,' said I. 'He shall go, or he shall leave the room, at any rate, before ten o'clock.'

"The young people wondered how I should accomplish this, but I would not tell them, and they looked anxiously for the accomplishment of my promise.

"Evening came; some friends who had dined with us went off at nine o'clock, and the usual party retired into the snuggery, Mr. John excepted. He was detained by his brother-in-law to talk over some family matters, and we thought that there would be no need to carry out my threat.

"At half-past nine a servant always placed a certain number of bedroom candlesticks on a side table in our apartment, for there was no gas in that country home.

"Just before ten o'clock in came Mr. John, more hurriedly than usual, as if to make up for lost time. He could hardly help glancing at the group of candlesticks as he entered, and quickly as possible I darted from my seat, seized one of them, and, having lighted the candle, presented it in the most insinuating fashion.

"You were looking for your candlestick, Mr. John,' I said. 'Allow me to give it to you, and say good-night.'

"He took the hand I offered, shook it, said good-night in turn, made his adieux to all the rest, and departed. Whether he went to bed or not I did not care to ascertain; but after having fulfilled my threat, I am afraid I felt some compunction of conscience for the trick I had played him. The youngsters laughed uproariously at my success, and began to gather round me to make a night of it, after our ordinary fashion. I could not join in their mirth, or feel properly triumphant and at ease. The thought of Mr. John's disappointed face, his longing glance at the expectant circle, his lingering departure, and of the shy nature which had not courage to assert its right to sit up another hour, or to sit down amongst the young guests, made me feel a little dissatisfied with myself. My listeners were also dissatisfied, and, with the frankness of children, told me that my stories were not half so good as usual. We broke up our sitting earlier than common, and——"

"And," interrupted Uncle Tom, "then *I* turned taleteller, and I managed to make Aunt Joe listen to me, though she had treated me so unjustifiably on the preceding evening."

"You! You! Why, you are not Mr. John!" shouted the young folks.

"Ah! do you not know that taletellers seldom give real names. The children called me Mr. Tom in those days."

"And what tale did you tell, Uncle Tom?" asked a small voice.

"I told Aunt Joe that she had the sweetest voice and the dearest face in the world. That no child amongst them liked to listen to the one, or look at the other, so well as I did. And, after all these years, I repeat *that* tale to-day. I told her she had stolen my heart away, and must give me hers instead; that my home was lonely, and she must come to cheer it, and make it and me bright with the sunshine of her dear presence. She listened— and, children, you know the rest. We are old husband and wife now, but nearer and dearer than ever. And, though Aunt Joe turned me out from her group of hearers once, I have had cause for thirty years or more to thank God that she listened kindly to my story."

Illustration from a Victorian Scrap Album, ca. 1887

"AND THERE AT THE DOOR STOOD OUR BRAVE SOLDIER LAD."

The Girl's Own Paper, 1883

THE RETURN.

By SYDNEY GREY.

'Twas close upon Christmas, the joy bells were ringing
   To tell of the story we fondly revere,
The snow to the earth like a mantle was clinging,
   The breath of the Frost King had frozen the mere;
'Twas the time that bids loving hearts love the more strongly,
   And kindly folks think of the poor and ill-clad,
When the step that we longed for was heard on the threshold,
   And back from the war came our brave soldier lad.

The mistletoe swung from the broad oaken rafter,
   The holly was ready to brighten the wall,
Yet we missed in our carols and even our laughter
   The voice of the one who was far from us all.
Good news had arrived of the enemy routed,
   But would *he* return to us eager and glad?
Ah! long had we trembled, and wondered, and doubted,
   When back from the war came our brave soldier lad.

Dear mother was seated, as well I remember,
   Quite snugly and warm in her old elbow-chair,
Just plucking the goose, for you know in December
   The housewives make ready their daintiest fare.
We girls mixed the pudding mid fun-seeking chatter,
   Though truly our hearts were a little bit sad,
When Bruno jumped up with a terrible clatter,
   And there at the door stood our brave soldier lad.

Swift welcome we gave him, half smiling, half tearful,
   The young ones were all nearly wild with delight;
And my father's worn face looked so happy and **cheerful**
   To see his forebodings put fairly to flight.
That evening how sweet was our song of thanksgiving,
   And oh! what a glorious Christmas we had,
When we knew that our loved one was still with the living,
   When back from the war came our brave soldier lad.

CHRISTMAS WITH OUR POETS.

For an account of Christmas, under its various aspects, we have only to refer to our poets of past and modern times. Indeed, this truly glorious festival of the Church has afforded our poets rich opportunities—which they have not failed to use—of depicting the beauties which its sacred teaching and associations suggest. Many of our poets, also, have bequeathed to us the most varied allusions to the mode of its observance in days gone by; a few of which may interest our readers in the present paper. Thus, amongst some of the well-known allusions to Christmastide, may be mentioned Milton's "Ode and Hymn on the Nativity"—

"It was the winter wild
  While the heaven-born child,
    All meanly wrapt, in the rude manger lies."

The Girl's Own Paper, 1883 (poem), 1885

In the twelfth book, too, of "Paradise Lost," we find a graphic account of the first Christmas night—

"His place of birth a solemn angel tells
To single shepherds, keeping watch by night;
They gladly thither haste, and by a quire
Of squadron'd angels hear his carol sung."

Speaking of carol-singing, it may be noted that, as Bishop Taylor remarks, the "Gloria in Excelsis" sung by the angels to the shepherds at our Lord's nativity was the earliest Christmas carol. George Herbert, it may be remembered, has some beautiful lines on this event, which are thoroughly appropriate at this season:—

"The shepherds sing, and shall I silent be?
My God, no hymn for Thee?
My soul's a shepherd too, a flock it feeds—
Of thoughts, and words, and deeds.
The pasture is Thy word, the streams Thy grace,
Enriching all the place.
Shepherd and flock shall sing, and all my powers
Out-sing the daylight hours."

In olden times, it would seem, our poets composed carols specially for Christmastide, and Warton, in his "History of English Poetry," notices a licence granted in the year 1562, to John Tysdale, for printing "Certayne Goodly Carowles to be songe to the glory of God;" and it will be further recollected how Goldsmith, in his "Vicar of Wakefield," describing the unsophisticated character of his parishioners, mentions the circumstance that "they kept up the Christmas carol." Again, referring to the words of the angels' carol, "On earth peace, goodwill towards men," we must not omit to notice the beautiful notion which represents the cock as crowing all night long on Christmas night, and by its vigilance dispelling every kind of malignant influence, and which has been so graphically described by our master poet—

"Some say that ever 'gainst that season comes
Wherein our Saviour's birth is celebrated,
The bird of dawning singeth all night long:
And then, they say, no spirit dare stir abroad;
The nights are wholesome, then no planets strike,
No fairy takes, nor witch hath power to charm,
So hallowed and so gracious is the time."

With these powerful lines we may compare the words of an old hymn said to have been composed by St. Ambrose, and formerly used in the Salisbury service.

"The cock, that is the trumpet to the morn,
Doth with his lofty and shrill-sounding throat
Awake the God of day, and, at his warning,
Whether in sea or fire, in earth or air,
The extravagant and erring spirit hies to his confine."

It is worthy of note, too, that the cock is not the only member of the animal creation whose natural instinct has, it is said, taught it to do honour to Christmas night. At Aberavon, in Monmouthshire, for instance, there formerly existed a superstition that every Christmas morning, and then only, a large salmon exhibited himself in the adjoining river, and permitted himself to be handled or taken up, although it would have been regarded as the height of impiety to capture it. At any rate, we know that in days gone by salmon was a very favourite dish at this festival, and Carew tells us how—

"Lastly, the sammon, king of fish,
Fils with good cheare the Christmas dish."

Once more, Howison, in his "Sketches of Upper Canada," relates how he met an Indian at midnight, on Christmas Eve, during a beautiful moonlight, cautiously creeping along, and beckoning him to silence, saying at the same time, "Me watch to see the deer kneel; this is Christmas night, and all the deer fall upon their knees to the Great Spirit, and look up."

Leaving the Christmas carol and its associations, we may briefly allude to the village waits, who, in many country places, may still be heard early in the evening, singing their rustic music, although midnight has generally been the more customary period for their nocturnal performances. Wordsworth, describing the village waits, clothes them with a spirit of romance, and tells us how—

"The minstrels played their Christmas tune
To-night beneath my cottage eaves."

Adding in the following verses—

"How touching, when at midnight sweep
Snow-muffled winds, and all is dark,
To hear—and sink again to sleep;
Or at an earlier call to mark,
By blazing fire, the still suspense,
Of self-complacent innocence.

"The mutual nod, the grave disguise,
Of hearts with gladness brimming o'er;
And some unbidden tears that rise,
For names once heard, and heard no more.
Fears brightened by the serenade,
For infant in the cradle laid."

Clare, again, in his "Shepherd's Calendar," speaks of this time-honoured custom thus—

"The singing waits, a merry throng,
At early morn, with simple skill,
Yet imitate the angels' song,
And chant their Christmas ditty still."

An important feature of our olden Christmas was the wassail-bowl, a compound consisting of ale, nutmeg, sugar, toast, and roasted crabs or apples. Many of the wassail-songs sung on the occasion still exist throughout the country. Washington Irving, in his charming account of "Christmas Merriment" in England, says, "There was much laughing and merriment as the honest emblem of Christmas joyfully circulated, and was kissed rather coyly by the ladies. When it reached master Simon, he raised it in both hands, and with the air of a boon companion, struck up the old wassail chanson—

"The browne bowle,
The merry browne bowle,
As it goes round about-a
Fill,
Still,
Let the world say what it will,
And drink your fill all out-a
The deep canne
The merry deep canne;
As thou dost freely quaff-a,
Sing,
Fling,
Be as merry as a king
And sound a lusty laugh-a."

In Devonshire and elsewhere it was customary to wassail the orchards, in allusion to which the husbandman is directed—

"Wassail the trees that they may bear
You many a plum and many a pear,
For more or less fruits they may bring,
As you do give them wassailing."

The poet Herrick, who has chronicled so many of our old usages, has bequeathed a pleasing account of the yule-log:—

"Come, bring with a noise,
My merry, merry boys,
The Christmas log to the firing,
While my good dame, she
Bids ye all be free
And drink to your hearts' desiring.

With the last year's brand
Light the new block, and
For good success in his spending,
On your psalteries play
That sweet luck may
Come while the cock is attending."

From time immemorial Christmas has been observed in this country with every mark of respect, but in modern times many of the old usages referred to in the literature of the past have passed away. As Mr. Sandys remarks, however, in his amusing little volume on "Christmastide," although there are no records that can be considered authentic of the way in which the early Britons kept Christmas, yet it was no doubt observed as one of their highest festivals. Probably, too, some of the Druidical ceremonies may have been introduced and embodied in the festive rejoicings observed on this occasion. The renowned King Arthur, according to the ballad of the "Marriage of Sir Gawaine"—

—"A royale Christmase kept,
With mirth and princely cheare;
To him repaired many a knighte,
That came both farre and neare."

But this, as Mr. Sandys remarks, "though ancient, is certainly of a date long subsequent to the far-famed hero." Coming to a later period, William the Conqueror was crowned on Christmas Day, 1066,—

"On Christmas Day, in solemne sort,
Then was he crowned here,
By Albert, Archbishope of Yorke
With many a noble peere."

But, coming down to a later period, one of the most spirited accounts of Christmastide rejoicings in days past is that by Sir Walter Scott in his "Marmion." After describing the many customs kept up with so much hilarity he sums up by telling us—

"England was merry England when
Old Christmas brought his sports again;
'Twas Christmas broached the mightiest ale,
'Twas Christmas told the merriest tale;
A Christmas gambol oft could cheer
The poor man's heart through half the year."

Old Moser, too, has some good and homely lines on Christmas festivities as kept up by our forefathers:—

"Of Christ cometh Christmas, the name with the feast,
A time full of joy, to the greatest and least;
At Christmas was Christ our Saviour born,
The world through sin altogether forlorn.
At Christmas we banquet, the rich with the poor,
Who then, but the miser, but openeth his door?
At Christmas of Christ many carols we sing,
And give many gifts in the joy of that King.
At Christmas in Christ we rejoice, and be glad,
As onely of whom our comfort is had;
At Christmas we joy all together with mirth
For His sake, that joyed us all with His birth."

Wither too, describing an old-fashioned Christmas, tells us:—

"Lo, now is come our joyful'st feast,
  Let every man be jolly;
Each room with ivy leaves is drest,
  And every post with holly.
Now all our neighbours' chimneys smoke,
  And Christmas blocks are burning;
Their ovens they with bak'd meats choke,
  And all their spits are turning."

Gay, noticing the use of evergreens used in Christmas decorations, remarks how—

"When rosemary and bays, the poet's crown,
  Are brawl'd in frequent cries through all the town,
Then judge the festival of Christmas near—
Christmas, the joyous period of the year!
Now with bright holly all the temples show,
With laurel green, and sacred misletoe."

Wordsworth, also, has some appropriate lines on church-decking at this season, and bids the reader

"Go, seek, when Christmas snows discomforts bring,
  The counter-spirit found in some gay church,
Green with fresh holly, every pew a porch,
In which the linnet or the thrush might sing,
  Merry and loud, and safe from prying search,
Strains offered only to the genial spring."

Poor Robin, again, whose almanac contains numerous allusions to our old usages, in a Christmas song of the year 1695, writes—

"With holly and ivy, so green and so gay,
We deck up our houses as fresh as the day;
With bays and rosemary and laurels complete,
And everyone now is a king in conceit."

Once more, we must not omit to notice Herrick's account of Christmas games in years gone by—

"Of Christmas sports, the wassail bowl,
  That tost up after fox-i-th'-hole;
Of blind-man-buffe, and the care
  That young men have, to shoe the mare.
Of Twelfth-tide cakes, of pease and beans,
Wherewith ye make those merry scenes,
When as ye choose your king and queen,
And cry out, 'Hey, for our town green.'"

The few illustrations we have given above are sufficient to show how fully our poets have entered into the spirit of Christmas. Thus, whilst reminding us on the one hand of its sacred teaching, they have not forgotten to refer to its festive side, thereby portraying our Christmas festival in its religious and social aspects.

T. F. THISELTON DYER.

CHRISTMAS AT COURT.

By the HON. MRS. H. ARMYTAGE.

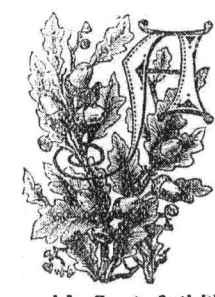

A RIGHT royal Christmas" is a traditionary expression very often put into the mouths of Englishmen, and yet when seeking materials on which to write an interesting paper under this heading, we find that at the present time there is not very much to relate respecting any special Court festivities at Christmastide. From the date of the Norman conquest we have records of the great feastings of our former sovereigns and their Court on each recurring season. The Norman kings held these feasts at York, at Gloucester, or at Windsor. William I. chose Christmas Day for his coronation. Richard Cœur de Lion once kept the feast with all his Court at Sicily. Edward I. is mentioned in history as being at Bristol among other places on a Christmas Day. In 1343 Edward III. renewed the famous tradition of the Knights of the Round Table, and instituted the Order of the Garter with great magnificence and unlimited feastings at Christmas. Henry V., during the lengthy siege of Rouen, would not let the day pass unheeded, but ceased hostilities and made it known by heralds that all of the enemy's force who would come to the English camp should be well fed at his expense. And again at the siege of Orleans a cessation of hostilities was requested that the day might be devoted to merriment and pleasure. A curious edict, dated 1461, forbid all diceing or playing at cards among the people except at Christmas. Henry VII. and VIII. both held splendid festivities during their respective reigns; neither did Queen Elizabeth fall short of them when she was on the throne, and the very serious tax of New Year's gifts is recorded in old documents which are most interesting. On the 1st January an usher knocked at the King's door (Henry VII.) and announced "A New Year's gift from the Queen." The messenger being admitted received the regulated number of marks for bringing Her Majesty's present. He was quickly followed by others, carrying gifts from all who would stand well in Royal favour, and to each a suitable payment was made from the King's exchequer. The catalogue of these gifts is extraordinary.

A purse containing gold was often given; valuable jewels and rare ornaments, while personal garments were not unfrequently presented. "A richly embroidered smock" to Queen Mary, and other articles of apparel, are noticed.

In return it appears that the sovereign made presents to his suite and others, and no doubt some of the gifts received by himself were passed on to others, as in one catalogue it is said a gilt cap given to His Majesty was presented to one of the courtiers.

There came a day in 1652 when, under the rigid rule of Puritanism, it was prohibited to commemorate the Holy Day of the Lord's Nativity in any manner; but with the restoration of Charles II. the Court broke out into the wildest amusements at Christmas as well as other times, masques and mummers, &c., having full swing.

There are now but few traces of the old English Christmas customs in any Royal gatherings. The wassail bowl is never served, and the splendid baron of beef which is always supplied to Her Majesty's table is almost the only special adornment of her Christmas board.

It is not many years since a very curious mess was served up at St. James's Palace to the Queen's chaplains. It was known as plum porridge, and from all accounts must have borne a strong resemblance to the original French idea of an English plum pudding.

It was always the duty of the poet laureate to compose an ode on the 1st of January, but the rule is not now enforced.

In Her Majesty's household, wherever she may be residing, the day is not observed in any special manner, nor have there been any very great Christmas festivities at Windsor Castle during her reign. The poor in all the parishes where Her Majesty has a Royal residence receive large gifts of clothing and of provisions. At Windsor this is always laid out in the large riding school, and the recipients assemble there on the day of distribution.

At Whippingham, in the Isle of Wight, the same is provided, and of late years the Court have generally passed the season at Osborne, so that Her Majesty takes a personal interest in the dole there given; but until the death of the Prince Consort, the Queen and Royal Family were generally present at the riding school at Windsor when the poor people assembled. At one time Her Majesty and the Prince were in the habit of having dramatic performances at Windsor Castle, and they generally took place at Christmas. Some additional guests were always included in the Royal dinner party on Christmas Day.

The German custom of Christmas trees on New Year's Eve or Day was certainly introduced, and though now it has been so extensively adopted in England as to have become almost an English custom, for many years it was seen in very few houses beyond the Court. Queen Victoria and her family keep the custom on New Year's Eve. A large tree, covered with lights and presents, is prepared for the servants of the Royal household, and the Queen herself distributes the gifts which surround the tree to each individual.

The ladies and gentlemen of the household are equally remembered, and receive a New Year's gift. In 1841 the Queen in her diary alludes to the dance given at Windsor, and that according to the German custom, as the clock struck twelve a flourish of trumpets sounded. Such family gatherings, with the addition of various members of the Royal household, and some chosen guests staying in the castle, have been the only festivities of the season.

T.R.H. the Prince and Princess of Wales since their marriage have generally spent their Christmas at Sandringham with their children and other guests. Seasonable gifts to the poor on the estate, with good cheer to all, are distributed as at Windsor in presence of the Prince and Princess and their family.

Within the last few years many of the minor commemorations of the season at Court have been done away with. Formerly all officials at any of the Royal offices received certain gifts. Mince pies of gigantic size, game, &c., were allotted to their use, but are so no longer.

"GOOD WISHES JUST NOW ARE IN SEASON."

The Girl's Own Paper, 1883

DISHES FOR A CHRISTMAS PARTY.

By PHYLLIS BROWNE.

OR this festive season, when so many people are on hospitable deeds intent, it is satisfactory to be able to add to our list of approved sweet dishes. It is hoped that the following suggestions and recipes will be acceptable.

Punch Torte.—Take half or three-quarters of a pound of Savoy finger biscuits—the quantity used must be determined by the size of the dish required. Make a syrup by boiling three or four lumps of sugar in half a teacupful of water, and adding the strained juice of a lemon. The amount of sugar needed will depend upon the acidity of the lemon. The syrup should be pleasantly acid and pleasantly sweet. Dip the finger biscuits into the syrup while it is hot, so that they may quickly soak through, and arrange them at once in a pyramid on the glass dish in which the *torte* is to be sent to table. The higher the pyramid the better, so long as it is not lop-sided. After the biscuits are in position, the syrup which drains from them should be taken up with a teaspoon and poured over the top, so that they may be thoroughly basted. Take the yolks of six fresh eggs, three wineglassfuls of sherry, and three tablespoonfuls of sugar. Put the yolks of eggs into a double pan, or if this is not at hand, into a jar which can be placed in a saucepan with boiling water round it. Pour the sherry over the eggs, and mix them a little, then add the sugar. There will not seem to be very much sauce, but before it is finished it will increase to three or four times its bulk. Put the saucepan on the fire, and whisk the mixture with an egg-whisk while the water boils round it, until it rises in a froth and begins to get thick and smooth. Take it off at once when it reaches this point, and let it go cold. A few minutes before the dish is served, pour the sauce by tablespoonfuls over and around the biscuits. Whisk the whites of the eggs to froth, sweeten them slightly, colour to a light pink with cochineal, and pile upon the preparation as a garnish. If more convenient, the biscuits may be soaked, and the sauce made some hours or even a day before the *torte* is wanted; but the sauce must not be poured over the biscuits until the last thing. Also, if preferred and for the sake of economy, good raisin wine may be used instead of sherry, as the process of boiling somewhat robs the wine of its distinctive flavour. This dish is very simple, very delicious, and not expensive when compared with preparations of a similar character, because no cream enters into its composition. The sauce was invented by Carême, the most celebrated cook of the present century, of whom it was once said that "if one were under the necessity of eating up either an elephant or our grandfather, it would be well that Carême should prepare the sauce." Some people think that this sauce was one of Carême's happiest efforts.

Bavarois.—(Half a dozen recipes in one.)—Blanch and bruise six bitter almonds, and put them, with the very thin rind of a fresh lemon, into a pint of milk. Let them infuse for a while until the flavour is well drawn out; then bring the milk to the boil. Sweeten it with five ounces of sugar, and pour it boiling upon the yolks of three eggs. Return the mixture to the jar or double pan, set it on the fire again and stir it till it is thick and smooth. Let it cool, then put with it one ounce of gelatine which has been soaked and dissolved, and half a pint of cream which has been whipped till firm. Put the preparation into a mould which has been rinsed first in hot, and afterwards in cold water: turn out and serve upon a glass dish.

The preparation now produced may be made into half a dozen sweets, according to the way in which it is finished, and flavoured, for the flavour may be varied in many ways. Vanilla and brandy, coffee, tea, fruit syrup, or what not, may be used instead of almonds and lemons; or two ounces of candied cherries and two ounces of candied citron cut small, or three ounces of preserved ginger, and one ounce of pistachio kernels blanched and chopped, can be stirred in when the cream is on the point of setting. Here we have variations of the Bavarois, every one of which is so unlike the other in taste, that no one would think they were made from the same recipe. The garnish also may be varied, because in no instance should the cream be put by itself into a mould; that would be a painful waste of good material. The cream will look very pretty if light coloured jelly, which will occupy space to the depth of about an inch, be allowed to set before the Bavarois (as the preparation of custard and cream is called) is poured in. It will look still prettier if the mould is completely lined with jelly before the Bavarois is placed within it. An easy way of doing this, and one which can be managed without ice, is to place a mould of a rather smaller size inside the mould that is to be used, and to fill the space between the two with liquid jelly. When this is set the smaller mould may be taken out, and the cream, which should be just on the point of setting, put in its stead.

When girls have a party on their minds, and intend to make a number of dishes of the sort described, it is an advantage to be able to calculate exactly how much material will be needed so that there may be no waste. If we get a clear idea of what we are aiming at before we commence proceedings, we shall save both time, labour, and money. Some girls would make each mould separately, but this would be a very wearisome business. Others would follow the recipe exactly, and take the chance of the quantities being right. The consequence would be either that their moulds would not be filled, which would be disappointing, or they would not contain all the cream which was made, which would involve loss. What they have to do, therefore, is to endeavour to make the exact quantity which will fill the moulds they have at command. To do this they must make their calculations from their moulds, which will, of course, vary in size and number in every household.

Collect the moulds that are to be used, therefore, in the first instance, no matter what their number, shape, and size may be. Half fill them with milk, then empty all the milk into one measure and measure it. It is to be used to make the custard, which will be the basis of each Bavarois. Next prepare the moulds, rinse them well first in boiling water, then in cold water, and remember they are to be left wet. Now decorate them in any approved way. The decoration ought to be done early, because it will need time to set. If coloured jelly is used it should have time to get firm before the cream is added; if any special decoration, such as preserved fruits, sliced pistachios, angelica, or silver or gold leaf is to be set in jelly, it should be placed in position, and then liquid jelly should be put gently over it with a spoon, so as to cover it entirely, and keep it from moving. This is a secret of successful decoration, to cover the garnish lightly with jelly, and to let the garnish become quite firm before the cream is placed upon it.

Measure the milk, and for each pint allow three-quarters of an ounce of gelatine in warm weather, and one ounce of gelatine in cold weather. Allow also for each pint of milk three eggs and half a pint of cream, and a tablespoonful of sugar for each egg. Put the gelatine to soak in good time. When giving recipes we are accustomed to say soak the gelatine for ten minutes; this is quite correct, as ten minutes will do for it; still, an hour is better, because the gelatine dissolves in a minute or two when it is thoroughly well soaked.

One way of saving time and trouble is to let the milk boil before pouring it on the eggs in making the custard. Many girls are afraid to do this. They think that it will make the eggs curdle. But if the milk is sweet and the eggs are good, there will be no fear of curdling, and if the ingredients are not good we should be fortunate if we discovered the fact now, before further mischief is done. The eggs should be lightly beaten and the boiling milk poured upon them, off the fire, and the two should be mixed very thoroughly before anything else is done. Also, after the eggs and milk are mixed, the custard should be thickened over the fire, but it should not on any account be allowed to reach the boiling point. If it did, it would curdle without doubt. To prevent this, it should be put into a double pan, or into a jug placed in a saucepan of boiling water, and stirred without ceasing until it becomes thick and coats the spoon. Then it should be taken off the fire at once, because if left it would become lumpy. Now every one who is accustomed to make custard knows that if milk and eggs are put when cool into a jug, and set in a saucepan of water to be stirred till thick, they are a long time before they become thick and smooth; indeed, they are so long, that oftener than not the individual who has to stand over the saucepan and stir, grows weary of her task, comes to the conclusion that the game is not worth the candle, and after a time in desperation pours the contents of the jug into an ordinary saucepan, sets it on the fire, and gets it burnt or curdled straight away. There is, however, no occasion for all this worry. If the milk is poured boiling over the eggs, and if the mixture is at once put into the double pan with boiling water round it, a few minutes will be sufficient to thicken it; and there will be no fear of spoiling it either, because being surrounded with boiling water it cannot boil, and custard spoils through being boiled. All we need to do is to be careful to keep the water boiling round it, and to keep on stirring it, making the spoon touch the bottom of the pan with every turn of the arm; then the custard will be everything that could be wished with no trouble at all. In making custard, as in many other of the more delicate operations of cooking, girls might avoid many an accident if they would but realise that no food can be brought up to the boiling point in a pan or jar that is surrounded with boiling water. This fact it is which makes a double saucepan so valuable.

Where a double saucepan is not available, however, and a jug has to be used instead, there is a danger ahead against which we need to be on our guard. It is this: the jug into which the hot custard is put must itself have been heated gradually, or it will be liable to crack and come in two pieces when put into the hot water. An accident of this kind is most annoying. When we have taken pains to make some excellent custard, we do not want to dilute it with a large quantity of hot water. More than once have I known this mischance to occur; and on one occasion the poor girl who had the custard in charge burst into a flood of bitter tears, wept long and loud, and refused to be comforted. One way to prevent the accident is to put the jug or jar which is to contain the custard, to get hot with the water which surrounds it; then it is hot enough to allow of hot custard being poured into it. A better way even than this is to provide ourselves with a porridge pan, or double pan. The inner pan of the utensil being made of white china, is so thoroughly sweet and clean that it is a satisfaction to use it, whilst it soon saves its price in preventing food being spoilt.

The custard being made, it may be left till cool; yet not left entirely, for it must be stirred every now and again to keep it from skimming on the top. The cream is the next consideration. I have before now spoken in detail of whipping cream, therefore the remarks made need not be repeated. It is, however, worth while to mention that when economy is a consideration, or when the richness of a large quantity of cream is considered objectionable, half the measure of cream may be taken, and white of egg used instead of the remainder. As the yolks only of eggs are needed for custard, whites of eggs are sure to be available. Of course, both the whites of eggs and the cream must be whisked till firm.

The order of making up the different creams is the same. The custard should first be flavoured. If brandy is to be introduced, a tablespoonful of the spirit will be sufficient for a pint of custard. If liqueurs are preferred, a wineglassful may be allowed. The custard must be cool, and the gelatine must be cool before the two are mixed; but neither must be cold, or they will not "come together" properly. The cream and white of egg should be added last of all, and the Bavarois should not be moulded until it is on the point of setting.

When preserved ginger is to be used as a flavourer, it should be cut into very thin slices and stewed for a few minutes in its own syrup, then allowed to cool before it is stirred into the cool custard. Ginger syrup is usually served with this cream as a sort of sauce.

Rice Cream is a very simple preparation, but it is much liked by those who know it. Soak half an ounce of gelatine in cold water to cover it. Put three tablespoonfuls of Carolina rice into a saucepan with a pint of cold water. Let it boil up, then drain away the hot water and wash the rice in cold water. Drain it again, and boil it very gently with a pint of milk, till the milk is absorbed. Sweeten it pleasantly, and flavour it as approved. Boil a quarter of a pint of milk, pour it upon the beaten yolk of one egg, and stir the custard over the fire in the usual way till it thickens. Add this with the gelatine dissolved, to the rice, and last of all add one gill of whipped cream. Set a gallipot with a weight in it in the centre of a plain round mould, and arrange the rice around. Turn it out when cold, and fill the space occupied by the gallipot either with cream, which has been whisked till firm and coloured pink, or with stewed fruit of some kind.

Apple Cream.—One or two very excellent though simple sweet dishes may be made with apples, and these are generally liked because they are refreshing to the palate. It is important, however, that the apples chosen should be of a fine flavour. Some people have an idea that baking-apples are simply apples not good enough for dessert apples. This is a mistake. The fact is that it is much easier to choose a good dessert apple than it is to choose a good baking apple, and when there is any doubt about the quality of those which are offered to us, it is much the best to take a known "dessert" variety, such as Blenheim, Flanders, or Ribston pippins, rather than to take apples simply because they will fall. To make the cream, pare and core the apples, and cut them into quarters, then weigh them. Soak half an ounce of gelatine in as much water as will cover it. Put the apples into a jar with the rind and juice of a small lemon, and a quarter of a pound of loaf sugar. Cover the jar closely, set it in a saucepan of boiling water, and steam the apples till they fall. Take out the lemon rind and beat the apple pulp in a basin. Mix thoroughly with it the gelatine which has been melted over the fire, and when nearly cool add half a pint of cream which has been whisked till firm. A few drops of cochineal may also be added for the sake of colour. Put the preparation into a mould which has been rinsed in hot and afterwards in cold water and left wet, and turn out when stiff. When wine is not objectionable, it makes a change of flavour to put a glass of port into the apples while they are steaming.

Oranges and Cream.—Peel six or eight St. Michael's oranges, and carefully divide them into sections, freeing them entirely from pith. Put the strained juice and very thin rind of one lemon, also a little of the orange rind, into an enamelled saucepan with a cupful of water, and a cupful of loaf sugar. Boil to a clear syrup, then put in the orange sections and let them boil a few minutes. Take the oranges out, and let the syrup boil a little longer till thick, and if approved put a teaspoonful of brandy into it. Let the sections become quite cold, then place them in layers in a glass dish; sprinkle desiccated cocoanut over each layer, and moisten with the syrup. Pile whipped cream on the top. The cream should be arranged last thing before serving, but the syrup should be poured over the cocoanut a little while before the dish is required.

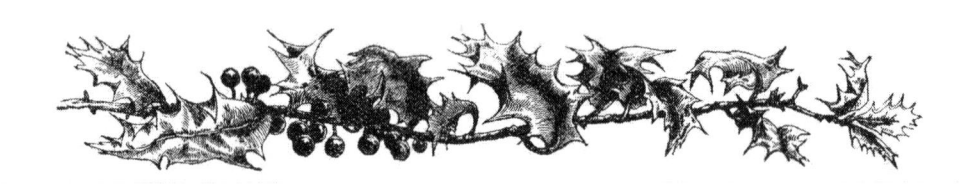

CHRISTMAS DAY ON DARTMOOR.
By CHARLES JOHNS.

GRANNY, and Annie, and Fanny went down
   From their home on the hill to the marge of the moor.
Granny was dressed in her best "Sind'y" gown—
   That very same gown at her wedding she wore
A prim little, trim little, sunny-faced soul,
With a laugh in her eyes and a smile that was droll,
   Was Granny.

Granny, and Annie, and Fanny went o'er
   The rough "vuzzy down" till they came to a cot.
Annie (aged ten) gave a "knack" at the door:
   "Aw, Nanny," she laughed, "if you knawed wot I've got,
You wou'dn' zit mumblin' an' grumblin'! No, fay!
But there! you'm stone deaf, an' can't yer wot I zay!"
   Said Annie.

Granny, and Annie, and Fanny went in.
   Nanny sat by the fire in her old easy chair.
"Lord love ey!" croaked Nanny, "ware evvy all bin?
   I thought you'd a-come in the mornin'. But there,
You be come in the aivnin'. Still, come wen you may,
I be main glad to zee ey, my dearies! Iss, fay!"
   Said Nanny.

Granny, and Annie, and Fanny all spoke:
   "Us knaws you be, Nanny. No doubt about that."
Fanny (aged eight) gave the fire such a poke
   That she "tipsized the kittle" and "upsit the cat!"
Then out on the table they spread the good cheer:
"'Tes C'rismasin', Nanny! 'Tes all vur you, dear!"
   Chirped Fanny.

Granny, and Annie, and Fanny kissed Nanny,
   For Nanny had been Granny's "nuss," years ago.
Nanny kissed Granny, and Annie, and Fanny;
   And just then Nanny's daughter came home through the snow.
More kisses and compliments. Christmas good-will.
Then home went the girls to their house on the hill,
   With Granny.

The Girl's Own Paper, 1885

HOW I SPENT CHRISTMAS IN THE FATHERLAND.

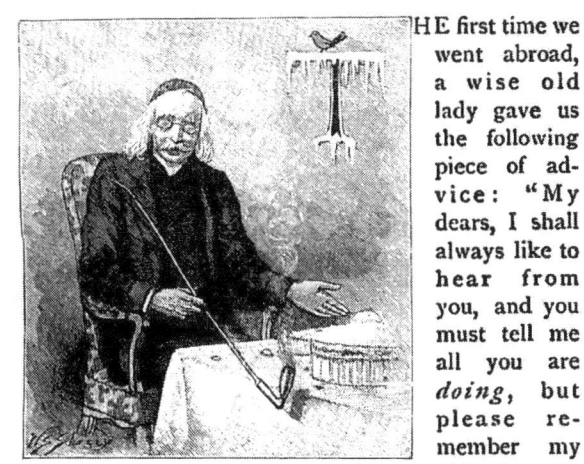

"'AH, MY CHILDREN, HERE IS WORK FOR ALL.'"

THE first time we went abroad, a wise old lady gave us the following piece of advice: "My dears, I shall always like to hear from you, and you must tell me all you are *doing*, but please remember my objection to the face of the country being described, as if we had not all been saturated with guide-books." Bearing these words in mind, I will not now "describe" the old German town where I passed the Christmas of 1882, but will only say that I was spending the winter in a German family, consisting of the Herr Vater, the Frau Mutter, Fräulein, her sister, little Lenchen, the eight-year-old daughter, and last, but by no means least, the dear old Herr Grosspapa. How well I remember the first night in my new quarters! A tremendous gale was blowing, but, tired out with the two days' journey, my head had literally no sooner touched the pillow than I was asleep. In the "dead waste and middle of the night" I was suddenly and rudely waked by the sound of glass smashing and crashing all around me. Terrified, and firmly convinced that thieves were breaking into the house, if not actually into my room, I leapt up, prepared to alarm the family. But all was now again still, and nothing to be either seen or heard until my door was opened, and Fräulein, who had been also awakened, made her appearance, and explained matters. It seems that on account of the violent storms and excessive cold the windows are all made double, and the noise I had heard was caused by my outer window being blown entirely away, and falling into the street below. "But it is nothing," concluded Fräulein cheerfully, as, smiling benevolently, she once more left my room. I returned to bed, but for a long time lay awake listening to the raging of the wind, and hearing at intervals the crashing of glass, now near, now far along the street, and thinking what a curious country it must be where the falling out of windows was looked upon so calmly as an everyday, or rather nightly, occurrence.

On the Sunday before Christmas Day, as we came home from service in the cathedral, I was surprised to find all the shops open, and the streets thronged with people laden with baskets and bags. It is the custom for the shops to be open on the two Sundays before Christmas, so that people who cannot get out during the week may do their Christmas shopping.

Christmas in Germany is a very serious business indeed, and everybody, young and old, is in an immense state of excitement about it for weeks beforehand. Lenchen could talk of nothing but what the "Christ-child" would bring her on Christmas Eve; and even the old Herr Grosspapa, when he went out in the afternoon to drink his coffee and read his paper, would come in with his pockets full of contributions for the Christmas-tree.

One evening, about a week before Christmas, we were all called from our usual occupations by the Herr Grosspapa to "come and help to prepare for the 'Christ-baum'" (Christmas-tree). There he sat at the table, his long silver hair peeping out from under his velvet skull-cap, as, with a triumphant smile on his kind old face, he pointed proudly to the well-filled table before him, exclaiming, "Ah, my children! here is work for all." And work indeed there was. There were walnuts and Brazil nuts to be covered with gold and silver paper, chocolate and cakes to be cut up into all imaginable shapes and wrapped in like manner in coloured paper, besides oranges, apples, and sweets of various and poisonous-looking colours, which were to be tied up with parti-coloured ribbons for

"THE TREE ARRIVED"

suspending to the tree. These preparations alone occupied us for three evenings, as nothing could be begun until little Lenchen was disposed of for the night; and as the whole party retired to bed at ten o'clock at latest, our time was very limited. The German children believe that if they are good the "Christ-child" will bring them presents, which they will find under the tree. Our custom of hanging up the stockings for Santa Claus to fill seemed quite a new idea to them, but one to which Lenchen took very kindly.

On the morning of the 23rd the tree arrived. It was bought by the Herr Vater at the "Jahr Markt," or great fair, which is held in the market-place at Christmas-time, and where any conceivable thing, from wearing apparel and furniture to ginger-bread and Christmas-trees, can be bought. From that moment every one appeared to be in a state of the wildest excitement and bustle. Frau Mutter was very busy in the kitchen, superintending the making of mysterious and unknown dishes, and the Herr Grosspapa and the Herr Vater set to work at once fixing all the candles and fruit on the tree. I offered my services, which were not accepted, as it is against all the rules and regulations for the "children" of the family to assist in the actual decoration of the tree itself, and from the moment of my arrival the Herr Grosspapa had numbered me among his "Kinder." So I retired to tie up and ticket, according to Fräulein's instructions, the various presents I had secretly prepared for the family. This done, they were all handed over to the Frau Mutter, to be seen no more until the long-wished for Christmas Eve arrived.

That evening a large skating party was given a short way out of the town, to which we were all invited. Well wrapped up in furs, we set forth about seven o'clock in a sleigh, and half an hour's swift gliding over the snow brought us within view of the lake. It is difficult to imagine what a bright, animated, un-English picture met our eyes. I felt for the first moment as though I must be dreaming—and dreaming of Russia. The whole lake was illuminated with numberless lanterns of all shapes and sizes; the white trees stood out, like giant spectres, against the starry sky, and as far as we could see stretched that "snowy coverlet" which the German poet says the "liebe Gott" lays over the sleeping earth. We were taken entirely round the lake in small, swan-shaped sleighs, which the skaters pushed before them, or tempted to the refreshment tent hard by, where hot coffee, spiced drinks, and cakes took the place of ices and champagne.

The 24th was a lovely bright day, and we were out all the morning skating in the park, as the "Bescherung," or the distribution of the presents, did not take place until after dark. Almost every one we met on our way home was laden with a Christmas-tree; sometimes they were quite little ones, not much bigger than dwarf azaleas, and worth about fourpence or fivepence. Every one, however poor, makes an effort to have a little household festival and a tree at Christmas-time. The afternoon, to Lenchen at least, crept slowly away, but about half-past four we were all assembled in the dining-room, telling one another stories, and speculating as to what the "Christ-child" would bring us, when the Frau Mutter came in to summon us. Suddenly the folding-doors into the drawing-room

"WE WERE TAKEN ENTIRELY ROUND THE LAKE IN SMALL, SWAN-SHAPED SLEIGHS."

were thrown back—the Herr Grosspapa played a brilliant march on the piano, and we were all ushered in. The "tree" stood in the middle of the room, all ablaze with lights, and sparkling with gold and silver. Beneath it and dotted about the room were many little tables covered with white cloths, and on these the presents were laid out. Each person had his or her own little table, and a prettier sight than this "Bescherung" I have seldom seen. Little Lenchen rushed about, showing us all her treasures, especially a large doll which Fräulein had dressed for her. Every one received a present from every one else, besides three large pieces of the "Pfeffer Kuchen," or gingerbread, which is almost universally eaten in Germany at Christmas-time. The servants had their tables also filled with presents, for the most part of a more useful kind, but with a liberal supply of gingerbread.

When the noise had a little subsided, we all settled down to "coffee and cakes," and then, too, we had an opportunity to examine the contents of each other's tables, to guess from whom the various presents came, and to return thanks accordingly. At supper appeared sundry awful compounds, called "Weihnachtsessen"—the Christmas dishes over which the Frau Mutter had been so busy for so long. She informed me that they were "national" dishes, and thinking it my duty to share thoroughly in the German Christmas, I conscientiously tried them all, though in much fear and trembling. Herring is the chief ingredient in these "national" dishes—*herring*, together with *apples* and *oil*. I felt it best not to inquire what else might be there, and breathed an inward thanksgiving that "Christmas comes but once a year." After supper we had music and merry-making till about half-past ten, at which hour little Lenchen was discovered sound asleep on a sofa, surrounded by her presents, and cuddling the new doll. She was waked to join in singing the Christmas hymn, "Stille Nacht" ("Still is the Night"), after which all trooped off to bed. On my way to my room I was waylaid by Lenchen, who begged me to come in when she was in bed, and show her "how Santa Claus liked the stocking to be put." I made her hang it on to the bed-post, and left her dreadfully afraid that Santa Claus "might have too much to do in England to make time to come to her." When she was asleep I filled the stocking with the sort of things we liked so much to find in ours when we were children, not forgetting a little purse with twenty-five pfennige in it. I did not, of course, see the fun of the stocking's being emptied, but was told next day by the Frau Mutter that at four in the morning she had been aroused by loud shrieks, and hurrying to see what was the matter, had found that all the noise came from Lenchen, who had waked and found her well-filled stocking, and was shrieking with delight and surprise. The best of it all was that she firmly believed it was Santa Claus who had brought the treasures to her, and that it was *I* who had told him to come. This I discovered as she

"SHOW HER HOW SANTA CLAUS LIKED THE STOCKING TO BE PUT."

proceeded to exhibit to me all my little gifts, with the greatest and most unsuspecting pleasure.

On Christmas morning, after a hasty cup of tea and a biscuit, we started off, a large party, to the nine o'clock Christmas service in the Lutheran Church, where some of Bach's music was to be played. I felt very strange and not a little homesick on this, my first Christmas Day away from home and England, and my thoughts were at first far from the great German building, now filled almost to overflowing. Two gigantic Christmas-trees, filled with candles, stood one on each side of the Communion table, and almost hid the portraits of Luther and Melanchthon. The exquisite Bach music did much to comfort and console me, and then the familiar Gospel and Epistle were read, and a hymn was sung, after which the address was given. The length of that address was something appalling—the author of the *Mikado* would have sympathised with us, for our "mystical German" seemed as if he really would go the length of preaching from "ten till four." The want of any proper breakfast, and our long trudge through the snow in the cold and early morning, made all this the more trying.

Owing to severe snow-storms, the English post had been delayed, and my disappointment was keen when I found I could have no Christmas greeting from home that day; but every one was so kind and anxious to make me happy, that I hid my depression, and joined a sleighing party into the country. In the evening, as we were all sitting at supper, a loud ring was heard at the front door, and a minute afterwards Augusta (the maid), entering the room, handed me—a telegram—a telegram from home wishing me "A Merry Christmas." Words could not express how pleased I was—the whole world seemed changed to me, for really Christmas so far from home *does* feel lonely, and the surprise only added to the pleasure. How often that telegram was read in the course of one evening I should be afraid to say.

As the night before we had sung the German hymns, so now my German friends insisted upon the dear old English ones, and with the last words of the "Herald Angels" still ringing in my ears, I went off to my room, to read the telegram yet once more, and to think over the many new and strange experiences of this Christmas-time. Suddenly twelve o'clock struck, and my first German Christmas was over. At this time of year there is certainly no lack of amusement in Germany—such as it is. My German friends heartily enjoyed their small "whirl of dissipation," and there was general rejoicing when new invitations arrived. On entering the breakfast-room the morning after Christmas, I was greeted by Fräulein with a kiss, and the news that "we had two more invitations," one to a "Kaffee" at the Frau Doktor's on the following day, and one to a party early in the New Year. "Now you will see a true German Kaffee," said the Herr Vater, "and we shall hear no more of your English five o'clock teas."

The next afternoon Fräulein and I set off to the Frau Doktor's, taking good care to arrive punctually at half-past four. To be late seems to be a very great breach of courtesy, and Fräulein was simply aghast at my remarking, "I suppose we must get there about five." "You did not then see Lieschen's letter," she said; "we are asked at half-past four." As we hurried along I endeavoured to explain that at home it was not the "fashion" to arrive on the stroke of the hour at which one was invited, but it was a hopeless task, and all I convinced Fräulein of was that "you English are certainly a curious people;" she was too polite to say *mad*, but I knew what was in her mind. We were introduced immediately on our arrival to the other guests—all young people—and there was a small amount of conversation till the "Kaffee" was brought in on a tray and handed round. We all took some, and I, naturally enough, thought we should remain where we were, dotted "casually" about the room. Much to my surprise, however, our hostess presently requested us "to take places round the table," which we accordingly did. It was a work of some time to get every one fitted into the right seat, as great complications had arisen when it was discovered that there were fewer gentlemen than ladies. But at last we were satisfactorily arranged—napkins were then dealt round—then plates—and then, all things being now ready, the eatables were brought in. One immense dish, crammed with all kinds of the most delicious and deleterious cakes and biscuits, was placed in the middle of the table, and we "fell to." After this really substantial meal, we occupied the time with various games—such as "What is my thought like?" and others of a similar kind to what one plays at home at children's parties—until about half-past six, when the tray again made its appearance, glasses of some hot drink having taken the place of coffee. After a short interval the command was once more given to "take our places at the table," which little ceremony was now much better managed, as every one knew where to go. Then a large iced chocolate cake was brought in, and as soon as it had been distributed, an apple tart appeared! Things were becoming more wonderful every minute. Think of an apple tart when you are invited out to afternoon "coffee"! It was a very good pie, however, and a considerable part of it soon disappeared. After this second meal, and a little more conversation, which by now had become rather more animated, I observed Fräulein "making the move" to go. I certainly thought it was late enough, being past seven o'clock, but she began by apologising to the Frau Doktor for "having to hurry away so early, as we expected a lady to supper, and must not be late back." The thought of supper, after having done nothing else but eat all the afternoon, was almost too much for me. I returned to the Herr Vater more English and a greater upholder of our five o'clock tea than ever.

This was almost the last of our Christmas festivities, and soon we settled down into the "quiet, working home life," as Herr Grosspapa called it, for which I had really gone out to Germany, but which gives still less to write about than my first Christmas in the Fatherland.

CHRISTMAS IN THE GERMAN FATHERLAND.

In the days of my youth it was my good fortune to have letters of introduction to some German friends of our family, and to be invited to spend the winter with them in their charming country house at the foot of the Riesengebirge.*

It was the 24th of December, and bitterly cold, when I emerged from the railway carriage upon the platform of a small country station, and was taken into friendly possession by a vivacious little dark-eyed baroness and her tall, flaxen-haired son, who, with many fears that I must be nearly frozen by my long journey from Berlin, wrapped me in an extra fur and supplied me with a third veil before allowing me to encounter the keen outer air and a long sledge drive.

To drive in a sledge at all was to me a novel and delightful experience, and the sledge to which I was now conducted was particularly pretty, with its body of light carved wood, its fur rugs lined with crimson, its pair of cream-coloured Russian ponies, with their harness studded with silver knobs, and arches of silver bells over their heads; and when once we were all warmly ensconced among the cushions and wrappers, and were gliding with noiseless swiftness over the well-kept sledge-way, it seemed to me that sledging was the very acme of luxurious motion, and I felt almost sorry when Baron Max checked his ponies to point out the high tower, now close at hand, which he said formed part of the main building of his home.

After passing through some fine pine-woods, we drove across the whilom moat, now planted with trees and called the Dark Walk, and, driving under a small archway, found ourselves in a spacious court laid out as a flower-garden, while facing us, and forming three sides of a hollow square, stood the schloss itself. The great entrance was approached by a long flight of steps, and upon these were several liveried servants awaiting our arrival, while at the sound of the sleigh-bells and the cracking of the driver's whip, two great wolfhounds rushed out to welcome their master, and were followed, more sedately, by the daughters of the house, who from their striking disparity in height were always known by the sobriquet of Tiny and Tall.

To Tiny's care I was immediately consigned, and, after a brief adjournment to my room, was led by her into the saloon, where we found Tall presiding over the coffee and cakes, which, as I discovered later on, she had herself prepared.

The Baroness had disappeared, leaving an apology for me that, as it was Christmas Eve, she had much to do, to which she must attend, and while we were waiting the signal to go and view the tree, Tiny and Tall proceeded to enlighten me as to many of their national customs in connection with this particular season.

In this village, for instance, as in many others of the Fatherland, and especially in Southern Germany, a veiled woman goes up and down the streets after nightfall, bearing in her arms a child chosen for his beauty and goodness to represent the Infant Saviour, and as they pass along they find the cottage windows discreetly left ajar, so that the Christ-child, as he is called, can leave upon the sill some token of the day. Every good child, upon awakening next morning, finds gifts — oranges, sweeties, or some such things; but, alas for the child who has been naughty! for him are no such delights; for him there lies only a pliant willow or birchen rod, suggestive of the chastisement he deserves. Into the towns the Christ-child seldom comes; he is there replaced by the Christmas tree; and it was to decorate such a tree that the mother of the family had now disappeared.

The room in which I was hearing all this was large and lofty, lighted by five windows, the remaining walls being hung with ancestral portraits; for these unassuming, domesticated young girls were the descendants of a noble and historical line, would not have changed their ancient barony for a modern dukedom, and with pardonable pride showed me the family portraits, and gave me slight sketches concerning the originals. The most striking of these was certainly the full-length picture of that old field-marshal of whom Carlyle thus graphically writes: — "With regard to Friedrich, the court-martial needs no amendment from the King. The sentence on Friedrich, a lieutenant-colonel guilty of desertion, is from president and all members, except two, death as by law."

From this portrait we turned to that of Frederic the Great himself—his own gift to the family; from that prince the transition was easy to the subject of the Seven Years War, and we had begun planning excursions to the different battlefields when a bell began to ring, and changed the current of our thoughts.

We rushed down a long corridor, being joined as we went by different other members of the household, and reached the room from whence the blaze of light betrayed the presence of the great tree. It was, indeed, a giant, and formed a most imposing spectacle, as it stood in the centre of the large room, dazzling with variegated waxen tapers, shimmering all over with ice-like crystals, and decorated with gilded fruits and sweetmeats. The base of this wonderful member of the vegetable world was covered by a pyramid of the tempting confectionery and gingerbread peculiar to the province, and for which lots had afterwards to be drawn.

Round the room, and overshadowed by the mighty branches of the central tree, stood tiny specimens of the same tribe, each standing upon a table laden with gifts, and each destined for a separate member of the family and household.

Even I, stranger as I was, had my own little tree and table of presents—pieces of fine Silesian linen, a huge surprise ball,* and a pretty gold brooch, embossed with roses and forget-me-nots, which I cherish still in remembrance of my first happy visit to Germany. There were so many pretty things to admire, so many thanks to tender, so many good wishes to exchange, that it was growing quite late before we could make up our minds to leave these "halls of dazzling light" for the more prosaic supper room.

Here—as in Germany the Eve is more celebrated (except as regards religious services) than the Christmas Day itself—we found the traditional dishes of Germany and of England. In honour of Germany I had to make acquaintance with real black bread—"Pumpernickel," as they call it in some parts of Germany, sauerkraut, and raw smoked ham, all of which at first I secretly thought odious, but eventually grew to like very much; and in honour of England we had plum pudding and mince pies—the former not at all badly cooked, the latter a dismal failure, as most English housewives will understand when I tell them that the cook, although adhering strictly to the proportions of an excellent recipe, had,—for some extraordinary reasons of his own—pounded the whole into a paste, and enclosed it in a very thick crust, the shape and size of a small pork pie.

We did not linger long after supper; for it had been a long and fatiguing day for everyone. As for myself, after so many interesting and novel incidents, and so long and wearying a journey, I was only too glad to find myself once more in my own room, and I slept without pause or wakening until the appearance of the young ladies' maid, Amalia, at my bedside next morning with a cup of coffee and the intimation that it was now 7.30, and that the sledge for church-goers would be at the door at nine o'clock.

We were off punctually to the time, and after about half an hour's drive over the hard-frozen snow, upon which the brilliant sunshine was streaming down, we reached the unpretending-looking little Lutheran church. Here, as the due of the Adel,* we sat in a gallery all by ourselves, and had high-backed velvet chairs, surmounted by the baron's coronet, and with footstools embroidered to match; and very strange it seemed to me to be looking down from this pinnacle of isolated grandeur upon the poorer congregation below.

Generally speaking, these wore the costume of the province, and a charming costume too—a short skirt of red, green, or blue serge, with five broad bands of black velvet round the lower edge; black velvet bodice, laced over a full chemisette, and sleeves of white cambric; pointed velvet cap (of the Stuart shape), in colour matching the skirt, adorned with heavy gold braiding, and edged with a fluting of Silesian lace. Long gold earrings and a broad gold plaque, set with garnets and suspended by a slender chain round the neck, were the ornaments worn with this costume, and were, as I was afterwards told, handed down as family heirlooms from mother to child.

The dress of the men was, of course, less elaborate. It consisted of dark-blue or grey cloth suits, much adorned with silver buttons. Both men and women wore long black stockings and buckled shoes as part of their Sunday garb, but on weekdays generally go barefoot.

Those among the congregation who abjured these picturesque costumes and went in for modern fashion, wore—like the gentle folk—black; and I found to my astonishment that black was also *de rigueur* for Confirmation and the Holy Communion. The clergyman, a tall, kindly-looking old man, wore a long black gown and a wide box-pleated ruff. There was an ebony and silver crucifix upon the altar, which had lighted waxen tapers burning upon it. The musical part of the service was led by a full brass band; and, to complete my surprise, I found it was against rule to kneel at any time; one either sat or stood.

All this seemed so utterly at variance with recognised ideas in England upon the same subject, that I am afraid I did not much profit by my first church-going in the Fatherland. Still, it was an interesting experience, and when time had familiarised me more with both the language and the customs, I found a great deal that I could honestly admire, though I never ceased to prefer our own bright and beautiful Liturgy to the somewhat ponderous nature of worship in the Fatherland.

---

* A lofty chain of mountains lying to the south of the province of Silesia.

* A ball of this kind is a favourite gift in Germany. It looks like a very unskilfully-wound ball of knitting wool. You are bound in honour to knit it up, and as you do so you disclose, one by one, a variety of gifts, the most precious being generally the innermost of all.

* Nobility.

CHRISTMAS IN A FRENCH BOARDING-SCHOOL.

CHRISTMAS morning of more than twenty years ago is breaking over a picturesque old town of fair France. The cold wintry sun touches upon the masts of the ships in her harbour and upon the crowded houses of the Lower Town, creeps up to the leafless trees upon the ramparts, and glints upon the steep roofs and stately cathedral of the Upper Town.

From the dormitory windows of a large boarding-school some dozen or more of girlish heads are peering into the feeble light, in the hope of seeing across the narrow "silver streak" the white cliffs of their English home. In vain. A cold, grey fog is rising from the sea, and baffles even their strong young eyes. The casements are closed, and as the big school-bell sends forth its summons, the English boarders hasten into the class-room below. It does not look very inviting at this early hour; there is no fire and little light, while the empty benches and the absence of the usual chattering throng of schoolgirls serve only to make those of them who remain the more depressed. They gather, from force of habit, round the fireless stove, and wish one another a "Merry Christmas"; but they neither look nor feel as if a merry Christmas could be theirs. With hands swollen with chilblains and faces blue with cold, they stand, a shivering group, comparing this with former anniversaries, and increasing their discomfort by reminding one another of the warm firesides, the ample Christmas cheer, and the lavish gifts with which the day is being ushered in at home.

At length the welcome sound of the breakfast-bell is heard, and our small party descends to the *réfectoire*. Here excellent hot coffee and omelettes, with the best of bread and butter, somewhat reconcile us to our hard lot, while the different mistresses are really very kind to *les petites désolées*, and do their best to enliven the meal. We are told that during the ten days' holiday now begun we shall be entirely exempted from the necessity of talking French, and shall be allowed to get up and go to bed an hour later than during the school terms; moreover, that after service in our own church that morning (for, to their credit be it said, these ladies, devout Catholics themselves, never tampered with our belief), we should have a good fire lighted in the small class-room, where we could amuse ourselves as we pleased for the rest of the day.

After such good news we set off, under the escort of the English governess, in revived spirits for church. It was a plain little building, but we always liked to go; it seemed a bit of old England transplanted into this foreign town; and to-day the holly and flowers, the familiar hymns, and our pastor's short and telling address, made the service particularly bright and cheery.

We were very fond of our good, gentle little clergyman, and always lingered a while after the services in the hope that he would speak to us, as he often did, especially upon any Church festivals; and to-day we had quite a long talk with him before, with many and hearty good wishes, we parted in the church porch.

As usual, after service, we went for a walk on the ramparts which encircle the Upper Town. The view was very fine, comprising on one side the Lower Town, the shining waters of the Channel, and, on very clear days, the houses as well as the cliffs of Dover; on the other, the hills and valleys, watered by the Liane; if we went further still, and passed the gloomy old château—now a prison —we could trace the roads leading to Calais and St. Omer; while on a bleak hill to the left rose Napoleon's Column.

This rampart walk was a great favourite with us all, and we generally liked to make two or three turns. To-day, however, we were to have an early luncheon, and, besides, were yearning for our letters; so we contented ourselves with *le petit tour*, and hurried home. Here we found an ample mail awaiting us, whilst among the pile each girl found a neat little French *billet* from mademoiselle, inviting us formally to dinner and a little dance that evening. Of course we sat down at once to write our acceptances, then, with a cheer for mademoiselle, turned our thoughts to the absorbing topic of what we should wear. Dinner was fixed for 5 p.m., so that after luncheon there was really not very much time left, especially as each girl, besides the difficulty of choosing and arranging her most becoming costume, had also to have her hair "done."

Hair-dressing was an elaborate science in those days, puffs and frisettes, curls and plaits, being all brought into requisition on state occasions, and if this—a dinner and a dance given by mademoiselle, the rather awe-inspiring though extremely kind mademoiselle, who reigned an undisputed autocrat in our little school-world—if this, I say, was not a state occasion, I appeal to every schoolgirl throughout the kingdom to tell me what was.

The *dortoir* was a gay and animated scene as we English girls repaired thither after luncheon to "lay out" (rather a dismal phrase, but one we always used) our best frocks and sashes, our open-worked stockings and evening shoes, and our black or white silk mittens. One of the girls was a capital hairdresser, as everyone else allowed, and as her services were eagerly entreated by the less skilful in the art, I can tell you her powers and her patience were put to the test that afternoon.

Oh, the plaiting and waving, the padding and puffing, the crimping and curling, that we gladly underwent on that memorable occasion! How openly we admired one another, and— more secretly—ourselves; and then how very funny it seemed to be walking into the drawing-room as mademoiselle's visitors!

Kind mademoiselle! how handsome she looked in her dark satin dress, with a little old French lace at her throat and wrists! How pleasantly she welcomed us all, while she gave extra care to the one child amongst us, who could only wear black ribbons even for Christmas Day.

Of course, all the under-mistresses were there, and one or two of the non-resident ones. I particularly remember the pretty singing mistress, and the head music mistress, whose brother I hear of nowadays as the first organist of Europe; whilst last of all to arrive was Monsieur l'Abbé, who was a frequent and honoured guest, and for whose coming we had all been waiting.

The dinner bell rang a few minutes after this important arrival, and we all descended to the *réfectoire*. How good that dinner was! A soup such as one never tastes anywhere but in France; the *bouilli*, which we were too English to care for; the turkey stuffed with chestnuts—delicious, but so unlike an English turkey; the plum pudding, very good again, but still with a foreign element about it somehow; and, as a winding up delicacy, the delicious *tourte à la crème*, a real triumph of gastronomy.

Then our glasses were filled with claret, and we drank the "health of parents and relations," a rather perilous toast for some of us, whose hearts were still tender from a recent parting; and finally coffee was served—not the coffee of everyday life, but the real *café noir*, which we girls drank with an extra dose of sugar, but which to seniors was served with a little cognac. Then, as we sat over our fruit and *galette*, mademoiselle and her mother, a charming old lady, with bright, dark eyes, and soft, silver hair, combined with Monsieur l'Abbé to keep us merry with a succession of amusing stories of French life and adventure, until the repeated ringing of the hall bell announced the arrival of some of the old pupils, who had been asked to join our dance. Tables were quickly cleared, superfluous chairs and benches removed, violin and piano set up a gay tune, and then we danced and danced away until nearly midnight, when the appearance of *eau sucrée* and lemonade, with a tray of tempting cakes, concluded the fun, and gave the signal for retiring.

The Girl's Own Paper, 1887

CHRISTMAS GIFTS.

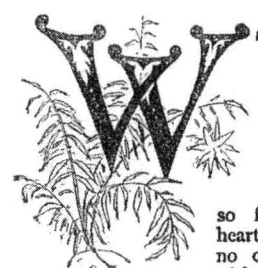

WITH the approach of Christmas and Christmas gifts, the cares of the girl members of a large family may be said to arrive at a crisis. There is no girl so friendless or so heartless that there is no one she loves or wishes to remind of that love at this season, while there are many surrounded by affectionate relations and true friends, whose love they warmly return, and whom they wish to please with a gift, and yet have but a small sum at command, and must think carefully over its division.

How many anxious calculations have to be made, what knitting of smooth brows, what hasty arithmetic on stray scraps of paper, what self-denial in personal matters to increase the little store, and then, when the materials are bought, what secret work is carried on behind father's chair, should he happen to be awake, and in this and that out-of-the-way nook of the house, so that the all-important, and generally extremely apparent, secret is not divulged until the Christmas or New Year's morning!

All honour to this secrecy, this planning and patient work! It is the true spirit of present-giving; and let not any of our readers despise it as childish; rather let them remember that that which costs no time, no thought, no self-sacrifice is but of little value in the eyes of affection, and pleases only where the gift is valued for itself, and not for the giver. The girl who can walk into a shop and select the first handsome article in it for mamma, and pay for it from an amply-supplied purse, neither awakens in herself or her mother the same holy feelings that are excited when baby works an impossible kettle-holder "all by herself," and which she "bided" out of the pennies given her for sweeties.

Admiring and sympathising as we do with girls who are generous-minded and do not count labour and time when anxious to please, we have brought together in this paper, with the idea of helping them, several useful and pretty articles that can be made without any great expense.

For a small present, costing at the utmost one shilling, the fashionable little "hold-all bags" are good. These bags are four in number, and are connected together only at the top; they are filled with odds and ends, such as buttons and silks, until they stand upright and all of a row, and they find a conspicuous place among drawing-room nick-nacks.

To make them, purchase one yard of good satin ribbon, in colour either ruby, navy blue, or chestnut brown, with the reverse side of a pale blue or old gold shade. The ribbon should be from two and a half to three inches wide. Divide the yard into four equal portions, sew over the sides, and hem the tops of two bags without decorating them, but work on one of the other bags a handsome and legible monogram containing the initials of the person for whom the present is intended. Work this with fine gold-coloured purse silk, and surround the chief outlines with Japanese gold thread. On the other bag work a small spray of flowers, either a branch of wild rose, a bit of heather, forget-me-not, or jessamine. Sew up these two bags, and hem them round like the others; then make sixteen eyelet-holes, four on each bag; make these round and not very big, and place them opposite to each other, and at the extreme corners of the opening. Sew the bags together by overcasting the first bag with its monogram turned outwards on the inner side of its opening to the outer side of the opening of one of the undecorated bags. Attach the second plain bag to the inner side of the first plain bag, and sew the fourth bag, with its decorated side turned outwards, to the inner side of the third bag. By this arrangement both the decorated bags are outside, and every bag at its base is separate. Finally, take a silk dress lace, the colour of the satin ribbon, and run that through the eyelet-holes to make a drawstring. Fill the bags, plant them out on the table, and draw their openings slightly together.

These "hold-all bags," instead of being filled with odds and ends, are sometimes turned into flower-vases. The smallest-sized penny tumblers are inserted into each bag and filled with cut flowers, or the smallest size flowerpot, filled with a tiny fern, is used. In the latter case, a piece of American cloth is fastened round the pot to prevent any moisture soiling the satin bag.

The present method for concealing flower-pots when required for drawing room decoration makes another simple but acceptable present. This is a bag of plush, into which the pot is put. To make this bag of plush, cut a round of millboard or stiff cardboard the size of the bottom of an ordinary flowerpot. Take a piece of plush, in width twice the circumference of the centre part of the pot, and in height the height of the pot; sew the two ends of the plush together, and make a hem an inch and a half wide. As a finish to the upper part, just below this hem, on the wrong side of the bag, run on a narrow piece of black tape to hold a draw-string, which make by running in a piece of strong elastic, that will draw in the fulness of the plush until it fits the upper part of the flower-pot tightly. Gather the lower ends of the plush, arrange evenly round the piece of millboard, and sew to the latter with the edges concealed, using strong thread for the securing stitches. When the plush cover is used, its millboard foundation keeps the bottom of the pot (which may be damp) from doing any damage to the furniture, and the wide hem beyond the draw-string stands out as a frilling a little below the edge of the pot. Half a yard of plush, which costs two shillings, will make a pair of flower-pot covers.

From America comes to us a novelty in bed-room decoration, and one very suitable as a present to a young lady who uses her bed-room as a sitting-room and likes it prettily decorated. This is known as a "pillow sham," and is a long strip of linen or cambric ornamented with lace and ribbons, and laid over the top part of the bed in the daytime only. It fits the width of the bed whatever size that is, and does not fall down the sides. If the worker is an adept at drawn-thread work, the pillow sham can be made very inexpensively and of material that will last through much wear, but when drawn-thread work is not used, Torchon and other strongly made lace is required. An easy way for making a pillow sham is to buy four new hem-stitched-bordered handkerchiefs, and upon the corner of one of the handkerchiefs to embroider the first letter of the owner's Christian name, making it four inches high and slanting it from the corner to the middle of the handkerchief. Join these handkerchiefs together, inserting between each an inch and a half wide strip of Torchon lace insertion, and bordering the handkerchiefs lengthways with a line of the same, so that each square of cambric is surrounded by insertion lace. Finish with a frill of Torchon lace edging, which carefully whip to the insertion lace. A careless bow of ribbon or one of Liberty's silk scarves tied in a bow is sewn to the corner of the pillow sham, just above the embroidered corner.

When using drawn-work instead of lace insertion, a piece of linen the length and width of the sham is taken, and the threads from this are drawn out as strips down the width, leaving five squares of plain linen between them. After working the strips over with linen thread into a pattern, narrow coloured ribbon is run down the centres of the drawn-work, and the linen squares embroidered with washing cotton of the same colour as the ribbon. An edging of lace finishes the border, and into this lace a line of narrow ribbon is threaded.

Another variety of pillow sham is made by sewing together five or eight pocket handkerchiefs with coloured borders, and ornamenting the same with a large knot of narrow ribbons of various shades of colour. The handkerchief borders in this case need not be alike, but should blend together, and their colours should be used as some of the colours in the knot of ribbons.

Palm-leaf fans still find favour as drawing-room fans, but are no longer left undecorated. The two newest ways of decorating them are as follows:—Take a well shaped and strong fan and paint it with oil-colours, with which a very little varnish has been mixed, either a very bright yellow or a brilliant scarlet. Give two coats of colour, and let the fan dry. Buy some ribbon half an inch in width; in colours, black, vivid green, sky-blue, and yellow-pink. Make a wide vandyke running down one of the lengths of ribbon by taking the running thread in diagonal lines across the ribbon from edge to edge. Draw the ribbon up so that it forms a number of pointed vandykes, sew the strips down the ribs of the fan at equal distances apart, and use black ribbon more than the other colours. Sew on a line of red gold tinsel between each strip of ribbon, and finish the handle with a knot of coloured ribbons.

The second make of fan requires a piece of plush, some narrow coloured silk cords, and various shades of tinsel. The cords are obtained by buying a yard of a twisted silk cord made up of various shades, and using the strands of this separately. Cut the piece of the plush the size of half the fan, so that it covers the fan on one side from the tip of leaf to the handle. Fasten this round the edge to the back of the fan, and ornament its straight edge on the fan with a line of tinsel on the uncovered side of the fan. Sew down each rib alternate lines of coloured silk cord and double lines of tinsel, using as many varieties of tinsel as possible, and arranging the cords with due regard to effect. Take three long peacocks' feathers, and fasten these across the piece of plush and sew their ends together close to the handle of the fan. Cover the handle with a piece of plush, and arrange a bow and ends of ribbon round the handle and to conceal the peacock feather ends. Line the back of the fan with thin silk or dark twill.

Blotting-book covers of velveteen are always acceptable presents. The foundation for these is a sixpenny blotter, size ten inches by eight inches, while three quarters of a yard of velveteen (price three shillings the yard) will make two covers, with a piece of brown holland or blue twill for the inside lining. The decoration for these covers is embroidery;

but this is only worked on the upper side of the blotter, the underside being left plain, so as not to interfere with its usefulness. The embroidery can be of any description of silk embroidery, either oriental embroidery with its quaintly-formed but impossible flowers and foliage, or sprays of naturally-tinted flowers worked in crewel silks, and both worked directly on to the velveteen foundation; or silk embroidery finished with a gold thread outline and worked upon a coloured rep silk foundation, and sewn on as an ornamental corner to the blotter; in fact there are many ways of ornamenting the cover, and the embroidery the worker is most proficient in should be selected. If church embroidery is within her capabilities, we advise the initials or coat of arms of the owner being worked in a frame on linen, cut out and couched down to the velveteen foundation with gold thread or gold cord; but such elaborate embroidery is not often obtainable. The way to make up the blotter is to cut the holland lining exactly the size of the sixpenny blotter, and the velveteen a little larger. Turn in the edges of both, and overcast them together, enclosing the stiff cover of the blotter between them, and sewing the blotting paper sheets in when the cover is made. Bradshaw covers are made like blotters, but naturally take less material, and are only embroidered in one corner.

Large photograph-holders can be easily made at home. These are used for the display of a number of cabinet photos, and are fitted with bands, into which the photograph is slipped and easily taken out. The size of such a stand is usually seventeen inches long by thirteen inches high, but they can be made of any size desired. The foundation is of millboard, to which a millboard support is fastened by its being glued to stout tape and the tape glued to the millboard, with sufficient width of tape left between the two pieces of millboard to allow the support to work. The upper side of the millboard is covered with quilted satin. The satin is selected of some bright colour, and the quilting lines are run as diagonal lines, not as making diamonds. Three tight bands of satin are sewn across the quilting; these are two inches in width, and require a lining of stiff net when made up. They are embroidered with coloured silks, either forming a running design, such as a spray of jessamine or celandine, or with some geometrical pattern constantly repeated. When finished and lined, the bands are placed as diagonal lines across the satin, not as horizontal lines.

For a photograph-holder the size given, the first band will be eleven inches in length, and will cross from the top of the holder to the left-hand side; the second band will be nineteen inches in length, and will cross from the extreme top corner of the frame on the right side to the bottom of the frame on the left; the third band will be twelve inches in length, and will be arranged beneath the last-mentioned, crossing from the right side to the bottom of the frame. Into these bands the photographs are stuck; therefore, they must be sewn firmly down at the sides where they end and commence, and stretch tightly across the quilted frame. On the right-hand bottom corner of the foundation, which is never covered with photographs, the owner's initials are sometimes worked in black silk over the quilting lines. This makes a good finish, but is not essential.

Bachelors' wall pincushions are useful presents for gentlemen. They are made of plush, and are ornamented with the perforated brass ornament used about the harness of cart-horses. These brass rounds are sold by all harness and saddle makers, and cost from sixpence to a shilling, and for the latter price the small brass handle by which they hang will be removed by the shopman, as it is not required for the pincushion. A quarter of a yard of plush, a quarter of a yard of house-flannel, and one yard of narrow satin ribbon are required for these cushions. To make them, tear up the house-flannel into an inch and a quarter wide widths. Roll these strips very tightly one over the other as a narrow wheel, and keep the strips firm by sticking pins through the wheel. When a round as large as the perforated brass is made, cut the plush into two rounds of the same size and a long strip an inch and a half wide. Cover one plush round with the perforated brass, and sew them both on the face of the wheel and well through to the back; turn the edges of the round of plush over the side, and sew on the round for the back of the cushion; conceal the edges of both pieces of plush with the narrow band, which turn in at its edges and secure tightly round the sides of the cushion. Make a loop of the ribbon to hang up the pincushion by, and sew the ends to the sides of the cushion, and with the remaining ribbon make a pretty bow, which fasten to the top of the loop.

The newest decoration for white wooden articles is the poker or burnt-wood work. This consists of burning down the background of any design so that the design itself is in relief. The fumes of the burning wood slightly colour the parts left untouched, and give an extremely soft and ivory-like appearance to the work, which, if carried out with the new apparatus introduced by Mr. Barnard, is quickly and easily accomplished.

The articles decorated with burnt wood work are all kinds of white wood photo frames, small wooden table screens, all kinds of boxes, bookslides, book cutters, drawing-room bellows, salt boxes, milking stools, tubs, paste rollers, etc. The best designs are those of large, single-petalled flowers, with their leaves, such as daffodils, daisies, and dog-roses. The design is drawn upon the wood, outlined with a burnt-in line, and its chief lines, such as divisions of flower petals, centres of flowers, veins of leaves indicated, and then the background burnt until it is depressed, and is of a warm brown deepening to black in colour. Mr. Barnard's apparatus consists of a platinum point connected by an indiarubber tube to a bottle of benzine, which is connected with another indiarubber tube to a small air pump. The latter held in the left hand is pressed, forcing air over the benzine to the platinum point and keeping that always red hot. The right hand holds the point and uses it like a broad pencil, keeping it steadily pressed on the wood until that is deeply burnt in. This apparatus costs twenty-five shillings, but if several girls join together to purchase it, there is no further outlay. Small pokers are used if the apparatus is not procurable. These are about eight inches long and an inch in circumference; they are sunk in wooden handles, and kept hot in a fire; four to six are required at once, as they soon become cold. The parts of the wood not burnt, such as the back of a screen, the legs of a stool, require to be stained, sized, and varnished, and the burnt wood is also varnished (not stained) as a finish. The paste rollers are used for holding whips, keys, etc. They are hung to the wall with coloured ribbons, and have a row of hooks screwed into them to hang keys, etc., to.   B. C. SAWARD.

CHOCOLATE DATES.

HAVE you ever tasted chocolate dates? If so, these directions will be almost needless to you, for I fancy that you will not have stopped at a taste, but will have tried and found out a way to manufacture them for yourself. But so far as I know, these dates are, as yet, quite a home-made sweet, and they are so delicious and so wholesome that they ought to be more widely known. Here then is the recipe. Any sort of dates and any sort of chocolate may be used, but the best results are got from the best materials in confectionary even more than in other work. Take then a pound of Tunis dates, either bought in the familiar oblong boxes or by the pound. Leave out any which are not perfectly ripe; the soapy taste of one of these paler, firmer dates is enough to disgust anyone with dates for ever. Wipe the others very gently with a damp cloth (dates are not gathered by the Dutch!), slit them lengthwise with a silver knife, but only so far as to enable you to extract the kernel without bruising the fruit. Then prepare the chocolate. Grate a quarter of a pound of best French chocolate, add an equal weight of fresh icing sugar, two tablespoonfuls of boiling water, and mix in a small brass or earthenware saucepan over the fire until quite smooth, only it must *not* boil; last of all add a few drops of vanilla.

Then put your small saucepan inside a larger one half filled with boiling water, just to keep the chocolate fluid until all the dates are filled. Take up a little of the mixture in a teaspoon, press open the date, and pour it neatly in. There must be no smears or threads of chocolate if your confectionary is to look dainty. When about a dozen are filled, gently press the sides together, and the chocolate should just show a shiny brown ridge in the middle of the date. Place on a board in a cool place to harden; they may be packed up next day.

Almost as nice as chocolate dates are nougat dates. The foundation for the nougat is the same as for American candies: the white of one egg and an equal quantity of cold water to half a pound of sifted icing sugar, all mixed perfectly smoothly together. Then chop equal quantities of blanched walnuts, almonds, Brazils, and hazel nuts together, mix with the sugar in the proportion of two thirds of nut to one of the sugar mixture, and leave until next day in the cellar. By that time the nougat will be firm enough to form into kernels by gently rolling between the hands; if it sticks, your hands are too warm. It is best to do this part of the work in the cellar. Having stoned and first wiped your dates, put in the nougat kernels, gently pressing the sides together; they will harden in a short time, and very pretty they look packed alternately with the chocolate dates in fancy boxes. Tunis dates do not keep good much longer than two months, the grocer tells me; we have never been able to keep them half that time to try! Of course, you can use the commoner dates, which are very good to eat, but hardly so nice to look at as the others, because on account of their more sugary consistency it is impossible to fill them so neatly as the moister Tunis dates. Tafilat dates are somehow too dry and solid to combine well either with nuts or chocolate.

THE GIRL'S OWN CAROL

JOSEPH BARNBY.

1. Holy night! peaceful night! Through the darkness beams a light; Holy night! peaceful night! Through the darkness beams a light, Through the darkness beams a light, Yonder, where they sweet

Where they sweet

The Girl's Own Paper, 1884

2.

Silent night! holiest night!
Darkness flies, and all is light!
Shepherds hear the angels sing—
"Hallelujah! hail the King!
Jesus the Saviour is here!"

3

Holiest night! peaceful night!
Child of heaven! O how bright
Thou didst smile when Thou wast born;
Blessed was that happy morn,
Full of heavenly joy

4.

Silent night! holiest night,
Guiding Star, O lend Thy light!
See the eastern wise men bring
Gifts and homage to our King!
Jesus the Saviour is here!

5.

Silent night! holiest night!
Wondrous Star, O lend Thy light!
With the angels let us sing
Hallelujah to our King!
Jesus *our* Saviour is here!

SWISS CAKES, AND HOW TO MAKE THEM.

The following recipes I have translated from a Swiss cookery book, recommended to me by a Swiss lady. Many of them are peculiar to the Bernese Oberland.

ALMOND SUGAR-BREAD.

Take half pound sugar-dust, quarter pound almonds (sweet) blanched and finely chopped, the rind of a lemon finely chopped, the weight of three eggs in flour, and five eggs. The yolks of the eggs and the sugar must be well beaten together until they begin to get white, then add the lemon-peel and the juice of the lemon, then the whites of the eggs (beaten till stiff), and lastly the flour and the chopped almonds, stirred in very lightly, and the whole well mixed. Pour into a cake-tin which has been previously well buttered and sprinkled with sugar. Sift sugar over, and bake.

SWABIAN BREAD.

Put thirteen ounces of flour on a paste-board, rub into it ten ounces of fresh butter, moisten with the white of one egg, and work them together; then add by degrees half pound sugar and half pound almonds, not blanched, the sugar and the almonds to be well pounded together before adding to the other ingredients, also half ounce pounded cinnamon and the rind of a lemon, with a little salt; work all together, and cut out into shapes with a cutter, brush over with the yolk of an egg, and bake on a floured tin.

LITTLE MACAROONS.

Quarter pound sifted sugar, quarter pound almonds (sweet) blanched and finely pounded, the rind of a lemon finely chopped, and the white of one egg beaten till stiff. Mix all together, and pour into little cakes; bake on a buttered paper.

TRONCHINES.

Three ounces sifted sugar, good weight, the finely chopped rind of a lemon, and the whites of three eggs beaten till stiff. Mix these together, and then stir in a good ounce and a half of flour. Spread this mixture on a buttered baking-tin, about the thickness of the back of a knife; when baked, while the cake is still hot, cut into small square pieces.

CHOCOLATE ROLLS.

Three ounces of sifted sugar, one and a half ounces good chocolate grated, the whites of two small eggs beaten till stiff; mix all well together, make into little heaps on buttered paper, and bake.

STEINERLI.

Take one pound of sifted sugar, one pound flour, and four eggs, the whites of which should be beaten a little; cinnamon according to taste, or the chopped rind of half a lemon; mix these ingredients together, roll out very thin, cut into shapes with a cutter, and bake on a floured tin; they should not be long in the oven, nor baked hard.

CHOCOLATE CAKE.

Quarter of a pound of chocolate grated, half a pound sugar pounded, with quarter of a pound blanched almonds, a little pounded vanilla or cinnamon; mix all together with the well-beaten whites of four eggs, then stir in a handful of flour; put the mixture into a well buttered mould; bake in a moderate oven, so that it is baked quite through.

EXCELLENT LITTLE CAKES.

Half a pound white sugar, half a pound blanched almonds. Half the almonds to be pounded, and the other half to be cut into strips; put the latter in a small saucepan with a very little water and the sugar, stir diligently over the fire until the sugar is melted and the almonds a little roasted; put this mixture in a bowl with the pounded almonds and the whites of three eggs well beaten, stir well together; then form into little cakes (flat) on a slightly buttered plate or dish, and bake till a golden brown. Great care must be taken that they do not burn.

FREEMASON BREAD.

Half a pound sifted sugar, and two whole eggs and two yolks to be beaten together for an hour; then stir in ten ounces of flour, and lastly one and a half ounces of lemon peel and one and a half ounces orange peel, and the rind of a lemon finely chopped or grated, together with a little pounded cinnamon, and, if liked, a little pounded clove. Make this mixture into little rolls as long and as thick as your finger; sprinkle a baking-tin with flour, and lay the fingers pretty far apart on it; make three little cuts across each with a knife, and bake in a slow oven.

SCHMELZBRÖDCHEN.

The whites of five eggs, the yolks of three eggs, the weight of four eggs in sifted sugar, the weight of two eggs in fresh butter, the weight of two eggs in flour, and the rind of a lemon grated or finely chopped. Beat the yolks of the eggs together with the sugar and lemon rind, until little bubbles appear on the surface, beat the whites till quite stiff, and stir in lightly, sift in the flour, and beat together; lastly add the butter a little melted. When well mixed, butter some small moulds, and fill them a little more than half full with the mixture, and bake a light brown.

TIRE-BOUCHONS.

The whites of three eggs beaten till quite stiff, two ounces of sugar, on which rub the rind of a lemon, two teaspoonfuls of red wine and three teaspoonfuls of ordinary white wine, and a tablespoonful of flour. First dissolve the sugar in the wine, then stir in the whites of the eggs well beaten, and lastly add the flour; when well mixed pour into a slightly buttered tin (flat), which ought to be large enough to allow of the mixture being quite thin; as soon as it is baked cut into long narrow strips, and while they are warm wind them round a stick, slip them off when cold.

L. STANTON.

THE PLEA OF THE TOM-TIT.

When gloomy and chill is the day,
   And the ground is all whitened with snow,
Forget not your songsters, I pray,
   But pay them the debt that you owe.
Scatter crumbs where the flowers once have been,
   Where all now is still and forlorn;
And when Robin Redbreast is seen,
   Turn not from his pleading in scorn!
From a balcony hang out a bone,
   Let it dangle at end of a string,
And it is not *one* tom-tit alone
   That you'll see round your charity cling.
A crowd of blue tits will appear,
   So dainty, with waistcoats of buff,
They're blest with good appetites, dear—
   In fact, one might say that they stuff.
Topsey-turvey, and thankful they'll cling,
   And nibble the meat off your bone;
The sparrows swoop by on fell wing,
   But the prize is the tom-tits' alone.
What though when your fruit is in bloom
   I may ravage and rob you a bit?
You've saved a poor bird from the tomb,
   And so I'm your grateful tom-tit.

                           Jetty Vogel.

The Girl's Own Paper, 1885

CHRISTMAS CARD POETS

By W. J. Wintle.

Illustrated by Portraits and special Autographs.

EVERY lover of the "Bab Ballads" will remember the sorrows of Ferdinando and Elvira, how in the midst of pulling crackers at Christmastide the lady's brow became clouded over with anxious thought, and presently her pent-up feelings found relief in an outburst of tears. The gallant Ferdinando was all anxiety, and in his eagerness to assuage the sorrows of his mistress, offered to go in search of the North Pole or explore the depths of Vesuvius, if such devotion could afford her any relief.

"But," she said, "It isn't polar bears or hot volcanic grottoes,
Only find out who it is that writes those lovely cracker mottoes."

Ferdinando set out upon a veritable voyage of discovery. He sought high and low, but failed to find the scent. Poets and "litterary gents" froze him with scorn and contempt when he inquired if they knew aught about it, and at last he gave way to despair. Then it was that he met with a gentle pieman, who admitted that in the intervals of making patties and polishing the silver he wrote "those lovely cracker verses."

We have been upon similar discovery bent, though we have not found a pieman amongst the poets. When the editor blandly suggested that a good deal of leisure time might be usefully occupied in finding out the writers of Christmas card verses, we first pulled a long face, then put on an air of well-assumed assurance, and sought help at the hands of two of the principal card manufacturers.

Our first call was at the establishment of Messrs. Raphael Tuck & Sons in Coleman Street, where the courteous director, Mr. Adolf Tuck, was good enough to talk about his experiences.

"We get very little usable verse from outsiders," he began; "nearly all our verse is written for us by our regular contributors, such as Miss Burnside and Mr. Cowan. Of course we get any quantity sent in, every post brings heaps of it, and," with a sigh, "we read it all. But very little is of any use."

"Then, I suppose, your waste-paper basket gets well filled?"

"Oh, no; not at all: we send it all back to the writers. You see we have no means of announcing that 'The Editor will not be responsible for the return of rejected contributions,' so it all has to go back again. What are the chief faults? Well, of course, much of it is mere nonsense, not poetry at all, written by persons who evidently know nothing whatever about verse-writing. But apart from mere faults of metre or rhyme, a great deal of it is far too sentimental and gushing. We often receive verses expressing sentiments which would only be appropriate in the case of an engaged couple, or of very near relatives. Now a Christmas card should be of such a character that any person may fitly send it to any other person, so that verses addressed to a mother, or to a lover, are quite inappropriate. Then a large proportion of the verse sent in is far too religious, and would not express the feelings of the general public. Many of the verses express the hope that the recipient may have a happy hereafter! Could anything be in worse taste than to remind a person of his latter end on a Christmas card?"

"What, then, are the qualities specially needed for a Christmas card verse, Mr. Tuck?"

"Well, in the first place, it should not be too poetical. By that I mean it should not be involved, or obscure in its allusions. We need verses that can be read at a glance and understood at the same time. They should read smoothly and rhyme correctly. Each should contain a simple appropriate sentiment of a friendly character. But the word 'friend' should be strictly tabooed. Then it is essential that they should be quite general in character. As I have already said, any sentiment which would only apply to special circumstances or relationships, would be fatal to the success of a card. The sentiment should not be especially Christmassy. We find practically no demand for the old-fashioned card, with a robin and a spray of holly. The favourite designs at the present day have no special reference to the season, and it goes without saying that the verse should agree with the design."

"You would hardly make much use of quotations from the poets then?"

"We do to a certain extent, but not very largely. Of course Shakspeare heads the list. You will be interested to know that about two years before Lord Tennyson's death I offered him a thousand guineas if he would write us eight Christmas card verses. He sent me a polite refusal, though I have reason to know that he did not resent the proposal. Talking of Tennyson reminds me that soon after the laureateship became vacant, I received a letter from a would-be poet in Edinburgh, enclosing yards of doggerel, and a photograph showing him to be a gentleman of the long-haired, wild-eyed variety. He explained in his letter that his friends so warmly admired his poetry that he had been encouraged to apply for the laureateship. Of course I wrote back a very polite letter, expressing the hope that he would get it! I may add that the bulk of our verses are written to order by our regular contributors. Curiously enough, our comic poet is a clergyman, the rector of an important English parish. No, you must not ask me his name. His verses are never signed, and he writes for us on the distinct understanding that his identity shall not be revealed."

"And now, Mr. Tuck, let me trouble you with only one more question. What is the latest step in the evolution of the Christmas card?"

"General beauty, undoubtedly. Considerations of season count for very little. Out of 1250 sets of cards we have only about a dozen that are Christmassy, and these sell the worst. Our special feature for the coming Christmas is a very chaste arrangement of flowers upon lace work, which I fancy will become popular. Of course, we have to work a long time in advance. The cards for the present season were completed last April, and we are now well on the way with those for 1897. I attribute all our success to the fact that each designer's work is executed at a factory specially selected for the purpose. We thus employ thirty factories in various countries, but for black and white work England is still supreme."

We next sought help from Mr. W. Macdonald Mackay, the manager of the card department of Messrs. Marcus Ward & Co.'s establishment at the Royal Ulster Works, Belfast.

"Of all writers of Christmas card verse," he observed, "the late Frances Ridley Havergal is still the most popular. For many years she wrote verses exclusively for our firm. None of her poems have touched the hearts of the people more than the familiar 'Bells across the Snow,' and of many celebrated poems in which the music of bells is brought back to our ears through the instrumentality of felicitous verses, I venture to think that none have struck happier or more resonant notes. The late Mrs. C. F. Alexander's few Christmas poems were also great favourites."

"You think, then, that religious verses still take with the public?"

"Most certainly that is the case in our experience, though I am aware that some firms do not find it so. But with us cards bearing verses of religious character have always proved to be the most popular, selling better even than the humorous ones. They are always the favourites. After all, the quantity of modern Christmas verse is by no means an extensive one. Indeed, the majority of our cards bear only the customary greeting, occasionally relieved with a quotation from Shakspeare, Burns, or Browning. We have issued some few cards each year bearing specially written poems by Sarah Doudney, the late Rev. J. R. Macduff, F. E. Weatherley, Eliza Keary, and others. Occasionally the artist who designed the cards wrote verses for them, as in the case of Walter Crane's well-known designs. The couplets were written by him."

"And what about the contributions of outsiders?"

"Do not mention it! Hundreds of verses are submitted to the firm during the year, all more or less of a very orthodox nature, and the majority of them quite unsuitable for publication."

"I understand that your firm has been recently endeavouring to raise the tone of Christmas card verses?"

"Yes, that is so. The want of Christmas verse of real merit was forcibly impressed on me some years ago when preparing mottoes and arranging verses for the season's cards. The idea of a series of literary cards arose in my mind, and, although time did not permit of an extensive series, we communicated with the best-known poets of the day, asking them to write us a poem or sonnet for the series. The number who favoured the idea was not large, but poems were secured from Richard Le Gallienne, Norman Gale, 'E. Nesbit,' and Mrs. C. F. Alexander, to which we added the carol by Canon Farrar and the well-known hymn by Sears. These were illustrated by a young South Kensington artist, Mr. F. Appleyard. The series was a great success, and was an attempt to raise the standard of paste-board verse. Last Christmas we arranged a competition to extend the series, and the first prize was awarded to 'Evan Keane,' whose verses were favourably noticed in the WINDSOR MAGAZINE for June. Mr. Keane's poem was considered a notable exception to the ordinary verse submitted to the firm, and since the competition he has written a good deal of Christmas verse for future use. This season we have secured poems from Mrs. Meynell, Mrs. Dollie Radford, and the use of Sir Lewis Morris's 'Christmas Carol.' I may add that Lord Tennyson's 'Christmas Bells,' and 'Ring out, wild bells,' were used many years ago on Christmas cards, by special arrangement with the late laureate, and have been immensely popular whenever issued."

"I notice that you include several of the minor poets among your contributors, Mr. Mackay."

"That is so, and I think the fact has its significance. According to the booksellers poetry is a drug in the market. Here then is a chance for our modern poets to exercise their gift of song. Their verses, through the medium of the Christmas card, would make their name and work more popular and widely known, and would help to introduce them to the general public. I hope that two of our contributors, for example, May Bateman and 'Evan Keane,' will be heard more of in the future. The latter may turn out another Byron, although a note of sadness is dominant in a lot of his work which has come under my notice."

"Do you find that Christmas cards are still largely used by the public?"

"Most certainly we do. Christmas cards have never been so popular as they are at the present time. The number of publishers is greater than ever, the majority of them showing productions more or less of German origin. Our own firm have this year a larger collection of cards than they ever had since they began to issue them in 1866."

Mr. Mackay was good enough to show us the principal series of cards for the coming season—a bewildering multitude of chaste designs, harmonious colouring and tuneful verse. By the courtesy of Messrs. Marcus Ward & Co. we are enabled to insert Miss Havergal's popular verses.

BELLS ACROSS THE SNOW.

O Christmas, merry Christmas!
  Is it really come again?
With its memories and greetings,
  With its joy and with its pain.
There's a minor in the carol,
  And a shadow in the light,
And a spray of cypress twining
  With the holly wreath to-night
And the hush is never broken
  By laughter light and low,
As we listen in the starlight
  To the "bells across the snow."

O Christmas, merry Christmas!
　'Tis not so very long
Since other voices blended
　With the carol and the song
If we could but hear them singing
　As they are singing now,
If we could but see the radiance
　Of the crown on each dear brow;
There would be no sigh to smother,
　No hidden tear to flow,
As we listen in the starlight
　To the "bells across the snow.

O Christmas, merry Christmas!
　This never more can be;
We cannot bring again the days
　Of our unshadowed glee.
But Christmas, happy Christmas,
　Sweet herald of good will,
With holy songs of glory
　Brings holy gladness still.
For peace and hope may brighten,
　And patient love may glow,
As we listen in the starlight
　To the "bells across the snow."

FRANCES RIDLEY HAVERGAL.

HELEN MARION BURNSIDE.

Amongst writers of Christmas card verse Miss Burnside stands in the foremost rank. Of Scottish origin, she was born at Bromley Hall, Middlesex, and is first cousin to Miss Charlotte Murray, the well-known writer of religious poetry. From a very early age she has written verses, her first volume of poems appearing in 1864. For many years she has been an untiring literary worker—tales, articles and poems without number having been produced month by month. The sweetness of her verse receives an added pathos from the fact that in childhood she permanently lost her hearing and has lived her life in an absolutely silent world. She was good enough to give us an interview at the house of Miss Rosa Nouchette Carey, the novelist, with whom she has lived and worked for the last twenty years.

"How did you first discover your gift of song?" we asked, with the aid of paper and pencil.

"Well it came about in this way. When I was twelve years old I became deaf after an attack of scarlet fever. Up to that time I was passionately fond of music, and when I could no longer hear the notes I used to love, all the music in me seemed to turn to song and I began to write verses. My first published verses were sent to Messrs. Marcus Ward, and were so severely handled by the reviewers that it spurred me on to the determination that I would write something

From a photo by]   *[Poole, Putney.*
MISS H. M. BURNSIDE.

worthy of their approval. I really think that I owe a great deal to my critics for the rough things they used to say about me."

"I suppose that your published verses must now amount to a very great number?"

"Yes, I have written card verses for upwards of twenty years, averaging perhaps about 400 verses in the year, inclusive of Christmas,

*A merry Christmas, take again
The old, old wish from me,
May it lead in a joyous train
Of happy years to be.*
　　　　Helen Marion Burnside

A CHRISTMAS VERSE BY MISS BURNSIDE.

New Year, Easter, birthday and valentine verses. In addition to the greater part of Messrs. Raphael Tuck & Sons' work I write verses for all the leading fine art publishers. But I am anxious not to be known as a writer of card verses merely, as this idea has been very injurious to me. I work hard all the year round, writing poems for booklets and calendars, daily text verses, songs, stories and magazine articles. I have just completed collecting and arranging a selection of my 'Poems and Lyrics' for publication in book form. You know, I suppose, that I used to be literary editor to Messrs. Tuck?"

"Yes, and I hope you will favour our readers with some of your experiences there."

"While I was with Messrs. Tuck many thousands of verses and poems used to pass through my hands every year. The greater part of the mornings was occupied in reading MSS. of this kind. Much of it was a real pleasure to read—such as would be sent in by clergymen, university men, and the minor poets. But these were in most cases totally unsuitable for the purpose. They were mostly too scholarly or too religious, whilst others were too high flown or sentimental. Of course one received a good deal which it was *not* a pleasure to read. Some of it was the silliest drivel imaginable. Many people seem to think they can write Christmas card verses."

"Can you give me an example how not to do it?"

"I only kept copies of a very few specimens, and some of these I have quoted in my reminiscences, which appear in the forthcoming Christmas number of *Hearth and Home*, but here is one that you may publish:—

    Hurrah! for at Christmas everybody
      Should eat and drink and merry make,
    And so I wish you lots of beef and toddy,
      For jolly Christmasses sake.

"But that is not half so bad as some of them were. I greatly enjoyed my editorial work, and I should like to add that I think card publishers are rather maligned by verse writers. I have had my little differences and difficulties, but have found them on the whole liberal and pleasant to deal with."

"And now, Miss Burnside, if one may venture upon the question, what do you think of the present standard of card verses?"

"It has from the first been my aim to raise the quality and standard of these verses, and certainly the verses which were published years ago would have no chance of acceptance to-day. In my own experience I find that what I consider my best work is generally rejected. Simple, pleasant verse is preferred to poetry. It is a curious fact that, after all my editorial experience, I am no judge of my own work. I can never tell which, out of any given set of my verses, will be accepted."

Miss Burnside did not mention, but it is right to say that she has gained no small reputation in other departments of art. The Royal Academy accepted one of her pictures before she was nineteen, and two on subsequent occasions. For some years she was designer to the Royal School of Art Needlework, where her drawings won the special approbation of the Princess Christian.

SAMUEL K. COWAN, M.A.

Major Cowan, M.A., is a son of the late Andrew Cowan, Esq., J.P., and he began to write poetry almost as soon as he

From a photo by]   *[Muir, Belfast.*
MR. S. K. COWAN.

could spell. In his pleasant country house near Belfast he is fond of telling how his first recorded piece—an address to the moon —was written at the age of eight. When a boy at school he established a trade in poetry on the old principle of barter, receiving remuneration for his efforts on somewhat after the following scale:—

One four-line verse for valentine = 2 sweets.
Two four-line verses for birthday card = 4 sweets.
One sonnet = stick of candy.
And so on, *pro rata*.

He is now well known as a leading Irish poet, nine volumes of collected verse having appeared from his pen, in addition to a vast amount of ephemeral matter. At our request he kindly spared time to talk of his Christmas card work.

"How was it, Major Cowan, that you turned your attention to this branch of literature?"

"It came about in this way. At the suggestion of the Rev. Frederick Langbridge, of St. John's Church, Limerick (who was familiar with much of my magazine work), I first submitted some Christmas verses, in March, 1883, to Messrs. S. Hildesheimer & Co., and Raphael Tuck & Sons, sending twelve verses to each. The former firm accepted four, and the latter seven. Mr. Adolf Tuck explained that he had rejected my other verses because their subjects appealed to too slender a market. And no wonder, for the subjects were: 'From a mother to her son at sea': 'To an absent friend': 'To a lady, come of age on Christmas Day': 'To a friend forbidden the house': and 'From a son at sea to his widowed mother.' Acting on his advice, I widened my sphere of subject, and discarded the use of several phrases, such as 'darling,' 'friend,' and 'love,' which narrowed the market for the verse."

"I suppose that your annual output since that time has been pretty considerable?"

"My first year's work totalled 146 verses, 101 of which I wrote for Messrs. Tuck. In 1884 my total increased to 661, and during the next year—my record one—1005 verses were accepted by eleven publishing firms."

"What do you consider to be the essential qualities for work of this kind?"

"The special qualities which make poetry suitable for Christmas cards are, in my opinion, simplicity and melody. Of course, a pretty sentiment is an essential requisite—the very *raison d'être* of the whole business—but the general public have not time, in the hurry of Christmas shopping, to fathom a pretty sentiment that is obscure, and their ear will be naturally offended by a rugged rhyme or rhythm. A verse to suit a Christmas card ought to be tender, tuneful, and simple; like Homocea, it should 'touch the spot' at once."

"And when and where does the Muse most favour you?"

"At any time and anywhere; both by day and night, at home, along the country lanes, and in camp. Nothing puts me off my work when I once make up my mind to do it. I have frequently sat up all night to complete

> Like music, set to happy words,
> May all your New-Year flow along;
> And may your heart, on all its chords,
> Accompany the happy song!
>
> *Samuel K. Cowan, M.A.*

AUTOGRAPH VERSE BY MR. COWAN.

an urgent order, my greatest achievement —from midnight till 6 a.m.—being twenty-five eight-line verses, written to design. For many years I made it a point to compose a few verses every day, and lay them aside for future contingencies; I have now, however, discontinued this system, and write only to order or design, principally the latter. My earlier practice gave rise to an odd mishap. Out of my accumulated stock, I sent in error to a French firm half a dozen condolence, instead of wedding verses. Strange to say, they accepted them all, save one, which they returned with the remark, 'Please you to make the enclosed wedding verse a little less *triste*.' As I stated before, the largest number of verses I ever composed in one year was 1005, classified as follows: 79 birthday, 46 valentine, 22 wedding, 13 Easter, and the remainder Christmas, New Year, and general verses. Since then valentine verses have entirely gone out of the market, but wedding verses have increased."

"How do you account for the change?"

"Well, perhaps the present bicycle craze may have something to do with it. The up-to-date young man and the New Woman, flying along at the rate of twelve miles an hour, have no sympathy with those who moon by the wayside, and moan, 'The time I've lost in wooing,' but rush headlong into matrimony without further ado, and thereby 'boom' the wedding-card market."

"Can you tell the readers of the WINDSOR MAGAZINE how many verses for cards you have written in all?"

"I estimate my entire Christmas work since I began writing in 1883, at 6500 verses, or an average of 500 verses per annum. At present I do not write for so many firms as formerly, as I consider that the value of one's work is lessened by a universal market; but as I am commissioned —in addition to some smaller work — by four houses (two of them 'comic' firms) to supply them with *all* their literary requirements, my yearly average output is fully maintained."

"I understand however that this does not represent the whole of your literary activity?"

"By no means. Since the year 1885 I have been entrusted with much work of a more important and abiding character, such as the beautiful floral albums and other similar volumes of the fine art publishers, including Messrs. Tuck's 'Jubilee Lyric to the Queen,' and many other books and booklets. I should like to add that for any success I may have achieved in the domain of Christmas card work, I shall always hold myself largely indebted to Mr. Adolf Tuck, whose sagacious counsel and advice in past years were only equalled by his hospitality, and I look back upon my many transactions with his firm as the pleasantest episodes in my literary career."

From a photo by]   *[Pannell, Brighton.*
MISS CHARLOTTE MURRAY.

CHARLOTTE MURRAY.

Among the writers of healthy religious verse few names are more popular with the general public than that of Miss Charlotte Murray. Hearing that she had entered the ranks of the card writers we sought her assistance in the preparation of this article, and on a certain wet day in the Highlands she was good enough to favour us with some of her experiences.

"Almost as far back as I can remember," she said, "verse has always been my outlet for deep emotion. One of my earliest attempts was after I had left babyhood and was old enough to lead others into mischief, which I had done on the day in question when we were engaged in a game of ball. The ball was being thrown by the younger children to me at an upper window. As might have been expected the ball missed its mark and went through a pane of frosted glass instead. My mother was out at the time: how should I tell her when she returned? To solve the difficulty I bethought me of verse, and began carefully composing my confession, which ran thus—

"Oh, mother dear, the window's broke!"
(Thus to her mother Charlotte spoke).
"I really am so very sorry
I'm sure you'll blame me for my folly.
I was playing with the children, mother,
When I just thought I'd have another
Throw with the ball . . ."

"At this point I had to fly suddenly to prose, for my mother appeared on the scene!

"Thus years went on and my doggerels flowed apace until at length, in the old literary institution at Hastings, I was suddenly fired with an irresistible longing to write verses that might help others, and that might be published. This with more or less power I was enabled to do from that time, month by month, through the kindness of Messrs. Drummond, of Stirling, who always allotted to me two corners in their magazines. Two hundred of these poems have since appeared in two separate volumes. The first one, 'Messages from the Master,' has just reached its twentieth thousand. After that came requests from London firms for Christmas card verses, etc., since which time I have been constantly writing."

"I presume your card verses must have reached a very high number by this time?"

"I cannot tell you exactly how many verses I have written, for that would require a lengthy calculation, but I can only express thanks to my friends that they have not wearied of my voice before this."

"And have you formed any decided opinion as to the qualities which a card verse should possess?"

"I should say that they are simplicity, directness, and a sympathetic tone; in fact, that every card should be a true message from one heart to another."

"Doubtless you have met with many interesting experiences in connection with this branch of your literary work?"

"I have never published anything of a purely secular character, therefore most of the incidents connected with my writings are of too private a nature to repeat. But just this I will say, that a young lady told me a short time ago that a card of mine, exposed in a shop window, was the means of arresting her in her intention to commit suicide. She was on her way to throw herself off the pier-head, when the question with which the poem on the card opened arrested her attention. It ran thus—

'Is life worth living?' are you sadly asking?

"She stopped, read the poem through, bought the card, and is now finding life quite worth living, from the highest standpoint."

We may add that Miss Murray last year brought out her first prose work, entitled "Morning Sunlight," and is this year issuing her third volume of poetry, called, "Eon the Good."

"EVAN T. KEANE."

The gentleman who writes under this pseudonym is a clergyman holding a public position, and is the author of an important school book, but as he prefers, for the present, to remain unknown, we are unable to publish his photograph, or to give any further details of his clerical and scholastic career. In answer to our inquiry, he kindly furnished the following statement about his verse-writing:—

"I have written verses since I was fourteen, but never attempted to publish them until last year, when I had an introduction to the acting editor of the *Pall Mall Gazette*. Since then I have been lucky enough to have verses accepted by the *Pall Mall Magazine*, the *Spectator*, and the WINDSOR MAGAZINE, at various times.

"My connection with Messrs. Marcus Ward began last February, when they gave me the first prize in a competition for verses suitable for a Christmas card, and

Behind our life, the Weaver stands
And works His wondrous will;
We leave it in His all-wise hands,
And trust His perfect skill.
Should mystery enshroud His plan,
And our short-sight be dim,
We will not try the whole to scan,
But leave each thread with Him.
                            Charlotte Murray

AUTOGRAPH POEM BY MISS MURRAY.

subsequently kindly gave me commissions for other verses. Some of the verses published are recent; others date as far back as the age of seventeen. Most of the verses written for Messrs. Marcus Ward are recent.

Sweeter than than southern air
Blowing over gardens fair
Milder than than dew that lies
On tired blossoms' drooping eyes.

AN AUTOGRAPH VERSE BY 'EVAN T. KEANE.'

"So many people write verse nowadays that I can only wonder at my good fortune in obtaining a small footing in the magazines."

By special permission of Messrs. Marcus Ward we are enabled to quote the first and last stanzas of "Evan Keane's" prize poem:—

White Star of Bethlehem, we come to thy manger,
  Little children singing in the frosty night:
White Star of Bethlehem, guide us from all danger,
  Keep our souls from darkness with Thy silver light.

* * *

Shepherd of Bethlehem, long is day a-breaking,
  Many of the children like sheep have gone astray:
Shepherd of Bethlehem, still watching and waking,
  Call us closer to Thee till the dawning of the day.

GERTRUDE E. SHAW.

Amongst the cards published by Messrs. Marcus Ward & Co., and by other firms, the initials of Mrs. Shaw will often be seen. Although away from home at the time, she very kindly spared time to tell us of her work. In answer to a question about the beginnings of her poetical career, she said:—

"It is difficult to fix the time when I began writing verses, for I was fond of attempting them as a child, but my first serious efforts in the direction of poetry were translations from French and German authors. Most of my earlier years were spent on the Continent, so that these languages were quite familiar to me.

"Like many youthful writers I published a small volume of poems anonymously, at my own expense, some years ago. The greater part of the issue was never sold, and has probably now been used for waste paper. To increase the difficulties of disposing of my little work, the literary concern which published it became bankrupt—whether due to touching my poetry or not, who shall say?

"I began writing Christmas verses between three and four years ago. I suppose that I was led to do so by the fact that a poet not only has a song to sing, but wishes for a little human sympathy in the singing of it. As, in spite of all my efforts, no one would take the slightest notice of what I was doing, it struck me that as the public were so casual in the purchase of Christmas verses, there was a chance in this field of striking up a passing acquaintance, which might here and there ripen into friendship. There is no doubt I am succeeding in this, and I believe there are now a few people who recognise my name and find time to read what I write. The fact that writers of Christmas verse are often looked upon as a lowly order in the literary profession did not trouble me, believing as I did, and do now, after considerable experience, that the literary value of a Christmas verse need not be an inferior one. On the contrary, the concentration necessary to condense what is practically a short poem into four or six lines is a very useful education in the art of writing verse, and in working on longer poems, I now find my facility for expressing much in a few

From a photo by]   *[Lewis, Clifton.*
MRS. SHAW.

words very greatly increased. To a conscientious writer of Christmas verses, redundant words are impossible.

"Of the first three publishers to whom I submitted card verses, Messrs. Marcus Ward & Co. accepted some, and further gave me a commission to write verses to special designs. Since then, out of fifty publishers of Christmas cards, thirteen have by degrees become purchasers of my verses. I suppose I have now written about a thousand verses for Christmas and birthday cards."

"What do you consider to be the essential qualities of a successful verse?"

"If by successful you mean saleable, I know of no standard. There is a great deal of trash printed, as well as good verses; in fact, probably far more trash than poetry. Personally, I consider that I have succeeded when in a few lines I have poetically or humorously expressed in a novel manner some kindly wish or thought. There are many different styles required by different publishers, varying with the public they cater for. A verse rejected by one will often be accepted at once by another, but there is often a difficulty in finding out precisely what a publisher requires. In a word, to sell his work to good publishers, a writer of verses must make them good: how much greater must be the difficulty of the writer of religious verses, who often has to make them 'goody' as well!

"Broadly speaking, there are three classes of Christmas verse—the humorous, the playful, and the serious. Of these, the first two meet with the best sale, but the last allows the best field for the poet."

CLIFTON BINGHAM.

It is scarcely possible to glance over a heap of music without encountering again and again the familiar inscription, "Words by Clifton Bingham." Few song-writers are better known to the public than the author of "The Promise of Life" and "The Dear Homeland." But Mr. Bingham is also a prolific writer of card verses, and it was upon this subject that we enjoyed a short chat with him, at the close of a day which had been diligently devoted to this branch of his work.

"Yes," he said, "I've been writing songs now for fifteen years, and have composed many hundreds in my time, some of which have become very popular. I have only written card verses during the past five years, but they already mount up to some thousands."

"What do you consider are the points of a good card verse?"

"Oh, simplicity, certainly; that is the main thing. They should not be elaborately poetical, nor too sentimental. It is essential that they should express a happy sentiment in a pleasant, flowing rhyme. Then they should always be short—a four-line verse is the most generally useful."

"And what are your methods of composition, Mr. Bingham?"

"Well, most of my work is written up to design. I do a great deal of verse-writing for Messrs. Nister, and I spend several hours every week in their office writing verses appropriate to the cards which have been designed by their artists. The great thing with me is to get a suitable idea, the

A CHRISTMAS WISH, BY MRS. SHAW.

versification is a mere matter of practice. Tell me what you want said and I will turn it into a verse while you are saying it. I often get ideas in this way from the poets, notably from Shakspeare. I do a great deal of this sort of work at odd moments—in the railway train, or anywhere in fact. Of course I had to learn the art; my present facility is the result of long practice. I cannot write songs in this fashion, they have to be done when I am in the humour."

"What is the present tendency in Christmas verse-writing?"

"The tendency is distinctly to improve. The standard is much higher to-day than it was years ago. I have tried to do my part to improve the taste of the public."

"Let me only ask you one more question. Do you think that people read the verses on Christmas cards?"

"I am sure that they do. The travellers frequently tell me that some verse of mine has taken with the public and sold well; or on the contrary, that it is not liked and has proved a failure. I assure you that the sale of a card depends quite as much upon the verse as upon the design; but it is impossible to gauge the popular taste."

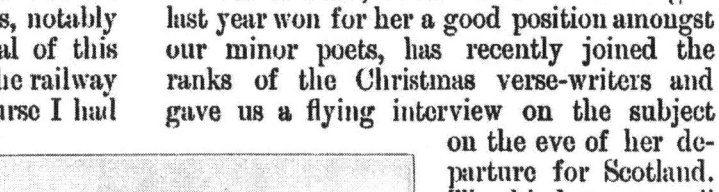

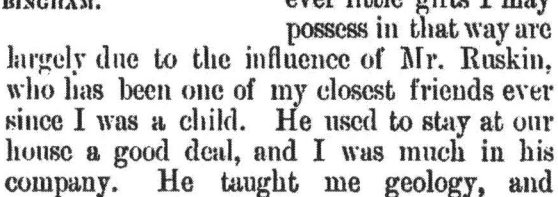

From a photo by]   MR. CLIFTON BINGHAM.   *[Alfred Ellis.*

MAY GERALDINE BATEMAN.

Miss Bateman, whose "Sonnets and Songs" last year won for her a good position amongst our minor poets, has recently joined the ranks of the Christmas verse-writers and gave us a flying interview on the subject on the eve of her departure for Scotland. The kindness was all the greater in view of the fact that she was very unwell and at the same time greatly pressed with literary work.

"Really I don't know what to tell you," she exclaimed. "You see I am only a beginner, and my story is not at all interesting."

"Well, perhaps you can tell me how you began?"

"Oh, I earned my first guinea for literary work, of a sort, when I was only seven years old. It was in connection with a competition in a children's magazine. But whatever little gifts I may possess in that way are largely due to the influence of Mr. Ruskin, who has been one of my closest friends ever since I was a child. He used to stay at our house a good deal, and I was much in his company. He taught me geology, and

A VERSE BY CLIFTON BINGHAM.

certainly he formed my taste in literary matters."

"Then his influence was certainly not lost, as witness your 'Sonnets and Songs?'"

"Well, that was more successful than I could have hoped. It was all written within six weeks. It came about in this way: I was ill and unable to use my eyes, and one day some lines were running in my mind and I asked my sister to write them down. When she had done so she said they made a sonnet. I could not believe it at first, but afterwards made some more attempts and

From a photo by]   *[Russell.*

MISS MAY BATEMAN.

discovered that I really could write verses. That is how 'Sonnets and Songs' came to be written, and now I have another volume ready."

"And you have lately commenced writing Christmas card verses?"

"Only this season, and but very few as yet. I chanced to see an advertisement by Messrs. Marcus Ward & Co. offering a prize for the best Christmas card poem. I did not care to compete, but wrote to the firm suggesting that I might be able to do some verses for them. Mr. Mackay replied that he had seen some of my work, and should be willing to consider contributions from me.

So I sent a few, which were accepted for next Christmas."

"You are now, I believe, very busy with literary work?"

"Yes, my hands are pretty full just now. I am editing a volume, 'The Children's Hour,' for Christmas, and I am engaged to write for a number of the leading magazines. I'm sorry I cannot say more about Christmas verses, but here is a funny tale about my 'Sonnets and Songs,' which may amuse your readers. Have you noticed the dedication? It is like this—

TO
*   *   *

Well, one day I called on an acquaintance, and found her sending off several copies of my book to her friends. On the dedication page of each she was writing the name of the recipient, and she said to me, 'It was *so* clever of you to arrange this page like they do on the Christmas cards, so that one can insert the name of the person one sends it to!' There, that has something to do with Christmas cards after all."

THE GREAT UNACCEPTED.

It was found quite impracticable to interview these, owing both to their multitude and their modesty. Their sentiments are said to be couched in language both "painful and free," and for that reason they will not be reproduced here. But we are enabled to give publicity to a few representative specimens of the contributions "which the editor much regrets that he is unable to use":—

A Meaningless Verse.
Oh! Christmas is coming, is coming, is coming!
  Pile up the faggots and let us be jolly;
The chestnuts are popping, the kettle is humming,
  The robins are whistling outside in the holly.
                         A. JINGLE.

A Gushing Verse.
My darling! I send you this sweet little card
  To tell you how fondly and dearly I love you,
When you pass from my vision all living seems hard;
  Oh! may angels keep watching and hov'ring above you!
                         V. FARGONE.

A High-Falutin Verse.
The gods on grey Olympus hailed the dawn
  When Phœbus with Aurora woke the day;
But brighter than them all this Christmas morn
  Art thou to whom I send this rhythmic lay.
                         CLASSICUS, M.A.

A "Good Old Times" Verse.
All hail to the glorious beef and plum pudding,
  The turkeys and geese and the snapdragon too;
Here's to the punch and the ice that it stood in!
  Bring in the holly and mistletoe true.
                         TITUS A. BRICK.

It goes without saying that all these are utterly unsuitable for the purposes of a Christmas card. They have this to commend them, however, that they scan fairly well and that the rhymes are pretty correct, save in the last example. But a worse torture awaits the Christmas card editor in the shape of yards upon yards of doggerel from persons who have yet to learn the first principles of verse-making. A glorious independence of all rules, an originality of rhymes and a limitless number of feet to each verse are a few of the leading characteristics of a large proportion of the "poetical" matter under which the postman staggers daily. We give some choice samples :—

I send this card to greet you on the blessed
   morning of Christmas,
  It only comes but once a year,
And when it comes I pray it may bring to you and
   your business
  A very happy time and plenty of good cheer.
                              W. PROSER.

Brightly the angels sang on Christmas morning
  When it came a good many years ago ;
May you have a season free from grief and moaning,
  And plenty of good cheer and feasting and kind
    friends too.   J. MEANWELL.

The method of manufacture appears to be a very simple one. You take a sufficient quantity of prose and then cut it carefully into lengths, not necessarily equal. It only remains to add that the above examples are quoted by special permission of their respective authors, and that all rights are strictly reserved.

AUTOGRAPH VERSE BY MISS BATEMAN.

IN THE OLDEN TIME.

Over the fields, past the half-buried hedge,
   Merrily glide the quaint couple—
Flaxen-haired Joan in her carved oaken sledge,
   And Ronald with limbs strong and supple.

In the cold wind and the snow and the rime,
   Finding for pleasure more reason—
Ah, youth was the same in the olden time,
   And snatched a new joy from each season.

                        S. E. G.

The Girl's Own Paper, 1885

USEFUL HINTS.

A WELSH PUDDING.—Well butter a pie dish, place at the bottom some slices of bread and butter, then a layer of black currant, raspberry, or any other jam which may be liked, then some more bread and butter, and repeat until the dish be filled. Bake in a moderate oven, and when done turn out on a dish, sift some powdered sugar over, and pour round the dish, not over, some sweet sauce, made of milk, flour, and sugar. This pudding may be also made with fresh fruit, instead of preserved, in which case some sugar must be sprinkled over it with every layer.

BAKING POWDER.—Tartaric acid, 6 oz., carbonate soda, 8 oz.; ground rice, 2 oz. Break up all lumps and well mix, put in a bottle, keep well corked, and in a dry place.

THREE MINUTES' PUDDING.—Bake in a very sharp oven three minutes only. 2 oz. flour, 1½ oz. sugar, 2 eggs, 2 small teaspoonfuls baking powder.

LEMONADE.—3 lb. loaf sugar, 2 oz. tartaric acid, 20 drops essence of lemon, 8 pints of water (boiling), dessertspoonful of yeast; bottle day after making.

LEMON SYRUP.—3 lb. loaf sugar, 2 oz. tartaric acid, 20 drops essence of lemon, 4 pints boiling water.

BOILED APPLE CUSTARD.—6 apples, 1 teacupful of flour, 5 drops essence of lemon, 2 eggs, small piece of butter, half-pint milk, quarter pound sugar:—Stew the apples, and when heated beat to a pulp, having added the essence of lemon and some sugar. Let it cool. Then mix the milk, eggs, butter, and flour, and beat all well. Then add the apples. Put all into a pudding mould, and let it boil one and a half hour. Serve cold with milk.

CRANBERRY TART.—The fruit must be washed through a colander several times, then put into a china-lined saucepan to stew gently for one and a-half hour. They must be perfectly cold before putting the crust on. To a pint of cranberries add a half pint of water and a pound of moist sugar. To make a nice crust you must use ¼ lb. of salt butter, ¼ lb. of lard, ½ lb. of flour. Take first the flour, and mix it with some filtered water sufficient to moisten it, then spread in with a knife the butter and the lard. Bake for an hour and a-half.

CHEAP ORANGE MARMALADE.—Six good-sized Seville oranges, quarter them and cut them into fine slices. Put the pieces into three quarts of water for 24 hours. Boil them for two hours slowly, but steadily, then add 5 lb. of sugar, boil them again as before for three-quarters of an hour or more if the syrup looks too thin. Add the juice of one lemon when taking off the fire. The pips to stand 24 hours.

DEVONSHIRE JUNKET.—To one quart of new milk, made just lukewarm, add a few drops of essence of lemon and four teaspoonfuls of essence of rennet. Mix well, and put into a glass dish; stand in a cool place until set, and serve with sifted sugar and clotted cream. The essence of rennet can be obtained of any chemist.

CARROT PUDDING. — Take ½ pound of raisins, ½ pound of currants, and the same of suet. 1 oz. of lemon peel, 2 tablespoonfuls of flour. Boil and pulp two large carrots, and add to the pudding, which requires two and a half hours of good cooking.

HEALTHY RECREATIONS.
NO. 1.—SKATING.
By the Author of "Skating and Scuttling."

I HAVE taught many girls of various ages how to skate, and it would be unjust to them not to say that they were far better pupils than boys of the same ages. They seem to have a better idea of balance, and they mostly do as they are told, which is more than can be said for boys in general. And, in consequence, when they are taught to be skaters they rarely degenerate into scuttlers, though they too frequently abandon the ice altogether.

Some years ago lady-skaters were at a disadvantage. Numbers of girls learned to skate very creditably, and if they had pursued their ice-studies steadily, they would have developed into good figure skaters. Now, even with male performers, figure skating is the very poetry of motion, and no more graceful sight could be imagined than the figures when performed by a "set" of eight accomplished lady skaters.

Yet, scarcely any of these girls ever learned even to execute the alpha of figure-skating, i.e., the figure 3, and I never yet saw a female skater who could take her part in a "set."

The reason for this decadence is to be found in Fashion. Young girls dressed in a way which allowed fair freedom to their limbs, and so they got on very well with their skates. But when they grew up, the tyrant Fashion seized upon them and put them into crinoline, within which metal or whalebone prison no human being could skate.

Now, however, female dress has assumed a much more sensible form, and costumes have been made expressly for skating as they have been made for bathing; and, as no true skater kicks the legs about, but always keeps the feet close to each other, the close-fitting and short skirt of the skating dress does not in the least interfere with the necessary freedom of the limbs.

And, if the sensible fashion of feminine skating dress will only continue for a few seasons, we may hope to see the poetry of motion in its most perfect and attractive form, and that the coveted "Silver Skate" may be worn at a lady's necklace as well as at a gentleman's button-hole.

As I hope that every girl who reads this magazine will either wish to learn the art of skating, or to improve her style even if she be a tolerable skater, I will give a few hints such as I always gave to my pupils, and begin with stating what to avoid.

Of course, a beginner will have her skates chosen for her by some one who knows how to skate, and she should never hire skates from the men who infest the ice.

Their skates are always of the worst possible kind, and made in the cheapest possible way. The edges are never sharp, so that there can be no hold of the ice, and the steel generally terminates before the screw instead of passing well behind it.

Then, their skates almost invariably have upturned points, which are not only useless but dangerous, and they have the heel cut off square instead of being rounded. In a good skate the steel barely projects beyond the wood in front, and is equally rounded at either end. The skate dealers will tell you that that these sharp heels are useful in stopping suddenly.

Do not believe them.

Certainly, by raising the toes and digging the sharp heels into the ice the skater *can* stop herself within a yard or two, and at the same time cut a couple of long, deep grooves in the ice; but she can stop herself in half the distance by simply spinning round, as every skater knows how, and without damaging the surface of the ice.

I must not be understood to recommend expensive skates for a young girl, especially if she be a beginner. Girls grow, and so do their feet, and it is very seldom that a pair of skates will last a growing girl more than a couple of seasons. Besides, a beginner would spoil a good pair of skates in a few days.

As to length, the skate should be just the length of the boot. It may be a trifle longer, but in that case, it must be set rather backward on the boot, so that it projects *behind* the heel, and not in front of the toe. Boots, of course, should be worn by the skater, and they should be laced and not buttoned or fitted with side springs. They should fit exactly but easily to the feet, so that their tightness can be regulated by the laces. Skating in loose boots is almost impossible, and a tight boot will cause indescribable agonies.

Avoid the straps which cross the instep. One broad strap, with double ends at the toe, and one heel strap, are all that are needed. Indeed, if the boots are perfectly fitting, the heel strap is scarcely needed. I use it myself, but merely employ it as a safeguard in case the screw should break, and I always have it drawn so loosely that a finger can be passed between the strap and the boot.

It will be an advantage to buy the skates for some months before the frost comes on, so as to soften the straps thoroughly before they are wanted. New straps are great nuisances, as they are stiff and apt to stretch, while a strap which has been repeatedly soaked in warm grease or oil, and then stretched, and pulled, and rubbed, will remains as soft and pliable as silk, will accommodate itself closely to the foot, and moreover, will be impervious to wet and consequent rotting.

Grease should also be rubbed daily into the junction of the steel with the wood, as in that case there will be no danger of weakening the steel by rust.

Do not employ any vegetable oil for the straps. Colza oil will do well enough for the skates, but neat's-foot oil is best for the straps. In default of neat's-foot oil, clarified lard, perfectly freed from salt, will answer very well if the lard be heated. Straps thus treated are almost indestructible. I have before me a set of straps more than twenty years old, which have been used in sixteen skating seasons. They are now as serviceable as ever, and will probably be used again this season.

If possible, a special pair of boots should be kept for skating, at all events during the season. Then the skates can be attached to them, the straps placed lightly over them, and thus they can be carried in the hand-bag, which every skater ought to possess. They can be slipped on in a moment, the straps and boot-laces tightened, and thus the tedious and troublesome operation of putting on the skates can be avoided.

The Girl's Own Paper, 1880, 1882 (Hints)

Boots last much longer in this way, because they are not pulled to pieces by the repeated insertion and removal of the screws. In a soft substance like leather, the hole soon becomes "screw-sick," and the screw has no hold. Then, either the hole must be plugged, or a new hole made, which will alter the bearings of the skate.

Moreover, when the skater comes off the ice, she has only to loosen the laces and straps and slip her feet out of the skate-boots. The comfort of changing the boots after skating is quite indescribable.

Should no such spare boots be available, the skates should always be fitted to them before they are on the feet. The screw-hole can then be placed exactly in the central line of the foot, which is a matter of no small importance. This hole should be filled in with tallow before starting, and when the skater arrives at the ice all that will be needed will be to clear out the grease.

In the bag should be carried a knife, a small gimlet, a brad-awl for making fresh holes in straps, a little bottle of oil, a large piece of old rag, and a pair of old leather gloves. These are to be worn while putting on the skates, and while drying, wiping, and oiling them after leaving the ice. Also, I very strongly recommend a piece of waterproofing, which can be spread as a seat. It often happens that the skater has to sit down, either to rest or to alter the skates, and if there should have been a slight thaw, or if the sunbeams should have melted the snow or hoar frost, sitting down is scarcely practicable.

Carry *nothing* in the pockets except a handkerchief.

We will now suppose that a young girl has been supplied with skates, &c., and has arrived at the ice. Although it is obviously impossible to teach the art of skating by means of the pen, it is possible to give a few useful hints which will save much time and trouble.

In the first place, use every means to be accompanied from the first by a really good skater, so that you may not acquire bad habits, which can scarcely ever be shaken off. Do not lean on the back of a chair, as is so often advised. You will get into a nasty, stooping, round-shouldered style, and will hardly ever be able to acquire the straight, but flexible form which distinguishes a good skater.

Still less depend on a stick. I regret to say that the skate dealers often sell sticks with spiked ends for the use of beginners. Learning to skate by means of a stick is as wrong as learning to swim with the aid of corks.

No good skater ever carries a stick on any pretence whatever. However skilled she may be a strap may break, or she may come against an unseen pebble or pinch of sand frozen into the ice, and in either case down she goes. Should she have a stick in her hand, she will instinctively grasp it as she falls, and will probably inflict a severe blow upon any one who happens to be near.

Do not allow yourself to be towed along by two skaters for the purpose of getting used to the ice. In the first place, you *must* stoop, and will stoop more and more as the pace increases. Moreover you will be sliding and not skating, and will be confirmed in the idea that ice is slippery. So it is to a slider, but not to a skater, who has a firm hold of the ice by the sharp edge of her skate.

Just at first, you may cling to the arm of your instructor, but, after a minute or two, depend entirely on yourself. You will feel the most helpless of beings; you will stoop forward; your feet will diverge, in spite of all endeavours to keep them together, and down you will come. You will not hurt yourself, as there is nothing hard in the pockets.

Being down, you will think that you will have to stay there, as getting up again seems impossible. There is, however, no difficulty about it. Kneel upright. Now put the right foot on the ice, lean forwards, and you will be on your feet. Most probably you will tumble down again almost before you are up. Never mind it, but get up again, and after two or three such harmless falls, you will find that your skates have edges, and that by means of these edges you can at all events prevent yourself from slipping sideways.

This is a most important point gained, and you will now be able to try locomotion.

Place the feet as in the "third position" in dancing, nearly at right angles to each other, | — thus, the perpendicular line representing the left foot, and the horizontal line the right.

Now, lean a little to the right, fix the inside edge of the left skate well into the ice, and so push yourself towards the right, bringing up the left foot as soon as you find yourself moving. When you can go towards the right with some certainty, reverse the position of the feet, and push yourself towards the left by pressing against the inner edge of the right skate.

TWO OF MY PUPILS.

The next step is to make these strokes alternately, and as regularly as possible, and if you persevere, in half-an-hour or so, you ought to get along with some little speed, and to direct your course as you like.

I strongly advise the beginner to continue the first day's practice as long as possible, for next day she will find herself so absurdly stiff that she will hardly be able to put one foot before another. Still, she ought to make her way to the ice, notwithstanding the stiffness, and will find that the best cure is the homœopathic principle.

It is remarkable, by the way, that when any one has become a really good skater he or she will never find themselves stiff, even though they may not have seen the ice for years. Neither do they forget the art.

I remember, many years ago, when the floods round Oxford were frozen, that an old gentleman who had in his time been the crack skater of Oxford, but who had abandoned the ice for some thirty years, could not resist the temptation of many miles of clear, black ice, hard as marble and as smooth as a mirror. So he put on his skates, and after half an hour or so was delighting the spectators with an exhibition of the old school of skating, in which the arms were raised and lowered alternately with the skates, something like the left arm of a fencer when standing on guard or thrusting.

Of course, he could not continue the exercise very long, but he was not in the least stiff, and came on the ice every day as long as the frost lasted.

It is the same with riding and swimming, neither accomplishment ever being forgotten after it has once been attained.

The foregoing instructions are quite sufficient to enable a girl to travel over ice and guide herself in her course. But, as I hope that none of my readers will be content with the mere alphabet of skating, but will desire to make progress in the art, I will give them a few hints.

The first point is to use the outer instead of the inner edge, and until this is done no one can even begin to learn the rudiments of true skating, which depends wholly on the outer edge.

Here I may observe there are just two kinds of legitimate skating, *i.e.*, "travelling on skates," and "figure-skating," both of which depend wholly on the outside edge.

Skate-travelling is seldom used in this country, owing to the brevity of the frosts, and the lack of long, narrow pieces of ice on which to travel. In Holland, however, where canals form almost the chief feature of the country, and the frosts last for a long time, skating forms the chief mode of locomotion in the winter, and the people learn to skate, not as a pastime, but as a mode of travelling. Children skate to their schools, market-women skate to the markets, bearing their laden baskets on their heads, and a young couple will skate twenty or thirty miles to be married, and then skate back again.

Naturally, a peculiar kind of stroke has come into use, and is popularly called the "Dutch roll." It is executed wholly on the outer edge, the strokes being long and sweeping, and each describing a slight curve some twenty yards in length. It is very deceptive in appearance. It appears to be slow, whereas it is only deliberate, and the swiftest English skater, if put on a Dutch canal, and matched against a Dutch market-woman, with a heavy basket on her head, will be hopelessly beaten in a long race.

At first he runs away from her, and leaves her far behind. But she keeps steadily on her course, with her long, steady, unchanging roll. After the first few miles, the distance between them gradually diminishes, and, strive how he may, the man will find his antagonist gradually creeping up to him, and at last forging ahead.

He may put on as many spurts as he likes, but they will be of no use. She will not alter her pace in the least, but swings herself along with the same unvarying roll, reaching the goal far ahead, and as fresh as when she began.

The skates are made for this mode of travelling, and are quite unfit for figure-skating. They are long in the steel, which projects far in front, and, in women's skates, curls over the toe. Mostly, they are fluted, and the edges are nearly straight instead of curved as in our English skates. Then, in the Dutch travelling roll, the knee is allowed to be bent, which is a heresy in a figure-skater. No matter how accurately a skater may be able to perform the most intricate figures, he will never obtain admission to the Skating Club if he allows the knee of the acting leg to be in the slightest degree bent.

Now for a little advice as to the outer edge. Some teachers advise that at each stroke the feet should be crossed, so that the outside edge *must* be brought into use. Certainly, it has this effect, but it has two serious defects. In the first place, it is impossible to keep a straight knee if you have to cross the right foot over the left or *vice versa*, and in the next place, you get into the habit of steering your course by the swing of the off leg, and not by the balance of the body as ought to be done.

The following plan will be found to answer admirably, and will give a good carriage to the body. Put on the ice some conspicuous object, and skate round and round it, keeping the right side towards it, the face always turned towards it, and the arms slightly hanging towards the right side.

In order to do this, the inside edge of the left skate and the outside edge of the right skate will be pressed against the ice.

When you feel yourself at home in this circle, take the left foot off the ice, and you will be on the outside edge. At first you will have to put down the left foot almost immediately, but in a little time you will be able to proceed for a yard or two on the right foot alone. Now go round in the opposite direction, keeping your left side inwards, and going on the outside edge of the left foot.

Now leave the circle and try to skate forwards, but instead of going on the inside edge of the skates as you did before, go on the outside edges. Do not be afraid of leaning well towards the outside edge. You will not fall, although at first you will feel as if you must topple over on your side.

Persevere in these movements, making your strokes longer and longer, and always keeping the knee of the active leg quite straight. When you can make these strokes long, even, and deliberate, which you ought to do after two or three days' practice, you will be fairly set upon your outside edge, and will be ready to begin a course of instruction in Figure Skating.

USEFUL HINTS.

WELCOME GUEST PUDDING.—Eight ounces of bread-crumbs, one half-pint of milk, four ounces of beef suet, three ounces of citron, four ounces of sugar, rind of one lemon, three ounces of almonds, four eggs, one grain of salt. Place four ounces of the bread-crumbs in a bowl, and, bringing the milk to a boil, pour it over them. Cover the bowl with a plate, and allow the bread-crumbs to soak in the milk for ten minutes. While the bread-crumbs are soaking, pour over the almonds some boiling water to blanch them, and remove their skins. Remove the skin from the suet and chop it very finely, and chop the almonds. Stir into the bowl with the soaked bread-crumbs the four remaining ounces of crumbs, add to this the chopped suet and almonds, also the grated rind of lemon, together with the sugar and citron, cut into very small pieces. Separate the yolks from the whites of the eggs very carefully, drop the yolks one by one into the bowl, and stir all well together. Whip the whites of the eggs to a stiff froth, adding the grain of salt. Mix this lightly with the other ingredients in the bowl, and, taking a quart mould, dry it thoroughly, greasing the interior with butter, pouring into it the mixture, and place securely over the top a greased sheet of kitchen paper. Place the mould, when filled, in a deep saucepan, containing enough water to reach halfway up the side, and let the pudding boil therein two hours. When done, the mould should be removed from the boiling water, allow two minutes for it to cool, and then turn the pudding out on the hot platter. This should be served with jam, or lemon sauce.

DUTCH GIRLS SKATING TO SCHOOL.

The Girl's Own Paper, 1880

GREETINGS.

By SYDNEY GREY.

CAN there be any greetings, I wonder,
  To feeling and friendship more dear,
Than the two that so seldom we sunder—
  "Merry Christmas and Happy New Year"?
When affection's whole force is paraded,
  A genial warfare to wage,
And each holly-crowned home is invaded,
  Like that on the frontispiece page.
Our artist has surely with reason
  Permitted his fancy to rove,
For good wishes just now are in season,
  And letter-bags bursting with love.

Here's a bit of young madcap's sweet folly,
  Which grandpapa's laughter will stir;
Here's a card to dear Ted from Aunt Molly,
  And somebody's missive to her.
Cousin Tom has a certain small token,
  The sender it fails to avow,
But I doubt not his thanks will be spoken
  Very close to the mistletoe bough.
Well—away on your mission, fair greetings,
  High embassy yours to fulfil;
Ever hailed amid joyous heart-beatings,
  The pledges of peace and good-will.

TOBOGGANING.

By RICHARD PATTERSON, J.P.

To most people in the United Kingdom, the above word is connected with a wooden structure which our ingenious American cousins introduced a few years since at all our important exhibitions, and which gave a vast amount of enjoyment to hundreds of thousands of our people. These "toboggan slides" have given way to the more exciting switchback railways, now so popular all over the country. Like rink-skating, these amusements are not likely to become permanent institutions with us, on account of the expense attendant on them; but at the same time they have given the public a taste for rapid travelling by gravitation.

At this season it may not be out of place to give some information about tobogganing on snow, which, if once commenced in any neighbourhood, is sure to become a most popular amusement with young and old, rich and poor. The writer having the honour to be the captain of the "Holywood Tobogganing Club," which is now in its third year of existence, and has upwards of three hundred members enrolled, he proposes to give a short account of the object and working of the club, which, as far as he knows, is the only one of the kind in Ireland, and possibly in the United Kingdom.

Holywood is a small town in the county Down, four miles from Belfast; it is situated on the southern shores of the Lough, at the base of a beautiful range of highly-cultivated and well-wooded hills. Here for some years tobagganing had been indulged in to a limited extent, but as there was no regular ground, nor any organisation, the snow would come and go before the people could avail themselves of it. It was therefore decided to establish a club, and, as the expenses connected with it were very trifling, the subscription was fixed at one shilling per annum, or family tickets five

The Girl's Own Paper, 1890

shillings. A portion of a large field was secured and fenced, so that none but members of the club and their friends from a distance should be admitted. The ground was cleared of all stones, and some rough places properly levelled; a number of "duck" lamps, such as are used about ship yards, were provided to mark out the track at night, besides a few of "Wells'" lamps for the top and bottom of the field. The club ground is about 450 yards long by about 100 yards wide, thus allowing ample room for several tracks being used simultaneously, which is quite necessary, as there will sometimes be upwards of one hundred sledges on the ground at the same time. The field is well adapted for the purpose, the upper part of the track for about 350 yards having a good steep gradient, so that a very high speed can be obtained before reaching the remaining 100 yards, which is nearly level. When the track is in good order it requires all the distance of the level ground to put on the break and stop the machines before reaching the bottom fence. Some idea of the speed to be attained can be had from the fact that the entire distance of 450 yards can be traversed in from forty to fifty seconds, including a slow start and slow finish, while this can be reduced to thirty seconds if there has been a slight thaw during the day and frost again in the evening. The maximum speed at the steepest part must be close on forty miles an hour; even with this high speed on there is little risk of accident with ordinary care and good steering.

Some description of the toboggans used by the club may be of service to those who desire to start this amusement in other parts of the country. All sorts and descriptions of machines have been tried, from old tea trays, or flat-bottomed baths, up to the light and graceful Canadian pattern. The last named is found unsuitable for this country, where the snow is seldom more than four or five inches deep, and it soon goes to pieces running over rough ground, although admirably adapted for deep snow. From experience it is found that the best pattern to meet local requirements is the ordinary hard sledge on runners. These runners may be from four to six feet long, five to six inches deep, made out of one and a quarter inch thick timber tapering down to one inch, and shod with strong hoop iron, fastened on with screws in countersunk holes; they must be well rounded off at both ends, so that they will easily pass over any obstacle with which they may come in contact; they should be about sixteen inches apart, and must be perfectly parallel, otherwise the machine will not run true. The deck or seat is formed of flat bars of three-quarter inch thick wood, twenty-one inches long by about four or six inches broad, with spaces of about three-quarters of an inch between; the bars are securely fastened down on the top of the runners by four strong screws in each, and the seat being wider than the runners gives a good edge by which to hold on. Some of the sledges are fitted with low bulwarks to prevent ladies' dresses getting over the edges and under the runners, which is severe on garments.

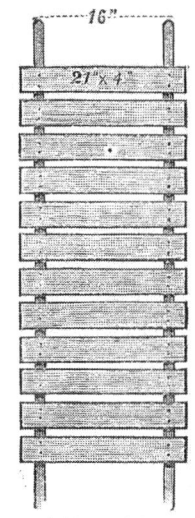

DECK PLAN.

Sledges of the above dimensions will carry from one to four persons, and will be found the most convenient sizes, as anything larger is very difficult to haul up a steep hill. Lever breaks are sometimes attached to each side for

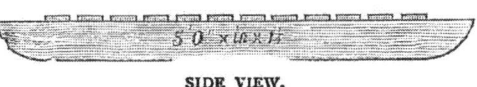

SIDE VIEW.

the purpose of either steering or stopping, but most tobogganers prefer using their heels lightly, or carrying two short pieces of stick in their hands.

The club has a number of field stewards,

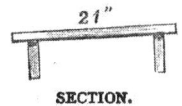

SECTION.

who make all arrangements on the ground for the comfort and safety of the members; all the regulations they make from time to time must be strictly conformed to. The one essential point to be observed is, that the moment the sledges reach the bottom of the track they should at once be pulled over to the "up tracks," which are situated at the extreme right and left of the ground, leaving all the down tracks in the centre. If this rule be strictly enforced accidents will be reduced to a minimum; as a matter of fact, very few serious accidents have happened, and if a collision or upset does occur, it is invariably the result of carelessness or want of steering knowledge.

A more animated or gayer scene it is impossible to imagine than that seen on a fine, calm winter's day, with the sun shining brightly on the pure snow, some hundreds of ladies on the ground in their cozy furs or gay-coloured wraps, while the men are suitably attired in their more sombre skating garments; the well-laden sledges, filled with merry young people or more sedate middle-aged or even elderly persons, tearing down the tracks at the rate of thirty or forty miles an hour, while the air resounds with hearty shouts and shrill whistling as a signal to others to keep the course clear. Then there is the uproarious fun and laughter when some ridiculous upset happens, and no one is hurt, though all may have had a good roll in the snow.

At each side of the ground there is a steady stream of toilers up the hill, dragging their sledges after them, all panting, and their faces aglow with the healthy exercise. To attempt to describe the scene at night, with the ground lighted by numerous lamps or, better still, by a full moon, with all her mellowing influences, would be quite beyond the writer's powers; suffice it to say that the amusement is of such an extremely social character that friendships are formed which are likely to prove much more enduring than the fickle snow.

Before concluding this very imperfect description of the Holywood Tobogganing Club, it may interest some lady readers to know that the most suitable materials for costumes for such severe work are the heavy (coloured) blankets, such as are used in Canada for all winter sports by both ladies and gentlemen. If these blankets cannot be easily procured, the common bright-coloured stable rugs will be found to make admirable skirts and jackets, as they will stand hard work, and do not show about like ordinary dress materials. As to headgear, ladies' fashionable hats are sure to come to grief; close-fitting caps or small hats will be found most suitable. And if ladies will disregard appearances and wear snow-boots over their ordinary boots or shoes, they will find that these add greatly to their comfort, keeping their feet always dry and warm, and enabling them to walk up hills with much greater ease.

In contributing this short article, the writer's sole object is to endeavour to popularise one of the best amusements he knows for both sexes. It can be indulged in at very little cost in a hilly country, and requires only two essentials — organisation and snow.

ON THE ICE.

WINTER.

Leisure Hour, 1860

OUR CHRISTMAS DECORATIONS.

THE style of decoration to be followed depends on a good many different circumstances. The size and nature of the room or hall, the locality, whether town or country, and the time which can be expended on the work, have all to be taken into account. The subject is so familiar to everyone, that there is no need for a detailed description of any style of decoration, and it is only necessary to give a few suggestions, to be adapted according to circumstances.

When holly and mistletoe are scarce, very pretty and effective varieties are made by introducing bulrushes, teazle heads, pampas grass, or any of the tall brown grasses to be found growing near water in the country. These should be gathered in the autumn, and well dried. If the bulrush heads are too ripe, and shed their seeds, they should be dipped in gum water. Mountain ash berries, and hips and haws should be gathered in the autumn too, and preserved for Christmas use by soaking in strong brine. Lichens are very useful as a background for red lettering, or to form the letters themselves on a coloured background edged with leaves. The grey lichen can frequently be torn off in large pieces from the trunks of trees, and this variety is the most useful for lettering; but twigs and branches covered with moss and lichen should be preserved just

The Girl's Own Paper, 1884

as they grow, as very quaint and effective decorations can be made by grouping these in masses, with trails of ivy hanging from them.

If artificial frost is wished for, crushed glass, sold under the name of "frost," answers the best, or it can be made at home by crushing white glass (old white bottles, or pieces of broken window panes) with a garden roller. It is more effective than Epsom salts, the coarse kind of which, however, such as is sold at oil shops, is often used when glass cannot be procured. In either case it is sprinkled over the surface of the leaves, or cotton-wool snow, which have previously been coated with strong colourless gum.

In small rooms it is not advisable to use artificial frost or snow of any kind, as it will not bear close scrutiny, and distance is necessary to give it a proper effect. A judicious use of grey lichen amongst glossy green leaves gives a very wintry appearance, and will not only bear close inspection, but does not look tawdry in the glaring light of day, which cannot be said for anything artificial.

Japanese fans, as well as those of ordinary shape made of paper, are very useful for brightening up sombre rooms. They are very cheap, and are made in all varieties of brilliant colours. They look particularly well over pictures, not only as a temporary, but a permanent decoration, as they break the monotonous straight lines of a number of picture frames, and add a touch of colour to the walls, where it is often very much wanted.

If it is absolutely necessary to employ imitation berries and flowers, the easiest plan is to buy bunches of artificial red berries, which are very inexpensive, and save a good deal of trouble in making them at home; but if there are plenty of helpers, they can easily be made either by dyeing peas or pellets of putty with Judson's dye, or by dissolving red sealing wax in spirits of wine, and dipping the peas into it so as to coat them with wax. Artificial Christmas flowers are not so easily purchased, as they are either expensive or very tawdry-looking; Christmas roses are not at all difficult to make at home. Have ready some white satin, or sateen, dark green paper, fine wire, greenish grey paint, and green crewels. Get a real flower to copy from, if possible, or, if not, good patterns of Christmas roses can often be obtained from old Christmas cards. Cut out the petals in satin; they are something of a pear shape, but flattened at the top, and wider in proportion at the upper part; leave half an inch of stalk at the base. A short length of fine wire is gummed up the back of each petal, to stiffen it. The stamens and pistil are of wire covered with crewels, and with a knot at the top; and these, with the stalks of the petals, are united by means of a fine wire twisted round them. This united stalk is then passed through a calyx, or little cup, of the green paper, and the flower is complete, except for the touches of greyish green shading on the petals, which are added with a paint brush. These look very delicate and pretty arranged amongst moss and dried ferns.

Be careful to avoid an air of heaviness in small rooms. It is better to use too little material than to let it appear overdone. Trails of ivy look light and graceful hanging at the sides of a picture or mirror, springing from a light bunch at the top. If the sprays are refractory, they should be wired. Laurel has a disagreeable smell, and should be used sparingly in small rooms.

A light trellis work of leaves looks very well to cover a blank space, or hide an ugly door. It is made by sewing single leaves on tape, or wiring them on thin laths of wood, with a cluster of leaves or berries where the bands cross each other.

In decorating schoolrooms, or any large hall with bare walls, one has to work on a different principle. Here quantity is of more importance than quality, as the general effect only is noticed while details are overlooked.

Flags are very useful. They are not used to the extent they well might be in such cases. The proper material for them is bunting, which hangs well and is durable, but it is expensive, and Turkey twill answers the purpose very well. The red and dark blue should be used. The small flags may be plain, but the larger ones should be elaborated by devices of contrasting colour, red or white upon blue, and *vice versâ*. Stars of gold and silver paper can be gummed on, and some of the flags edged with the tinsel paper, cut into a fringe and folded to a good thickness. The larger devices in twill and calico are more durable if stitched into place. Shields, anchors, and other emblems can be cut out in millboard, and covered with red twill, and are useful as centre pieces for masses of green, or, as connecting links for festoons.

Wreaths and garlands are easier to make, and show up better if arranged in a flat form, instead of round like a rope. They should be fastened on to a strip of any bright red material, which shows on either side; this not only enhances the effect of the garland, but preserves the wall from being scratched or discoloured by the stalks.

For a large bare room, on which little time can be expended, an effective centre-piece for the end wall can be obtained by making a very large circle of thin wood or strong cardboard, covered with some bright colour, with a spreading bunch of green upon it, and a star of tinsel or straw in the middle, and four or six garlands springing from behind it, carried to the side-walls of the room, where each ends in a short hanging bunch of green—a sort of tassel.

Mission rooms and wards which have a wooden or painted dado can be brightened by making a heading to the dado of a long strip of red lining, about a quarter of a yard wide, and edged with a band of gold-paper pasted on, or else overlapping leaves stitched on. At intervals, say a yard apart, stitch or paste on one of the Japanese paper pictures, sold at a halfpenny each. In addition to the pictures, a motto, the letters cut out in white, may be applied, a word, or two if short, between each picture. If texts of Scripture are preferred, the pictures should be omitted or less curious ones substituted, as the two are hardly suitable together. An easy way of applying letters is by stencilling. Take a piece of stiff card, large enough to contain a single letter besides a margin of two inches or more all round. Draw and cut out the letter, taking care to have it in the middle of the card, and of a plain clear shape. In letters such as B, where there are fragments which would fall out if the whole letter were cut, little strips of cardboard must be left here and there to connect them. Place the frame of cardboard from which the letter has been cut in position on the red strip, and paint over with paint or whitewash. On removing the frame, the letter will, of course, remain clear and white, and the marks left by the connecting strips of card must be filled in afterwards. The cardboard shapes are easily made and can be used over and over again.

Mirrors, and even windows, are sometimes pressed into the service of decoration by having mottoes and devices painted on them in whitening. A branch of a tree or spray of flowers is usually painted coming down from the left-hand top corner of the glass, and partially encircling the motto which is near the bottom of the mirror, where it can be easily read. The whitening is easily wiped off, and rather improves the glass than otherwise, and if a tasteful design is selected, the effect is exceedingly pretty.

USEFUL HINTS.

FIG PUDDING.—One half-pound of figs, one half-pound of bread-crumbs, one half-pound of sugar, one half-pound of beef suet, three eggs. Remove the skin from the suet, chop it very finely, put it into a bowl, and, chopping the figs very finely, mix both together. Stir into this the bread-crumbs, beat in a separate bowl the eggs and sugar, mix this with the figs, suet, and bread-crumbs, and, greasing the interior of the mould, pour this into it, put on the cover, and plunging it into a large saucepan of boiling water, let it, with its contents, boil for two hours.

LEMON SAUCE.—One lemon, six pieces of cut loaf sugar, one teacupful of cold water. Pare the rind from the lemon, and cut this into strips the size of a straw. Put these strips of lemon-rind into a small saucepan, together with the lumps of sugar, and, covering these with the cold water, squeeze into the mixture the juice of the lemon. Put the saucepan over the fire, and stir the contents until boiling. When this takes place, cover the saucepan, and drawing it to one side of the fire, let all simmer slowly for twenty minutes. This sauce should be poured over the pudding with which it is served, in order that the straws of lemon-rind may garnish the top of the pudding.

LEMON CHEESE CAKES.—Take 3 lemons,—grating the rind and squeezing out the juice—6 eggs, well whisked, and 1 pound of sifted or lump sugar. Put all into a jar, stand and boil in a pan of water till thick, stirring occasionally, for about three-quarters of an hour. Then cover and keep in a cool place.

LEMON SPONGE.—One ounce of gelatine, one pint of water, two lemons, one half-pound of cut loaf sugar, whites of three eggs. Put the gelatine into a bowl, cover it with cold water, and let it soak for twenty minutes. At the end of this time add to it the rind of the lemons, squeeze over the lemon-juice, throw in the sugar, and pour all into a copper or porcelain-lined saucepan, place the saucepan over the fire, and stir its contents until boiling, after which it must be allowed to boil for two minutes. At the end of this time pour the mixture through a sieve into a bowl, and let it remain therein until cold, but not long enough to set. Beat the whites of eggs slightly, pour them into the mixture in the bowl, and stir all together, when all must be whisked until thick and white. Pour the sponge into a mould, stand it in a cool, dry place, and when "set," turn it out upon, and serve in, a crystal dessert dish.

CHUTNEY.—English chutney may be made thus:—Take half-pound of mustard seed, half-pound of salt, half-pound of raisins (stoned), half-pound of brown sugar; six ounces of garlic, six ounces of cayenne pepper, one quart of gooseberries, one quart of the best vinegar. Dry and bruise the mustard, make a syrup of the sugar with half a pint of the vinegar, dry the gooseberries and boil in half a quart of the vinegar, and well bruise the garlic in a mortar. When cold, gradually mix and thoroughly amalgamate the whole in a mortar, and then tie down well. The longer preserved the better.

The Girl's Own Paper, 1880

THE ILLUSTRATED LONDON ALMANACK.

DECEMBER.

THE YULE BLOCK.*
A CHRISTMAS CAROL.

*A cross-grain'd block of elm we'll take
And by his light hold merry wake!*—OLD BALLAD.

When holly leaves and ivy green,
With berries bright and dark between,
Around the cottage room are seen,
 The simple place adorning—
What joy before the cheerful blaze,
The almost conscious fire displays,
To sit in Christmas' merry days
 Ay! sit up till the morning!

And hear the early carillon
Of village bells—while old and young
Are mingled in that festal throng,
 Through life we aye remember!
To feel the heat of Summer's glow,
In frosty depth of Winter's snow
And think we're *Maying it,* although
 'Tis flowerless December!

To join the hearty laugh around,
When some coy damsel's feet are found
To thoughtless tread the fairy-ground
 The Mistletoe that's under;—
And see some longing lover steal
A kiss from cheeks that ill conceal
The secret joy they inward feel,
 'Neath frowns and blushing wonder!

What face with summer s sun embrown'd
Was ever half so joyous found
As those in ruddy gladness 'round
 The YULE-BLOCK's† cheerful gleaming!
Romance may seek wild solitudes,
By waterfalls in lonely woods—
But Mirth and Love, with happier moods,
 O'er Christmas hearth are beaming!
  W.

* *Yule* from the Saxon *yeol* or *yehul,* the Christmas time.
† In many parts of the country it was a practice to preserve a portion of the *yule block* to the next year in order to light the new Christmas log.

CHRISTMAS is now no longer marked by that fervid hospitality which characterised its observance among our forefathers. At present, Christmas meetings are chiefly confined to family parties. The wassail bowl, the yule clog, and the Lord of Misrule, with a long train of sports and customs, which formerly prevailed at this season, are nearly forgotten: even Christmas carols are nearly gone by; and the decking of churches and of a few houses of people in humble life, with holly and other evergreens, forms now almost the only indication that this great festival is at hand, if we except the distribution of warm clothing and creature comforts among the poor by those whom heaven has blessed with "the luxury of doing good." In olden times—

On Christmas Eve, the bells were rung;
On Christmas Eve, the mass was sung;
That only night in all the year,
Saw the stoled priest the chalice rear.
The damsel donned her kirtle sheen;
The hall was dressed with holly green;
Forth to the wood did merry men go,
To gather in the mistletoe.
Then opened wide the baron's hall,
To vassal, tenant, serf, and all.

The pursuit of the fox may be now enjoyed in perfection; the fox, the hounds, and the horses having, by exercise, obtained good wind and good running condition altogether. Hares which by previous over-feeding were rendered somewhat sluggish will now stand up well before their pursuers, and afford as good runs, if not better, than at any other period of the season.

ANGLING.

USE the same baits as last month. In favourable weather, pike, roach, and chub, may sometimes be taken; but all other fish have retired to their winter retreats, to screen themselves till the voice of Spring again re-animates, and calls them forth to their old haunts.

The Illustrated London Almanack, 1845

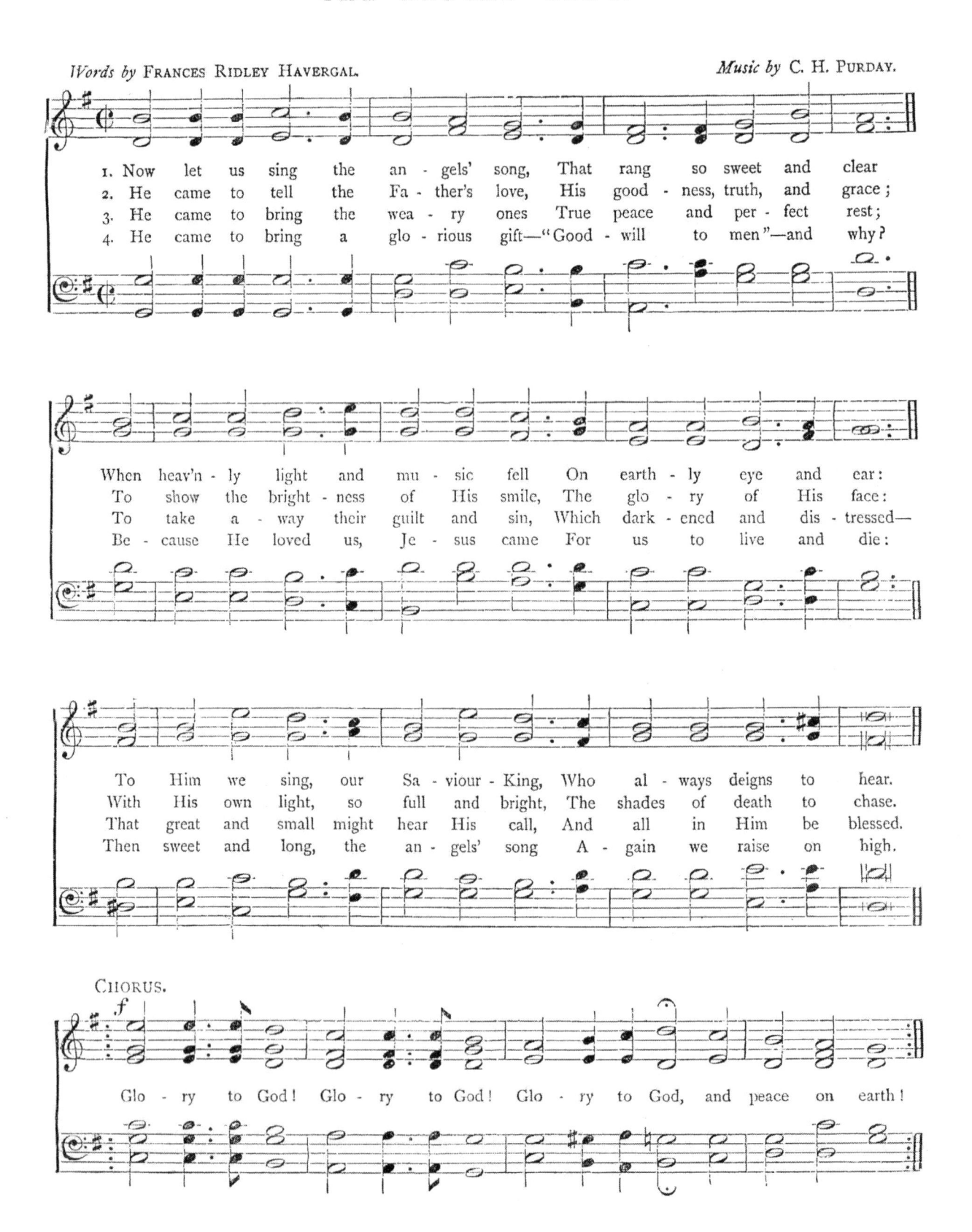

THE ANGELS' SONG.

Words by FRANCES RIDLEY HAVERGAL.   *Music by* C. H. PURDAY.

1. Now let us sing the angels' song, That rang so sweet and clear
When heav'nly light and music fell On earthly eye and ear:
To Him we sing, our Saviour-King, Who always deigns to hear.

2. He came to tell the Father's love, His goodness, truth, and grace;
To show the brightness of His smile, The glory of His face:
With His own light, so full and bright, The shades of death to chase.

3. He came to bring the weary ones True peace and perfect rest;
To take away their guilt and sin, Which darkened and distressed—
That great and small might hear His call, And all in Him be blessed.

4. He came to bring a glorious gift—"Good-will to men"—and why?
Because He loved us, Jesus came For us to live and die:
Then sweet and long, the angels' song Again we raise on high.

CHORUS.

f Glory to God! Glory to God! Glory to God, and peace on earth!

The Girl's Own Paper, 1883

MERRY CHRISTMAS.

MERRY CHRISTMAS! Through the tumult
    Of earth's Babel manifold,
Through its eager strife for honor,
    O'er its restless cry for gold;
Through the fever and the fretting,
    Through the sorrow and the sighs,
List! the chorus of the seraphs!
    List! the greeting of the skies.

MERRY CHRISTMAS! Angels brought it
    From the opened door of heaven;
Never gift so great to mortals,
    Largess so divine was given.
High above Judean mountains,
    Flamed the torch of Bethlehem's star!
Patient over Syrian deserts,
    Came the wise men from afar.

MERRY CHRISTMAS! Virgin Mother,
    With the Holy on thy knee,
Every woman, babe that beareth,
    Blesséd is, because of thee.
Still the mother's joy is riven
    By the mystic sword of pain;
Still in love's supreme evangel,
    Comes the Child in peace to reign.

EVERMORE around the cradle
    Hardest hearts grow soft and mild;
Every human babe is dearer
    Since He lived, the undefiled.
And the GLORIA IN EXCELSIS
    Overflows our doubt and scorn,
Brims the world's deep heart with sweetness,
    In the flush of Christmas morn.

CHILDREN'S SONG.

THE blossoms were over, oh! long ago,
    And now it is falling, the fleecy snow;
It sifts o'er the branches, it powders the eaves,
And over the meadows its mantle weaves.
Oh the merriest, merriest time o' the year,
Is Christmas! and good Santa Claus is near.

HE speeds along in his reindeer sledge,
    Piled with pretty things clear to the edge;
Dolls from Germany, dolls from France,
Dolls that can walk, and talk, and dance,
Castles from Switzerland, English drums;
Hurrah for Santa Claus! hither he comes.

HIS bells go jingling over the snow,
    As swiftly he rushes to and fro;
But only the fairies can see him pass,
Quick as a ripple, over the grass,
Quick as the lightning across the sky,
He has so much to do that he *has* to fly.

AND this of Santa Claus must be told,
    He is ever so young, though so awfully old;
And he knows every child in the big round earth,
Lofty its name, or lowly its birth;
And we think a child would be dreadfully bad,
If Santa Claus couldn't make him glad.

Demorest's Monthly Magazine, 1880

THE streets like gardens laugh,
    The windows are so gay;
Folks carry their own bundles home,
    When to-morrow's Christmas day.

AND oh! such gems of price,
    Such silver frost of lace;
And such a light of happiness
    On every passing face.

WHAT SHALL I GET FOR JOHN?

GIVE me your advice, my dear, it's *so* hard to choose for men;
    And my husband's had already paper-knife, and fountain pen,
Slippers, dressing-gown and cap, yes, my picture in a frame,
    And, just let me whisper, dear, himself has paid for all the same.

I'VE never felt the pleasure that I want, when giving things to John,
    Because he knows just every cent I spend, for all that I have on;
And then I hate to go to him for money, every little while—
    Indeed, it's bitterness to me. Now, Cora dear, you needn't smile.

BUT now I've *earned* my Christmas fund; that china set I painted Lou;
    Has paid me for it, and I've got a purse that is not tinged with rue;
And *now* the question in my brain is, what to buy for darling John?
    And surely you can help me, love, your own good thinking-cap put on!

THE CHRISTMAS TREE.

OVER *the sea, there's a wonderful tree,*
*   We heard of it first in Germany;*
But now old England gathers its fruit,
*   And here in our soil it has taken root.*

IN GERMAN HOMES.

HERE is the day when we cast away
    The weight of our cumbering cares;
And this is the sign of the Child Divine,
    Such marvelous beauty who wears.

THERE'S blowing of bugles, and beating of drums,
    There's dancing of dear little feet;
The children are jumping, and shouting, and trooping,
    The children so merry and sweet.

"A multitude of the heavenly host, praising God, and saying: Glory to God in the Highest, on Earth Peace, Good Will toward Men."

CHRISTMAS SHOPPING.

WHO cares for nipping wind,
    Who cares for sullen cold,
When everybody's copper
    Is sudden turned to gold?
When crusty men grow cordial,
    And fretful women mild,
And once more all the world is grouped
    Around a little child.

AND there's nobody old, for the ringlets of gold
    So mix with the tresses of gray,
That the grandsire forgets, as he plays with his pets,
    The years which have vanished away.

CHRISTMAS COMFORT.

LIKE to rest after toil, like to ease after labor,
    Like trilling of flute, and like piping of tabor;
Like hand-clasp of friend, and like greeting of neighbor,
    Is the day of the Child Divine.

MIDNIGHT ON CHRISTMAS EVE.

IN Albion, when the midnight falls
O'er roofs of thatch and storied halls,
The old cathedral chimes send forth
Their message, far to South and North.
    And hark! O hark!
      Through the thickening gloom
    How sudden the silence
      Seems breaking in bloom.
    There are lights on the highway,
      And fires on the height,
    And men go with singing
      To blazon the night.
    Ring, bells in the steeple,
      Gleam, lamps in the spire,
    And waken good people,
      And build the yule fire.

ADVICE AT CHRISTMAS.

OUT of the Black Forest, there stole a wolf one day,
    And he carried a pretty maiden far and far away;
O, list, my own fair daughter, the fierce wehr-wolf beware,
    And fortify thy innocence each day with fervent prayer.

SO to the child the mother
    Still talks on Christmas night;
And to the father listens
    The son, with blushes bright;
For simple souls and loving
    Abide anear the wold,
And worship God with honest faith,
    As in the days of old.

IN HOLLAND:

COME hither, Marie, let me string thy cap
With the shining coins I have in my lap;
For the boats went out in the summer time,
And the sound of the oars was smooth as rhyme.
Come hither, and let thy mother pray
Christ bless her child on Christmas Day.

HANGING UP THE STOCKINGS.

HANG the stockings in the corner!
    Santa Claus will come to-night;
Baby's little sock, and brother's,
    Though he's grown to manly height.
And the children in between—
Pretty Gertrude's, sweet sixteen,
Maud's, and Reginald's, and Bess's,
Little Tom's, who never guesses
    Anything about the day,
    But that it is jolly. Say,
What shall fill these dainty hose?
Bulging them from knee to toes:
Candies, sashes, toys, and furs,
    Books and puzzles, pictures bright,
Just what each had wanted; hers
    And his too, and all is right.
Somehow, in the wildest weather,
Santa Claus and love together,
    Fill the happy house with light.

HANG the stocking in the corner?
    Here, where want is gaunt and grim?
Where the wolf is ever stalking,
    In the shadows fierce and dim,
Where the fire is failing, dying,
    Where the cold must freeze the blood,
Where the feeble faith grows feebler,
    Wondering if God is good?
Shall they hang the stocking here?
What have they of mirth and cheer,
In this ending of the year?

YES, wan mother, hang the stocking,
    Bid the children go to sleep;
For the Christmas angels see you
    When you watch, and when you weep.
And already up the stairway
    Climbs a messenger, to bring
Christmas gifts to those who need them,
    Till the weary heart shall sing.
Ah! let none forget the power
Given by God at Christmas hour:
Love must not despise its dower.

MERRY CHRISTMAS.

MERRY CHRISTMAS! Merry Christmas!
    Deep and solemn, far and wide;
Let the old-time music thrill us,
    Let it still our clamorous pride.
Peace on earth! Let raging passion
    And its folly be subdued,
While we chant, in thankful fashion,
    Praise the Lord, for He is good.

The following genuine bills of fare may be interesting to plain housekeepers who are puzzled in regard to their menu for a Christmas dinner.

A Christmas dinner for a large party, all belonging to one family, included the following list of good things:

OYSTER SOUP.
OYSTERS RAW IN THE HALF SHELL.
CELERY.
ROAST BEEF—ROAST TURKEY.
GRATED HORSE-RADISH—CRANBERRY JELLY.
MASHED POTATOES—SPINACH.
OLIVES—PICKLES.
WILD DUCKS ROASTED—PRAIRIE HENS BROILED.
CURRANT JELLY—CELERY—CHEESE.
BREAD—BUTTER.
PLUM PUDDING—MINCE PIES.
ORANGES—APPLES—NUTS—ETC.

A PLAIN CHRISTMAS DINNER.

BOILED HAM
ROAST GOOSE WITH POTATO STUFFING.
APPLE SAUCE.
BOILED CABBAGE—MASHED POTATOES.
PUMPKIN PIE—CHEESE.
APPLES—NUTS—COFFEE.

A CHRISTMAS DINNER on a limited purse is the rule in large cities, and the following genuine bill of fare provided by a careful housewife was satisfactory to the hungry family of boys and girls who had long looked forward to their meeting on the day around the home table. The joint was a leg of fresh pork, stuffed. The stuffing was made of bread, seasoned with pepper, salt, onions, and sage. There were boiled white potatoes, boiled onions, boiled turnips, and apple sauce to make the first course. The pudding, which was voted delicious, was a rowley-powley, made of rolled paste covered with prunes, over which ground spices were shaken. It was served with butter and brown sugar. Ground cinnamon, ginger, and cloves, when boiled with either raisins or prunes, give a fine flavor to a pudding. Apples and hickory-nuts carefully cracked completed the bill of fare.

The two following Christmas dinners are from English sources:

CHRISTMAS DINNER—EIGHT PERSONS.

FIRST COURSE.

OXTAIL SOUP.
CRIMPED COD AND OYSTER SAUCE.
Entrées.
SAVORY RISSOLES—FOWL—SCOLLOPS A LA BECHAMEL.

SECOND COURSE.

SADDLE OF MUTTON—BOILED CHICKENS.
CELERY SAUCE.
BACON CHEEK, GARNISHED WITH BRUSSELS SPROUTS.
VEGETABLES.

THIRD COURSE.

QUAILS—SALAD.
ORANGE JELLY—APPLES A LA PORTUGAISE.
MINCE PIES—APRICOT JAM—TARTLETS.
SOUFFLE OF RICE.
Dessert.

CHRISTMAS DINNER—TEN PERSONS.

FIRST COURSE.
MULLIGATAWNEY SOUP.
BOILED CODFISH—LOBSTER SAUCE.
WHITEFISH A LA CREME.
Entrées.
CROQUETTES OF FOWL—CUTLETS AND TOMATO SAUCE.

SECOND COURSE.
ROAST RIBS OF BEEF—BOILED TURKEY AND CELERY SAUCE—TONGUE, GARNISHED.
VEGETABLES.

THIRD COURSE.
GROUSE—SALAD.
PLUM PUDDING—MINCE PIES.
CHARLOTTE A LA PARISIENNE—CHEESE-CAKES.
APPLE TART—NESSELRODE PUDDING.
Dessert and Ices.

Here are two from the famous *chef de cuisine*, Francatelli.

DINNER—SIX PERSONS.

FIRST COURSE.
JULLIENNE SOUP.
FRIED SOLES—ANCHOVY SAUCE.
FOWL AND RICE—ROAST LEG OF WELSH MUTTON.
Entrées.
SALMIS OF PARTRIDGES A L'ANCIENNE.
FRICANDEAU WITH PUREE OF SORREL.

SECOND COURSE.
ROAST SNIPES.
THREE EXTREMETS.
SPINACH WITH CREAM—BLANC-MANGE.
APPLES A LA PORTUGAISE.

DINNER—TWELVE PERSONS.

FIRST COURSE.
BISQUE OF LOBSTER SOUP.
CRIMPED COD WITH OYSTER SAUCE, GARNISHED WITH FRIED SMELTS.
PATTIES A LA MOUGLAS.
ROAST TURKEY A LA PERIGORD.
BRAIZED HAM WITH SPINACH.
Two Entrées.
FAT LIVERS A LA FIANCIESE.
FILLETS DE PARTRIDGES A LA LUCULLUS.

SECOND COURSE.
ROAST BLACK COCK—ROAST TEAL.
SOUFFLE OF APPLES A LA VENITIENNE.
FOUR EXTREMETS.
MECCA LOAVES, WITH APRICOTS.
BRAIZED CELERY.
ITALIAN CREAM—MACARONI AU GRATIN.

PUDDINGS AND PIES FOR CHRISTMAS.

Cup-Puddings for the Old and Young.—1. Soak stale bread in hot water till soft, drain it off, mash it, and add some cream, nutmeg, and currants, sugar to taste, pour in a dish and bake, lay a small piece of butter on the top.

2. Pour boiling milk over the crusts of bread, and let them remain till soft; beat them smooth and add three eggs well beaten, the grated rind of a lemon, and sugar to taste; also a little cream. Pour this in small buttered cups, and bake a light brown; turn them out, and strew sifted sugar over.

Scotch Pudding.—Butter a mold and put cut raisins to ornament; mix quarter pound suet very fine, quarter pound breadcrumbs, one and a half ounce ground rice, pinch salt, three ounces marmalade, three ounces white sugar, three eggs, rind of lemon grated; beat well, pour in mold, boil one hour; sauce.

Demorest Monthly Magazine, 1880

Cocoa-nut Puddings.—Half pound grated cocoa, one ounce butter, half the juice of one lemon and the rind grated, four eggs, the whits of one left out, half pound grated lemon; mix all together; then put into cups and bake them.

Amber Pudding.—Five eggs, two whites left out, half a pound lump sugar pounded fine, not quite half pound of butter melted and mixed with the sugar, then the eggs mixed in, and a little candied peel, and flavored according to taste. Make a paste, line a pudding dish with it, pour the mixture in, and cover with paste. When baked, turn it out in a glass dish, strew over with sugar, and eat cold.

Ice Pudding.—Take one pint and a half of clarified syrup and the strained juice of three lemons. Put the mixture in the freezing pot, and when nearly frozen add essence of citron to taste, and one ounce of pistachio-nuts blanched, and split in half lengthwise; finish freezing, put into a mold, and lay it on ice till wanted.

Marlborough Pudding.—Cover a pie dish with a thin puff paste, then take an ounce of candied citron, one of orange, and the same of lemon peel, sliced very thin, and lay them over the bottom of the dish. Dissolve six ounces of butter without water, and add to it six ounces of pounded sugar, and the yolks of four well-beaten eggs. Stir them over the fire until the mixture boils, then pour it over the sweetmeats, bake the pudding in a moderate oven for three-quarters of an hour, and serve it hot or cold.

Coffee Ice Pudding.—Pound two ounces of freshly-roasted coffee in a mortar, just enough to crush the berries without reducing them to powder. Put them into a pint of milk with six ounces of loaf sugar, let it boil, then leave it to get cold; strain it on the yolks of six eggs in a double saucepan, and stir on the fire till the custard thickens. When quite cold, work into it a gill and a half of cream whipped to a froth. Freeze the mixture in the ice pot, then fill a plain ice mold with it, and lay it in ice till the time of serving.

Cocoa-nut Pudding.—Put a half pound packet of desiccated cocoa-nut, or grate a large one with brown skin pared off, into a pudding dish. Break in pieces two penny sponge cakes. Pour over the cocoa-nut and cake a quart of boiling milk with one tablespoonful of butter melted in it and four tablespoonfuls of sugar. Let it stand an hour, covered close. Beat four eggs, and stir into the mixture; then bake in a slow oven, like custard pudding. To be eaten either warm or cold.

Dartmouth Pudding.—Mix one quart of Indian meal with four ounces of butter or finely minced beef suet, and four ounces of brown sugar, or one pint of molasses; add two teaspoonfuls of powdered cinnamon and one pint of milk; add two eggs well beaten, then pour over the whole three pints of boiling milk; stir a few minutes, then pour it into a pudding pan, and bake it four or five hours in a moderate oven. Every hour pour a little cold milk on the top of the pudding to prevent its becoming tough. Serve hot.

Nantucket Pudding.—Fill a pudding pan with apples pared, quartered, and cored. Cover the top with a crust rolled out of light bread dough, make a hole in the lid, and set the pan in a brick oven. After it has cooked lift the crust and add molasses or brown sugar, a little powdered cinnamon and nutmeg to taste, also one tablespoonful of butter. Stir it well, cut the crust into square bits, mix all together, cover it with a large plate, return it to the oven for three or four hours. Serve hot.

The Boys' Own.—Mix three gills of Indian meal, one gill of wheat flour, one gill of molasses, one teaspoonful salt, half teaspoonful of powdered ginger, one teaspoonful powdered cinnamon, and the grated peel of one lemon. Pour over all one quart of boiling milk, stir well, and when a little cooled, add six eggs beaten separately, and one pound of stoned raisins, dredged with flour; or dried peaches or apples, well washed and dried in the sun, may be substituted. Scald a bag, flour it, and boil the pudding in it, leaving plenty of space for it to swell. Boil five hours, and serve with wine sauce.

Mince-meat.—1. Two pounds raisins, two pounds currants, two pounds sugar, one pound suet, half a pound mixed candied peel, rind and juice of three lemons, if liked; chop the suet and raisins fine, add currants, candied peel, etc.; pare, core, and cut the apples, bake them till soft, beat up as for sauce, and mix them well with the other ingredients; add pint of sweet cider boiled with half the sugar.

2. Mince very finely one and a half pounds beef suet, one and a half pounds of currants, one and a half pounds chopped raisins, one and a half pounds good apples; mix well in a basin, adding one pound of moist sugar, half a pound of mixed peel finely minced, squeeze the juice of a lemon in the mixture, and, lastly, put in the thin rind of it finely chopped. Put half a tablespoonful of salt, a cup of melted currant jelly, and powdered mixed spice and ginger to taste. Add this to the mince, work it a little now and then to get it well mixed, and put it by in a covered jar.

3. To two pounds of lean beef, taken from the under side of the back loin, add the same weight of beef suet, four and a half pounds of currants, one and a half pounds of raisins stoned and chopped, the juice and peel of three lemons, one pound powdered sugar, two large nutmegs, cloves and mace (pounded, of each quarter ounce), quarter ounce of cinnamon, one quart of boiled cider, about eighteen apples, and quarter pound candied lemon peel. The apples and candied peel must not be mixed with the other ingredients to keep in a jar, or the mince-meat will go moldy; they must be added to each portion when the pies are made, the candied peel cut in thin strips and laid across the mince-meat in each pie. This recipe has been in family use for sixty years. Cut the meat hot, when half cooked, from the fresh roasted sirloin.

Paste for Pies.—One pound butter, one pound flour; break the butter up with the flour, add cold water sufficient to make paste, roll out, and then fold it; roll it twice more. Be careful to roll it from you, and not back again. Have a nice hot oven, and bake for thirty minutes without opening the oven door. Brush over with egg, which improves the look. Half a pound of butter and half a pound lard, with one pound of flour, will make nice paste.

Pumpkin Pie.—Pare some pumpkin or squash, stew it with very little water, drain it, mash it smoothly. To one pint of mashed pumpkin add two cups of sugar, four beaten eggs, a little salt, the grated peel of one lemon, a little essence of rose, one small tablespoonful of butter, one teaspoonful of mixed cinnamon and ginger; mix well, then add one quart of hot milk. Bake it in deep soup plates lined with paste, without any upper crust.

Swiss Pie.—Three pounds rump steak, six mutton kidneys; cut the steak in moderate pieces, and split the kidneys, and put both on the fire, with enough water to cover them, with a Spanish onion cut in small rings, and seasoned with pepper and salt. Have some potatoes ready boiled, but not too much; cut them in quarters, brown them, and put round dish in rows on the top of the meat. A pretty way of dishing this is to put it in a game pie-dish.

Mince Pies without Meat.—Take six large lemons, squeeze out all the juice, then boil all the rinds and pulp in three or four waters, until the bitterness is quite extracted and the rinds are very tender. When cold, beat or chop it very fine, and add to it two pounds currants, one pound raisins chopped, two pounds sugar, and one pound beef suet chopped very fine; put to it the juice of the lemons, two wineglassfuls sweet peach pickle syrup, two ounces candied lemon and orange peel. Add, if liked, six apples chopped, a little more sugar, and a little nutmeg, mace, cloves, and cinnamon.

Delicious Mince-meat.—Two pounds of currants, well washed, carefully picked, and rubbed dry, half of them slightly chopped; two pounds of raisins, stoned and finely chopped; three-quarters of a pound of candied peel, chopped; one pound of good apples, carefully cored, peeled, and chopped; one pound of fresh beef suet, chopped; three-quarters of a pound of the under side of the sirloin of beef (roasted, but not over-done), or fillet of veal, chopped; the grated rinds and strained juice of two lemons and one Seville orange, one and a half pound of moist sugar, half a nutmeg grated, half a teaspoonful of powdered cinnamon, half a saltspoonful of powdered ginger, two grains of powdered cloves, and a pint of cider; mix these ingredients well together, put the mince in stone jars, tie them over with bladder, and keep in a cool, dry place till wanted. It will keep a year or longer, and should be made a few weeks before it is wanted: *new* fruit must be made.

An old Recipe.—Two pounds Valencias stoned and chopped, two pounds currants washed and dried, two pounds Sultanas whole, two pounds cooking apples chopped fine, two pounds brown crystallized sugar, one and a half pounds best beef suet chopped fine, three-quarters of a pound mixed peel cut into small pieces. Mix the whole well together, then add the juice of two lemons and the rinds of the same chopped very fine; grate a whole nutmeg, and sprinkle a penny packet of mixed spice into it, after which stir well, and put it into a large earthenware jar; pour enough boiled cider to moisten over it, and tie down until wanted. This is a good quantity to make for a family of ten persons. It is very useful for rolled suet puddings, as well as for mince pies. It may be interesting to housewives to know that ancient mince pies were made in the form of a cradle, and the mixture they contained was supposed to be emblematic of the gold, frankincense, and myrrh.

A Plain Christmas Pudding.—One pound of flour, one pound of breadcrumbs, three-quarters of a pound of stoned raisins, three-quarters of a pound of currants, three-quarters of a pound of suet, three or four eggs, milk, two ounces of candied peel, one teaspoonful of powdered allspice, half a teaspoonful of salt. Let the suet be finely chopped, the raisins stoned, and the currants well washed, picked, and dried. Mix these with the other dry ingredients, and stir all well together; beat and strain the eggs to the pudding, stir these in, and add just sufficient milk to make it mix properly. Tie it up in a well-floured cloth, put it into boiling water, and boil for at least five hours. Serve with a sprig of holly placed in the middle of the pudding, and a little pounded sugar sprinkled over it, and also with a rich sauce.

Plum Pudding without Eggs.—Half a pound of flour, six ounces of raisins, six ounces of currants, quarter of a pound of chopped suet, quarter of a pound of brown sugar, quarter of a pound of mashed carrot, quarter of a pound of mashed potatoes, a tablespoonful of molasses, one ounce of candied lemon peel, one ounce of candied citron. Mix the flour, currants, suet, and sugar well together; have ready the above preparations of mashed carrot and potatoes, which stir into the other ingredients; add the molasses and lemon peel, but put no liquid in the mixture, or it will be spoiled. Tie it loosely in a cloth, or, if put in a basin, do not quite fill it, as the pudding should have room to swell, and boil it for four hours. Serve with rich sauce. This pudding is better for being mixed over-night.

Maryland Plum Pudding.—One pound of grated breadcrumbs, one pound of raisins stoned, one pound of currants, half pound of citron, nine eggs beaten light, leaving out the whites of three; one large teacup of brown sugar, a teacup of cream, a tablespoonful of flour; cloves, mace, and nutmeg to your taste; all well mixed together. Scald your cloth in which it is to be boiled, let the water boil, and stir it about a few minutes after it goes in; three hours are sufficient to cook it. When ready to serve, ornament the pudding with spikes of almond and a sprig of holly, and sprinkle sugar over it. Serve with sauce.

A well-tried Plum Pudding.—The yokes of five eggs and the whites of three beaten up with quarter pint of cream, two ounces of fine dried flour, half pound fresh beef suet chopped very fine, half pound currants washed and picked over, half pound of best raisins stoned and chopped small, one ounce candied citron, one ounce orange, one ounce lemon ditto, shredded thin, one ounce of fine sugar, half a glass of brandy, a little nutmeg. Mix all well together, butter a large mold or basin, and drop the mold into boiling water, and keep it boiling many hours, say eight or nine hours, if possible.

Molasses Pudding.—Six ounces suet, teaspoonful of salt, three-quarters pound flour, half pound stoned raisins, one tablespoonful sugar, one pint of molasses, half cup milk. Mix as stiff as possible, and boil four hours.

A Richer Pudding.—One pound each of suet, currants, stoned raisins, two pounds flour, cup of molasses, a small cupful of milk, three tablespoonfuls of moist sugar, citron, ginger, and cloves to taste; boil eight hours.

A Tried Recipe.—A well-tried recipe for plum pudding: Three-quarters pound each of raisins, currants, and suet, half pound each of flour and breadcrumbs, quarter pound moist sugar, one-third of a nutmeg, almond flavoring to taste, two ounces candied peel, as much milk as will moisten it well, about one pint or less, as it must be fairly stiff. Chop the suet very fine, and mix all well together; boil ten hours—six when made, and four when required for use. Eggs in a plum pudding are virtually wasted. It is quite as good without.

Family Pudding.—Half pound beef suet finely chopped, half pound currants, half pound raisins stoned and chopped, half pound breadcrumbs, quarter pound moist sugar, one pound of treacle, two ounces candied peel, chopped finely, half a nutmeg grated, the juice of one lemon, the rind grated, half ounce of powdered cinnamon, one tablespoonful salt, one gill of milk, four eggs well beaten. Boil the milk and pour at once on to the breadcrumbs; add the suet, fruit, sugar, spice, etc.; moisten with the eggs and spirit; stir well, and if too stiff add a little milk, or if too moist add a little flour. Press into buttered mold, tie tightly, put into boiling water, and boil four hours; serve with sauce.

Aunt Margaret's Pudding.—Stone and cut in halves one and a half pound of raisins, but do not chop them; wash, pick, and dry a half pound of currants, and mince the suet (three-quarters of a pound) finely; add salt, cut a quarter of a pound candied peel into thin slices, grate down bread into three-quarters of a pound of fine crumbs. When all these dry ingredients are prepared, mix them well together; then moisten the mixture with six eggs, which should be very well beaten;

add one glassful of cider, stir well that everything may be really thoroughly blended, and *press* the pudding into a buttered mold; tie it down tightly with a floured cloth, and boil for six hours. When the pudding is taken out of the pot, hang it up immediately, and put a saucer underneath to catch the water that drains from it. The day it is to be eaten, plunge it into boiling water, and keep it boiling for two hours; then turn it out of the mold. The raisins should be rubbed in flour.

A Very Good Pudding.—Chop very finely one pound of suet, extremely fresh, and carefully picked from all skin, three-quarters of a pound of flour, one-quarter of a pound of breadcrumbs, half pound moist sugar, two ounces candied mixed peel chopped fine, half a nutmeg grated, one teaspoonful salt, one pound of currants carefully washed and dried, one pound of raisins well stoned, half an ounce of bitter almonds, one ounce of sweet almonds chopped, six eggs well beaten, whites and yolks together. Mix it all well up together with as much milk as will make it too thick to be poured, but not thick enough to be handled as paste. It requires no kneading or beating, and should be made six hours before putting it into the mold. Line the basin or mold with a buttered paper, tie a thick pudding cloth tightly over it, and boil it six hours. Serve with sauce.

"Every Christmas" Pudding.—It is not too rich, and very inexpensive. Half a pound of Valencia raisins stoned, half a pound of currants, three ounces of flour, half a pound of beef suet chopped very fine, half a pound of breadcrumbs grated, two ounces soft sugar, two ounces candied peel, the rind of a small lemon chopped very fine, and half a nutmeg grated; mix all well in a bowl, and add a wineglass of rum or brandy, and four eggs well beaten. Cover over with a plate, and let it stand all night; in the morning stir it up well, and add a teacupful of cider; mix thoroughly, and put it into a well-buttered mold. Lay a buttered and floured paper over the top, and tie all in a large cloth. Boil six hours, a week or more before it is wanted, and then at least four hours the day the pudding is required; serve with sauce.

Unrivaled Plum Pudding.—One and a half pound of raisins, one and a half pound currants, one pound of Sultana raisins, half pound of sugar, one and a quarter pound of breadcrumbs, three-quarters of a pound of flour, two pounds of finely chopped suet, six ounces of mixed candied peel, the rind grated and juice of one lemon, one ounce of sweet, half ounce of bitter almonds, pounded; quarter of a grated nutmeg, a teaspoonful of mixed spice, fourteen eggs, and a wineglass of brandy; all to be mixed together, and the flour dusted in at the last. Put in molds, and boil eight hours. To be mixed the night before boiling; sufficient for three puddings, and will keep for months. A plain flour-and-water paste to be put over the basins before the cloth.

Mocha Pudding.—Beat up the yolks of four eggs with quarter pound of powdered loaf sugar, add gradually two ounces of flour and two ounces of potato flour; lastly, the whites of four eggs whipped to a stiff froth. When the whole is well mixed, put it in a buttered plain mold and bake. Turn out the cake when done, and when it is quite cold cover it evenly all over with the following icing, ornamenting it with piping of the icing pushed through a paper cone. This last operation must be done with care, lest the heat of the hand warm the icing. When the cake is finished it should be put in a cold place, or on ice till the time of serving. THE ICING.—Take half a pound of fresh butter and a quarter of a pound of powdered loaf sugar, and beat them to a cream in a bowl, adding drop by drop, during the process,

half a teacupful of the strongest coffee that can be made.

A Pound Pudding.—The ingredients are as follows, for a pound pudding: One pound of best Valencia raisins, stoned and cut in half; one pound of best currants, rubbed in a damp cloth and then in a dry one, all little stalks and rough bits being picked from them, after which sprinkle them with flour slightly, to prevent them from clinging together in lumps; one pound of nicely shred beef suet, chopped as fine as to look like flour; one pound of brown sugar, freed from all lumps, not the crystallized; one pound of finely grated breadcrumbs, off a stale loaf; quarter pound of candied peel, mixed orange, citron and lemon; the rind of a fresh lemon, cut thin, so as not to touch the white skin, chopped very fine; a good pinch of salt; a dessertspoonful of spices, well pounded, viz., cloves, mace, whole allspice, and cinnamon (very little mace, it is so strong, if good), and half a nutmeg grated, also a little ginger; one glass of fresh cider; eight eggs and a little flour, not more than six or seven moderate-sized dessertspoonfuls; no milk, as that would ruin the pudding. The pudding is mixed thus: Have a large paushon or bowl, to give plenty of room for stirring, and place the five articles in pounds round it, thus: raisins, sugar, currants, suet, and bread. If placed in this order, the mixing is greatly facilitated. Stir them round from the center until all are well mixed together; then add the candied peel, cut up into small pieces, and sprinkled all over; then the fresh lemon peel, and the mixed spice, stirring after each sprinkling, the spoonful of salt over all. Then break four eggs, and beat them separately, sprinkle them in a state of froth over the mixture in the bowl, and stir again. Now add four dessertspoonfuls of flour, stirring it in, and then add the cider; always stir the ingredients as lightly as possible, lifting it and breaking any close, heavy lumps. Cover the bowl over, and leave it in a cool dry place for one night. When required for use, beat up the other four eggs, and add two or three spoonfuls of flour. You can judge when you have sufficient flour by the ingredients adhering together lightly, not in heavy lumps. Have your water boiling ready, and dip your pudding cloth (which should be a sound new one) into it, place it, when wrung as dry as possible, in a bowl, dredge it with flour, and drop your pudding into it in light spoonfuls; do not press them together, as that makes the pudding heavy; then gather up the cloth, a very small portion at a time, as small gathers make the pudding a nicer shape. Have a yard of new tape to tie it with, and leave plenty of room for the pudding to swell; it should be tied tight enough to prevent the water from getting in. The pudding should be kept boiling for eight hours, and care taken that it does not set to the bottom of the pan. To serve the pudding, crushed loaf sugar should be piled on the top to imitate snow, and also over the sprig of berried holly that is stuck in it; and, when desired, flaming spirit may be added in the dish.

Sauce for the Pudding.—Put into a small saucepan two ounces of butter—not "cooking butter," but the very best of table butter. To this add a large tablespoonful of fresh and sweet flour. Mix these well together, while they are cold; do this with a wooden spoon. Pour in half a pint of cold water; add a little salt. Place these over the fire and stir until it has *almost* reached the boiling point, but not *quite*. Now add a glass of the best currant or lemon jelly. Add some pulverized sugar. Do not spoil the sauce with coarse sugar; add a dust of cinnamon and the grated peel of half a lemon, the outside rind. Make the sauce hot and sprinkle another dash of cinnamon on the surface. Now ornament the pudding with a miniature American flag stuck on the top.

CHRISTMAS THROUGHOUT CHRISTENDOM.

THOR.

THE angels in the *Gloria in Excelsis* have probably given us the best definition of Christmas, "On earth peace, good-will toward men." This Christian idea of Christmas, with its love, charity, and forgiveness, has probably found its most striking realization in the *Julafred*, or Yule-peace of the Scandinavians—a custom, though ancient as the Runic stones, still existing in Sweden, by virtue of a Christian baptism, as a Christian institution. Extending from Christmas-eve to Epiphany, and solemnly proclaimed by a public crier, any violation of the Yule-peace is visited with double or treble punishment. The courts are closed; old quarrels are adjusted; old feuds are forgotten; while on the Yule-evening the shoes, great and small, of the entire household, are set close together in a row, that during the coming year the family may live together in peace and harmony.

To this pacific, Christian conception of the Christmas-time not a few pagan elements have been added, which are clearly traceable, as we shall see, to the old German "Twelve Nights" and the Roman Saturnalia. Hence its mirth and festivity, its jesting and feasting, its frolic and license. The decoration and illumination of our Christian churches recall the temples of Saturn radiant with burning tapers and resplendent with garlands. The "merry Christmas" responds to the "*bona Saturnalia*," and our modern Christmas presents to the *dona amicis*.

During the Saturnalia, which were intended to symbolize the freedom, equality, and peaceful prosperity of the golden or Saturnian age, all labor was suspended. The schools were closed; the Senate adjourned; no criminal was executed; no war proclaimed. Slaves exchanged places with their masters, or, seated at the banqueting tables wearing badges of freedom, jested with them familiarly as their equals.

All these customs have found their counterpart during the Christmas holidays in modern society. In Italy, at the present day, masters and servants not unfrequently meet and are seated at a common Christmas table; while among the English aristocracy the "huge hall table," at least in the times when Scott sang of the Christmas-tide,

"Bore then upon its surface broad
No mark to part the squire and lord."

Nor do we fail to find the outcroppings of the freedom and license of the old Saturnalia even in Protestant England and Puritanic Scotland. In the stalwart times of "good Queen Bess" the Christmas holidays lasted over a month. Those were the palmy days of the Christmas-tide, when the mystic mistletoe bough, as now, conferred upon amorous swains a charter for kissing as "broad as the wind," when the Christmas-logs flamed and roared, when boars' heads and barbecues smoked, and fun and frolic and boisterous mirth raged furiously through the "wee short hours" until the sky turned round. Then it was that the Lord of Misrule or Abbot of Unreason was the autocrat of the Christmas-time, when, clothed with the same powers as the lord of the Feast of Asses in France, he enjoyed the right to say with impunity whatever he chose, to whomsoever he pleased, even to hooting the minister during divine service, when the congregation would frequently desert the church in a body to join the roistering revelers under his capricious command.

Although Epiphanius dates back the custom of commemorating the birthday of Christ to the days of the apostles, its origin is to be referred with greater probability to the latter part of the fourth century. The primitive Christians, it is true, celebrated the birthdays of Christian martyrs, only they selected the day of their death as their real birthday—the birthday of their eternal life. When, however, Constantine proclaimed the Christian faith as the predominating religion of the Roman empire, the Christian Church, relieved from persecution throughout both Orient and Occident, began to solemnize, under the ægis of imperial authority, Christmas as the birthday of Christ. One prominent feature, however, of Constantine's political propaganda of Christianity was the adoption under Christian forms not only of pagan rites and ceremonies, but also of pagan festivals. In order to reconcile heathen converts to the new faith, these relics of paganism, like antique columns transferred from ancient temples to adorn Christian churches, were freely incorporated into the Christian ceremonial. Thus it was that Christmas, though formerly observed on the 6th of January, was transferred to the 25th of December, the time of the Roman Saturnalia, and became invested with much of the paraphernalia of the heathen festival. This transfer became the more easy from the fact that, although the early Christians had fixed upon the 6th of January in their symbolic calendar as the day of Christ's birth, the date could never be satisfactorily determined. Piper, however, rather curiously explains the adoption of the day we now celebrate from the fact that the conception of the Virgin Mary was supposed to have taken place on the day corresponding to the creation of the world, which must have been upon the 25th of March, as the days and nights are then equal, and consequently that Christ must have been born on the 25th of December.

The custom thus established in the Occident spread rapidly, particularly through the efforts of St. Chrysostom, who makes mention of it in one of his sermons as early as 386. Fifty years later it was introduced into Egypt. Here, however, it came into collision with the feast of Epiphany, which was already celebrated, as the feast of the birth and baptism of Christ, on the 6th of January, the birthday of Osiris, the Egyptian sun-god.

In Germany the Christmas holidays appear to have been substituted for the old pagan festival

ODIN AS THE WILD HUNTSMAN.

of the "Twelve Nights," which extended from the 25th of December to the 6th of January. The Twelve Nights were religiously observed by numerous feasts, and were regarded by the ancient Germans as among the holiest and most solemn of their festivals. Regarding, in common with other pagan nations, the active forces of nature as living personifications, they symbolized the conflict of natural forces by the battle of the gods and giants. Thus in the old German mythology Winter is represented as the ice-giant, heartless, inexorable, the enemy of all life, and the relentless foe of gods and men. By the aid of his powerful steed Swadilfari, the all-stiffening north wind, he constructs a formidable castle of ice, which threatens to inaugurate the reign of Night and Winter, of Darkness and eternal Death. Then follows the conflict of giants and gods, of Winter with Spring, of North Wind with South Wind, until Thor, the god of the thunder-storm, demolishes with his thunder-stone the castle of the ice-giant, when Freija, the beautiful goddess of spring, resumes her former sway, and life and light and prosperity return.

But the restless giants ever invent new stratagems to regain their lost supremacy. Thrym, the prince of the giants, robs the sleeping Thor of his dreaded sledge-hammer, and hides it eight leagues under the earth. This insures the reign of Winter for the eight months of the year when the thunderstorm slumbers, until Thor, accompanied by Loki, the spring wind, again demolishes with his recaptured hammer the castle of the ice-king, when the Winter Storm is again compelled reluctantly to retire. This eternal conflict of the opposing forces of summer and winter frequently occurs under various forms in the German mythology, and constituted one of the most striking features of the old German poesy, as the beautiful legend of Idunna and her apples and the giant Thiassi, in the poem of "Edda."

FRAU HOLLE, OR BERCHTA, AND HER TRAIN.

In the midst of this struggle of the conflicting forces of nature the Germans and other Northern peoples celebrated the festival of the Twelve Nights. This festival, as already stated, commenced on the 25th of December. Though in the depth of midwinter, when the ice-king was in the full flush of victory, it was nevertheless the turning-point in the conflict of natural forces. The sun-god having reached the goal of the winter solstice, now wheeled his fiery steeds, and became the sure precursor of the coming victory of light and life over darkness and death.

But while a pagan festival might be transformed into a Christian holiday, there was no place in a system of theism, unless in its poesy, for the pantheon of pagan gods. These were therefore either relegated to oblivion, or, metamorphosed into demons, witches, and ghosts, are now supposed to have special power to work mischief, particularly during the Christmas-time. Hulda, once the producing night of spring, now bewitches the distaff of lazy spinner-girls. Odin, the god of fecundity, who formerly pursued with impetuous ardor the fair and beautiful Freija, now, as the wild huntsman of hell, sweeps through the air with his devilish crew, foretelling future wars or portending coming calamity. The once-resplendent Berchta, now a malevolent witch, hung with cow-bells and disguised with a horrid wooden mask, has become the bugbear of children, as she mutters from house to house,

"Children or bacon,
Else I don't go away."

A singular rumor of sea-birds, during the nights of November and December, in the island of Schonen, is still known as the hunting of Odin.

In the Bavarian and Styrian Alps the Twelve Nights are called "Rumor Nights," on account of their visions of ghosts and hobgoblins, when priests and prudent housewives, with prayer and invocation, holy-water and burning incense, fumigate dwelling and outhouse, and sprinkle their cattle with salt. Hence these nights were also called "Fumigating Nights." As an additional protection against "witches' feet" and "devils' paws," the initials of the holy magicians were formerly inscribed upon the door-posts. On the dreaded Twelfth-night, when Frau Holle, or Berchta, issues with her fearful train from her wild mountain home, where she dwells among the dead, she is generally preceded by the faithful Eckhart, an old man with a long beard and a white wand, who warns every one of her terrible approach.

There is a pretty legend related by Von Reinsberg in his "Festliche Jahr" (to which we are indebted for much of the material and a number of the illustrations for this article), that on one occasion the good Eckhart met two little children, who, coming out of a beer shop with a pot of beer, were overtaken by the fearful troop, who drank all the beer. Having no money to buy more, and apprehensive of punishment, they cried bitterly, when the faithful Eckhart comforted them with the assurance that if they would never tell what they had seen, their pot would always be brimful of beer. And so it was, until their parents prevailed upon the children to divulge the mysterious secret, when the miraculous gift disappeared.

As with Christmas as a holiday, so with many of its characters and customs. If not of pagan origin, they constitute a curious medley of paganism and Christianity. This is particularly true among the Germans, who were strongly attached to their old religious ceremonies. The Christchild with his gifts and masked attendant all belong to the German antiquity. In the procession of the star-singers the three kings replace the pagan gods. Only the names have been changed, while the custom has received the rites of a Christian baptism. The German custom of some one going, in a state of nudity, at midnight on Christmas-eve, to bind the fruit trees with ropes of straw, or

THE FAITHFUL ECKHART.

Devil.   Pharisees.   Angel Gabriel.   Star-bearer.

CHARACTERS IN THE CHRISTMAS PLAYS.

of frugal housewives shaking the crumbs from the table-cloth around their roots in order that they become more fruitful, clearly points to the mysterious influence attributed by the ancient Germans to the time of the Twelve Nights. In the Tyrol the fruit trees, for a similar reason, are soundly beaten. In Bohemia they are violently shaken during the time of the midnight mass; while in other localities they are regaled with the remains of the Christmas supper, to which they had been previously and specially invited.

A similar custom, probably of German origin, still prevails in some parts of England. In Devonshire a corn cake and some hot cider are carried into the orchard, and there offered up to the largest apple-tree as the king of the orchard, while those who take part in the singular ceremony join lustily in the chorus,

"Bear good apples and 'pears enough'—
Barns full, bags full, sacks full!
Hurrah! hurrah! hurrah!"

Mistletoe and holly, Yule-log and Yule-candle, belong to the same category. The mistletoe was regarded by the Druids with religious veneration, and its berries of pearl, as symbolic of purity, were associated by them with the rites of marriage. From this the transition was but slight to the lover's kiss beneath its mystic bough during the Christmas-tide. At this festive season also they kindle bonfires upon the hill-tops. Nor must we forget that our pagan progenitors burned a great log and a mammoth candle upon the 21st of December, which, being the shortest day in the year, was regarded as the turning-point in the conflict between the contending forces of winter and spring.

Advent is the herald of Christmas. In Protestant as well as Catholic countries choristers and school-boys during the "holy-nights" go from house to house singing songs or Christmas carols, with which to usher in the auspicious day. In the south of Germany they accompany the singing by knocking at the doors with a little hammer, or throwing pease, beans, or lentils at the windows. Hence the origin of the name of "knocking nights."

In Bohemia, Styria, Carniola, and other German provinces it is customary for a number of persons to associate themselves together in a dramatic company, and perform Christmas plays during Advent. The story of the Saviour's birth, his persecution by Herod, and the flight of the Holy Family into Egypt constitutes the simple plot. The *dramatis personæ*, as well as the performance, vary somewhat according to the locality. Usually, however, they consist of the Christ-child, St. Nicholas or St. Peter, St. Joseph and the Virgin, Herod, the varlet Ruprecht, several angels, together with shepherds and other less conspicuous personages. The devil is notably the merriest character in the play. Before the representation begins he capers about through the village—a sort of peripatetic play-bill—furiously blowing his horn, and frightening or bantering both old and young. During the performance, though figuring in the rather humble rôle of a messenger, he does not cease to joke with the players or rail at the public. A handsome youth of the strictest morals is usually selected to represent the Virgin Mary.

The rehearsal is usually accompanied by a certain rhythmical movement, the players going four steps to and fro, so that a metre or foot corresponds to every step, and on the fourth, which includes the rhyme, the performer turns quickly around. The holy personages sing instead of rehearsing their parts, but accompany their singing with the same rhythmical movement. On the first Sunday in Advent the play is inaugurated by a solemn procession, headed by the master singer bearing a gigantic star, followed by the others drawing a large fir-tree ornamented with ribbons and apples; and thus they go singing to the large hall where the play is to be performed. On arriving at the door they form a half circle, and sing the star-song; then, after saluting sun, moon, and stars, the emperor, the government, and the master singer, in the name of all the "herbs and roots that grow in the earth," they enter the hall, and the performance begins.

The prologue and epilogue are sung by an angel. As the whole stage apparatus often consists of only a straw-bottomed chair and a wooden stool, every change of scene is indicated by a procession of the whole company singing an appropriate song; after which only those who take part in the next act remain standing, while the remainder go off singing.

These dramatic representations are often very simple, or only fragmentary, consisting, it may be, of a troop of boys and girls disguised as shepherds and shepherdesses, who go about singing shepherd songs, thus announcing the approaching advent of our Saviour. At other times they are performed from house to house, and are associated with the distribution of Christmas presents. In such cases they are made the occasion of a solemn inquest into the conduct of the children, and constitute in Germany—which appears to be at once the paradise and purgatory of Christmas-loving juveniles—a potential auxiliary of pedagogic and parental discipline.

The archangel Gabriel, it may be, first appears upon the scene, and thus announces his advent:

"May God give you a happy good-evening! I am his messenger, sent from angel-land. My name is Gabriel. In my hands I bear the sceptre which the Son of God has given me. On my head I wear the crown with which the Son of God has crowned me."

Thereupon the Christ-child, wearing a gilded paper crown, and carrying a basket full of apples and nuts, enters, singing the song commencing,

"Down from the high heaven I come,"

and greets the company with a similar salutation. In the course of his song he informs the children that the object of his coming is to learn whether they have been good and obedient, and if they "pray and spin diligently." If so, they are to be rewarded with gifts from his golden chariot which stands at the door; if not, their backs are to be belabored with rods. St. Peter or St. Nicholas, as the case may be, is then called in to furnish a faithful account of the children's deportment. If it be St. Nicholas, he enters with a long staff or crozier in his hand, and a bishop's mitre of gilt paper upon his head. His report is not usually a flattering one. On their way from school the children loiter in the streets, they tear their books, neglect their tasks, and forget to say their prayers; and as a penance for all this evil-doing, he recommends a liberal application of the rod. The Christ-child interposes, almost supplicatingly,

"Ah, Nicholas, forbear. Spare the little child. Spare the young blood!"

The two then join with the angel in singing a song, when St. Peter is summoned, who promptly enters, jingling his keys. The saint, who rather plumes himself on his high office of heavenly janitor, carries matters with a high hand. He examines the children's copy-books, it may be, bids them kneel down and pray, and then, by virtue of his high prerogative, pronounces sentence upon the unfortunate delinquents, and calls upon the black Ruprecht, who stands waiting outside the door, to execute his orders.

"Ruperus, Ruperus, enter!
The children will not be obedient."

The frightful bugbear, dressed in fur, and covered with chains, with blackened face and fiery eyes, and a long red tongue protruding out of his mouth, stumbles over the threshold, brandishing an enormous birch, and as he falls headlong into the room, roars out to the children, "Can you pray?" Whereupon they fall upon their knees and repeat their prayers at the top of their voices. The five heavenly visitors, standing in a half circle, then sing another song or two descriptive of the heavenly joys, or freighted with wholesome advice to both children and parents. The latter give them in return a few farthings, while the Christ-child scatters apples and nuts here and there upon the floor for the further edification of the children, and then Christ-child, St. Nicholas, St. Peter, the archangel Gabriel, and devil *exeunt*.

St. Nicholas, as all the world knows, is the patron of children, with whom he is the most popular saint in the calendar. Bishop of Myra, in Lycia, in the time of Constantine the Great, if we are to credit the Roman breviary, he supplied three destitute maidens with dowries by secretly leaving a marriage-portion for each at their window. Hence the popular fiction that he is the purveyor of presents to children on Christmas-eve. He usually makes his appearance as an old man with a venerable beard, and dressed as a bishop, either riding a white horse or an ass, and carrying a large basket on his arm, and a bundle of rods in his hand. In some parts of Bohemia he appears dressed up in a sheet instead of a surplice, with a crushed pillow on his head instead of a mitre. On his calling out, "Wilt thou pray?" all the children fall upon their knees, whereupon he lets fall some fruit upon the floor and disappears. In this manner he goes from house to house, sometimes ringing a bell to announce his arrival, visits the nurseries, inquires into the conduct of the children, praises or admonishes them, as the case may be, distributing sweetmeats or rods accordingly.

St. Nicholas is the Santa Claus of Holland, and the Samiklaus of Switzerland, and the Sönner Klås of Helgoland. In the Vorarlberg he is known as Zemmiklas, who threatens to put naughty children into his hay-sack; in Nether Austria as Niklo, or Niglo, who is followed by a masked servant called Krampus; while in the Tyrol he goes by the name of the "Holy Man," and shares the patronage of his office with St. Lucy, who distributes gifts among the girls, as he among the boys. Sometimes he is accompanied by the Christ-child.

In many parts of Switzerland, Germany, and the Netherlands St. Nicholas still distributes his presents on St. Nicholas's Eve— the 5th of December—instead of on Christmas-eve. In the Netherlands and adjoining provinces he is especially popular, and is perhaps the only saint who has maintained his full credit, even among the Protestants. For days previous to his expected advent busy housewives have been secretly conspiring with the bakers in gilding nuts, cakes, and gingerbread, and torturing pastry, prepared with flour, sugar, honey, spices, and sweetmeats, into the most fantastical forms, from which the good saint may from time to time replenish his supplies. As to the children, St. Nicholas or Sünder Klaas is the burden of their prayers, the staple of their dreams, and the inspiration of their songs. As they importune him to let fall from the chimney-top some pretty gift into their little aprons, they go on singing with childish fervor,

"Sünder Klaas du gode Bloot!
Breng' mi Nööt un Zuckerbrod,
Nicht to veel un nich to minn
Smiet in mine Schörten in!"

In Belgium, on the eve of the good bishop's aerial voyage in his pastoral visitation of his bishopric of chimney-tops, the children polish their shoes, and after filling them with hay, oats, or carrots for the saint's white horse, they put them on a table, or set them in the fire-place. The room is then carefully closed and the door locked. Next morning it is opened in the presence of the assembled household, when, *mirabile dictu!* the furniture is found to be turned topsy-turvy, while the little shoes, instead of horse's forage, are filled with sweetmeats and toys for the good children, and with rods for the bad ones. In some places wooden or China shoes, stockings, baskets, cups and saucers, and even bundles of hay, are placed in the chimney, or by the side of the bed, or in a corner of the room, as the favorite receptacles of St. Nicholas's presents.

In France, though New-Year's is generally observed rather than Christmas for the distribution of presents, it is the *Jésus bambin* who comes with a convoy of angels loaded with books and toys with which to fill the expectant little shoes, that tiny hands have so carefully arranged in the fire-place. In Alsace he is represented by a young maiden dressed in white, with hair of lamb's wool hanging down upon her shoulders, and her face whitened with flour, while on her head she wears a crown of gilt paper set round with burning tapers. In one hand she holds a silver bell, in the other a basket full of sweetmeats. She is the messenger of joy to all children, but that joy is usually changed into terror on the appearance of Hans Trapp, the Alsacian Ruprecht. The bugbear, on entering, demands in a hoarse voice which of the children have not been obedient, walking up toward them in a threatening manner, while they, trembling and crying, seek to hide themselves as best they may from the impending storm. But the Christ-child intercedes for them, and, upon their

CHRISTMAS IN FRANCE.

promising to become better in the future, leads them up to the brilliantly illuminated Christmas-tree loaded with presents, which soon make them oblivious of the frightful Hans Trapp.

In the Erzgebirge it is St. Peter who, dressed as a bishop, and accompanied by the dreadful Ruprecht, is impatiently expected by the children on Christmas-eve. The character of his visit does not differ materially from that of the Christ-child, only that, on leaving, he delivers a short sermon, lays on the table a rod dipped in chalk, and then departs as noiselessly as he came. The children, relieved from the presence of Ruprecht, now breathe free again. They hasten to take off their shoes, polish them, and then tie them together, when the most daring among them, after listening if Niglo's bell has ceased tinkling, runs out into the garden and puts them under a bush. The others, plucking up courage, follow his example. They now pass the time until the clock strikes ten in telling stories, in which the black Ruprecht plays a principal part, when, having reconnoitred the situation through the key-hole to see that the coast is clear, they go noise-

THE CHRIST-CHILD AND HANS TRAPP.

lessly on tiptoe to their shoes under the bush, to find them filled with apples, nuts, and all sorts of sweetmeats.

From what precedes, it will appear that the bugbear Ruprecht, under different names and disguises, plays a conspicuous part among German-speaking populations in the Christmas festivities. In the Tyrol the terrible Klaubauf accompanies St. Nicholas, who kidnaps naughty children and stows them away in his basket. In Lower Austria it is the frightful Krampus, with his clanking chains and horrible devil's mask, who, notwithstanding his gilded nuts and apples, gingerbread and toys, which he carries in his basket, is the terror of the nursery. In the Bohemian Netherlands Rumpanz figures as the bugbear in the train of the Christchild. Three young men disguise themselves, one as an angel, another as the devil, and the third as a he-goat. The latter catches and holds wicked children, who do not say their prayers, upon his horns, in order that the devil may beat them with his rod. In Alsace Ruprecht, as already intimated, is represented by Hans Trapp. In Suabia the Christ-child is accompanied by the Pelzmaert, who carries an old bell, and an earthen pot containing the presents; while throughout Northern Germany it is customary in the rural districts for a blackbearded peasant, wrapped in straw, to go from house to house asking the children if they know how to pray, rewarding those who can with gingerbread, apples, and nuts, and punishing unmercifully those who can not. In Hanover, Holstein, and Mecklenburg he is known as Clüs. In Silesia his name is Joseph.

Sometimes the Christmas bugbear carries a rod, at the end of which is fastened a sack full of ashes, with which he beats the children, and is therefore called Ashy Claws. At others he rides a white horse, called in some localities the "Spanish stallion," and not unfrequently he is accompanied by a bear wrapped in straw. On the island of Usedom three figures belong to the procession of Ruprecht. One wrapped in straw bears the rod and cinder-bag, or ash-sack.

CHRISTMAS MASKS.

The second appears as the rider of the "Spanish stallion." The third carries the *Klapperbock*. This consists of a pole over which is drawn a buckskin. To the extremity of the pole a ram's head is attached, from the nether jaw of which a cord passes through the upper jaw and thence into the throat, so that when the bearer pulls the cord the jaws rattle or clatter. With this Klapperbock, which in Denmark, under the name of the *Julbock* or Yule-buck, is the unfailing accompaniment of the Yule-time, they threaten and frighten the children. In the Harz a similar scarecrow, called the Habersack, consists of a hay-fork, between the prongs of which a broom is attached so as to present the appearance of a head with horns, while the body is made up of a sheet with a man under it.

In former times there was also a female bugbear. In Lower Austria she was called the Budelfrau. In Suabia it was the Berchtel, who chastised children that did not spin diligently with rods, but rewarded the industrious with dried pears, apples, and nuts. In the environs of Augsburg the Buzebercht, with her blackened face and streaming hair and flaunting rags, accompanied St. Nicholas, besmearing every one she met with the contents of her starch-pot; while in the Böhmerwalde, or Bohemian Forest, St. Lucy, under the form of a goat covered with a sheet, through which the horns project, is to this day the terror of lazy or undutiful children.

On Sylvester's-day or New-Year's Eve the procession of the "Spanish stallion," cinder-bag, and Klapperbock is supplemented in Faterland by the *Wêpelrôt*. This consists of a wheel made of willow, in the centre of which there is a gilded ornament that flashes like a star. At the extremity of the spokes on the exterior of the rim there is a succession of spikes, upon which apples are stuck. Just after midnight the bearer throws it into the house of his lady-love, demanding a token in return. He then fires a pistol, and runs away at the top of his speed, pursued by the inmates of the house, who, if he is caught and brought back, compel him to drink *Rôtwasser*, and ride astride of the pot-hanger. Christmas masks of a somewhat similar character are in vogue in Naples, and, unless we are mistaken, also in Sicily.

Time would fail to speak of the many singular customs and quaint superstitions associated with the Christmas holidays. In some places, as in Suabia, it is customary for maidens, inquisitive as to their prospective lovers, to draw a stick of wood out of a heap to see whether he will be long or short, crooked or straight. At other times they will pour melted lead into cold water, and from the figures formed will prognosticate the trade or profession of their future husbands. If they imagine they see a plane, or last, or a pair of shears, it signifies that he is to be a carpenter, or shoe-maker, or tailor; while a hammer or pickaxe indicates a smith or a common laborer. The maidens of Pfullingen, when they wish to ascertain which of them will first become a wife, form a circle, and place in their midst a blindfolded gander, and the one to whom he goes first will soon be a bride; while the Tyrolese peasants, on the "knocking nights," listen at the baking ovens, and if they hear music, it signifies an early wedding, but if the ringing of bells, it forebodes the death of the listener. Among many others a favorite method of forecasting the future is to sit upon the floor and throw one's shoe with the foot over the shoulder, and then to predict from the position it assumes what is about to transpire.

The superstition that cattle kneel at midnight on Christmas-eve, in recognition of the anniversary of the Saviour's birth, is still said to exist even in some parts of England; while the belief that water drawn at twelve o'clock on Christmas-night is miraculously turned into wine is no less widely diffused. In Mecklenburg it is not allowable to call certain animals by their right names, and he who does not say "long tail," for example, for fox, pays a forfeit.

In Poland, and elsewhere, it is believed that on Christmas-night the heavens are opened, and the scene of Jacob's ladder is reenacted, but it is only permitted to the saints to see it. Throughout Northern Germany the tables are spread and lights left burning during the entire night, that the Virgin Mary, and the angel who passes when every body sleeps, may find something to eat. In certain parts of Austria they put candles in the windows, that the Christ-child may not stumble in passing through the village. There is also a wide-spread opinion that a pack of wolves, which were no other than wicked men transformed into wolves, committed great havoc upon Christmas-night. Taking advantage of this superstition, it was not unusual for rogues disguised in wolf-skins to attack honest people, rifle their houses, sack their cellars, and drink or steal all their beer. As a specific charm, no doubt, against these wolfish depredations, it was customary in Austria, up to a recent date, after high mass on Christmas-night, to sing in a particular tone, to the sound of the large bell, the chapter of the generation of Jesus Christ.

The Christmas-tree is doubtless of German origin. Though in its present form it is comparatively of recent date, yet its pagan prototype enjoyed a very high antiquity. The early Germans conceived of the world as a great tree whose roots were hidden deep under the earth, but whose top, flourishing in the midst of Walhalla, the old German paradise, nourished the she-goat upon whose milk fallen heroes restored themselves. Yggdnafil was the name of this tree, and its memory was still green long after Christianity had been introduced into Germany, when much of its symbolic character was transferred to the Christmas-tree. At first fitted up during the Twelve Nights in honor of Berchta, the goddess of spring, it was subsequently transferred to the birthday of Christ, who, as the God-man, is become the "resurrection and the life." The evergreen fir-tree, an emblem of spring-time, became the symbol of an eternal spring. The burning lights were to adumbrate Him who is the "light of the world," and the gifts to remind us that God, in giving His only Son for the world's redemption, conferred upon us the most priceless of all gifts. This symbolism extended also to the most usual of Christmas presents, apples and nuts; the former being considered as an emblem of youth, the latter as a profound symbol of spring, while the "boy's legs" relate to Saturn, who devoured his own children, and the *Kröpfel* to the thunder-stone of Thor.

Until within the present century the

THE CHRISTMAS-TREE.

Christmas-tree was regarded as a distinctive Protestant custom. The Reformers, in order to separate themselves more completely from the Catholic Church, dispensed with its rites, ceremonies, and customs, and those of the Christmas holidays among the rest. The *Krippe*, or holy manger, which was considered a distinctively Catholic institution, strangely enough, was supplanted by an old pagan custom of immemorial antiquity and kindred significance. To invest the festival with additional importance in the eyes of children, the distribution of holiday presents was transferred from the 5th to the 24th of December, or from St. Nicholas's Eve to Christmas-eve. Such was its origin. Now the Christmas-tree, radiant with light and loaded with its rich variety of golden fruit, is not only to be found every where throughout Germany, but has taken root and become acclimated from the Alps to the Ural, and from the Kiölen to the Apennines; beneath Italian suns and amidst Lapland snows; alike on the banks of the Neva and the Po, the Mississippi and the Thames—in truth, wherever German civilization has penetrated or German Protestantism prevails.

The *presepio*, or manger, has, however, maintained its pre-eminence in Roman Catholic countries. It is said to owe its origin to St. Francis, who constructed the first one in 1223. Subsequently the custom spread throughout Italy, and afterward Germany and the Netherlands. The *presepii* vary in size and expensiveness from the rude wooden figures of the Alpine goat-herd, cut out with his own hands during the long winter evenings, to the pretentious representation of the wealthy burgher, with its exquisite carving and gilding, velvet drapery and cloth of gold, costing thousands of crowns. In many churches the whole parish contribute to the expense of fitting up the *presepio*, while moribund misers do not forget to endow it with a legacy in their last will and testament.

One of these representations in a church of the Capuchins near by has become more familiar to the younger members of our household than the Christmas-stocking scene around the old familiar fireside. The Holy Family occupy the foreground. In the manger reposes the *Bambino*, over whom St. Joseph, holding a bouquet, and the Virgin, dressed in satin and lace, with blue veil and silver crown, bend admiringly. Around kneel sundry shepherds in the act of adoration; while overhead, angels with golden wings float among the clouds and chant the *Gloria in Excelsis*. A silver star with its comet-like

THE PRESEPIO.

trail directs the approach of the Eastern magi, who, with their brilliant retinue of horsemen and attendants, dazzle the eyes of the juvenile spectators with their Oriental pomp and pageantry. Here a ragged beggar stretches out a beseeching palm, and there a devout hermit kneels before a rustic chapel. In the background rise the mountains, dotted with villas and *chalets*, with flocks of sheep and goats grazing here and there upon their grassy slopes, while peasants are everywhere seen approaching, bearing the products of the farm, the dairy, and the chase as their simple offerings to the new-born child. Just opposite a tribune has been erected, from which dapper little boys and dainty little girls, greatly to the edification of indulgent parents, recite, or rather intone, selections of poetry and prose appropriate to the festive occasion.

In some places in Bohemia they use the *Krippe*, or manger, as the receptacle of the presents which the Christ-child, drawn through the air by four milk-white horses, is fabled to bring in his chariot laden with all sorts of toys and sweetmeats. So, too, the representation is frequently accompanied with dramatic performances, styled *Krippenspiele*, or manger plays. In the Bohemian Forest the Christ-child, after announcing his approach in the deepening twilight by the tinkling of his little bell, throws in the children's Christmas presents through the partially opened door, or else, in token of displeasure, he substitutes a rod, or a handful of pease, the former suggestive of punishment, the latter of penance. The kneeling on pease during prayer appears to be still in some Catholic countries a favorite method of doing penance, and an Italian friend relates as an unpleasant item of his boyhood's experience that it was formerly a cherished mode of administering discipline in the schools.

The *Bambino* is the Santa Claus of Italy. It is not unusual, however, among the Italians for the children to accompany their parents in their "shopping" during the week preceding Christmas, with a view of selecting their own presents. Meanwhile the streets are transformed into fairs, and every public square becomes a bazar. Then there is the *presepio* in the churches and private families, and the midnight mass on Christmas-eve, when the *Bambino*, held up in front of the high altar by the officiating priest, is devoutly kissed by the faithful, while old and young emulate the choir in singing that beautiful pastoral hymn, commencing,

"Fra l' orrido rigor di stagion cruda
Nacesti mio Gesù nella capanna."

Of the services in the churches, however, it is not our purpose to speak, unless incidentally, as our main object has been to illustrate Christmas in its social aspects.

One of the principal features of the holiday is the grand Christmas dinner, which begins early and lasts late, so that Christmas-night in Italy is fairly entitled to the not very elegant epithet of *Vollbauchsabend* as applied by the Holsteiners to their Christmas meal after the midnight mass. The rich feast right royally, and the poor, who can afford to eat meat but once a year, must have it for the Christmas dinner. In anticipation of this, it is customary for every one who has turned a hand for you during the year to call upon you in advance of the Christmas holidays for their *buona festa*. It is simply a generalization of what is true of our newspaper carriers on New-Year's Day. This a resident foreigner especially finds out to his sorrow. If he be a consul, so much the worse. He is not only expected to fee his own employés, but those of the health office, of the captain of the port, of the prefect, of the chief of police—in fact, of all the authorities with whom he has held official intercourse. Then come the telegraph messenger, the penny postman, the scavenger, the washer-woman, the baker's boy, who alone returns you an equivalent by bringing you a *pane dolce*, together with the servants of your friends, where you have called frequently, especially if you have dined with them at any time during the year. The *buona festa* varies from two to fifty francs, and occasionally more. Sometimes, instead of calling in person, the more aristocratic, as the *portiers* of the Bourse, will send you their *carte de visite*, with the compliments of the season, but they would consider it as rather a grim joke if you were simply to send yours in return.

A similar custom prevails in England. The bellman goes round at midnight ringing his bell, and rattling off a stanza or two, for the gratuity which he confidently anticipates; while watchmen, firemen, rate-collectors, postmen, chimney-sweeps, street scavengers, the errand-boys of your baker, butcher, poultry merchant, and green-grocer, even to the hired singers in the churches, all expect their Christmas-box.

In Spain Christmas is observed, we understand, very much as it is in Italy, the Christmas dinner playing a very conspicuous part. In Russia, though St. Nicholas is a special favorite, and they have the Christmas-tree, and services in the churches, all special ceremonies are reserved for the Easter holidays and Epiphany.

On the other hand, throughout the Scandinavian countries, the Yule-time is the gayest and merriest season of the year. It begins on Christmas and continues until Epiphany, and is given up, for the most part, to feasting, dancing, and merry-making. During this time no heavy work is to be done. The watch-dog is unchained. The cattle receive an extra allowance of fodder, and the birds some generous handfuls of seed. In the rural districts the tables are spread and left standing, loaded with the substantial good cheer of the season, together with the indispensable national dishes, Yule-groats and Yule-buck or Yule-boar — a species of bread, on which is represented a boar or ram. Every visitor is expected to partake of something, otherwise he is believed to take away with him the Yule-joy. In many places the floor of the festive hall is strewn with rye straw, called Yule-straw, which possesses the miraculous property of preserving poultry from witchcraft and cattle from distemper. Over the dining-table hangs suspended from the ceiling an ornamental straw cock. The family go singing to and from the table, while a light is left burning the entire night, and should it accidentally go out, some one in the house will surely die during the coming year.

In Lapland and Norway it is still customary to set out a cake in the snow as a Christmas offering, intended originally, in all probability, to propitiate some pagan divinity, as it dates back to the times of Thor the Thunderer. Nor must we omit to speak of the Yule-club, which was formerly suspended by a ribbon over the table, to be played by the guests in order to decide about the drink, nor of the Yule-cock, a cock made of the Yule-straw, which was played in a similar manner.

In Sweden and Denmark the *Julklapp*, or Christmas-box, inclosed in innumerable wrappers, and labeled with the name of the person for whom it is intended, is suddenly thrown into the room by some unseen, mysterious messenger, who accompanies it with a loud rap upon the door. No little ingenuity is frequently exhibited in the selection of the envelope inclosing the present. Sometimes an elegant vase is inclosed in a monster bale, or a costly brooch in a great straw boot, or some valuable ornament in an earthenware hen. During the evening all sorts of messengers, in all possible and impossible disguises, some in masks, some in female attire, some as cripples on crutches, others as postilions on horseback, hurry hither and thither, and deliver the presents in the most unexpected and mysterious manner. The Yule-klapp is not unfrequently accompanied by a biting epigram or satirical allusion, like the valentine. Thus, a lady extravagantly fond of dress is liable to be presented with a ridiculously dressed doll, or a newly married couple who are rather demonstrative in their billing and cooing with a pair of young turtle-doves.

In the larger towns and cities, as in Stockholm, they hold a great fair. The shops are richly decorated and splendidly illuminated. There are family reunions, where children receive their presents and adults their Yule-klapps, while in the midst of the festive scene rises a Christmas-tree with its rich burden of flowers, fruits, and sweetmeats, and brilliant with burning wax-lights.

UNDER THE MISTLETOE.

BRINGING IN THE BOAR'S HEAD.

Christmas in England is scarcely the shadow of its former merry, brilliant self, when all classes of society, united around a common banquet-table, indulged in the most unrestrained joviality and merriment. The wassail* bowl, that once played so conspicuous a part at the Christmas banquet, has become obsolete, while the old-time toasts of "*Drinc heil*," or "*Was hail*," from which the bowl derives its name, has given place to the modern "Come, here's to you," or "I'll pledge you." Then, too, the singing of Christmas carols, which was once so popular even at court, has greatly fallen into disuse, and is now principally confined to the lower classes. Even the traditional mistletoe, around which gathers so much of poesy and romance, and under which coy maidens coquettishly courted the kiss of their present or prospective lovers, now excluded from the churches as a relic of paganism, has been banished by slow degrees from its high post of favor; while the Yule-block, or Christmas-log, with its warm welcome, extending even to the poor and the stranger as they gathered around the hospitable board, is being gradually supplanted by the Christmas-tree, whose introduction into England is comparatively of recent date.

But if the Lord of Misrule has been the loser, Christian civilization has been the gainer, in a more rational observance of the Christmas festivities in England. The Christmas-tree sheds its mellow radiance over a more quiet but not less enjoyable scene. Churches and home sanctuaries robe themselves in evergreen holly, ivy, and laurel. Generous rations of beef and bread are distributed to the parish poor on Christmas-eve by jeweled hands, while the Christmas bells still ring out their silvery chimes on the crisp morning air joyfully and cheerfully. Nor is there wanting a spicy flavor of the old-time feasting and frolic, when there

"was brought in the lusty brawn
By old blue-coated serving man;
Then the grim boar's head frowned on high,
Crested with bays and rosemary,
 *   *   *   *   *   *
While round the merry wassail bowl,
Garnished with ribbons, blithe did trowl."

To say nothing of the roast beef and plum-pudding, Christmas pies, furmity,* and snap-dragons, the Yule-log and the mistletoe have not finally abdicated, while the boar's head, decorated with rosemary or prickly holly, maintains its place at the English Christmas dinner, and is still served up in great state at the royal Christmas table.

The "bringing in of the boar's head" was formerly attended with no little ceremony. At Oxford it was carried in by the strongest of the guardsmen, singing a Christmas carol,

---

* *Wassail*—warm ale with apples floating therein.

* A kind of thick and highly flavored barley-water.

and preceded by a forester, a huntsman, and a couple of pages dressed in silk and carrying the indispensable mustard, which at that time was regarded not only as a great luxury, but an infallible digester. The following celebrated carol of the "Boar's Head" may be found in the book of "Christmasse Carolles" published in 1521 by Wynkyn de Warde:

"Caput apri defero,
Reddens laudes Domino.
The bore's head in hande bring I,
With garlandes gay and rosemary,
I pray you all synge merely,
Qui estis in convivio.

"The bore's head, I understande,
Is the chefe servyce in this lande.
Loke wherever it be fande,
Servite cum cantico.

"Be gladde, lordes, both more and lasse,
For this hath ordayned our stewarde,
To chere you all this Christmasse,
The bore's head with mustarde."

A somewhat similar custom appears to have prevailed in Genoa in the times of the Dorias, since we learn from Carbone that a boar decorated with branches of laurel, and accompanied by trumpeters, was annually presented to the Doria family by the Abbot of San Antonio at Pré, at mid-day of the 24th of December.

Formerly the Yule-log, a huge section of the birch, was cut from a tree selected on Candlemas-day, which so late as the time of Queen Elizabeth was the last day of the Christmas holidays. On the following Christmas-eve it was dragged in and placed upon the hearth with great ceremony, the merry-makers pulling with a will, and singing the while the modernized Christmas carol commencing,

"Come, bring with a noise,
My merrie, merrie boys,
The Christmas-log to the firing."

It was then kindled with a brand from last year's Christmas fire, which, if it was not thus kept continually burning, still linked the merry-making of one Christmas-time to that of another.

In Ramsgate, Kent, and the Isle of Thanet, the custom styled "hodening" is still in vogue. The "hoden," which appears to be a cross between the "white horse" and the Klapperbock of the Germans, is accompanied by a number of youths in fantastic dress, who go round from door to door ringing bells and singing Christmas carols.

The Christmas *mummers*, that carry us back to the old Morality Plays, the origin of the modern English drama, may yet be found in Cornwall and Gloucestershire. The players are for the most part plow-boys or country "bumpkins," variously masked and grotesquely dressed, who, tricked out with swords and gilt paper hats, go about on Christmas-eve from house to house, and, wherever received, giving a rude dramatic performance styled a Mystery.

Until the time of Charles I. it was customary in England to proceed in solemn state and present the king and queen with a branch of the celebrated Glastonbury thorn, which was said to bud on Christmas-eve and blossom on Christmas morning. A popular legend relates that this thorn-bush, which once flourished in the church-yard of Glastonbury Abbey, but was subsequently cut down during the time of the civil wars, was a shoot of the staff of Joseph of Arimathea, stuck into the ground with his own hands; that it immediately took root and put forth leaves, and the day following was covered all over with snow-white blossoms, and that it thus continued to bloom for a long series of years, great numbers of people visiting it annually to witness the miracle. When, however, in 1753, a shoot of the Glastonbury thorn in Buckinghamshire refused to blossom, though thousands of spectators with lights and lanterns had assembled as usual to see it, the people declared thereupon that the 25th of December, new style, was not the true Christmas, and refused to observe it as such, most of all as the whitethorn continued to blossom on the 5th of January as usual. To put an end to the dispute, the clergy of the neighborhood issued an order that both days, old style and new, were to be similarly kept.

Our limited space will not permit us to speak of Christmas customs in Scotland, which, however—making due allowance for difference in temperament—are quite similar to those of England. There are the Yule-log and carol singers, the mummers, or guisarts, the mince-pies and plum porridge, with the added "Yule-dow" and "wad shooting." Nor may we, for the same reason, enlarge upon those of the Emerald Isle, where "purty colleens" seek four-leaved shamrocks on "Christmas-ave;" where the haggard banshee, sure precursor of impending evil, with wrinkled visage and great melancholy eyes, and white hair streaming in the wind, sweeps through the glen or gleams out of the darkness; where parish priests brew the whisky punch and bless it with a grace, while the lads and the lasses "fut" the merry jig with mirthful uproar, until the burning lights grow pale and the glowing peat burns low.

Of Christmas in the New World we need not speak at all, since its customs, for the most part, have been transplanted from the Old. Even the negroes of Jamaica elect themselves a king and queen of misrule, and indulge in Christmas masks and mummers. Our own Christmas-tree comes from Germany, our Santa Claus from Holland; the Christmas stocking from Belgium or France; while the "Merry Christmas and happy New-Year" was the old English greeting shouted from window to street, and from street back to window, in the "long, long ago."

134   *A Victorian Christmas Treasury*

OLD FATHER CHRISTMAS

Godey's Lady's Book, 1867

CHRISTMAS HYMN.

Say what offering can we
Bring to Jesus lovingly
   On His birthday morn;
As by faith we softly tread
Where on lowly manger-bed
   Lies the Babe new-born.

We would bring our life this day
Humbly at His feet to lay,
   For His will to use;
Though so poor a gift it be,
What is offered willingly
   He will not refuse.

Gold of love we'll offer there
Incense, too, of praise and prayer,
   Brought with reverence due.
And, for all the sins which He
Bore for us upon the tree,
   Myrrh of sorrow true.

All our selfishness and pride
We would strive to lay aside,
   And our pattern take
From His life, who long ago
Came into this world of woe
   For His brethren's sake.

J. E.

USEFUL HINTS.

To make Bread Quickly and Easily.—Weigh 2 lbs. of the best flour, and rub in one teaspoonful of salt, then mix gradually a pennyworth of German yeast with a pint and a half of lukewarm water; work this into the flour, and let it stand for a couple of hours to rise, after which you can slightly knead and make up into loaves, place in your tins, and bake in a quick oven. The above quantity will make four good loaves.

Beef Tea.—To 1 lb. of leg or shin of beef, minced up small, add three half-pints of water and let it stand all night; in the morning put it in a nice clean saucepan and let it come slowly to the boil, watching that it only simmers gently; then put in a little salt to flavour, and a top crust which has been toasted a dark brown. Keep the lid close, and simmer gently for three hours, then pour it off, and when cold remove the fat; it is then ready for use.

To Fry Fish or Cutlets Economically.—Dry your fish thoroughly with a cloth, then roll it in flour; next make a batter of flour and water, dip your fish in on both sides, dredge over some fine raspings—which you can procure from your baker; fry quickly in boiling lard or oil.

Steak-Pie or Pudding.—In making, sprinkle about half a teaspoonful of moist sugar over the steak along with the pepper and salt; it not only improves the flavour, but makes the meat very tender.

Coffee made in a Jug without Boiling.—Warm your jug, then measure out the coffee, say a good teaspoonful for each cup, pour the *boiling* water on to it, stir it round well, cover it over, and let it stand for five minutes; then stir it round again, put a tablespoonful of cold water and a good pinch of salt in to fine it, cover up, and let it stand for ten minutes, when it will be ready for use. Serve with hot milk.

To Make Tea and Preserve the Flavour.—First warm your teapot, then fill it with water *boiling* from the fire, and having the quantity of tea required measured out in a cup, put it into teapot on the top of the water, cover it up quickly and put the cosy over, letting it stand for ten minutes.

Lemonade.—Peel three lemons, squeeze the juice into a jug, and add part of the peel, pour a quart of boiling water over the lemons, and sweeten to taste, either with barley-sugar or sugar.

When Roasting Meat, sprinkle a little salt and flour over it; it adds to the flavour of the meat and helps to brown the gravy, which should be made from the dripping-pan, after the dripping is removed.

Tonic.—1 oz. of Peruvian bark, 1 oz. of gentian root, 1 oz. of coriander seeds, 1 oz. of Seville orange peel; pound these ingredients, and put them into a bottle of good French brandy; infuse for one week before using. Dose, one teaspoonful in a wineglass of water half an hour before dinner.

OUR YULE-TIDE EVERGREENS.

THOUSANDS of busy hands are, year by year, engaged in gathering and arranging the evergreen boughs and blossoms of the winter season; and much good taste is exhibited in their graceful distribution in our homes and places of worship. But a large proportion of those young people who gather and form these treasures of the woods and gardens into beautiful decorations, know nothing of their properties and uses, and the historical interest attached to them. Now, it is both pleasant and profitable to learn something more of the things we so commonly handle than their mere names, form, or colour; and thus, what little additional information I possess in reference to these Christmas greeneries shall be placed at their service.

I have adopted the old name "Yule-tide" because the custom of decorating with evergreen boughs was of ancient date in Britain; and, by a curious coincidence, the season which was made one of rejoicing and festivity on account of the sun's revolution at the "winter's solstice" by our heathen ancestors, was that period when in after years the advent of our blessed Lord was commemorated, and made the time for family reunions, giving of love-tokens, alms, and hospitality.

The name "Christmas," which succeeded "Yule-tide," was derived from the Saxon word *Masse*, a "feast," and so may be rendered "Christ-feast." *Yule* likewise means "a feast," of which term there are several very similar ones, derived from the same primitive root in the Danish and Swedish as well as Saxon and Anglo-Saxon languages. I will not enter further into the question of the meaning and origin of the quaint old name "yule," because in a former article I made some observations thereupon, but pass on to the main subject under consideration.

The shrubs and evergreen trees chiefly in use for the decorations of the above-named festival are the bay, box, cypress, holly, ivy, laurel, laurestina, mistletoe, and yew; and to supplement these, there are winter flowers, such as Christmas roses, monthly roses, crocuses, snowdrops, daisies, bachelor's buttons, dried lavender, together with ferns, furze, parsley leaves, pine cones, &c. I will confine my observations, however, to the few evergreens which are above-named, and within the reach of all.

The Bay-tree (*Laurus nobilis*) is a native of Europe, Asia, and Africa. It is a highly aromatic shrub, and is much esteemed, as most of you know, for culinary purposes, and the decorative trimming of dishes; but, already familiar with the tree and its uses, some of you may like to know something of its classical history. The curious traditions connected with it date back to very early times, long prior to the Christian era, when it was designated the "tree of Apollo." The story was that the heathen deity, Jupiter, was credited with having transformed Daphne into a bay-tree to save her from the pursuit of the former. On this account we learn that peculiar virtues were attributed to it; and, amongst others, it was believed to be a preservative against injury from lightning.

Probably on this account it was that some of the Roman emperors, including Tiberius, selected the bay to form the wreath which they wore round the head, just as they would have worn an amulet. It was also employed to make those with which poets were crowned, and the successful competitors in some of the ancient games—then as a symbol of victory. The bay was also credited with gifting those who tasted its leaves with prophetic inspirations, and thus the Pythian Priestess used to chew them, because, after a season of abstinence, they produced some degree of excitement. Besides being regarded as a symbol of victory, the withering of the tree was considered or evil omen, and a presage of death. An allusion to this superstition is to be found in one of the plays of Shakespeare, viz.—

"'Tis thought the king is dead. We'll not stay;
The bay-trees in our country are withered."
—*Richard II.*

The Box-tree (*Buxus*) follows next on my list. There was some traditional virtue or significance attached to it, evidenced in the discovery of the twigs found in some old British barrows in Essex. There are dwarf species as well as forest trees; and in the neighbourhood of Dorking there is some high ground called "Box-hill," which was at one time covered with this valuable tree, most of which was cut down at the beginning of the present century (1815), and sold for £10,000. The grain of the wood is exquisitely fine and close, and is found superior to all others for engraving and wood-carving, the manufacture of musical and mathematical instruments, and chessmen, &c., its delicate, pale yellow colour rendering any use of a dye not only superfluous, but destructive of its beauty. There are splendid forests of this tree both in north-western Russia and Persia; but in this country they now grow singly as a rule; but the dwarf kind (*Buxus sempervirens*), which is a Dutch variety, is much employed as a border for flower-beds, and in carpet-gardening. In country villages you may often observe the quaint shapes into which box-trees are cut, an idea borrowed by our ancestors from the Romans. The latter clipped them into the shapes of gigantic birds and beasts. No blossoms appear on this tree until the month of April; but its small and pointed leaves, somewhat resembling those of the myrtle, contrast well with the broad and brighter leaves of the laurel. It was a great favourite amongst our forefathers for the decoration of their houses on festal occasions, and it is one of those named by the prophet Isaiah to flourish in the land of Israel, when the waste places shall resume their ancient fruitfulness, and become "the garden of the Lord"; and, again, we are told, "He shall plant in the desert the fir-tree, the pine-tree, and the box-tree together" (Isaiah lxi. 19), and also in chap. lx. 13, "The glory of Lebanon shall come unto thee; the fir-tree, the pine-tree, and the box together; to beautify the place of my sanctuary."

The Cypress stands third in alphabetical order, and may be utilised amongst our Christmas decorations. It is true that this peculiar and beautiful tree is much connected with cemetery plantations, owing to its dark and sombre hue; but it is likewise associated with births and weddings from ancient times in the East. When a daughter was born amongst the inhabitants of the Greek archipelago, a grove of cypress trees was planted by the father as her future portion, her fortune augmenting as her years were multiplied. And thus we may trace the origin of the name by which these groves were designated—viz., "daughters' dowers." The tree is one characterised by extreme longevity. Its duration of life is computed at from five to six hundred years, some proportion reaching from eight to nine hundred. But Strabo names one example in Persia which had attained the wonderful age of 2,500 years. They rise to a height of about 120 feet, and measure from twenty-five to forty feet in circumference. One cypress, seen by De Candolle in Mexico, measured as much as 120 feet round at the base, and was considered by him to be older than Adamson's and Humboldt's famous baobab, or baobab tree, of Africa, which tree is the patriarch of living organisations. By calculating its circles the specimen which they especially name was estimated at an age of 5,700 years. The cypress of Montezuma is forty-one feet in circumference, and, grand as it is, it is quite diminutive in comparison with that in Mexico, before-named. It is said that, when the roots of this tree are for six months under water, it is observed to grow to a gigantic size.

The Holly (*Ilex aquifolium*) is a special favourite amongst our Christmas greeneries, for it is not only employed on walls, windows, and pillars, but is awarded a place of distinction on the dinner-table, to beautify with its scarlet berries the historical and characteristic "plum pudding," the "standing dish" of the season. There is considerable variety exhibited in the colour of the leaves, some trees producing them of an ivory-white, and some a beautiful and delicate shade of pink, while on others we find them variegated. The most remarkable specimens of this description which I have myself observed were some in the County Carlow. Perhaps the deep shade of the splendid avenue of ancient yew-trees with which these hollies were surrounded may have had some influence in the colouring, at least, of the ivory-white variety.

Perhaps it may be regarded as having a special claim to recognition, not alone for its bright appearance but as one of the limited number of trees indigenous to Great Britain. The name has been erroneously supposed to be a corruption of the word "holy," but it has, however, been dignified in Germany and throughout Scandinavia by the distinctive name of "Christ's Thorn," possibly because of its putting forth its berries at the nominal season of our Saviour's birth, the time-honoured custom of its use in the decoration of churches in commemoration of that event, and as a natural result of many of the ancient traditions connected with it. For instance, according to legendary history, it was the bush in which God appeared to Moses in a flame of fire; and when the latter turned aside to see why the bush was not burnt, "God called unto him out of the midst of the bush," and told him that the place whereon he stood was "holy ground." There is also another legendary history attached to the holly tree, and that is that the cross on which our Saviour was crucified was made of its wood, on which account it was known as the *Lignum Sanctæ crucis*. But not alone since the Christian era has it been held in such esteem; for in Eastern nations, as well as in the West, and dating back to early heathen times, it was valued, not merely for its beauty, but for some fancied medicinal virtues, and as possessing some characteristics connected with the supernatural. It was dedicated to Saturn by the ancient Romans, whose feast, held in his honour, was observed at the same period of the year as the Christian festival, and commemorated, among other ways, by the sending of sprigs between friends and relatives, accompanied by good wishes, just as we send pictorial cards and kindly greetings. The flowers of the holly were regarded, according to Pliny, as an antidote to poison, and a decoction produced from the leaves was supposed to convey the gift of wisdom by the Persians, for which reason they sprinkled their children with it. Our own Druids, pitying the sylvan sprites when, during the season of frost and snow, there was no shelter provided for them by the leafless branches of the oak, used to garnish the walls of private dwellings with branches of holly, in which they could find a place of refuge suited to their taste.

I now pass on to the Ivy (*Hedera helix*), which is seen in perfection at this season, the blossoms being amongst the very few that gladden the eye in winter. There are various kinds of ivy, some being of a reddish purple, resembling the colour of the Virginia creeper; others of an ivory-white, and others variegated, having irregular markings and streaks of green and white; and perhaps no other plant can show so great a variety in the formation of the leaves and in their respective dimensions. What is known as "Irish ivy" was imported from the Canary Islands as a covering for an old wall or a border for a flower-bed; and even as an evergreen substitute for flowers in the same, as well as to serve as a climber over a wire trellis on a house, or an archway over a garden walk, it is of much beauty and value. It is also suitable as hanging greenery from a garden vase or a basket suspended in a room.

But it clings with only too "cruel kindness" to a tree, and absorbs much of the nourishment which should go to it from the soil, depriving it of air, light, and sunshine, and strangling it in its deadly grasp. Never allow it to grow as a parasite on any tree, and wherever found so doing, saw the stem through at the base, that it may wither, and release its hold, and then pull up the root, for it will kill whatever it entwines. Ivy will live to a stupendous age, ranging from five to six hundred years. As a decoration for the pillars of a church it could not be surpassed in suitability and elegance; and as regards any symbolic significance it is one of the emblems of eternal life. In reference to its classical history and ancient associations, it was dedicated by the Egyptians to Osiris, and by the Greeks and Romans to Bacchus, or the god of wine, who was represented as crowned with ivy, as it was supposed by the ancients to neutralise the intoxicating influence of any excess in wine-drinking.

But this graceful evergreen had a second symbolic significance in the old-world times, derived from the tenacity with which it clings to whatever it once entwines. On this account it was presented by the heathen priests to persons newly married, to represent the "Gordian knot," by which they were bound one to the other. Hence the motto, "We flourish or fall together." Ivy was presented in the form of wreaths and garlands to the victors at the Isthmian games, afterwards superseded by pine-branch garlands. It bears round clusters of dark purple berries, which succeed the blossoms, in the depth of the winter season.

The Laurel, one of the most beautiful of our winter evergreens, was famous in classic times, and in the Christian art of the middle ages. It was introduced into Europe from the East in 1679. The name is derived from the Celtic *blaur*, pronounced "lor," and signifying "green." The plant is of the genus *Laurus nobilis*, or bay tree, of which there are many species, and all valuable, including the camphor, cinnamon, bay (before-named), and sassafras. A considerable difference in character is shown in the tree called the American laurel, a shrub of the genus *Kalmia*. Other kinds are known as the cherry laurel, or *Prunus laurocerasus*; and also the great laurel, or *Rhododendron maximum*. No plant has a finer glaze on its beautiful pointed broad leaves. Early in the year they turn to a fine yellow hue, and fall off; but they are completely replaced by the middle of April. The blossoms are small and white, growing in clusters. As to its classical associations, it was famous amongst plants. In the Pythian games the victors were rewarded by wreaths of laurels, while those in the Olympic were formed of green parsley. It was supposed to possess extraordinary virtues, endowing those who slept under its branches with poetical inspirations, and likewise to be a safeguard against the power of lightning, as it could never be struck by it. I have myself seen the group of laurels around the tomb of Virgil at Baia, near Naples, who died there on his way to Greece, and these laurels are the successors of those parent trees which were planted there by Petrarch.

The *Laurestinus*, or *Viburnum tinus*, was known to the ancients as the *Tinus*, the leaves of which, as you know, are smaller, darker, and less glazed than those of the laurel. It is not a native of this country, and was introduced here at about the time of Bacon, having been introduced into Europe from the East in 1596. It is now common everywhere; but in the south of Europe it even forms extensive hedgerows. Its berries are of a dark purple colour, and the tiny blossoms grow in large clusters, presenting a flat, even surface of a pinkish-white tint. I am not aware that the *Laurestinus* has any classical associations, and only name it as an admirable addition to the greeneries which the winter season affords.

Next in order on our list of evergreens is the Mistletoe.

This curious plant, which owes its existence and borrows its nutriment from another, and not direct from the soil, is a parasite of the oak, crab-apple, pear, locust, and lime-trees, that on the oak being the rarest kind. In Anglo-Saxon it was called *Mistelta*. A popular song, well known by many of our readers, bears the name of "The Mistletoe Bough," and the unfortunate young bride, who constitutes the heroine of a very tragic history, has been multiplied, like William Tell, and claimed by more than one distinguished family, but, I have reason to believe, was one of the Copes of Bramshill, although the catastrophe took place during a residence of her family in Italy. With reference to the mistletoe, I must remind you that the Druids selected it to do honour to their great festival in the winter solstice. They called it "All-Heal," and, according to some accounts, they used to cut it from the trees with their brazen celts, or upright hatchets, fastened to the ends of their staves; but, according to others, it was cut by the chief of the Druids with a golden sickle, kept for that purpose only. These branches were carried by them in procession, and laid upon their altars. (See Stukeley's account—"Medallic History of Carausius.") It is said that the medicinal properties of this curious and beautiful plant were universally believed in, and that wonderful cures were effected by its use in cases of epilepsy and various other disorders of a like character. In the year 1729 a treatise was published on its virtues as a medicine by Sir John Colbach; and, more especially in reference to its use in epilepsy, another appeared in 1806 by a Dr. Fraser. The genuine plant is the *Viscum album* of botany; but there is one very nearly allied to it—the *Loranthus Europæus*—which may often be found on the oak, as on the other trees named. This species is to be found near Vienna, in the garden of Schoenbrunn, but does not appear in a more westerly direction. It has been thought that this, and not the *Viscum album*, was the sacred mistletoe of the Druids. A description of birdlime is made from its fruit.

The use and veneration of the mistletoe was peculiar to the Celts and Goths, who alike introduced it into their religious rites as the sun approached the winter solstice. It forms the solitary exception amongst our evergreens in reference to the decoration of churches, and is, by common consent, altogether confined to our private homes. The poet Gay, in his "Trivia," names it amongst the other greeneries set up in our churches; but he did so through some oversight, for the plant so peculiarly connected with ancient heathen worship in this country, having been, by a mistake of a country sexton, brought into a Christian place of worship, it was expelled on account of its heathen associations, which rendered its use inappropriate.

The last evergreen respecting which my space will permit me to speak, is the Yew, or *Taxus baccata*. Emblematic as it is of death, it is also recognised as one of immortality. In olden times the wood was especially valuable as the best for the manufacture of bows and cross-bows, and those of you who are well-informed in English history may remember that with the bows of yew the battles of Cressy and Poictiers were won; the best in use for modern archery, and a variety of articles, such as arm-chairs, are likewise manufactured from it. The trunks of these venerable-looking trees resemble a number of rods bound together, looking like "fluted" pillars. I have seen an avenue of such at Fenagh, co. Carlow, which presented the appearance of a dim cathedral aisle. The yew is famous for its great longevity. One found in a bog had 545 rings, each marking an annual growth, although the diameter measured only 18 inches—100 rings to an inch. Those at Fountain's Abbey are about 1,200 years old; one at Crowhurst of 1,500; at Fortingal, another upwards of 2,000; and at Brabourne, in Kent, and at Hedson, Buckinghamshire, there are patriarchs of from 2,500 to 3,000 years of age, being the oldest specimens of still living vegetation existing. Yew trees seem to have been favourites with our forefathers. We see them not only in churchyards, but in the little gardens in front of country cottages and farmhouses, very usually clipped into grotesque forms like box-trees. They were also much employed for garden hedgerows, of which a very remarkable specimen is to be seen at Battle Abbey, in Sussex. They are also much employed in the same way in Holland.

I will not now speak of the gorse, ferns, and other evergreens that also help to deck our homes at this great season of family reunions; my notes, composed of facts and fables, are concluded; but I must raise your thoughts to higher considerations: the unfading blooms and eternal reunions, where He is Lord of the feast, whose birth, as the "Son of Man," we feebly commemorate here.

The evergreen plants, which ancient custom has connected with that wondrous event, may typify in your mind the never-fading "Tree of Life," in the paradise of God. The incomprehensible "ages of ages" are spoken of, in connection with it, as if divided by months and years; but only to convey to your minds the idea that through the long course of that blissful existence will be granted successively new delights. Nor is this all. For the sick and suffering what is the feast? to the blind, the loveliest garden? But with the ever-varying joys will be granted the power of enjoyment, for "Then shall the blind see out of obscurity; the lame man shall leap as a hart; and the tongue of the dumb shall sing," for "the leaves" of that tree are "for the healing of the nations."

S. F. A. CAULFEILD.

THE STORY OF THE EVERGREENS.

THE FROST SPIRIT.

He comes—he comes—the Frost Spirit comes
  From the frozen Labrador;
From the icy bridge or the northern seas,
  Which the white bear wanders o'er;
Where the fisherman's sail is stiff with ice,
  And the luckless forms below,
In the sunless cold of the atmosphere,
  Into marble statues grow!

He comes—he comes—the Frost Spirit comes!
  And the quiet lake shall feel
The torpid touch of his glazing breath,
  And ring to the skater's heel;
And the streams which danced on the broken rocks,
  Or sang to the leaning grass,
Shall bow again to their winter chain,
  And in mournful silence pass.

He comes—he comes—the Frost Spirit comes!
  Let us meet him as we may,
And turn with the light of the parlour fire
  His evil power away;
And gather closer the circle round,
  When that firelight dances high,
And laugh at the shriek of the baffled fiend,
  As his sounding wing goes by!

                        Whittier.

The Girl's Own Paper, 1889

THE TOUCHING TALE OF A PLUM-PUDDING.

Written and Illustrated by BEATRICE MOLYNEUX.

"WELL, my dear, if you do not make a noble appearance at the Christmas dinner to-morrow, I don't know who will," chirped a big, tempting-looking plum-pudding, walking on tiptoe round an equally toothsome ditto, the object of her admiration, who was surveying himself in a diminutive hand-glass with perfect self-satisfaction depicted on every plum in his shining countenance. "Why," she added, "it isn't safe for you to go out alone."

"My love," said the other, holding his plum-pudding head high in the air, "I should like to behold the hand daring enough to pluck so much as a currant from off my brow. Where's the boy?" he asked, brushing away at a roguish little hat. "Oh, you're there, are you!"—as a dirty pasty pudding (a milk and watery production of stale groceries) dressed in page-boy garments, and carrying a liliputian plum-pudding robed in a long white dress, and who was howling lustily, came cringing into the room.

"That child is always bellowing," said Mr. Plumpudding, wrathfully glaring at the page, who forthwith became more pasty than ever.

"It's the almonds, sir, please."

"The what!" screamed Mr. and Mrs. Plumpudding.

"The almonds," repeated the page, in an awestruck voice. "He's been an' swallowed of 'em, an' they're sticking out tremendous like, all over him."

"Oh, why does that boy exist!" cried Mr. Plumpudding, waving with tragic gesture a scented handkerchief. "Oh, why is he allowed to torment me thus!"

"It warn't me," sobbed the small page.

"Cease, wretched youth; attire thyself instantly and follow me," said his master. "Wife, what's for supper?"

"Sparrow-pie—de-licious," answered Mrs. Plumpudding, smacking her lips.

"Ahem! Wife!"

"Yes, love?"

"Don't pick."

The pasty page, who meanwhile had enveloped his pale features in a huge muffler and sun-bonnet, now stood respectfully awaiting his master's pleasure.

"Boy, where's the infant?"

The page in utter bewilderment stared into vacancy, and muttered that "It might be up the spout!"

Mrs. Plumpudding sank in a fainting condition on a chair, murmuring feebly for something "hot and strong, and quick." While Mr. Plumpudding, having boxed the page's doughy ears, which stuck in flabby despair to his plumless head, tore in frantic alarm round the room, in his efforts to obtain all utensils that contained liquid, the contents of which he poured over his swooning spouse.

This remedy having the surprising effect of bringing her to in no time, there ensued a search for the missing heir, who was shortly discovered heels up in the coal-scuttle, making a hearty meal off the coal.

"I give that child up as a bad job," cried Mr. Plumpudding; "he will be the death of somebody when he comes to table, that's certain. Boy, attend me. Adieu, wife; I would salute you, but you have a dirty face." So saying, Mr. Plumpudding strutted to the door, followed by the pasty page.

"What a magnificent night!" observed his master, proceeding to walk at a brisk pace down the brilliantly-lighted street, with the small boy trotting breathlessly behind.

"Making a hearty meal."

The outward and visible sign of the season was seen everywhere that bright Christmas Eve—in the shape of sweets and savouries of all descriptions. Big plum-puddings, little plum-puddings stepped along with jaunty airs, well knowing their own value, for were not their brown bodies filled to bursting with groceries of the clearest water and warranted not gritty? Dainty mince-pies tripped by, whispering merrily of the coming festivities, in which they would bear no small part; ruddy bottles of wine, descended from the finest bin, were to be seen walking arm in arm, laughing gaily; saucy little hazel-nuts hopped up and down on the pavement, getting in everyone's way in their excitement, and being threatened by kingly joints that they would have their cheeky heads cracked if better respect was not shown to superiors. Lordly sirloins beamed upon all through golden collars of fat, while numbers of turkeys, already stuffed and roasted, passed, talking genteelly together.

"What an august spectacle!" exclaimed Mr. Plumpudding, pausing for a moment with folded arms to watch the animated scene. "Ha!" he continued. "It requires a mind such as mine to appreciate with sufficient admiration so magnificent a sight. What have you to say to this, boy?" he asked, looking down with lofty dignity at the pasty page.

"I should say, Mister," replied that pale youth, "that if so be as the human party as were a-lookin' at this 'ere 'ad no stomick like, 'e might hobserve without a-wantin' to stick a knife and fork into 'im."

"Oh, the vulgarity of the lower class!" cried Mr. Plumpudding. "They creep and they crawl in their ignorance, but never soar to more elevated regions. Oh, you—you—you animal!" roared he, backing away from the page, who meekly asked what he had "been an' gone an' done."

But Mr. Plumpudding at that moment was unable to speak, for he had come in violent collision with a bottle of port wine that was leaning upside down against a lamp-post, and nearly sent him sprawling on his aristocratic nose. Meanwhile the bottle of port wine, having with difficulty reared himself the right end up, reeled up to Mr. Plumpudding, and waving his arms to support his balance, said, with a tipsy giggle—

"My head'sh qui' cleash, but my legs are deshidedly intoxicated." Here he sank in a confused heap upon the pavement.

"Master," said the page in a tragic whisper, "I believe he's drunk and incapable."

At this remark the bottle of port wine once more staggered to his feet, and standing with inebriated legs very wide apart, glared indignantly in Mr. Plumpudding's face, and roared forth, "Notch so tipshy as you!" Here he again fell to the ground, for the forty-ninth and last time, where he remained, swearing horribly at the world in general, and his own tipsy limbs in particular.

"What a degrading exhibition!" said Mr. Plumpudding, turning away in disgust, and motioning to the small boy to follow; but the page could not resist waiting a minute to screw his face into a hideous grimace and stare at the recumbent form of the bottle of port, at the same time emitting

"My legs are deshidedly intoxicated."

a kind of whirring noise from his mouth, which appeared to have an extremely irritating effect on that gentleman, for he bubbled and frothed, and foamed in indignation, and certainly would have burst if the cork had not given vent to his outraged feeling by popping out with a bang, and hitting in the eye a huge round of beef, who happened at that moment to be driving past on a dish. The beefy monarch rose to his feet and shrieked out, "He'd be dished if he stood that!" But as he was dished already, it would be rather undignified to descend, chastise the offender, and then dish himself again; so he took the wisest course of remaining where he was, taking a little comfort by fixing his one uninjured orb fiercely on the bottle of port, who was rapidly disappearing in a cataract of foam.

The pasty page, alarmed at the result of his game, sneaked after Mr. Plumpudding.

"Why did you not come at once, boy?" he was sternly asked.

"Because, Mister," meekly replied the page, "I could not 'elp a-giving that 'ere degrader a bit of my mind, an' I told 'im you was so noble, as you did not know what it was to fetch a drop of water to wash your own 'ands, and as 'ow you 'ad 'caps and 'caps."

"Oh," said Mr. Plumpudding, somewhat mollified, "and what did the wretched creature say to that?"

"'E didn't say nothin'," answered the pasty page—"it seemed to squench 'im."

"Well, well," returned his master, "I must endeavour to forget him. We will now wend our way homewards; it is on the point of seven. At what hour did your mistress say the dinner would be served?"

"She said as 'ow at seven o'clock *precise* the sparrer-pie 'll be took out of the hoven," replied the page.

"By jabbers, she'll pick!" exclaimed Mr. Plumpudding, in an agitated whisper, striding rapidly in the direction of his home, while the pasty youth, smiling a bilious smile, hurried after him. This speed was continued in silence until they had traversed several streets, when Mr. Plumpudding, in turning a corner, stumbled over what appeared to be a grimy heap of rags squatting on the pavement.

"Why, bless my soul!" cried Mr. Plumpudding, holding up his eyeglass. "What is this?"

"It's me," said a voice.

"Dear me, how very extraordinary!" ejaculated Mr. Plumpudding.

The heap of rags slowly rose, and disclosed a little loaf of bread, attired in an old top hat and high-lows very much the worse for wear.

"Please," whined the small loaf, "I ain't got nothing in my inside."

"Poor forlorn one," said Mr. Plumpudding, adjusting his eyeglass. "Page, my money-purse. This is sad, very sad indeed," he muttered. "Christmas-time and not even a currant in him. Here, forlorn one, take this and fill yourself instantly."

In great glee the small loaf commenced turning head over heels down the street, in the direction of the nearest grocer's, while Mr. Plumpudding and page went on their way, the former's heart expanding with warmth at having performed so magnanimous an act.

"I wonder if anybody saw me," he thought. "Boy, did you observe any pedestrians perambulating the street during my little deed of kindness?"

"No, sir; not one human bean."

"Of course not," said Mr. Plumpudding in an injured tone—"of course not. Slave," he added, stopping and listening, "hear you a strange fluttering in mid-air?"

"I do," replied the page in a frightened voice.

"Good gracious!" cried Mr. Plumpudding, as a number of sparrows alighted on the pavement and popped gravely up to him.

"*I ain't got nothing in my inside.*"

"I believe," said the foremost bird, who was dressed in deep mourning, "that I behold my enemy—the wretched creature who stole my beloved wife." Here he wept copiously in a black-edged handkerchief.

"This is very fearful!" exclaimed Mr. Plumpudding, streaming with perspiration. "Boy, stand in front."

"Oh, sir, I dursn't," whimpered the horrified page, retreating.

"See," continued the small bird, "he pales—my enemy pales. Oh, my sweet Maria Jane, to think that you should end your days in pie-crust. But I will be avenged!"

"Oh, dear," said Mr. Plumpudding, "this is getting frightful! Boy, defend your master!"

"Oh, sir, I can't, my legs are so slender," sobbed the page.

"Then there is nothing for it but flight; we must flee."

So saying, he commenced tearing down

"I believe that I behold my enemy."

the street, followed by the page holding tight to his master's coat-tails.

"Mates," called out the sparrow, "charge!"

"Loose me, loose me!" screamed Mr. Plumpudding to the page; but that pasty youth only clung tighter.

Away flew the sparrows after Mr. Plumpudding, and each as they came up to him picked out a currant.

"I shan't have a morsel left!" shrieked Mr. Plumpudding.

"Oh, oh, oh!" roared the page, as a sparrow alighted on his master's head and pecked out a huge almond.

"The pride of my life gone," wailed Mr. Plumpudding. "I will give in and die like a Briton!"

"No, no, sir!" panted the pasty youth. "Remember your hoffspring. I'm a-begging of you on," he gasped, clinging in desperation to the coat of his unfortunate master; and thus in horror-stricken silence they raced on.

The revengeful sparrow with his mates fluttered excitedly about Mr. Plumpudding, twittering loudly as they fought over the fruity contents of his cranium; while the pasty page inwardly rejoiced that his own pale pate was so utterly devoid of the like delicacies.

The roast joints of meat they encountered in that headlong flight started aside in wonder and alarm. as Mr. Plumpudding with the page tore past, surrounded by angry birds; the rich cakes and mince-pies thought their last hour had come; and the stuffed turkeys screamed hoarsely as they fluttered away in terror. I regret to say the little hazel-nuts were cracked most prematurely in the general confusion.

"I feel that fainty 'ot, Mister," whined the page, as at last they reached home and visions of nice resuscitating drinks rose before him; but Mr. Plumpudding answered never a word, but bursting open the door—which the pasty youth quickly barred and bolted—tumbled into the arms of his wondering wife.

"I shall never hold up my head again," he wept.

"It was them sparrers, Missus," said the page, who was not hurt in the least; "an' if it 'adn't been for me a-shoving of 'im on he wouldn't 'ave so much as a bit of peel left, though I just did 'ave queer feels a-doing of it."

"Oh, dear," wept Mr. Plumpudding, "to think how noble I looked when I sallied forth, and see me now!"

This was too much. Mrs. Plumpudding began to sob, the small infant also howled dismally in some remote region, and the pasty page who wanted—for the first time in his meagre life—to laugh, exploded in a dish-cover, which had the effect of extreme grief.

The sparrows, fully satisfied with their revenge, chuckled as they heard the lamentations within, and the bereaved one, leaving his mates to finish the carols of jubilation, flew away to seek another bride.

Mr. Plumpudding slowly emerged from his handkerchief, embraced his wife, and

"A sparrow pecked out a huge almond."

extending a hand to the page said—

"I bear no malice, and I hope all the readers of my direful tale will not pick the few remaining currants left me, and like the sparrows will spare my page."

A Victorian Christmas Treasury

USEFUL HINTS.

Lemon Drops.—Grate the peel of three good sized lemons, add to it half a pound of castor sugar, one tablespoonful of fine flour, and beat well into it the whites of two eggs. Butter some kitchen paper and drop the mixture from a teaspoon into it and bake in a moderate oven on a tin sheet.

Sultana Drop Cakes.—Mix one pound of dry flour with half a pound of butter; after you have rubbed it well in, add a quarter of a pound of castor sugar, half a pound of sultanas well-washed and dried, one egg and two tablespoonfuls of orange flower water, and one tablespoonful of sherry or brandy; drop on a baking sheet well floured.

Gherkin Pickle.—Cut some nice young gherkins or small cucumbers, spread them on a dish and sprinkle the ordinary cooking-salt over them, and let them lie in the salt for seven or eight days. Drain them quite free from salt and put them in a stone jar, covering them with boiling vinegar. Set the jar near the fire and cover over the gherkins plenty of nice fresh vine leaves, and leave them for an hour or so, and, if they do not become a pretty good colour, pour the vinegar back again and boil, and cover them each time with fresh vine leaves; after the second time they will become a nice spring green. Tie it up with parchment or use a good cork, and keep it in a dry place.

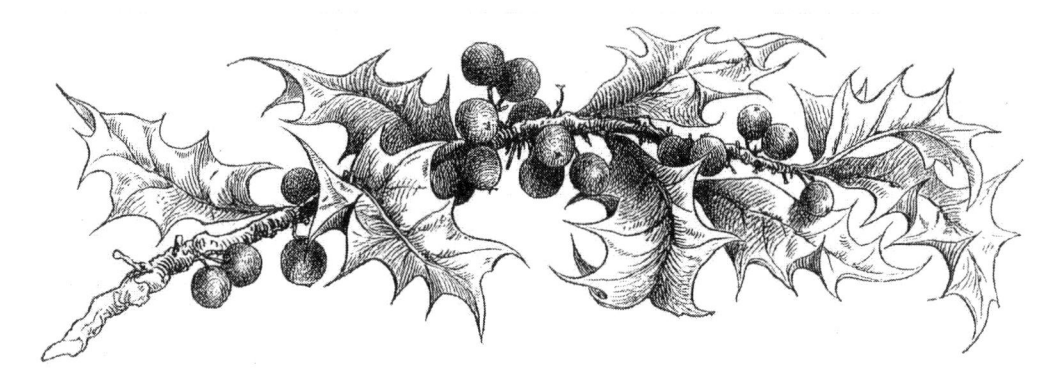

SEE, THE DAWN FROM HEAVEN IS BREAKING!

A CHRISTMAS CAROL.

Words by Thomas Moore.
Music by W. G. Cusins.

Andantino. p

See, the dawn from Heav'n is break-ing O'er our sight, And earth, from sin a-wak-ing,............ Hails......... the light! See those groups of an-gels, wing-ing

The Girl's Own Paper, 1886

From the realms a-bove, On their brows, from E-den, bring-ing Wreaths of Hope and Love! See those groups of an-gels, wing-ing From the realms a-bove— wing-ing From the realms a-bove, On their brows, from E-den, bring-ing Wreaths of Hope and Love! Hark, their hymns

A Victorian Christmas Treasury 145

146   *A Victorian Christmas Treasury*

HINTS FOR CHRISTMAS DECORATIONS

In the pleasing hope of rendering some little assistance towards making bright and joyful the Christian's great anniversary of the proclamation, "Peace on earth, good will towards men," we venture to offer a few hints for Christmas decorations.

The pleasant work of decorating in the country is comparatively easy compared to the same thing in town. There, when one's stock of materials is exhausted, a run into the garden or a stroll along the lane is all that is required to replenish it; while in the town every branch of evergreen, every trail of ivy has to be paid for, and the price is high enough to make a large purchase a very expensive matter. Therefore it behoves us, the "pale-eyed denizens of the city," to avail ourselves of any and every means of practising economy.

Pre-eminent amongst our materials is the holly. Unfortunately, it is always dear in towns, and sometimes this time-honoured friend of decorators fails altogether as far as its chief attraction—its berries—is concerned. It is quite unnecessary to pay more than a trifling sum for the berries, as imitations can be made which answer all the purposes of the real ones, and at a very small cost.

Amongst the many methods adopted the following will be found the easiest: ivy berries or dried peas dyed red (a sixpenny bottle of dye will be sufficient for a very large quantity); or putty, rolled into little balls and coloured either in the same way or in a solution of sealing-wax mixed with spirits of wine; or red wax, to be bought at an oil shop, and shaped into berries, after slightly softening before the fire. There are many different sorts of red berries to be had in the autumn, which, by soaking in strong salt and water, will keep till Christmas time, and may well pass for holly. And, lastly, easiest of all, artificial berries are sold in bunches very cheaply at most toy shops.

With all this choice at our disposal and a little judicious management a great deal can be done with a few of the commonest evergreens; a room may be made to look very pretty with only a little laurel, ivy, and holly; but any others which may be obtainable will be useful in giving a variety of effect; amongst them may be mentioned the box, arbor vitæ, bay, variegated holly, ivy, and laurestinus.

Some artificial berries are too hard to admit of stalks being added, and will only be available for gumming on to a flat surface. Where stalks are required the soft berries must be chosen, and a little fine wire inserted.

The decorator must not fail to provide herself with some of the bunches of dry moss which is sold at all florists'; also with the necessary implements—string, wire, and strong glue.

The effect of snow is easily obtained, and gives a very seasonable air to the decorations. For a flat background white wadding, bought at sixpence a yard, answers very well, but for an object standing out, such as a statuette, the fine soft wool called jeweller's cotton is required. The wool should be first tied on with thread all over the top edges and wherever snow would be likely to lodge. It must then be pulled out, and made to look as light and natural as possible, hanging down in irregular points and masses over any projecting parts. The effect of snow may be obtained on branches and leaves of evergreens with less trouble by coating the upper surface with gum, and then sprinkling thickly with flour.

Trees sparkling with hoar frost are always a lovely sight in winter, and this effect of frost or rime can easily be procured by artificial means. Drop gum upon the wool, wherever frost would naturally form, and sprinkle coarse Epsom salts over it. The surfaces of leaves and twigs may be coated in the same way, and, as an alternative for Epsom salts, frosted glass, ready crushed, is sold; but a much less expensive contrivance is to pound roughly, or crush with a garden roller, any pieces of glass, such as old bottles, which have been saved up during the summer for this purpose. Cardboard letters, for mottoes, can be crystallised in the same way, and look well on a background of leaves or coloured flannel.

Another method of crystallising, which is more useful for some purposes, is to dip the objects in a solution of alum. On one pound of alum, pour a quart of boiling water. Whilst still warm, suspend the leaves in it by a string tied round the stalks; leave them in for twenty-four hours and then hang them up till dry. Large and beautiful crystals are formed, but the effect is less like real frost than by employing the other means. If a wreath or festoon is to be thus crystallised, it must be made up first, and then immersed in the alum, as it is impossible to handle it much afterwards, without breaking off the crystals.

Everlasting flowers are very useful indeed in adding colour to our devices. If a suitable natural colour cannot be obtained, the flowers may be easily dyed; red, violet, or yellow being the most useful colours. Mixed with the green in wreaths and garlands, or sewn thickly over cardboard shapes for letters, these are very effective. Grasses dyed in the same way will also be useful, particularly the splendid heads of Pampas grass. These latter, dyed crimson, are most beautiful objects.

If one has time and patience to make a number of them, the paper rosettes, which were used so much for little picture-frames a year or two ago, are very pretty and useful, and are so durable that they will serve for years, with care. Those made of brown paper and varnished are much used in church decoration, as at a little distance they look exactly like carved oak. Large ones, made of red paper, are very handsome on devices made of yew, or dark green leaves, while small ones, in creamy white, may well pass for ivory. Their uses are almost endless, and they will quite repay one's trouble. The way to make them is too well known to need description here, but the various colours, especially red, are rarely seen, though most effective.

Letters and borderings should be first cut out in strong cardboard, and then ornamented in various ways. A novel method is to coat the letter thickly over with gum, and then sprinkle it with pieces of broken walnut shells, or to fasten them on whole in rows. A similar effect is produced by cutting up old corks, and sprinkling their fragments on a gummed surface.

The methods of making ornamental letters for mottoes or monograms are innumerable, and the choice will depend upon the position they are to occupy. If near the eye they must be carefully and neatly done. Cardboard letters, with small leaves sewn thickly all over them, look well, but it is a long task; the background should be first covered with green or red paper or cloth, to show through between the letters. Silvery letters, too, are pretty, made of tinfoil. Cut a piece of the tinfoil to something like the shape of the letter, but larger, and crumple it up in the hand; then straighten it out slightly, but so as still to preserve the crinkled appearance, and lay it lightly over the card letter, fastening it at the back. Others are covered with everlasting flowers, sewn firmly on to a foundation of cardboard; or if they are required strong enough to last for future occasions, of perforated zinc.

Very pretty letters, in imitation of coral, are made by coating the shapes with gum, as above, and sprinkling them with rice or, better still, tapioca; they will generally require two coats to give them the proper rough look. Sometimes the rice is first dyed red, which looks very pretty; for a monogram it is a good plan to have each letter a different colour, which will make them more legible than they usually are.

A word as to cutting out the letters may be useful. It is most important that they should all be the same size; this is not so much a matter of course as would appear to the uninitiated, but is easily managed. Decide first how many inches in height and width each letter is to occupy, then cut out a number of pieces of paper or cardboard of these dimensions, and all of exactly the same size, and by taking one of these for each letter they are sure to be correct. The smaller they are the simpler they should be in design, as if elaborately-formed letters are used for small mottoes they will not be legible, and their chief charm will be lost.

The border of mottoes will depend on the colour and texture of the background and letters; but it must not be so obtrusive as to detract from the effect of the sentiment it frames. A simple and pretty border is easily made of a double or treble row of holly leaves stitched or nailed on according to the material; the point of each leaf must overlap and hide the stalk of the last one. A more durable one can be made with cork or nut shells, as described for the letters.

Red is the favourite colour for the background of mottoes and scrolls; Turkey twill, cheap flannel, or glazed lining being generally employed for the purpose; but where the position is too high up for close inspection coloured paper does equally well.

For devices such as an anchor, shield, or Maltese cross, moss makes a capital foundation for further ornamentation. It must be stitched on in tufts, and afterwards arranged with the fingers till the surface looks uniformly covered. Letters of bright everlasting flowers or small red rosettes on a background of moss are very pretty. The Cape silver leaves, too, of which there are such beautiful wreaths on the Prince Imperial's tomb at Chislehurst, look charming laid on bright green moss, but, as they are rather expensive, they should be reserved for small wreaths or mottoes in a conspicuous position.

Before beginning to decorate it is well to have a plan in one's mind, more or less matured, for the general arrangement. In forming this design, be careful not to over do it, or the result will be a heavy and crowded effect, which is anything but beautiful. A little tasteful decoration is much more pleasing than an excessive amount.

Wreaths and garlands in a room should not be too thick, but a light, graceful effect must be aimed at. In making them, there should always be two persons at work together. Having cut the rope to the required length, one should hold it and bind on the twigs which the other arranges and hands to her; if there is only one worker, she has constantly to lay down the rope while she seeks out suitable pieces, which not only hinders her very much, but probably mars the symmetry of the wreath. For churches and public rooms a number of large, rough wreaths and ropes of green are usually required for adorning pillars and windows. These should be left to the last, as the *débris* from the small wreaths and more delicate devices will do for them. They should be made on stout rope, and the bunches of green tied round it with string.

If it is wished to ornament a pier glass or other article of furniture likely to be injured by the green, a thin lath of wood should be obtained to fit the top of the glass, to which all the decorations are fixed, thus preventing their contact with the gilt frame or glass. If possible some long trailing pieces of ground ivy or other creepers should be fastened on to this lath, as their reflection in the mirror is exceedingly pretty; these should be quite short in the middle, getting longer towards each side, till the outside ones should be long enough to reach to the bottom of the frame.

A lath may be arranged in the same way over doors, but in this case, of course, there must be trailing pieces at the sides only. This is a suitable place too, for a motto, as it can rest on the ledge over the door, and so avoid injuring the wall with nails.

In decorating a chandelier, only light materials should be chosen, and few of them, or their weight is likely to drag it down, besides casting an unpleasant shadow. A graceful effect may be obtained by twisting round the stem of the chandelier a very slight wreath of ivy, made on thin wire, and having a few of the leaves frosted.

If there is a large space of bare walls, wreaths can be made, light enough to be affixed with strong pins instead of nails, by stitching laurel, other large leaves, or dried fern leaves on a length of tape. The leaves should be sewn on two at a time, one pointing to the right and the other to the left, and they must slightly overlap each other where the stalks meet, or, better still, let the juncture be hidden by a good-sized red rosette.

We venture to urge the desirability of not leaving decorations up too long, but of

USEFUL HINTS

SCONES.—Prepare the flour for them thus:—To 5lbs. of flour, add 1oz. of carbonate of soda, and 1½ozs. cream of tartar. This flour, ready mixed, will keep for weeks in a dry place. For making the scones—take one pound of the prepared flour, as above, and rub in 2ozs. of butter, take sufficient milk to moisten to a stiff paste, and a little salt; roll out in rounds, and bake immediately, marking the quarters before baking, or cutting them into quarters as desired.

A PLAIN PUDDING.—Weigh ¾ lb. of any scraps of bread, crust or crumb, cut them into small pieces, and pour boiling water upon them, allowing them to become well soaked. After standing until the water be cool press it all out, and mash the bread smooth with the back of a spoon. Add a teaspoonful of powdered ginger, sweeten with moist sugar, and add ¼ lb. of cleaned and well-picked currants. Mix well, butter a pan, and lay the mixture in it. Flatten all down with a spoon, lay some pieces of butter on the top, bake in a moderately hot oven, and serve hot.

removing them before either the occasion has passed by, or the least symptom appears suggesting the perishable nature of the materials; for, in every circumstance in life, there is nothing much more objectionable than faded finery.

CHRISTMAS IN ITALY.

WE were spending a winter on the Riviera, and, after trying various hotels in town and country, had finally established ourselves in a pretty little Italian villa, *palazzino*, as the peasants called it, not many miles from Genoa.

From the terraced garden there was a wide and splendid view. On our left, as we looked seawards, was the city herself, her marble palaces and churches rising crescentwise behind the bay, which on the eastern side is bounded by the headland of Porto Fino. Facing us was the shining sweep of the Mediterranean; while to the right hand the Alpes Maritimes trended away into the far distance, their giant peaks and hollows an ever-present, ever-changing feast of colour—whether seen at early dawn, a glory of rose and gold; or at sunset, a gorgeous vision of amber and crimson, and softest, tenderest violet; or under the southern moonlight, a study in oxydised silver.

For me mountains have always had a peculiar fascination, and no landscape ever seems complete without them. I could spend, and, indeed, did spend, when in Italy, many an hour in watching their changing hues. But to-day none of our party had time for indulging in mere sentiment. Throughout the week we had been rambling among the hills and valleys in quest of mosses, ferns, and other greenery wherewith to decorate the house; for this was Christmas week, and the day after to-morrow would be Christmas Day itself.

How difficult it was, even as we worked at the familiar mottoes and rejoiced over the holly, which, after a seemingly hopeless search, we had at last found in a remote corner of the Doria woods—how difficult it was, I say, to realise the fact that this was the 23rd of December. Why, the garden was full of roses, camellias, and heliotrope; the air was as soft as upon a summer's day in England; and we were out of doors in thin woollen dresses and large, shady hats, rejoicing in the brilliant sunshine.

We had to give up our pleasant work early that afternoon, as we had engaged to help at a children's party given by a kindly English doctor in the neighbouring village. He had hired a large room at the hotel, and invited about forty children to a sumptuous tea; and, though wintering abroad for health's sake, and with doubtless many an anxious thought for wife and little ones at home, he most unselfishly catered upon this evening for the amusement of "other folks' children."

The long table was covered with dainties such as little folks love, while assiduous waiters handed round cups of delicious-looking coffee and chocolate.

Tea over, there was an adjournment to another room in which all kinds of merry romps were carried on for an hour or two, a general distribution of presents took place, a hearty cheer was raised for the kind doctor, and the young flock trooped gaily home.

Christmas Eve we spent in really hard work over our decorations. The dining-room was made festive with mottoes in pine sprays and trophies of orange-boughs laden with fruit, while the drawing-room was adorned with maidenhair fern, lycopodium moss, arbutus-berries, and the much-prized holly before mentioned. Then, about six p.m. we started to spend the evening with some charming neighbours.

The host was German, his wife English, and their two children spoke both languages with equal facility, adding thereto no mean proficiency in Italian. An Italian marquis and his younger brother, a married sister of our hostess, with her husband and little girl, a German composer, with our own quartet, made up the party. We were at once ushered into the room in which the Christmas tree had been placed; for the children, at least, were on the tiptoe of excitement as to their gifts; and thence, after due distribution thereof, we adjourned to the dining-room for high tea.

The table was a picture, with its bowls of crimson or pale-pink china roses. Each couvert had its own bouquet of heliotrope, fern, and camellia; while the profusion of handsome silver and of ancient Nuremberg glass combined still further to set off the tasteful appearance of the whole. What with the many German dishes, and the chatter of the German tongue all around me, I seemed to be transferred bodily from the shores of the Mediterranean to the dear and well-remembered Fatherland—an illusion which was not dispelled until an hour or so later on, when we found ourselves walking homewards under the brilliant, starlit sky of the south. On this particular night, too, the stars were shining with a radiancy which in England would betoken a hard frost; only that in this case the stars themselves looked so much larger, and in many instances shone with such intensity as to make themselves the centre of a distinct halo.

We met numbers of people on their way to midnight mass, either at the various shrines in the mountains or at favourite churches in Genoa, and at about eleven p.m. the bells began to ring, and went on at intervals for four hours, when they ceased for a time, to recommence at five a.m., and summon the worshippers to early mass.

I inaugurated Christmas in Italy by dressing with open windows, then joined the younger members of our party in carol-singing outside our hostess's bedroom door; after which we all descended to the dining-room—not, as it would have been, in England, to spread out icy hands and feet to the welcome blaze of a roaring fire, but to open the long French windows and to stand awhile upon the balcony watching the lizards flitting swiftly in and out among the crevices of the marble, and the green frogs jumping about the boughs of the orange-trees.

Breakfast in Italy was never a heavy meal; but to-day, in honour of the day, polenta cake and chestnut bread were added to the usual omelette and roll, to which due attention having been paid, we returned to the balcony and eagerly awaited the postman.

He brought a goodly supply of letters for each of us, and with thankful hearts we set out for morning service.

The church was full of roses—red, white, and yellow. Arbutus and fern wreathed the east window and the chancel arch; and designs of roses upon a mossy ground filled in the panels of lectern and reading desk and the wide window-sills. There was, of course, a good attendance, and all joined with spirit in the service; but our clergyman rather damped the conclusion of it by preaching a very long and exceedingly dolorous sermon, in which he harped upon "vacant chairs," absent friends," "broken circles," and "dear invalids," until he had reduced two-thirds of the congregation to tears.

Our dinner-party included a few English friends staying at the hotel, and one or two Italians, the latter being as much interested in our national customs as we were in theirs. It was certainly quaint enough to find that the Eastern Counties doggerel had its counterpart among the shepherds of Sardinia, with whom it is generally used as a cradle song.

" Lu letto meo est de battor cantones,
Et battor anghelos si bei ponem,
Duos in pes, et duos in cabitta.
Nostre Segnora a costazu m'istu.
Ea mie narat: Dormi e reposa,
No hapas paura de mala cosa."

In Upper Italy they sing—

"Dormi, dormi, O bel Bambin,
Rè divin.
Dormi, dormi, O fantolin,
Fa la nanna, O caro giglio,
Rè de Ciel."

And a gentleman who joined us later on wound up our charming evening by singing to a strange old chant the following Burgundian carol, written, as my readers will perceive, in alternate lines of French and Latin:—

" Voici la Roi des Nations,
Natus ex sacra Virgine :
Ce fils de bénédiction,
Ortus de David seminæ ;
Voici l'Etoile de Jacob,
Quam prædixerat Balaam :
Ce Dieu qui détruisit Jéricho,
In clara terra Chanaam."

The Girl's Own Paper, 1887

CHRISTMAS DAY FESTIVITIES IN ITALY.

CHRISTMAS DAY in every country of the world where the great festival is solemnised is more or less associated with feasting and a general feeling of conviviality, and although the Christmas dinner is not quite such a solemn thing in sunny Italy as in England and Germany, still the natives of this fair land are by no means behindhand in their appreciation of the various delicacies of the season. The huge sirloin of beef and the flaming plum pudding, whose memory is apt to linger in the form of indigestion, are unknown items in the *menu* of an Italian Christmas dinner, their place being taken by the goodly capon stuffed with chestnuts, and the gala dish of Italy, *panna montata* or whipped cream.

The following is a fairly typical *menu* of a Roman dinner-party on 25th December. It varies occasionally according to taste, but this is the general order of the courses. Clear soup, with *capelletti* floating in it, viz., little hat-shaped pieces of maccaroni filled with forced-meat; this is followed by the *lesso*, or meat of which the soup has been made, and which is an inevitable feature on the majority of Italian tables, and is served with a piquant sauce and vegetables. The next course is the *misto frito*, a dish of brains, liver, potatoes and various vegetables all fried that rich golden colour which seems to be only obtainable in a foreign frying-pan. Bologna sausage, a *specialité* of the season, is then partaken of, no Christmas dinner being considered complete without its somewhat garlicy presence. Now appears the capon in all its substantial glory, surrounded by sippets of fried bread and pounded anchovies, and accompanied by a fresh green salad. Then follow the sweets: ices and *panna montata*, for which I will give the recipe, judging by my own experience that it will be appreciated by my readers.

Boil and pulp about a pound or a little over of chestnuts, skin and pound them to the consistency of very fine flour, sweeten with powdered sugar and place in a glass dish. Whip and sweeten a quart or so of rich cream, the quantity depending on the size of the dish required, and heap it over the chestnuts. Serve with ice wafers. In Italy, the cream can be bought already whipped and sweetened, which is an immense saving of labour. With the dessert, the Italian substitute for plum pudding, *pan forte*, makes its appearance. This delicacy, of which a very little goes a long way, is something of the description of soft hardbake, and pounded almonds enter largely into its preparation. The schoolboy term "stickjaw," which I have heard applied to it, is a singularly appropriate one. At this season it occupies a prominent place in the confectioners' shops, which are indeed worth regarding from an artistic point of view, with their ethereally-tinted bon-bons in gaily-hued satin bags, and their variety of cakes frosted over with sugar icing in white and pink.

Very tempting also are the grocers' and provision shops, with their array of comestibles and delicacies artistically arranged, with the inevitable sausages tied up in frilled papers and adorned with coloured ribbons.

As for the jewellers' and fancy shops, etc., it would take up far more space than I am permitted were I to dilate upon their charms, and as this article is devoted more to the solemn business of feeding than to æsthetic considerations, let us return to our capons.

The great idea at Christmas-time in Italy in the present-giving line is to send off enormous cakes called *panettoni* to your absent friends and relations. These are much esteemed, though the reason of such appreciation is, and will ever remain to me, one of the unsolved enigmas of existence. They are unwieldy to pack, and they are not particularly nice, being distinctly plain in character. The principal ingredients are eggs, flour and yeast, forming a sort of very light dough, with here and there a solitary currant, separated by a painful distance from its companions. Such are the *panettoni*, and yet, every postman staggers under their weight, and aunts, and cousins, mothers-in-law, and uncles despatch them to various members of their family, receiving the self-same souvenir in return. By the way, the recipient of a gift in Italy finds it rather expensive, as one of the unwritten laws of Italian etiquette decrees that a present shall be immediately sent off to the giver, with the evident intention of shaking off the irksome load of obligation and crying quits as soon as possible.

In Naples, the Christmas-Eve dinner is almost as important as the banquet partaken of on the day itself. Being a fast, there are naturally no meat dishes, but the changes are rung on boiled, roast and fried fish, the *pièce de résistance* consisting of a dish of stewed eels, which are considered such a luxury, that many a happy-go-lucky Neapolitan cheerfully starves for a week beforehand in order to secure this delicacy for Christmas-Eve.

Many family gatherings are held about this time, dancing and the *tombola* taking the place of our Christmas trees and snapdragon. On New Year's Eve the majority of Italians invite their relations and intimate friends to spend the evening. It is amusing at these reunions to observe the formality and propriety which reigns supreme at the beginning of the proceedings, gradually melting away under the combined influences of the *tombola*, a game like a miniature lottery, and a *recherché* supper. On first arriving, the women portion of the guests range themselves on one side of the room and talk chiffons, servants and babies, while the men, after making elaborate bows, congregate together on the opposite side, somewhat after the manner of the lost and saved in Michael Angelo's "Last Judgment." A chastened solemnity lingers upon all present until the entrance of the supper, after which the social atmosphere becomes buoyant, choruses are sung, glasses are clinked, and everyone talks at once. It is harmless, innocent mirth, however, that one witnesses at these family *festas*, for these sons and daughters of the South are slow to banish the memory of their childish days, and are fortunate in possessing that capacity for the enjoyment of the moment, which is rarely seen beyond the limits of our English nurseries and schoolrooms.

New Year's Day itself is not such an important festival in Italy as it is in France. Members of families usually meet to dine together, but no presents are given, and instead of the boxes of bonbons, fans, jewellery, etc., which are exchanged between friends and relations, in Paris and New York, visiting-cards, with the owner's good wishes, are sent round to all one's acquaintances, which practice, if not so pleasing, is decidedly more economical.

VERA.

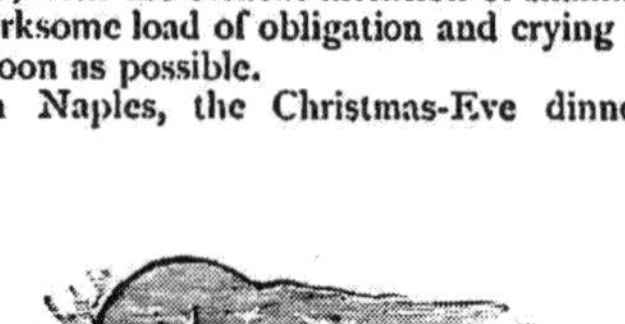

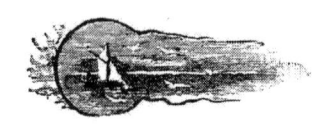

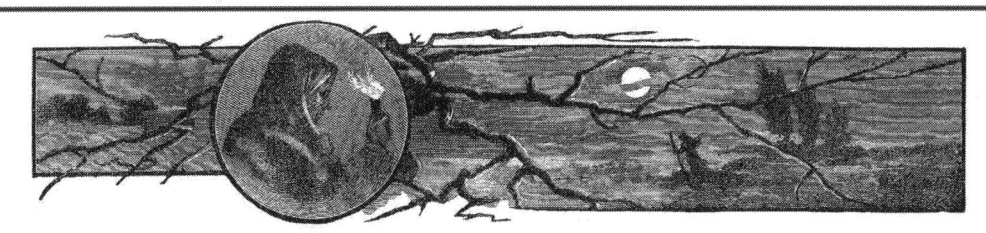

POPULAR CHRISTMAS FESTIVITIES IN NAPLES.

By the middle of December preparations for Christmas are in full swing. The streets are all animation, and one meets with hurry, jostling and noise wherever one goes. Too often also the ear is pained by the pitiful bleating of poor little lambs as they are carried to their fate. In many of the by-streets vehicles of all descriptions, paniered donkeys, half hidden by artistically arranged loads of fruit or vegetables, throng the thoroughfare, and gaily-dressed country-women, usually squatting on the ground, may be seen in picturesque groups behind their baskets of eggs, in the midst of a nondescript crowd of persons hurrying to and fro, many of them carrying the usual Christmas presents made by clients to their doctors and lawyers. These presents consist principally of lambs, kids, capons, and coffee and sugar, the weight of sugar being always double that of the coffee.

The shops too are already dressed, but the only ones worthy of notice are the fruit and cake shops and the butterman's. The first-named, besides their piles of fruit arranged in various ways and ornamented with flowers and greenery, generally display inscriptions and designs formed of dried fruit, figs, raisins, etc. The windows of the cake shops exhibit wonderful structures in *struffoli* in the shape of castles, houses and churches. These *struffoli* are one of the special Christmas sweets. They are made of a stiff paste of eggs and flour cut into small round pieces, and delicately fried in oil. When cooked they are tastefully arranged on a dish, and sprinkled over with honey and tiny coloured comfits. But most surprising of all is the butterman's display, for his window generally contains the figure of a man all complete, with hat, collar, shirt, jacket, trousers, and even boots, made of dried sausages and bacon fat and rind.

A week before Christmas, along both sides of the principal street in Naples, the Toledo or Via Roma, to give it its modern but by the Neapolitans little used name, the *bancherelli* are put up. These *bancherelli* are stalls for the sale of toys, glass and china, books, brushes, and all sorts of small articles. In the two squares, "Piazza Dante" and "Piazza della Carita," a great display of baskets and tin-ware is always to be seen. Here and there an aged peasant in his old-fashioned costume has an old sack or piece of cloth spread on the pavement before him, upon which he has set out his wares, evidently of his own manufacture ; spoons, egg-cups, whistles, and a few other trifles, all made of wood. Of course, in fine weather the scene is gay and cheerful enough, but when the season is wet and cold (and rain nearly always does set in as soon as the *bancherelli* are put up) the scene presented by the covered stalls and the unfortunate vendors, often consisting of whole families, crouching under the poor shelter or huddling together round a pan of kindled charcoal for warmth and comfort, is disconsolate in the extreme.

On the ninth day before Christmas the *Novena* begins, that is to say, a nine days devotion to the child Jesus. It consists of the recital, on those nine consecutive days, of an invitation to shepherds to join in visiting and adoring the newborn Babe, to the accompaniment of bagpipes and flageolet. Very often, however, the words are omitted, only the music being executed by the *zampognatori* or bagpipe players, such as one occasionally sees in England.

They are shepherds still wearing their ancient costumes, who come up to Naples yearly for this purpose, sometimes from great distances, and have to live all the year on the gains of these few days. The sum they carry home may amount to four or five pounds, each *Novena* being paid for at the rate of from half a franc to five francs, according to the purse and the inclination of the devotee. Besides the money, the *zampognatori* take back with them a small provision of Christmas fruits, cakes and liquor, for the reception of which they always carry a big bag and a wooden bottle.

Both in private houses and in churches the *Novena* is performed either before a picture or a little figure in wood, wax, or chalk, of the infant Jesus ; and this little figure may be alone or it may form the central point of a *presepe* (manger). These *presepi* may be described as a species of *tableaux vivants*, representing more or less fancifully and on a more or less elaborate scale, by means of a cork background and figures of persons and animals, the birth of the Holy Child, and the incidents attendant on it. These figures are known by the generic name of *pastori* (shepherds). They are either carved in wood or moulded in stucco, and many of them are of such beautiful workmanship—real works of art. The finest of all is the one in the museum of San Martino. The whole is so arranged as to represent rustic scenery, generally including some ancient ruin, and the centre of every *presepe* is, of course, the grotto or stable of Bethlehem, and the holy family with the ox and the ass. Immediately in front are generally placed some *zampognatori*, and the wise men of the east in posture of adoration. A shepherd with his dog, asleep under a thatched hut, while his sheep are grazing around, must not be left out, nor the inn with its array of eatables, maccaroni, ham (eaten raw with fresh figs), and fruit. In a well-got-up *presepe* a lake, stream, or fountain, contrived out of pieces of looking-glass, is essential, while scattered here and there are single figures or groups, all wending their way to the manger in which the Holy Babe lies. There is the woman on a donkey with her baby in her arms and her husband following, carrying their offering of eggs, poultry, etc. There is the turbaned Moor with his tray of precious coins, a tribute from his master. There is the Eastern prince on horse-back, his dress sparkling with jewels, and his retinue of servants and camels, all laden with presents for the Holy Child. Above the grotto shines the star of the East ; groups of angels hover about in the air, and so on, according as the *presepe* properties (if I may be allowed the term) permit. Few, of course, are the very extensive *presepi* got up every year, and the minor ones are gradually being replaced by the Christmas-tree, whilst in many families a combination of both is found, a diminutive *presepe* being arranged round the base of the tree.

On the evening before Christmas Eve it is usual to pay a visit to "Via Santa Brigada," one of the finest streets in the town, which, on this occasion, becomes a perfect fish-market. The scene presented there is thoroughly Neapolitan and most picturesque, with its stalls and baskets of various kinds of fish, conspicuous amongst which is the Christmas *capitone* or large eel garnished with green sea-weed, and lit up with innumerable little lamps, while the vendors, often dressed in a sort of fisherman's costume, and actively gesticulating, keep up a continual cry, sometimes in harsh and discordant tones, though more often in long and melodious cadences, resembling more the notes of some fisher's song than the cry of an ordinary salesman.

And now the great day has arrived, for in Naples the greatest festivities take place on the evening of Christmas Eve. They begin with the dinner, which, even in families used to an early dinner, is put off till after dark ; and an invitation to dinner on this day is generally understood to extend both to Christmas and to Boxing Days. The average dinner consists of maccaroni with a fish or a garlic and parsley sauce. Then come various sorts of fish, dressed in different ways, and the never-failing *capitone*, a pie of endive with capers, raisins, and anchovies intermixed, a *caponata*, or compound salad, fruit and *struffoli* with various other sweets. Dinner over, the Christmas games are played, lasting till about eleven o'clock at night, when the religious ceremonies begin. They may take place either in church or in private houses, a special permission being accorded on such occasions. The spectacle in the Cathedral is, of course, the most brilliant ; and the service on this night is peculiar in this, that, at a certain point in it, a shining star is drawn across the church, an emblem, of course, of the star of Bethlehem. In private houses the ceremony consists of sacred music, Mass being celebrated three times, after which a little figure of the infant Jesus is presented to each person to be kissed. Refreshments are then partaken of while fireworks are let off, and Bengal lights are burnt on the balconies, after which the guests are at liberty to retire.

Only a very few years back it was by no means pleasant walking through the streets on this night, for as soon as the church solemnities ended, such an explosion of squibs and great crackers commenced, that the noise was simply deafening, and numerous accidents were invariably reported in the newspapers afterwards. In the theatres there is a special performance for this evening called *The Song of the Shepherds*, being, of course, a representation of the birth of Christ, though now corrupted by the introduction of some purely Neapolitan characters. These entertainments, however, often come to a somewhat riotous end, owing probably to the late and unusually abundant dinner both of the actors and the spectators.

And here the Christmas festivities may be said to end, for on Christmas Day itself nothing particular takes place. The dinner, of course, is a holiday one, in which the capon, turkey, or goose, forms an item ; but the habit of giving Christmas presents is by no means universal in Naples, and Father Christmas is unknown to Neapolitan children.

THE DOGS' CHRISTMAS DINNER.

Illustration from a Victorian Scrap Album, ca. 1887

OUR NOVEL CHRISTMAS-TREE

CHAPTER I.

THOSE youngsters of ours were all agitating for a Christmas party. Of course, "Mother," being the weaker vessel, they attacked her first, and equally, of course, secured her as an ally. Father, being popularly supposed to be framed of sterner stuff, did not give in quite so easily. The paternal mind generally shrinks from anything that is suggestive of, metaphorically, "turning the house out of the windows," and the head of our family proved no exception to the rule.

All at once, on the 5th of January, he yielded, just when the elongated faces of the children showed that they were giving up hope; just, too, when they were within ten days or so of the end of the Christmas vacation. All our preparations must be made, our invitations sent out as quickly as possible, and our party itself must be over in eight days; so we lost no time in beginning.

In several cases when we invited children, we told elder brothers and sisters what sort of gathering it would be, and that if they would join us we should be glad to see them. But it was distinctly understood that this was to be a "children's party," to begin and end within reasonable hours—namely, to commence at five and conclude at ten o'clock.

Most of our elder young friends seemed to like the idea of it very much, and declared there was nothing they enjoyed more than a juvenile party. So the result was that our party was a decidedly mixed one as regarded ages, which commenced at eight and went up to anything you like to imagine.

"Now," said papa, when we had sent out our invitations, "how are you going to amuse the youngsters? You must have some definite plan; because if you simply bring together forty or fifty young people whom you know, but many of whom are unacquainted with each other, your gathering will be a failure."

"O yes," said one of the girls, "such parties are never pleasant. The rough ones romp about and often make things uncomfortable; and the shy, quiet, little people get into corners, enjoy nothing but the supper, and are glad when somebody comes to fetch them home."

My motherly experience corroborated this statement, and I agreed with papa that we must have a proper plan for our evening. We would write out a programme and adhere to it, but must first consider our resources, as we were resolved to have no professional aid in the way of "drawing-room magic" or "dissolving views."

"There are games, charades, music, and, papa, best of all, a Christmas-tree."

"What! when Christmas will be more than a fortnight old! What an unseasonable suggestion. Besides, you had your tree on Christmas Day, at the proper time, and I cannot pretend to give you a second edition."

"As though we wanted anything for ourselves when you have been so good already. But really, papa, a Christmas-tree is never out of season, at least until the holidays are over, for nearly all the children's parties we go to are in January or quite at the end of December. People are too busy entertaining their own families at that time to trouble about outside friends until Christmas itself is actually over."

"Well, if your mother thinks she can manage it, I am agreeable," says papa, and goes off to the City after showers of kisses, and amid a chorus of thanks from the youngsters.

So games, charades, and a Christmas-tree were to be the component parts of our evening's amusement. But all these must be nicely arranged and fitted one into another, so that all might run smoothly, pleasantly, and punctually.

"What charades have you decided upon?" I inquired, and at this question the faces of the girls fell a little. True, charades had been a very favourite amusement during the long evenings. They and some schoolfellows who lived conveniently near, had spent many a play-hour in improvising word-pictures, which were often extremely amusing to the audience—namely, papa and myself.

Our children, I am thankful to say, always like us to be associated with them, even in their games, if possible, and I have never yet known what it was to see their faces brighten at the prospect of our leaving them for an evening to their own devices. When boys and girls begin to wish for the absence of the parents it is not a good sign, either for the young folks or their elders.

When these word-pictures were going on, as soon as the first syllable was ready, a deputation would proceed to the dining-room to escort us into the play-room, where, from the "reserved seats"—a sofa—we might be entertained by the performance, and have our minds exercised in guessing the word.

A "school scene" was almost sure to occur in each charade. And how severe was the youngster who played teacher! And how woefully stupid were her pupils!

I noticed, too, that the little girls always preferred *very grown-up parts*, especially such as could only be properly represented in long dresses; and that to be attired in one of mine which had rather an extra "tail" to it gave peculiar satisfaction.

Of course my own wardrobe was regularly rummaged, and everything, from a dressing gown upwards, put into requisition. But the children really did no harm to anything, and it was part of the bargain that every article should be put back tidily into its place, even to chairs and tables, so that neither mamma nor servants might be vexed by clothing or rooms left at sixes and sevens.

However pleasant and droll these improvised charades might be, it was evident we should want to get up something with a little more care to please a number of young guests, and the girls had been searching their books of games for a suitable charade, but in vain. When I asked what was chosen, the reply was not quite a cheery one.

"There are charades enough, mamma," said Mary, "but some of them want a great many preparations, and are too much like 'plays' to please papa and you. Others have such very long, learned words in them that they are quite unsuitable for children, and though nice to read, would be very difficult to commit to memory."

"Then what do you propose in place of charades?"

"O, mamma, we must not give them up; but couldn't you write one for us?" she added this *very coaxingly*.

This suggestion was rapidly seconded and carried by the juveniles, whose elasticity of conscience in expecting one to do such a thing on such short notice, could only be surpassed by their unlimited faith in the maternal powers.

I considered a moment, and then said, "I will try what I can do," a reply which called forth clappings of hands, hugs, and a species of wild Indian dance executed around me by the juveniles then assembled, who seemed to think their difficulties were at an end.

CHAPTER II.

OUR PREPARATION.

WE first of all laid our heads together and wrote our programme, which ran as follows:—

January 13th.

5 P.M.—Tea and coffee in hall.

6.—Games in breakfast-room, music in drawing-room.

6.45.—First charade in drawing-room; to be followed by recitations, music, and singing, games in breakfast-room, after the charade is concluded, and until supper.

8.30.—Supper in dining-room.

9.30.—Christmas-tree in drawing-room.

10 to 10.30.—"Good-night."

We bought fifty little forms for writing the programmes upon, and the children did this very quickly and neatly, and put them carefully away until the evening, when they would be required.

We had asked our guests for five o'clock, but we calculated that fully an hour would be occupied in dispensing tea and coffee amongst them, and making them acquainted with each other; that some would like the merry games, and others music and quieter amusements. So these were to go on at the same time, but in different rooms, without any clashing, the youngsters passing from one to another as inclination prompted.

I want in this chapter to tell you about our Christmas-tree, and to show any young folk who may not know how to manage such a thing that it may be done easily, inexpensively, and in such a manner as to please guests of various ages, and yet without introducing any elements that the most "particular" of parents could object to.

Fortunately our Christmas-day-tree was still standing in the pot, though a great many of the leaves were off, owing to the warmth of the room in which it had stood.

It was a tall, well-shaped fir, which reached nearly to the top of the dining-room. Even in its present condition it would be very useful, as I had determined on turning a triangular slice of the drawing-room into a little winter scene; so I shook off all loose leaves, and then watered the tree with a watering-pot until it was dripping. Then, whilst it was still damp, with a large basin of flour and a dredging-box, I floured it all over.

When this was done, the tree looked very pretty, just as if it were covered with snow; and being floured whilst it was damp, the flour did not fall off again, except where it was very thick. A gentle shake took off what might have otherwise dropped on the carpets during conveyance upstairs.

(N.B.—Always be as *neat* as possible, even in arranging for games. As the little rhyme says: "let putting away be part of the play." It encourages us fathers and mothers to give our girls and boys as much pleasure as we can, when it does not cause needless work for grumbling servants.)

We wished the tree could have remained just as it looked after the night's frost; for, owing to the shower-bath it had undergone there were dear little glittering icicles from every bough, but we were obliged to have these melted off in a warmer atmosphere before it went upstairs.

Beside this *white* tree, we had two other young firs and some plants; but these were not floured, as a great number of little ornamental articles were fastened to the boughs. On the white tree were only lights—little coloured candles which can be bought in half-pound boxes, and there are now suitable candlesticks, with tiny springs which clip the boughs and fasten in a moment, keeping their places much better than the old sort did.

These will last year after year, and as we had procured several dozens before Christmas, we had no need to include them in our purchases. But we needed a number of articles, so we took a morning for shopping.

Here is our list of requisites, though, as I have told you, we had some in hand; but I must make it complete for the guidance of those who may this winter do what we did last year:—

Young fir tree or trees, according to space available for snow-scene.

At least three dozens of candlesticks and candles.

As many little articles for the tree as you have guests.

Two pieces of white cotton wadding.

This may be purchased at about four shillings the piece of a dozen yards, and we had the quantity named; but, if only a small space is available, less would do.

Four or six ounces of pounded glass, called "frost." It is the thing you often see on those Christmas Cards which glitter, as if frozen, and, though made of glass, it does not cut your fingers when you pick it up.

Beside the articles intended for presents, such things as little banners, balls of coloured glass, china dolls, and any light ornaments that can be mustered will be required, and these must be fastened to the boughs. I bought, amongst other things, twelve pretty little coloured glass kettles, filled with perfume, for half-a-crown; and these were very effective for hanging on the trees, and required no fastening with wire.

A little bunch of snowdrops—these may be either real or imitation, according to circumstances. Two remnants of tinselled gauze, one white, the other black, and each about two yards in length. One dozen of imitation silver buttons.

I had to arrange the dresses for four characters. Father Christmas, Snow, Frost, and Fog, who were to be associated with our Christmas Tree. Now, about the first there was no difficulty. For his long flowing robe we utilised a new scarlet flannel dressing-gown, with the addition of a belt, collar, cuffs, and large square pockets covered with cotton wadding.

We hired a flowing wig and beard of snowy whiteness, added a wreath of holly, artificial to spare the prickles—it cost threepence, and was rich in berries—a staff with a bough of fir tied to the top and twisted round with cotton wadding, and the costume of Father Christmas was complete.

It sounds very unpoetical; but Father Christmas's staff was a broom-stick—long, straight, and strong, which the youngsters borrowed from the kitchen, and honourably restored when done with.

Snow's dress was made of cotton wadding, and was cut out, fitted, and made in two hours. I cut a lining of coarse book muslin, the shape of a child's princess pinafore, but enlarged to fit a girl of thirteen, who was to be "Snow." On this I placed cotton wadding—the real dress material, stitched up the seams inside as slightly as possible with the sewing-machine, and put in sleeves three quarters length. Then I hemmed by hand, and very slightly, each side of the front—which was open from top to bottom—and the bottoms of the sleeves, and put a band round the throat.

On the left side the imitation silver buttons were placed—the button-holes were very small, and only cut, not worked. The bottom of the dress was not hemmed, or the seams felled, and if a stitch showed through anywhere it was only necessary to ruffle the surface of the wadding and it was covered. We did this down the back and side seams, so that the dress looked just like unbroken snow.

The white silver tinselled gauze made a glittering sash, tied at one side, and little pleatings for neck and wrists.

The cap or turban had for its foundation part of the paper in which our parcel of wadding had been wrapped. A round of paper—six thicknesses—doing duty for cardboard, and giving a better effect, formed the crown, and a strip, two inches wide, for the brim, both covered with cotton wadding. The brim was sewed, outside, to the crown—the stitches hidden, as in the dress, and joined at one side. The seam, or rather joining, was covered by a little bunch of snowdrops, fastened with an *imitation* silver brooch and tassel. Another little bunch of snowdrops was also held by a silver brooch at the throat of the dress, and a little necklet of imitation coins formed a pretty finish.

But Snow's dress was not quite complete. We wanted it to sparkle as well as to look white, so we touched it and the cap here and there very carefully with white liquid gum, and sprinkled it with the frost or powdered glass, and left it to dry.

The effect of this dress in the gas-light was most beautiful, and those not in the secret thought it was made of fine white fur. I need hardly add that shoes and stockings were white, and that a fair child should represent Snow.

All these silver ornaments may be done without, though they look pretty, and a few more snowdrops substituted. But, as silver is so much used now, there are few houses in which it is not to be found, and mammas or elder sisters will always help the young folks by lending the needful ornaments. If purchased in imitation silver, the brooches cost sixpence each, the necklet—quite a beauty—eighteen pence.

Our Frost was a boy of ten. For him we made a little blouse of black tinselled gauze—no fells or bottom hems, but put together lightly, and buttoning at the throat; leather belt and satchel liberally frosted, steel buckles, and buttons. For the head an old Scotch cap, gummed all over, and then so frosted that you could not tell what it was made of; with a rook's feather at the side, fastened by a steel clasp. For the steel clasps any very common ones will do, or anything that glitters may be substituted, such as glass, only it must suit the other articles. We happened to have good cut steel ones.

As to Fog, he only requires a long veil of any half-transparent material that will allow him to be dimly seen through it.

Frost's satchel was filled with small articles for presents, and a large carpet bag, and sundry parcels duly labelled, "Father Christmas, passenger," held the larger gifts.

All these things were ready, and put carefully aside, and as our party was to assemble on Monday, we prepared our little scene on Saturday in one corner of the drawing-room. We made a rocky background with all sorts of odds and ends, a log or two, and a small empty tea-chest, helped, I remember, our object being to make it as up and down as we could. These things we covered with cotton wadding, which also carpeted the triangular portion of the floor that was to be snowy. On this the trees were placed; the tall white one with the tapers, in the corner, the others decorated and more to the front. Then all were sprinkled with the powdered glass and we had a beautiful little snow scene around our Christmas Tree.

When papa saw our preparations and heard that Father Christmas, Frost, Snow, and Fog, were to be represented, he wanted to have a finger in the business, and said, "Cannot you find something for me to do?"

The children, of course, insisted that the sight of their finery had excited his envy,

WAITING TO BE FED.

and that he wanted to be "dressed up," which he protested was an undeserved accusation—he was merely pleased to see how nicely and simply things were managed and he wanted to be useful, if he could, and, if mother could contrive a part for him. In consequence of this it was agreed that papa and I, in our natural places as master and mistress of the house, should have a few words to say in order to make the whole affair seem more homely and real.

I can hardly tell you how or when, during that busy week, the lines were composed to suit our characters. I just had pencil and paper at hand and scribbled bits down as they came into my head. More than once papa grumbled at being waked up by the striking of a match, and the sudden lighting of gas in the night time, in order that a happy thought might not be lost or vanish in the land of dreams.

Somehow all was done in good time, and the youngsters mastered their parts, though there was only one MS. for them all to join at. On Saturday evening we had a full-dress rehearsal, and found that all went well.

I should not forget to say that the presents were labelled beforehand with the names of the guests, and that Father Christmas had a list to refer to as they were given out by Frost and Snow or by himself.

We took great care to arrange the dresses and every article required or likely to be wanted so that, when the children stole away from the supper table, the dressing might be accomplished very quickly, and the youngsters be ready to appear by the time their guests were seated in the room. Great caution was also observed in lighting the tapers, so that no spark might fall on the wadding carpet, and as the one illuminated tree was in the back-ground, there was no danger to the children from the many candles on the lower branches. (The candles should be thick enough to last more than half an hour, and some one should be deputed to take special notice of their condition, and to extinguish them at the proper time.)

An easy chair was placed near the snow-scene, and facing the audience, and a table with refreshments, which a servant was ready to supply, stood near the door. These little matters completed "our preparations."

Father Christmas was represented by a tall girl of fourteen, who wore spectacles.

Snow.—A girl of thirteen.
Frost.—A boy of ten.
Fog.—A boy of any age you like who can speak in a thick and grumpy voice. *Our* Fog was a young lady.
Host.—Papa.
Hostess.—Mamma.

These two parts could be taken equally well by a girl and boy dressed in *grown-up garments*, and looking as old as possible.

(To be Continued.)

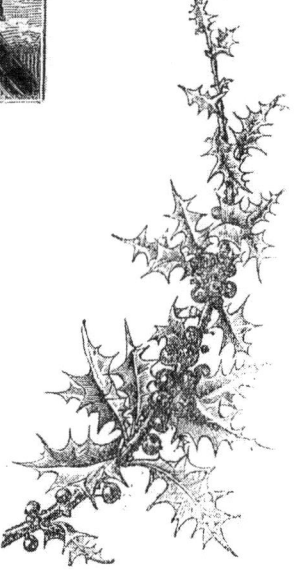

OUR NOVEL CHRISTMAS-TREE.

My wife will be delighted. See, my dear,
Here's one *you* little thought could be so
  near."

(*Hostess advances, and Host, turning again to Father Christmas*)—

"We hardly hoped to see your face again
So soon, but trust you will remain
And share our pleasures."

FATHER CHRISTMAS (*shaking hands with Hostess, and addressing her*)—
  "Shall I not intrude?
In coming thus will *you* not deem me rude?"

HOSTESS—
"My husband's friends are mine, but I, as well,
Have known *you* longer than I care to tell.
Where are the children? Kiss me, little
  Snow."

(*Kisses her, and turns to Frost*)
"Shake hands, my boy. Dear, dear, how
  they do grow!"

(*Fog, who has been hanging back, here steals into the room and hides, as well as he can, behind one of the* unlighted *trees, as if afraid of being seen by Father Christmas, who is now seated. The Hostess, assisted by servant, hands refreshments to Father Christmas, Frost, and Snow, but does not observe Fog in his hiding-place.*)

CHAPTER III.
THE TREE!

A LOUD knock is heard at the door. Host rises to open it, and holds up his hands in great astonishment at seeing Father Christmas, who enters, followed by Frost, Snow, and a servant carrying, *apparently*, heavy carpet-bag and parcels which are put down near the trees.

HOST (*shaking hands with Father Christmas*)—
"My very oldest friend! I do declare!
A thousand welcomes! take this easy chair.

HOSTESS (*addressing Father Christmas*)—
"I am *so* grieved that such an honoured guest
Was not in time to sup with all the rest."

FATHER CHRISTMAS—
"Don't name it, pray, I only can be blamed,
And, at so late an hour, I feel ashamed
To trespass on your kindness by a call."

HOSTESS—
"A hearty welcome meets you from us all;
We're only too delighted you have come,
And that you find us, with our friends, 'At
  Home.'"

FATHER CHRISTMAS (*accepting refreshments*)—
"Thanks, thanks. Some lemonade, I take no wine.
Ah! Frost, my boy, I'm sure that cake is fine.
You are a biting fellow, people say,
And I have watched you, as you bit your way
Through that large hunch, and made it disappear.
True, Winter is a hungry time of year;
But if there's famine, you will be to blame;
'Tis well that others supped before *you* came."
(*They push away their plates and refuse more.*)
HOST—
"Our friends are begging that you'll say a word
Or two to them, you are so seldom heard
Amongst us."
FATHER CHRISTMAS—
"Certainly, though I did not *expect* to speak,
But still I'll try."
(*He rises, and leaning on his staff, addresses the guests, Frost and Snow standing, one at each side of him.*)
FATHER CHRISTMAS—
"I'm Father Christmas, as no doubt you know;
I made your first acquaintance long ago.
And, since that time, have paid an annual call,
True to the minute, upon one and all;
And as I've journeyed on from place to place,
Could read a welcome upon every face.
No cold rebuff, or, 'Master's not at home,'
Has ever greeted me when I have come;
But all the children—bless each little dear!
Counted each hour a day when I drew near,
And whispered, as they helped to stone the plums,
'Shan't you be glad when dear old Christmas comes?'
(*Slowly and solemnly spoken.*)
"Still Father Christmas must one trial bear,
Sometimes he comes and finds an empty chair;
Finds that the hand lies cold that used to clasp
His own in friendship's warmest, kindest grasp."
(*Here Father Christmas's voice must tremble. He sighs, puts his hand before his face for a moment, and pauses. Then, apparently recovering himself, he continues.*)
"Away these tears, we meet now to rejoice,
And, while I paused a moment, sure a voice
Said 'Gone before, not lost; in realms above
You'll meet to part no more with those you love.'"
(*Slight pause.*)
"Perhaps you wonder I am here to-night,
Think New Year had put Christmas out of sight?
And so it had; but hearing there was fun
Going on amongst you, I just thought 'I'll run
In for an hour or two to make a call,
And in my wallet take a gift for all.'
Besides, I do declare until to-night
I've had no time to see the electric light.
If I am late blame those two chicks of mine;
One (*points alternately to Frost and Snow, who laugh and chuckle*) froze the road, the other blocked the line.
I'll introduce you to these children two.
You see them, my son Frost, my daughter Snow."
(*As their names are mentioned, Frost and Snow bend politely to the guests, whose instinctive good manners, of course, suggests the proper acknowledgment, and Father Christmas continues, shaking his fist at Frost.*)
"Frost is a sharp young rascal, full of tricks,
Famous for putting housewives in a fix;
He stops their pipes, makes their gaslights go jump,
Leaves not a drop of water in the pump.
He numbs your fingers, pinches red each nose,
And scatters chilblains upon all your toes."
(*While Father Christmas tells of his doings Frost should shrug his shoulders and laugh quietly, as if enjoying the recital of his tricks. Father Christmas then points to Snow and describes her.*)
"My daughter Snow is a much milder child;
But even she is just a little wild.
When Frost and Fog and she get out together
I cannot say that they improve the weather:
They whirl about like elves, in maddest glee,
And will not heed a single word from me.
Wind gives a howl, Snow slaps you on the back,
Fills your eye corners, covers up your track;
Bewildering Fog then leads you such a dance
You can't tell Ludgate Hill from Spain or France."
(*Father Christmas glances round, catches sight of Fog, whose half-subdued laugh has interrupted him, and exclaims in astonishment.*)
"Why Fog is here! Come out, sir; make your bow."
(*Fog gives a sulky nod, but does not come any nearer.*)
"He is so thick you scarce can see him now;
I'm glad to say he is no child of mine;
He dulls our sports, and nightly takes the shine
Out of our revels, throws his ugly cloak
On all things—like the blackest smoke;
Soils Nature's face, and I've no doubt that he
Would like to cover up our Christmas Tree.
But here, mid brightness, joy, and social glee,
(*Shakes his fist at Fog*)
We bid defiance, Master Fog, to thee.
Now I must stop; Frost has a tale to tell;
And Snow perhaps may say a word as well."
FROST—
"Our father is like fathers everywhere;
He has no word of praise for us to spare.
He shakes his head (*imitates Father Christmas*), tells all we do amiss,
And shows his sore displeasure by—a kiss!
He will say nothing for us when we're nigh,
So, to defend my character I'll try:
I froze the streams. Speak now, ye skaters, tell
If Frost in Winter does not serve you well?
Boys! I appeal to you who love to glide
O'er frozen surface—Who prepared the slide?"
(*Snow now begins, and, at the proper places, points to portions of the little winter scene to illustrate her words.*)
SNOW—
"I threw a carpet of the purest white
O'er Nature's barrenness, and, out of sight
Hid desolation—clothed the leafless trees
With beauty, till the lightest breeze
Brought glittering showers like diamonds all around.
I warmed the roots that lay beneath the ground.
Ye boys and girls, I pray you, let me know
Where would have been your snowballs but for Snow?"
FROST—
"I fairy pictures drew, with cunning hand,
And flung them, broadcast, over all the land."
(*Fog growls out from his corner, from which he will not stir.*)
FOG—
"I hid a thief that ran from the police."
FATHER CHRISTMAS (*indignantly*)—
"A pretty thing to boast of, rascal! Peace!"
FOG (*eagerly, and as if to re-establish his reputation*)—
"I hid a bridge the robber should have crossed."
FROST—
"And but for me his life would have been lost.
On the firm ice a safe retreat he found;
But for that frozen brook he'd have been drowned."
FOG—
"I made old fogies cough and moan and wheeze;
Crept up their noses, forced them all to sneeze."
SNOW—
"I did my best to save them from all harm,
Snowed up their thresholds, and so kept them warm."
FATHER CHRISTMAS—
"Enough, my children, we have work to do,
Our little gifts to share, dear friends, with you;
They are but trifles, still, a straw will show
To each observer how the wind doth blow;
And these, though straws, to each and all will prove
From Father Christmas they are marks of love."
(*Father Christmas unlocks his carpet-bag, and begins to take out the articles and lay them in order upon the table, from which the refreshments have been quietly removed. Hostess comes forward and offers to assist him in unpacking the various parcels.*)
HOSTESS—
"Shall I unpack your wallet? Sure 'twill ease
Your task a little."
FATHER CHRISTMAS—
"Madam, if you please."
(*When all are arranged, Father Christmas takes a paper in his hand, on which are written the names of the guests. In a line with each name is that of the article to be given, and a little couplet is to be said, as it is handed over, by one of the characters—Father Christmas, Frost, or Snow, as the case may be.*)
FATHER CHRISTMAS—
"Girls to my son, boys unto Snow draw near,
You'll find for each I've brought a souvenir."
(*As soon as the distribution of presents is commenced, Fog, feeling himself one too many, slips quietly away, and is seen no more in character, but gets rid of his cloak, and returns to the room in his own proper person to see the conclusion.*)
(Pretty needle-case and needles for a girl.)
FATHER CHRISTMAS—
"A stitch in time, some wise old people say,
May save your taking nine another day."
(Bottle of perfume for boy.)
SNOW—
"Who sprinkles this upon his Sunday clothes
Will scatter sweets around where'er he goes."
(Baby doll for little girl.)
FROST—
"A baby! This of children is the best,
I'll guarantee she ne'er disturbs your rest."
(A very harmless box of parlour fireworks, but with a terrible name.)
FATHER CHRISTMAS—
"A Diabolical Box! For Fog alone
This can be meant (*turns round to look for Fog, who is no longer visible*). I vow the rascal's gone!"
(*Gives it to the boy who has taken the part, and who is now amongst the guests.*)
(Woollen muffler, for a gentleman.)
SNOW—
"East wind, a spiteful, throat-attacking wight is;
With this you may defy him and—bronchitis!"
(Bottle of perfume for a girl.)
FROST—
"'Sweets to the sweet.' That saying sure is true,
I prove it when I hand this gift to you."
(Packet of ornamental note paper for young lady.)
FATHER CHRISTMAS—
"Some pretty note paper, my dear, for you;
The very thing to use for billets-doux!"
(Chinese puzzle, for a boy.)
SNOW—
"'A Chinese Mystery.' Ah well! No doubt
A clever lad like you will find it out."

(Photographic album, for girl.)
FROST—
"A photographic album here you see;
Put in your friends, but keep a place for me."
(China box, shaped like a loaf, and containing perfume, either for boy or girl.)
FATHER CHRISTMAS—
"Only a small one; but I've heard it said
That half a loaf is better than no bread."
(Gentleman's purse.)
SNOW—
"If you put money in and take none out
You'll be a millionaire in time no doubt."
(Pair of China figures, for a little girl).
FROST—
"These children never quarrel, scold, nor fight;
No need for you to put them out of sight."
(Book, for either boy or girl.)
FATHER CHRISTMAS—
"Within this little volume you will find
Something to please and to inform the mind."
(Box of bon-bons, for a child.)
SNOW—
"Don't eat too fast, for fear you should be ill,
And need to take a powder or a pill."
(A lady's purse, for Hostess.)
FROST—
"I hope you'll find in this, where'er you live,
Money to lend, and spend, and some to give."
(Game—"Go-bang" or "draughts"—for a boy.)
FATHER CHRISTMAS—
"This is a game, my lad, which you may play
In any place, at any time of day."
(Toy pistol, for a boy.)
SNOW—
"When out of use, upon your highest shelf
Deposit this, and—do not shoot yourself!"
(Pincushion, for girl.)
FROST—
"Pick up a pin where'er you see it lie,
Or you will want a pin before you die."
(Miniature hat-box, full of chocolate creams, for boy.)
FATHER CHRISTMAS—
"If you have planned a summer trip to go,
This will be ready for your best *chapeau*."
(Lace tie, for girl.)
FATHER CHRISTMAS—
"A dainty tie, my dear; you'll put it on,
But wait till Frost, and Snow, and I are gone."
(Box of toy soldiers, for a boy.)
SNOW—
"Would that all battles might begin and end
As when you fight with these, my little friend."
(Writing case, for a girl.)
FROST—
"When using this to ask your friends to tea,
Please don't forget to send a card for me."
(*Father Christmas looks about as if he has lost something, then rummaging his carpet-bag once more he discovers the missing article.*)
(A pair of worked slippers for the Host.)
FATHER CHRISTMAS—
"These for our kindly Host, before we go,
And may they ne'er enclose a gouty toe."
(*Father Christmas, Frost, and Snow then throw handfuls of crackers and bon-bons to the young guests, saying*)—
"Though Father Christmas cannot bring you flowers,
He does his best, and sweets around you showers."
(*Father Christmas alone, and fastening up his empty carpet-bag.*)
"Our pleasant task is ended—we must go;
So, children, say 'Good-bye' to Frost and Snow."
CHILDREN, HOST, and HOSTESS—
"Don't go, don't go."
FATHER CHRISTMAS—
"Alas! we must away.
Time flies, and time forbids a longer stay.
(*A general hand-shaking ensues, during which* HOST, HOSTESS, FROST, SNOW, and FATHER CHRISTMAS *all say, alternately*)
"Good night to all. Glad days; bright health, good cheer,
And may we meet again another year."
(*Father Christmas resumes his staff and goes out with his companions as the last words are uttered, and the "Christmas Tree" is over.*)

In our particular case the youngsters who took the parts were immediately recalled by a tremendous storm of applause, and a great many kind things were said about the simple entertainment provided for our young guests. We had reason to think the elder ones enjoyed it quite as much as the juveniles; and I hope, if the same scene should be enacted in other homes, it will go as cheerily and leave as pleasant a memory as it did in ours.

I have given a few couplets to suit little articles that are commonly found on Christmas trees; but these are only samples, as I cannot, even in imagination, choose your gifts for you and fit them all with rhymes.

I think, however, that any intelligent girl could compose simple rhymes to suit the articles selected, the cost of each of which should be duly calculated, so that the money allotted for this purpose may not be exceeded.

Perhaps, if you like this, I may be tempted to write out some of our "Fireside Charades."

RUTH LAMB.

GOOD AND ECONOMICAL CAKE. — ½lb. flour, ¼lb. white sifted sugar, ¼lb. butter, ¼lb. currants, ½oz. candied lemon, a little freshly grated lemon rind, two eggs, a small cup of warm milk, and a teaspoonful of baking powder. Beat milk and eggs together. Rub butter into dry flour; add sugar, currants, peel cut into chips, and grated lemon. Stir in the eggs and milk and lastly the baking powder. Bake *immediately*, in a well buttered mould in a moderate oven. The paste must not be *too* soft, or the currants will settle to the bottom of the mould. This cake may be varied in several ways, *all nice*. Leave out fruit and peel, and stir in a teaspoonful of carraway seeds—you have a light seed cake. With only chips of candied citron a nice citron cake. With no fruit or peel, and only almond flavouring, you get yet another variety.

TO MAKE GOOD BAKING POWDER.—Take 1lb. of ground rice, ¼lb. of carbonate of soda, ¼lb. of tartaric acid. Mix them thoroughly together, and the powder is ready for use. Must be kept in a covered tin or jar and in a dry place.

CRYSTALLISED FRUIT.—To every pound of fruit allow 1 lb. of loaf sugar and a quarter pint of water. For this purpose the fruit must be used before it is quite ripe, and part of the stalk must be left on. Weigh the fruit, rejecting all that is in the least degree blemished, and put it into a lined saucepan with the sugar and water, which should have been previously boiled together to a rich syrup. Boil the fruit in this for ten minutes, remove it from the fire, and drain the fruit. The next day boil up the syrup and put in the fruit again, and let it simmer for three minutes, and drain the syrup away. Continue this process for five or six days, and the last time place the fruit, when drained, on a hair sieve, and put them in an oven or warm spot to dry. Keep them in a box, with paper between each layer, in a place free from damp.

QUICKLY-MADE AND SIMPLE PUFF PASTE.—Take 1 lb. of dry flour, rub into it 8 or 10 oz. of butter and lard, in thin flakes, placing them on a plate, until nearly all the shortening has been absorbed; mix a little water with the remaining flour, until it is a stiff paste; roll this out as thin as possible, arrange the flakes of butter and lard over it evenly, fold it up and roll it out; fold and roll till the pastry is thoroughly mixed; line your tins, put in mince, or preserve, cover, place in a quick oven, and in about ten minutes they will be of a delicate brown, and will rise to the twenty flakes, which is the ambition of most cooks to attain. The whole affair will be over in half-an-hour, if the artiste has a quick light hand.

SOFT GINGERBREAD.—One cup of sugar, one cup of molasses, one half-cup of butter, one cup of sour milk, two eggs, one tablespoonful of cinnamon, one teaspoonful of cloves, one-half of a nutmeg, one tablespoonful of ginger: do not mix very stiff; two teaspoonfuls of soda (dissolved in a little hot water); put this in last; bake in a quick oven in a square tin.

QUEEN OF PUDDINGS.—One pint of fine bread crumbs, a piece of butter the size of an egg rubbed in, a teacupful of fine sifted loaf sugar, the rind of one lemon grated, yolks of four eggs, and a pint of milk. Mix these ingredients together in a pie-dish, and bake in a quick oven until well set, but be careful not to let the pudding get leathery; it will take only a short time. When cool, spread a layer of apricot or strawberry jam over the top. Whip the whites of the four eggs with a teacupful of sifted sugar and either the juice of the lemon or a *small* teaspoonful of essence of lemon into a very stiff froth and throw lightly over, making it as rocky as possible, and piling it up higher in the centre. Very slightly brown it by putting it into the oven for a few minutes or passing a salamander over it.

LEMON MINCE-MEAT.—Boil four lemons until quite tender, then pound them in a mortar or chop them up while warm; adding to them two pounds of pounded loaf sugar. Let this stand till next day, then add two pounds of suet, two pounds of currants, one pound of raisins chopped, a little brandy, one ounce of mixed spices, and port wine to taste, say half a pound of brandy and wine together.

PLAIN BREAD-AND-BUTTER PUDDING.—Cut the bread-and-butter in rather thick slices, lay them in a dish, strew a few currants over them, then another layer of bread and currants, and so on until the dish be filled. Beat two eggs, with one pint of hot milk, and add a little allspice and nutmeg, sweeten to taste, pour over the bread in dish. Be careful to let it soak for half-an-hour before baking. Bake for half-an-hour.

APPLE TANSY.—Pare some apples, cut into thin round slices, and fry in butter. Beat up half a dozen eggs in a quart of cream, and pour them upon the apples.

Hints - The Girl's Own Paper, 1880-1882

A CHRISTMAS MYSTERY IN THE 15TH CENTURY

BY THEODORE CHILD

LET us go back in imagination some six hundred years. It is Christmas night. In every town in Europe the bells are ringing merrily, and the people, noble and simple alike, are streaming toward the church or cathedral, each family or group preceded by its lantern-bearer, for street lights are few and far between. We will suppose ourselves in Chester, in Rouen, in Verona, or in Seville—the name and the place matter little, the mediæval Christmas usages from the eleventh to the sixteenth century being the same all over western Europe. Matins have just ended with the "Te Deum," and there is a movement of expectation in the church and a rustling of feet, for before the celebration of mass we are to assist at the dramatic Office of the Shepherds. Behind and above the altar is placed the manger or *crèche*, and beside it an image of Saint Mary. Five canons of the first rank, or at least their vicars, wearing the sacerdotal tunic, and over it the amice, or linen gown, represent the shepherds, and form a group in the transept in front of the entrance to the choir. The shepherds carry crooks, and have with them real sheep and dogs, and attendants with musical instruments and rustic offerings of fruit. We may imagine how picturesque and impressive this Office of the Shepherds must have been in some Lombardian church where the architecture lent itself to effective pantomime. We may figure to ourselves the shepherds, feigning

CHILDREN AS ANGELS SINGING IN THE CLERE-STORY.

some to sleep and some to watch their flocks, when suddenly in the stillness of the church, all richly decorated with tapestry, drapery, garlands of evergreens, and with a profusion of candles, a boy dressed as an angel mounts, artlessly with the aid of a ladder, the wall beside the ambon, or small pulpit, and there, after the musicians have sounded a long and piercing trumpet blast, the angel intones in Latin these verses from St. Luke: "Fear not: for, behold, I bring you good tidings of great joy, which shall be to all people. For unto you is born this day in the city of David a Saviour, which is Christ the Lord. And this shall be a sign unto you: Ye shall find the babe wrapped in swaddling clothes, lying in a manger." Thereupon a number of singing boys, posted in the galleries in the clere-story of the cathedral—*aux voûtes de l'église*, says an old Rouen manuscript—and representing the "multitude of the heavenly host," begin to sing, "Glory to God in the highest, and on earth peace, good will toward men." And from the indications of the old manuscripts, and from the judgments of competent critics, we may conclude that the music which accompanied this Office was very grand and simple, for the plain song was supplemented by special melodies, and the music of brass and of stringed instruments was employed besides that of the organ.

Meanwhile the shepherds enter by the great gate of the choir, and advance slowly toward the altar and the manger, chanting a rhymed Latin hymn, "Pax in terris." Arrived at the manger, they are met by two priests of the first rank, wearing the long white dalmatica and figuring two midwives, who ask them, "Quem quæritis in præsepe, pastores dicite?" (Say, shepherds, whom seek ye in the manger?) And the shepherds reply, "Salvatorem, Christum Dominum." (We seek the Saviour, Christ the Lord, the babe wrapped in swaddling clothes, according to the angel's words.) Thereupon the two priests figuring midwives draw a curtain and show the child Jesus to the shepherds, and bid them announce the Nativity to the people. The shepherds kneel in adoration, and salute the Virgin with a rhymed Latin hymn. After which they return processionally through the choir, singing: "Alleluia! Alleluia! sing all his coming, and say with the prophet, Unto us a child is born." These words form the Introit of the Christmas mass, which begins immediately, the shepherd-priests directing the choir—*pastores regunt chorum*, says the Rouen manuscript—and reading the lessons from the lectern.

This detail is interesting because it shows that the bond which united the above and similar dramas to the liturgy was so close that the personages of the drama remained in view, and even in action, during the course of divine service. It was, as it were, an Office of the Shepherds intercalated in the usual Office of Christmas. But some may think how impious to introduce these mummeries into the very sanctuary, and to set up the scenery of a stage play behind the high altar. Let us not judge too harshly, but having reconstituted the material aspect of a liturgical drama, let us endeavor to realize the spirit in which our mediæval ancestors witnessed such spectacles.

Nowadays we are accustomed to consider a church simply as a "house of prayer," according to the terms of the gospel. But there was a time when the church was not only a house of prayer, but also the principal and almost the only centre of intellectual and moral life. As the historian Michelet has put it, "The church was then the domicile of the people. The dwelling-house, the miserable hut, to which man returned at night was only a momentary shelter. In plain truth, there was only one house, and that was the house of God. It was not a vain word that the church possessed the right of asylum; it was then the universal asylum; social life had taken refuge there entirely." In the times of which we are speaking, about the twelfth century of our era, to employ the poetic phrase of an old chronicler, Raoul Glaber, it seemed "as if the whole world had shaken off the rags of antiquity to put on the white robe of the church," and that white robe took the splendid form of the cathedrals of Reims, Rouen, Cologne, Salisbury—edifices whose storied walls expounded with all the charm and sincerity of primitive art the history of the Fall and of the Redemption of man, the lives of the saints, the images and actions of heroes. The religion which presided over the construction of these edifices had the pretension not only of guiding man to his salvation in the world to come, but also of penetrating his whole nature in this present world, of enlightening his mind, of comforting his soul, and of charming his eyes. Hence the arts of sculpture, of painting, and of music became tributary to the church, and helped to enrich the exterior and public forms of worship, or, in other words, the liturgy. And, in order still further to fascinate and charm the worshipper, the delicate and poetic symbolism of the liturgy was materialized: the frescoes and bass-reliefs on the cathedral walls were animated, and the latent dramatic elements of the church ceremonial were developed in the form of naïve dramatic representations, such as the Shepherds, the Adoration of the Magi, the Massacre of the Innocents, the Resurrection, and other similar pieces, which were enacted in churches and monasteries, especially during the feasts of Christmas and Easter.

As the victory of Christianity became more complete, and the wealth and influence of the church more extended, the service of the church grew more pompous, and the dramatic element more considerable. At first this dramatic element takes the form of a simple trope interpolated in the liturgy, the words in Latin being borrowed from Scripture or from the canonical tradition. In the next phase of the liturgical drama short pieces of verse are intercalated in the sacred prose. Then gradually the verse gains ground, the prose diminishes in quantity, the purely liturgical elements disappear, and refrains and catch lines in the vulgar tongue are introduced. Finally the liturgical drama, in France at least, develops into a composition of very complicated and varied versification, written half in Latin and half in French or Provençal. Thus we see that in western Europe, as in ancient Greece, the stage was born of the ceremonies of public worship; and far from proscribing the theatre, religion may be said not only to have adopted it, but even to have created it; for the liturgical drama is the precursor of the Mystery play, and the Mystery is the first form of the serious national stage in England, France, Italy, Spain, and Germany.

Let us now repair in fancy to the good town of Rouen, in the year 1473, we will say. Seven citizens of high degree have met in the house of one of their number, a canon perhaps of the cathedral, or, at any rate, a great clerk, doctor in one of the universities of the kingdom, and a most religious and learned person, celebrated in the city and the whole surrounding country for his literary labors both in the Latin and in the vulgar tongue. The object of the meeting is most grave. It is nearly twenty years since the inhabitants of the city have been edified and rejoiced by the representation of a Mystery play. The souvenir of the last triumphant and magnificent spectacle of the Nativity given on the market-place is waxing feeble in the minds of the people, and it might be desirable to stir up their devotion by a new representation. The times are peaceful, the city is rich, the municipal finances are in a good state. Perhaps a humble and pathetic petition to the sheriffs might enable them to obtain not only the necessary authorization, but also a subvention of money. The chapter of the cathedral, too, and that of Saint Maclou, cannot refuse to contribute with purse and person to the success of a work so useful to religion. Several citizens have also promised to help with money and drapery; and some of the old costumes and scenery still exist. Thereupon these citizens of high degree bind themselves to pursue their project in spite of all obstacles, and the learned, eloquent, and scientific doctor agrees to furnish the text of a Mystery, say of some ten thousand verses—in short, a Mystery that can be played comfortably in two days.*

The sheriffs, after having been waited upon by the seven citizens who have taken the initiative in this pious work, deliberate, and decide to grant the authorization demanded, vote a handsome

---

* I have chosen the instance of a French Mystery in preference to an English one because the *mise en scène* was evidently more elaborate and more curious, and also because researches made during the past thirty years in French provincial archives have brought to light many new documents which enable us to conceive with considerable certitude the aspect of the mediæval theatre and the manner in which a Mystery play was mounted. For that matter the history of the Mystery plays of Coventry, Chester, York, London, Cornwall, and Cambridgeshire has been fully treated by many distinguished English writers whose works are easily accessible. In general we may say that the mediæval Mystery plays were much the same in England and in France, only in France the stage, although temporary, was fixed, whereas in England, where the performance of the Mysteries seems to have been the monopoly of trade companies and guilds, who played regularly every year, especially on Corpus Christi Day, the stage was movable, as is described in an old account of the Chester plays; that is to say, "every company had his pagiant, a high scafold with 2 rownes, a higher and a lower, upon 4 wheeles. In the lower they apparelled themselves, and in the higher rowme they played, beinge all upon the top, that all beholders might heare and see them." These pageants or scaffolds were wheeled from street to street for the better advantage of spectators, and the subject of the plays was the story of the Old and the New Testaments " composed into old English rithme."

The texts which I have consulted in the preparation of this essay are too numerous to be cited, but I must especially recognize obligations to M. Marius Sepet and M. Petit de Julleville. The latter author, in his erudite volumes on the mediæval stage, has published the essence of almost every document hitherto discovered which throws any light on the French Mysteries. But my heaviest debt is to M. Luc Olivier Merson, whose profound knowledge of the costumes, usages, life, and spirit of the epoch has enabled him to reconstitute in the illustration of this article a representation of a Mystery in its most minute details. M. Merson might justly add to his name the proud mediæval title of *docteur ès drames sacrés*.

HEROD PLAYING WITH HIS SCEPTRE.

subsidy from the municipal funds, and appoint a number of commissioners to act, so far as concerns the financial and police departments, in concert with the citizens who have conceived the scheme. The chapter of the cathedral and that of Saint Maclou have both responded warmly to the appeal of the committee, and have vied with each other in gifts of money, and loans of albs, stoles, dalmaticas, and copes; while the most learned of the canons of both chapters have promised to play the rôles of God the Father, the Saviour, the Virgin Mary, the twelve apostles, the prophets, the Sibyl, Saint John, Herod, and others of considerable importance. Meanwhile the learned doctor, whom we see at work in the initial letter of this essay, has made great progress with his piece, which is an ingenious compilation of the works of his predecessors, adorned with a few new rhymes and a few favorite quotations from Aristotle and the Venerable Bede; and all things being thus far satisfactory, the initiatory committee decide to have a public cry and *monstre* on the coming Sunday, and separate, after having appointed the learned doctor *meneur du jeu*, or master of the ceremonies, and having nominated its members "superintendents."

The *monstre* was a great event. On the appointed day we may be sure that the streets swarmed with people, and that the crowd was particularly thick in front of the town-hall, whence the cortége was to issue. At eight in the morning the gates were thrown wide open, and there rode forth on prancing horses first of all six trumpeters, who flourished valiantly upon their long brass trumpets, from which hung silken banderolles emblazoned with the arms of the town. Then followed the ordinary town trumpeter and his coadjutor the town crier, commodiously mounted on appropriate steeds, and after them a group of mounted sergeants and archers, wearing the livery both of the king and of the municipality, whose duty it was to preserve order, and to prevent the crowd from breaking in upon the goodly order of the procession. Next came, mounted on fine horses, two heralds, dressed in black velvet, with satin sleeves of gray, yellow, and blue, and their duty was to make the "cry," or proclamation. Behind them, on their mules, two by two, gravely rode those canons of the cathedral and of Saint Maclou who had accepted rôles in the play; and after them, on horses richly caparisoned, rode the learned doctor, *meneur du jeu*, author of the Mystery. In his hand he carried the roll of his precious manuscript, and his visage was radiant with the pride of authorship. At a short distance he was followed by his two lieutenants, and by the superintendents, clad in black velvet doublets and crimson coats, and mounted on horses richly harnessed. The cortége was closed by a number of notable citizens and people of the town, all well mounted, according to their estate and capacity. At each crossing the procession halted, and two of the superintendents rode up to the ordinary town trumpeter and his coadjutor the town crier; the six trumpeters thereupon sounded three times, and after the usual exhortations in the name of the king and the mayor, the proclamation was delivered in pompous and detestable verse, after which a simpler and more intelligible announcement was made in vulgar prose, to the effect that a Mystery was to be represented, and that those who wished to act in the said Mystery were to come on such and such a day to the church of Saint Maclou, where, in the hall of the chapter, they would find commissioners deputed to hear the voices of all candidates. God save the king!

The parts were distributed without further difficulty than attended the selection of those candidates whose voices were strongest and whose pronunciation was clearest, for as the performance was to take place in the open air, it was necessary that the actors should have far-reaching voices in order to make themselves heard by the thousands of spectators who were naturally expected.

As for the actors, we have seen that the leading rôles were undertaken by the clergy, and the rest were accepted by members even of the richer bourgeoisie, but especially by members of the minor bourgeoisie and of the artisan class, which latter supplied the actors for the secondary and mute rôles. All the feminine parts were of course filled by men, according to the usage, and great care was shown by the superintendent in picking out youths with soft voices. It is curious to note that young men often obtained astonishing success in such rôles.

All the documents having been duly signed, and the two or three hundred actors necessary for the performance of the learned doctor's Mystery having been enrolled, the rehearsals began in the hall and in the cloisters obligingly lent by those excellent canons of Saint Maclou; and at the same time the costumes, scenery, and accessories were made, or, where possible, the old accessories were furbished up and the old costumes repaired.

It was decided that the representation should begin on December 24th, and that eight days before there should be made a second *monstre* by all the actors in full costume, in order to warn the public. And so the last touches were given to the accessories by the scene-painters, the costumes were tried on, the old palm-trees were freshened up, labels were posted to mark the sites of Bethlehem and Nazareth, and Herod, while amusing himself with his new sceptre, was obliged to endure the counsels of that tiresome though learned doctor, who thought only of his text, and cared little about the splendor of Herod's costume. Poor Herod!

However, on the appointed day the trumpeter and the crier rode through the streets, and summoned all who had parts to play in the Mystery to assemble at the hour of noon in the cloister of Saint Maclou, each one in the costume of his rôle. After which "cry" the players met at the said place, where they were set in order, one after the other, all clad, accoutred, armed, appointed, and mounted so very well that better were impossible. And so great and triumphant was the procession that when God and His angels, who closed the cortége, issued from the cloister, Satan and his devils, who headed the parade, had already reached the cathedral Close, which is no small distance away. And so the cortége traversed the town in all directions, amidst the acclamations of the crowd, which gazed with astonishment on the fine trappings and splendid costumes; for, in despite of historic and dramatic truth, even those who played the parts of beggars and valets in the Mystery were dressed sumptuously and magnificently. Considerations of local color and of archæological exactitude were then unknown, both in scenery and in costume, and in this grand parade we must figure to ourselves that God was dressed in the paraphernalia of a pope, and the Magi in the richest costumes that the wardrobes of the churches and the armories of the town could offer; while

CASPAR, ONE OF THE MAGI, WITH HIS SON, A PAGE.

the shepherds of Bethlehem wore doublets and slashed sleeves of the most approved fifteenth century cut.

In our illustration (page 164) will be seen one of those three kings of the East—Melchior, Caspar, and Balthazar—who came to see the infant Jesus and to offer Him gifts. This is Caspar, impersonated by a wealthy merchant prince of Rouen, who is attended by his son dressed as a page. Caspar is clad in armor, over which he wears a magnificent dalmatica lent by the chapter of the cathedral; around his waist is tied a rich Oriental scarf, which, together with the scimitar, is spoil brought home by some crusader; although his armor and spurs denote a horseman, he carries, for decorative purposes, the round buckler or *rondache* of the foot-soldier; around his neck are chains and jewels, the gala ornaments of his wife; over his hat is placed a spiked crown and a turban laced with strings of pearls; in one hand he carries a golden censer borrowed from the treasury of Saint Maclou, and with the other he grasps a fantastical sceptre, whose Gothic design is intermingled with souvenirs of imperial Rome. His little son, who stands in front of the family greyhound, and holds on his fist a hooded hawk, and on his left shoulder his mother's pet monkey, is worthy of our attention as being the very pink and mirror of fifteenth century fashion. The only fantastical detail in his costume is the turban, studded with big stones, which is wound round his felt hat, with a view to giving him an Eastern air. The rest of his dress—his velvet coat, his fur-trimmed mantle of stout silk brocaded with pomegranates, his hose, and his one long boot of doeskin—all this is the height of *chic*.

The shepherd whose image is here depicted, like King Caspar, has been decked out in superfine clothing, high-life shoes, soft doeskin hose, a dalmatica of rich brocaded silk, a fur-lined cape, a wallet trimmed with fur, and a felt cap starred with a big jewel; while on his fingers he wears rings in profusion—all of them doubtless lent by the treasury of the cathedral. His crook is adorned with streamers of ribbon and a branch of holly, and the Druidical mistletoe has been honored with a place on the bagpipes. But who is that little maiden so quaintly dressed, who is arraying a patient ewe with garlands of Christmas roses? This is Madelon, the little shepherdess, whose history has been prettily told by a modern French poet, Émile Blémont. Madelon came with the shepherds to adore the infant Jesus, but being poor, she had no present to offer, and so she stood back behind the shepherds and the Magi and wept and prayed. And the angel Gabriel came down from heaven and said to Madelon, "Little shepherdess, why do you weep and why do you pray?" And Madelon answered, with quavering voice: "Alas! I have no present to offer to the infant Jesus. If I could only give Him some roses. He has not a single flower. But it is freezing, and spring is far away. Good angel, woe is me!"

And Gabriel took Madelon by the hand and led her out; and when they were outside a golden light seemed to float around them. Then Gabriel struck the frozen earth with his rod, and behold the ground was covered with fresh flowers, of which Madelon gathered a posy and gave to the infant Jesus. In memory of this miraculous origin of the Christmas rose, Madelon is decking her ewe with fresh garlands, and she herself is tricked out with brocades and jewelled kirtles, and her headdress is composed of a tall peaked *hennin*, the very height of the fashion, and of a starched muslin veil, which happily shelters her lovers from the too vehement ardor of her beauteous eyes. How artlessly and sincerely these good shepherds must have played their parts, and how quaint must have been the effect when they approached the manger, Primus Pastor playing the pipes, while Secundus and Tertius Pastor sang, as in one of the Coventry pageants:

" Doune from heaven, from heaven so hie,
    Of angels there came a great companie.
    With mirthe and joy and great solemnitye
    They sange, terly, terlow;
    So mereli the sheppards ther pipes can blow!"

As for little Madelon, she would doubtless join her voice to those of the women who sang a lullaby-lament in this strain:

" Lully, lulla, thow littel tine child;
    By, by, lully, lullay, thow littell tyne child;
        By, by, lully, lullay.
    O sisters too! how may we do
        For to preserve this day
    This pore yongling, for whom we do singe
        By, by, lully, lullay.

" Herod, the King, in his raging,
        Chargèd he hath this day
    His men of might, in his owne sight,
        All yonge children to slay.

ILLUMINATIONS IN THE STREETS.

"That wo is me, pore child for the!
 And ever morne and day,
For thi parting nether say nor singe,
 By, by, lully, lullay."

The day after the final parade the scaffolds were taken possession of by the actors and the stage-managers, and by the citizens who had undertaken to fit out the stage with hangings and furniture. The mayor caused to be published such police measures as he judged necessary in the circumstances; notably, he prohibited the exercise of all mechanic trades during the two days of the play, and ordered that all shops should be closed, except those of the sellers of food and drink, who were requested to set up temporary counters on the market-place for the convenience of the spectators, both during and after the representation. And in order to enable people to go to see the Mystery without fear for their property, the mayor announced that during the hours of the representation of the Mystery the gates of the city would be closed, armed patrols of

SCENE IN THE MYSTERY PLAY—THE ARRIVAL AT BETHLEHEM.

archers would parade the streets to watch over the empty houses and catch the thieves, and two watchers would be posted on the tower of the belfry. The crier also published the desire of the mayor and of the sheriffs that on the eve and during the three days of the representation citizens would hang lanterns on their houses in sign of rejoicing, and also in order to light up the streets for the greater convenience of the multitude of visitors who were expected from the neighboring towns and villages. Finally the bishop caused to be announced in all the churches of the diocese that the hours of divine service would be changed during the two days of the representation, in order that the faithful might be deprived neither of their accustomed prayers nor of the edifying spectacle of this Mystery of the "Incarnacion et Nativité de nostre saulveur et redempteur Jesuchrist."

At last, we will suppose, the great day has come; it is between seven and eight in the morning, and there is an immense crowd in the New Market-place when the seventy-eight leading actors, and the hundred and fifty figurants—angels and devils—preceded by the learned doctor, and accompanied by the music of trumpets, clarions, drums, organs, harps, and other instruments, make their appearance in procession, and take up their position on the stage.

But first of all, in order that we may better comprehend and follow the performance of this famous Mystery, let us examine the construction of the theatre, and the sitting and other accommodation provided for the spectators. The New Market-place formed a vast quadrilateral, from the sides of which radiated the quaint and narrow streets of old Rouen. Along the northern side were erected the *establies*, or stage, or "skafhold," as it is called in English Mysteries; and along the southern side, facing the stage, stand other scaffolds, or "pentes," forming an amphitheatre, and surmounted by a row of private boxes. On these pentes were the reserved seats, and in the centre was a richly decorated box, emblazoned with the arms of the town, and adorned with a canopy of gold and purple, beneath which sat the mayor, the sheriffs, the bishop, and the deans and the canons of the chapters of the cathedral and of St. Maclou. The common people, who were not rich enough to pay for reserved seats, swarmed in the intermediate space between the tribunes and the fence which enclosed the northern side of the market-place reserved for the stage and the actors; and in order that the public might sit down at ease, all this intermediate space was strewn with straw. Finally, every window in the market-place and in the neighboring streets, every gable, and every cozy vantage-point near a warm chimney, was of course occupied, and from this crowd of spectators, which numbered some sixteen thousand people, there rose a terrible clamor and murmuring, and only those who were near the stage could hear the supplication of the learned doctor, shouting in his prologue:

"Silete! Silete! Silentum habeatis,
Et per Dei Filium pacem faciatis."

The stage may be figured as an immense floor, sloping slightly, like a modern stage, and about one hundred feet square, thus presenting a superficies of ten thousand square feet. This space comprises two distinct parts—the "mansions," "lieux," "sieges," or "loges," and the stage proper, or *parloir*, or, in other words, the open space in front of the "mansions." These "mansions" figured the edifices or towns where the action successively took place, for in a Mystery play all the scenery was set when the public arrived, and remained, together with the actors, simultaneously and uninterruptedly visible until the end of the performance. Nowadays, when we play a piece in five or six acts, the scenery is changed five or six times, but successively. In a Mystery the different scenes or places, however numerous, were set and disposed in advance all together and at the same time. The stage was, so to speak, the materialization of those mediæval frescoes, pictures, and bass-reliefs where we see represented in the different planes of the same expanse the different phases of the life of a man, or the different incidents of some event, which, though happening successively, are grouped in such a manner that the spectator embraces them all at a glance. The stage on which the Mysteries were performed was arranged in a similar manner; the scenery was permanent and the action mobile. Twenty times in a single day's performance the action changed place, and passed successively to the different localities where it was supposed to happen. The problem of having so many scenes set simultaneously on a single stage gave rise to the hypothesis that the stage of the Mystery plays was several stories high, and that it resembled a tall house from which the front had been removed. The absurdity of this hypothesis has been demonstrated recently by M. Paulin Paris, and from the ingenious conjectures of this *savant*, and from the examination of documents—not only written documents, but especially tapestries, pictures, miniatures, sculptures in ivory, and even iron-work—we can now explain the general construction of the mediæval stage with considerable certitude.

We may imagine that the "mansions" were disposed as follows: in the centre Paradise, and then, beginning at the west end of the stage, Nazareth, with the house of the parents of Our Lady and the oratory where the Virgin says her prayers. By the side of Nazareth, separated by a distance of a few feet only, was Bethlehem, and the inn, bearing the name and sign of the Fleur-de-Lis, where Joseph will come to beg hospitality for Our Lady, and doff his cap respectfully to the surly innkeeper, who will appear at the window, lantern in hand, to indicate that the time is supposed to be night. In our illustration M. Merson has depicted this episode of the play with charming naïveté, and shown us also the ubiquitous doctor standing with his manuscript unrolled, ready to prompt the various actors. The doctor might or might not be visible to the public; he would in all probability be masked by the next "mansion," which represented the stable and the manger, near which were placed an ox and an ass, ingeniously contrived with mechanism to allow them to kneel before the infant Jesus at the given moment. Next to the stable were "mansions" representing the receipt of customs, the field where the shepherds guard their flocks and make believe to play upon pipes. Then followed Jerusalem with the Temple, Herod's palace, the golden gate, the houses of Simeon, Joseph of Arimathea, Nicodemus, Zacchæus, etc.; and beyond was Rome, the Temple of Apollo, where a pagan bishop was seen adoring idols, the home of the Sibyl, the lodging of the princes of the synagogue, the chamber of the Roman emperor and his throne, and finally the Capitol. Next came Hell, in the guise of an immense mouth opening and closing with a curtain as need required, and the limbo of the fathers in the form of a square tower with iron gratings. In all, the scenery of this Mystery comprised some thirty different places, disseminated over four towns, namely, Nazareth, Jerusalem, Bethlehem, and Rome.

Now it must not be supposed that the stage town was a large structure. A wall and a gate and a few gables sufficed to indicate Nazareth; the Temple was figured by a pavilion surrounded by a balustrade, and containing the altar and the ark of the covenant, in the shape of a reliquary lent by the chapter of the cathedral; Herod's palace was likewise a pavilion, such as we see in primitive German and Flemish pictures, raised a few steps from the ground, and showing through large open windows, upon a dais, the throne where Herod sat crowned and sceptred. Beside Herod was his son Antipater, and at his feet were his guards, clad in armor, helmeted, and bristling with long lances and formidable swords; the oratory of the Virgin was provided with stoles and cushions, and before it, as before most of the "mansions," were hung curtains, and only when the action required would these curtains be drawn, and the "mansions" "sodeynly unclose," as the English texts say. All the mansions were very fair to see, gayly painted, richly furnished, and draped by the munificence and diligence of notable citizens, and in front of them, running the whole length of the stage, was a good free space or promenade, which is called the *parloir*.

Of Paradise and of Hell we must speak more at length, for a fine Paradise was the triumph of the fifteenth-century stage carpenter, and the Paradise of this present Mystery was very finely disposed in a grand pavilion two stories high and dominating the whole stage; the upper floor was open to the sky, and in the middle was a golden throne surrounded by golden rays, in which God sat, an attentive and

CANNON FIRING BEHIND THE SCENES.

INSIDE THE MOUTH OF HELL.

permanent spectator of the play. At his feet were Peace and Mercy on the right, and Justice and Truth on the left, each figure allegorically arrayed. And God, who was impersonated by the tallest of the canons of Saint Maclou, was dressed like a pope; on his head was a tiara, in his right hand he held a sceptre, and in his left the globe surmounted by the cross, symbol of the universe. Around and behind the throne were arranged semicircularly in tiers, one above the other, nine orders of angels, clad in albs and stoles,* and with wings attached to their shoulders; and behind the angels, and concealed by them from the public, were the organ and the musicians and singers, for these angelic choirs were naturally charged with the musical parts of the performance. But as most of the angels were chosen for their beautiful faces from amongst the youths and boys of the town, it happened that few of them had musical talent, and that was why the real players of instruments and singers were hidden behind the scenes, while the beautiful angels were only to make believe (*font manière de jouer*).

As for Hell, it was figured by a square battlemented tower, the entrance to which was in the shape of a hideous and grimacing dragon's head, provided internally with braziers and chimneys, so that fire and smoke might be vomited from the mouth, nostrils, eyes, and ears. The inside of Hell was partly visible through lateral gratings, and the devils were constantly making a terrible noise with drums, trumpets, cannons, barrels full of stones, and other noisy engines. The French Hell mouth was most hideous, and corresponded exactly with the Hell mouth of the English Mysteries, as described in Sackville's Induction to the *Mirrour for Magistrates*:

"An hideous hole all vaste, withouten shape,
  Of endlesse depth, orewhelm'd with ragged stone,
With ougly mouth, and griesly iawes doth gape,
  And to our sight confounds itself in one."

This time the Hell mouth was most terrible, and our learned doctor had suggested many details, which the painter had most excellently carried out. The costumes of Lucifer and of his attendant devils had also been particularly attended to. Some were clad in skins of wolves, calves, and rams; some had sheep's heads, and others the heads of oxen skilfully imitated by an ingenious artificer; while round their waists they wore belts hung with grelots and bells, and some carried black rods full of squibs, and others smoky firebrands; and both big devils and little devils were very active and nimble, and

---

* Itm payd for waschyng yᵉ angells albs, ijd. Itm pd for mendynge yᵉ angells surplices & wasshyng, iijd.—*Coventry Leet-Book.*

THE THUNDER BARREL—BEHIND THE SCENES.

many were said to be excellent tumblers and leapers, so that the interludes of *diableries* were expected impatiently by the public.*

Indeed there is no exaggeration in saying that for the grosser majority of the spectators the tricks and antics of Satan and his attendants formed the chief attraction of a Mystery, and for the actors themselves the noise and fun that went on inside Hell mouth behind the scenes appear to have been singularly fascinating. What joy for the boys to blow up the charcoal fires for burning the pitch and brimstone, and to hold baskets of fire in the eye holes of the Hell head! With what glee the devils bounded through the clouds of smoke that rolled forth from Hell mouth! Even Lucifer himself, and Saint Peter, must come to see the firing of the wooden cannons bound round with iron rings, and so absorbed are they in this interesting spectacle that they pay no heed to the voice of the scientific doctor, who is calling to them to hurry on to the stage to play their parts. As for the thunder barrel, even the white angels come down from Paradise to hear the stones rattle inside it; and for some reason or other the grown-up actors find the noisy vicinity of the thunder machine a convenient place for taking a drink and a bite.

Yet a word or two concerning the management of the stage. Dominating the whole was Paradise; on the level of the stage proper, and distributed over it, were the "mansions"; at one end was Hell mouth and the pit of Hell, which rested on the pavement of the market-place, while the level of the stage was about eight feet above the ground. Below the stage thus formed a vast room, where was installed the machinery for the traps, counterpoises, and other strange engines and "secrets," as they were called; and behind the stage also were windlasses and counterpoises, for the stage carpenters of Rouen were very skilful, and not only did they make mechanical kneeling oxen and asses, but very curious *voleries*, or *voulleryes*, for ascensions or flying visits of angels; wheels *secrètement faictes dessus un pivot à vis*, for raising souls into Paradise; and many sorts of traps, called by metonymy "apparitions," and used for sudden appearances or disappearances, for the substitutions of persons, and for passing up the manikins to be tortured or beheading, as we often read in old account-books, *Item un faux corps pour la decollation*. As a rule, the actors remained in view and *en scène*, even when their rôles were interrupted or finished, the principal characters abiding in their "mansions," and the secondary characters grouped on each side of the stage in convenient places, and standing "pour honorer le jeu," according to the directions of the learned doctor. Only those actors disappeared through the traps

---

* In the expenses of the English Mysteries in the old Leet-Books, Hell mouth invariably figures. Thus in the Coventry books for the Drapers' Pageant of Doomsday we read: "1537. Itm paide for payntyng and makyng new hell hede, xijd. 1538. Itm payd for mendyng new hell hede, vjd. 1565. p'd to Jhon Huyt for payntyng of hell mowthe, xvjd. 1567. p'd for makyng hell mouth and cloth for hyt, iiijs. Itm payd for kepyng of fyer at hell mothe, iiijd."

AN ENTR'ACTE FOR DINNER, SHOWING THE STAGE.

whose presence would too directly interfere with the dramatic illusion. Finally we have a few *écriteaux*, or placards, bearing the name of Jerusalem, Nazareth, or Bethlehem, in order to indicate the principal "mansions," and to explain the general geography of the stage.

But the *protocolle* or *acteur*, that is to say, the author or arranger of the text, our friend the learned doctor, steps forward to speak his prologue. He bows and gesticulates, but amidst the roar of the crowd his voice is not heard, and a good half-hour passes before the doctor becomes intelligible and honey-mouthed.

> "Doulces gens, un peu de silence
> Doulces gens, un peu escoutez
> Pésiblement, sans noise faire."

Thus he begins a long sermon in verse, full of quotations from the Bible, Virgil, Saint Thomas, Boethius, Hippocrates, and Aristotle of course; and in this discourse he explains the scenes that are about to be represented, draws the useful moral from them, sketches a plan of the drama, exhorts the people to virtue and piety, and after devoutly reciting an Ave Maria, he turns to the actor who holds the rôle of Balaam, and signifies to him to begin the play. Balaam, mounted on his ass, advances and prophesies in verse, and after him David, Isaiah, Jeremiah, Ezekiel, and Daniel — the testimony of the prophets of Christ having remained the traditional beginning of the Mysteries of the Nativity. After having finished his prophecy, each prophet is seized by the devils, carried off, and respectfully precipitated into the Limbo of the Patriarchs. Finally comes the Sibyl, who steps upon the stage, and prophesies the coming of the Son of Man and the last judgment, *teste David cum Sibylla*. Next comes a scene in Limbo, where Adam laments his fate, and a scene in Heaven, where the four virtues, Truth, Justice, Mercy, and Peace, dispute with such vivacity over the lot of man that Peace at last cries to them to be calm, for it is not becoming to see such noise and storming amongst virtues. However, the redemption of mankind through the death of the Son of God is decided upon. Thereupon a solemn chorus of angels celebrates the approaching salvation of man, the choruses singing a verse, the air of which the players of instruments repeated after them, and many complicated and beautiful variations being executed by the tenor, the counter-tenor, and by duos, trios, and quartettes, alternating with the choruses and the instruments, which are the violin, the trumpet, the harp, the rebec, and the organ. After this beautiful harmony the learned doctor, *meneur du jeu*, coming forward as protocolle, announces the half-hour *entr'acte* for dinner, begging that all will remain in their places, and eat and drink heartily while the minstrels play.

After dinner the learned doctor delivered only a very short versified sermon, and the Mystery continued with the Annunciation and the Visitation, which, with the musical and other interludes, ended the first day's programme.

The second day of the Mystery begins with the order of Augustus to number the inhabitants of his empire, which causes Joseph to quit Nazareth and go to Bethlehem. At this point Ludin, the "fol pasteur," comes upon the stage, and Anathot, the "pasteur niays," who performs all sorts of antic tricks and pleasant inventions, and speaks many grotesque histories and farces, to amuse the public. Then, together with the other shepherds, they sing rustic songs. Next we see Mary and Joseph enter the stable, and Joseph expresses his sorrow to think that Mary will have to give birth to the Saviour in such a miserable spot. But the Virgin resignedly replies, "It pleases God that it be so" (*Il plait à Dieu qu'ainsi se face*). "Alas!" continues Joseph, "where are those grand castles, those fine towers with battlements, so pleasantly built? And the Son of God is here so poorly lodged." And Mary replies, "*Il plait à Dieu qu'ainsi se face.*" Then Joseph resumes, "Where are those halls so finely painted with diverse colors and paved with tiles, and so pleasant that it is a consolation to behold them?" And Mary: "*Il plait à Dieu qu'ainsi se face.*" And to each regret of Joseph, who enumerates the delights of chambers hung with gold-embroidered tapestry, and of beds richly decked with rare furs, Mary replies, with sweet resignation, "*Il plait à Dieu qu'ainsi se face.*"

Meanwhile Jesus is born; the angels salute him with songs; his mother adores him; the idols fall down in the pagan temples, and Hell mouth opens to display the rage of the demons. Lucifer asks Asmodeus news of the false gods, and the fury of the devils is manifested by fire and brimstone, and a horrible din of cannons, culverines, and diabolical engines. And after that the angels come into the stable and adore Christ; the shepherds and the Magi follow with their gifts and homage, and the Mystery ends at Rome with the sacrifice that Augustus, by order of the Sibyl, offers to an image of the Virgin. Whereupon the doctor delivers an edifying final sermon, and the chorus sings the *Te Deum*.

The representation having been thus happily concluded, we find that the performers descended from their scaffolds, and, accompanied by the mayor and sheriffs and other notabilities, went on horseback in solemn procession to the church of Saint Maclou, where a "Salut," followed by the *Te Deum*, was sung to thank God for the success of this triumphant Mystery of the "Incarnation and Nativity," the souvenir of which remained long graven in the memory of the inhabitants.

PASTOR PRIMUS AND MADELON.

DECEMBER.

I AM come! the Winter hoar,
Latest of the seasons four;
Wrapped around with thickest furs to keep me from
    the cold.
Many pleasant songs I sing,
Many joys with me I bring;
Happy, cheerful times, are they when I my revels
    hold.

Hear ye not the chiming bells,
And full many a sound, which tells
Pleasure is a-foot without, and gaiety within?
I have evergreens to wear,
And rich bounteous gifts I bear.
For all comers that may seek my countenance to
    win.

Robin Redbreast waits on me;
And though leafless is the tree,
There are berries crystalline, and of a crimson hue.
I have stores of garnered wealth,
I have gladness, I have health,
I can please, and entertain, and give instruction,
    too.

H. G. A.

Chatterbox, 1873

CHRISTMAS SWEET DISHES.

Now that the festive season is once more approaching, and with it the gathering together of scattered families, the anxious housekeeper begins to worry about providing for the numerous tea and supper-parties which are a part of the festivities, and so now I will try and give directions how to make some new and suitable dainties in the way of cakes (the joy of the children home for the holidays), and also of some sweets for the supper-table.

I will begin by giving directions how to make two things which we always have here in Scotland at Christmas, namely, "Christmas Currant Bun," and "Shortbread."

For the *Currant Bun* you have two lots of ingredients, one for the crust and the other for the inside. For the crust, you require a breakfastcupful and a half of flour, quarter of a pound of butter, half a teaspoonful of baking-powder, and enough water to make a paste. For the cake, take one pound of fine flour, half a pound of sugar, two pounds of raisins, two pounds of currants, quarter of a pound of orange peel, quarter of a pound of almonds, half an ounce of ground ginger, half an ounce of ground cinnamon, half an ounce of Jamaica pepper, half a teaspoonful of black pepper, one teaspoonful of carbonate of soda, one teaspoonful of cream of tartar, and one breakfastcupful of sweet milk. Stone the raisins, have the currants well cleaned, the orange peel finely cut, and the almonds blanched, and left whole or halved, as desired. Take the first lot of ingredients, flour, butter, etc.; rub the butter into the flour, add the baking-powder, and enough cold water to make a nice firm paste. Roll out to a thin sheet. Take a square tin, not too large, grease it well inside, and line it neatly with the paste, leaving enough for a cover, and be sure and join it neatly. Cut the cover the size of the tin, and lay it aside while you mix the cake.

Put the fruit, sugar, and all the dry ingredients into a large bowl or basin and mix them well together, so that the spices may get well incorporated; then add the milk, good measure, and with the hand well mix it in till all is thoroughly moistened; this must be carefully done or else you will find the mixture quite dry at the bottom of the basin. The mixture will be a stiffish dough. Now put it carefully into the paste-lined tin, and with your fingers, previously wet in milk, smooth it on the top to make it level, then put on the paste cover, moisten the edges to join them, pinch them all round, brush over the top with egg, prick all over with a fork, and bake for three and a half hours in a good oven. Put a thick paper over the top to prevent its burning while it is baking.

Shortbread.—This is a Scotch delicacy that is a universal favourite with our friends "over the Border," and is well worth the patient kneading it requires. When once the art is acquired it does not seem nearly such hard work. Put on the baking-board three and a half ounces of sifted sugar and three quarters of a pound of butter; work in the sugar to the butter, then knead in gradually a pound and three quarters of fine flour into which has been sifted one teaspoonful of Borwick's baking-powder. When all the flour has been kneaded in it will be rather a dry paste. Take about an eighth of the paste, and with the palm of the hand knead it out slowly into a round cake about a quarter of an inch thick, pinch round the edges, and bake on paper in a moderate oven to a pale brown. When done take them out, and while hot strew over them thickly sifted sugar. I have given one eighth of the paste as the quantity for each cake, because it will be found easier at first to make them smaller, as the dough is so difficult to keep from crumbling; but six cakes is really the number that should be made with the quantity of flour, etc. Whatever you do, don't make the shortbread thick—it is not nearly so nice to look at nor to taste.

If kept in a tin box it will keep a long time, and only requires to be toasted in the oven for a few minutes, and when cool will be as crisp as though newly made.

The following cake is usually a favourite one to make amongst the supply at this time, and the one thing to be careful about is the baking, as owing to the syrup in it it is very easily scorched. Be sure and bake it with a stout paper over the top of it. *Spice Cake* requires three quarters of a pound of flour of rice, quarter of a pound of ground rice, half a pound of flour, three quarters of a pound of fine flour, one pound of castor sugar, a pound and a half of golden syrup, nine eggs, one ounce of ground ginger, one ounce of ground cinnamon, and one nutmeg grated. Beat in a basin the eggs and sugar till light and white, then add the butter previously beaten to a cream, and beat all together for a little while, then add the flour with two teaspoonfuls of baking-powder mixed in, then the ground rice, flour of rice, spices, and syrup; beat all well together, then pour into a buttered and paper-lined tin and bake till dry in the centre when tested with a knife run into it.

Peel Cake.—One pound of sugar, a good three quarters of a pound of butter, a pound and a half of flour, twelve eggs, a pound and a half of orange, lemon, and citron peel mixed, two teaspoonfuls of baking-powder. Beat sugar and butter for half an hour together, then put in the peel finely shred, then the eggs and flour alternately, till all is in, beating all the time. Bake in paper-lined and well-buttered tin.

Dundee Cake.—Five ounces of butter, six ounces of sifted sugar, five ounces of flour, three eggs, two tablespoonfuls of milk, quarter of a pound of sultana raisins, quarter of a pound of blanched whole almonds, and two ounces of peel. Beat sugar and butter to a cream, add one egg and a spoonful of the flour, beat well; add another egg and more flour, beat again; then third egg and flour, then the remainder of the flour and milk, and beat well. Put in the fruit and half of the almonds, mix and pour

Christmas-time.

into a well-buttered tin; sprinkle the rest of the almonds cut in halves on the top, and bake in good oven for three quarters of an hour.

For *Dessert Cakes*, whisk till light and white half a pound of castor sugar and six eggs; add six ounces of ground almonds, grated rind of half a lemon, and lastly, sift in half a pound of fine flour. Place in small well-buttered tins and bake in a good oven.

Croquettes.—Mix a pound and a half of fine sugar, three quarters of a pound of ground almonds, and three quarters of a pound of fine flour. Make to a stiff paste with eggs, roll out thin, and bake. Or else, take one pound of fine sugar and the same quantity of ground almonds, make to a stiff paste with the beaten yolks of three eggs, make into small shapes, lay them on paper sprinkled with sugar, and bake in a cool oven to a nice pale brown.

New Year's Cakes.—A pound and a quarter of sugar, one pound of butter, half a pint of cold water, three eggs, three pounds of fine flour, one teaspoonful of carbonate of soda dissolved in a very little hot water, four tablespoonfuls of carraway seeds sprinkled in the flour. Rub the butter or chop it up into the flour, dissolve the sugar in the water, mix all well with the beaten eggs, cut into small square or round cakes, and bake in a quick oven. This is a large quantity.

Rose Biscottines.—One pound of fine flour, eight ounces of sifted sugar, eight ounces of butter, half an ounce of baking-powder, one wineglassful of rose-water, and two eggs. Sift the baking-powder into the flour, rub in butter and sugar, make a hole in the centre, and into it put the eggs and rose-water; stir together and make into a stiff, firm paste, roll out to one eighth of an inch thick, and then cut out into small rounds or fancy shapes. Lay on buttered baking-tins, and bake in a warm oven.

And now that I have, I think, given you enough variety in cakes to choose from, I shall pass on to the sweet dishes suitable for supper at small musical or evening parties. Some of the above small cakes are suitable for the supper-table to serve when tea and coffee are provided.

Everyone likes *Meringues*, so be sure and have a heaped dish of them; they are not troublesome nor expensive to make. Whisk on a large plate the whites of six eggs to as stiff a froth as possible, then put them into a basin, and with a wooden spoon stir in as quickly as possible twelve ounces of castor sugar. Have ready strips of paper laid on boards, put the mixture out in spoonfuls as nearly egg-shaped as possible; do not let them touch each other; sprinkle some sugar over each, and bake in a moderate oven to a very pale brown. Take them out, turn them over on their backs on fresh paper, and with a teaspoon take a spoonful of the soft mixture out from the middle, taking care not to break them; return to oven to harden, then take them out, and when cold they will be quite crisp. Fill with whipped cream sweetened with sugar and flavoured with vanilla essence. The secret of success in the making is to get them quickly into the oven after the sugar is stirred in, otherwise it melts, and they lose their shape before they are set by the baking. If the eggs are large a little more than the twelve ounces of sugar may be used.

Fig Compôte.—One dozen figs cut up put on in a pan with a sixpenny packet of gelatine, two ounces of sugar, and enough water to cover all. Simmer for two hours. Pour into a mould previously wet with cold water, and when set turn out and serve with whipped cream round it. Prunes can be done in the same way, using half a pound of prunes to the packet of gelatine. Stone the fruit; and half a glass of port wine added after they are cooked and before putting into the mould is a great improvement.

French Oranges.—Cut four oranges in halves, take out the pulp carefully and nick out the edges of the rind and leave to soak in water. Squeeze the juice of the pulp through a sieve and add water to make up two breakfastcupfuls. Put it in a pan with one ounce of gelatine, quarter of a pound of sugar, white and shell of one egg, juice and rind of small lemon; whisk over the fire till it boils, let it settle a minute, then strain through a jelly bag. Fill the rinds with the jelly, and when set whip up one teacupful of thick cream with a little sugar and a few drops of vanilla essence, and pile over the jelly roughly.

Orange Cream.—One ounce of isinglass, six large oranges, one lemon, sugar, water, and half a pint of cream. Rub sugar on rind of orange, put in a pan with the strained juice, the isinglass, and enough water to make up a pint and a half. Boil for ten minutes, strain, and when cold beat up with it the half pint of thick cream. Pour into a wet mould, and when set turn out.

Pineapple Jelly.—Take one tin of preserved pineapple, cut the fruit in small pieces, and put it in a pan with its own juice with sugar to taste, a spoonful of lemon juice and one ounce of gelatine, and a good half pint of water. Simmer about one hour, and strain through a jelly bag into a wet mould.

Russian Pudding.—One quart of claret, one ounce of isinglass, three quarters of a pound of loaf sugar, juice of a lemon, one breakfastcupful of damson jam, and one glass of brandy. Soak the isinglass in the claret, brandy, and sugar, then add the jam, and stir over the fire. Let it boil for five minutes, and then strain into a wet casserole mould. When set, turn out and serve with whipped cream in the centre.

Pudding à la Métropole.—Cut a round or oval shilling sponge cake in slices, spread each with lemon preserve, and pile upon each other in a glass dish. Pour over two tablespoonfuls of sherry wine, and glaze with the following mixture: Two good tablespoonfuls of apricot jam, three of water, and one of sugar. Boil till the jam is quite dissolved, put through a strainer, and add a quarter of an ounce of dissolved gelatine. When half cool pour over the cake, and let it stand till set. Ornament round the edge and top with dried cherries and strips of angelica, and round it place spoonfuls of whipped cream.

Apricot Cream.—One dozen and a half of tinned apricots; stew with a little of the syrup and an ounce of sugar till a soft pulp, and rub through a strainer. Boil a pint and a half of milk with three tablespoonfuls of sugar. Let it cool, then add the yolks of eight eggs well beaten. Put into a jug set in a pan of water, and stir till mixture thickens; add an ounce and a half of isinglass which has been boiled in a little water, and when the cream is cold add the apricots and mix well. Pour into a mould, and put in a cool place till set.

Greengage Compôte.—Take a round sponge cake, and cut a slice off the top about an inch thick; then cut out the centre of the cake, leaving the sides quite an inch thick. Fill the hole with stewed greengages (or any kind of fruit), and place the slice on again as a lid; pour over the syrup, and leave an hour to soak. Make a thick custard; pour it over the cake, and ornament with split blanched almonds and angelica. The centre of the cake can be used as cake, or else to make a small Trifle or Tipsy Cake.

Orange Fool.—The juice of four large sweet oranges, three eggs well beaten, one pint of good cream, a scraped nutmeg, cinnamon, and sugar to taste. Set it on the fire till it is as thick as lemon preserve, and do not let it boil. Pour into a glass dish or custard glasses, and serve when cold.

Lemon Snow.—Dissolve three quarters of an ounce of isinglass in one pint of boiling water, add half a pound of loaf sugar, and the rind of two lemons cut very thin. Boil ten minutes, strain, and while hot add the strained juice of the two lemons. When nearly cold, whisk till it looks like snow. Pour into a wet mould and turn out the next day.

Those creams, etc., with gelatine can be made the day before they are wanted, which, besides being a saving of labour, ensures their being quite set before they are turned out; indeed, if kept as they ought to be, in a cool place, they will keep for two days. Of course where whipped cream is used to put round, it must not be done till the day it is used. The meringue cases keep for several days if kept dry, and can be filled as required.

All the foregoing "sweets" are also suitable for dinners, as hot puddings are not so much used now, except for more informal dinner-parties.

I hope amongst the recipes I have given my readers may be able to find something new; and I know all are good, and quite worth a trial

"CONSTANCE."

REMINISCENCES OF CHRISTMAS

By AN ANGLO CANADIAN.

IN one of the numerous suburbs of London, where so many tasteful and pretty villas abound, I was once the guest in a small household during the Christmas week; and pleasant indeed were the days I passed, sometimes running up to town to select some little offering for one of my friends, or working at the finishing stitches of some fine piece of fancy work, to add to the numerous gifts. My friend had a large party gathered under her small roof, and for each of them some trifle was made or bought; also each of the servants was to be a recipient of a gift, for in English homes none are forgotten, from the least to the greatest, at that glad season; and I looked in amazement as parcel after parcel arrived, and wondered how and where they were all to be distributed; and I was more puzzled than ever when my friend said: "Now I must get the greengrocer to give me a nice clean hamper and cord."

Well, we went to church on the Christmas morning, and heard a delightful sermon preached by the vicar; he dwelt long and lovingly on Christ's own childhood, and ended up by saying Christmas was the children's day, and that all should join in trying to make the day happy to them, that they might therefore be brought to love Christ the more. I grieved over the fact that there were no children in our party, and wondered how my friend would feel at the constant mention of the little ones, not knowing that she was deeply interested in a young fatherless and motherless lad, and had long promised him, if he did well at school, that at some future time she would give him a watch, and she had already invited him to join in our evening's festivity. I might have known her loving nature would not be content till she found some young person to brighten us up, and upon whom she could shower her loving kindness; and after our dinner, which was an excellent one, had been partaken of, and one and all had drunk to the health of our absent friends, we returned to the drawing-room, and there found the little lad smilingly awaiting us.

Having quietly sipped our coffee, and enjoyed a little music, we were suddenly aroused by one of those loud and solemn single knocks that come so unawares to strangers unused to London ways, and directly a maid entered, and said: "If you please, ma'am, there is a carrier at the door with a hamper for you," and my friend smilingly asked her guests, as it was Christmas time, might she bring it in and open it there? and one replied, "Indeed, yes; it is a pleasant surprise for you to get a Christmas hamper so late; and you had better open it at once, for no doubt it is fruit or game from the country." But I had my doubts. I thought it looked strongly like *the hamper* with its green cord that I had noted a few days since. My friend said nothing, but asked the servant to bring her a knife, and, throwing off the lid, displayed innumerable white and brown parcels; and even then few understood that each in the room had a treasure packed away somewhere in the depths of the basket till our friend began to distribute them.

One gentleman got the most lovely knitted silk socks, tied down in a charming little toy hamper so closely with blue ribbons that he never thought of looking into it to see what lay beneath, till some elderly lady said, "Untie the ribbons," and as he did so there lay the pretty soft silk socks; the colour rose into his face as he glanced with a pleased look across to a kindly-looking young lady who sat with her unopened gift in her hand. Her parcel was so tiny that surely nothing but some valuable gem could be inside it; and so it was, for I caught just one glimpse of it, and it shone like gold, and she looked happy.

Our little school-boy, who had stood near the hamper all this time, and handed each parcel as the name was read out, was in a great state of excitement. I had watched his fine open countenance, and his soft grey eyes open with expectancy, as package after package passed through his hands and none came for him. He eyed every little parcel more earnestly than the last, and presently his name was called. But alas! it was a large, bulky package—no precious watch for him this Christmas. But all the same, boy-like, he had soon torn off the wrappings. But behold! inside was another paper, and that was addressed to his friend; and when she had thrown that aside, there was another, this time with my name upon it; and so it changed hands many times, but at last came back to its first owner, and throwing down the last brown paper, a good sized wooden box was displayed, and the lad's face fell more and more as he pulled out wool and paper and paper and wool, till at the very bottom was found a wee case, and opening it, with a cry of joy he held up high above his head the long-wished-for watch! There was a sound of kisses and smothered laughter, and my poor friend was being hugged till she had to cry for mercy.

The servants, who had been told to remain in the room, and had stood together at the door, had each received a gift most suitable, besides all of them getting a sealed envelope, which, from the shape and apparent weight of it, I concluded contained at least five shillings: and one of the maids whispered to me as she passed: "Oh, ma'am, is not the mistress most kind?" And I most heartily agreed with her, for was I not so laden with all sorts of gifts that when at last our gay evening was over I could scarcely climb the stairs to my comfortable bedroom? but when once there stood long looking into the glowing coals, and chanting quietly to myself an old poem that I had once learned as a child of "The Merry Homes of England." And I do not know where my stupid thoughts might have led me if one of my pretty gifts had not fallen from my arms, and in my efforts to save it from the fire recalled my wandering thoughts to the present; and I was not long in getting into my nice warm bed, when I was soon sent fast asleep by the jangling of the Christmas chimes.

Another Christmas, and the sun had just set in one of our small Canadian villages, leaving a trail of beautiful colours behind it on the usual grey-tinted sky of evening, and the one village street was just being lighted with its oil lamps, which burnt most dimly, and were at best few and far between. But though the lights were dim the hearts were light, for it was Christmas Eve. In the little wooden church, by the dim light of a few lanterns and an odd lamp, a number of young people were sticking here and there, in holes bored in the different seats, small branches of the mountain ash, with their scarlet berries, and two or three of the most venturesome spirits had gone so far as to put a few bits in the corners of the sombre old pulpit. But much decoration was deemed unseemly, and not allowed in those primitive times. In the vestry beyond were assembled the doctor's young son, a stalwart young butcher, and a short, bald-headed old man, who on ordinary days mended the villagers' boots and shoes, but who at this time was bringing forth the most doleful groans from a big bass viol in his efforts to keep time with the above-named young gentlemen, who were practising their respective parts in the Psalms and hymn tunes on a flute and violin. These, with a few young girls' voices, comprised the choir; but to-night the young maidens were too busy to join them, and only peeped in as they passed to and fro bearing their little branches to their destination.

In the little frame cottages the mothers were more or less busy preparing the good things for the week, for these kindly people laid in such a store of cakes and pies as would astonish ordinary mortals nowadays. There was the great stone oven to be heated for the dozen of pumpkin pies, and how recklessly the golden cream had been stirred in none but the good mother knew, for had she not a fine brindled cow of her own? and the pies must be extra good this Christmas time, when all the children would be coming home. Then the turkey was well stuffed with savory herbs that she had picked and dried out of her own nice garden, the apple-cream placed in the big glass dish, and the pudding tied ready for the pot. I was watching our good housewife as she went back and forth in her spotless kitchen, when suddenly I heard the light flying steps of children, and two young creatures, a boy of about five years of age and a little girl of seven, came in so covered with snow that but for their rosy cheeks and chattering tongues I should have taken them for two snow images. They had been out with their sled, as they called it; and had tumbled from it so often in their sliding down hill that all their garments had a firm coating of the glistening snow. As each laid aside comforter, cap, and hood, I saw that the boy had curly brown hair, but the girl's wavy locks were as fair as her face almost, and you could see that she had a sensitive, clinging nature, and I could not help wondering what her future might be. Well, they sat themselves down by the great kitchen fire, where a pot hung on a long crook, or crane, full of boiling lard, waiting for the few remaining crullers to be dropped in it. A great platter of the crisp brown doughnuts was already on the table, which the children eyed so lovingly that their mother gave them each one, and, telling them to go to bed, said—

"For you know, dears, that Christkindchen never comes to fill the stockings of the good little children till they are all asleep."

Then you should have seen the awe that stole into the little girl's face as she turned her fluffy head, and looking up into the broad chimney, said—

"Christkindchen! Christkindchen! we have been good; please put something nice into our stockings, but be very careful of the fire when you come down, or it will burn you."

And Christkindchen heard her and came carefully down, for in the morning both children's stockings were full. But you little people nowadays, who have so many toys, gay picture books, and French sweets, and no end of valuable gifts besides, will laugh when I tell you what trifles gave those little ones of that household long ago so much pleasure. First, in the toes of the little stockings were a few sticks of candy, twisted tightly in paper, a package of blanched almonds, and raisins, and a dolly made of the doughnuts, with allspice eyes, cloves for ears and nose, and a raisin for the mouth; this was prized the most, and carried about all day; and I saw tears shed when one was broken, though comfort was found afterwards in a degree by the eating of it.

One more Christmas and I have done. This time I was in old London again, and it seemed busier and more full than ever—big folk, little folk, fat folk, thin folk, all seeming to vie with each other as to which could hurry over the ground the fastest. There seemed only one place in all that vast city where anyone stood still or where quiet reigned, and that was opposite the Marylebone Soup Kitchen, where groups of emaciated men, a few bedraggled and wan-looking women, and poor little ragged, shivering children, sat upon the curbstone, or leaned against the side of the building or a lamp post, waiting till some belated passer-by would of their plenty give them a penny to get a basin of soup. I had already given away a number of tickets to the man in charge of the place, but it being Christmas Eve, my heart was very pitiful toward the poor hungry creatures, though I had been told that the men were mostly drunkards, who only came there when they had no pence for the publichouse. But as I passed along on the pavement I saw a poor little boy crouching near the wall to shield himself from the wind, looking so cold and miserable, and crying bitterly; so I spoke to him and gave him a sixpence. But just as I gave it to him, a tall, gaunt man reached his hand over us and snatched it from him, and before I had quite realised what had happened he had rushed at a mad pace quite out of sight. I was with a friend who knew more of the ways of London than I did, so she urged me to come away at once, or she said we would be mobbed, as by this time several grimy hands were extended in supplication to me; so I walked rather quickly, to be out of their way. But I earnestly hoped some braver spirit than mine would see that the poor little child got his supper before the night fairly closed in. It was very hard to think that in the very midst of such great wealth and comfort hundreds of poor creatures lay cold and unfed when such a trifle would help them.

Christmas morning came, but no bright sun awakened me, for it was foggy; and as we walked to church the fog seemed to penetrate even through our warm cloaks. We found the gas burning in the street, and though all lighted in the church, it seemed very poor and dim. But I forgot all about it in the beautiful service and grand singing, for I supposed the day would clear up later; but instead of doing so the fog became more dense than ever. As we walked home I could not but congratulate myself that I had not to go out to get my Christmas dinner, though several friends were to dine with us. As the hour for dinner approached we observed an anxious look upon the faces of the servants as they came and went about the house. We waited an hour, then another, for our expected guests, and after all our small party of three had to sit down alone; and we even could not have the satisfaction of grumbling, for there was the solemn footman handing dish after dish with as much solemnity as if our eight stranger guests were all there. It was bad indeed for us, but our poor friends had the worst of it, for they all had made the effort to come, and had driven round and round in the pitch darkness of the terrible fog, the gentlemen having even got out of their carriages and carried lights before the coachman. But all to no purpose, for at ten o'clock they found themselves back in the near neighbourhood of their own homes, and were thankful to refresh themselves with cold beef and mutton, and whatever good thing might be found in the larder. But as for a merry Christmas, few had really had it, for the elements had conspired together to prevent it; and almost all the dinner parties on that Christmas day ended more or less as ours had done.

CHRISTMAS PARTIES.

By the Rev. T. F. THISELTON DYER, M.A.

CHRISTMAS gatherings a hundred years ago were not unlike those at the present day. However much the manners of modern society may have altered during the past century, we find little variation in the programme of merrymaking arranged for the parties of the young in olden times. Indeed no change of fashion could alter the leading feature of a Christmas party, namely, the idea of affording both old and young as much laughter and enjoyment as possible. Although dancing formed an attractive element of the evening's proceedings, yet it was not by any means the prominent diversion as nowadays, games of all kinds having been in popular requisition.

There was one advantage, however, which most Christmas parties in years gone by possessed, and which one would like to see introduced into the merrymakings of the present day—they commenced and ended early. The late hours to which even our juvenile gatherings are prolonged, would have found no favour with our forefathers, who believed in no exception to the rule "Early to bed," especially when young folk were concerned. This was a good old-fashioned arrangement, and precluded any objections that even the most rigid moralist might raise against such periodical scenes of dissipation. It should be remembered, too, that the times were more simple and unconventional, and the mode of procedure on such occasions was far less elaborate than nowadays. This, again, was worthy of our imitation, and in striking contrast with the costly and unnecessary extravagance which so often mars the homely simplicity of the Christmas party. And yet let it not be supposed that they were less hearty or inferior in thorough good merriment to the modern entertainments. If the preparations were less extensive, and the programme not so attractive as at the present day, there was, nevertheless, a greater amount of unstudied enjoyment—everyone deeming it right to contribute as far as possible to the evening's amusement. Hence looking back on the social history of years past, as recorded in contemporary literature, we get a clear insight into the manner that juvenile gatherings were usually conducted.

An amusing little book, called "Round About Our Coal Fire; or, Christmas Entertainments," gives a quaint account of the arrangements at such times. The rooms, we are told, were embowered with holly, ivy, cypress, bays, laurel, and mistletoe; and "a bouncing Christmas log in the chimney, glowing like the cheeks of a country maid." The servants were running here and there "with merry hearts and jolly countenances. Everyone was busy in welcoming of guests, and the maids were as blithe and buxom as in the days of good Queen Bess." In short, cheery good nature was the order of the day; and an earnest desire on all sides to make each little guest feel welcome and happy more than fully compensated for the lack of those amusements which are nowadays supplied by professional establishments.

Among the pastimes mentioned were the masqueradings, which were the signal for the utmost excitement. The young people dressed themselves up in the most ridiculous attire, and borrowed from every conceivable quarter any article of dress which might add to the eccentricity of their appearance. As may be imagined, there was no small rivalry as to who should most cleverly conceal or disguise his or her identity, all manner of artful contrivances being resorted to for this purpose. Occasionally, too, when their "make up" was complete and generally approved of, some of these juvenile masqueraders would slip out of the house and pay a visit to a neighbouring family, their approach being heralded by many a merry peal of laughter. It was a happy time, full of good nature and harmless fun, and cheered the old as well as the young. Of the many allusions to entertainments of this kind may be noticed the "Paston Letters," wherein we find a letter dated December 24th, 1484, which relates how Lady Morley, on account of the death of her lord, directing what pastimes were to be used in her house at Christmas, gave orders that "there were none disguisings, nor harping, nor luting, nor singing, nor none loud disports; but playing at the tables, and chess, and cards; such disports she gave her folks leave to play, and none other."

In modern times, perhaps, the nearest approach to these amusing "makes up" of past years are either charades or "tableaux vivants," in which young people ransack the wardrobes, laying their hands on anything which they consider suitable for the occasion. Indeed, it is the preparation for their juvenile display which oftentimes causes the greatest fun, besides affording an opportunity for the exercise of originality of design and ingenuity in utilising the most awkward and unpropitious materials.

At the conclusion of such entertainments dancing has generally formed the chief diversion, or as it was formerly nicknamed, "hopping;" for, as the same old writer says, "these dances stir the blood;" while those unable to join in this pastime have never failed to find equal pleasure in one of the many time-honoured English games, in which even "children of a larger growth" have whiled away many an hour. But in the course of years some of these harmless and once popular amusements have become almost obsolete, being nowadays rarely seen. Some of them might well be revived, and would doubtless prove as attractive in our modern juvenile gatherings as they did in days of long ago.

A game, for example, which often caused a considerable amount of laughter and excitement was known as "Dun in the Mire." The mode of procedure was somewhat after the following fashion:—A log of wood was brought into the middle of the room; this was nicknamed "Dun," or the carthorse, and a cry was made that he had stuck hopelessly in the mire. Instantly two of the young people, responding to the appeal, advanced, either with or without ropes, to draw him out. When unable to do so they in turn called for further help, and finally all the party joined in the game; poor Dun, of course, being eventually extricated. Meanwhile, however, no small merriment was caused by each person's sly efforts to let the log fall on his neighbour's toes. The popularity of this Christmas pastime may be gathered from the frequent allusions to it by old writers. Thus Shakespeare, it may be remembered, in *Romeo and Juliet* (Act i. scene 4), speaks of it, where Mercutio says to Romeo—

"Tut, dun's the mouse, the constable's own word:
If thou art dun, we'll draw thee from the mire."

Beaumont and Fletcher also, in *The Woman Hater* (Act iv. scene 3), refer to it:—

"Dun's in the mire; get out again how he can."

Chaucer, too, probably alludes to this old game in the *Manciples Prologue*, where the host, seeing the cook asleep, exclaims—

"Syr, what dunne is in the mire?"

Another diversion which was in request at Christmas parties was "hot cockles." This was a species of blindman's buff, in which the person kneeling down, and being struck behind, was to guess who inflicted the blow.

According to Strutt, in his "Sports and Pastimes," this pastime received its name from the French "hautes-coquilles," and is thus described by Gay in the following lines—

"As at hot cockles once I laid me down,
And felt the weighty hand of many a clown,
Buxoma gave a gentle tap, and I
Quick rose, and read soft mischief in her eye."

Then there was the old phrase "to sit upon hot cockles" which probably meant to be very impatient, as in the subjoined extract from a work of the beginning of the seventeenth century: "He laughs and kicks like Chrysippus when he saw an ass eat figs; and sits upon hot cockles till it be blazed abroad, and withal intreats his neighbours to make bone-fires for his good hap, and causeth all the bells of the parish to ring forth the peal of his own fame."

Again, oftentimes, "Handy-dandy" was the signal for a merry romp at the Christmas party. One of the party concealed something in his or her hand, making the others guess what was concealed. If the latter guessed rightly, he or she won the article; but if wrongly had to pay a forfeit of an equivalent value. Sometimes it would appear the game was played by a sort of sleight of hand, the article being rapidly changed from one hand into the other, so that the looker-on was easily deceived.

Such old games as snap-dragon and hide-seek are, however, as popular at our juvenile gatherings as in years past, although unfortunately some survive only in name. A game twice mentioned by Herrick, but not once explained, is "Fox i' th' hole," the allusion being thus—

"Of Christmas sports, the wassail bowl,
That's tossed up after fox i' th' hole."

After the young people were fairly tired with dancing and romping, round games were next in request, these in their turn affording immense excitement. Then there are numerous allusions to the diversion known as "Questions and Answers," or as it was sometimes called "Questions and Commands," when, says the author of "Round About Our Coal Fire," "the commander may oblige his subject to answer any lawful question, and make the same obey him instantly, under the penalty of being smutted, or paying such forfeit as may be laid on the aggressor." The more intellectually inclined would play at "cap-verses," wherein one gave a word, to which another of the party gave a rhyme, and so on, much amusement being caused by the difficulty some would have of finding the suitable rhyme, and the foolish mistakes others would make; for which, of course, they had to pay in each case a forfeit.

Card-games, once more, have from time immemorial been an endless source of laughter at Christmas parties; a highly popular one having been known as "Post and Pair," an allusion to which Ben Jonson makes in his "Masque of Christmas."

"Now Post and Pair, old Christmas's heir,
Doth make a gingling sally;
And wot you who, 'tis one of my two
Sons, card-makers in Pur-alley."

This game is included among the pastimes enumerated by Sir Walter Scott in his famous and graphic picture of Christmas Eve, given in "Marmion." It was played thus: Three cards were dealt to all, the excitement of the game consisting in each of the young people vying, or betting, on the goodness of his own hand. A pair royal of aces was the best hand, and next any other three cards according to their order. If there were no threes, the highest pairs might win. But round games of this kind were numerous, the forfeits being paid with sugar-plums. It is unnecessary to quote further instances of these harmless modes of merrymaking, which were the life and happiness of the young at Christmastime, and many of which might be with advantage revived at the present day. They had, too, this additional recommendation—they united old and young together; and whilst the former forgot for a few hours the more prosaic matters of life, the latter were proud of, and flattered by, the hearty interest displayed by their elders.

DRAWN BY REGINALD B. BIRCH. ENGRAVED BY R. G. TIETZE.

THE LITTLE CHRISTMAS SPY.

THE LITTLE CHRISTMAS SPY.

By Helen Gray Cone.

Our Madge, in growing tall and wise,
   Has reached that most befogged of tracts,
The Land of Half-Belief, that lies
   Between the Fairies and the Facts.

Her little heart's a crowded nest
   Of faiths and fancies, dear and shy;
The dearer, since she somehow guessed
   They'd flutter from her by and by.

Her doubts are pains, yet pleasures, too,
   With which her timid thoughts will play;
How sad the chill, "It may n't be true"—
   How sweet the thrill, "But, then, it may!"

On Christmas Eve she long had lain
   With sleepless eyes, like owlet's bright;
She rose, and rubbed the frosted pane,
   And stared into the starry night.

She saw the moon laugh round and clear
   From smoky wreaths of cloud, and throw,
In shapes like branching horns of deer,
   The sharp tree-shadows on the snow.

Oh, would he come, the jolly Saint
   Whom everybody talked about?
"It may be so—and yet, it may n't;
   If I should watch, I might find out!"

She turned; her pulses wildly beat;
   She'd like to spy—but should she dare?
Yes! Pat, pat, pat, with stealthy feet
   She passed adown the winding stair.

The great hearth glowed; the grave old cat,
   With fixed, expanded, emerald eyes,
Erect, before the chimney sat;
   He seemed to wear a waiting guise.

The andirons shone; the clock ticked on;
   Each moment made her more afraid.
"Oh, if he comes, I'll wish I'd gone—
   But if I go, I'll wish I'd staid!

"Perhaps he is n't real at all—
   But—if he is—perhaps he'll mind!"
A sudden soot-flake chanced to fall—
   She fled, and never looked behind!

She throbbed with fright, she flushed with shame,
   Her pillowed head she closely hid;
She said, "I don't believe he came!"
   She sighed, "Oh, dear—suppose he did!"

St. Nicholas, 1888

DECEMBER.—CHRISTMAS-DAY ON THE PAVEMENT.

OF the festivals and anniversaries which we are wont, in the course of the year, to celebrate with especial honour, there is scarcely one which, had it escaped our recollection, we should not be able, on its arrival, to detect, from some feature peculiar to itself in the aspect of the public streets. When merry bells are ringing from every steeple, and flags are waving from the summits of public buildings; when skeleton crowns, and as yet, untransparent transparencies, salute us on every side, and all the town seems wending westward, we do not require a reference to the last Gazette to satisfy us that it is the day appointed for the celebration of Her Majesty's Birthday. When, on a dark morning, towards the close of the year, we find ourselves unable to penetrate to our City engagements through the host of sight-seers who are pressing eastward, regardless of fog and mud, we do not require to be told that the day has arrived for the annual apotheosis of Civic Majesty. The Feast of St. Valentine, is in its turn legible as print, in the window of every stationer's shop we approach; the most unobservant street wanderer can require no warning of Twelfth Day: while the unwonted gloss of novelty which pervades the apparel of the holiday-makers one encounters on Whit-Monday, proclaims that Feast, as clearly as though every garment were a public advertisement of the fact. Even Christmas-day—so peculiarly the festival of home feelings and fireside joys, that it would seem to possess but little in common with the turmoil and bustle of the external world—is as distinguishable in its out-door dress, as any of the anniversaries which have preceded it in the year. Should we entertain any doubt upon the subject, we have only to sally out and satisfy ourselves.

It is on the stroke of eleven as we turn our steps eastward: yes! eastward it must be, for it is in the working-day world of town that we must look for the characteristics of which we are in search. Hyde-park-gardens and Belgravia turn not out of the even tenor of their every-day existence, be the occasion ever so moving. It is the misfortune of Fashion—ill-starred goddess that she is—that what is the relaxation and enjoyment of the ordinary world, is her daily toil and labour: she has no holidays. As we turn our steps, then, Cityward, the bells are ringing a cheery welcome to church, and streams of happy faces are responding to their bidding. Were it not for the branch of red berries which the green-grocer's boy is carrying down the area next door, and the apparition of the postman—that wanderer who seems to know no rest—we might fancy that we had retraced the course of time to some genial Sunday in the spring of the year. There is, however, something not altogether Sabbath-like in the aspect of things around us. Railway carts are busied in delivering hampers, which, it is to be feared, ought to have reached their destination on the preceeding day; and the grocers' shops in by-streets continue to exhibit, in opulent profusion, masses of currants and stacks of raisins, for the convenience of improvident housewives, who may have failed to lay in the needful supply of those delicacies on the previous night. If such there be, however, they have no time to lose in completing their purchases; the church bells have ceased ringing, services have commenced throughout the length and breadth of the land, and myriads of voices are at this moment raised in accents of praise and thanksgiving for this holy day. We shall, however, observe nothing of that half-deserted appearance which characterizes the streets during morning service on a Sunday; for, as twelve o'clock approaches, the public thoroughfares are as crowded as they were at eleven. Clerks of genius, great-coated, comfortered, and railway-wrappered, as though bent on a polar expedition, are luxuriating in the fragrance of the "justly-celebrated havannahs at seven for a shilling," and wondering at the air of novelty which being out at so unwonted an hour imparts to the streets they know so well. Attenuate mechanics and sturdy labourers are doing their best, by a walk in the fresh air, to acquire an additional zest for the twelve pounds of roasting beef, etc., which twenty weeks' self-denial, and subscription to their club procures for them to-day. These, after all, are the genuine enjoyers of the season—to them the Sunday of the year. They have no bills to make up, with book debts of dubious value, like the worthy tradesman before them; nor is their enjoyment of the day impaired by any visions of similar unliquidated liabilities of their own, as may be the case with the gentleman with the rough coat and short meerschaum who is now passing. They are too well used to the uncertainties of life to have any solicitude about the future; they have a good dinner before them to-day, and with that knowledge are abundantly satisfied. How different is the deprecating manner with which yon old man seems to appeal for excuse even for the liberty of participating in the free air of heaven. Who could mistake him?—a pauper from the neighbouring workhouse, enjoying, if enjoyment it can be called, his only holiday in the year. There are few, however—and it might be some consolation, could he but know it—even of those whom Fortune has used most kindly, who will see out this anniversary without their share of its shade as well as of its sunshine. To all of us, Christmay-day is as it were a resting place between the stages of a weary march; one of a series of landmarks on a lengthened journey, so prominent and conspicuous that we can cast our eyes back from one to the other to within a short distance from our original starting-place. The companions who travelled with us, the varied vicissitudes of our march—nay, even the feelings and hopes associated with each stage of our pilgrimage—rise up before us with startling distinctness as we look back upon it. That life has been a happy one indeed, in which such a retrospect brings with it only pleasure. We shall be safe in affirming that the party ahead of us has not yet arrived at this point in the day's experiences. They are on the "sunny side o' the wall." It cannot, surely, be one family! No. Those two respectable, middle-aged gentlemen are evidently both heads of houses; so we will divide the rest of the party between them, taking care, for the sake of the picturesque, to apportion on opposite sides the younger male and female members who compose it. The youngest male unit, that urchin with his hand in his pocket, is, I imagine, somewhat in the way; his ebullitions of delight at the prospect of total idleness and late hours for three good weeks to come, have been but feebly responded to by his companions; nay, the damsel has snubbed him twice distinctly. He will, no doubt, retreat, to bestow his society upon the old folk; their conversation must be far less important, and they can, therefore, better afford to be tolerant. The mamma, it is to be observed, is not in either case visible; she, probably, "on hospitable thoughts intent," is busily occupied with the important domestic avocations of the day, and will be beheld by no mortal eye, till she makes her appearance, just before dinner, in all the glories of her best black satin.

As one o'clock strikes, the morning idlers begin to wend their way homewards, while those who have been employing their time more profitably, and have just come out of church, occupy, for a time, the walks they have begun to desert.

As two o'clock approaches, the streets begin to assume their busiest aspect, and we come upon one of the most important features of the day—the Diner Out! There is the first we have met, yon thrifty lady, with dress tucked up and basket in hand; she is probably an intimate friend invited to come early, and receive the guests; or a poor relation, perhaps, with a genius for custards. Soon we notice one or two more provident seizers of time by the forelock, coming intermittently, like the first drops of a shower of rain, till the stream becomes continuous. Nearly every one we now meet seems bent on testing the hospitality of every one else; the mystery is, who are the entertainers. The diner out of Christmas-day is markedly distinguishable among the ladies, from the circumstance of their always presenting themselves, cap in hand, like a debtor to a dun. What distinctions of taste in this important article of female costume should we not discover if those whity-brown coverings could only be removed for a moment. Every variety, doubtless, we should find, from the cap that really is a cap, and means something, with a proper allowance of net-work and yellow flowers, such as we may imagine to be the object of care, with that respectable matron over the way; to the coquettish contrivance of wire and ribbon, studiously designed to look as little like what it is as possible.

Another marked feature of the day in the streets is, that there is scarcely one of the people we meet who is not the bearer of some substantial evidence of the genial influences of the season:—they are all carrying gifts, like the Kings of Sabœa. There are the donors of albums, pencil-cases, and similar conventional testimonials of regard, who seem desirous only of marking their general sense of the duties of the day by a gift of some sort, without deeming it necessary to exercise any peculiar discrimination in its selection. Others there are—but they are chiefly ladies—who exhibit considerably more judgment in the matter; and as of this class we may set down the bearer of that large tea-pot, which, though ingeniously muffled, presents its features with a distinctness wholly independent of concealment. The gift is one which, under ordinary circumstances, would hardly suggest itself as a Christmas present; and yet we might venture to affirm that there are deficiencies connected with the tea equipage of the friend for whom it is intended, which, could we know them, would satisfy us of the appropriateness of the gift. The papier mâché work-table, which the young gentleman before us is bearing with so much care, would also at first sight appear a rather out-of-the-way tribute of regard. It is awkward to carry, and inconvenient for the purpose of presentation. But how good-humouredly he toils under his burden, and how carefully he guards it from injury: were it his own offspring it could scarcely receive more tender treatment. Stay! That is the secret! It is one of a description of gifts very common at the present day, a present in kind—a specimen of his own handiwork—the result, no doubt, of many a weary hour's labour, and many an anxious hour's thought. Is it intended for a married sister, or destined to serve as a propitiatory offering to the mother of some one in whom he takes a nearer interest? This question, must remain unsolved.

The strokes of each successive quarter after three o'clock, warn us more and more distinctly that we have accomplished the object of our walk, and shall now find little to amuse us abroad. The day, which has been bright and genial, begins to draw in, and looks as dark and cheerless as the most enthusiastic admirer of seasonable weather could desire. The pedestrians have, comparatively speaking, disappeared, and the limited business operations of which the day admits, almost exclusively connected with the *agremens* of the table, will, during the next two hours be entirely suspended. The period for the delivery of those humbler delicacies which are dependent for their perfection upon the baker has gone by; and the tray of the confectioner, with its *entremets*, has not yet commenced its circulation.

Now and then some delinquent *early* diner that should be, hurries by, fiery red with haste, in all the agonizing conciousness of being twenty minutes late, with a punctilious hostess; or a perturbed lady, for whom we stop a Paddington omnibus, causes us a moment's disquietude, by persisting in depositing herself in an "Elephant and Castle:" but, with these exceptions, the monotony is almost unbroken. From five to seven there will be an increased bustle in cabs and carriages conveying the late diners to their engagements; and then, save the occasional vagaries, leniently to be judged, of some worthy who has enjoyed the day, "not wisely, but too well," all will be quiet for the rest of the evening.

The Illustrated London Alamanack, 1855

THE QUEEN'S CHRISTMAS.

THERE is no more happy home in all the realms over which our Queen reigns than that at Osborne at Christmas time. If loving thought and careful, earnest preparation can make happy hearts, the Queen secures this for all her children, grandchildren, and servants at Christmas time. For weeks before, manufacturers of toys have been busy planning and presenting to Her Majesty the latest and most wonderful productions of Toyland. Tables have simply been littered with toys, jewels, costly furs, and the hundred and one things that people are wont to give to their friends at that happy season. Every present is selected by the Queen herself. As the toys are unpacked, she sees a marvellous horse that neighs and shakes its head; at once it is put aside with the words, "That will do for Edward." A doll's house, the dolls all dressed in furs, and the ground outside covered with snow, next comes to view; "That's just the thing for Olga," says the Queen. Thus every present is carefully selected, the wants of each one lovingly thought of, until not a servant in the whole of the royal household has been forgotten.

The Christmas programme begins on Christmas Eve. By this time the whole of the palace has been thoroughly decorated with holly, mistletoe, evergreens, and flowers. Waggon-loads of these have come from Windsor, and from the estate of Osborne. In the afternoon the schoolchildren of St. Mildred's, Whippingham, which is the parish church—in fact, was built by Her Majesty—will come up to the palace for their treat. This is a great event, and has been looked forward to for many weeks. At this function the Queen is not present. This is Princess Ena's opportunity; she plays the lady of the house and receives the Queen's little guests with all the dignity of her position. It is true that Princess Beatrice and Princess Louise are present to see that all goes well, and they are assisted by the little cousins who may be staying for Christmas at Osborne.

Then presents of beef and pudding are given to the labourers on the estate, and Christmas doles to aged, sick, and disabled persons, recommended by the clergymen of the selected parishes. But the evening is the great time in the Queen's home. Then there are tremendous romps round the royal Christmas tree in the banqueting-hall. The tree is a fine young fir after the German custom, and it is loaded with all the presents, and illuminated with myriads of coloured tapers. One need not describe the scene, for the hearts of royal princes and princesses are just the same as those of commoners. Little eyes sparkle, little feet dance, little hands clap, and little hearts are full of gladness; just like those we have seen in other rooms. No one is better pleased, no one is happier in all this festive group, than the Queen herself.

On the morning of Christmas Day, the Queen gives her grandchildren their presents, and they offer her their little gifts of their own handiwork, which have cost them no little thought and trouble. These presents the Queen prefers to any that can be bought at shops. Then there are letters to read, and cards to delight over, and the Queen enjoys the young people's pleasure quite as much as they do themselves.

The Queen, her family, and suite attend divine service at the Chapel Royal in the palace. This is simply decorated with holly and white chrysanthemums, arranged by the Princess Beatrice, her daughter, and the other young people at Osborne. One of the clergy of the Isle of Wight officiates. Christmas hymns are sung, and the same simple service is held as that in every other church thoroughout the land. Lunch takes place at one o'clock in the private dining-room. The baron of beef, woodcock-pie, and boar's head are much in evidence for those who like a cold lunch. In the afternoon the Queen drives out with one or two of her daughters, and leaves the young people to amuse themselves after their own fashion. Not a few of the latter mount their bicycles, and go for a scorch round the royal domain, making a laughing, racing troop of young people. The great event, however, is the Christmas dinner. For this all the children have a special dispensation to stay up, and those of us who can remember our own childhood's days can imagine the feeling of fun created by this extra dissipation. Dinner takes place in the banqueting-hall; the sideboard is loaded with plate—salvers, flagons, cups, goblets, beakers, and ewers—the accumulation of many reigns—all polished until they twinkle in the light. Very pretty is the effect of the red and green holly contrasting with the subdued Oriental colouring of the decorations. On the fire is a huge yule-log, a portion of the trunk of a young tree, crackling in the most Christmassy fashion. A band plays in the gallery; and when, the lights being lowered, the pudding is brought in, hissing and steaming with its lighted brandy, one can realise that the mirth has reached its height, and the children feel that Christmas is the very merriest and brightest time in all the happy year. After dinner is dessert of all kinds of fruit, walnuts, French bonbons, and German cakes, etc., just as in any ordinary house. After more games, tired heads and tired little bodies sleep and dream in Royal Osborne with the same feelings as in our simple homes.

God give our Queen and all her family a happy Christmas this 1898! So say we all of us.

The Home Magazine, 1898

A Christmas Carol.

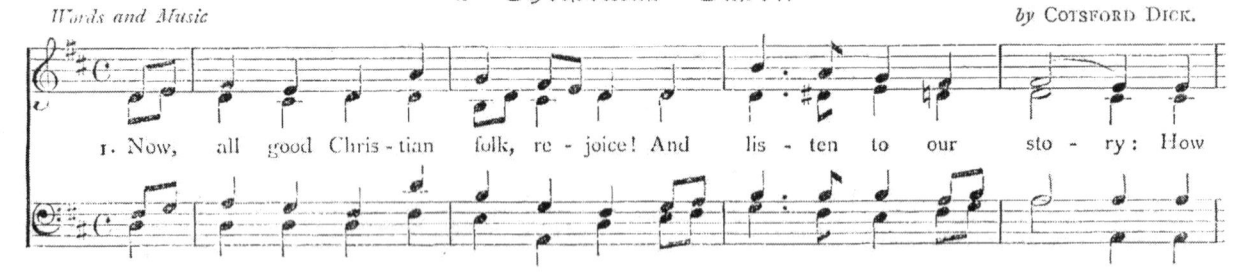

Words and Music — *by* COTSFORD DICK.

1. Now, all good Christian folk, rejoice! And listen to our story: How watchful shepherds saw one night The heavens filled with glory.

II.
Amazed, they heard the Angels call,
  "Good tidings are we bringing,
For Christ is born in Bethlehem,
  His praise let all be singing."

III.
With joy they hastened there to find,
  Within a manger lying,
A little Child, who to the world
  Should tell of Love undying;

IV.
Of Love, all fear to cast away,
  Though life be dark and dreary;
Of Love to welcome Home at last
  The wandering and weary.

V.
To God, who sent this Love to us,
  Be honour, praise, and glory;
And peace, good-will be unto you
  Who listen to our story.

The Girl's Own Paper, 1882

Receipts, &c.

PLUM PUDDING AND OTHER RECEIPTS FOR CHRISTMAS.

We give a number of receipts for puddings, pies, cakes, etc., that will be of great use to our lady friends during the Christmas holidays.

A Christmas Plum Pudding, with or without Eggs.—Take two pounds of bread crumbs that have been well sifted through a colander; two tablespoonfuls of flour; half an ounce of ground allspice, and one pound of brown moist sugar; rub these ingredients thoroughly well together; chop one pound of suet very fine, and thoroughly mix in with the other things. Wash well in tepid water a pound and a half of raisins, and stone them, or two pounds of Sultana raisins, which require no stoning, and are equally good, though more expensive; chop these, not too fine, and well mix in; then a pound of well-washed currants, and a quarter of a pound of candied peel, cut into lumps, *not slices*. Having mixed all this together well, make the whole sufficiently moist with a little milk; well butter one or more large basins; well press the mixture into the bottom of each (or they will not turn out in good shape), and when filled to a trifle above the brim of the basin, spread some flour on the top, and tie the basin down with a well-wetted cloth; place the pudding in boiling water, let it boil up rapidly, and so continue for four hours; then take it up, remove the cloth but do not turn it out of the basin. The next day, or when wanted for use, put the pudding to warm, with the basin still on, for two hours, in a moderately warm oven, then take it out, turn it from the basin on to the dish in which it is to be sent to table. With the handle of a teaspoon, or the blade of a fruit-knife, make incisions in different parts of the pudding, and pour on some sherry wine, then sift powdered sugar over. It is obvious that this pudding must be made the day before it is required for use, and it is much better for being so. Eggs are not necessary to give either richness or flavor, or to "bind the pudding;" the milk and the flour will do that. Eggs render the mass thoroughly indigestible; but if they must still be had—and *we again repeat that they are not needed*—eight eggs, well beaten and strained, can be used instead of the milk. Great care is necessary in all puddings of the kind, not to make them too wet, or they will be heavy; and to thoroughly mix the ingredients separately.

Christmas Plum Pudding.—A pound of suet, cut in pieces not too fine, a pound of currants, and a pound of raisins stoned, four eggs, half a grated nutmeg, an ounce of citron and lemon-peel, shred fine, a teaspoonful of beaten ginger, half a pound of bread-crumbs, half a pound of flour, and a pint of milk; beat the eggs first, add half the milk, beat them together, and by degrees stir in the flour, then the suet, spice, and fruit, and as much milk as will mix it together very thick; then take a clean cloth, dip in boiling water, and squeeze dry. While the water is boiling fast, put in your pudding, which should boil at least five hours.

Another way.—Seven ounces raisins, seeded and a little chopped; seven ounce currants, well washed and picked; one and a half ounce citron; three ounces of beef suet, chopped very fine; three-quarters of a nutmeg, grated; one-quarter of a teaspoonful of cinnamon; five eggs well beaten up; four tablespoonfuls of sugar; five tablespoonfuls of wheat flour; half a lemon-peel, grated; one glass of brandy and one glass of Madeira; a little milk to mix, sufficient to make rather a thick batter. The whole must be well mixed. The above mixture to be put into a well-buttered basin. Tie a pudding cloth over, and pin the four corners over the top. Put into boiling water, and to be kept boiling without ceasing for five hours. We have tried this receipt, and know it to be excellent.

Currant Cake.—One cup of butter, three eggs, one cup of water or milk, half a teaspoonful of saleratus, nutmeg, cup of currants.

Light Cakes.—Put a small quantity of flour into a mug, mix it with very good milk, with a lump of butter the size of an egg, a little barm, an egg, a teaspoonful of honey, and a little ginger; beat them well, and let them rise before baking.

Little Plum Cakes to keep long.—Dry one pound of flour, and mix with six ounces of finely-pounded sugar; beat six ounces of butter to a cream, and add to three eggs well beaten, half a pound of currants nicely dried, and the flour and sugar; beat all for some time, then dredge flour on tin plates, and drop the batter on them the size of a walnut. If properly mixed, it will be a stiff paste. Bake in a brisk oven.

Rich Plum Pudding.—Stone carefully one pound of the best raisins, wash and pick one pound of currants, chop very small one pound of fresh beef suet, blanch and chop small or pound two ounces of sweet almonds and one ounce of bitter ones; mix the whole well together, with one pound of sifted flour, and the same weight of crumb of bread soaked in milk, then squeezed dry and stirred with a spoon until reduced to a mash, before it is mixed with the flour. Cut in small pieces two ounces each of preserved citron, orange, and lemon-peel, and add a quarter of an ounce of mixed spice; quarter of a pound of moist sugar should be put into a basin, with eight eggs, and well beaten together with a three-pronged fork; stir this with the pudding, and make it of the proper consistence with milk. Remember that it must not be made too thin, or the fruit will sink to the bottom, but be made to the consistence of good thick batter. Two wineglassfuls of brandy should be poured over the fruit and spice, mixed together in a basin, and allowed to stand three or four hours before the pudding is made, stirring them occasionally. It must be tied in a cloth, and will take five hours of constant boiling. When done, turn it out on a dish, sift loaf-sugar over the top, and serve it with wine-sauce in a boat, and some poured round the pudding.

The pudding will be of considerable size, but half the quantity of materials, used in the same proportion, will be equally good.

Boiled Plum Pudding.—The crumbs of a small loaf, half a pound each of sugar, currants, raisins, and beef-suet shred, two ounces of candied peel, three drops of essence of lemon, three eggs, a little nutmeg, a tablespoonful of flour. Butter the mould, and boil them five hours. Serve with brandy-sauce.

A Good Pound-Cake.—Beat one pound of butter to a cream, and mix with it the whites and yolks of eight eggs beaten apart. Have ready, warm by the fire, one pound of flour, and the same of sifted sugar; mix them and a few cloves, a little nutmeg and cinnamon, in fine powder together; then by degrees work the dry ingredients into the butter and eggs. When well beaten, add a glass of wine and some caraways. It must be beaten

Godey's Lady's Book, 1863

a full hour. Butter a pan, and bake it an hour in a quick oven.

The above proportions, leaving out four ounces of the butter, and the same of sugar, make a less luscious cake, and to most tastes a more pleasant one.

A RICH CHRISTMAS PUDDING.—One pound of raisins, stoned, one pound of currants, half a pound of beef-suet, quarter of a pound of sugar, two spoonfuls of flour, three eggs, a cup of sweetmeats, and a wineglass of brandy. Mix well, and boil in a mould eight hours.

A GOOD CHRISTMAS PUDDING.—One pound of flour, two pounds of suet, one pound of currants, one pound of plums, eight eggs, two ounces of candied peel, almonds and mixed spice according to taste. Boil gently for seven hours.

COMMON CRULLERS OR TWIST CAKES.—Mix well together half a pint of sour milk, or buttermilk, two teacupfuls of sugar, one teacupful of butter, and three eggs, well-beaten; add to this a teaspoonful of saleratus dissolved in hot water, a teaspoonful of salt, half a nutmeg grated, and a teaspoonful of powdered cinnamon; sift in flour enough to make a smooth dough: roll it out not quite a quarter of an inch thick; cut in small oblong pieces; divide one end in three or four parts like fingers, and twist or plait them over each other. Fry them in boiling lard. These cakes may be cut in strips, and the ends joined, to make a ring, or in any other shape.

SOFT CRULLERS.—Sift three-quarters of a pound of flour, and powder half a pound of loaf-sugar; heat a pint of water in a round-bottomed saucepan, and when quite warm, mix the flour with it gradually; set half a pound of fresh butter over the fire in a small vessel; and when it begins to melt, stir it gradually into the flour and water; then add by degrees the powdered sugar and half a grated nutmeg. Take the saucepan off the fire, and beat the contents with a wooden spaddle or spatula till they are thoroughly mixed; then beat six eggs very light, and stir them gradually into the mixture. Beat the whole very hard till it becomes a thick batter. Flour a pasteboard very well, and lay out the batter upon it in rings (the best way is to pass it through a screw funnel). Have ready, on the fire, a pot of boiling lard of the very best quality; put in the crullers, removing them from the board by carefully taking them up, one at a time, on a broad-bladed knife. Boil but few at a time. They must be of a fine brown. Lift them out on a perforated skimmer, draining the lard from them back into the pot; lay them on a large dish, and sift powdered white sugar over them.

CHRISTMAS CAKE.

To two pounds of flour well sifted unite
Of loaf-sugar ounces sixteen;
Two pounds of fresh butter, with eighteen fine eggs,
And four pounds of currants washed clean;
Eight ounces of almonds well blanched and cut small,
The same weight of citron sliced;
Of orange and lemon-peel candied one pound,
And a gill of pale brandy uniced;
A large nutmeg grated: exact half an ounce
Of allspice, but only a quarter
Of mace, coriander, and ginger well ground,
Or pounded to dust in a mortar.
An important addition is cinnamon, which
Is better increased than diminished;
The fourth of an ounce is sufficient. Now this
May be baked four good hours till finished.

DOUGH-NUTS.—Take three pounds of flour, one pound of butter, one and a half pound of sugar; cut the butter fine into the flour; beat six eggs light, and put them in; add two wine-glasses of yeast, one pint of milk, some cinnamon, mace and nutmeg; make it up into a light dough, and put it to rise. When it is light enough, roll out the paste, cut it in small pieces, and boil them in lard.

FRUIT CAKE.—Take one pound of butter and one pound of sugar, and beat them together with the yolks of eight eggs; beat the whites separately; mix with these one and a half pound of flour, one teacupful of cream, one wineglassful of brandy and one of wine, one nutmeg, one teaspoonful of mace, one teaspoonful of cloves, two teaspoonfuls of cinnamon, one salt-spoonful of salt, three-quarters of a pound of raisins, stoned, three-quarters of a pound of currants, half a pound of citron; mix with the flour two teaspoonfuls of yeast powder.

WASHINGTON CAKE.—Beat together one and a half pound of sugar, and three-quarters of a pound of butter: add four eggs well beaten, half a pint of sour milk, and one teaspoonful of saleratus, dissolved in a little hot water. Stir in gradually one and three-quarter pound of flour, one wineglassful of wine or brandy, and one nutmeg, grated. Beat all well together.

This will make two round cakes. It should be baked in a quick oven, and will take from fifteen to thirty minutes, according to the thickness of the cakes.

QUEEN CAKE.—Mix one pound of dried flour, the same of sifted sugar and of washed currants; wash one pound of butter in rose-water, beat it well, then mix with it eight eggs, yolks and whites beaten separately, and put in the dry ingredients by degrees; beat the whole an hour; butter little tins, teacups, or saucers, filling them only half full; sift a little fine sugar over just as you put them into the oven.

LEMON GINGERBREAD.—Grate the rinds of two or three lemons, and add the juice to a glass of brandy; then mix the grated lemon in one pound of flour, make a hole in the flour, pour in half a pound of treacle, half a pound of butter melted, the lemon-juice, and brandy, and mix all up together with half an ounce of ground ginger and quarter of an ounce of Cayenne pepper.

SEED CAKE.—Beat one pound of butter to a cream, adding gradually a quarter of a pound of sifted sugar, beating both together; have ready the yolks of eighteen eggs, and the whites of ten, beaten separately; mix in the whites first, and then the yolks, and beat the whole for ten minutes; add two grated nutmegs, one pound and a half of flour, and mix them very gradually with the other ingredients; when the oven is ready, beat in three ounces of picked caraway-seeds.

PUMPKIN PUDDING.—Take one pint of pumpkin that has been stewed soft and pressed through a colander; melt in half a pint of warm milk a quarter of a pound of butter and the same quantity of sugar, stirring them well together; one pint of rich cream will be better than milk and butter; beat eight eggs very light, and add them gradually to the other ingredients alternately with the pumpkin; then stir in a wineglass of rose-water and two glasses of wine mixed together, a large teaspoonful of powdered mace and cinnamon mixed, and a grated nutmeg. Having stirred the whole very hard, put it into a buttered dish, and bake it three-quarters of an hour.

LEMON CAKE.—Beat six eggs, the yolks and whites separately, till in a solid froth; add to the yolks the grated rind of a fine lemon and six ounces of sugar dried and sifted; beat this a quarter of an hour; shake in with the left hand six ounces of dried flour; then add the whites of the eggs and the juice of the lemon; when these are well beaten in, put it immediately into tins, and bake it about an hour in a moderately hot oven.

CLOVE CAKE.—One pound of sugar, one pound of flour, half pound of butter, four eggs, a teaspoonful of saleratus, a cup of milk, a teaspoonful of powdered mace, same of cinnamon, same of cloves; fruit, if you choose.

MINCEMEAT.—Six pounds of currants, three pounds of raisins stoned, three pounds of apples chopped fine, four pounds of suet, two pounds of sugar, two pounds of beef, the peel and juice of two lemons, a pint of sweet wine, a quarter of a pint of brandy, half an ounce of mixed spice. Press the whole into a deep pan when well mixed.

Another way.—Two pounds of raisins, three pounds of currants, three pounds of beef-suet, two pounds of moist sugar, two ounces of citron, one ounce of orange-peel, one small nutmeg, one pottle of apples chopped fine, the rind of two lemons and juice of one, half a pint of brandy; mix well together. This should be made a little time before wanted for use.

MINCE PIES.—Take a pound of beef, free from skin and strings, and chop it very fine; then two pounds of suet, which likewise pick and chop; then add three pounds of currants nicely cleaned and perfectly dry, one pound and a half of apples, the peel and juice of a lemon, half a pint of sweet wine, half a nutmeg, and a few cloves and mace, with pimento in fine powder; have citron, orange, and lemon-peel ready, and put some in each of the pies when made.

MOLASSES PIE.—Four eggs—beat the whites separate—one teacupful of brown sugar, half a nutmeg, two tablespoonfuls of butter, beat them well together; stir in one teacupful and a half of molasses, and then add the white of eggs. Bake on pastry.

CREAM PIE (*fine*).—Half pound of butter, four eggs, sugar, salt, and nutmeg to your taste, and two tablespoonfuls of arrowroot wet; pour on it a quart of boiling milk, and stir the whole together. To be baked in deep dishes.

GINGER SPONGE-CAKE.—One cup of molasses, one cup of butter, two cups of sugar, four eggs, three cups of flour, one cup of milk, soda, and ginger.

FRENCH JUMBLES.—One pound and a half of flour, one pound of sugar, three quarters of a pound of butter, three eggs; dissolve one teaspoonful of soda in one-half cup of milk; add this, also one nutmeg, and roll out the dough, and cut into small cakes of any shape, and bake them in a quick oven.

HOW TO COOK POULTRY.

To BOIL A TURKEY.—Make a stuffing as for veal; or if you wish a plain stuffing, pound a cracker or some breadcrumb very fine, chop raw salt pork very fine, sift some sage and any other sweet herbs that are liked, season with pepper, and mould them together with the yolk of an egg; put this under the breast, and tie it closely. Set on the turkey in boiling water enough to cover it; boil very slowly, and take off the scum as it rises. A large turkey will require more than two hours' boiling: a small one an hour and a half. Garnish with fried forcemeat, and serve with oyster or celery sauce.

Or: Fill the body with oysters, and let it boil by steam without any water. When sufficiently done, take it up, strain the gravy that will be found in the pan, and which, when cold, will be a fine jelly; thicken it with a little flour and butter, add the liquor of the oysters intended for sauce, also stewed, and warm the oysters up in it; whiten it with a little boiled cream, and pour it over the turkey.

To ROAST A TURKEY.—Prepare a stuffing of pork sausage-meat, one beaten egg, and a few crumbs of bread: or, if sausages are to be served with the turkey, stuffing as for fillet of veal; in either, a little shred shallot is an improvement. Stuff the bird under the breast; dredge it with flour, and put it down to a clear, brisk fire; at a moderate distance the first half hour, but afterwards nearer. Baste with butter; and when the turkey is plumped up, and the steam draws towards the fire, it will be nearly done; then dredge it lightly with flour, and baste it with a little more butter, first melted in the basting ladle. Serve with gravy in the dish and bread sauce in a tureen. It may be garnished with sausages, or with fried forcemeat, if veal stuffing be used. Sometimes the gizzard and liver are dipped into the yolk of an egg, sprinkled with salt and Cayenne, and then put under the pinions before the bird is put to the fire. A very large turkey will require three hours' roasting; one of eight or ten pounds, two hours; and a small one, an hour and a half.

To ROAST A GOOSE.—Geese seem to bear the same relation to poultry that pork does to the flesh of other domestic quadrupeds; that is, the flesh of goose is not suitable for, or agreeable to, the very delicate in constitution. One reason, doubtless, is that it is the fashion to bring it to table very rare done; a detestable mode!

Take a young goose, pick, singe and clean well. Make the stuffing with two ounces of onions (about four common sized), and one ounce of green sage chopped very fine; then add a large coffee cup of stale breadcrumbs and the same of mashed potatoes; a little pepper and salt, a bit of butter as big as a walnut, the yolk of an egg or two; mix these well together, and stuff the goose. Do not fill it entirely; the stuffing requires room to swell. Spit it, tie the spit at both ends to prevent its swinging round, and to keep the stuffing from coming out. The fire must be brisk. Baste it with salt and water at first, then with its own dripping. It will take two hours or more to roast it thoroughly.

A green goose, that is, one under four months old, is seasoned with pepper and salt instead of sage and onions. It will roast in an hour.

SAUCE FOR A ROASTED GOOSE.—Put into a saucepan a tablespoonful of made mustard, half a teaspoonful of Cayenne pepper, a glass of port wine, and a gill of gravy; mix, and warm, and pour it through a slit in the apron into the body of the goose, just before serving.

CHRISTMAS AND NEW YEAR'S DINNERS.

BOILED turkey with oyster sauce, roast goose with apple sauce, roasted ham, chicken pie, stewed beets, cole-slaw, turnips, salsify, winter squash; mince pie, plum pudding, lemon custard, cranberry pie.

Roast turkey with cranberry sauce, boiled fowls with celery sauce, boiled ham, goose pie, turnips, salsify, cole-slaw, winter squash, beets; mince pudding boiled, lemon pudding baked, pumpkin pudding.

Mock turtle soup, roast turkey with cranberry sauce, boiled turkey with celery sauce, roasted ham, smoke-tongue, chicken curry, oyster pie, beets, cole-slaw, winter squash, salsify, fried celery; plum pudding, mince pie, calf's-foot jelly, blanc-mange.

CHRISTMAS TABLE DECORATIONS.

To decorate the house for the Christmas festivities is always a pleasing task, cheerfully undertaken by the junior members of the family, and very clever and ingenious are the designs into which they not infrequently weave the somewhat heavy winter greenery. This year, however, their task will be lighter, and its effect gain in brightness from the masses of berries with which the holly branches are clothed. Not for many years have we had so plentiful a store; even the hips and haws still remain a glowing crimson on their bare branches, while in some places the leaves of the holly can scarcely be seen, so covered is it with berry. Whether or not the old saying that this plethora portends a hard winter be true or not, it is certain that it will be productive of great joy amongst those who are mainly responsible for the effective decoration of the home, the church or the Sunday school.

Yet perhaps in the zeal which is expended upon the transformation of the hall, staircase, sitting-rooms and dining-room walls, it may happen that the table itself is somewhat neglected. The menu, of course, has received the greatest care and forethought, and been in preparation for some days; possibly also a few of the choicest sprays of berried holly or blooms of chrysanthemums have been reserved for the vases which usually adorn it, but this is scarcely enough, for the gaiety and merriment of the Christmas feast will be greatly enhanced by the cheering influence of a bright and harmonious setting.

It is true that nowadays at this time of the year we are able to procure a profusion of foreign flowers for a very moderate sum, narcissi, violets, hyacinths, roses, tulips, etc., but the old familiar evergreens are the most appropriate to the season, and carry our memories back to Christmases of long ago. I will give you one or two suggestions which will be a variation to the vase arrangement.

On the fine damask cloth a strip of crimson satin should be laid down the centre of the table, and round the edge may run a border of small trails of the clinging variegated ivy, the sharply-pointed leaves of which will embrace many shades of colour, from white to tender green and brown. If there are no silver bowls we may take china flower pots and arrange in them branches of berberis, holly or mistletoe, to look like miniature trees sprinkled with snow. To do this, when the bowls are arranged, we take a fine-rosed watering can and dew them over with weak gum and water, and when it has drained off a little we dredge them over with the finest white flour and afterwards with sparkling salt. Both the salt and the flour must be well dried and sifted before using. The bowls are placed down the length of the table on the crimson satin, the spaces here and there being filled with little silver or china holders for sweets and fruits, and a tiny spray of mistletoe is placed in each dinner napkin.

Care must be taken that the lights burn brightly, whether they be candles or lamps, and that the shades should harmonise with the scheme of decoration. Red shades are always cheerful in winter time, and red candles add another touch of colour. If the table is very large and this does not seem to be enough, a wreath is easily made of sprigs of berried holly fastened on a slender wire which can be wound in and out amongst the smaller dishes. This kind of wreath is most useful for twining around picture frames which are too valuable to warrant the intrusion of a nail or tack.

A more dainty and delicate combination of colour for those to whom the above may seem too vivid can be carried out with the time-honoured mistletoe alone. This too will require a table centre to throw up its subtle colouring, but it should be of a delicate leaf-green satin, with a pattern of gold and silver running through it, such as Liberty so frequently shows us. A border of Christmas roses will be very effective if they can be procured, if not the ivy trails are always at hand and are easy to arrange. A copper bowl hung from a tripod of wrought iron, with similar smaller ones, stand upon this groundwork, and are lightly and gracefully filled with branches of freshly-cut mistletoe arranged to spread outwards in light feathery masses. The sweetmeat holders should if possible be of copper, and a similar wreath made of mistletoe sprigs may be twined in and out amongst them if necessary. If the lamp or candle shades are of a reddish pink they will cast a rich warm glow over this delicately-tinted table. Where copper receptacles are not to hand, some good old brass, well-polished, produces an almost equally good effect, and failing that, the blue Delft ware or green Nuremberg glass will best harmonise with the tints of the mistletoe.

An original and inexpensive decoration for an oval table can be carried out with a centre strip of crimson cloth, rather wide, and bordered with the motto "Wishing all a Merry Christmas and a Happy New Year;" the letters, about three inches long, are cut out of brown paper and covered with leaves of the variegated holly sewn on, they are then sprinkled with gum and water and afterwards with frosting powder. A tiny wire must be placed at the back to raise them a little from the table so that the motto may be more easily read. In the centre of the cloth a large bowl should be filled with frosted branches of berried holly, with smaller bowls on either side, and the candlesticks of white china holding red candles and shades are arranged on the crimson cloth. The motto and the bowls could easily be prepared a day or two beforehand if they are kept in a cool place where the leaves are not likely to shrivel, and indeed they may be used on more than one occasion, being easily adapted for the decoration of a long supper-table if need be.

Speaking of supper-tables reminds me that if the table stands back against the wall its front should be ornamented with trails of greenery and loops of ribbon. High handled baskets filled with flowers and tied with bows to match are a favourite decoration, although there is now a new design which is very charming and is specially arranged for supper buffets.

It is a light stand made of gilded wire, in various heights, tall and slender, its top branching out in sprays holding little tubes which are filled with flowers. When lightly arranged with a mixture of flowers, grasses, and trails of fine green they closely resemble a miniature waterfall and are very graceful; their height too is a great advantage, as they are well above the dishes on the table. These wire frames are also made in other designs, arches, columns, towers, etc.

For the decoration of a supper-table for a children's party nothing will delight them more than tiny Christmas trees. They should glitter with "frost" and be well lighted up with candles fitted to their branches, but they need not have many ornaments except coloured sweetmeats and oranges.

There is a very quaint custom in vogue in the north-country at children's birthday parties which might with advantage be more generally known. The birthday cake—with the child's name and age engraved thereon in sugar—is placed in the centre of the table and surrounded with lighted candles, the number corresponding to the age of the child. Much merriment is caused by the efforts of the guests to count these twinkling lights, and the child feels great with the importance of an added candle at each recurrence of its holiday party. This same custom was recently carried out with intense delight at a gathering of children, and children's children, to celebrate the birthday of a great-grandfather. The ninety dazzling lights seemed to illustrate with peculiar force the long, long road of life which he had trodden.

But whatever suggestion we may adopt let us not forget the true spirit of Christmastide—love, peace and goodwill—to one another.

CHATS ABOUT THE CALENDAR.

DECEMBER, according to the calendar of Romulus, was the tenth month, as the name implies (*decem* being the Latin word for ten); but by the Julian calendar it was made the twelfth, and is the last month in our year. Among the Romans this month was devoted to various festivals. The peasants kept the feast of Vacuna, after having got in the fruits, and sown their corn. During this time all orders of the community were devoted to mirth and festivity. Friends sent presents to one another; the schools kept a vacation, and pleasure was the order of the day.

Our Anglo-Saxon ancestors called December the *Winter-monath*, but after their conversion to Christianity they called it *Heligh-monat*, or holy month, in commemoration of the feast of the Nativity, which is always celebrated in this month. There are few remarkable days to be noticed. Perhaps it may interest some to know that in this month the poet Gray and the painter Rubens were born; and Richelieu, John Wycliffe, Flaxman, Mozart, Dr. Johnson, Washington (names you should surely know something about) died. The 21st day is the shortest day, and from this time we may begin to look forward with some hope to the passing away of the dreary days of winter. But by far the most remarkable festival occurs on the 25th, commonly called Christmas Day. Happy Christmas! The time of family reunions, of joyous greetings, and of welcome presents. Out of doors there may be rain and wind, snow and ice; but indoors the scene is very different, with the merry games, the kisses under the mistletoe, Sir Roger de Coverley, not to mention the roast beef and turkey, the plum-pudding and the mince-pies, without which, in the opinion of many young people, Christmas would not be Christmas at all! The mistletoe is so associated with the festivities and decorations of Christmas that a word or two about it may not be uninteresting. It grows luxuriantly upon apple-trees, and upon the oak, and the fruit is made by the Italians into a kind of birdlime. The mystic uses of the mistletoe are traced to the pagan ages; it has even been identified with the golden branch referred to by Virgil in the lower regions. The Druids called it *all heal* or *guidhell*. They had an extraordinary veneration for the number three, and chose the mistletoe because its berries grow in clusters of three united to one stalk. They celebrated a grand festival on the annual cutting of the shrubs, on which occasion many ceremonies were observed; the officiating Druid being clad in white, and cutting the branches with a golden sickle. But when did mistletoe become recognised as a Christmas evergreen? We have Christmas carols in praise of holly and ivy of even earlier date than the fifteenth century; but allusion to mistletoe can scarcely be found for two centuries later, or before the time of Herrick.

"Down with the rosemary, and so,
Down with the baies and mistletoe,
Down with the holly, ivie all,
Wherewith ye dressed the Christmas hall."

And Shakespeare describes—

"The trees, though summer, yet forlorn and lean,
O'ercome with moss and baleful mistletoe."

The seeds of the mistletoe ripen late, between February and April, and birds do not willingly feed upon them as long as they can procure the berries of hawthorn, hollies, ivies, and other winter food. No sooner, however, does a late frost set in, and the ground become covered with snow, perhaps for the first time, then the little food-seeking warblers fly to the mistletoe, and find the sustenance in its berries which is denied them elsewhere. If the ripe berries are rubbed upon the branches of trees they may thus be readily cultivated.

The 28th day of this month is celebrated as the slaughter of the Innocents by Herod, and there is a strange superstition which affirms that it is unlucky to begin any work upon this day.

A good many people still keep up the custom of seeing the old year out and the new year in, and I daresay many of our young readers have done so. At first it is considered fine fun, and the old year is gladly pushed aside, in order to make room for the more welcome incoming one. But as you grow older, you will not be in such a hurry to get rid of the old years, but cling more lovingly to them, as you begin to feel the truth that they can never be recalled. Hence you will treat their exit into the land where all things are forgotten, more tenderly, and perhaps even sorrowfully.

December is allegorically represented by the Ancients as an old man, with a severe countenance, clothed in a coarse (but, let us hope, warm) garment; his hands, which are encased in gloves, hold a hatchet, emblematical of the season, which is the time for felling timber. Instead of his head being surrounded by a garland, it appears to be wrapped in three or four nightcaps, with a Turkish turban over them; his mouth and beard are thickly icicled over; at his back is a bundle of ivy, holly, and mistletoe, while by his side is the sign of the goat, Capricornus, symbolical of the sun entering that constellation on the 21st.

Christmas long ago.

Chatterbox, 1878

CHRISTMAS IN THE OLDEN TIME.

BY HENRY J. VERNON.

CHRISTMAS is much more generally observed, in the United States, than it was a generation ago, and its observance is annually extending. But it is not kept, even yet, with anything like the universality, much less the enthusiasm, of the olden time in England.

Three hundred years ago, Christmas was, emphatically, the great festival of the year. It was the one that appealed, more eloquently than any other, to that feeling of a common brotherhood in man, which is the very essence of true Christianity. On Christmas day, rich and poor were drawn together, as they were at no other time. The mendicant was sure of his alms, no matter at what gate he knocked. The lord of the Manor saw that every one, who took his hire, had a joint for dinner. In the houses of the wealthy, relatives of every degree met, as they meet now at Thanksgiving in New England: the son from across the sea, the married daughter from another county, the widow, the orphan, the heir, the repentant prodigal. The chimneys blazed, the boards groaned, the minstrels piped. The young danced the long evenings through. The aged looked on, thought of the past, and smiled. While many a bashful lover, who had sighed in vain all the year, took courage, when he caught his sweetheart under the evergreen, and availing himself of the old-time license, kissed her, and found tongue to speak.

But that which hallowed Christmas, especially, was the sacred memory connected with it. The story of the Babe in the manger was a story that melted the hardest hearts to love and reverence. It was kept vividly before the mind, on every recurring Christmas season, by the words of Holy Writ, by poetry, by legend, by pictorial representations even. The lowly stable, the Wise Men offering gifts, the actual Star in the East were real to the men of that day, in a sense that can hardly be understood in this material age. The times were, essentially, imaginative. People saw the steps of fairies in the rings of blighted grass. The devout believed, as Milton believed long after, in spiritual presences all about them. What wonder, therefore, that, in the quiet, starlit night, the carol-singers, wandering homeward, almost fancied they heard, in the sough of the wind among the trees, the rush of angels' wings, as the celestial messengers chanted, far up, and out of sight, "Glory to God in the Highest!"

"With folded hands, in stoles of white,
On sleeping wings they sail."

For Christmas was ushered in invariably by carol-singers. The custom has now disappeared, almost entirely, even in England. Here we only know it, as practised in the domestic circle, when a mother, or elder sister, gathers the little ones around her, and sings carols with them. But as evening drew on, in the old times of which we write, the picked singers of the vicinage, both men and women, came together, and going from house to house, sang carols until long after midnight. Many of these carols are still extant, the oldest being a Norman one of the thirteenth century, of which we give the first stanza:

"Lordlings, listen to our lay—

"We have come from far away,
To seek Christmas.
In this mansion we are told
He his yearly feast doth hold:
'Tis to-day:
May joy come from God above,
To all those who Christmas love."

Sometimes the music was wholly vocal; sometimes a viol only accompanied the voices; sometimes there were musical instruments of every variety then known. But the carol, in the main, depended for its success, on the voice; and wisely, for vocal music was as universally cultivated, in England then, as in Germany now. This carol-singing was a beautiful custom, and might be revived to advantage, if not abused. Fancy the long prolonged notes, rising and falling, melodiously, on the night-air, and dying away, at last, in the distance, as if seraphic choirs echoed them from heaven. As Milton, in his "Hymn to the Nativity," rapturously exclaims;

"Such music (as 'tis said)
Before was never made,
But when of old the sons of Morning sung,
While the Creator great
His constellatations set,
And the well-balanced world on hinges hung."

While the carol-singers were thus going from house to house, the Yule log, at the Manor House, was being brought in. Those were the days of capacious chimneys, and fire-places, wide enough to roast an ox. For this ceremonial, the butt of some huge tree was selected; for it was expected to act as back-log the week out; and it was dragged in by ropes, the whole household attending, with shouts, and often with music. The master, or mistress, sat by the hearth, looking on. When the mighty piece of timber was fairly in its place, and the lesser logs snapping and burning, musically, in front, the servants were sent back to the kitchen, where they kept Christmas Eve with song and dance, while the heads of the family, gathering around the blaze, with their children, and grandchildren, and other near relatives, "held high festival."

But if bringing in the Yule log was indispensable on Christmas eve, not less was the going to church, for morning service, on Christmas day. Every one, high or low, was expected to be present. Woe to him or her, Goodman Hodge, or Goody Joan, who failed to appear. If not provided with an excellent excuse, scant was the dole that would be his, or hers, when Christmas came around again. The church, for this festive day, was decked out with holly, ivy, bay, and other evergreens. The lord of the Manor was there, prominent in his pew; the rest of the congregation had suitable, but ruder, seats.

Church over, everybody went home: in the earlier times to a late breakfast, afterwards to dinner. The dinner was the dinner of the year. Every one was happy, or tried to be so. All yielded to the genial spirit of the season. Smiles were on the faces of rich and poor alike. It was under the influence of these festivities, that old George Withers broke out into his famous verses:

"So now has come our joyf'lest feast,
 Let every man be jolly.
Each room with ivy leaves is drest,
 And ev'ry post with holly.
Though some churls at out mirth repine,
Round your foreheads garlands twine,
 And let us all be merry.

Now all our neighbors' chimneys smoke,
 And Christmas blocks are burning;
Their ovens, they with baked meats choke,
 And all their spits are turning.
Without the door let sorrow lie
And if for cold it hap' to die,
We'll bury it in a Christmas pie,
 And evermore be merry."

In the houses of the nobles, the greatest state was observed; and the principal feature of the festival was the bringing in the boar's head. No Christmas dinner there, was considered complete without this famous dish. The preparation and adorning of the boar's head tasked the head-cook's utmost skill; each *chef* tried to outdo his rival, each strove to excel his former triumphs. It was an age when spices were used, in preparing food, to an extent utterly unknown now. Almost the only dish that has descended, unimpaired, from those times, is the Christmas mince-pie. What it is to other pies, all dishes, at that period, were to modern dishes. The boar's head was a marvel of spices, and was served up decked with holly, and with an apple in its mouth. A servitor of distinction, attired in his best, and preceded by heralds blowing trumpets, the jester leading all, carried in the dish; while minstrels, in a gallery overlooking the apartment, played on the viol, harp, and other instruments.

One of our illustrations depicts such a scene. The apartment is not unlike the banquet room, in Haddon Hall, where such revels were held for generation after generation. The old place is deserted now and desolate. The knights who fought at Crecy and Agincourt, and who kept their Christmas at Haddon afterwards, have been in their graves for centuries. No longer are there feastings in kitchen or solar; gay laughter is heard no more beneath holly and ivy; the long gallery echoes not to the feet of dancers. But we have been there, when, in the fading twilight, everything assumed a shape so shadowy, that, for a moment, the antique rooms seemed to be peopled again, and we almost fancied we could hear the light step of Dorothy Vernon, as she lifted the tapestry, and stole out of the little postern door, to elope with her forest lover, who was of the Manners family, since Dukes of Rutland, a "squire," as she found afterwards, of "high degree," in disguise.

At this dinner each one had a place in keeping with his rank; for distinction of caste was, in those days, scrupulously observed. The head of the household sat at the upper end of the board, often on a raised platform called a *dais*; while inferiors were placed at the lower end, and below the salt. A Lord of Misrule, chosen annually for the twelve days of the Christmas festivities, was always present, with his assistants, and they jested, mimicked, cut antics, and often danced the famous Dance of Fools. Practical jokes were greeted with roars of laughter. The food, like the fun, was rather coarse. Beef, mutton, boar's meat, and wild fowl were the dishes. It was a jovial, merry age, but not a refined one. Yet never, since, has any people, perhaps, so heartily KEPT CHRISTMAS.

CHRISTMAS POULTRY AND GAME, AND HOW TO COOK IT.

THERE are many persons who regard poultry and game, but especially the latter, as expensive luxuries, that should be indulged in only at rare intervals or on special occasions. Of all great occasions there are none equal in importance to the present. Of all birthdays that we celebrate none can compare with *the* birthday. Of all feasts that we keep, how do they sink to insignificance when contrasted with *the* feast! When, too, we cast our eyes over the world, and remember that this day all nations, peoples, and tongues unite in homage and praise to One Who, meek and lowly, 1900 years ago, first preached the gospel of mercy and compassion, love and forgiveness of sins, who can doubt the divinity of the Author and Founder of the feast?

There are other persons who consider either poultry or game as necessary to their daily dinner, and who order them regardless of the variation in price which they undergo at different seasons of the year. For instance, a couple of chickens, weighing a little over a pound each, will cost more in early spring than a couple of substantial fowls weighing, perhaps, four pounds each, would in July or August. Early spring chickens are undoubtedly expensive luxuries, and so are grouse at 12s. a brace. On the other hand, a couple of fowls, weighing, perhaps, eight pounds, if they can be bought at 6s. a couple, are as cheap, if not cheaper, than butcher's meat, especially if we take into account the very important use to which the bones of the fowls can be applied. Game also varies considerably in price, especially in very hot weather, when there is a large supply, and the danger of the game getting too high if not sold off quickly; and we must also take into account the increased importation of foreign game from Russia, Norway, and even America.

Probably the two standard dishes at the present season are the humble goose and the patrician turkey. How many a poor family there is to whom poultry, like Christmas, comes but once a year!

At the season of Christmas there is an enormous demand for geese; and, thanks to Free Trade and the laws of supply and demand, the supply is equal to the occasion. Hundreds of thousands of geese are sent over from the Continent, and can be bought at times as cheap as 6d. per pound; and many a poor household, like Bob Cratchet's of old, are enabled to "make merry with the goose," while no doubt the children, like his, get steeped in sage and onion up to their eyebrows. We will commence our few practical hints on poultry and game by giving a few words of advice on "How to cook the poor man's goose," more especially as there is an old saying that a goose is too much for two but not enough for three. If there is any truth in this, it is certainly very important to know how, in cooking the goose, to make the most of it. And the difficulty increases somewhat as, practically, too often many persons are dependent upon the baker's oven. Besides, there are many of our readers who would gladly advise their poorer brethren how to improve their Christmas dinner if they only knew how, notwithstanding the fact that the poor too often resent any interference in their domestic arrangements, never mind how kindly or how wisely such advice may be given.

The poor man's goose is generally sent to the bakehouse as follows: — The goose is placed, just as it is, in the middle of a large tin, and a heap of sage and onions is placed on one side and potatoes peeled and cut up for baking on the other. The idea of placing the sage and onions inside the goose evidently is an advancement in the art of cooking which they have not yet reached. First, a few words on the sage and onion stuffing. It is not every one, perhaps, that is aware of the fact that French cooks, who are generally, and justly, supposed to be superior to the English, differ altogether in their ideas of sage and onion stuffing from our own cooks. In England it is customary to make our sage and onion stuffing as follows: Supposing we have a large goose, we should take, say, six good-sized onions, parboil them till they are nearly tender, and then chop them up fine with either six fresh sage leaves or twelve dried, the allowance being one fresh leaf or two dried to each onion. In addition to this, we should add a tablespoonful of dried breadcrumbs to each onion, and a little pepper and salt. Some cooks add an egg. The whole of this stuffing is put inside the carcase of the goose, and is of course securely fastened in with a skewer or string, and roasted with it. If a Frenchman were going to stuff a goose, he would take, say, six onions, but would add nearly twenty times the quantity of sage. In France the proportion is in quantity three-parts onion and one part sage. The sage leaves are parboiled for a couple of minutes, and then stewed with the onions in a little butter. Those who have ever eaten ducks or geese abroad—in France—will probably remember that the sage entirely overpowered every other flavour, and the stuffing resembled in appearance dark spinach. Of course this variation of stuffing is entirely a matter of taste, and perhaps some persons may be disposed to try the French method as an experiment. There is one thing to be said in its favour. Supposing a duck or goose has been kept in a damp or close larder, and consequently has reached that stage which is generally described by housekeepers as "it ought to be cooked immediately." In this case the French stuffing is very useful. If we wish to make a goose go as far as possible we must have plenty of stuffing, and have the stuffing mild, and we would recommend, in cases where a small goose is cooked for a large family, two tablespoonfuls of breadcrumbs to every onion instead of one; and in this case we may add a little butter in order to avoid the possibility of the stuffing being too dry.

Another point to be borne in mind, if we wish to make our goose go as far as possible, is to have plenty of apple sauce. This is especially important where there are children, who as a rule enjoy the sage and onion stuffing and the apple sauce more than the meat itself. Boiled potatoes are much more suited to be eaten with goose than baked, and probably it is only amongst quite the poorer classes that baked potatoes are ever served in conjunction with it.

There is always a charm in novelty, and we might ask ourselves the question, "Is there any other method of cooking a goose besides roasting it? We wonder how a goose would taste boiled. It is an experiment we never tried, nor did we ever hear of its being boiled." But the idea provides material for thought. In France it is a very common thing to meet with a goose that has been braised. For this purpose we should require a large oval stew-pan, and in private households an ordinary fish-kettle would answer every purpose. We must first of all take a couple of large onions, half a dozen fresh sage leaves, and a teaspoonful of fresh thyme, or double that quantity of dried thyme, and having parboiled the onions, chop them up very fine first, and mix them all together with the herbs. Many French cooks add rosemary—a teaspoonful will be enough; add about half a grated nutmeg, pepper, and salt. We then stew these onions and herbs in about a couple of ounces of butter for about ten minutes. You then place this in, say, the fish-kettle, with half a pound of butter, a small handful of parsley, a small head of celery cut up, and a carrot sliced. Add a quarter of a pint of sherry, and place the goose in the fish-kettle; put on the lid (which ought to fit very tight), and let it what is called braise for nearly two hours. The goose must be turned from time to time over and over, in order that it may acquire a good colour. When the goose is thoroughly cooked, if any portions lack colour, the light coloured parts may be browned with a salamander or red-hot shovel. Next take a pint of good stock or gravy and throw it into the fish-kettle, and let it boil up, and scrape off all the brown sediment that may have collected on the sides and bottom of the fish-kettle, exactly in the same way that we pour boiling water into a tin that has roasted a large joint of meat in order to make the gravy. This very rich gravy must now be poured off, strained, skimmed, and thickened with a little brown roux or browned flour. Some must be poured over the goose, and the rest served separately in a tureen. The goose is generally sent to table with a border of glazed turnips or glazed onions, and in Italy small heaps of boiled macaroni are placed between each. A goose cooked this way is extremely nice. Foreign geese are much coarser, but fortunately much cheaper, than English ones. The fumes arising from the herbs and wine impregnate the meat, and render it exceedingly nice. A very cheap common wine is quite good enough for the purpose. It is a good plan to put a heavy weight on the lid of the fish-kettle, though of course a long oval braising pan is still better adapted for the purpose, as in that case when used abroad they always put hot charcoal on the lid.

In Belgium, when a goose has been braised in this manner, and some of the rich bright gravy poured over it, it is sent to table surrounded by a border of glazed vegetables such as turnips, onions, carrots, and Brussels sprouts.

Glazed vegetables make a very pretty border to a variety of dishes, but there are many English cooks who do not even know what glazed vegetables mean. To make glaze for vegetables is so simple and so cheap, that we would strongly recommend a trial, especially at the present season of the year, when it is customary to indulge in a little extra hospitality. What we want is a little gelatine and a little caramel. Caramel, as you probably know, is burnt sugar dissolved in water, and should be of the consistency of treacle. It is a great saving of both time and trouble to buy a small bottle for eightpence, which will probably last you for months. It is sold by grocers under the somewhat grand name of Parisian Essence. To make glaze, all we have to do is to open a packet of gelatine and put a large pinch into a tea-cup—we will say half a tea-cup. Now pour sufficient water over the gelatine to rather more than cover it. Let this stand, and in about an hour's time the gelatine will swell and absorb the water, and the cup will appear nearly full. Put the cup in the oven, and in five or ten minutes we shall have rather more than half a cupful of what looks like white glue. Add about half a teaspoonful of Parisian Essence, or caramel, and stir it up, and we have what looks like dark, old-fashioned treacle, very nearly black. Suppose you have some young carrots, turnips, or Brussels sprouts, drained off from the boiling water and quite dry; dip a paste brush into this glaze, and paint them over. The difference in their appearance is almost magical. You can paint over some small baked onions, and indeed almost any kind of vegetables. A roast turkey can be surrounded by these glazed vegetables, as we shall show by-and-by, in describing that very *récherché* dish, turkey *à la chipolata*. If you have this glaze ready, it is a great improvement to paint the breast of the goose with it, and pour some of the gravy round the base.

In the case of having cold roast fowls for luncheon or supper, it is well worth while to make a little of this glaze in order that they may be properly decorated. Brush the outside of the fowl, and it will assume the appearance of a well-polished Spanish mahogany table. Fill in the crevices with bright green parsley, and put plenty of parsley round the base. A few small red tomatoes, placed on the parsley make the dish look exceedingly pretty.

Supposing we are going to give a little supper party. It is wonderful what a difference half a teacupful of this glaze will make, although it only costs a few pence. Supposing we have a cold tongue, or a piece of cold pressed beef; its appearance, after it is glazed and before, makes all the difference between a dish fitted for a wedding breakfast and a homely one that we may meet with in a cottage; or perhaps a better simile would be, the difference between a plank of mahogany just planed in a carpenter's shop and the top of a well-kept mahogany table.

The Christmas turkey is as standing a dish among the well-to-do classes as the goose is amongst their poorer brethren. In high-class cooking, where expense is no object, few dishes rank higher than the turkey stuffed with truffles *à la chipolata*. It is exceedingly expensive, chiefly on account of the truffles; and in London there are many who, at Christmas time, send over to Paris and have their turkey sent back ready stuffed. The *chipolata* ragoût by which the turkey is surrounded is also somewhat expensive, as, properly speaking, it should contain cockscombs, button mushrooms, truffles, quenelles of forcemeat, besides carrots and turnips cut into pretty shapes, small round balls of streaky bacon, and chestnuts. If we leave out the cockscombs, quenelles, and the truffles, this ragoût ceases to be really expensive, as a tin of mushrooms can now be bought at a, comparatively speaking, trifling cost.

First of all, we must give up stuffing the turkey with truffles; but a very good substitute can be made with chestnuts. A turkey can be stuffed with chestnuts only, but it is better and more customary to mix the chestnuts with some ordinary veal stuffing: half of each is the usual proportion. Suppose we are going to have roast turkey *à la chipolata*, we should want some of the chestnuts whole, to go round the turkey by way of garnish. If the turkey is a large one, we should want, say, six dozen chestnuts, half of which will be required for the stuffing. We must first of all peel the chestnuts; and to do this easily (as otherwise it would be a very long job), put them in a saucepan or stewpan with a little butter, put them on the fire, occasionally shaking the saucepan. In a very short time the peel will come off without any trouble. The chestnuts should then be boiled till tender in a little good stock, and half the quantity taken out and pounded, and mixed with a similar quantity of ordinary veal stuffing. With this we will stuff the turkey. The next point is the ragoût. We shall want a small tin of button mushrooms, and some carrot and turnip. These must be cut into little round balls, about the size of a small walnut. They must be boiled till tender in a little good stock; and we must remember that the stock improves their flavour, while they improve the flavour of the stock. A piece of streaky bacon should also be cut up into round balls, about the same size, and fried brown on the outside. We already have three dozen chestnuts, boiled tender. Some good, rich, brown gravy must be made from the stock in which we have boiled the carrots, etc., and to which should be added the water in the tin of mushrooms. The gravy must be made thick with brown roux, made of a rich dark colour with a few drops of the Parisian Essence, and a wine-glass of sherry should be added to it. A little of this gravy should be poured over the turkey and a little round the base, while the bulk should be served separately in a tureen. The button mushrooms, the chestnuts, the round balls of carrot, turnip, and bacon, should be dipped in the thick bright glaze we have been speaking of. Little heaps of each should be piled up round the dish, so that a little heap of vegetable, either carrot or turnip, is placed alternately right round the dish. Thus a heap of chestnuts, mushrooms, or bacon will always have a little red heap on the one side and a little white heap on the other. The turkey itself should be ornamented with a couple of imitation flowers, one cut out of a carrot and the other from a turnip. These colours will of course match with the colours round the base.

There are many ways of utilising the remains of a cold turkey. Of course the drumsticks can be grilled, and we can have from the remainder minced turkey, in making which we can use up the remains of the gravy, mushrooms, chestnuts, and fried balls of bacon, while the vegetables, carrot and turnip, if any are left, should be placed round the edge. A very nice dish for supper can be made from cold turkey, in the shape of a mayonnaise salad. We will not enter into the details of making an ornamented mayonnaise salad, beyond pointing out the very pretty decoration that can be made if any of the white part of the breast of the turkey is left sufficient to be cut into slices. Cut some thin slices off the white meat of the turkey, and get a few slices of red tongue. Now, with a cutter or knife cut these red and white slices into the shape of a cockscomb, and dip them into the glaze, which should be made rather thinner for the purpose. When they are cold they will be bright and shiny. These should be placed alternately round the base of the mayonnaise salad; the pieces cut off should of course be added to the meat, and placed underneath the lettuces.

In conclusion, a few words on Game. In England, it is customary to serve game plainly roasted, with some good gravy and bread sauce, or fried breadcrumbs, as the case may be. English game is so superior to foreign that we can well afford to do without any accessory to flavour, and trust to the game itself. There is one point worth mentioning in connection with game, and that is, what are we to do with a grouse or brace of pheasants when they are undoubtedly regular old stagers. These very old birds, even if hung a long time, are hardly worth eating, they are so tough. We will suppose we have got an old grouse, too tough to be roasted in the ordinary way; what can we do with it? An old bird like this will make half a gallon of really first-rate game soup, and will well repay the trouble of making. We shall want, say, a couple of pounds of knuckle of veal, or rather more. Chop up the bone of the veal into little pieces, and put it with the veal in a stock-pot with a couple of onions, in which have been stuck half a dozen cloves, a carrot, a turnip (small), and a head of celery (also small). Let all this boil for six or seven hours, and keep adding water, so that the quantity is about half a gallon. In the meanwhile, partially roast the grouse. Now strain off the stock, cut up the grouse into little pieces, and put it in the stock to boil. Do not forget to pour a little of the stock into the tin in which the grouse is roasted, so as to catch the drippings. Let the whole boil till the bones come out quite bare, add a small teaspoonful of aromatic flavouring herbs. These are sold by grocers under the name of herbacious mixture. Now rub the whole of the meat of the grouse through a wire sieve, with the soup, after first removing the dry bones. Thicken the soup with a little brown roux, and add a claret glass of sherry to the soup before sending it to table. This is a far better method of treating old game than trying to keep birds till they are very high in order to get them tender. We may add that game soup should be dark in appearance, and in order to attain this object we can add about a teaspoonful of our Parisian Essence. The thickness of the soup should as much as possible depend upon the meat rubbed through the sieve, and very little roux should be added; in fact, only sufficient to give it consistency. When sent to table in the tureen, whoever helps the soup should bear in mind to give it a stir before each helping, as the meat rubbed through the sieve is a sort of powder, and has a tendency to sink to the bottom of the tureen.

Game soup can be made from partridges, pheasants, and Norwegian grouse. These latter should be kept a long time before being used for the purpose. If game soup is made from hare, or the remains of roast or jugged hare, an exactly similar method should be pursued, including the addition of the aromatic herbs; only, in the case of hare soup it is a great improvement to add a teaspoonful of red currant jelly to every quart of soup. Game soup should not be thick, like pea soup, but of the consistency of ordinary good mock-turtle, as if too much roux is added it overpowers the flavour of the game.

CHRISTMAS CUSTOMS HERE AND ELSEWHERE.

WE shall soon be celebrating the most glorious festival of the Christian year, the only festival, we may say, that receives almost universal recognition. Wherever the Christian religion has been preached, Christmas is the joy-time of the year.

Let us say a few words about the origin of this great festival. It was first inaugurated as a festival in the year 98; but it was not till about thirty years after that Pope Telesphorus, in the reign of Antoninus Pius, ordered its annual observance by all true Christians on the 25th December, 137, which then fell on the day we now call the 6th January. From that time it seems to have been constantly and devoutly celebrated throughout the Church.

Christmas was called Yuletide by our Saxon ancestors, and meant literally the festival of the sun. One of their names for the sun was Yule, hence the great feast, which was always held at the winter solstice, was called the Yule feast. Yule was the greatest festival in the countries of Scandinavia. Yule bonfires blazed everywhere to scare witches and wizards, offerings were made to the gods, the boar dedicated to Freyr was placed on the table, and over it the warriors vowed to perform great deeds. Pork, mead, and ale abounded, and the Yuletide passed merrily away with games and mirth of our Saxon forefathers. The houses were decorated with holly, ivy, and mistletoe, the churches were decked with evergreens. Gay says—

"Now with bright holly all the temple strow
With laurel green and sacred mistletoe."

Standards covered with greenery were set up in the streets and on the village greens, and there the people danced and made merry. Great fires of wood were kindled in their huge chimneys, and the blazing of the Yule-log is supposed to have been intended to signify the light and heat of the sun. In the king's palace, and in nearly every great house was a personage called the "Lord of Misrule," or the "Master of Merry Disports," whose business it was to see that the fun was kept up with spirit. Disguisings, masks, and mummeries were also held accompanied by all sorts of fun and frolic, men and women dressed in each other's clothes, and gave themselves up to the wildest merriment.

"Now Christmas is come,
Let us beat up the drum,
And call all our neighbours together;
And when they appear
Let us make them such cheer
As will keep out the wind and the weather."

In addition to the sports and feasting of Christmastide, there were many singular customs associated with the season to which we must briefly refer. Crowds of people used to assemble on Christmas Day in the burial ground at Glastonbury in Somersetshire to see the thorn bud in bloom, which was said to have sprung from a staff planted by Joseph of Arimathea, to whom tradition attributes the introduction of the Gospel into Britain. It was long a popular belief that this famous thorn would produce flowers in full bloom every Christmas Day; and when the spectators were disappointed in seeing the miracle they ascribed the failure to the alteration of the style, and watched again on old Christmas Day. There was, however, no miracle in the case, as the thorn was one of that species which frequently blows in mild winters.

In this article we desire more to speak of the customs associated with this season in other countries. The Dutch, a slow and phlegmatic race, made their Christmas-keeping a somewhat prolonged festival, often taking more than a week to celebrate it, indulging the whole time in all the good things they could procure, and consuming an amount of "strong waters" that would have meant excess to any temperament less cold and phlegmatic than their own. The old Dutch recipe books contained rules for many compounds requiring delicate manipulation on the part of the cooks. Indeed, one can but conceive the greatest respect for the mental powers of the woman whose "crullers" and waffles were always light and crispy notwithstanding that baking powders and egg-beaters were things unknown, that even "pearl ash" was of home manufacture, and the right quantity of sour cream which was to balance the alkali as well as its due degree of acidity, had to be determined in each individual case.

The French were even more temperate than their neighbours, and very early displayed the talent which has made them what we may call the tutors of the rest of the world in all matters relating to culinary art. To the French Huguenots Christmas was a day of rejoicing, family festivity, and neighbourly greeting. They drank very little strong liquors, and their mild pure wines served but to aid digestion and impart gaiety to the spirits. Rarely was drunkenness known among them. The giving of gifts was a more prominent feature of Christmas-time with them than with others. And their gifts, unlike those of the English and Dutch, which were nearly always of something to eat and drink, were of permanent value. They were poor in this world's goods, most of them having had to flee from their country and leave their possessions behind them, owing to the cruel intolerance of Louis XIV., so that their gifts were seldom costly; but some have survived even to this day in the possession of their descendants—cobweb laces made by delicate fingers, pointed fans and screens, and embroidered foot-stools and cushions.

Christmas is celebrated with great pomp and ceremony throughout Italy, and especially in Rome and Naples. In these cities, all through the night of the 23rd, the screaming of fish vendors resounds in the streets, for eels are the favourite fish for the day. It is said the Pope receives many tons of this indigestible though savoury dish as a present at this season. In the eternal city the festivity assumes something more of a religious character. The Piazza di Navona with its beautiful fountain is the centre of attraction, and there all sorts of comestibles are to be bought. The people, full of animation, move hither and thither, and in their bright gay dresses present a lively and joyous scene. Among the religious ceremonies which take place at this time, the midnight mass at the church of Santa Maria Maggiore is the chief attraction. In the old days ere the sword of Garibaldi cut away the temporal sovereignty of the Pope, His Holiness was always present at this high mass attended by his brilliant court. In connection with this service there used to be a very curious usage called Blessing of the Sword and Cap, which succeeded a usage still more ancient, namely, that of sending the standard of St. Peter to some sovereign undertaking a crusade in the interests of the Church. Then followed the procession of the sacred "relic," a portion of Christ's cradle set in a magnificent shrine of crystal with the figure of the Divine Infant in gold. This ceremony, like many others, is now a thing of the past. When the light comes the shadows flee away. After the midnight mass it was usual for the Pope to invite the cardinals and high dignitaries of the city to partake of a sumptuous supper. And the example set by so high an authority was followed by all orders of the people. The Christmas festivities at Rome seemed to comprise two parts, the religious rites and the heavy *cenone* or supper.

Every Neapolitan would think he failed in his duty if on Christmas Eve he did not dine with his family. On all the other days of the year he might dine at his club or at the café, or wherever he pleased, but on Christmas Eve it was obligatory that he should dine at home, when the traditional *vermicelli con vougli* (periwinkles), the succulent *capitone* (eel) appear on the table. The poorest people sell or pawn all they have to celebrate the Santa Natale with a good supper. The balconies display every kind of illumination, fireworks, bombs, etc., and lively talk and boisterous laughter indicate the happiness and good temper of all. On the evening of Christmas Day, on the other hand, the greatest quiet prevails in the streets. All are in-doors, and one might traverse the whole city and not meet with a living soul, or hear a sound unless it be the ringing of a church-bell calling to vespers. The amount of sweets and cakes consumed at the Christmas festival is enormous. Families have been known to order as much as half a ton, out of which they send presents to their friends. The chief sweet is a species of almond toffee, and the cake most in favour is what is called the *panegallo*, which somewhat resembles plum-pudding.

In some of the country villages every *contadino* brings two small oak trees into his house, throws them into the fireplace, covers them with grain and leaves them until all are consumed. In some places these oaks are covered with flowers, red silk ribbons, and gold thread. Large logs of wood are put on the hearth, as the Yule log is in this country, but with this difference that when it is half burnt it is taken out of the fireplace and religiously preserved, the superstitious people believing that it will keep them from all misfortune during the coming year.

In Sicily the feast of onions used to be the chief peculiarity about Christmas. A fight with onions took place between the villagers, and the victor was presented with a bull. But the most curious custom of all was that which prevailed in a certain province of Italy. The women dragged all the old bachelors they could find into the village church, running them round the sacred edifice and beating them well with their fists. This was done that they might feel ashamed, and take to themselves wives before Christmas came round again.

In Denmark there are strange ceremonies which have come down from pre-Christian times. In those days Odin and Thor and other deities were worshipped by our Saxon ancestors. At Christmas a sheaf of corn was tied to the gables of the houses as a feed to Odin's mighty horse, Sleipner. It was the last sheaf cut in the field. And at the present day, every Yule-tide, the sheaf is still hung out, but now it is for Santa Claus's horse (for the colt of Odin has given place to the patron saint of children) and a person convalescent after a dangerous illness is said to have "given a feed to Death's horse."

In Germany every house has its Christmas-tree, and there is much music and carol singing. There is a pleasant custom all over the fatherland which we must not omit to notice. On Christmas Eve two figures may frequently be seen making their round among the houses of a selected neighbourhood. They are Knecht Ruprecht (Knight Rupert) and Father Christmas. At the door of the house a great bag of fruit, toys, and other good things, is handed to Knecht Ruprecht. Then he enters and inquires after the conduct of the children, and if the parents "give them a good report," Father Christmas, who wears a white dress and a pink or gilt belt, orders the contents of the bag to be emptied on the floor, and while the attention of the children is centred in the scramble, the two figures disappear to perform a similar office at other houses.

In Burgundy, for some weeks before Christmas, the young men and women who can sing, meet together and practice those carols whose chief theme is the coming of the Messiah. They sometimes meet at one house and sometimes at another, taking turns in paying for the chestnuts and white wine, but singing with one common voice the praises of *le petit Jesus*. More or less until Christmas Eve all goes on in this way, and thousands of chestnuts are consumed and gallons of wine are drunk. But to-night supper is provided on a grand scale, and everyone goes in for hearty enjoyment. After supper a circle gathers round the hearth on which an enormous log has been placed, called the *Suche*, or Yule-log. And they say to the children, "Look you, if you are good this evening Noel will rain down sugar plums in the night." Meantime little parcels of them are placed under each end of the log, and the children come and pick them up, believing in good faith that the *Suche de Noel* has borne them. Carols are sung to the miraculous Noel. Noel! Noel! Noel! resounds on all sides; it seasons every sauce, it is served up with every course. Of the thousands of canticles which are heard on this famous eve, it is said that ninety-nine in a hundred begin and end with this word. The merry-making and feasting are prolonged into midnight. And then as the bells ring out on the frosty air, the company, who are furnished with a little taper streaked with various colours (the Christmas candle), go through the crowded streets where the lanterns are dancing the Will-o'-the-wisp at the impatient summons of the multitudinous chimes. It is the midnight-mass. And after hearing the Mass they return homeward in tumult and great haste; they salute the Yule-log, they pay homage to the hearth, they sit down at table, and amid songs that reverberate louder than ever feast far into the morning hours. But all things have an end, and so is it here. The Yule-log burns out, the merry company separate, and each goes to his domicile and his bed.

In south-eastern Europe there are various singular customs observed on Christmas Day. Among the mountaineers of Servia and Montenegro it is a general custom for each family to choose some goodly youth of their acquaintance as a dropper-in for the Christmas Day festivities. He is called the "Polaznik," or Christmas guest. As he approaches the threshold he calls out, "Christ is born," and scatters some corn from his hand inside the dwelling house. "Welcome," cries the housemother who stands at the door to meet him, "of a truth He is born," and she throws at the same time a handful of corn in his face. The Polaznik now draws near the Yule-fire, and taking up the remains of the chief log, which is burning on the hearth, knocks it against the cauldron hook above so as to make the sparks fly, saying as he does so, "So may our Domachin (house-father) have all good luck and happiness." He then, with the same log, strikes the embers below, saying as the sparks fly again, "Even so may our brother the Domachin, have oxen and cows and goats and sheep and all good luck." After this he places an orange on the end of the log and on the orange a small coin, which the Domachitz (housewife) promptly takes possession of. In return for this gift she presents the Polaznik before he leaves with the leggings and socks in use among these mountaineers, and along with them a Christmas loaf, or "pogatch," as it is called. The Polaznik now asks his host, the Domachin, what kind of Christmas he has, and whether he is merry? To which he replies, "Christmas has come as a kind guest, never better, my brother; all have enough and all are merry." Immediately the new-comer exchanges the kiss of peace with every member of the family, and then, sitting down beside the hearth, is pledged with wine and raki to his heart's content. Other ceremonies of an elaborate and singular character are gone through, and so the day ends. A Montenegrin song says,

"Without eyesight there is no day!
Without Christmas no true feast!
The flame shoots up brighter than 'tis wont,
Before the fire the straw is strewed,
The Yule-logs are laid across the fire,
The guns are fired, the roast meat turns,
The guzlas twang, and they play the kolo.
The grandsires dance with the grand-children,
Three generations turn round in the dance.
You would say they were all the same year's children!
For the joy and the mirth levels all.
But what most falls to my taste
Is that each must be toasted!"

On New Year's Day, which is called by the serfs "Little Christmas," the head of the roasted pig or sheep, which was the chief dish of the Christmas feast, is eaten. A particular kind of cake is made for this day called in the cities and towns "St. Basil's cake," but in the villages "the cake for the she-bear," for what reason we cannot tell. The evening is spent by the young people in various modes of divination, especially in forecasting their marriage future—a source of great interest and amusement to all.

In the Highlands of Scotland (to come back to our own country) curious out-of-door games were played on Christmas Day, and peculiar sorts of cakes and thick broth were eaten. In some places a carp was the chief dish at supper, and a boar's head served on a silver platter for dinner, and the festivities were often kept up from Christmas to Twelfth Night. In the Isle of Man people sat up all night, and the next morning they hunted and killed a wren, and carrying the little bird to church, buried it with mock solemnities. This custom still prevails in the Celtic parts of Ireland, only instead of carrying the dead wren to church, they carry it round, tied on a bough to the principal houses, singing at each the doggerel lines—

"The wren, the wren, the king of all birds,
St. Stephen's Day was caught in the furze;
Although she is small, her family is great,
Rise up, landlady, and give us a treat."

It would be easy to add a variety of suggestive customs from other lands pertaining to this joyous season of Christmas, but to do so would be to prolong our paper to an inordinate length. And therefore we here make an end by wishing all our readers a "Merry Christmas and a Happy New Year."

WILLIAM COWAN.

A CHRISTMAS-TIDE REMEMBRANCE.

Words by MRS. NORTON.　　　　　　　　　　　　　　　*Music by* C. A. MACIRONE.

Do you re-mem-ber all the sun-ny pla-ces, Where in bright days...... long past we played to-ge - - - ther? Do you re-mem-ber all the old home fa-ces That ga-thered round the hearth.... in win-try wea - - ther?

The Girl's Own Paper, 1888

Do you re - mem - ber all the hap - py meet - ings, In sum - mer ev - - 'nings,
pp
round the o - pen door? Kind looks, kind words,.............
cres.
.... and ten - der greet - ings, And cling - - - - - - - ing hands, whose
pp
pul - ses beat no more?............. Do you re - mem - - ber
these?............. Do you re -
rall.
tempo.

-mem - -ber all the sun - ny pla - ces, Where in bright days long past we played to - ge - - - ther? Do you re - mem - ber all the old home fa - ces, That ga-ther'd round the hearth in win - try wea - - ther, That ga - ther'd round the hearth? Do......... you re - mem - ber these?..........

DECEMBER.

December fell, baith sharp and snell,
Makes flowers creep in the ground;
Then man's threescore, both sick and sore,
No soundness in him found.
His ears and een, and teeth of bane,
All these now to him fail;
That he may say, both night and day,
That death shall him assail.

OLD POEM; 1653.

THE FINE OLD ENGLISH GENTLEMAN WELCOMING AT HIS GATE A BAND OF MUMMERS, TO SHARE WITH HIM, AND ENLIVEN, THE FESTIVITIES OF CHRISTMAS.

DECEMBER, the tenth (from *Decem*), and last month of the Alban and early Roman Calendars, is also the last month of the modern year. In this month, the Romans celebrated their *Saturnalia*, when slaves were on an equal footing with their masters. The Saxons, before their conversion to Christianity, called December *Winter-Monath*; but, after that, added to it the appellation of *Haligh*, or Haly, in commemoration of the Nativity, which has always been celebrated in this month; although the true time of our Saviour's birth is placed in August.

St. Nicholas's (Dec. 6) legends relate such marvellous instances of his early conformity to the observances of the Roman Church, as entitled him to the appellation of the Boy Bishop. The choice of his representative in every cathedral church in this country continued till the reign of Henry VIII.; and, in many, large provision of money and goods was made for the annual observance of the festival of the Boy Bishop, which lasted from this day until *Innocents' Day* (Dec. 28), during which the utmost misrule and mockery of the most solemn rites were practised and enjoined. Of these customs, the *Montem* at Eton is a corruption: it is celebrated triennially; the last Montem was in June, 1844.

Christmas Eve (Dec. 24) is celebrated because, Christmas Day, in the primitive Church, was always observed as the Sabbath Day, and, like it, preceded by an Eve, or Vigil. Superstition, ever sweet to the soul, was doubly prompted by the sanctity of the season. It was once believed that, at midnight, all the cattle in the cow-house would be found kneeling; that bees sang in their hives on Christmas Eve, to welcome the approaching day; and that cocks crowed all night with same object: to the latter, Shakspeare alludes in *Hamlet*:—

Some say that even 'gainst that hallow'd season
At which Our Saviour's birth is celebrated,
The Bird of Dawning croweth all night long.

The ceremonies and amusements of this season are too numerous for us to describe. The Waits, or more properly Wakes, usually commence their nocturnal serenades about the middle of the month, and play nightly, till Christmas Day. Although the music now played is secular, the custom originated evidently in commemoration of the early salutation of the Virgin Mary before the birth of Jesus Christ, or the *Gloria in Excelsis* the hymn of the angels—the earliest Christmas Carol: the word Carol is from the Italian *Carola*, a song of devotion, (*Ash*); or from *cantare*, to sing, and *rola*, an interjection of joy, (*Bourne*.)

Carols are yet sung at Christmas in Ireland and Wales; but, in Scotland, where no Church fasts have been kept since the days of John Knox, the custom *is* unknown. On the Continent it is almost universal: during the last days of Advent, Calabrian minstrels enter Rome, and are to be seen in every street, saluting the shrines of the Virgin-mother with their wild music. Within the present century, the singing of Carols began on Christmas Eve, and were continued late into the night. On Christmas Day, these Carols took the place of Psalms in all the churches, the whole congregation joining; and at the end the clerk declared in a loud voice, his wishes for a merry Christmas and a happy new year to all the parishioners. Still these Carols differed materially from those of earlier times, which were festal chansons for enlivening the merriment of Christmas, and not songs of Scripture history; the change having been made by the Puritans.

The decking of churches and houses with laurel and other evergreens, at this period, may be to commemorate the victory gained over the powers of darkness by the coming of Christ. The gathering of Mistletoe is a relic of Druidic worship; and Holly was originally called the *holy* tree, from its being used in holy places.

CHRISTMAS DAY has been set apart, from time immemorial, for the commemoration of our Blessed Saviour's birth; when, "though Christ was humbled to a manger, the contempt of the place was took off by the glory of the attendance and ministration of angels." Christmas is named from *Christi Missa*, the mass of Christ; it was, however, forbidden to be kept as a fast by the Council of Braga, A.D. 563; which anathematised such as did not duly honour the birthday of Christ, according to the flesh, but pretended to honour it by fasting on that day; a custom attributed to the same conception which led to the practice of fasting on the Lord's day namely, the belief that Christ was not truly born in the nature of man. Since this Canon, we do not find any positive regulation specially affecting the observance of Christmas.—(*Feasts and Fasts*.)

To detail the hospitalities of Christmas would fill a volume, though our artist has grouped the most characteristic celebrities of the season. Here is "The Fine Old English Gentleman" welcoming to his gate a band of Mummers, (masked persons,) and Minstrels, with their ludicrous frolics, not forgetting the Hobbyhorse Dance:—

We are come over the Mire and Moss: A Dragon you shall see,
We dance an Hobby-horse;   And a wild worm for to flee.

The Loving-cup was borrowed from the Wassail-bowl, though the latter was carried about with an image of Our Saviour. Here, too, is the *bore's head*, "the rarest dish in all the lande, and provided in honour of the King of bliss." Nor must we omit the Yule-log burnt on Christmas Eve; though the bringing it in with "Christmas Candles" is forgotten. Even the mince-pies are assumed to be emblematical—their long shape imitating the cratch, rack, or manger wherein Christ was laid—(*Selden*). Christmas boxes are of Pagan origin.

Although much of this custom of profuse hospitality has passed away, Christmas is yet universally recognised as a season when every Christian should show his gratitude to the Almighty, for the inestimable benefits procured to us by the Nativity of our Blessed Saviour, by an ample display of good will toward our fellow men. "Hospitality is threefold: for one's family; this is of necessitie: for strangers; this is of courtesie: for the poore; this is charity."—(*Fuller*.)

St. Stephen's Day, (December 26,) is first in the days of Martyrdom: St. Stephen being a Martyr both in *will* and *deed*. *St. John* (December 27,) being a Martyr in *will*, but not in *deed*, is placed second.

The Innocents, (December 28,) being Martyrs in *deed*, though not in *will*, are, therefore, placed last.—(*Elementa Liturgica*.)

I. T.

The Story of Santa-Claus.

THE STORY OF SANTA-CLAUS.

"'Twas the night before Christmas, when all through the house
Not a creature was stirring, not even a mouse.
The stockings were hung by the chimney with care,
In hopes that St. Nicholas soon would be there ;
The children were nestled all snug in their beds,
While visions of sugar-plums danced in their heads ;
When out on the lawn there arose such a clatter
I sprang from the bed to see what was the matter.
Away to the window I flew like a flash,
Tore open the shutters and threw up the sash;
When what to my wondering eyes should appear
But a miniature sleigh and eight tiny reindeer,
With a little old driver ! I'd no need to pause,
I knew in a moment 'twas good Santa Claus !"

ALMOST all our little English folks have of late years made the acquaintance of that celebrated but mysterious personage known here as Santa-Claus. His annual visit is eagerly watched for and reckoned upon in many a home, though when, whence, how he comes—whether down the chimney; by the road, in Germany and France; or in the invisible "miniature sleigh with eight tiny reindeer," with which, under the name of Kris Kringle, he rattles across the snow in America—they neither know or care; so that he fills their long stockings for them they are satisfied. This same Santa-Claus is no new per- sonage. In old times he was much honoured in England as the patron saint of boys and scholars; and on the 6th of December,

Little Folks Magazine, 1878

Little Folks.

St. Nicholas' Day, in each year, a boy bishop was elected in Salisbury Cathedral, with many ceremonies, who, with his boy dean and prebendaries, held a kind of jurisdiction, which lasted until Childermas Day, December the 28th. St. Nicholas appears to have been very popular in most countries. He is the patron saint of Russia, and most of the Czars are named after him. He is also the patron of New York city, which was first settled by the Dutch, who hold him in high esteem in their own country; while in England, I am informed, there are three hundred and seventy-two churches named in his honour.

Wonderful tales are told of the doings of this saint, who, by his piety and industry, rose from the position of humble citizen to that of Archbishop of Patara, in Asia Minor. Should you one day visit other lands, you will find in the Continental churches many pictures commemorating his kind deeds, and particularly the one to which he owes his character as the children's friend. Over the altar of St. Nicholas, at Ghent, he is represented standing in full episcopal dress, and crozier in hand, holding two fingers up in solemn warning; close by are three youths in a tub, who appear to be praising him. These, the quaint old legend goes on to relate, were three little scholars who were cruelly murdered and hidden in a tub; by means of the good man's supplications they were brought back to life, and, as the picture shows, at once sat up, and would have thanked him had he not bidden them worship none but God Himself.

Later on he became very rich, but he gave all his money to the poorest and most deserving of his fellow-citizens. He was so truly charitable and unostentatious that he always tried to do this in such a fashion that the recipients of his gifts should not know who was the giver, going about at night, and secretly leaving his alms where they were most wanted.

So you see St. Nicholas is an old friend to the young people; though, in his new character of Santa-Claus, he has only been known to us of late years. I think he came from Germany, when our Queen first had her little children to please—at least, I never heard of him or of Christmas-trees before.

Here is a notice of the new trees from a letter written from Ratzeburg, in North Germany, about that time. It alludes, not to Christmas Eve, but to St. Nicholas' Day, which falls on the 6th of December. "There is a Christmas custom here which pleased and interested me much. The children make little presents to their parents and to each other, and the parents to the children. For three or four months before Christmas the girls are all busy, and the boys save up their pocket-money to buy these presents. What the gifts are to be is kept a profound secret. The girls have a world of contrivances to conceal it: such as working when out on visits, or getting up early in the morning. Then on Christmas Eve, or rather St. Nicholas' Day, one of the rooms, into which the parents must not go, is lighted up by the children. A great yew bough is fastened on to the table at a little distance from the wall, and a number of little tapers are fixed on the bough, but not so as to burn it, and coloured paper hangs from the twigs. Under this bough the children lay out in order the presents they mean for their parents, still concealing what they intend for each other. Then the parents are introduced, and each presents his little gift, and then they bring out the remainder one by one from their pockets to offer them to their brothers, sisters, and friends, with kisses and embraces."

I must say I like this simple fashion of each child really "making" a little present. I would rather have the clumsiest pen-wiper or the roughest of ties, put together by loving fingers, than the grandest of bought ornaments—unless, indeed, as sometimes happens, the buying involves self-denial. I fancy all parents and real friends would be of the same opinion. There are so many things neat-handed young people can make—fancy needle-books, pen-wipers, neckties, warm knitted or crocheted cuffs, or spectacle-cases for the older ones. With a little gum, a few coloured scraps, and plenty of patience, any old cardboard box, being first neatly covered with black paper, can be transformed into quite a handsome collar or handkerchief box for papa's dressing table. A few skeins of bright wool or braid become a pretty mat or tidy for mamma; while any little cheap doll will look charming, and be sure to please the other youngsters, if they see that its clothes have been neatly put together by their big sister; any roughly home-rigged carved boat will please better than any bought one—at least, it ought to do so; and those who think otherwise are, to my mind, not worth a present at all. I have heard of some lucky children who have so many toys they don't know what to do with them. All I can say is, remember that there are always a great many young folks who would highly prize the oldest and most battered of toys. Think, if you do not know, of some such that Santa-Claus most likely has never visited, and do you then be his representative, kindly and unobtrusive as he was, and, if possible, help to make this a happy Christmas-time to them, as your kind friends will, I doubt not, try to make it to you.

THE ANCIENT AND ORIGINAL MUMMERY OF ST. GEORGE AND THE TURKISH KNIGHT.

"Then came the merry masquers in,
And carols roared in blythesome din;
If unmelodious was the song,
It was a hearty note and strong.
Who lists may in their mumming see
Traces of ancient mystery.
White shirts supplied the masquerade,
And smutted cheeks the visor made.
But, oh! what masquers richly dight
Can boast of bosoms half as light?
England was merry England when
Old Christmas brought his sports again."—SCOTT.

EVERY Christmas, in old times, and even in more modern ones, a strange motley party would arrive at the doors of well-to-do country folks, and loudly demand the privilege of the season for Old Father Christmas, St. George of England, and their merry men. Almost always these mummers were admitted, and family and friends, household and neighbours, gathered round to stare, and laugh, and wonder at the strange new-comers.

There was venerable Father Christmas, with a long white beard made of tow; there was St. George, in armour as bright as silver paper and tinsel could make it, and as fierce as burnt cork and red lead could make him; there was a turbaned Turk, with moustachios that curled so fiercely that it was a wonder they did not lift his head off; there was a dismal doctor, white with chalk and blue about the spectacles, which were of the biggest and heaviest; there was a solemn Oliver Cromwell, in a tall hat and wrapped in a big cloak; there were a pretty little girl or two, carrying a large bunch of mistletoe; there was—let me see—a whole troop of masquers, a kind of awkward squad, I believe, who kept in the background, but were generally supposed to represent the English nation assembled to watch and wonder at the feats of her great champion.

AN AMPHIBIOUS MUMMER.

Once admitted into kitchen or parlour, the performance began by Father Christmas advancing and addressing the company generally, in these words:—

"Here come I, Old Father Christmas!
I hope Old Father Christmas
Will never be forgot.
A room—make room here, gallant boys,
  [*Clears space with his holly wand.*
And give us room to rhyme.
We've come to show activity
Upon a Christmas time.
Acting youth or acting age,
The like was never acted on this stage.
If you don't believe what I now say,
Enter St. George, and clear yourself the way!"

Enter ST. GEORGE, *flourishing his spear.*

"Here come I, St. George the valiant man,
With naked sword and spear in hand.
I fought the dragon and brought him to slaughter,
And for this won the King of Egypt's daughter.
What man or mortal will dare to stand
Before me with his sword in hand?
I'll slay him and cut him as small as flies!
And send him to Jamaica to make mince pies!"

The Turkish knight steps up and says haughtily—

"Here come I, a Turkish knight,
In Turkish land I learnt to fight;
I'll fight St. George with courage bold,
And his hot blood I will make cold!"

St. George.—"If thou art a Turkish knight
Draw out thy sword and let us fight."

Here a desperate encounter follows, continued until the Turk falls prostrate, mortally wounded, to all appearance. St. George, like a noble foe, kneels down and tries to assist him, then rising, addresses the audience, pointing proudly downwards:

"Ladies and gentlemen,
  See what I've done.
I've cut this Turk down
  Like the evening sun.
Is there any doctor that can be found
  [*Looking about.*
To cure the knight of his deadly wound?"

DOCTOR *advances.*

"Here come I, old Doctor Grub,
Under my arm I carry a club.

Little Folks.

"I have a bottle in my pocket   [*Produces large bottle.*
Called hokum shokum, alicampane.
I'll touch his eyes, nose, mouth, and chin,
And say ' Rise, dead man, and fight again ! ' "

He touches the prostrate hero on each feature as he speaks, and at the last word the Turk leaps up, and stands prepared for battle. Of this, however, St. George takes no present notice, but addresses the audience in a boastful strain :—

"Here am I, St. George, with shining armour bright;
I am a famous champion, also a worthy knight.
Seven long years in a close cave was kept,
And out of that into a prison leapt ;
From out of that into a rock of stones,
There I laid down all my poor grievous bones.
Many a giant did I subdue,
And ran a fiery dragon through.
First, then, I fought in France,
Second I fought in Spain,
Thirdly I came to ——
    [*Any place where the party are assembled.*
To fight the Turk again."

He turns to the Turk, and a desperate encounter again takes place, in which the Turk is, of course, defeated, and falls at St. George's feet, who once more cries—

"Is there any doctor that can be found
To cure this knight of his deadly wound ?"

And once more the doctor advances and says—

"Here come I, old Doctor Grub," &c.

Once more he touches the eyes, nose, mouth, and chin of the patient with the contents of the big bottle, and then the Turk again rises, and stands in order of battle, when another character advances, who announces himself as Oliver Cromwell, though what brought him here or what his errand is seems rather difficult to explain. He himself does not do so, though he says—

"Here come I, Oliver Cromwell,
    As you may suppose ;
Many nations have I conquered
    With my copper nose.
I made the French to tremble,
    And the Spanish for to quake,
I fought the jolly Dutchmen,
    And made their hearts to ache ! "

He then drops his cloak and declares himself in altogether a different character.

"Here come I, Rub a dub dub !"

Then producing a bag or cap, he adds, taking off his hat and bowing—

"Ladies and gentlemen, our story's ended,
Our money box is recommended.
Five or six shillings will do us no harm,
Silver or copper, or gold if you can."

While the cap or hat passes round, the actors fall in line and file out, generally singing some quaint old carol or seasonable song.

I myself saw the whole of this droll "mummery," as it is wrongly called (for a real mummery is all dumb show), performed in the kitchen of a gentleman's house in Dorset, and the next week the boys of the family gave us the whole thing over again in the nursery, which had been prepared for the occasion. They had learned their parts—the words of which are handed down orally, though I met with them afterwards in a book called " Traditions of Tenby "—from the dairy-maid's brother, who, it appeared, was no less a personage than St. George ; and by the aid of silver paper, feathers, cardboard, and borrowed finery, they made quite a show. I think some of my young readers might amuse themselves and others one of these long winter evenings with this little mummery, which is so very, very old that it would most likely be quite a novelty to many.

THE CHILDREN'S PARTY-SUPPER.

THE children clamoured for a party; father groaned as he thought of the call it would make upon his already overstrained pocket, and mother sighed at the prospect of having her orderly house turned into a bear-garden; neither encouraged the project, although it must be said in their favour that they did not actually quash it. The children turned to Pollie—she was always a refuge and strong tower to them; if there was a way of possibility Pollie could always find a means of treading in that way, she had an open sesame wherewith to charm apparently closed doors. In this instance she was entirely on the children's side; a frolic on a winter's evening was quite to her own taste, and she even initiated the proposal of a party-supper. This was attacking the enemy's camp with a boldness that was almost effrontery, but she gained her point all the same.

"Have it your own way, only don't turn me out-of-doors entirely, and make that cover all your expenses," father said, and "that" proved to be a five-pound note. Pollie gave him a grateful kiss and the others ventured a cheer.

Approached on the subject of supper, mother said, "You are quite able to manage it yourself, Pollie; I will give you what help I can, but don't ask the servants to do more than their regular share of work." So, left to her own resources, Pollie, as directress, wisely pressed everyone, even the little ones, into service.

After much debating it was decided that supper should be laid in the nursery upstairs, partly because this was one of the largest rooms in the house, and as everything save the chocolate would be served cold, the table could be left finished in every detail before the guests' arrival; also, as the supper was to conclude the festivities there seemed something appropriate in mounting upwards in order to reach it.

The staircases were to be lighted with Chinese lanterns, as the subdued light from these quite hid from view the shortcomings of well-worn carpets, while a few plants here and a draped curtain there, completed the illusion. In the banqueting-hall itself a good deal of this illusory work was required, but it was wonderful how much was accomplished by a few yards of art muslin, some flags and evergreen boughs, when ingenuity set to work upon them.

The long table down the middle of the room consisted of boards laid over trestles, the barrenness of these was hidden by having a blanket laid over before the cloths were put on. Over the white cloth to form a lattice-work pattern, ribbons were laid in diagonal lines crossing each other, very cheap ribbons and very narrow ones, but of bright colours—scarlet, green, and yellow, and the effect was brilliant. Small feathery ferns and palms in white and green pots broke up the uniformity. Two dozen cane chairs had been hired for this room, also a little crockery and glass.

The maids were by no means unwilling to help in waiting upon the guests, so the business of serving coffee and chocolate was left to their hands; the boys being pressed into service, were drilled by their sisters, and became deft at removing and carrying plates, etc.

Home-made lemonade with split ice in it filled several glass jugs on the table, and was found refreshing by even those fascinated by sweet chocolate in dainty blue and white cups. Ices were vetoed, not only for their unwholesomeness, but for the difficulty of making them, as the establishment did not boast a freezer, but there were two iced puddings, besides jellies on the table, so the absence of other kinds was not noticed.

As the viands were all cold they were all placed upon the table, but when meat plates were removed the principal meat dishes were taken away also, and the sweets which required serving were taken in their place. These latter were a Crystal Palace pudding, a Duchess *gateau*, a chocolate mould with cream, and a prune jelly. In the spaces between came moulds of jelly of different colours, some with fruits and some without, mince pies, and cheesecakes, *éclairs*, custards, and small cakes. A beautiful dish of fruit, bright oranges, apples, bananas, and grapes, tastefully arranged, was in the centre of the table.

The plain gas brackets belonging to the nursery had their ugliness veiled by crinkled paper covers of different shades, while the lighting of the table itself was done by the somewhat old-fashioned but ever-charming fairy lamps. The soft light which these afforded gave just the touch of mystery that was needed to make an enchanting whole when all arrangements were completed, and even father was compelled to admiration when he peeped in and saw what a transformation had been effected.

Mother had helped to choose the more substantial dishes belonging to the feast, and she undertook to make the galantines of rabbit and the chicken patties, also seeing to the boiling of the ham. A tongue was purchased ready cooked, as its cost thus was not any more and was a saving of trouble. Perhaps we might note down the way in which mother proceeded with regard to the—

Galantine.—One rabbit cut into joints was gently stewed with seasoning and a little salt bacon until just tender, then the flesh was removed from the bones and sliced. A pound of lean veal cutlet was also sliced after being sufficiently cooked, and two eggs were boiled hard, then shelled and cut through. A large breakfastcupful of clear strong gravy was made from stock and bones, and in this half an ounce of isinglass was dissolved; then a fluted mould was taken, a little gravy put in the bottom, some strips of egg to form a star pattern next, then slices of rabbit, veal and ham alternately; more egg whenever it seemed well, and the rest of the meat until all was used up. The remainder of the gravy was poured over, then a cover to fit inside the top of the mould and a weight upon that, after which it was set in the oven and very gently cooked for about an hour. This was left undisturbed until thoroughly cold, when, after removing weight and cover it could be turned out on to a dish and garnished. Cut into very thin slices this was most savoury.

For the *Chicken Patties* a little veal and ham were minced with the flesh of a boiled fowl, some grated lemon peel, a few bread-crumbs and a pinch of aromatic seasoning, then sufficient white sauce to moisten the whole. Some patty-pans were lined with very light pastry, but not "puff," a spoonful of the mince and an upper crust to cover, brushed over with milk, then baked for thirty minutes in a moderate oven.

The sweets were all left to Pollie's care, and she strove to excel herself in their making, and the result was almost—if not quite—professional. The first thing to be made was the

Duchess Gateau.—The cake part of this consisted of four ounces of ordinary flour and two ounces of Paisley, three ounces of fresh butter, three ounces of castor sugar, the whites of four eggs beaten to a snow, and a few drops of almond essence. The butter and sugar were beaten together, then the mixed flour and the whites of eggs were beaten in alternately, the cake was then baked in a buttered tin in a quick oven for twenty minutes. The tin was a round one, and, when the cake had grown cold, it was cut into three and spread first with apricot jam, then with a layer of cream whipped until stiff between each division, the whole covered with cream just before taking to table and ornamented with crystallised fruits.

The *Crystal Palace Pudding* was simple enough.—A mould was filled with alternate layers of macaroons, sponge fingers and ratafias, a layer of greengage jam between each layer of biscuits. A custard made with the yolks of the four eggs used for the *gateau*, with a pint of new milk, half an ounce of isinglass and two spoonfuls of sugar, and the strained juice of half a lemon added after the custard had been boiled. This was poured into the mould and set aside in a cold place for several hours.

The *Chocolate Mould* was made at the same time as this pudding as it also required a good while to set. A pint and a half of new milk, an ounce of cornflour and two of ground rice, two ounces of grated chocolate and as much sugar, were all boiled together for five minutes after boiling-point was reached, then the saucepan was taken from the fire, the yolk of an egg was stirred in together with an ounce of fresh butter and a spoonful of lemon-juice, then the mixture was poured into a fancy mould previously made wet with cold water. When turned out this was surrounded with fresh cream. So also was the

Prune Jelly, which took a place on the opposite side of the table. The prunes for this had been soaked overnight in cold water, then cooked very slowly for several hours, and afterwards rubbed through a sieve until a pulp was obtained. This pulp was sweetened with sufficient lump sugar, flavoured with lemon-juice, a little water added to it and a good ounce of isinglass, then it was boiled for a few minutes and poured into a wet mould.

The mince pies and cheesecakes belonged to the Christmas batch, and simply required re-heating to make them fresh. The orange and lemon jellies were made from fresh fruit with gelatine to stiffen them, but the currant and raspberry jellies were made from Rizine flakes. The smaller cakes and biscuits with other sweetmeats were bought, as they scarcely paid for the time and trouble entailed when made at home. Some plates of fruit, oranges cut in halves, sliced pine-apples, figs, and nuts, were laid ready down-stairs for passing about while games were in progress and between the dances, but these had apparently not spoiled the appetites which the company brought to the feast when at last the signal was given to go up higher. Although the hour was still early as ball hours go, it was perhaps as well for some of the guests that a sharp trot in the air awaited them when supper was over, for Pollie's sweets found many an appreciative "tooth."

L. H. YATES.

"Christmas Morning, at Mother's Bedroom Door"

Peterson's Magazine, 1883

The Christmas Snow.

It was Christmas Eve, and the snow fell fast,
   For the clouds had met together,
And they whispered softly, "Come, now, let's brew
   Some rare old Christmas weather.

And we must be quick! there is much to do
   Ere the Christmas bells be pealing,
And all must be ready ere over the east
   The rosy red dawn comes stealing."

Then there went a stir through the soft, gray clouds;
   For the beautiful flakes were forming
In starry hosts, while a loving thought
   Each pure little heart was warming.

And the wind went hurrying here and there
   In his noisy, blustering fashion,
And hustled things so that he really seemed
   To be in a terrible passion.

But that was only his way, you know;
   At heart he was honestly striving
To help the good clouds in their work of love
   With all his rushing and driving.

   So he whirled the flakes at a flying pace,
      And hurried them hither and thither,
   Some high in the air, and some low on the ground,
      It seemed that he cared not whither.

   And yet, in spite of his madcap tricks,
      And spite of his airs and graces,
   The sweet flakes quietly found their way
      Just into their own right places.

   Some rested lightly on bare, brown roofs,
      And covered their peaks and gables,
   Till they looked like the sculptured marble domes
      We read of in Eastern fables.

   Some nestled lovingly down to earth
      In curving drifts of beauty,
   Nor stayed to grieve o'er their lowly lot,
      If that was their place of duty.

   Rare, frosted nettings of lace they wove,
      And looped o'er the slender larches,
   And twisted them over the somber firs
      In gay, fantastic arches.

   They hung the boughs of the oaks and elms
      With fine and feathery fringes,
   And scattered themselves into diamond dust,
      A-sparkle with silvery tinges.

   And some slipped quietly from the rest,
      With tender, sweet pretenses,
   To hide the patch on the poor man's roof,
      And cover his fallen fences.

   "For O!" they said, "for this one sweet time
      We will brighten these homes so dreary,
   And try as hard as ever we can
      To make them look glad and cheery."

   All night they sped through the silent air
      On their mission loving and tender,
   Till the earth was dressed like a fairy bride,
      In her robes of sheeny splendor.

   And people gazed through their crystal panes
      On the white and wondrous vision,
   And said, "What a beautiful fall of snow!
      It looks like a world elysian."

   Yes—that was all; and they turned away,
      No deeper thought bestowing;
   It was only a "beautiful fall of snow"
      To the careless or unknowing.

   But to you and me it would mean far more;
      For the secret is in our keeping,
   And we know how the white flakes waked and worked,
      While the rest of the world were sleeping.

   We know the thought of love in their hearts,
      And their pure, sweet sense of duty,
   As they silently fell from their home in the clouds,
      To cover the earth with beauty.

LOUISE W. TILDEN.

THE FLIGHT OF WINTER.

Adeste, fideles,
Læti triumphantes,
Venite, venite in Bethlehem;
Natum videte
Regem angelorum.
Venite adoremus, venite adoremus,
Venite adoremus dominum.

"Hither, ye faithful, haste with songs of triumph;
To Bethlehem haste, the Lord of life to meet.
To you this day is born a Prince and Savior;
O come and let us worship,
O come and let us worship,
O come and let us worship,
At his feet."

The Flight of Winter.

"Hi! Old Winter! off you go!
Take your frost and ice and snow;
Wrap your cloak around you quick,
Grasp your gnarly walking-stick—
See the old man quake with fear!—
Hurry, hurry! Spring is near!

Long enough you've nipped each nose,
Pinched our fingers and our toes;
Come, be off, before your feet
Find no pathway for retreat—
Spring is coming in a trice,
She will break your bridge of ice."

Winter halts a moment while
His grim mouth begins to smile,
Eyes the youngsters with a laugh,
Crying, "Come now, stop your chaff!
Why, you little rogues, 't was I
Brought you turkey, cakes, and pie.

Would you have a Christmas-tree
Ever—were it not for me?
And I crammed the stockings, too,
Full of lovely toys for you!
Snow-balls, coasting, sledding, ice—
Sure you found these rather nice.

You ungrateful little scamps,
When Spring comes with mists and damps.
When her treacherous melting breezes
Bring you colds and coughs and sneezes,
And you pine through weeks of rain,
You'll want Winter back again."

Then, instead of laugh and jeer
Every child lets fall a tear;
And they kiss their chubby hands
To the old man where he stands,
Crying, "Good-bye, Winter, dear!
Come to us again next year."

Young People's Scrapbook, 1884

SCIENCE RAMBLES

THE MISTLETOE

CHRISTMAS is here, and the houses are decked with evergreens; round the picture frames the red-berried holly is wreathed; over the chimney-piece are the soft branches of the fresh green fir; and hanging from the lamp in the hall is a fine bunch of the mystic mistletoe. How well we know the thick forked stem with its branching twigs, bearing the small rounded green leaves, and the opaque yellowish berries. We know it was beloved of the Druids, and most of us perhaps have a vague idea that it grows upon oak trees, which it sometimes does, only I think most of us might visit all the oak trees within a radius of ten miles, and not find a single clump of mistletoe on the whole lot; because it is very scarce in mosts parts of England, and does not grow upon the oak if it can find any other of its favourite trees handy. It is an unscrupulous plant, this mistletoe which we make free of in the house every Christmas-tide, and even wear in our buttonholes; it is one of those vegetables which does not obtain its living honestly, by taking root in the soil and using up the carbon contained in the air in the form of carbonic acid gas, but it lives as a parasite, that is to say, it sponges upon another plant, robbing it of the sap which is its source of life and strength.

Like the interloping cuckoo, who lays her eggs in the nest of the hedge-sparrow, so that they may flourish at the expense of their unconscious hosts, the mistletoe settles upon the apple tree or hawthorn, without so much as by your leave or with your leave, and calmly commences to deprive its unfortunate entertainer of the very juices which it has stored up in his woody tissues for its own profit.

You will always find the mistletoe growing in a great bush from the forked branch of a tree, and it is in the centre of this fork that the roots of the parasite take hold. Here the bark is thinner and more delicate, and the long fibres of the parasite can more easily penetrate through the woody coating down to the soft tissue and juicy sap below. Now perhaps you will wonder how the seed of the mistletoe ever got to this convenient fork, and found a resting-place just at the point where two apple stems unite. You may think that perhaps the seed was blown thither by the wind, or carried by those great gardeners, the insect family.

No, this time it is a bird who is responsible for planting the mistletoe just where it will thrive the best.

This bird is called the missel-thrush, because he is so fond of the berries of the mistletoe, and commonly feeds upon them. These berries contain the seed of the plant, for you know that all plants which bear berries are propagated by this means. The berry consists of some eatable stuff surrounding the seed, which is usually hard—in the case of the plum, you know, it has a stony coat which is strong enough to protect it from the digestive juices of any animal that chances to eat the fruit. The missel-thrush, attracted by the sticky pulp of the mistletoe berries, eats away, but does not swallow the hard, nut-like seeds which lie safely embedded in the viscid mass; they, being sticky, are gummed to the feet and bill of the bird, and when he has finished his repast he flies away with them safely attached to him. By-and-bye he grows hungry again, and visits other trees in search of food, perhaps a healthy apple tree on which he hopes to find a good crop of mistletoe berries; but alas! he is disappointed, and having perched on a branch only to find none of the fruit which he so dearly loves, he begins—not as the old man in the rhyme, to "scratch his head and think" what he shall do next, but—to rub off the uncomfortable adhesions against a forked branch, which is the very spot which best suits the young mistletoe for sprouting.

So the bird and the plant are really a small co-operative society, each having a share in the profits; while, I am afraid, the apple tree represents the unfortunate shareholder, who supplies the capital and receives no dividends; because the mistletoe, whom we must regard as the sleeping partner in this concern, is as fraudulent and dishonest a one as could be found in the whole length and breadth of the vegetable kingdom.

The missel-thrush is pursued by a singular nemesis for his unconscious share in this swindling of the defenceless apple tree, because from the berries of the mistletoe man makes the very bird-lime which so often lures him to destruction.

SUTHERLAND WALKER.

The Home Magazine, 1898

A Vision of St. Nicholas

A POEM FOR CHILDREN.   BY C. C. MOORE.

'TWAS the night before Christmas, when all through the house
Not a creature was stirring, not even a mouse;
The stockings were hung by the chimney with care,
In hopes that St. Nicholas soon would be there;
The children were nestled all snug in their beds,
While visions of sugar-plums danced in their heads;
And mamma in her kerchief, and I in my cap,
Had just settled our brains for a long winter's nap—
When out on the lawn there arose such a clatter,
I sprang from my bed to see what was the matter.
Away to the window I flew like a flash,
Tore open the shutters, and threw up the sash.
The moon, on the breast of the new-fallen snow,
Gave a lustre of mid-day to objects below;
When, what to my wondering eyes should appear,
But a miniature sleigh and eight tiny reindeer,
With a little, old driver, so lively and quick,
I knew in a moment it must be St. Nick.
More rapid than eagles, his coursers they came,
And he whistled, and shouted, and called them by name;
"Now, Dasher! now, Dancer! now, Prancer and Vixen!

The Strand, 1891

On, Comet! on, Cupid! on, Donder and Blitzen!
To the top of the porch, to the top of the wall!
Now dash away! dash away, dash away all!"
As dry leaves that before the wild hurricane fly,
When they meet with an obstacle, mount to the sky,
So, up to the housetop, the coursers they flew,

A bundle of toys he had flung on his back,
And he looked like a pedlar just opening his pack.
His eyes how they twinkled! His dimples how merry!

With the sleighful of toys—and St. Nicholas too.
And then in a twinkling I heard on the roof
The prancing and pawing of each little hoof.
As I drew in my head, and was turning around,
Down the chimney St. Nicholas came with a bound.
He was dressed all in fur from his head to his foot,
And his clothes were all tarnished with ashes and soot;

His cheeks were like roses, his nose like a cherry;
His droll little mouth was drawn up like a bow,
And the beard on his chin was as white as the snow.
The stump of a pipe he held tight in his teeth,
And the smoke, it encircled his head like a wreath.
He had a broad face and a little round belly,
That shook, when he laughed, like a bowl full of jelly.
He was chubby and plump—a right jolly old elf;
And I laughed when I saw him, in spite of myself.
A wink of his eye, and a twist of his head,
Soon gave me to know I had nothing to dread.
He spoke not a word, but went straight to his work,
And filled all the stockings; then turned with a jerk,
And laying his finger aside of his nose,
And giving a nod, up the chimney he rose.
He sprang to his sleigh, to his team gave a whistle,
And away they all flew, like the down of a thistle;
But I heard him exclaim, ere they drove out of sight—
"Merry Christmas to all, and to all a good night!"

A VISION OF SANTA CLAUS.

By CHRISTIAN BURKE.

Through the keen air crystal snowflakes are flying,
   Drifting in heaps in the garden and glen,
Cyril and Mark in their cosy beds lying
   Plan they will make some tremendous snow-men!
Loud wails the wind, rising higher and higher,
Drowsily crackles the nursery fire.

Dreaming, and faster asleep they are falling—
   Mark is a soldier gone off to the wars—
Suddenly Cyril awakes him by calling,
   "What a bad night for that poor Santa Claus!
'Tis such a pity it's turned so much colder,
Each year, you know, he grows older and older!

"Mark, if you only would rouse up and listen!
   This time perhaps we may catch him at last;
Here by the firelight his white beard will glisten—
   He is too old and too stiff to walk fast.
Maybe he'd ask us to help him unpacking,
Then we could tell him if anything's lacking.

"There is your boat—that's a heavy thing, rather—
   Then there's my sledge, to bring all through the snow!
Does Santa Claus get a letter from Father?
   Else I can't think how he always should know.
Mark, keep awake; I am getting quite creepy!
Oh, how I wish that I wasn't so sleepy!"

Then his voice fails, and, as shadows grow deeper,
   Someone steals in like a beautiful ghost—
Kisses the brow of each warm little sleeper,
   Leaving the treasures each wanted the most.
"But we *did* see him!" next day cry the brothers—
"Santa Claus' eyes are *exactly* like Mother's!"

SOME CURIOUS CHRISTMAS PIES AND OTHER PASTIES.

By LINA ORMAN COOPER, Author of "We Wives," etc.

Ever since the day that immortal Mr. Weller lived with a pie-man, we have been cautious and suspicious about the inside of pies—"kittens seasoned as beefsteak, veal or kidney, accordin' to the demand, at a minut's notice" have been by him suggested, but in this paper I want to talk about some real historical pasties, and give a few recipes for preparing modern ones.

We all know that the voluble Home Secretary—Master Pepys—allowed his wife to spend all one Christmas Day in preparing a pie for his Christmas dinner. We would not rule with such a rod of iron. But since the days of long ago, pasties and pies have been the fare of the merrie season.

A writer in *The Gentleman's Magazine* for 1733, in an essay on Christmas, recognises the fact. He says, "This dish is most in vogue at this time of the year. Some think it owing to the barrenness of the season, and the scarcity of fruits and milk to make tarts, custards and other desserts. The pie being a compound that furnishes a dessert of itself. But I rather think it bears a religious kind of relation to the festivities from which it takes its name. Our tables are always set out with this dish at this time, and probably for the same reason that our windows are adorned with ivy. I am the more confirmed in this opinion from the zealous opposition it meets with from the Quakers, who distinguish their feasts by an heretical sort of pudding known by their name, and inveigh against Christmas pie as an invention of the Scarlet Lady of Babylon, an hodge-podge of Popery, superstition, the devil and his works."

This extract lifts the pie proper from a domain of unwholesomeness to one of heresy! From the regard of the gourmand to that of the enthusiast. However, it is perfectly true that the Christmas pie has often been mixed up with religion; enthusiastic Presbyterians in 1720 "under the censure of lewd customs included all sorts of public sports, exercises and recreation, how innocent soever, nay, rosemary, bay, and the Christmas pie was made an abomination!"

A favourite dish at the tables of our forefathers was this same iniquitous pie. Sometimes it was made a vehicle for surprising guests round the festive board. Such was the case in 1630 when Charles I. and his Queen were entertained by the Duke and Duchess of Buckingham, at Burleigh on the Hill—for ever immortalised by Lord Tennyson. A huge pie was placed in the place of honour. Out of this pie stepped the first dwarf of whom we have any authentic record. Geffrey Hudson was only eighteen inches high at the time, and must have been a fearsome spectacle after confinement under a pastry roof. Shakespeare says of such surprise pies, *via* Hamlet as a medium, that their introduction was "to set on a quantity of barren spectators to laugh." These pies were filled with living birds, like the four and twenty in "Sing a song for sixpence." But in 1540, a *bonâ fide* recipe was given in a pamphlet, for "making pies that the birds may be alive in them and fly out when it is cut open." Poor fledgelings! plucked and baked and yet not killed.

"Little Jack Horner" has been perhaps a more well-known character than any of his contemporaries; that is saying a good deal, for he lived in the time of King Hal VIII. It was his robbery of the contents of a pie which made him so. We all know that he

"Sat in a corner
Eating a Christmas pie;
He put in his thumb and pulled out a plum,
And said what a good boy am I."

But few of us know what the "plum" was.

It appears that during the reign of the eighth Henry all monasteries and religious houses in England were suppressed. One of the richest of these was Glastonbury Abbey, and amongst the possessions of this priory, was a place of great value called the Manor of Wells. When the title-deeds held by the abbey were demanded by the King's Commissioner, in order to give them into other hands, the abbot made up his mind to send them to a place of safety. It was Christmas-time. What more suitable gift could the wealthy abbot send a friend in London than a pie? Accordingly, Jack Horner, a trusty messenger, was given this pie, along with many injunctions to guard it safely, and only to deliver it into the hands of the person to whom it was directed. But Jack Horner might have been Fatima judging by the curiosity he possessed. At one part of the journey, he raised the crust and "put in his thumb." Forthwith came a rustle of parchment, and then a couple of fingers more brought to light the title-deeds of Wells.

The authorities in London were very angry at the reception of an empty pie, for to them the wily messenger eventually carried the dish and crust. They soundly rated the poor monks of Glastonbury for their supposed deception, and made them suffer severely for it. Jack Horner said never a word; but, when peaceable times came, he produced the title-deeds and stepped into possession of the beautiful Manor of Wells. Truly this was a case of,

"Treason in a December pye,
And death within the pot."

Jack Horner's escapade, however, only enhanced the popularity of the Christmas pie. Misson, in his *Travels in England*, has his word to say about it: "Every family against Christmas makes a famous pye which they call Christmas pye. It is a great nostrume the composition of this pastry. It is a most learned mixture of neat's tongue, chickens, eggs, sugar, raisins, lemon and orange peel, various kinds of spicery, etc."

This description would suit far better a Cornish pasty of the present day. In it everything from a salt herring to jam finds shelter, and yet, I am told, it is a toothsome article!

A stately pie, indeed, was one made by a certain Mrs. Dorothy Patterson, housekeeper, in the year 1770. It measured nine feet in circumference, weighed twelve stone, took two men to present it at table, and was supplied with wheels to enable each guest at Howick Castle to help themselves. In its manufacture two bushels of flour and twenty pounds of butter were employed. It was filled with "four geese, four turkeys, two rabbits, four wild ducks, two woodcocks, six snipes, four partridges, two neats' tongues, two curlews, seven blackbirds, and six pigeons." Pies of these dimensions were always heavily spiced so that they kept for weeks. They rested generally on the side-board, and all comers could cut and come again as they listed.

A more modern pie was that one made in commemoration of the Queen's Jubilee. Of it the following jingle spoke:—

"This pie contained as much rump steak
    As would half supply the Navy,
With bullocks' milts enough to make
    Ninety gallons of gravy.

Forty ducks, two stone a-piece,
    Enough for any glutton,
With ninety-five large legs of beef
    And a hundred legs of mutton."

This wonderful pie, which took ninety ploughmen to serve it up to the table, was prepared by the inhabitants of Denby Dale. They followed the American plan of commemorating famous events by pie-making, for they baked one at King George III.'s jubilee in 1788, after the Battle of Waterloo, and upon the repeal of the Corn Laws in 1846. The mammoth pie I have told about above, however, was the biggest of their efforts. It contained three thousand and seventeen pounds of potatoes and meat, and had to be baked in an oven specially built for it.

I think it is now time for us to talk a little about pasties. I wonder how many folk know what constitutes the difference between a pie and a pasty! Our dictionary defines the former as a "crust baked with fruit, etc., in it," and the latter as "a pie of crust raised without a dish." Well, men made dictionaries, and it requires a woman to make their explanations intelligible.

A pasty is distinguished from a pie or tart because it has pastry under as well as over the meat or fruit. So our three-cornered jam-puffs and mince-pies, containing " that mixture strange of suet, currants, meat, where various tastes incline," are really, properly speaking, mince pasties. In Queen Elizabeth's time they were called "minched pies," and, even earlier than that, "shrid pies."

It has been thought that the mince pasties —a combination as it is of the choicest products of the East—may have originally had in view the offering made by the wise men who came from afar to worship, bringing spices, etc. I think the idea is rather a taking one—as are all theories that link habit on to the sweet story of Bethlehem.

There is an old superstition that Christmas without a mince pie is unlucky. In 1656, the Puritans condemned this "idolatrie in crust," and very wisely. It would be far more unlucky to taste thereof if it disagreed with one!

It is generally conceded that Americans countenance "piety"—forgive the scandalous pun!—more than any other nation. It is popularly supposed that squash and apple pie, cranberry pasties and every other kind can be bought at every corner in New York; but there is one kind I should like to see more universally provided than it is both in America and England. The pie I refer to is covered with a cardboard crust and has an interior of indigestible bran. Like the surprise pies of our ancestors, from the bowels of the bran pie should come all sorts of queer and useful presents. "Every face which we set sparkling at Christmas is a reflection of that goodness of nature which generosity helps to unclose." And how the children's faces light up round the bran tub! In another article I should like to give instructions how to make many inexpensive articles which we can, to quote an eighteenth-century poet:

"Hash and smash as small as flies
And send to help these bran mince pies."

I have not space for them in this article.

The recipe for a merry Christmas is to shelter the homeless, clothe the naked, feed the hungry, and make the children's heart leap for joy. The way to enjoy our Christmas luxuries is to share them with others. Listen to Nehemiah's sound advice.

"Go your way, eat the fat and drink the sweet, and send portions unto them for whom nothing is prepared. For this day is holy unto our Lord; neither be ye sorry, for the joy of the Lord is your strength (Neh. viii. 10).

I must close this paper by giving a recipe or two for mince-pastes and meat-pies, as I promised; I will not, however, burden this article with many, as every cookery-book teems with especial directions for their evolution. A very useful dish in a large family is made from poultry of any sort—game more especially. After plucking, singeing, and drawing, cut up the birds into fair-sized pieces, and pack a pie-dish with them; layer over them some nice fat bacon or ham, and cover with a sheet of sweet herbs, bread-crumbs, chopped parsley, bound into force-meat with a beaten egg. The gravy must come from some wedge-shaped lumps of raw beef-steak laid here and there. Cover with a good, wholesome crust, and bake in a moderate oven. If the pastry "catches" before the birds are cooked, veil it with a sheet of buttered paper.

Just before taking this pie from the oven, brush over the hot crust with yolk of egg, and, if intended to eat cold, lift off the lid before serving, and place some cubes of savoury aspic jelly under it.

A plain chicken pie made as above is a very economical side-board dish when the "boys" are home for the holidays. The bones must be well broken, and even without the addition of aspic, the dish will be found filled with jelly.

Mince-meat is made in many different ways, so I will not give minute directions for the same, only lay down one or two broad rules about it. Let the beef suet be bought early, or you will have to pay a big price for inferior stuff. Let the meat be partly cooked before using. The mince will keep better. Always, when using, take from the bottom of the jar, or all will grow mouldy. Make it a month before it is wanted for table, as it will then have time to mellow. Exclude air by tying it down tight with bladder.

Honesty in pie-making is one of the smaller "diamonds" in culinary work that I recommend. None of us would like to have our names handed down to posterity as has been done to one Thomas Pepys—"cosen" of the famous Home Secretary. He placed before the fastidious diarist "a venison pasty, which was palpable mutton." "This was not handsome," comments the master curtly and pregnantly.

A fourteenth-century recipe, by insisting on good ingredients and work has lived to this day by reason of its honesty. I copy it. "Tak gode applys and gode spycis and gode figgs and reysons and perys (pears?) and wan they are wel ybrazed, colourd wyth safron wel, do yt in a cofyn, and do yt forth to bake wel." You see six injunctions to excellence are here given. We can imagine how much this apple-tart must have been esteemed by those privileged to taste it.

Though Christmas plum-pudding and mince-meat are the better for being made a long time in advance, pies and pasties are best eaten fresh. The good housewives, at the beginning of the last century recognised this. One of them sings:—

"Now, mistress Betty, get up and rise
If you intend to make your Christmas pyes,
And let your ingenuity be seen
In decking all the windows up with green."

In Venice a very queer kind of pye is eaten at the feast of the nativity. It is crust filled with pottage called *Torta de Casagne*, and is composed of oil, onions, paste, parsley, pine nuts, raisins, currants and candied peel. With this curious recipe I must close this paper. The Queen of Hearts still makes her tarts, her pyes, and her pasties, whilst the yule log burns on the hearth, and holly boughs with lumps of shining berries adorn the ingle-nook. As she weighs the flour, fruit and spices let her not forget to send portions to those for whom nothing is prepared. Then, indeed, like the Israelites of old, she will be able "to eat and drink and make great mirth," for she will have understood and carried out the directions given her.

CHRISTMAS DAY AT SEA.

TO some of the readers of LITTLE FOLKS who have always spent their Christmas Days in their quiet homes, it may be interesting to hear how we spent ours on board ship on our voyage to New Zealand, down in latitude 44° south. We had had a beautiful voyage, no storms, but now and then rather long calms, which are very tantalising when you want to get quickly to the end of your voyage to see the dear friends who are waiting for you. We had had some amusements on the voyage—concerts, either on the main deck or in the saloon, sometimes twice a week. But the great entertainment was to be for Christmas, and it was decided, with the captain's permission, that a Christmas-tree should be prepared, and that a very nice tea, with plenty of plum-cake, jam, and other good things, should be given in the saloon to the nineteen children who were on board. Christmas Eve was fixed on as the night for the festivity.

But little folk on land will perhaps say, "How could they have a Christmas-tree on board ship? Fir-trees don't grow in the sea." No, little folk, they certainly do not; but some people are very clever in contriving. Now I will tell you how we managed. Some ingenious passenger twisted wire rope into the shape of branches, and cunningly fastened tufts of tow on to them to make some resemblance to leaves; then another clever person knew how to make little candles, and we fastened on a great many that the tree might be very brilliant. It was wonderful how many devices were thought of, and how useful many little things generally thrown away were found to be. One young lady embroidered flags with the gold thread that she had taken off a packet of chocolate, and holly was made by cutting leaves from an old green calico blind, and the berries were made of red sealing-wax.

People were very busy before Christmas getting ready their presents, and the sailors, who were a very nice set of men, took a great interest in the tree, and often came to those who had the charge of it, sometimes bringing a knife, a foot rule, a set of draughts, or something else which they had carved, to be placed on or round it.

At last Christmas Eve arrived, but the day had been too stormy to allow any hope of having the tree that evening, and the pleasure had to be put off; but still there was Christmas Day to be prepared for.

On Christmas Eve a notice was placed on the mainmast that the post-office would be open for letters up to nine p.m., and that there would be an early delivery on Christmas morning; so all posted their little presents and Christmas cards. At midnight we were awakened by the waits coming round and singing Christmas hymns. That sounded very sweet; there were five singers and one performer on the cornet. Christmas Day was a most lovely day, bright blue sky overhead, and bright blue sea below, with little white crests to the waves. We all put on our best dresses in honour of the day, and on going on deck had very kind good wishes from the sailors. Then at breakfast-time we heard the postman's horn and double knock, and he (one of the steerage passengers) came into the saloon with a large bag and delivered round his letters; then he delivered those which were addressed to the second and third class passengers, and then those intended for the sailors. One of the young ladies had sent each sailor and each child in the steerage a Christmas card, with which they were much pleased. At eleven o'clock there was church service in the saloon, and we sang a number of Christmas hymns. So we had much to remind us of Christmas Day in dear old England. Some of the sailors and a good many passengers were present, and the singing was very hearty.

The next day all was excitement about the Christmas-tree. About four o'clock in the afternoon the children were mustered in the saloon, and the piles of cake, bread-and-butter, and bread-and-jam soon disappeared. Many an eager little pair of eyes looked about, and many an eager little voice asked, for the tree, but patience, patience was the word. At last they go on deck; behold, a tent has been made there, ornamented with the ship's flags! In the centre of the tent stands the long-expected tree, covered with presents and glittering with lights. But who is this who stands by the tree? A tall old man with a red face and a long white beard; he is muffled in a long cloak, and see, his cloak is sprinkled with snow! It is—yes, it must be—Father Christmas! Imagine the delight of the little ones when Father Christmas turns out to be the captain! Then there is the distribution of the presents; every child gets four or five, and every passenger and sailor gets one or more. All are pleased; then three cheers, and then three cheers more for the captain and the promoters of the entertainment; and so end the Christmas festivities at sea.

Little Folks Magazine, 1878

"O'ER NATURE'S FUNERAL PALL IT THROWS
A MANTLE RICH AND RARE TO SEE."

The Girl's Own Paper, 1883

CHRISTMAS FARE FOR RICH AND POOR.

HERE are two plum-puddings that cost so little as to be within the reach of all, but so good-looking and good-tasting are they, the rich man's table would be graced by them both.

A Baroness Plum-Pudding.—Take equal quantities, say, three quarters of a pound of flour, finely-chopped beef suet, and good raisins stoned and cut small, a small teacupful of golden syrup, half a teaspoonful of salt, and a small teacupful of milk. Mix all very thoroughly together, working them to a stiff dough and kneading it for several minutes. Butter a pudding basin, line it with raisins and shred lemon-peel, then put in the pudding mixture, which must not quite fill it, cover with a buttered paper, and boil this pudding, or rather steam it by standing the mould in boiling water for four hours. Turn out of the mould without allowing it to stand more than a moment or two, and serve with simple sweet sauce. This is, or should be, dark, rich, and luscious, and very easy of digestion.

A Vegetable Plum-Pudding.—Cheap but good.

Mix very thoroughly together one pound of mashed potatoes, half a pound of carrot boiled and beaten to a smooth paste, one pound of flour, one pound of currants, one pound of stoned raisins, three quarters of a pound of brown sugar, half a pound of chopped suet, a large teaspoonful of mixed spice, and half a teaspoonful of salt. No eggs and no milk.

The mixture should be prepared a fortnight before it is required, and stirred up vigorously every day.

Buttered moulds should be filled to within half an inch of the top, then tied over with cloths, plunged in boiling water, and boiled for nearly five hours. If boiled, these puddings may be kept for a long time, giving them another hour's boiling when occasion calls for their eating.

The above quantities will make a pudding large enough for sixteen persons, and will not exceed half a crown in cost.

The Rich Man's Pudding.—Will make four quart-mould puddings.

One pound and a half of bread-crumbs, half a pound of flour, two pounds of currants, one pound and a half of raisins, stoned, one pound and a half of suet, one pound of sugar, quarter of a pound of shred candied peel, nine eggs, one pint of milk, and half a pint of brandy. This pudding is not expensive but is almost perfect in flavour; it should boil for four hours also.

There are many persons who cannot be tempted to touch plum-pudding at all, however tempting it may be; for them it is well to have a contrasting one of which they can have the choice at festive times, and either of the following recipes will be found well worth trying.

Exeter Pudding.—Ten tablespoonfuls of bread-crumbs, three ditto of sago, six of suet, four of sugar, a pinch of salt, half a lemon-rind grated, and two or three well-beaten eggs, with two ounces of dissolved butter. Mix these ingredients well together, adding a little milk if needful; have ready half-a-dozen penny sponge cakes split in half and spread with raspberry jam, also a few ratafias. Butter a mould and lay a row of sponge cakes at the bottom, filling up the spaces with the biscuits, then cover with a layer of the mixture, then more cakes and biscuits, and repeat until the mould is full, keeping the mixture at the top. Cover with a buttered paper, and either bake in a gentle oven, or steam the pudding for an hour and a half.

For sauce a small pot of red-currant jelly is dissolved and the liquid poured over the pudding after it has been turned out.

Alpine Pudding.—A rather shallow, fluted, fireproof china dish should be buttered and sprinkled with brown sugar, then a mixture made from the following ingredients is poured in and baked until it is firmly set, after which it is spread with apple or apricot jelly and a *méringue* made with the whites of three eggs beaten stiff, three-pennyworth of cream also beaten, and a teaspoonful of castor sugar, also heaped lightly over the preserve. Ingredients:—Three ounces of stale sponge-cake crumbs, half an ounce of ground almonds or desiccated cocoanut, two ounces of castor sugar, a pinch of salt, yolks of three eggs, and half a pint of boiled milk.

A very inexpensive yet pretty dish is the following, it is suitable for a poor children's party, as it will please the eye and taste, and is wholesome, while but small trouble to prepare.

Peel as many fine apples as are desired, taking the cores out with a scoop, so as not to injure the shape. Put the apples into a deep baking-dish with three glasses of cheap wine, a quarter of a pound of loaf-sugar, and the peel of a lemon. Cover the dish and let the apples cook gently, but do not allow them to break. Place them on a pretty dish, boil the syrup longer until it is thick, and let it get cold. Place between the apples tiny heaps of well-boiled rice, pour over all the syrup, and fill up the holes in the apples with bright-coloured preserve. Decorate with strips of green angelica and crystallised cherries.

Apple Snow.—Half-a-dozen large apples that will cook well; let them be pared and cored, and cooked quickly in a very little water, then when perfectly soft beat them lightly with a fork; add, when nearly cold, three tablespoonfuls of castor-sugar and the whites of three eggs whisked to a stiff froth. Whisk all well together. Line a plain mould with sponge fingers, placing them close together at the bottom, and wider apart at the top. Fill up the mould with the "snow," taking care not to disturb the biscuits. Set the mould on ice or in a freezer until it is firm, then turn the shape out on to a glass dish, and heap bright apple jelly around the base of the shape, on the top pile a few spoonfuls of thick whipped cream, and sprinkle that with pink granulated sugar.

ALL ABOUT ORANGES.

"Oh, that I were an orange tree—
　That busy plant!
Then should I ever laden be,
　And never want
Some fruit for Him that dresseth me."

So wrote good George Herbert more than two hundred and fifty years ago, and we can easily understand the ground of his wish. Orange trees are indeed, under favourable circumstances, exceedingly prolific. Some live to a great age, and they bear fruit from fifty to eighty years. One which was planted at Versailles, near Paris, lived more than four hundred years, and there are orange trees growing at Cordova, in Spain, which are said to be more than six hundred years old. A good tree will produce a large quantity of fruit; and as many as a thousand oranges have been know to grow on one tree. There is no wonder that the poet said an orange tree was "a busy plant."

Oranges are amongst the most delicious of fruits. They are exceedingly wholesome, and are enjoyed by the sick and the hale. It is well for us that we have them in such abundance, for we should sorely miss them if we were deprived of them. Large as the demand for them has been of late years, it is steadily growing, and some idea of the quantity imported may be gained from the fact that a fruit-broker of whom enquiries were made a few months ago said that during the previous year there were 453,000 cases of oranges shipped to England from Valencia alone, and that each case weighed over a hundredweight, and contained from 400 to 700 oranges. That is to say, that averaging them all round at 500, there were imported from Valencia alone 226,500,000 oranges, weighing about 32,000 tons. After hearing this, no one can say that oranges in England are not appreciated.

When oranges are ripe, sweet, and sound, it is scarcely possible to do better with them than eat them *au naturel*. The individuals who care for the fruit most are generally most averse to cooking it. This is a mistake, for in many forms it is most excellent when cooked. For the benefit, therefore, of those who feel disposed to experiment in this direction, it is proposed to give a few suggestions for dainty dishes, into the composition of which the orange may be allowed to enter. Girls acquainted with these dishes would be able to introduce a most agreeable variety into the daily fare of the household.

Before, however, speaking of oranges in cookery, it will be well to say a word or two about the choice of oranges, and the best way of buying the fruit.

Within the last few years oranges have been obtainable in England very nearly all the year round. Until a very recent date, however, they were in season only from November till May or June, so that during the autumn months we had to do without them. Every year, however, the fruit appears earlier and stays later, so that it may almost be said that oranges are always with us. Two or three years ago it was hoped that Australian oranges would be available during the autumn months; but we cannot congratulate ourselves that the orange trade between England and Australia is as yet thoroughly developed, because the cost of freightage is so heavy, and this makes a difficulty. Even the most enthusiastic lover of the juicy fruit does not care to pay threepence or fourpence each for oranges when plums, pears, and blackberries are to be had in perfection, especially if the said costly treasure is not quite up to the mark, creating the impression that it is past date, and has lived through the prime of its life. If, however, Australian oranges are not always quite what one would wish them to be, it is to be remembered that they have been brought from a very long distance, and that their importation can scarcely be said to have passed as yet beyond the experimental stage. Fruit merchants say that when the difficulties have been surmounted there is a great future before Australian oranges, and that they will arrive here in excellent condition if only they are

The Girl's Own Paper, 1896, 1892

properly packed. It is to be hoped that this prediction will be fulfilled.

Of the oranges which come to us from parts nearer home, probably the best of all are the *St. Michael's*. This variety comes chiefly from the Azores, and not many years ago it used to be thought that no other orange was worth mentioning by the side of it. Of late it has somewhat gone out of fashion, and dealers tell us that of the five islands of the Azores which used to supply us, only one now sends it; the trees therein have ceased to bear, and have not been renewed. "Why have they not been renewed?" girls will perhaps ask. The answer is that other varieties are preferred by orange buyers. The fact is that St. Michael's oranges do not keep well; also they are not handsome, and the public of to-day is very eager for what looks beautiful. Curiously enough the more speckled and battered a St. Michael's orange looks—so long as it is sound—the more likely it is to be sweet and juicy. This orange is light-coloured, and has a thin, smooth rind, and it usually comes to market packed in the long, dried leaves of Indian corn, whereas Valencia oranges and other Spanish sorts come wrapped in thin paper. If, therefore, girls see at the greengrocers cases of light-coloured oranges, with long, thin, dried leaves about them, it will be fairly safe to conclude that the oranges contained therein are real St. Michael's.

For two or three years *Valencia* oranges have held the market. They are very excellent, very juicy, and very good; they are generally to be had in perfection towards the end of January. *Jaffa* oranges are a recent importation; they are most excellent, large, juicy, substantial, and delicious. Heretofore the chief objection to them has been their price; but they are getting cheaper. The small *Tangerine* oranges are usually approved as a dessert dish. They are excellent for decorative cookery, because they can be freed so entirely from the white pith. The skin of these oranges has a delightful fragrance; and one of the most delicious ice creams of which we have any knowledge is made of cream flavoured with the rind of Tangerines. Maltese oranges are quite unlike all others. The pulp is streaked with red, and is very soft and juicy, and there is a sweet bitterness in the taste which is quite confined to this variety. It is said that Maltese oranges owe their peculiarity to the fact that they have been grafted on the pomegranate tree. *Seville* oranges are of course not fit to eat, being very bitter. They are used for making marmalade, wine, and bitters. They generally come in towards the end of February, and are at their best during March. Girls who think of making marmalade should not defer the business over long.

Now let me give a few recipes for dishes made of oranges. First in popularity comes—

Orange Marmalade.—This preparation is known and approved all over the civilised world. It is understood to be the pet dainty of the people of Scotland, and Scottish housekeepers are particularly expert in making it. The great Thomas Carlyle spoke eloquently in its praise, and said that it was "a delicious confection, pure as liquid amber; in taste and look most poetically delicate." Students and men of letters are almost invariably partial to it; and it is so wholesome, so excellent, and so satisfactory, that it would scarcely be possible to speak extravagantly in its praise. There are in existence scores of recipes for making it, and many of these are very good; indeed, the majority of proved recipes are good, and the difference between marmalades made by one and by another is as the difference between tweedledum and tweedledee. The objection usually brought against them is that they are very troublesome, and girls who have made marmalade once or twice, and who have other work on hand, feel tempted, when March comes round, to shirk the business, and buy their marmalade of the grocer.

Now there is no denying that much of the marmalade offered for sale is very pure and good; still, there is a charm about home-made produce which commercial products can never boast. Girls, therefore, who have become a little out of patience with the elaborate methods usually followed, are recommended to try the following recipe. The marmalade made from it is most delicious, and also very economical, and the method easy indeed. Marmalade made thus with lump sugar at threepence per pound cost me twopence three-farthings per pound.

Recipe.—Slice six Seville and one sweet orange. Cut the fruit into very fine strips and remove nothing but the pips. Put pulp, fruit, and everything into three quarts of water, and leave for twenty-four hours. Turn into a preserving pan and simmer for two hours; at the end of this time add five pounds of white sugar and boil for one hour, or longer if necessary. When the marmalade is quite clear it is done, but the thing is to boil it enough. Stir all the time after the sugar is put in.

Orange Jelly is a very pleasant change from marmalade. Take three pounds bitter oranges, three pounds sweet oranges, and six lemons. To each pound of fruit allow three pints of water. Cut the fruit in round slices, and boil the pips and all until the liquor is reduced to one half. Strain through a jelly-bag, and to every pint of juice put a pound and a half of lump sugar. Boil about an hour, until the preparation jellies. This confection is more easily made than the last, because one does not need to stand over it at all. Yet it is most excellent.

Orange Pudding.—There are three or four ways of making the dish which is served with this name.

No. 1.—Take three ounces of stale cakecrumbs (ratafias, or stale sponge-biscuits will do; cake with currants in it is not suitable). Rub them through a sieve and put with them two ounces of sugar, the grated rind of two oranges, and the juice of three. Pour on half a pint of milk, the yolks of three and the whisked white of one egg. Line a pie-dish with a little good pastry, pour in the mixture, and bake till set and a light brown colour.

No. 2.—Boil the rind of a Seville orange till a pin will pierce it easily, then pound it to paste in a mortar. Put with it a quarter of a pound of fine breadcrumbs which have been passed through a sieve, the strained juice of the fruit, a piece of butter the size of half an egg, a teacupful of white sugar, and the beaten yolks of two eggs. Whisk the whites of the eggs separately till they are firm, and just before the pudding is to be cooked dash them lightly in. Turn the preparation into a buttered mould, put a piece of buttered paper on the top, and steam it for an hour, or till firm in the centre. Let it stand a few minutes before turning it out.

No. 3.—Peel and cut three or four oranges into thin slices, free them entirely from the white pith (which, if left, will swell and quite spoil the pudding), lay them in a pie-dish, and sprinkle white sugar thickly over them. Boil a pint of milk, mix a tablespoonful of flour smoothly with a little cold milk, add it to the boiling milk, and stir till thick. Add also two tablespoonfuls of sugar and the yolks of three eggs well beaten. Pour the preparation over the sliced oranges, bake it in the oven, and serve hot or cold.

An *Orange Sauce* for any of these puddings may be made by soaking thin orange rind in syrup till the latter is pleasantly flavoured, adding orange juice, and thickening the preparation with arrowroot.

Francatelli's Orange Pudding (very rich).—Put the strained juice of ten oranges and the rind of three rubbed on lumps of sugar into a basin with six ounces of bruised ratafias, six ounces of sugar, a pint of cream, ten yolks of eggs, and six whites whipped. Add a pinch of salt and a little grated nutmeg. Work these ingredients together for five minutes with a whisk, and then pour the mixture into a piedish already furnished with a thin border of puff-paste round the rim of the dish and reaching half way to the bottom. Shake some bruised ratafias over the surface, set the pudding in a baking-tin, and bake for about half an hour, till it is a light fawn colour.

This recipe, it is very evident, is the original of which recipe No. 1 is a humble modification. Francatelli's pudding is intended for people who can use cream and eggs galore; it would be regarded as most extravagant by ordinary individuals.

Orange Soufflée.—Girls who have succeeded in making soufflées know that they are not costly, and are both elegant and good. The chief points to be careful about with regard to them is, first, to cook the sauce very well, to whisk the egg-whites very stiffly, and to steam the pudding very gently and regularly. Prepare a quart tin mould with straight sides by greasing it well, and by twining a broad band of double paper, greased, round the outside, to make the sides of the mould several inches deeper. The paper must be fastened securely with twine, and must be close to the top of the tin, not low down, or the water would touch it. Put the thin rind of a small Seville orange into a basin with half a pint of milk, and set in a warm place till pleasantly and rather strongly flavoured. Melt an ounce of butter in a stewpan over the fire, stir in two dessertspoonfuls of flour and one dessertspoonful of arrowroot; mix and cook thoroughly, then add gradually the flavoured milk, with sugar to sweeten the preparation. Stir the mixture with a wooden spoon till it boils and thickens. When it leaves the sides of the stewpan quite clean it is enough. Draw it from the fire, let it cool a little, then drop into it (still off the fire) one by one the yolks of three eggs. Just before it is to be cooked whisk the whites of four eggs to a firm froth, stir these lightly into the batter, taking care not to break down the foam, and lay a piece of greased paper on the top to keep out the moisture from the steam. Place the tin in a deep saucepan with boiling water to reach half way up the sides, and steam steadily and gently for three quarters of an hour. When the soufflée is very light, and feels firm to the touch when pressed in the centre, it must be turned out carefully and served on the instant.

Orange Cream is an excellent and easilymade sweet. Soak an ounce of gelatine in a gill of milk. Put the thin rind of two or three oranges (without any of the white pith) in three quarters of a pint of milk, and sweeten with four ounces of loaf sugar. Boil and strain over the soaked gelatine, stirring well the while. Let the milk get cold; then mix with it half a pint of orange juice and the juice of one lemon. Mould when the cream is beginning to get firm. Of course this cream will be all the richer if cream, or a portion of cream, be used instead of milk. In this case the cream should be whipped stiffly before being added to the other ingredients. A pleasant change may be made by adding egg yolks to the milk, and thus converting it into custard. This will give it the yellow tinge which suggests oranges.

Orange Jelly for immediate use is of course simply jelly flavoured with orange juice. It is easily made because it does not need to be clarified. It makes variety to introduce sections of orange into the jelly, instead of having it quite plain. The oranges should be freed entirely from pith, and cut into small pieces with a sharp knife. They should then be stirred into the jelly just as it is beginning to set. If put in while the jelly is liquid they would sink to the bottom; and what is wanted is that they should permeate the mass.

Chartreuse of Oranges is a most elegant and tasty preparation. Line the inside of a plain round mould with straight sides with sections of Tangerine oranges by dipping the sections into jelly just ready to firm, and fixing them on the tin. If the mould has been rinsed in cold water and left damp, the sections will attach themselves instantly. When the lining is firm fill the mould with orange cream, made as above, or made by whipping half a pint of double cream, sweetening it with two ounces of sugar, flavouring it with the juice of three oranges, and adding to it a tablespoonful of gelatine dissolved in a little milk.

Orange Tarts.—Line a shallow dish or tartlet tin with pastry, spread some orange paste upon it, and bake till the pastry is done. To make the mixture put the grated rind and strained juice of three oranges upon the beaten yolks of three eggs, and add an ounce of butter and a quarter of a pound of sugar, or less if the oranges are sweet. Mix the ingredients thoroughly, and put them in a small stewpan; keep stirring one way till the paste is as thick as honey.

Orange Compôte.—Divide oranges into sections; free them from pith, and boil them for a few minutes in thin syrup flavoured with orange juice. Drain them and boil the syrup till thick. When cold lay the orange sections in a compôte dish; sprinkle desiccated cocoanut over them, and also a little of the syrup. Repeat until the ingredients are used. If the employment of alcoholic beverages is approved, a little sherry or brandy may be added to the syrup.

Orange Fritters.—Sections of orange freed from pith and fried in batter constitute a most excellent and elegant dish for the pudding course. Probably girls know well how to make these, so it is not necessary to give the recipe in full. Good batter may be made with a quarter of a pound of flour, a pinch of salt, two tablespoonfuls of salad oil, a gill of lukewarm water, and the whites of two eggs whisked to a firm froth and dashed lightly in last thing. The batter will be all the lighter if made some hours before it is wanted. It is to be noted that oil used instead of milk makes the batter crisp instead of leathery. If liked, three tablespoonfuls of oil might be used instead of two—then the whites of the eggs could be omitted altogether. Batter thus made would be too rich for everyone.

Orange Jelly set in Orange Peel.—Gouffé's Recipe.—Oranges thus prepared look very pretty when they are a success; and they are not as difficult to make as one would imagine. Girls with clever fingers, who would bestow a little pains upon them, could make them well enough. Choose some even-sized oranges, and with an inch plain cutter make a hole in the top of each. Remove the inside of the oranges carefully and completely, partly with a fruit knife and partly with the fingers, and be very careful not to tear the rind. When the skins are clear put them into cold water to soak for awhile; then drain and dry them. Afterwards set them on pounded ice, and fill them with orange jelly. When the jelly is firmly set cut each orange in four pieces, and arrange them on a graduated stand with laurel leaves between the pieces. They will look better if the jelly with which the skins are filled is of different colours. Sometimes the orange rinds are cut into the shape of baskets with handles, and the jelly, instead of being set in the baskets, is set separately, then coarsely chopped and set in last thing. The handle of the basket should be marked evenly across the stalk end of the fruit, and should be about half an inch thick. If the peel should be broken at all when cleaning it for the jelly, the hole can be stopped with a little butter, which can be removed when the jelly is set. If the rind has become thin, a little butter may be run over the inside to make it hold. The pulp can be most easily detached after the basket is cut out.

Rice Balls with Orange.—Wash a teacupful of rice in one or two waters; drain it, and cook it slowly in a pint and a half of milk, with five or six almonds, till the rice is quite tender and has absorbed the liquid. Beat it vigorously for three or four minutes to make it smooth, sweeten it with sifted sugar, and pack it tightly into small cups which have been rinsed in cold water and left wet. Cut the thin rind of an orange into neat shreds. Boil these in half a pint of water till soft. Take them out, and put into the water three ounces of white sugar, and boil to a clear thick syrup. Turn out the rice. Pour the syrup over the balls, and baste them with it in order to glaze them; sprinkle the cut rinds over them, and serve with cream.

Orange Marmalade Pudding.—Take six ounces of fine breadcrumbs, a pinch of salt, six ounces of finely-shred suet, two ounces of flour, two tablespoonfuls of sugar, six ounces of orange marmalade, half a teaspoonful of baking-powder, and two eggs. Put the mixture into a greased mould, lay a buttered paper over the top, and steam for four hours. Serve with sweet sauce.

Orange Baked Custard.—Take the very thin rind of a Tangerine orange (if this is not to be had, an ordinary orange may be used), boil it till tender, pound it to a paste, and mix with it a tablespoonful of brandy. Beat the yolks of four eggs in a basin, and pour on them a pint of boiling milk; stir well. Add two tablespoonfuls of sugar, a little salt, and the orange paste. Turn into a buttered dish or mould; set this in a tin containing warm water, and bake in a moderate oven till the custard is firm in the centre. Do not move it or shake it in any way. When cooked lift it out as gently as possible, and let it remain till cold. If necessary, put more water into the tin in which the pudding stands, but be very careful not to shake the pudding itself. Standing in water thus will ensure moderate cooking, and will make the pudding firm and smooth throughout without the holes which spoil the appearance of baked custard. When the pudding is quite cold turn it out carefully; pour orange syrup round it, and garnish with whipped cream. Orange custard may be converted into a very excellent sweet by turning the custard upon a layer of orange jelly, made according to the directions for the second of the jellies. (The first jelly is intended for storing.) The layer of jelly should be a little larger than the custard pudding, and should be stiff enough to support it. The orange sauce is made by boiling a quarter of a pound of sugar with a gill of water, adding three tablespoonfuls of orange juice and the rind of the orange, which has been boiled till tender and cut into thin strips. If four eggs are considered extravagant in making this dish (and eggs, be it remembered, are always dear when oranges are in season), two whole eggs may be used instead of four yolks. The eggs must, however, be fresh; and it is to be noted that though, when this number of eggs is used, the custard will taste good, it will not look as rich, and it will need to bake more than twice as long as if the larger number of eggs were employed. As, however, it is to be served cold, this does not signify. The custard can be put in the oven and left till firm; and if baked in water, it will be smooth and even throughout.

Such are a few of the recipes for dishes of which oranges are the distinguishing feature. It is to be hoped that girls who make them will succeed with them, and will enjoy them.

PHYLLIS BROWNE.

An Old Christmas Carol.

1. The first Nowell, the Angel did say, Was to certain poor shepherds in fields as they lay; In fields where they lay keeping their sheep, On a cold winter's night that was so deep.
2. They looked up and saw a Star Shining in the east, beyond them far, And to the earth it gave great light, And so it continued day and night.
3. And by the light of that same Star Three wise men came from country far; To seek for a king was their intent, And to follow the Star wherever it went.
4. This Star drew nigh to the north-west— O'er Bethlehem it stayed to rest, And there it did both stop and stay Right over the place where Jesus lay.
5. Then entered in those wise men three, And made due homage on their knee; And offered there, in His presence, Rare gold, and myrrh, and frankincense.
6. Then let us all, with one accord, Sing praises due to our Heavenly Lord, Who hath made Heaven and earth of nought, And with His Blood mankind hath bought.

CHORUS.

Nowell! Nowell! Nowell! Nowell! Born is the King of Israel!

The Girl's Own Paper, 1881

AN ORIGINAL CHARADE.

HOLIDAY AFTERNOONS.

One Monday morning, Marian and Clara Lane asked to speak to Miss Walker before school commenced. They had a request to prefer, and Marian was the spokeswoman.

"As next Saturday will be our last half-holiday before we break up, we should very much like to get up a charade or two, if you will allow us. I have the words of a simple one which we had at a juvenile party at Westwood last Christmas, and you know, dear Miss Walker, that if mamma herself took a part there *could* be nothing wrong in it."

"I am quite sure of that, dear, but charades generally require more preparation than we should have time for; especially during examination week."

"Our charades are very simple affairs, what we call 'fireside charades,' and demand nothing but what our every day resources will supply. Then examination week being all occupied in going over old work, we really have as much spare time as when we are preparing fresh lessons, if not more. You know, Miss Walker, you *do* make us learn things thoroughly the first time, and, at any rate, there is not much chance of our forgetting them before the end of the term."

"I hope not," replied their teacher, smiling at Marian's arguments. "I cannot, however, discuss the plan fully now, but come to me when afternoon school is over; explain everything, and I will see what can be done."

The girls went off, abundantly contented with this reply. Miss Walker's promise to see what could be done did not mean what similar words do in the mouths of many people, and especially in dealing with children—namely, that the matter would pass away from the thoughts and memory as if *it* had never been mentioned.

They knew their teacher would consider it fairly, help them if possible, and, in any case, give them an answer without needless delay. They left their manuscript charade in her hands, wondering how she would manage to read it and decide as to its suitability during the short time at her disposal, and with all the business of school going on, almost without intermission for her.

Amid these various occupations Miss Walker did find time to read the charade, and we will imagine that we are looking over her shoulder whilst she is thus occupied.

"SHOWING CONSIDERABLE INDEPENDENCE WITH REGARD TO TIME."

CHARADE.
Word—"Holidays."

A slight orthographical liberty being taken with the first two syllables in the opening part, which represents " Holly."

Characters.

Mamma (Mrs. Keith).
Four Children (Annie, Tom, Hilda, and Harry).
Aunt Alice.
The Parlour Maid (Mary).

Party of carol singers, or waits, not less than four in number, but as many more as you like.

Scene I.

A lady is sitting in a drawing-room with young children about her. On the floor is a large open basket, or tray, containing sprigs of holly, which the children break into suitable pieces and hand to the mamma. She twists them into a wreath and binds them together with fine wire.

Time—December 21, Evening.

(*Youngest child, Tom, yawns, drops his hands on his lap with a weary look, and says*)—
I think it must be nearly time for bed.
Was it *this* morning that the gardener said
 "We've reached the shortest day"? He must be wrong.
I'm sure I never knew one half so long.
Mamma, mamma, when will these wreaths be done?
At first this garland work was famous fair;
But all the funny part is long since past,
And each tough stem seems tougher than the last.
I tried a knife, when, ah, unlucky elf!
I meant to cut a twig, but cut myself.
Ivy and laurel wreaths were well enough;
But, oh, this holly is such prickly stuff!
Look at my fingers. (*Holds them up.*)
 Second Child (Harry).—Yes, and look at mine. (*Holds up his hands.*)
 Third Child (Annie, the eldest of the four).—And poor mamma has had them to all twine.
We've only cut the sprays for her to use.
A trifling task, and yet you would excuse
Yourselves from further labour. Fie, for shame!
 Mamma.—Hush, Annie, dear, you really must not blame
These tiny workers; they have done their part,
And done it well; though little fingers smart
With many a thorn, and each dear weary head
Longs for old nurse's summons, "Come to bed."
 Fourth Child (Hilda).—Annie, it was not kind to say "For Shame."
I'm sure papa *quite* wondered when he came
And saw how much we'd done. I know he said,
Putting his hand upon Tom's curly head,
And cuddling me quite close upon his knee—
"These willing hands make labour light. I see
You've changed my study to a fairy bower;
And these small folks have helped with all their power."
He kissed us then with such a merry smile,
And asked how much we'd done? Tom said, "A mile."

(*Aunt Alice enters in out-door costume, shakes hands with all, and kisses the children; then, at Mamma's request, takes off her jacket and sits down with little Tom upon her knee.*)
 Aunt Alice.—I had to pass the gate, so thought I'd come
And ask when all the rest are to be home.
Have you had news?
 Mamma.—Yes; letters came to-day
From Winifred and Mabel, just to say
That on the twenty-third they will be here,
And Winny adds, "Mamma, we've such a dear
Sweet darling schoolfellow, the best of girls;
She is *so* good. And she has *lovely curls!*
Her parents are abroad; too far away
For her to join them; and she was to stay
The holidays with friends who love her well,
When, all at once, a letter came to tell
Of sickness in their home. She cannot go:
And what to plan our teacher does not know.
Do ask if she may come to us instead;
Now don't say No. She may have half my bed.
I've heard you say our house was full before,
Still there was always room for just one more.
Write by return. You really must say Yes.
And I'll the postage pay with many a kiss;
I cannot write one-half that's in my head,
So close, with love to all, from
 WINIFRED."
 Aunt Alice.—So like that loving child. What shall you do?
 Mamma.—Write her the "yes" she asks for; one or two
The more amidst our merry, noisy clan
Will only make us happier.
(*Turns to Tom, and shows him the wreath completed.*)
 Little man,
Our task is done; this wreath is quite the last.
Now I must write, or post time will be past.
(*Mamma lays finished wreath on the basket, and sits down to answer Winifred's letter, in which she encloses a second note; then, having closed the envelope, she hands it to Harry, saying*)—
Tell John to post this letter, and not wait
A moment, or I fear it may be late.
(*Child goes out of the room with the letter.*)
 Aunt Alice.—My own dear boys have sent a line to me
Saying they bring a comrade, who will be
Like sunshine in the house; no time to tell
More than this much, "You're sure to like him well."
 Mamma.—Guests add a little to our household cares;
But love makes light of this, and, unawares,
We may have angel guests in earthly guise.
In any case, it surely must be wise
To help our children when they wish to share
Their joys with others and to lighten care.

(*At this moment singing is heard. Mamma, Aunt Alice, and the children, including Harry, who is come back after taking the letter, go to the window and look out, but cannot see the singers.*)
 Mamma.—They must be in the hall; I'll ring the bell.
(*Does so, and Mary, the parlour maid, appears.*)
Who are those singers, Mary; can you tell?
 Mary.—They are the waits, and will be glad to know
If you will hear them sing before they go.
(*Voices come nearer, and words can be distinguished by the listeners in the drawing-room.*)
 Chorus.—Heigho, sing heigho unto the green holly!
Most friendship is feigning, most loving mere folly.
Then heigho! the holly, the holly!
This life is most jolly, most jolly,
This life is most jolly.*

(*Enter Waits, in thick coats and shawls and woollen comforters, the males hats in hand. They bow awkwardly, and ask leave to sing.*)

---
* This is a part of the chorus to a beautiful glee, called " Blow, Blow, Thou Winter Wind," published, at a very trifling price, by Novello & Co., and forming a number of their Standard Glee Books.

On receiving permission they sing the glee all through, and then the leader says, after the children have clapped and applauded the singing)—
Please, ma'am, we'd like to sing a carol too.
 Mamma.—A carol! No, indeed, that will not do.
It is too soon. But come on Christmas Eve Again, and I will gladly give you leave.
(*She gives money to the leader, and the singers go out, led by the parlour-maid, saying all together as they make their bows and curtseys*)—
Good night! Good night! Good luck to all,
Right soon we'll make another call.
(*Aunt Alice resumes her out-door dress, saying*)—
Now I *must* go.
 Mamma.—And these must all to bed,
Or I shall hear of many an aching head.
(*They all go out, the little ones led by Mamma and Aunt Alice, the elder children following.*)

END OF FIRST SCENE.

Scene II.

Characters.

Governess and School Girls (named Winifred, Maggie, Emma, Nellie, Louie, &c.)

Word—"Days."
Time—December 22nd, 11 a.m.
A Schoolroom.

(*A number of girls sitting at desks or tables, and occupied in various ways, with books, slates, maps, &c., scattered up and down. One girl takes a pen, opens a small memorandum book and carefully crosses out something, then closes the book with an air of great satisfaction, and puts it in her pocket.*)
 Maggie.—What are you doing, Winny?
 Winifred.—That's the last
But one. The tedious days are nearly past;
Just a few hours of work, and then, away
To weeks and weeks of home and joy and play.
No tiresome bell to ring us in to school,
No crosses, or bad marks for breach of rule,
Nor anything to do that is not nice.
 Maggie.—What were you marking?
 Winifred (*taking book out of her pocket again*).—Listen, in a trice
I'll tell you all about it. 'Tis a way
I have of marking off each tiresome day
That comes between mamma, and home, and me.
I started it six weeks ago. You see
(*Opens book and points to the page.*)
I drew six rows of strokes — in each was seven—
And every morning when it struck eleven
I crossed one off. Now there is only one;
By twelve to-morrow we shall all be gone.
 Maggie.—Not all. Alas! not all. I shall be left.
The hour which brings *you* joy leaves *me* bereft
Of all my playfellows.
(*Puts her hand before her face and appears to be weeping.*)
 Nellie.—O Maggie, dear,
I am *so* sorry we must leave you here;
It grieves me, too, to think that you will be
Alone and sad, in this dull house, while we
Are scattered north, and south, and east, and west,
To pass our time with those we love the best.
I'd like to take you with me, but we spend
The next ten days with father's oldest friend.
But dry your tears, my darling.
(*Draws Maggie's head lovingly on her shoulder, wipes her eyes and kisses her, then*

turns sharply round to a little girl who approaches, slate in hand, and with a beseeching look at NELLIE.)

Little Dunce,
What do you want?
    LOUIE.—Please, just this once
To help me with my sum; *it won't come right*,
Although I did it seven times last night;
And it was always wrong.
    WINIFRED.—And likely, too,
It should be wrong. The stupid things you do,
You careless child, would almost drive me mad.
I tell you, Louie, I am very glad
I'm not your teacher. See, now; there are seven,
Six, five, two, three! *You* say they make eleven!
And, out of seven, three, six, and just one more,
You nicely calculate an even score!
    MAGGIE.—She's such a little thing—at six years old
We don't know much of figures; do not scold
A weeping child. Come hither, little mite,
And do your sum with me; 'twill soon be right.

(*Takes the slate from* LOUIE *and makes little groups of strokes upon it, corresponding with the numbers the child has to add, then says to her*)—
Count all these strokes and see what they will make.
Put down the six. The one we onward take
To the next line, and add it with the rest:
They make eighteen. All's done.
    LOUIE.—You are the best
Of friends to little girls who want to play;
I do so hate to be kept in all day.

(LOUIE *runs off joyfully, and as she does so the schoolroom door opens and the Governess enters with a number of letters in her hand.* GOVERNESS *distributing the letters as she speaks*)—
Annie, there's one for you. For Winny three.
    MAGGIE (*aside*).—I'm very sure there will be none for me.
    GOVERNESS.—Louie's mamma a message sends in mine
To say her train will start at five to nine,
And that, two stations on, she will be met
By Uncle Tom. Nellie must not forget
To take her waterproof, for fear of rain,
As brother James will bring the car again.
The brougham is engaged for grandmamma,
But Nellie will not mind, it is not far,
And wraps and rugs in plenty will be sent.
    NELLIE.—I like the open car, and am content
With anything that bears me quickly on.
    MAGGIE.—I knew there was no letter.
    WINIFRED.—Here is one
Enclosed in mine for you. Why do you stare?
As though it could not be. Come, take your share
Of postal spoils, and, if you care for me,
Pray read it quickly, Mistress Marjorie."

(MAGGIE *takes the letter held out by* WINIFRED, *opens it, and reads as follows*)—
"My dear Girl,
  "I have heard from one of my children that something has occurred to prevent your spending the vacation with the friends who hoped to welcome you. It will give my young people and myself great pleasure if your governess, who, I understand, arranges everything for you in the absence of your parents, will allow you to pass the next few weeks with us. She has known us so long that I do not think she will say 'no,' and I trust, my dear girl, you will accept this invitation in the loving spirit in which it is given.
  "I shall be delighted to count you as one amongst my rather large flock of youngsters, and for the time, and in order to make our house more like home, you must look upon me as your own, dear mamma's deputy. Ask anything of me that you would ask of her; come to me when you please, and try to think of me as representing, to the best of my power, that dear mother who is longing to have you with her again.
  "Hoping to see you arrive with my daughter Winny, and with love and kindest wishes,
    "Believe me, yours affectionately,
            "ELEANOR KEITH."

    MAGGIE (*with a look of bewilderment*).—
Winny, you've played a trick. It can't be true,
Your mother asks me to go home with you!
She has not even seen my face.
    WINIFRED.—As though
That mattered, Maggie darling. You *must* go.
I spoke beforehand to our teacher. She
Is quite agreeable, and certainly
We shall take no denial. Not a word
Of doubt or protest, it will not be heard.

(WINNY *puts her fingers to her ears, as if determined not to listen to a word from* MAGGIE, *and the teacher, laying her hand affectionately on* MAGGIE'S *shoulder, says*)—
I can rejoice with you, my child; no fear
That I shall say you nay, or keep you here.
Go and be happy with these friends, and when
The days of rest are past, come back again,
With roses on your cheeks, once more to find
A welcome here.
    MAGGIE.—You always are so kind.
(*Another girl comes to the governess and says*)—
Please may we put our work and books away?
We really cannot think of them to-day.
    GOVERNESS.—No wonder, dear; I know
your thoughts will roam,
However you may strive, to friends at home.
Clear all away, and when this task is done
Put on your garden hats and take a run
For half an hour; then come and do your part—
To make all ready for to-morrow's start.

(*All the girls jump up, and, with thanks to the governess and exclamations of delight, rapidly clear away all school articles, and then run out, followed more quietly by the governess, who has been watching them with an amused face.*)

END OF SECOND SCENE.

SCENE III.
COMPLETE WORD—"Holidays."
TIME — Evening, December 23rd.
CHARACTERS.

MAMMA, PAPA, ANNIE, HILDA, TOM, HARRY, AUNT ALICE, UNCLE JAMES (her husband), FRED and JACK, their two boys, and their school friend, CHARLIE FREEMAN, WINIFRED and MAGGIE, and MABEL, an elder sister of WINNY's.

(*The drawing-room as in scene first.* MAMMA, AUNT ALICE, *and the four children are together. Nobody seems able to settle to any employment. First one and then another goes to the window, draws aside the curtains, and looks out, or appears to be listening for something.* Mamma *rises from her seat, goes to the fire, and stirs it vigorously.*)
    ANNIE.—Mamma, you surely mean to roast us quite!
See what a blaze! I do not think the night
Is very cold.
    MAMMA.—My child, *you* do not know
How cuttingly this fierce, north wind can blow,
Clothed, fed, and sheltered, all your happy past
Has been so bright. *You* never felt the blast
Piercing your half-clad limbs, or hunger knew,
Or suffering, from which love could shelter you.
    AUNT ALICE.—True, but we have no starving people here.
I wish with all my heart that we could cheer
Each homeless wanderer with such a sight
As waits our children when they come to night.
They will be glad enough to gather round
This fireside. Hark! was not that a sound
Of coming wheels? It surely must be time.
    MAMMA.—I hear no sound except the merry chime
Of evening bells, ringing, so soft and sweet
Through the clear air.
    AUNT ALICE.—I'd rather hear the feet
Of trampling horses and the shout of boys.
To me sweet music now were only noise
And hateful discord. All my listening ear
Is for my children. Would that they were here!

(*Looks at her watch, then puts it to her ear to listen if it is going; then compares it with* MAMMA'S *watch*).
    MAMMA (*holding out hers*).—See, sister, they are both alike. 'Tis only we
Whose thoughts are in advance of Time, and he
Goes hobbling on with the same lagging feet
Now as of old, when joy we fain would meet.
But, O the change! No sooner do we grasp
The happiness we longed for, than our clasp
We tighten round it, and would gladly tie
The feet of Father Time, lest he rush by
Too rapidly; and, all unpitying, tear
From loving hearts what most we cherish there.

(*The children are now all standing at the windows and peeping behind the curtains, hoping to catch the first glimpse of the expected travellers*).
Enter PAPA *and* UNCLE JAMES.
    MAMMA.—What! Are you here? We really thought you went
To meet the children.
    PAPA.—We must be content to wait with you.
    AUNT ALICE.—I think the train is late.
    TOM (*shouts, while all the others clap their hands*)—
I see a carriage. It is past the gate.
    HARRY.—And there's another, both are coming round.
    ANNIE.—I see the girls.
    HARRY.—And don't you hear the sound
Of boys hurrahing? Yes they come, they come.
    UNCLE JAMES.—And lads approaching home are never dumb.
The door is open; now the frosty air
Steals in.
    AUNT ALICE.—And now their feet are on the stair.

(WINIFRED, MAGGIE, *an elder girl*, FRED, JACK, *and* CHARLIE FREEMAN *all come clattering in, and there is a general shaking of hands and embracing between parents and children. All the travellers are in out-door costume and warmly wrapped.* MAGGIE *is led forward by* WINNIE *and introduced to* MAMMA, *who kisses her affectionately.*)
    WINIFRED.—Here is the child you wrote for.
    MAMMA.—Maggie, dear,
I'm very glad indeed to see you here.
I trust, my child, we shall find many ways
To make you happy through the holidays.
I cannot show you all my flock to-night:
It is not often they are all in sight.
    PAPA (*shaking hands with* MAGGIE).—Our
Children by instalments you must see;
They sometimes very nearly frighten me—
There's such a tribe of little Keiths. Ah well!
They're dearer to our hearts than lips can tell.

Some are upstairs, the smallest are in bed,
(*Points to the elder youths, who have just arrived, and have been specially welcomed by* AUNT ALICE *and* UNCLE JAMES)
These are Aunt Alice's, both Jack and Fred.
UNCLE JAMES (*introducing* CHARLIE FREEMAN)
And this *our* visitor, who comes, like you,
To make another home the happier too.
(MAGGIE *starts, then darts forward towards* CHARLIE FREEMAN.)
MAGGIE.—My cousin Charlie, if I may believe
My eyes! but think they surely must deceive.
CHARLIE.—There's no mistake at all; just then I was
Wondering what brought *you* here, my little coz.
UNCLE JAMES.—This is a glad surprise; but you, our guest,
Must with these boys go to our proper nest.
AUNT ALICE.—Yet, happily, though you must part to-night,
'Twill be to meet again with morning light.
(*All the boys and girls here begin to sing the following verses, making a great deal of noise, and showing considerable independence with regard to tune, their principal object being to make the performance as vigorous as possible. The elder people laugh, and pretend to stop their ears. As the song draws to a close,* MAMMA *leads out the two little ones, while* ANNIE, HILDA, WINNIE, MAGGIE, *and the elder sister follow. Papa accompanies* AUNT ALICE *and* UNCLE JAMES *with the three boys to the door. The last four lines should be sung as they are going out of the room, and the sound should at last die away in the distance.*)

HOLIDAY SONG.

Hurrah! Hurrah for the holidays!
 Shan't we be having some fun?
Won't we be having some jolly days
 Now the vacation's begun?

We'll turn the house out of the windows,
 And turn it in back at the doors;
We'll empty the dairy and larder,
 And eat up the chickens by scores.

Hurrah! Hurrah for the holidays!
 Which bring us such pleasure and fun;
We hope to have nothing but jolly days
 Now the vacation's begun.

No doubt we shall wear out the carpets,
 With clattering upstairs and down;
Some parents might grumble, but "Mother"
 Won't give us the ghost of a frown.

Hurrah! Hurrah for the holidays!
 This is the first of our fun;
This is the best of all jolly days,
 For the vacation's begun.

END OF CHARADE.

DIAMOND CUT DIAMOND.

A CHRISTMAS ENTERTAINMENT.

BY SOMERVILLE GIBNEY, Author of "A Friend in Need," "By Parcel Post," "Speaking Likenesses," &c.

IN recent years there have appeared in these pages, about Christmas-time, entertainments suitable for a small number of performers, with a limited space at their command; but, as I have each time owned, they have not been absolutely new, in that they were performed at the house of Mrs. Greyden before they appeared in the "G.O.P." This year, however, I propose giving you one that is absolutely new, as it has never been performed anywhere. They say there is a charm about novelty, and on this account it may be acceptable. I have framed it on the same lines as the previous ones, viz., that it requires only a small number of performers, that no large platform is requisite, and that it provides for the distribution of presents. It is therefore applicable to school treats as well as private parties, where young people always appreciate their gifts more if accompanied by a certain amount of mystery in their production.

Let me start by saying there is no real difficulty in what I am going to set before you that cannot easily be overcome by fertile brains and active hands, and, acting on the rule I have hitherto followed, I will first give you the words and directions for performance, and then such further hints as may be necessary.

Performers:
 WINTER.
 DISCONTENT.
 GOODWILL.
 And two Pages or Attendants to GOODWILL (if preferred).

SCENE.

(*A rocky cavern, with opening at back. The lights are low and blue. On the curtain being raised* WINTER *is discovered seated on a piece of rock in the cave.*)

WINTER. There is a saying "Each dog has his day,"
 And if that's true, well, then, perhaps, I may
 Be fortunate in this respect as well;
 Though why I should thus draw a parallel
 Between myself, being Winter, and a hound
 I cannot give a reason really sound,
 Although I know a sad dog some folks dub me;
 Still low abuse does not the wrong way rub me.
 I'm Winter, and as such have my employment,
 And with it what to me is great enjoyment.
 My stay in England always is but brief,
 And my departure some think a relief.
 The way last Spring and Summer lingered here
 Most anxious made me, and caused me to fear
 That I should be excluded altogether,
 And Christmas would be spent in scorching weather.
 But here I am, and my intention now is
 To make up for lost time, and show my prowess.
 I'll let folks know, and knowing they shall rue,
 What Winter, when he's put to it can do.
 I'll rain, I'll hail, and vary this with snow;
 And in between times, for a change, I'll blow,
 Not genial airs, but downright blinding blizzards;
 For as to storms I've all the skill of wizards.
 I'll start this minute, just to let folks see
 What they, poor souls, may now expect of me.

[*Rises, and taking his staff, waves it slowly in all directions during the following, which he speaks slowly.*]

 Black clouds arise,
 Blot out the skies.
 Blow high, blow low,
 Come hail! come snow!

The Girl's Own Paper, 1896

        Stern warfare wage,
        And tear and rage.
  And in an icy shroud, and cold,
  The shivering, trembling world enfold.

[*Sounds of a fierce tempest with rain and hail are heard outside.* WINTER *stands quite still for a time, listening, then seating himself.*]

  That's set them going, what a noise! Oh dear!
  It's glorious the howling wind to hear,
  I must be in it. [*Rises to go out.*]

(*A voice heard outside.*) Hollo, there, I say!

WINTER (*laughing*). There's some poor wretch——

(*A voice.*)   Who's that? I've lost my way.
  Where am I? Give me shelter. I'm half dead
  With cold and snow and wet.

WINTER (*at entrance and speaking off*). Come straight ahead.
  There's shelter here. Now mind that rock.

(*A voice.*)   All right,
  I see. My word! it is an awful night.

[*Enter* DISCONTENT *shaking a cloud of snow off her head and shoulders.*]

  So unexpectedly it came on, too.
  Why, Winter! you don't mean to say that's you?

WINTER. What, Discontent! It's you, my lady, is it,
  Upon your way to pay your yearly visit?
  We always meet.

DISCONTENT.   Now, Winter, it's too bad
  To play a trick like this, and send half mad
  The elements about my ears to-night;
  A joke's a joke, but this is far from right,
  There's no fun in it, none at least for me.

WINTER. I'm sorry, Discontent; but then you see
  I'd no idea——

DISCONTENT.   Oh, nonsense! No excuse,
  You know with me they're not the slightest use.
  I'm up to all your ways——

WINTER.   But, Discontent,
  I didn't mean——

DISCONTENT.   No matter what you meant,
  Just stop this noise, and let me speak in peace;

WINTER (*waving his wand*). Wind, storm, snow, hail, shut up,
  your turmoil cease.   [*Instant silence.*]

DISCONTENT. That's better; now then, what's all this about?
  And why this dreadful atmospheric rout?
  You've got a finger in it, come now?

WINTER.   Yes;
  You're not so very far out in your guess.
  The fact is simply this, last spring and summer
  Were so superb, I feared the latest comer.

DISCONTENT. You mean yourself?

WINTER.   Just so; might underrated
  Be, or scoffed at, so I contemplated
  A little taste of what I really *could* do,
  And what, as days and weeks went on, I should do.

DISCONTENT. Quite right, for mortals very uppish get,
  And fancy they must have, now dry, now wet,
  Just as it suits them.

WINTER.   No, it will not do
  To pander to their fancies; but then you
  Don't do it.

DISCONTENT. No. I act up to my name,
  I'm Discontent, and make some mortals blame
  Most things.

WINTER (*laughing*). You do; your nature is not sweet,
  For disagreeableness you're hard to beat.
  Now I'll be bound that in your bag you've got
  Of ills and trials quite a pretty lot.

DISCONTENT. You're right, I have, a really choice collection,
  There are some outside, quite worthy your inspection.

[*She undoes a bag she is carrying, and takes from it parcels, as required.*]

  Look here (*holding up parcel*), this is a gross or two of colds,
  And this sore throats and influenza holds, (*holding up another*)
  Chilblains and hotaches for the hands and toes, (*another*)
  And this is for young ladies, marked "red nose"; (*another*)
  Burst water-pipes, which mortals do not much like, (*another*)
  And here are frozen greenhouses and such-like; (*another*)
  This one is loss of work (*another*), and this, you see, (*another*)
  Contains a mass of want and misery.
  I've here a batch of falls and accidents,
  And broken limbs make up this one's contents;
  Besides all these——

WINTER.   Oh, thank you, that will do,
  I shall receive, I see, much help from you.
  And we shall little difficulty find
  In making these poor mortals keep in mind
  For years to come this season, as the one
  In which they'd all the kicks and little fun.

DISCONTENT. Let's start at once, I'm sheltered now and warm,
  So just turn on again that awful storm,
  'Twill set some people shivering.

WINTER.   All right,
  We'll start our season with an awful night!

[*Rising and waving his wand as before.*]

      Black clouds arise,
      Blot out the skies,
      Stern warfare wage,
      And tear and rage;
      Blow high, blow low,
    Come hail, come snow,
  And in an icy shroud and cold,
  The shivering, trembling world enfold.

[*The noise of the storm is heard outside as before.*]

DISCONTENT. That's grand, I love the sound when I'm in shelter,
  Just hark how it is hailing helter-skelter.

WINTER. Yes, listen to the hurricane too! This
  A real good storm is (*sounds cease suddenly*). Hollo! what's amiss?
  There's something wrong; they've stopped!

DISCONTENT.   What can it be?

WINTER. I can't conceive. I'll just run out and see.

[*Going, when he is met at the door by* GOODWILL, *at the same moment the lights are turned up, and change from blue to rose, and the scene becomes bright and warm-looking, and* WINTER *and* DISCONTENT *huddle together in the farthest corner away from* GOODWILL, *as if in terror.*]

GOODWILL. Ah, yes! just what I thought might be the case.
  No wonder you don't like to see my face.

WINTER (*aside to* DIS.). Goodwill! We're done for!

GOODWILL.   Raising such a storm,
  And you yourselves in shelter, snug and warm.
  However, Winter, I have scotched your spite
  And bottled up your malice for to-night.

DISCONTENT (*aside*). Just like her impudence, this domineering.
  I hate Goodwill, she's always interfering.

WINTER (*aside*). It is too bad.

GOODWILL.   Who have you with you there?
  What, Discontent! A very pretty pair!
  No wonder mischief was abroad! No doubt
  You quite expected not to be found out.
  But I won't have it, Winter. Do you hear? (*decidedly*)
  It's perfectly disgusting! you appear
  To fancy you can do just what you please,
  Send snow and hail in showers, blow, and freeze,
  As if the place belonged to you. But I
  Won't have it, as I said; I'll tell you why—
  You're sent here to do good, not ill, and so
  I don't object to now and then some snow,
  And ice in reason, also wind and rain,
  When through them Earth can some advantage gain;
  But if you send them only out of spite,
  At once I'll stop them, as I've done to-night;
  And further, you will give of all you do
  A strict account——

WINTER (*sullenly*).   What! give account to you?
  I'll not.

GOODWILL. You will, or else, my friend, you'll rue it.
  You'd better settle once for all to do it;
  For if you don't—but there—— Now, Discontent,
  A word with you. You're not like Winter, sent——

DISCONTENT.   No, rather not.

GOODWILL. But come of your free will,
Yet when you come you bring no good, but ill.

DISCONTENT (*aside*). Just listen to her.

GOODWILL. Now then, I'll be bound
A mass of trouble might on you be found.
What have you in that bag?

DISCONTENT (*impudently*). What's that to you?
The bag's my own.

GOODWILL. Hollo! This will not do (*looks fixedly and sternly at* DISCONTENT, *who cowers back and slowly opens the bag she carries*).
Now, Discontent, be careful; you know well
You're powerless before my potent spell.
Produce what you have there, and if I see
That you have tried to steal a march on me,
Then woe betide you. Quick now, hand them out.
What's this? (*Taking a packet which* DISCONTENT *hands her*.)

DISCONTENT. Bad colds.

GOODWILL (*taking another*). And this sore throats, no doubt.

DISCONTENT (*handing another*). Chilblains and hotaches.

GOODWILL. One might well suppose
You would not spare the young. What's this (*reading*) "Red Nose,"
You wretch! (*to* DISCONTENT).

DISCONTENT (*handing another*). Burst water-pipes.

GOODWILL. It's clear.
You've——

DISCONTENT (*handing another*). Frozen greenhouses.

GOODWILL. No business here.
Give me them all, and those you left outside

[DISCONTENT *turns out her bag, and brings in the other parcels, putting them all down together.*]

You needn't think that I can be defied.
Your spite I'll bring to naught (*standing over the parcels with outstretched hands*). It is my will
That each and all be changed to good from ill.
They're harmless now; indeed they each contain
Something that pleasure will afford, not pain—
Now, Discontent, begone. At this glad season
Your presence here is nothing short of treason.

DISCONTENT. But may I not?——

GOODWILL. At once begone, I say,
Nor dare to linger longer.

[*Exit* DISCONTENT, WINTER *is following.*]

Winter, stay,
Your time's not up, and as a punishment
For what you did in spite, you shall present
These gifts to those for whom they are intended.
And take care that henceforth your ways are mended,
So that in future mortals may have reason
To speak of Winter as a merry season.

DISTRIBUTION OF PRESENTS.

And now then for the *modus operandi*. As to the curtain and the proscenium, I have recently in "Speaking Likenesses" given full instruction with regard to them, so that I need only refer my readers to that article. For the scene itself a rocky cavern will be most effective, and there is no difficulty in this. I gave instructions how it was to be managed in an article in one of the Christmas Numbers, headed "A Friend in Need," but as some of my present readers may not have seen it, I may say that the rocks are formed by sheets of brown paper crumpled up and sewn on to canvas, which is either nailed to frames or hung from cords, stretched out of sight above the proscenium. The brown paper can be made more effective by being painted here and there to deepen the shadows, when the canvas is hung in its place. A roof can also be formed in the same way, but this should not be stretched too tightly, but allowed to sag down in the middle, thus giving the effect of naturally uneven rockwork. In the present case an opening can be left at the back through which the performers may enter, but then a back cloth must be painted with a wintry scene. This would not be a difficult task to some, for the opening need not be a large one; and the effect would be greatly enhanced. The floor of the cavern should be covered with brown canvas or holland to represent sand, and a few stones or rocks lying about would help the illusion.

The lights should be hung as described in the entertainment "Speaking Likenesses," with the addition of one behind the canvas on which the rocks are fastened, pointing on the back cloth, otherwise this would hardly be seen. Sheets of blue gelatine or pieces of blue glass fixed in front of the lamps will give the cold, dim light requisite during the first portion of the entertainment, and these can be quickly changed for red ones on the entrance of Goodwill, when the lights will of course be turned up to their full. Several careful rehearsals of the lighting should be held before the performance, when the best effects will be discovered, for it may be that it will be found sufficient to have only one of the lamps lighting the interior of the cave with the red glass in front, and the other merely the plain white light.

The sound of the hail is obtained by allowing peas to fall upon a sheet of cardboard from some little height, and the moaning of the wind is managed by a piece of silk stretched over a wheel.

Of course these effects must be carefully rehearsed, as a good deal of the picturesqueness of the performance will depend upon their being well executed; they should attain their full power when the characters are silent, and gradually sink so as not to interfere with the words. Use them at all rehearsals so that those who manage them may be fully up to their duties, and the performers may grow accustomed to the noise and not be distracted by it.

Winter should be represented by a male, and should be clad in a grey robe down to his feet, edged with ermine or fur, and tied with a girdle round his waist. His head should be covered by a hood, part of the garment also edged in the same way. He should have a wig of straggling grey hair, and grey eyebrows made, as I have often previously described, of *crepe* hair, but no beard or moustache. His face should be made up old, lantern-jawed, and sallow. You will find grease paints the best to work with, and the easiest to get rid of after the performance if the face is well rubbed with vaseline before washing in warm water. Winter's nose should be decidedly red towards the tip, and you may make this more or less pointed by the aid of spirit-gum and cotton wool. I may here mention that there is a book published on making up, which may be obtained through any bookseller's, in which you will find directions for representing any class of face that may be desired. Care must be taken that Winter is not confused with Father Christmas, but this can be avoided by giving him a thin, pinched, miserable look, instead of a jovial, merry, good-tempered one. In this performance it will be seen that the worst side of Winter's character is brought to the front, and his face must be a reflex of it.

Discontent may be represented by either a male or female as may be found most convenient, but if by the latter she must not hesitate to sacrifice every atom of her good looks to the character. Discontent, as her name implies, is a disagreeable, vixenish old hag, soured in temper and looks. She also should be in grey with bare skinny arms, and a hood or cloak over her head, beneath which grey elf locks should appear, falling partly over her face, which should be very sallow and withered-looking, the corners of the mouth must be shaded to give the appearance of being drawn down, and the forehead must be well wrinkled, while two short, dark lines going straight upwards from the inner ends of the eyebrows will give a cross, ill-tempered expression. Her disagreeable appearance may be heightened by depriving her of most of her front teeth. There will be no need of a dentist to effect the operation, it will be quite sufficient to stick black court plaster on those you wish to disappear, and at a few feet distant the effect will be complete.

In direct contrast, in every way, to these two characters must be Goodwill, who will be sure to carry off the sympathies of the audience. Her representative should be young and nice-looking. She must dress in any flowing robe of white (of course not of a modern fashion), which may be relieved by a gold belt or some gold embroidery, but not put on too heavily. Her hair should be worn down her back and a diamond star in the front would heighten the effect. Her arms and neck should be bare. The only jewels she should wear must be diamonds, and not too many of them. Her character is a bright and happy one, and this should be reflected in her dress and appearance. A little rouge should be used, and the eyelashes lined as I have given directions in former articles.

The snow which Discontent shakes off on her entrance is formed of coarse powdered salt, sprinkled over her just before she appears. The parcels of "troubles" which she carries are of course the presents intended to be given to the guests, and they may be done up in any way most convenient.

And now what more is there to say, save my oft-repeated direction, rehearse, rehearse, rehearse, till the whole thing goes like clockwork. Let the representatives of Winter and Discontent remember that they are not to expect a particle of sympathy from their audience, and that if they get it they may know they have not performed their part properly. They are the villains of the piece, and the greatest compliments they can receive is to be soundly hissed. Goodwill may have two pages attending her if it is found convenient, and space is sufficiently large, but if she has them, they should also attend rehearsals though they have not a word to say, because they must learn where to stand so as not to get in the way of the others; as to their dress I may leave that to the taste of my readers, only imploring them not to allow them to appear in anything in modern fashion; and now then go to work, and may success attend your efforts.

THE CHRISTMAS KALENDS OF PROVENCE.

BY THOMAS A. JANVIER,
SÒCI DÒU FELIBRIGE,
Author of "An Embassy to Provence," etc.

WITH PICTURES BY LOUIS LOEB.

Fancy you 've journeyed down the Rhône,
   Fancy you 've passed Vienne, Valence,
Fancy you 've skirted Avignon—
   And so are come *en pleine* Provence.

Fancy a mistral cutting keen
   Across the sunlit wintry fields,
Fancy brown vines, and olives green,
   And blustered, swaying cypress shields.

Fancy a widely opened door,
   Fancy an eager outstretched hand,
Fancy—nor need you ask for more—
   A heart-sped welcome to our land.

Fancy the peal of Christmas chimes,
   Fancy that some long-buried year
Is born again of ancient times—
   And in Provence take Christmas cheer.

I.

IN my own case, this journey and this welcome were not fancies but realities. I had come to keep Christmas with my friend M. de Vièlmur according to the traditional Provençal rites and ceremonies in his own entirely Provençal home: an ancient dwelling which stands high up on the westward slope of the Alpilles, overlooking Arles and Tarascon and within sight of Avignon, near the Rhône margin of Provence.

The Vidame—such is M. de Vièlmur's ancient title, derived originally not from a minor overlord but directly from the sovereign counts of Provence—is an old-school country gentleman who is amiably at odds with modern times. While tolerant of those who have yielded to the new order, he himself is a great stickler for the preservation of antique forms and ceremonies; sometimes, indeed, pushing his fancies to lengths that fairly would lay him open to the charge of whimsicality, were not even the most extravagant of his crotchets touched and mellowed by his natural goodness of heart.

The château of Vièlmur has remained so intimately a part of the middle ages that the subtle essence of that romantic period still pervades it, and gives to all that goes on there a quaintly archaic tone. The donjon, a prodigiously strong square tower dating from the twelfth century, partly is surrounded by a dwelling in the florid style of two hundred years back, the architectural flippancies of which have been so tousled by time and weather as to give it the look of an old beau caught unawares by age and grizzled in the midst of his affected youth.

In the rear of these oddly coupled structures is a farm-house with a dependent rambling collection of farm-buildings, the whole inclosing a large open court to which access is had by a vaulted passageway that on occasion may be closed by a double set of ancient iron-clamped doors. As the few exterior windows of the farm-house are grated heavily, and as from each of the rear corners of the square there projects a crusty tourelle from which a raking fire could be kept up along the walls, the place has quite the air of a testy little fortress—and a fortress it was meant to be when it was built three hundred years ago (the date, 1561, is carved on the keystone of the arched entrance) in the time of the religious wars.

But now the iron-clamped doors stand open on rusty hinges, and the courtyard has that look of placid cheerfulness which goes with the varied peaceful activities of farm labor and farm life. Chickens and ducks wander about it chattering complacently, an aged goat of a melancholy humor stands usually in one corner lost in misanthropic thought, and a great flock of extraordinarily tame pigeons flutters back and forth between the stone dovecote rising in a square tower above the farm-house and the farm well.

This well—inclosed in a stone building surmounted by a very ancient crucifix—is in the center of the courtyard, and it also is the center of a little domestic world. To its curb come the farm animals three times daily; while as frequently, though less regularly, most of the members of the two households come there too; and there do the humans—notably, I have observed, if they be of different sexes—find it convenient to rest for a while together and take a dish of friendly talk. From the low-toned chattering and the soft laughter that I have heard now and then of an evening I have inferred that these nominally chance encounters are not confined wholly to the day.

The château stands, as I have said, well up on the mountain-side; and on the very spot (I must observe that I am here quoting its owner) where was the camp in which Marius lay with his legions until the time was ripe for him to strike the blow that secured southern Gaul to Rome.

II.

IN the dominion of Vièlmur there is an inner empire. Nominally, the Vidame is the reigning sovereign; but the power behind his throne is Misè Fougueiroun. The term «Misè» is an old-fashioned Provençal title of respect for women of the little bourgeoisie—tradesmen's and shopkeepers' wives and the like—that has become obsolescent since the Revolution and very generally has given place to the fine-ladyish «Madamo.» With a little stretching, it may be rendered by our English old-fashioned title of «Mistress»; and Misè Fougueiroun, who is the Vidame's housekeeper, is mistress over his household in a truly masterful way.

This personage is a little round woman, still plumply pleasing, although she is rising sixty, who is arrayed always with an exquisite neatness in the dress—the sober black and white of the elder women, not the gay colors worn by the young girls—of the Pays d'Arles; and although shortness and plumpness are at odds with majesty of deportment she has, at least, the peremptory manner of one long accustomed to command.

By my obviously sincere admiration of the château and its surroundings, and by a discreet word or two implying a more personal admiration,—a tribute which no woman of the Pays d'Arles ever is too old to accept graciously as her due,—I was so fortunate as to win Misè Fougueiroun's favor at the outset; a fact of which I was apprised on the evening of my arrival—it was at dinner, and the housekeeper herself had brought in a bottle of precious Château-neuf-du-Pape—by the cordiality with which she joined forces with the Vidame in reprobating my belated coming to the château. Actually, I was near

DRAWN BY LOUIS LOEB.

AT THE WELL.

a fortnight behind the time named in my invitation, which had stated expressly that Christmas began in Provence on the feast of Saint Barbara, and that I was expected not later than that day—December 4.

«Monsieur should have been here,» said the housekeeper with decision, «when we planted the blessed Saint Barbara's grain. And now it is grown a full span. Monsieur will not see Christmas at all!»

But my apologetic explanation that I never even had heard of Saint Barbara's grain only made my case the more deplorable.

«Mai!» exclaimed Misè Fougueiroun, in the tone of one who faces suddenly a real calamity. «Can it be that there are no

Christians in Monsieur's America? Is it possible that down there they do not keep the Christmas feast at all?»

To cover my confusion, the Vidame intervened with an explanation which made America appear in a less heathenish light. «The planting of Saint Barbara's grain,» he said, «is a custom that I think is peculiar to the south of France. In almost every household in Provence, and over in Languedoc too, on Saint Barbara's day the women fill two, sometimes three, plates with wheat or lentils, which they set afloat in water and then stand in the warm ashes of the fireplace or on a sunny window-ledge to germinate. This is done in order to foretell the harvest of the coming year, for as Saint Barbara's grain grows well or ill so will the harvest of the coming year be good or bad; and also that there may be on the table when the Great Supper is served on Christmas eve—that is to say, on the feast of the winter solstice—green growing grain in symbol or in earnest of the harvest of the new year that then begins.

«The association of the Trinitarian Saint Barbara with this custom,» the Vidame continued, «I fear is a bit of makeshift. Were three plates of grain the rule, something of a case would be made out in her favor. But the rule, so far as one can be found, is for only two. The custom must be of pagan origin, and therefore dates from far back of the time when Saint Barbara lived in her three-windowed tower at Heliopolis. Probably her name was tagged to it because of old these votive and prophetic grain-fields were sown on what in Christian times became her dedicated day. But whatever light-mannered goddess may have been their patroness then, she is their patroness now; and from their sowing we date the beginning of our Christmas feast.»

It was obvious that this explanation of the custom went much too far for Misè Fougueiroun. At the mention of its foundation in paganism she sniffed audibly, and upon the Vidame's reference to the light-mannered goddess she drew her ample skirts primly about her and left the room.

The Vidame smiled. «I have scandalized Misè, and to-morrow I shall have to listen to a lecture,» he said; and in a moment continued: «It is not easy to make our Provençaux realize how closely we are linked to older peoples and to older times. The very name for Christmas in Provençal, Calèndo, tells how this Christian festival lives on from the Roman festival of the winter solstice, the January Kalends; and the beliefs and customs which go with its celebration still more plainly mark its origin.»

III.

IN the early morning a lively clatter rising from the farm-yard came through my open window, along with the sunshine and the crisp freshness of the morning air.

In the courtyard there was more than the ordinary morning commotion of farm life, and the buzz of talk going on at the well and the racing and shouting of a parcel of children all had in it a touch of eagerness and expectancy. While I still was drinking my coffee—in the excellence and delicate service of which I recognized the friendly hand of Misè Fougueiroun—there came a knock at my door, and, upon my answer, the Vidame entered, looking so elate and wearing so blithe an air that he easily might have been mistaken for a frolicsome middle-aged sunbeam.

«Hurry! Hurry!» he cried, while still shaking both my hands. «This is a day of days—we are going now to bring home the *cacho-fiò*, the Yule log! Put on a pair of heavy shoes—the walking is rough on the mountain-side. But be quick, and come down the moment that you are ready. Now I must be off. There is a world for me to do.»

When I went down-stairs, five minutes later, I found him standing in the hall by the open doorway. «Come along!» he cried. «They all are waiting for us at the Mazet,» and he hurried me down the steps to the terrace and so around to the rear of the château, talking away eagerly as we walked.

«It is a most important matter,» he said, «this bringing home of the *cacho-fiò*. The whole family must take part in it. The head of the family—the grandfather, the father, or the eldest son—must cut the tree; all the others must share in carrying home the log that is to make the Christmas fire. And the tree must be a fruit-bearing tree. With us it usually is an almond or an olive. The olive especially is sacred. Our people, getting their faith from their Greek ancestors, believe that lightning never strikes it. But an apple-tree or a pear-tree will serve the purpose, and up in the Alp region they burn the acorn-bearing oak. What we shall do to-day is an echo of Druidical ceremonial—of the time when the Druid priests cut the Yule oak and with their golden sickles reaped the sacred mistletoe; but old Jan here, who is so stiff for preserving ancient customs, does not know that this custom, like many others that he stands for, is the survival of a rite.»

While the Vidame was speaking we had

turned from the terrace and were nearing the Mazet—which diminutive of the Provençal word *mas*, meaning farm-house, is applied to the farm establishment at Vièlmur partly in friendliness and partly in indication of its dependence upon the great house, the château. At the arched entrance we found the farm family awaiting us: Old Jan, the steward of the estate, and his wife Elizo; Marius, their elder son, a man over forty, who is the active manager of affairs; their younger son Esperit, and their daughter Nanoun; and the wife of Marius, Janetoun, to whose skirts a small child was clinging while three or four larger children scampered about her in a whir of excitement over the imminent event by which Christmas really would be ushered in.

When my presentation had been accomplished we set off across the home vineyard, and thence upward through the olive-orchards, to the high region on the mountain-side where grew the almond-tree which the Vidame and his steward in counsel together had selected for the Christmas sacrifice.

Nanoun, a strapping red-cheeked, black-haired bounce of twenty, ran back into the Mazet as we started, and joined us again, while we were crossing the vineyard, bringing with her a gentle-faced fair girl of her own age, who came shyly. The Vidame, calling her Magali, had a cordial word for this newcomer, and nudged me to bid me mark how promptly Esperit was by her side. «It is as good as settled,» he whispered. «They have been lovers since they were children. Magali is the daughter of Elizo's foster-sister, who died when the child was born. Then Elizo brought her home to the Mazet, and there she has lived her whole life long. Esperit is waiting only until he shall be established in the world to speak the word. And the scamp is in a hurry. Actually, he is pestering me to put him at the head of the Lower Farm!»

The Vidame gave this last piece of information in a tone of severity; but there was a twinkle in his kind old eyes as he spoke which led me to infer that Master Esperit's chances for the stewardship of the Lower Farm were anything but desperate, and I noticed that from time to time he cast very friendly glances toward these young lovers, as our little procession, mounting the successive terraces, went through the olive-orchards along the hillside upward.

Presently we were grouped around the devoted almond-tree, a gnarled old personage, of a great age and girth, having that pathetic look of sorrowful dignity which I find always in superannuated trees, and now and then in people of gentle natures who are conscious that their days of usefulness are gone.

Even the children were quiet as old Jan took his place beside the tree, and there was a touch of solemnity in his manner as he swung his heavy ax and gave the first strong blow, that sent a shiver through all the branches, as though the tree realized that death had overtaken it at last. When he had slashed a dozen times into the trunk, making a deep gash in the pale red wood beneath the brown bark, he handed the ax to Marius, and stood watching silently with the rest of us while his son finished the work that he had begun. In a few minutes the tree tottered, and then fell with a growling death-cry, as its brittle old branches crashed upon the ground.

Whatever there had been of unconscious reverence in the silence that attended the felling was at an end. As the tree came down everybody shouted. Instantly the children were swarming all over it. In a moment our little company burst into the flood of loud and lively talk that is inseparable in Provence from gay occasions, and that is ill held in check even at funerals and in church. They are the merriest people in the world, the Provençaux.

IV.

MARIUS completed his work by cutting through the trunk again, making a noble cacho-fiò near five feet long—big enough to burn, according to the Provençal rule, from Christmas eve until the evening of New Year's day.

We returned homeward, moving in a mildly triumphal procession that I felt to be a little tinctured with ceremonial practices come down from forgotten times. Old Jan and Marius marching in front, Esperit and the sturdy Nanoun marching behind, carried between them the Yule log slung to shoulder-poles.

Our procession took on grand proportions, I should explain, because our Yule log was of extraordinary size. But always the Yule log is brought home in triumph. If it is small, it is carried on the shoulder of the father or the eldest son; if of a goodly size, these two carry it together; or a young husband and wife may bear it between them—as we actually saw a thick branch of our almond borne away that afternoon—while their children caracole around them or lend little helping hands.

Being come to the Mazet, the log was stood

on end in the courtyard in readiness to be taken thence to the fireplace on Christmas eve. I fancied that the men handled it with a certain reverence; and the Vidame assured me that such actually was the case. Already, being fully destined for the Christmas rite, it had become in a way sacred; and along with its sanctity, according to the popular belief, it had acquired a power which enabled it sharply to resent anything that smacked of sacrilegious affront.

On the other hand, when treated reverently and burned with fitting rites, the Yule log brings upon all the household a blessing; and when it has been consumed even its ashes are potent for good.

The home-bringing ceremony being thus ended, we walked back to the château together—startling Esperit and Magali standing hand in hand, lover-like, in the archway; and when we were come to the terrace, and were seated snugly in a sunny corner, the Vidame told me of a very stately Yule log gift that was made anciently in Aix—and very likely elsewhere also—in feudal times.

In Aix it was the custom, when the counts of Provence still lived and ruled there, for the magistrates of the city each year at Christmas-tide to carry in solemn procession a huge cacho-fiò to the palace of their sovereign; and there formally to present to him—or, in his absence, to the grand seneschal on his behalf—this their free-will and good-will offering. And when the ceremony of presentation was ended the city fathers were served with a collation at the count's charges, and were given the opportunity to pledge him loyally in his own good wine.

Knowing Aix well, I was able to fill in the outlines of the Vidame's bare statement of fact, and also to give it a background. What a joy the procession must have been to see! The gray-bearded magistrates, in their velvet caps and robes, wearing their golden chains of office; the great log, swung to shoulder-poles and borne by leathern-jerkined henchmen; surely drummers and fifers, for such a ceremonial would have been impossibly incomplete in Provence without a *tambourin* and *galoubet;* doubtless a brace of ceremonial trumpeters; and a seemly guard in front and rear of steel-capped and steel-jacketed halberdiers. All these marching gallantly through the narrow, yet stately, Aix streets; with comfortable burghers and well-rounded matrons in the doorways looking on, and pretty faces peeping from upper windows and going all a-blushing because of the overbold glances of the men-at-arms! And then fancy the presentation in the great hall of the castle; and the gay feasting; and the merry wagging of gray-bearded chins as the magistrates cried all together, «To the health of the count!» and tossed their wine!

DRAWN BY LOUIS LOEB.
BRINGING HOME THE «CACHO-FIÒ» (YULE LOG).

V.

As Christmas day drew near I observed that Misè Fougueiroun walked thoughtfully and seemed to be oppressed by heavy cares. It was the same just then with all the housewives of the region; for the chief ceremonial event of Christmas in Provence is the *Gros Soupa* that is eaten upon Christmas eve, and of even greater culinary importance is the dinner that is eaten upon Christmas day—wherefore does every woman brood and labor that her achievement of these meals may realize her high ideal. Especially does the preparation of the Great Supper compel exhaustive thought. Being of a vigil, the supper necessarily is «lean,» and custom has fixed unalterably the principal dishes of which it must be composed. Thus limited straitly, the making of it becomes a struggle of genius against material conditions.

Because of the Vidame's desolate bachelorhood, the kindly custom long ago was established that he and all his household every year should eat their Great Supper with the farm family at the Mazet—an arrangement that did not work well until Misè Fougueiroun and Elizo (after some years of spirited squabbling) came to the agreement that the former should be permitted to prepare the delicate sweets served for dessert at that repast. Of these the most important is *nougat*, without which Christmas would be as barren in Provence as Christmas would be in England without plum-pudding or in America without mince-pies.

But it was the making of the Christmas dinner that mainly occupied Misè Fougueiroun's mind—a feast pure and simple, governed by the one jolly law that it shall be the very best dinner of the whole year. What may be termed its by-laws are that the principal dish shall be a roast turkey, and that nougat and *poumpo* shall figure at the dessert. Why poumpo is held in high esteem by the Provençaux I am not prepared to say. It seemed to me a cake of only a humdrum quality; but even Misè Fougueiroun spoke of it in a sincerely admiring and chop-smacking way.

Ordinarily the Provençal Christmas turkey is roasted with a stuffing of chestnuts, or of sausage-meat and black olives; but the high cooks of Provence also roast him stuffed with truffles, making so superb a dish that Brillat-Savarin has singled it out for praise.

Of the minor dishes served at the Christmas dinner it is needless to speak. There was nothing ceremonial about them; nothing remarkable except their excellence and their profusion. Indeed, the distinctiveness of a Provençal Christmas—unless the New-Year ceremonial be considered as a part of it—ends on Christmas eve with the midnight mass.

VI.

But in spite of their eager natural love for all good things eatable, the Provençaux also are poets, and along with the cooking, another matter was in train that was wholly of a poetic cast. This was the making of the *crèche*, a representation with odd little figures and accessories of the personages and scene of the Nativity, the whole at once so naïve and so tender as to be possible only among a people blessed with rare sweetness and rare simplicity of soul.

In a way, the crèche takes in Provence the place of the Christmas tree, of which Northern institution nothing is known here; but it is closer to the heart of Christmas than the tree, being touched with a little of the tender beauty of the event which it represents in so quaint a guise. Its invention is ascribed to Saint Francis of Assisi. The chronicle of his order tells that this seraphic man, having first obtained the permission of the holy see, represented the principal scenes of the Nativity in a stable, and that in the stable so transformed he celebrated mass and preached to the people. All this is wholly in keeping with the character of Saint Francis; and certainly the crèche had its origin in Italy in his period, and in the same conditions which formed his graciously fanciful soul. Its introduction into Provence is said to have been in the time of John XXII, the second of the Avignon popes, who came to the pontificate in the year 1316, and by the fathers of the Oratory of Marseille: from which center it rapidly spread abroad through the land until it became a necessary feature of the Christmas festival both in churches and in homes.

Obviously, the crèche is an offshoot from the miracle-plays and mysteries which had their beginning a full two centuries earlier. These also survive vigorously in Provence in the «Pastouralo,» an acted representation of the Nativity that is given each year during the Christmas season by amateurs or professionals in every city and town and in almost every village.

In the farm-houses, and in the dwellings of the middle class, the crèche is placed always in the living-room, and so becomes an intimate part of the family life. On a table set in a corner is represented a rocky hillside rising in terraces tufted with moss and grass and little trees, and broken by foot-paths and a winding road. This structure is very like a Provençal hillside, but it is supposed to represent the rocky region around Bethlehem, and it is dusted with flour to represent snow. At its base, on the left, embowered in laurel or in holly, is a wooden or pasteboard representation of the inn; and beside the inn is the stable: an open shed in which are grouped little figures representing the several personages of the Nativity. In the center is the Christ-child, either in a cradle or lying on a truss of straw; seated beside him is the Virgin; Saint Joseph stands near, holding in his hand the mystic lily; with their heads bent down over the Child are the ox and the ass—for those good animals helped with their breath through that cold night to keep him warm. In the foreground are the two *ravi*—a man and a woman in awed ecstasy, with upraised arms—and the adoring shepherds. To these are added on Epiphany the figures of the Magi—the kings, as they are called always in French and in Provençal—with their train of attendants, and the camels on which they have brought their gifts. Angels (pendent from the farm-house ceiling) float in the air above the stable. Higher is the star, from which a ray (a golden thread) descends to the Christ-child's hand. Over all, in a glory of clouds, is the figure of Jehovah attended by a white dove.

These are the essentials of the crèche, and in the beginning, no doubt, these made the whole of it. But for nearly six centuries the delicate imagination of the Provençal poets and the cruder, but still poetic, fancy of the Provençal people have been enlarging upon the simple original—with the result that twoscore or more figures often are found in the crèche of to-day.

Either drawing from the quaintly beautiful medieval legends of the birth and childhood of Jesus, or directly from their own quaintly simple souls, the poets from early times have been making Christmas songs—noëls, or *nouvè* as they are called in Provençal—in which new subordinate characters have been created in a spirit of frank realism, and these have materialized in new figures surrounding the crèche. At the same time the fancy of the people, working with a still more naïve directness along the lines of associated ideas, has been making the most curiously incongruous and anachronistic additions to the group.

To the first order belong such creations as the blind man, led by a child, coming to be healed of his blindness by the Infant's touch; or that of the young mother hurrying to offer her breast to the New-born (in accordance with the beautiful custom still in force in Provence), that its own mother may rest a little before she begins to suckle it; or that of the other mother bringing the cradle of which her own baby has been dispossessed, because of her compassion for the poor woman at the inn whose Child is lying on a truss of straw.

But the popular additions, begotten of association of ideas, are far more numerous and also are far more curious. The hilltop, close under the floating figure of Jehovah, has been crowned with a windmill, because windmills abounded anciently on the hilltops of Provence; and to the mill, naturally, has been added a miller who is riding down the road on an ass with a sack of flour across his saddle-bow that he is carrying as a gift to the Holy Family. The adoring shepherds have been given flocks of sheep, and on the hillside more shepherds and more sheep have been put for company. The sheep, in association with the ox and the ass, have brought in their train a whole troop of domestic animals—including geese and turkeys and chickens and a cock on the roof of the stable; and in the train of the camels has come the extraordinary addition of lions, bears, leopards, elephants, ostriches, and even crocodiles! The Provençaux being from of old mighty hunters (the tradition has found its classic embodiment in Tartarin), and hillsides being appropriate to hunting, the figure of a fowler with a gun at his shoulder has been introduced; and as it is well, even in the case of a Provençal sportsman, to point a gun at a definite object, the fowler usually is so placed as to aim at the cock on the stable roof. He is a modern, yet not very recent, addition, the fowler, as is shown by the fact that he carries a flint-lock fowling-piece. Drumming and fifing being absolute essentials to every sort of Provençal festivity, a conspicuous figure always is found playing on a tambourin and galoubet. Itinerant knife-grinders are an old institution here, and in some obscure way—possibly because of their thievish propensities—are associated intimately with the devil; and so there is either a knife-grinder simple, or a devil with a knife-grinder's wheel. Of old it was the custom for the women to carry distaffs and to spin out thread as they went to and from the fields or along the roads (just as the women nowadays knit as they walk), and therefore a spinning-woman always is of the company. Because child-stealing was not uncommon here formerly, and because Gipsies still are plentiful, there are three Gipsies lurking about the inn all ready to steal the Christ-child away. As the innkeeper naturally would come out to investigate the cause of the commotion in his stable-yard, he is found with the others, lantern in hand. And, finally, there is a group of women bearing as gifts to the Christ-child the essentials of the Christmas feast: codfish, chickens, *carde*, ropes of garlic, eggs, and the great Christmas cakes, poumpo and *fougasso*.

Many other figures may be, and often are, added to the group, of which one of the most delightful is the Turk who makes a solacing present of his pipe to Saint Joseph. But all of these which I have named have come to be now quite as necessary to a properly made crèche as are the few which are taken direct from the Bible narrative; and the congregation surely is one of the quaintest that ever poetry and simplicity together devised.

VII.

ON the morning of the day preceding Christmas a lurking, yet ill-repressed, excitement pervaded the château and all its dependencies. In the case of the Vidame and Misè Fougueiroun the excitement did not even lurk: it blazed forth so openly that they were as a brace of comets—bustling violently through our universe and dragging into their erratic wakes, away from normal orbits, the whole planetary system of the household and all haply intrusive stars.

Although the morning still was young, work on the estate had ended for the day, and about the door of the kitchen more than a score of laborers were gathered.

Misè Fougueiroun—a plump embodiment of Benevolence—stood beside a table on which was a great heap of her own fougasso, and big baskets filled with dried figs and almonds and celery, and a genial battalion of bottles standing guard over all. One by one the vassals were called up—there was a strong flavor of feudalism in it all—and to each, while the Vidame wished him a « Bòni fèsto! » the housekeeper gave his Christmas portion: a fougasso, a double handful each of figs and almonds, a stalk of celery, and a bottle of *vin cue*, the cordial that is used for the libation of the Yule log and for the solemn Yule cup; and each, as he received his portion, made his little speech of friendly thanks—in several cases most gracefully turned—and then was off in a hurry for his home.

VIII.

As we passed the Mazet in our afternoon walk we stopped to greet the new arrivals there, come to make the family gathering complete: two more married children, with a flock of their own little ones, and Elizo's father and mother—a bowed little rosy-cheeked old woman and a bowed lean old man, both well above eighty years. There was a lively passage of friendly greetings between them all and the Vidame; and it was quite delightful to see how the bowed little old woman kindled and bridled when the Vidame gallantly protested that she grew younger and handsomer every year.

A tall ladder stood against the Mazet, and the children were engaged in hanging tiny wheat-sheaves along the eaves—the Christmas portion of the birds.

IX.

OUR march, out through the rear door of the château and across the courtyard to the Mazet, was processional. All the household went with us. The Vidame gallantly gave his arm to Misè Fougueiroun; I followed with her first officer, a saucebox named Mouneto, so plumply provoking and charming in her Arlesian dress that I will not say what did or did not happen in the darkness as we passed the well! A little in our rear followed the house servants, even to the least; and in the Mazet already were gathered, with the family, the few work-people of the estate who had not gone to their own homes. For the Great Supper is a patriarchal feast, to which in Christian fellowship come the master and the master's family and all of their servitors and dependents on equal terms.

A broad stream of light came out through the open doorway of the farm-house, and with it a great clatter and buzz of talk, that increased tenfold as we entered, and a cry of « Bòni fèsto! » came from the whole company at once. As for the Vidame, he so radiated cordiality that he seemed to be the veritable spirit of Christmas (incarnate at the age of sixty, and at that period of the present century when stocks and frilled shirts were worn), and his joyful old legs were near to dancing as he went among the company with warm-hearted greetings and outstretched hands.

X.

THE crèche, around which the children were gathered in a swarm, was built up in one corner, and our coming was the signal for the first of the ceremonies, the lighting of the crèche candles, to begin. In this all the children had a part, making rather a scramble of it: for there was rivalry as to which of them should light the most, and in a moment a constellation of little flames covered the Bethlehem hillside and brought into bright prominence the Holy Family and its strange attendant host of quite impossible people and beasts and birds.

The laying of the Yule log followed—a ceremony so grave that it has all the dignity of, and really is, a religious rite. The buzz of talk died away into silence as Elizo's father, the oldest man, took by the hand and led out into the courtyard where the log was lying his great-grandson, the little Tounin, the youngest child: it being the rule that the nominal bearers of the cacho-fiò to the hearth shall be the oldest and the youngest of the family—the one personifying the year that is dying, the other the year new-born. Sometimes, and this is the prettiest rendering of the custom, the two are an old, old man and a baby carried in its mother's arms, while between them the real bearers of the burden walk.

In our case the log actually was carried by Marius and Esperit; but the tottering old man clasped its forward end with his thin, feeble hands, and its hinder end was clasped by the plump, feeble hands of the tottering child. Thus, the four together, they brought it in through the doorway and carried it thrice around the room, circling the supper-table and the lighted candles; and then, reverently, it was laid before the fireplace, that still sometimes is called in Provençal the *lar*.

There was a pause, while the old man filled out a cup of vin cue, and a solemn hush fell upon the company, and all heads were bowed, as he poured three libations upon the log, saying with the last: « In the name of the Father, and of the Son, and of the Holy Ghost! » and then cried with all the vigor that he could infuse into his thin and quavering old voice:

Cacho-fiò,
Bouto-fiò!
Alègre! Alègre!
Dièu nous alègre!
Calèndo vèn! Tout bèn vèn!
Dièu nous fague la gràci de vèire l'an que vèn,
E se noun sian pas mai, que noun fuguen pas mens!

Yule log,
Catch fire!
Joy! Joy!
God gives joy!

Christmas comes! All good comes!
May God give us grace to see the coming year,
And if we are not more, may we not be less!

As he ended his invocation he crossed himself, as did all the rest; and a great glad shout was raised of « Alègre! Alègre! » as Marius and Esperit, first casting some fagots of vine-branches on the bed of glowing coals, placed the Yule log upon the fire. Instantly the vines blazed up, flooding the room with brightness; and as the Yule log glowed and reddened everybody cried:

Cacho-fiò,
Bouto-fiò!
Alègre! Alègre!

again and again—as though the whole of them together of a sudden had gone merry-mad!

In the midst of this triumphant rejoicing the bowl from which the libation had been poured was filled afresh with vin cue, and was passed from hand to hand and lip to lip,—beginning with the little Tounin, and so upward in order of seniority until it came last of all to the old man,—and from it each drank to the new fire of the new year.

One of my Aix friends, the poet Joachim Gasquet, has described to me the Christmas-eve customs which were observed in his own home: the Gasquet bakery, in the Rue de la Cépède, that has been handed down from father to son through so many hundreds of years that even its owners cannot tell certainly whether it was in the fourteenth or the fifteenth century that their family legend of good baking had its rise.

In the Gasquet family it was the custom to eat the Great Supper in the oven-room: because that was the heart, the sanctuary, of the house; the place consecrated by the toil which gave the family its livelihood. On the supper-table there was always a wax figure of the infant Christ, and this was carried just before midnight to the living-room, off from the shop, in one corner of which the crèche was set up. It was the little Joachim whose right it was, because he was the youngest, the purest, to carry the figure. A formal procession was made. He walked at its head, a little chap with long curling golden hair, between his two grandfathers; the rest followed in the order of their age and rank: his two grandmothers, his father and mother, Monsieur Auguste (a dashing blade of a young baker then) with the maid-servant, and the apprentices last of all. A single candle was carried by one of his grandfathers into the dark room—the illumination of which, that

AT THE STROKE OF MIDNIGHT.
Drawn by Louis Loeb.

night, could come only from the new fire kindled before the crèche. Precisely at midnight—at the moment when all the clocks of Aix striking together let loose the Christmas chimes—the child laid the holy figure in the manger, and then the candles instantly were set ablaze.

Sometimes there would be a thrilling pause of half a minute or more while they waited for the bells: the child, with the image in his hands, standing before the crèche in the little circle of light; the others grouped behind him, and for the most part lost in dark shadow cast by the single candle held low down; those nearest to the crèche holding matches ready to strike so that all the candles might be lighted at once when the moment came. And then all the bells together would send their voices out over the city heavenward; and his mother would say softly, «Now, my little son!» and the room would flash into brightness suddenly—as though a glory radiated from the Christ-child lying there in the manger between the ox and the ass.

upon the fireplace, and replaced the pots and pans for a final heating upon the coals.

The long table had been set before our arrival and was in perfect readiness, covered with a fine white linen cloth, sacredly reserved for use at high festivals, that fairly sparkled in the blaze of light cast by the overhanging petroleum lamp. Yet the two ceremonial

«ELIZO'S OLD FATHER.»

DRAWN BY LOUIS LOEB.

XI.

WHILE our Yule-log ceremonial was in progress, the good Elizo and Janetoun, upon whom the responsibility of the supper rested, evidently were a prey to anxious thoughts. They whispered together, and cast uneasy glances toward the chimney, into the broad corners of which the various cooking-vessels had been moved to make way for the cacho-fiò; and barely had the cup of benediction passed their lips when they precipitated themselves candles, one at each end of the table, also were lighted.

Beside these candles were the harvest harbingers, the plates on which was growing Saint Barbara's grain, so vigorous and so freshly green that old Jan rubbed his hands together comfortably as he said to the Vidame, «Ah, we need have no fears for the harvest that is coming in this blessed year!» In the center of the table, its browned crust slashed with a cross, was the great loaf of Christmas bread, *pan Calendau;* on which was a bunch of holly tied with the white pith of rushes—the «marrow» of the rush, that is held to be an emblem of strength. Old Jan, the master of the house, cut the loaf into as many portions as there were persons present, with one double portion over to be given to some poor one in charity—« the portion of the good God.» It is of a miraculous nature, this blessed bread: the sailors of Provence carry morsels of it with them on their voyages, and by strewing its crumbs upon the troubled waters stay the tempests of the sea.

For the rest, the table had down its middle a line of dishes—many of them old faïence of Moustiers, the mere sight of which would have thrilled a collector's heart—heaped with the nougat and the other sweets over the making of which our housekeeper and her lieutenants so soulfully had toiled. And on the table in the corner were fruits and nuts and wines.

Grace always is said before the Great Supper—a simple formula ending with the prayer of the Yule log that if another year there are no more, there may be no less. It is the custom that this blessing shall be asked by the youngest child of the family who can speak the words—a pretty usage which sometimes makes the blessing go very queerly indeed. Our little Tounin came to the front again in this matter, exhibiting an air of grave responsibility which showed that he had been well drilled; and it was with quite a saintly look on his little face that he folded his hands together and said very earnestly: « God bless all that we are going to eat, and if we are no less next year, may we be no more!» at which everybody looked at Janetoun and laughed.

In our seating a due order of precedence was observed. Old Jan, the head of the family, presided, with the Vidame and myself on his right and with Elizo's father and mother on his left; and thence the company went downward by age and station to the foot of the table, where were grouped the servants from the château and the workmen on the farm. But no other distinction was made. All were served alike and all drank together as equals when the toasts were called. The servers were Elizo and Janetoun, with Nanoun and Magali for assistants; and these four, although they took their places at the table when each course had been brought on, had rather a Passover time of it: for they ate, as it were, with their loins girded and with full or empty dishes imminent to their hands.

As I have said, the Great Supper must be «lean,» and is restricted to certain dishes which in no circumstances can be changed; but rich leanness is possible in a country where olive-oil takes the place of animal fat in cooking, and where the accumulated skill of ages presides over the kitchen fire. The principal dish is the *raïto*—a ragout made of delicately fried fish served in a sauce flavored with wine and capers—whereof the tradition goes back around twenty-five hundred years, to the time when the Phocæan housewives brought with them to Massalia (the Marseille of to-day) the happy mystery of its making from their Grecian homes. But this excellent dish was not lost to Greece because it was gained by Gaul: bearing the same name, and made in the same fashion, it is eaten by the Greeks of the present day. It usually is made of dried codfish in Provence, where the cod is held in high esteem; but is most delicately toothsome when made of eels.

The second course of the Great Supper also is fish, which may be of any sort and served in any way—in our case it was a perch-like variety of dainty pan-fish, fresh from the Rhône. A third course of fish sometimes is served, but the third course usually is snails cooked in a rich brown sauce strongly flavored with garlic. The Provençal snails, which feed in a *gourmet* fashion upon vine-leaves, are peculiarly delicious, and there was a murmur of delight from our company as the four women brought to the table four big dishes full of them; and for a while there was only the sound of eager munching, mixed with the clatter on china of the empty shells. To extract them we had the strong thorns, three or four inches long, of the wild acacia; and on these the little brown morsels were carried to the avid mouths and eaten with a bit of bread sopped in the sauce; and then the shell was subjected to a vigorous sucking, that not a drop of the sauce lingering within it should be lost.

To the snails succeeded another dish essentially Provençal, carde. The carde is a giant thistle that grows to a height of five or six feet, and is so luxuriantly magnificent both in leaf and in flower that it deserves a place among ornamental plants. The edible portion is the stem—blanched like celery, which it much resembles, by being earthed up—cooked with a white sauce flavored with garlic. The garlic, however, is a mistake, since it overpowers the delicate taste of the carde; but garlic is the overlord of all things eatable in Provence. I was glad when we passed on to the celery, with which the first section of the supper came to an end.

The second section was such an explosion of sweets as might fly into space should a comet collide with a confectioner's shop—nougat, fougasso, a great poumpo, compotes, candied fruits, and a whole nightmare herd of rich cakes on which persons not blessed with the most powerful organs of digestion surely would go galloping to the country of dreadful dreams. Of the dessert of nuts and fruit the notable features were grapes and winter melons.

With the serious part of the supper we drank the ordinary small wine diluted with water; but with the dessert was paraded a gallant company of dusty bottles containing ancient vintages which through many ripening years had been growing richer by feeding upon their own excellence in the wine-room of the Mazet or the cellar of the château.

XII.

BUT the material element of the Great Supper is its least part. What entitles it to the augmenting adjective is its soul—that subtle essence of peace and amity for which the word Christmas is a synonym in all Christian lands. It is the rule of these family gatherings at Christmas-time in Provence that the heartburnings and rancors which may have sprung up during the year then shall be cut down; and even if sometimes they quickly grow again, as no doubt they do now and then, it makes for happiness that they shall be thus banished from the peace-feast of the year. When the serious part of the supper had been disposed of and the mere palate-tickling period of the dessert had come, I was much interested in observing that the talk, mainly carried on by the elders, was turned with an obviously deliberate purpose upon family history, and especially upon the doings of those who in the past had brought honor upon the family name.

The chief ancestral glory of the family of the Mazet is its close blood-relationship with the gallant André Etienne, that drummer of the fifty-first demi-brigade of the Army of Italy who is commemorated on the frieze of the Panthéon, and who is known and honored as the «Tambour d'Arcole» all over France. It was delightful to listen to old Jan's telling of the brave story: how this André, their own kinsman, swam the stream under the enemy's fire at Arcola with his drum on his back and then drummed his fellow-soldiers on to victory; how Bonaparte awarded him the drumsticks of honor, and later, when the Legion of Honor was founded, gave him the cross; how they carved him in stone, drumming the charge, up there on the front of the Panthéon in Paris itself; how Mistral, the great poet of Provence, had made a poem about him that had been printed in a book; and how, only two years ago, they set up his marble statue in Cadenet, the little town, not far from Avignon, where he was born!

Old Jan was not content with merely telling this story—like a true Provençal he acted it: swinging a supposititious drum upon his back, jumping into an imaginary river and swimming it with his head in the air, swinging his drum back into place again, and then —*zóu!*—starting off at the head of the fifty-first demi-brigade with such a rousing play of drumsticks that I protest we fairly heard the rattle of them, along with the spatter of Austrian musketry in the face of which André Etienne beat that gallant *pas de charge!*

It set me all a-thrilling; and still more did it thrill those other listeners who were of the Arcola hero's very blood and bone. They clapped their hands and they shouted. They laughed with delight. And the fighting spirit of Gaul was so stirred within them that at a word. I verily believe they would have been for marching in a body across the southeastern frontier!

Elizo's old father was rather out of the running in this matter. It was not by any relative of his that the drumsticks of honor had been won; and his thoughts, after wandering a little, evidently settled down upon the strictly personal fact that his thin old legs were cold. Rising slowly from the table, he carried his plate to the fireplace, and when he had arranged some live coals in one of the sconces of the waist-high andirons he rested the plate above them on the iron rim; and so stood there, eating contentedly, while the warmth from the glowing Yule log entered gratefully into his lean old body and stirred to a brisker pulsing the blood in his meager veins. But his interest in what was going forward revived again—his legs being, also, by that time well warmed—when his own praises were sounded by his daughter in the story of how he stopped the runaway horse on the very brink of the precipice at Les Baux; and how his wife all the while sat steady beside him in the cart, cool and silent and showing no sign of fear.

When Elizo had finished this story she whispered a word to Magali and Nanoun that sent them laughing out of the room; and presently Magali came back again arrayed in the identical dress which had been worn by the heroine of the adventure—who had perked and plumed herself not a little while her daughter told about it—when the runaway horse so nearly had galloped her off the Baux rock into eternity. It was the Provençal costume, with full sleeves and flaring cap, of sixty years back; but a little gayer than the strict Arles dress of that period, because her mother was not of Arles, but of Beaucaire. It was not so graceful, especially in the head-dress, as the costume of the present day; nor nearly so becoming—as Magali showed by looking a dozen years older after putting it on. But Magali, even with a dozen years added, could not but be charming.

By long experience, gained on many such occasions, the Vidame knew that the culminating point of the supper would be reached when the family drummer swam the river and headed the French charge at Arcola. Therefore had he reserved until a later period, when the excitement incident to the revival of that honorable bit of family history should have subsided, a joy-giving bombshell of his own that he had all ready to explode. An American or an Englishman never could have fired it without something in the way of speech-making; but the Vidame was of a shy temper, and speechmaking was not in his line. When the chatter caused by Magali's costuming had lulled a little, and there came a momentary pause in the talk, he merely reached diagonally across the table and touched glasses with Esperit and said simply: «To your good health, Monsieur the Superintendent of the Lower Farm!»

It was done so quietly that for some seconds no one realized that the Vidame's toast brought happiness to all the household, and to two of its members a lifelong joy. Esperit, even, had his glass almost to his lips before he understood to what he was drinking; and then his understanding came through the finer nature of Magali, who gave a quick, deep sob as she buried her face in the buxom Nanoun's bosom and encircled that astonished young person's neck with her arms. Esperit went pale at that; but the hand did not tremble in which he held his still raised glass, nor did his voice quaver as he said with a deep earnestness: «To the good health of Monsieur le Vidame, with the thanks of two very happy hearts!»—and so drained his wine.

A great danger puts no more strain upon the nerves of a man of good fiber than does a great joy; and it seemed to me that Esperit's absolute steadiness, under this sudden fire of happiness, showed him to be made of as fine and as manly stuff as went to the making of his kinsman who beat the pas de charge up the slope at Arcola at the head of the fifty-first demi-brigade.

But nothing less than the turbulence of the whole battle of Arcola—not to say of that whole triumphant campaign in Italy—will suffice for a comparison with the tumult that arose about our supper-table when the meaning of the Vidame's toast fairly was grasped by the company at large. I do not think that I could express in words, nor by any less elaborate method of illustration than a kinetoscope, the state of excitement into which a Provençal will fly over a matter of absolutely no importance at all; how he will burst forth into a very whirlwind of words and gestures about some trifle that an ordinary human being would dispose of without the quiver of an eye. And as our matter was one so truly moving that a very Dutchman through all his phlegm would have been stirred by it, such a tornado was set a-going as would have put a mere hurricane of the tropics to open shame.

Naturally, the disturbance was central over Esperit and Magali and the Vidame. The latter—his kind old face shining like the sun of an Easter morning—gave back with a good will on Magali's cheeks her kisses of gratitude, and exchanged embraces and kisses with the elder women, and went through such an ordeal of violent hand-shaking that I trembled for the integrity of his arms. But as for the young people, whom everybody embraced over and over again with a terrible energy—that they came through it all with whole ribs is as near to being a miracle as anything that has happened in modern times!

Gradually the storm subsided, though not without some fierce after-gusts, and at last worked itself off harmlessly in song, as we returned to the ritual of the evening and took to the singing of noëls—the Christmas canticles which are sung between the ending of the Great Supper and the beginning of the midnight mass.

XIII.

THE Provençal noëls—being some real, or some imagined, incident of the Nativity told in verse set to a gay or tender air—are the crèche translated into song. The simplest of them are direct renderings of the Bible narrative. Our own Christmas hymn, «While Shepherds Watched their Flocks by Night,» is precisely of this order; and, indeed, is of the very period when flourished the greatest of the Provençal noël-writers; for the poet laureate Nahum Tate, whose laurel this hymn keeps green, was born in the year 1652 and had begun his mildly poetic career while Saboly still was alive.

But most of the noëls—*nouvè* they are called in Provençal—are purely imaginative:

quaintly innocent stories created by the poets, or taken from those apocryphal scriptures in which the simple-minded faithful of patristic times built up a warmly colored legend of the Virgin's life and of the birth and childhood of her Son. Sometimes, even, the writers stray away entirely from a religious base and produce mere roistering catches or topical songs.

The Provençaux have been writing noëls for more than four hundred years. One of the oldest belongs to the first half of the fifteenth century and is ascribed to Raymond Féraud; the latest are of our own day—by Roumanille, Crousillat, Mistral, Girard, Gras, and a score more. But only a few have been written to live. The memory of many once famous noël-writers is preserved now either mainly or wholly by a single song.

The one assured immortal among these musical mortalities is Nicolas Saboly,[1] who was born in Monteux, close by Avignon, in the year 1614; who for the greater part of his life was chapel-master and organist of the Avignon church of St. Pierre; who died in the year 1675; and who was buried in the choir of the church which for so long he had filled with his own heaven-sweet harmonies.

Saboly's music has a «go» and a melodic quality suggestive of the work of Sir Arthur Sullivan; but it has a more tender, a fresher, a purer note, even more sparkle, than ever Sullivan has achieved. In his gay airs the attack is instant, brilliant, overpowering,—like a glad outburst of sweet bells, like the joyous laughter of a child,—and everything goes with a dash and a swing. But while he thus loved to harmonize a laugh, he also could strike a note of infinite tenderness. In his pathetic noëls he drops into thrillingly plaintive minors which fairly drag one's heart out—echoes or survivals, possibly (for this poignant melody is not uncommon in old Provençal music), of the passionately longing love-songs with which Saracen knights once went a-serenading beneath castle windows here in Provence.

Nor is his verse, of its curious kind, less excellent than his music. By turns, as the humor takes him, his noëls are sermons, or delicate religious fancies, or sharp-pointed satires, or whimsical studies of country-side life. One whole series of seven is a history of the Nativity (surely the quaintest and the gayest and the tenderest oratorio that ever was written!) in which, in music and in words, he is at his very best. Above all, his noëls are local.

This naïve local twist is not peculiar to Saboly. With very few exceptions all Provençal noëls are packed full of the same delightful anachronisms. It is to Provençal shepherds that the herald angel appears; it is Provençaux who compose the *bregado*, the pilgrim company, that starts for Bethlehem; and Bethlehem is a village always within easy walking-distance here in Provence. Yet is it not wholly simplicity that has brought about this shifting of the scene of the Nativity from the hill-country of Judea to the hill-country of southeastern France. The life and the look of the two lands have much in common; and most impressively will their common character be felt by one who walks here by night beneath the stars.

XIV.

It was with Saboly's «Hòu, de l'houstau!» that our singing began. It is one of the series in his history of the Nativity and is the most popular of all his noëls: a dialogue between Saint Joseph and the Bethlehem innkeeper, that opens with a sweet and plaintive long-drawn note of supplication as Saint Joseph timorously calls:

O-o-oh, there, the house! Master! Mistress! Varlet! Maid! Is *no* one there?

And then it continues with humble entreaties for shelter for himself and his wife, who is very near her time; to which the host replies with rough refusals for a while, but in the end grants grudgingly a corner of his stable in which the wayfarers may lie for the night.

Esperit and Magali sang this responsively; Magali taking Saint Joseph's part—in which, in all the noëls, is a strain of feminine sweetness and gentleness. Then Marius and Esperit, in the same fashion, sang the famous «C'est le bon lever,» a dialogue between an angel and a shepherd, in which the angel, as becomes so exalted a personage, speaks French, while the shepherd speaks Provençal.

«It's high time to get up, sweet shepherd,» the angel begins; and goes on to tell that «in Bethlehem, quite near this place,» the Saviour of the world has been born of a virgin.

«Perhaps you take me for a common peasant,» the shepherd answers, «talking to me like that! I am poor, but I'd have you to know that I come of good stock. In old times my great-great-grandfather was mayor

---

[1] The admirable edition of Saboly's noëls, text and music, published at Avignon in the year 1856 by François Seguin, is to be reissued for this present Christmas by the same publisher in definitive form. It can be obtained through the Librairie Roumanille, Avignon.

of our village! And who are you, anyway, fine sir! Are you a Jew or a Dutchman? Your jargon makes me laugh. A virgin mother! A child god! No, never were such things heard!»

But when the angel reiterates his strange statement the shepherd's interest is aroused. He declares that he will go at once and steal this miraculous child; and he quite takes the angel into his confidence—as though standing close to his elbow and speaking as friend to friend. In the end, of course, he is convinced of the miracle, and says that he «will get the ass and set forth» to join the worshipers about the manger at Bethlehem.

There are many of these noëls in dialogue; and most of them are touched with this same quality of easy familiarity with sacred subjects, and abound in turns of broad humor, which render them not a little startling from our nicer point of view. But they never are coarse, and their simplicity saves them from being irreverent; nor is there, I am sure, the least thought of irreverence on the part of those by whom they are sung. I noticed, though, that these lively numbers were the ones which most hit the fancy of the men; while the women as plainly showed their liking for those of a finer spirit in which the dominant qualities were pathos and grace.

Of this latter class is Roumanille's rarely beautiful noël, «The Blind Girl» («La Chato Avuglo»), that Magali sang with a tenderness which set the women to crying openly, and which made the older men cough a little and look suspiciously red about the eyes. Of all the modern noëls it has come closest to and has taken the strongest hold upon the popular heart—this pathetic story of the child «blind from her birth,» who pleads with her mother that she also may go with the rest to Bethlehem, urging that though she cannot see the «lovely golden face» she still may touch the Christ-child's hand.

And when, all thrilling, to the stable she was come
She placed the little hand of Jesus on her heart—
And saw him whom she touched!

I am persuaded, so thoroughly did they all enjoy their own caroling, that the singing of noëls would have gone on until broad daylight had it not been for the intervention of the midnight mass. But the mass of Christmas eve—or, rather, of Christmas morning —is a matter not only of pleasure, but of obligation. Even those upon whom churchly requirements at other times rest lightly rarely fail to attend it; and to the faithful it is the most touchingly beautiful, as Easter is the most joyous, church festival of the year.

By eleven o'clock, therefore, we were under way for our walk of a mile or so down the long slope of the hillside to the village.

Presently some one started a very sweet and plaintive noël, fairly heart-wringing in its tender beseeching and soft lament, yet with a consoling undertone to which it constantly returned. I think, but I am not sure, that it was Roumanille's noël telling of the widowed mother who carried the cradle of her own baby to the Virgin, that the Christchild might not lie on straw. One by one the other voices took up the strain, until in a full chorus the sorrowingly compassionate melody went thrilling through the moonlit silence of the night.

And so, singing, we walked by the white way onward, hearing as we neared the town the songs of other companies coming up, as ours was, from outlying farms. And when they and we had passed in through the gateways—where the townsfolk of old lashed out against their robber infidel and robber Christian enemies—all the black, little narrow streets were filled with an undertone of murmuring voices and an overtone of clear, sweet song.

XV.

ON the little Grande Place the crowd was packed densely. There the several streams of humanity pouring into the town met and mingled, and thence in a strong current flowed onward into the church. Coming from the blackness without,—for the tall houses surrounding the Grande Place cut off the moonlight and made it a little pocket of darkness, —it was with a shock of splendor that we encountered the brightness within. All the side-altars were blazing with candles, and as the service went on, and the high altar also flamed up, the whole building was filled with a soft radiance—save that strange luminous shadows lingered in the lofty vaulting of the nave.

After the high altar, the most brilliant spot was the altar of Saint Joseph, in the west transept; beside which was a magnificent crèche, the figures half life-size, beautifully modeled and richly clothed. But there was nothing whimsical about this crèche: the group might have been, and very possibly had been, composed after a well-painted «Nativity» by some artist of the late Renaissance.

The mass was the customary office; but at

the offertory it was interrupted by a ceremony that gave it suddenly an entirely medieval cast, of which I felt more fully the beauty, and the strangeness in our time, because the Vidame sedulously had guarded against my having knowledge of it in advance. This was nothing less than a living rendering of the adoration of the shepherds, done with a simplicity to make one fancy the figures in Ghirlandajo's picture were alive again and stirred by the very spirit that animated them when they were set on canvas four hundred years ago.

By some means only a little short of a miracle, a way was opened through the dense crowd along the center of the nave from the door to the altar, and up this way with their offerings real shepherds came—the quaintest procession that anywhere I have ever seen. In the lead were four musicians, playing upon the tambourin, the galoubet, the very small cymbals called *palets*, and the bagpipe-like *carlamuso;* and then, two by two, came ten shepherds wearing the long, brown, full cloaks, weather-stained and patched and mended, which seem always to have come down through many generations and which never by any chance are new; carrying tucked beneath their arms their battered felt hats browned, like their cloaks, by long warfare with sun and rain; holding in one hand a lighted candle and in the other a staff. The two leaders, dispensing with staves and candles, bore garlanded baskets; one filled with fruit—melons, pears, apples, and grapes—and in the other a pair of doves, which with sharp, quick motions turned their heads from side to side as they gazed wonderingly on their strange surroundings with their bright, beautiful eyes.

Following came the main offering—a spotless lamb. Most originally, and in a way poetically, was this offering made. Drawn by a mild-faced ewe, whose fleece had been washed to a wonder of whiteness and who was decked out with bright-colored ribbons in a way to unhinge with vanity her sheepish mind, was a little two-wheeled cart—all garlanded with laurel and holly, and bedizened with knots of ribbon and pink paper roses and glittering little objects such as are hung on Christmas trees in other lands. Lying in the cart placidly, not bound and not in the least frightened, was the dazzlingly white lamb, decked like the ewe with knots of ribbon and wearing about its neck a red collar brilliant to behold. Now and then the ewe would turn to look at it, and in response to one of these wistful maternal glances the little creature stood up shakily on its unduly long legs and gave an anxious baa. But when a shepherd bent over and stroked it gently, it was reassured; lying down contentedly again in its queer little car of triumph, and thereafter through the ceremony remaining still.

Behind the car came ten more shepherds, and in their wake a long double line of country-folk, each with a lighted candle in hand. There is difficulty, indeed, in keeping this part of the demonstration within bounds, because it is esteemed an honor and a privilege to walk in the procession of the offered lamb.

Slowly this strange company moved toward the altar, where the ministering priest awaited its coming; and at the altar steps the bearers of the fruit and the doves separated, so that the little cart might come between them and their offering be made complete, while the other shepherds formed a semicircle in the rear. The music was stilled, and the priest accepted and set upon the altar the baskets; and then extended the paten that the shepherds, kneeling, might kiss it in token of their offering of the lamb. This completed the ceremony. The tambourin and galoubet and palets and carlamuso all together struck up again, and the shepherds and the lamb's car passed down the nave between the files of candle-bearers and so out through the door.

Within the last sixty years or so this naïve ceremony has fallen more and more into disuse. But it still occasionally is revived—as at Barbentane in 1868, and Rognonas in 1894, and repeatedly within the last decade in the sheep-raising parish of Maussane—by a curé who is at one with his flock in a love for the customs of ancient times. Its origin assuredly goes back far into antiquity; so very far, indeed, that the airs played by the musicians in the procession seem by comparison quite of our own time: yet tradition ascribes the composition of these airs to the good King René, whose happy rule over Provence ended more than four centuries ago.

XVI.

WHEN the stir caused by the coming and going of the shepherds had subsided, the mass went on, with no change from the usual observance, until the sacrament was administered, save that there was a vigorous singing of noëls. It was congregational singing of a very enthusiastic sort,—indeed, nothing short of gagging every one of them could have kept those song-loving Provençaux still, —but it was led by the choir, and choristers took the solo parts. The most notable number was the famous noël in which the crowing of a cock alternates with the note of a nightingale; each verse beginning with a prodigious cock-a-doodle-d-o-o! and then rattling along to the gayest of gay airs. The nightingale was not a brilliant success; but the cock-crowing was so realistic that at its first outburst I thought that a genuine barnyard gallant was up in the organ-loft. I learned later that this was a musical *tour de force* for which the organist was famed. A buzz of delight filled the church after each cock-crowing volley; and I fancy that I was alone in finding anything odd in so jaunty a performance within church walls. The viewpoint in regard to such matters is of race and education. The Provençaux, who are born laughing, are not necessarily irreverent because even in sacred places they sometimes are frankly gay.

Assuredly, there was no lack of seemly decorum when the moment came for the administration of the sacrament, which rite on Christmas eve is reserved to the women, the men communing on Christmas day. The women who were to partake—nearly all who were present—wore the Provençal costume, but of dark color. Most of them were in black, save for the white *chapelle*, or kerchief, and the scrap of white which shows above the ribbon confining the knotted hair. But before going up to the altar each placed upon her head a white gauze veil, so long and so ample that her whole person was enveloped in its soft folds; and the women were so many, and their action was with such sudden unanimity, that in a moment a delicate mist seemed to have fallen and spread its silvery whiteness over all the throng.

Singly and by twos and threes these palely gleaming figures moved toward the altar, until more than a hundred of them were crowded together before the sanctuary rail. Nearest to the rail, being privileged to commune before the rest, stood a row of black-robed sisters—teachers in the parish school —whose somber habits made a vigorous line of black against the dazzle of the altar, everywhere aflame with candles, and by contrast gave to all that sweep of lustrous misty whiteness a splendor still softer and more strange. And within the rail the rich vestments of the ministering priests, and the rich cloths of the altar, all in a flood of light, added a warm color-note of gorgeous tones.

Slowly the rite went on. Twenty at a time the women, kneeling, ranged themselves at the rail, rising to give room to others when they had partaken, and so returning to their seats. For a full half-hour those pale, lambent figures were moving ghost-like about the church, while the white-veiled throng before the altar gradually diminished until at last it disappeared, fading from sight a little at a time, softly, as dream-visions of things beautiful melt away.

Presently came the benediction, and all together we streamed out from the brightness of the church into the wintry darkness, being by that time well into Christmas morning, and the moon gone down. But when we had left behind us the black streets of the little town, and were come out into the open country, the star-haze sufficed to light us as we went onward by the windings of the spectral white road; for the stars shine very gloriously in Provence.

We elders kept together staidly, as became the gravity of our years; but the young people, save two of them, frolicked on ahead and took again with a will to singing noëls; and from afar we heard through the night stillness, sweetly, other home-going companies singing these glad Christmas songs. Lingering behind us, following slowly, came Esperit and Magali, to whom that Christmas-tide had brought a lifetime's happiness. They did not join in the joy-songs, nor did I hear them talking. The fullest love is still.

And peace and good-will were with us as we went along the white way homeward beneath the Christmas morning stars.

Thomas A. Janvier.

NEW YEAR'S EVE.

By NORA CHESSON, Author of "Ballads in Prose," "Under Quicken Boughs," "Songs of the Morning," etc.

EVERYTHING comes to her who knows how to wait, and from the patient inquirer who seeks to lift the curtain of the future upon Near Year's Eve, there shall surely be but few things hidden.

Does she want to know the exact appearance of the man she is to marry? Let her eat a hard-boiled egg, whose yolk has been extracted and replaced by salt, and go to bed (not fasting but thirsting), and she will dream of someone who brings her water to drink. The face she sees in her dream will be the face of her future husband! Such a spell needs some courage and endurance in the worker of it, as does the following one; but old wives will tell you that, like Somebody's patent pills, "they have never been known to fail." This is an omen that has nothing to do with marriage, but only with good fortune to come. Whosoever desires this must put under her pillow for nine nights running—beginning with New Year's Eve—a dead ember and a piece of coal that the fire has never touched. Having done this, she may be sure of good luck for a year to come, and also of the ill-will of her bed-maker and laundress!

It is said that the house-mother should rake her fire out carefully on New Year's Eve, and spread out the ashes smoothly on the kitchen floor. Next morning, when she rises, she may (or may not) find a footmark in the ashes. Turned towards the door the footmark bodes that one of the family will die early in the year; but if the print is turned as if entering the room, there will shortly be a birth. Who eats herrings on New Year's Eve will be prosperous all the year; and who chances to receive money on New Year's morning will be in luck's way as long. Those who have a dark man for their firstfoot may rejoice; and so may those who see a man first from their windows on New Year's morning. Floors must not be swept until the sun has shone on this day, lest the luck of the house be swept out with the dust. This is an Oriental as well as an Occidental superstition, and one may find it in Japan and Anglesey.

All water becomes wine between eleven and twelve on New Year's Eve, but no one must be so curious as to go out to stream or well at this time, or, like Peeping Tom, he will be blinded for his indiscretion. On this night, too, as on Christmas Eve, the cattle are supposed to receive the gift of human speech for an hour, and the bees hum midnight Mass in their hives! Mummers and masquers choose the New Year for their especial season; and New Year carols were once as popular and as pretty as those sacred to Christmas.

Men and women with blackened faces, much be-ribboned and carrying brooms, go about from house to house on New Year's Eve offering to sweep out the Old Year, and are paid in kind with eggs and butter, and New Year cakes baked in the shape of a crescent. The master of a house, before he bolts and bars the front door for the last time in the old year, will lay down in the doorway the largest silver or the smallest gold coin in his possession. If it remains in the doorway untouched until the New Year is rung in, and the door is re-opened, the house will not want money all the year.

It is very lucky to be paid money on New Year's morning (Northamptonshire), and luckier to give away food (Ireland), but industry is misplaced at this season, and those who want good fortune to come their way must not bake or brew to-day, must not wash clothes, mend clothes or make clothes. Wheels must not turn at all during the twelve nights of Christmas, and the knitting-needles may rust if they will (Saxony), for—

"Who knits, with sorrow sits;
Who spins, adds three to her sins;
Who weaves, the Virgin grieves;
Who nets, God forgets;
Who fishes, against heaven wishes."

A dream dreamed on New Year's Eve is sure to come true; but a New Year's Morning dream comes through the Gates of Ivory instead of the Gates of Horn, and is not to be believed in.

A New Year's Day child will be always lucky, if a boy; if a girl, she will have no luck but much beauty, according to a Hungarian superstition, and men's hearts will be poured out like water before her.

The Wassail Bowl is as much a New Year as a Christmas custom. Here is a Gloucestershire Wassailing song.

"Wassail, Wassail, all over the town,
Our toast it is white and our ale is brown;
Our bowl is made of a maple tree;
We be good fellows all; I drink to thee.
Be here any maids? I suppose here be some;
Sure they will not let young men stand on the cold stone.
Sing hey, O maids, come troll back the pin,
And the fairest maid in the house let us all in."

Country folk used to observe the quarter whence the wind blew on New Year's Eve with much attention. "As it is calm or boisterous; as the wind blows from the south or north; from the east or the west; they prognosticate the nature of the weather till the end of the (coming) year. The wind of the south will be productive of heat and fertility; the wind of the west of milk and fish; the wind from the north of cold and storm; the wind from the east of fruit on the trees." (Sinclair's Statistical Account of Scotland). When the New Year fell on a Sunday, "a pleasant spring and a rainy harvest were promised by the calendars, also many wars"; on a Monday, "little fruit and the death of great men"; on Tuesday, "a bad harvest and much rain in spring and summer"; on Wednesday, "many wars" but "a good harvest"; on Thursday, "many winds and floods, but much fruit"; on Friday, "earthquakes and much free giving of money"; on Saturday, "hot summer, late harvest, much fruit, and rumours of wars."

Truly these superstitious customs are amusing reading, but every true reader of this magazine will, we feel sure, rather respond, in their hearts, to the sentiment of the following lines—

"Father, let me dedicate
All this year to Thee,
In whatever worldly state
Thou wilt have me be;
Not from sorrow, pain or care
Freedom dare I claim,
This alone shall be my prayer
Glorify Thy Name."

A HAPPY NEW YEAR.

By HELEN MARION BURNSIDE.

TRUST in the Lord, let no future affright thee,
    Thine is the present to deal with to-day;
The lamp of God's love is uplifted to light thee,
    And step after step 'twill illumine the way.

Leave thou the past in the Angel's safe keeping,
    And gratefully take the New Year that He gives;
Sow broadcast good seed for some future's glad reaping,
    And work thou His will in the present that lives.

One day thou shalt know what thy Lord is preparing
    For all who have lived for, and trusted in Him;
One day thou shalt know, when His joy thou art sharing,
    The Light that led on, when Earth's sunshine grew dim.

Far in the East see the grey dawn is breaking;
    Trust in the Lord, let thine heart hold no fear!
The bitter and sweet He will mingle for making,
    What He deems in wisdom, "A Happy New Year."

Recipe Index

No Victorian Christmas was "complete" without a feast—and magazines offered recipes for feasts for both rich and poor. For today's reader, it's important to remember that the Victorian term "pudding" applied to a very different dish than what we (at least in America) call "pudding" today. Think of plum pudding and you'll have the basic idea. What Americans call "pudding," Victorians (and Brits today) call "custard."

Almond Simnel Cake 16
Almond Sugar-Bread 85
Almond Toffee............................... 61
Alpine Pudding 221
Amber Pudding............................ 115
Apple Cream 74
Apple Custard Pudding.................. 22
Apple Custard, Boiled................... 101
Apple Snow 221
Apple Tansy 158
Apricot Crème 178
Aunt Margaret's Pudding.............. 116
Baking Powder.................... 101, 158
Barley Sugar 61
Baroness Plum Pudding 221
Bavarois.. 73
Beef a la Mode 16
Beef Tea............................... 28, 135
Biscottines, Rose.......................... 178
Boiled Apple Custard................... 101
Boy's Own Pudding..................... 115
Bread-and-Butter Pudding 158
Butter Scotch 61
Cake
    Almond Simnel 16
    Cherry 16
    Almond Sugar-Bread 85
    Chocolate 85
    Christmas 188
    Clove..................................... 189
    Currant 187
    Dessert 178
    Duchess Gateau..................... 209
    Dundee 177
    Economical 158
    Freemason Bread 85
    Fruit...................................... 188
    Ginger Sponge 189
    Lemon 188
    Light...................................... 187
    New Year's 178
    Peel....................................... 177
    Plum..................................... 187
    Pound 187
    Queen 188
    School-Treat........................... 16
    Schmelzbrödchen 85
    Seasonable 16
    Seed 188
    Spice 177
    Steinerli.................................. 85
    Sultana Drop 143
    Swabian Bread 85
    Tire-Bouchons 85
    Tronchines 85

    Washington.......................... 188
    Yeast Plum 16
Carrot Pudding 101
Castle Puddings.............................30
Chartreuse of Oranges 223
Cheese Cake, Lemon.................... 108
Cherry Cake 16
Chestnut Panna Montata............... 150
Chestnut Stuffing.......................... 198
Chicken Patties............................ 209
Chocolate Cake 85
Chocolate Creams 61
Chocolate Dates............................. 82
Chocolate Mould 209
Chocolate Pudding 22
Chocolate Rolls 85
Christmas Cake 188
Christmas Plum Pudding 187
Christmas Pudding 115, 188
Chutney................................ 28, 108
Clear Soup 29
Clove Cake 189
Cocoanut Pudding 22, 115
Cocoanut Tablet 61
Cod à la Genoise, Cutlets of 30
Coffee 135
Coffee Ice Pudding...................... 115
Compôte, Fig............................... 178
Compôte, Greengage 178
Compôte, Orange 223
Cranberry Tart 101
Cream Pie 189
Cream
    Apple..................................... 74
    Orange 178, 222
    Rice 74
Creams, Chocolate 61
Crème, Apricot............................ 178
Croquettes 178
Crullers/Twist Cakes 188
Crystal Palace Pudding................ 209
Crystallized Fruit......................... 158
Cup-Puddings 114
Curates' Pudding 22
Currant Bun 177
Currant Cake 187
Curry Powder 28
Curry Vinegar............................... 28
Custard, Orange Baked................ 223
Cutlets of Cod à la Genoise 30
Dartmouth Pudding 115
Dates, Chocolate............................ 82
Dates, Nougat................................ 82
Dessert Cakes 178
Devonshire Junket 101

Drop Cakes, Sultana 143
Duchess Gateau (cake)................ 209
Dundee Cake............................... 177
Economical Cake 158
Everton Toffee............................... 61
Every Christmas Pudding 116
Excellent Little Cake 85
Exeter Pudding...................... 22, 221
Family Pudding........................... 116
Fig Compôte 178
Fig Pudding......................... 22, 108
Fig Rock 61
Fig-Pudding, Turkish 16
Francatelli's Orange Pudding....... 222
Freemason Bread (Cake)............... 85
French Jumbles 189
French Oranges........................... 178
Fritters, Orange 223
Fruit Cake 188
Fruit, Crystallized 158
Galantine.................................... 209
Game Pie 16
Game Soup 198
Gherkin Pickle 143
Ginger Sponge-Cake 189
Gingerbread 28
Ginger-Bread Pudding 22
Gingerbread, Lemon 188
Gingerbread, Soft........................ 158
Glazed Vegetables 198
Goose, Roasted 189
Goose, Sauce for 189
Goose, various recipes 197
Gravy.. 197
Greengage Compôte 178
Grouse... 198
Gruel 28
Ice Pudding................................. 115
Indian Curry Powder..................... 28
Jelly
    Orange 222
    Orange, in Orange Peel 223
    Pineapple.............................. 183
    Prune 209
Jumbles, French 189
Lemon Cake 188
Lemon Cheese Cake 108
Lemon Drops 143
Lemon Gingerbread 188
Lemon Meringue Pudding 22
Lemon Mince-Meat 158
Lemon Sauce 108
Lemon Snow............................... 178
Lemon Sponge 108
Lemon Syrup 101

Lemonade 101, 135
Light Cakes 187
Macaroons 85
Marlborough Pudding 115
Marmalade Pudding 22
Marmalade, Orange 27, 101, 222
Maryland Plum Pudding 116
Marzipan 61
Meringues 178
Mince Pies 189
Mince Pies, Meatless 115
Mincemeat 16, 115, 189
Mince-Meat, Lemon 158
Mocha Pudding 116
Molasses Pie 189
Molasses Pudding 116
Mould, Chocolate 209
Nantucket Pudding 115
New Year's Cakes 178
Newark Pudding 22
Nougat Dates 82
Orange Baked Custard 223
Orange Compôte 223
Orange Cream 178, 222
Orange Fool 178
Orange Fritters 223
Orange Jelly 222
Orange Jelly in Orange Peel 223
Orange Marmalade 27, 101, 222
Orange Marmalade Pudding 223
Orange Pudding 222
Orange Sauce (for pudding) 222
Orange Soufflé 222
Orange Tarts 223
Oranges and Cream 74
Oranges, Chartreuses of 223
Oranges, French 178
Panna Montata, Chestnut 150
Patties, Savoury 16
Peel Cake 177
Pembleton Pudding 22
Pickle, Gherkin 143
Pie
    Cream 189
    Game 16
    Mince 189
    Mince, Meatless 115
    Molassess 189
    Pumpkin 115
    Swiss 115
    Steak 135
Piecrust 115
Pineapple Jelly 178
Plain Pudding 149
Plum Cakes 187
Plum Pudding 30
    Baroness 221
    Boiled 187
    Christmas 187
    Maryland 116
    Rich 187
    Unrivaled 116
    Vegetable 221
    Well-Tried 116

Without Eggs 115
Potatoes Tossed in Butter 30
Poultry, how to cook 197
Pound Pudding 116
Pound-Cake 187
Prune Jelly 209
Pudding
    à la Mètropole 178
    Alpine 221
    Amber 115
    Apple Custard 22
    Aunt Margaret's 116
    Boy's Own 115
    Bread-and-Butter 158
    Carrot 101
    Castle 30
    Chocolate 22
    Christmas 115, 188
    Cocoanut 22, 115
    Coffee Ice 115
    Crystal Palace 209
    Cup 114
    Curates' 22
    Dartmouth 115
    Every Christmas 116
    Exeter 22, 221
    Family 116
    Fig 22, 108
    Francatelli's Orange 222
    Ginger-Bread 22
    Ice 115
    Lemon Meringue 22
    Marlborough 115
    Marmalade 22
    Mocha 116
    Molasses 116
    Nantucket 115
    Newark 22
    Orange 222
    Orange Marmalade 223
    Pembleton 22
    Plain 149
    Plum – see "Plum Pudding"
    Pound 116
    Pumpkin 188
    Queen of 22, 158
    Raisin 22
    Rich Man's 221
    Russian 178
    Scotch 114
    Steak 135
    Swiss Apple 22
    Three Minutes' 101
    Turkish Fig 16
    Various 116
    Welcome Guest 103
    Welsh 101
    Winter Raspberry 22
Pudding à la Mètropole 178
Pudding Sauce 30, 116
Pudding Sauce, Orange 222
Puff Paste 158
Pumpkin Pie 115
Pumpkin Pudding 188

Punch Torte 73
Queen Cake 188
Queen of Puddings 22, 158
Raisin Pudding 22
Rice Balls with Orange 223
Rice Cream 74
Rich Man's Pudding 221
Rose Biscottines 178
Russian Pudding 178
Sardines, Tomatoes and 28
School-Treat Cake 16
Schmelzbrödchen (Cake) 85
Scones 149
Scotch Pudding 114
Seasonable Cake 16
Seed Cake 188
Shortbread 177
Soufflé, Orange 222
Soup Brunoise 28
Soup, Clear 29
Soup, Game 198
Spice Cake 177
Sponge, Lemon 108
Spruce Beer 27
Steak Pie or Pudding 135
Steinerli (Cake) 85
Stuffing, Chestnut 198
Stuffing, for turkey or goose 197
Sugar-Bread, Almond 85
Sultana Drop Cakes 143
Swabian Bread 85
Swiss Apple Pudding 22
Swiss Pie 115
Tarragon Vinegar 28
Tarts, Orange 223
Three Minutes' Pudding 101
Tire-Bouchons (Cake) 85
Toffee 61
Toffee Balls 61
Toffee, Almond 61
Toffee, Everton 61
Tomatoes and Sardines 28
Tonic 135
Torte, Punch 73
Tronchines (Cake) 85
Turkey with Turnips
    and Potato Snow 30
Turkey, Boiled 189
Turkey, Roasted 189
Turkey, various recipes 197
Turkish Fig-Pudding 16
Turnips 30
Twist Cakes (Crullers) 188
Vegetable Plum Pudding 221
Vegetables, Glazed 198
Vinegar, Curry 28
Vinegar, Tarragon 28
Washington Cake 188
Welcome Guest Pudding 103
Welsh Pudding 101
Winter Raspberry Pudding 22
Yeast Plum Cake 16

Printed in Great Britain
by Amazon